Ius Comparatum – Global Studies in Comparative Law

Volume 18

More information about this series at http://www.springer.com/series/11943

Académie Internationale de Droit Comparé
International Academy of Comparative Law

Rossella Bottoni • Rinaldo Cristofori
Silvio Ferrari
Editors

Religious Rules, State Law, and Normative Pluralism - A Comparative Overview

Springer

Editors
Rossella Bottoni
Università Cattolica del Sacro Cuore
Milan, Italy

Rinaldo Cristofori
Università degli Studi di Milano
Milan, Italy

Silvio Ferrari
Università degli Studi di Milano
Milan, Italy

Chapter - APPLICATION OF RELIGIOUS LAW IN A MULTI-RELIGION NATION STATE. THE ISRAELI MODEL; Asher Maoz signed non exclusive consent form

ISSN 2214-6881 ISSN 2214-689X (electronic)
Ius Comparatum – Global Studies in Comparative Law
ISBN 978-3-319-28333-3 ISBN 978-3-319-28335-7 (eBook)
DOI 10.1007/978-3-319-28335-7

Library of Congress Control Number: 2016938789

Printed on acid-free paper

This Springer imprint is published by Springer Nature
The registered company is Springer International Publishing AG Switzerland

Contents

Contributors

Mohamed Azam Mohamed Adil International Institute of Advanced Islamic Studies Malaysia/Universiti Teknologi MARA, Kuala Lumpur, Malaysia

Paulo Pulido Adragao Law Faculty, University of Porto, Porto, Portugal

Nisar Mohammad Ahmad Universiti Sains Islam Malaysia, Nilai, Malaysia

Ino Augsberg University of Kiel, Kiel, Germany

Louis-Léon Christians Université Catholique de Louvain, Louvain-la-Neuve, Belgium

Pieter Coertzen University of Stellenbosch, Stellenbosch, South Africa

Jabeur Fathally University of Ottawa, Ottawa, Canada

Silvio Ferrari Università degli Studi di Milano, Milan, Italy

Michele Graziadei Università degli Studi di Torino, Turin, Italy

Søren Holm University of Manchester, Manchester, UK

Nurjaanah Chew Li Hua University of Malaya, Kuala Lumpur, Malaysia

Arif A. Jamal Faculty of Law, National University of Singapore, Singapore, Singapore

Merilin Kiviorg School of Law, University of Tartu, Tartu, Estonia

Stefan Korioth University of Munich, Munich, Germany

Anabela Leão Law Faculty, University of Porto, Porto, Portugal

Asher Maoz Peres Academic Center, Rehovot, Israel

Javier Martínez-Torrón Unversidad Complutense de Madrid, Madrid, Spain

Roberto Mazzola Università degli Studi del Piemonte Orientale, Vercelli, Italy

Javier García Oliva University of Manchester, Manchester, UK

Adriaan Overbeeke Free University of Amsterdam, Amsterdam, The Netherlands

Balázs Schanda Pázmány Péter Catholic University, Budapest, Hungary

Jane Reis Gonçalves Pereira Universidade do Estado do Rio de Janeiro, Rio de Janeiro, Brazil

Vicente Prieto Universidad de La Sabana, Bogotá, Colombia

Martin Ramstedt Max Planck Institute for Social Anthropology, Halle, Germany

Jacques Robert Panthéon Assas University, Paris, France

Russell Sandberg Cardiff Law School, Cardiff University, Cardiff, UK

Bryan S. Turner The Graduate Center CUNY and ACU (Melbourne), University of Western Sydney, Sydney, Australia

Sophie Van Bijsterveld Radboud Universiteit Nijmegen, Nijmegen, The Netherlands

Wolfgang Wieshaider University of Vienna, Vienna, Austria

Chapter 1
Religious Rules and Legal Pluralism: An Introduction

Silvio Ferrari

Abstract This chapter analyzes the interplay between religious rules and State law from the angle of legal pluralism, discussing how State recognition of religious rules can affect the degree of legal diversity that is available to citizens. This issue is approached through an examination of religious law, that is rules that are considered to be different from secular rules, particularly in those legal traditions that have been more strongly influenced by the Christian religion. As the latter rules are frequently identified with State law, religious laws are regarded as a challenge to the State monopoly of law. First, the chapter defines what is meant by religious rules; second, it examines the tensions between religious and secular rules; and finally discusses the different strategies and tools implemented and used by States to govern these tensions.

Introduction

This chapter, and most of the book, concerns the interplay between religious rules and State law. This issue can be approached from different angles. I shall consider it from the angle of legal pluralism, discussing how State recognition of religious rules can affect the degree of legal diversity that is available to citizens. I am aware that religious rules and State law are two normative systems among many others, and their interaction cannot be fully understood outside this wider horizon. As incisively highlighted by Martin Ramstedt (2016, p. 57), "the existence and interplay of multiple written and unwritten normativities in a certain social field, their scalar range, their spatialization and temporalization, and the worldviews they are embedded in" need to be carefully taken into account to make sense of the global pluralism of today. However, as any good legal anthropologist knows, focusing on a tessera can help to shed light on the entire mosaic, provided that the part which is the object of the analysis is not mistaken for the whole. In this particular case, focusing on the intertwinement and interplay of State law and religious rules can help to answer two

S. Ferrari (✉)
Università degli Studi di Milano, Milan, Italy
e-mail: silvio.ferrari@unimi.it

R. Bottoni et al. (eds.), *Religious Rules, State Law, and Normative Pluralism - A Comparative Overview*, Ius Comparatum – Global Studies in Comparative Law 18, DOI 10.1007/978-3-319-28335-7_1

questions. First, scholars have observed that "opposition to political power and to the law based on religious grounds is notoriously difficult to overcome or to override, for a variety of reasons, including the possibility that many religions have to call upon beliefs relating to an after world, or to a supernatural world, to take position on every aspect of social life" (Graziadei 2016, p. 32). This remark seems to imply that the transcendent character of religious rules gives them a particular strength vis-à-vis State law. This issue will be discussed in the two following sections of this chapter. Second, scholars debate "whether and how the bond of citizenship can be reconciled with the bonds deriving from adherence to a religion, and in particular whether religion is to be considered different from other cultural phenomena in this respect" (Graziadei 2016, p. 30). This question is connected to the relationship between religious equality and liberty, that is, the problem of how equal treatment of non-believers and believers of different religions can be reconciled with the respect of the different beliefs and practices connected to each religion or non-religious worldview. This issue will be discussed in the two final sections of this chapter. The data and information contained in the chapters devoted to specific countries provide the materials on which the answers to these two questions are based.

There is a growing consensus that, all over the world, legal pluralism is on the rise. Although the expression 'legal pluralism' can have many and different meanings (Turner 2016; Ramsted 2016; Twining 2000, pp. 82–88), it is generally claimed that legal centralism –a system based on the State monopoly of law – is declining and that, as a consequence, State legal systems are becoming more pluralistic. Support for this conclusion comes from different circles. Lawyers point to the extension of human rights provisions over States and at the limits posed by international law to State sovereignty; anthropologists underline the increasing importance of customary laws and the rights of indigenous people; sociologists observe that mass migration has increased cultural, religious and therefore also legal diversity; economists highlight the impact of financial globalization in reducing State independence in economic issues and in making them weaker vis-à-vis transnational corporations; political scientists look with interest at the de-centralization of nation States and the transfer of law-making power from central authority to local and regional entities.[1] They all conclude that legal pluralism is an inevitable consequence of these processes (Turner and Possamai 2015, p. 12).

This picture can be one-sided and overlook the fact that some of these transformations can encourage a re-centralization trend as well: in Belgium the "uncertainty about the position of Islam (even a fear of "Islamisation") have progressively destabilized" the "traditional pluralist policies" (Christians and Overbeeke 2016, p. 110) and in the US "a number of state legislatures passed amendments to pre-empt the use of non-state legal principles in private dispute resolution, specifically singling out both Shari'a law and international law as competing normative orders that must be avoided" (Shachar 2015, p. 327). However, it is to be expected that, in the long

[1] The evolution of Belgium from a unitary State into a federation, mentioned in the chapter written by Louis-Léon Christians and Adriaan Overbeeke in this book, is an example of this process.

run, this fear-driven attitude will lose ground, so that it is reasonable to take the growth of legal pluralism as a sound working hypothesis for this chapter. My introduction will focus on the following questions: is this development to be welcomed as a recognition of individual and collective freedom or is it to be feared as a threat to equality of citizens before the law?; Is it to be interpreted as a manifestation of inclusion of diversities in the social fabric or as a step towards segregation and civil unrest?; Is it to be understood as a way of allowing citizens to manage their life according to their own choices? These are very broad questions that cannot have clear answers without taking into account the historical and cultural background of each country. However, it is possible to identify some conditions that the legal systems of different countries should meet in order to achieve a positive outcome from this process.

These questions will be approached through an examination of religious law: namely, rules that – for some reasons still to be determined[2] – are considered to be different from secular rules, particularly in those legal traditions that have been more strongly influenced by the Christian religion. As the latter are frequently identified with State law, religious laws are regarded as a challenge to the State monopoly of law. First, I shall define what I mean by religious rules; second, I shall identify the tensions between religious and secular rules; and third, I shall examine the different strategies and tools implemented and used by States to govern these tensions, in this way returning to the questions posed earlier in this section.

Religious Rules

As stated in the Belgian report, "courts very often use the concept of "religious rules", but its precise content remains undefined" (Christians and Overbeeke 2016, p. 93).[3] There are various criteria that in abstract could be helpful to distinguish religious from secular rules.[4]

The first is based on the distinction between spiritual and temporal matters, which is one of the central features of the Christian doctrine. Religious rules, as opposed to secular rules, have a religious content. But, although not unknown in many religions, this secular-religious distinction has different borders and contents in each of them. A matter that is considered to be secular in a religious legal system (for example, inheritance laws in contemporary Roman Catholic Canon law[5]) is

---

[2] See the next section.

[3] The ambiguity of the notion of "religious rules" is also noted by Paulo Adragão and Anabela Leão (see pp. 305–07) with reference to Portuguese law.

[4] For a discussion of the different meanings of the expression "religious law" see Sandberg (2011, pp. 170–82).

[5] Consequently, in compliance with Canon 22, the 1983 Code of Canon law refrains from regulating inheritance and refers on this matter to State laws as long as they are not contrary to divine law.

regarded as religious in another (the same laws in the Islamic legal system[6]). To say the least, their content does not always offer a precise yardstick to separate religious from secular rules or, to be more precise, the distinction between the two is far from being consistent once we try to transplant it from Christianity (where this distinction has a long and strong theological and philosophical background) to other religions (where it has weaker roots and plays a much lesser role). Moreover, even limiting the analysis to the law of the Christian Churches and of the States with a Christian background (where the distinction should be stronger), it is easy to observe that religious matters are the subject of State law and secular matters are the subject of Church law: as noted by Sandberg, "there is considerable overlapping between the subject-matter of religious law and that of other forms of regulation, such as State law" (Sandberg 2011, p. 177).

A second method to identify a religious rule is based on its source, and is grounded on the idea that religious rules are enacted by authorities different from the State.[7] This argument is partially true for the Roman Catholic Canon law,[8] but it is already questionable with reference to the law of other Christian Churches: if we take as an example the Church of England, the ordination of women to priesthood became an applicable law only after the English Parliament endorsed the measure approved by the General Synod.[9] When we come to other religions that do not have a centralized authority, like Islam and Judaism, the State quite frequently enacts and enforces rules that are considered to be religious in their content and nature: in the chapter devoted to Malaysia, Chew Li Hua underlines that "Islamic law is implemented via the numerous state legislations and rules passed by the State Legislative Assemblies on Islamic Law matters".[10] A different version of this argument underlines that religious rules are not part of the sources of State law,[11] which is basically

---

[6] Consequently, in a number of countries with a Muslim background, State laws make reference to Islamic law for the regulation of inheritance. See Rohe (2015, pp. 263–66).

[7] See Mazzola (p. 234): "En ce qui concerne les normes religieuses, la nature confessionnelle de celles-ci dépend, en général, de l'autorité d'où elles proviennent, c'est-à-dire que le caractère confessionnel de l'autorité législative donne la substance à la règle religieuse, quel que soit le contenu de celui-ci". See also Augsberg-Korioth (2016, p. 179) where, speaking of the self-determination of religious groups by means of religious rules, the latter are defined as "rules which derive from religious authorities and form a set of rules strictly separated from the law of the state": while "they mostly concern religious items", they "do not necessarily have a direct religious content". In the same vein see Martinez-Torrón (2016, pp. 358–59), Adragão and Leão (2016, pp. 305–07, with some nuances), Wolfgang Wieshaider (2016, pp. 80–81), and Fathally (2016, p. 315).

[8] It does not come as a surprise, then, that in countries such as Colombia, where the Catholic religion has had a strong influence on the development of the State legal system, the relationship between the State and the Catholic Church (and to a lesser degree also with other religious organizations) "is understood as a relationship between autonomous legal systems", so that Canon law is seen as "a legal system independent from the State" (Prieto 2016, p. 139). However, as correctly noted by Coriden (1991, p. 47) State laws and concordats are important sources of Canon law.

[9] See Holm-Oliva (2016, p. 380).

[10] See Chew Li Hua (2016, p. 253).

[11] See Martinez-Torrón (2016, p. 358): "the sources of the Spanish legal system are of secular nature, and no religious law – Catholic or other – is per se a legal source for State law". See also Fathally (2016, p. 319).

true for most Western countries, due to the secularization of their State legal systems, but is not a tenable statement for many countries with a Muslim majority population, where *shari'a* is frequently listed among the sources of State law.[12]

On a general line, these content- and source-based criteria seem to reflect too closely the dualistic approach that is typical of Christianity, and insist upon a distinction between God and Caesar, religion and politics, Church and State, which does not have the same importance in other religious and legal traditions.

Aware of this problem, some legal experts prefer to focus on the organizational purpose of the religious rules and affirm that they are "the rules that religions develop for their own internal functioning".[13] This may be partially true for the modern Roman Catholic Canon law and for the law of other Christian Churches, that progressively reduced their scope to the discipline of the clergy and the activity of the ecclesiastical institution (see Ferrari 2002, p. 75 ff.). But Jewish and Islamic law did not experience the same shrinking process undergone by the law of many Christian Churches, and continued to discipline matters that affect almost all facets of the individual and collective life of the faithful and go well beyond the borders of a regulatory system of religious personnel and institutions.

Confronted with these difficulties, other legal experts claim that religious rules frequently have a supernatural and transcendent goal (the attainment of salvation, spiritual illumination, eternal life, etc.) that is extraneous to secular rules (see Ferrari 2002, p. 275 ff.; Sandberg 2011, pp. 172–74). While this statement is correct in many cases (the last provision of the Roman Catholic Code of Canon law says that "the salvation of souls […] must always be the supreme law in the Church"), sometimes it is difficult to see this supernatural character in rules that are normally regarded as religious and vice versa. The Koran *suras* devoted to the inheritance shares due to men and women are not so different from the provisions that could be found in many States' civil codes, while the Constitution of Ireland opens by stating that "all actions both of men and States must be referred […] as our final end" to "the Most Holy Trinity", a statement that could easily find place in a religious legal text.

Finally, many authors of this book underline that it is difficult – sometimes impossible – to disentangle religious from cultural rules (see, for example, Maoz, p. 215). Christians and Overbeeke (2016, p. 93) write that "courts do not seem to clearly distinguish culture and religion nor make a coherent distinction between cultural customs and religious traditions". This inability is not without consequences. The same authors go on to note that "it is possible to observe a strategy of balancing between a *cultural* understanding for previous dominant religious customs (e.g. Sunday rest) and an accentuation on *religious* aspects to describe any minority

[12] See Ferrari 2013, pp. 437–478. The same remark applies to Israel: although Jewish law is not explicitly mentioned among the sources of Israeli State law, it "serves as an important source of legislation and adjudication" (see Maoz 2016, p. 215).

[13] See Coertzen 2016, p. 345. Contra, Sandberg 2011, p. 174, who underlines that "in addition to fulfilling the purpose of order […], religious law also fulfils the deeper purpose of facilitating religious life".

practice. This variation of either cultural or religious understanding pushes the judge to deem neutral the former but not the latter" (Christians and Overbeeke 2016, p. 93). In this way, the classification of a rule as cultural or religious entails a different degree of acceptation (and therefore of legal protection) of a religious group in the public space. In some chapters of this book it is acknowledged that many State recognized holidays have a religious origin and their enforcement as general days of rest in a secular society and by a secular State is supported with the reference to their cultural significance. But this justification applies only to the majority religious festivities and days of rest and cannot be employed to recognize the festivities of minority religions without strong cultural roots in the country. It would be naïve and also dangerous to think that it is possible to draw a clear-cut distinction between religious and cultural rules: we need to accept the existence of a middle ground where these rules overlap and blend, and learn how to deal with this intermingling on a pragmatic basis (for example, maintaining the State recognition of the holidays based on the religion of the majority but allowing minorities to abstain from work on their religious holidays[14] or replacing some majority religious holidays that have a weak religious significance –think of Easter Monday in the Christian tradition – with holidays of different religions[15]), without denying the role and significance of cultural heritage but considering it as a living entity open to change.

What conclusion can be drawn from these remarks? Religious rules cannot be defined in a comprehensive and clear-cut way because religion itself – its nature, content, characteristics – cannot be defined in abstract from the cultural setting of which each religion is part (see Asad 1993, pp. 27–54; Cavanaugh 2009, pp. 57–122). This conclusion does not mean we cannot understand what religion and religious rules are: it means that our understanding is inevitably embedded in history and culture. More precisely, while there are a number of rules that are regarded as religious in many cultural and geographical regions of the world (the rules concerning liturgy, for example), there is also an equally wide grey area where the distinction between religious and non-religious rules depends on the cultural traditions prevailing in a specific part of the world and in a specific period of time. The operative indication stemming from this conclusion is that we need to apply a fairly wide and comprehensive criterion, qualifying as religious rules all the "commands and injunctions […] posited by conscious manifestations of belief that may or may not have to do with traditional religions (as Roman Catholicism, Protestantism and Judaism), but that play, in the lives of people, a role analogous to that played by traditional religious commandments".[16] Although not exempt from criticisms,[17] this concept is the "most suited to the dynamic character of religious phenomena" and,

[14] As it happens in a number of countries, including Belgium, Austria and Italy.

[15] An experiment that, to my knowledge, has been carried out nowhere in the world.

[16] Reis 2016, p. 120. Also Christians and Overbeeke (2016, p. 93) note that "«religious rules» are often (and even wrongly) referred to norms coming only from recognized religion", while "the judiciary seems to be reluctant to take into account religious "rules" affirmed by non-recognized churches or traditions".

[17] Mainly based on the fact that, in this scenario, traditional religions would provide the yardstick to assess the religious nature of new religious doctrines or practices.

encouraging the inclusion of different religious experiences and manifestations, "is most adequate to the requirements of neutrality on the part of law and the state in an increasingly plural and diversified social scenario" (Reis 2016, p. 120).

Tensions

The chapters of this book show that the widespread tensions between religious rules and State law do not have a recognizable pattern: tensions emerge in different areas of the State-religions relationship and do not depend on variables such as the existence or absence of a system of religious jurisdiction or of religiously based personal laws. These tensions can have different manifestations according to national historical backgrounds and legal systems, but affect equally secular and confessional States as well as countries with different religious majorities and State-religion systems. It is then natural to wonder whether religious rules have some structural characteristics that can help to explain these tensions with State rules. I am aware it is a dangerous question that can easily be regarded as tainted by an "essentialist" approach. However, branding this question as one of essentialism and dismissing it without further consideration is not the right answer. I am not arguing that the tensions between religious and State rules can be explained with exclusive reference to their different "essence" or "nature": I am saying that the particular features of religious rules cannot be ignored when taking into account the various historical, social, and cultural factors that explain the country-specific manifestations of these tensions. Two examples can be helpful to elucidate this statement.

Personal-Territorial

This tension stems from the fact that most State laws have a territorial area of application while most religious norms have a personal area of application. Religious norms follow the member of the religious community wherever he/she is: from their point of view national borders are scarcely relevant. On the contrary, State norms do not apply beyond the borders of the State, except in limited and carefully circumscribed cases. Of course there are exceptions to this rule on both sides: Islamic law knows the difference between *dār al-Islām* and *dār al-Ḥarb* and in certain circumstances Israeli law can be applied to Jews living outside Israel (see Maoz 2016, p. 218). Nevertheless, these exceptions have a limited scope and do not affect the general validity of the principle that religious laws, like human rights law, "are able to transcend the law of the land and to survive the crisis of traditional State-based sovereignty" (Ventura 2015, p. 162).

This personal-territorial tension is an ancient one. In nineteenth century England Catholics were called "papists" because they obeyed an authority, the Pope, who lived outside the State: as a consequence they could not be fully trusted as English citizens and their political rights were curtailed. Something analogous happened in France, where the most conservative Catholics were called "ultramontanists" because they looked for guidance beyond the mountains (the Alps) to the Roman Pontiff. After the First World War this mistrust declined[18] but recently it revived again: many European States are uneasy with their Muslim citizens or residents who listen to *fatwas* pronounced in Cairo or Mecca and tend to consider this behavior a threat to national security (see Laurence 2012, p. 132 ff.). The same happens in some predominantly Muslim States of North Africa and Middle East. Arab Christians are looked upon with suspicion by part of the Muslim population, which thinks that it is impossible to be truly Arab without being Muslim.

For a long time this tension was successfully governed through the secularization of the State legal system and, in a small number of residual cases, through the tools provided by international private law (IPL). Now the secular character of the State is increasingly questioned and the IPL tools are becoming less and less effective because the people who are giving rise to these tensions are no longer foreigners but citizens. National States feel threatened by the ability of the great religions to overcome national borders and to provide citizens of different States with a supranational bond and identity. Governments are in search of new tools to grant social cohesion but are uncertain between two different strategies: reaffirming the exclusiveness of State law as a way to recreate a strong national identity, or accommodating religious laws within the State legal system as a way to "domesticate" religions and exploit their new power in favor of the State.[19] How much room is left to the application of religious rules in a State legal system depends on the choice between these two strategies.

Autonomous-Heteronomous

This second tension attains an even deeper level as it directly questions the foundation of law itself. The problem had already been underlined, more than a century ago, by Max Weber, who pointed to the fact that it is impossible to proceed to a full rationalization of religious rules (see Weber 1978, p. 809 ff). Just because their foundation is heteronomous and is attributed to an authority that is external and superior to human beings, in the legal systems of most religions there is a core set of rules that cannot be explained in purely rational or ethical terms. The strength of this set of rules does not reside in their ethical or rational foundation, nor can it be explained by reference to tradition and customs only: they are obeyed simply because they are dictated by God (for some religions) or rooted in the cosmic order

[18] For an analysis of this change see Ferrari 2006, pp. 625–639.

[19] The State-supported creation of representative organizations of "moderate Islam" in many European countries is an example of this strategy. See Laurence (2012).

(for others).[20] To give a few examples, the Jewish prohibition of eating meat and milk together may have been supported, at its origins, by reasons of practical nature, but today it is respected only because observant Jews consider it an expression of God's will, not because it has a rational basis or responds to an ethical imperative; the debate on the ordination of women to priesthood has been closed by the Roman Catholic religious authorities with the statement that no human being, not even the pope, can modify what is taught on this point by the Tradition, which is part of divine revelation.[21] From this perspective, the compelling strength of a religious precept is based on its origin from a power that comes from outside, and is accepted because of this origin. Although these remarks apply only to a limited number of religious rules (while the majority of them can easily be defended on rational and/or ethical grounds), there is a difference with secular rules, whose legitimacy, at least in the States inspired by liberal constitutionalism, is based on the will of citizens and is explained with reference to their rational or ethical nature. This lack of rational or ethical justification explains the suspicion with which some religious rules are considered in contemporary Western society, as shown by the recent and heated debates on Jewish circumcision, ritual slaughtering or the Roman Catholic ban on female priesthood.

This tension between the heteronomous and autonomous foundation of religious and non-religious rules should not be exaggerated. Elements of heteronomy can be found in the law of some non-religious organizations (the military, for example), while religious organizations have always strived to find ethical and rational explanations for the observance of their divine or cosmic law. But a margin of diversity remains: the ultimate foundation of the religious rules can be found neither in reason nor in human conscience, but in a reality that is external to both. Sometimes – perhaps even most of the time – there is no conflict between what is dictated by reason and human conscience on the one hand and what is commanded by this transcendent reality on the other. But the latter is never fully reducible to the first two. This tension also has an impact on the recognition of religious rules within the State legal systems as States are afraid that broadening the space for religious laws paves the way to uncontrollable dynamics based on principles and values that are incompatible both with State law and with human rights.[22]

[20] An echo of this conception can be found in Maoz (2016, p. 215) where he refers to the clashes between State and religious organizations due to the fact that the latter "regard their powers as emerging from God Almighty".

[21] See the Apostolic letter *Ordinatio Sacerdotalis* 22 May 1994, http://www.vatican.va/holy_father/john_paul_ii/apost_letters/1994/documents/hf_jp-ii_apl_19940522_ordinatio-sacerdotalis_en.html, n. 4.

[22] The somewhat disproportionate reactions to the Archbishop of Canterbury's invitation to make room for Islamic law within the borders of the UK legal system are a good example of these fears. See Williams (2008, pp. 262–82) and, for the ensuing debates Bradney (2010, pp. 299–314).

Strategies and Tools

The States deal with these tensions through different legal strategies and tools that reflect the different historical, social, and cultural background of their country. In most cases various strategies overlap, at least partially, in the same country. However, it is frequently possible to identify a prevalent trend that largely determines the choice of legal tools. Strategies can be classified according to the different importance given to community and individual rights[23] on the one hand and to religious freedom and equality on the other. Some strategies favor group rights and collective religious freedom, giving a lesser position to individual rights and equal treatment of citizens. Others give the precedence to the rights and freedoms of individuals in a framework dominated by the notions of equality and non-discrimination.

Community Oriented Strategies

A first set of strategies is focused on group rights and obligations. The community takes center-stage and rights and obligations are attributed to the group. Individual rights may be limited as a consequence of group membership, and the emphasis is placed more on the respect of religious diversity than on the protection of citizens' equality, irrespective of their religious convictions. Different examples of community-oriented strategies are provided in the chapters of this book.

1. *Minority rights*. Minority rights can come in different forms but they all are grounded on the idea that religious minorities (whose definition and identification is not a simple matter in itself: see Rivoal 2010, pp. 718–25) are entitled to enjoy a set of rights aimed at making up for the disadvantages inherent in their minority status. A first example is provided by Greece, where the Muslim community living in Thrace enjoys certain privileges concerning family and inheritance law. Disputes on questions related to these matters are solved on the basis of Islamic law and are attributed to the jurisdiction of the religious leaders of the Muslim community, the Muftis. In Greece's case, minority rights have been granted through international law instruments: the status of the Muslim community of Thrace is defined in the Treaty of Lausanne, concluded in 1923.[24]

   A second example is provided by Singapore where Art. 152 of the Constitution grants State protection of the (*inter alia*) religious interests of the Malay community, which consists overwhelmingly of Muslims (see Thio 2012, pp. 446–69; Thio 2008, pp. 73–103). This protection extends primarily to

[23] The new centrality acquired by the tension between individual and collective freedom of religion is underlined by Casanova (2012, pp. 140–41).

[24] On the minority rights system governing the Muslim community of Thrace see Akgönül 2009, pp. 279–292.

matters of family law (like in Greece) that are regulated by the Muslim community itself, through the operation of special *Shari'a* courts. The analogy with Greece is quite obvious and is reinforced by the fact that, like in Greece, "no other religious community has a structure for its religious law established by statute"[25] or special courts in charge of the application of its religious laws. However, there is a difference concerning the tools adopted to implement this strategy. In Greece they are provided by international law, while in Singapore the protection of the Islamic religious minority is based on constitutional law. It is not a small difference. The special regime for the Muslim community in Thrace has been largely imposed upon Greece as part of a larger settlement concerning the definition of the borders with Turkey after the collapse of the Ottoman Empire. This fact explains the "exceptionalism" of the Greek case, as religious minority protection systems are unusual in Western European countries (see European Consortium for Church-State Research 1994; Bastian and Messner 2007). The special regime for the Muslim community in Singapore is a domestic-found solution to the problem of the Muslim/Malay community, which represents "the indigenous people of Singapore" (Art. 152 Cost.).

Minority rights systems are not exempt from criticisms. In particular, they are sometimes blamed for fostering segregation and preventing the consolidation of a tradition of shared and equal citizenship. These criticisms are based on the conviction, strongly rooted in the post-Second World War declarations of Human Rights, that recognizing individual rights is sufficient to provide members of minorities with all the freedoms they need. In line with this approach, Art. 27 of the 1966 International Pact on Civil and Political Rights addresses the issue of minority rights in terms of rights of individuals who belong to a minority, without considering minorities as subjects of collective rights. Only in the last 20 years has this individualistic perspective been partially balanced against the recognition of States having the obligation to protect the existence and identity of minorities,[26] but this protection has been much more effective in relation to racial than to religious groups. In conclusion, while the issue of minorities has gained importance since the last decade of the twentieth century, minority rights have never become the main tool to protect religious minorities, whose problems have been and still are largely addressed through the general provisions on freedom of religion (see Ghanea 2012, pp. 57–79).[27]

[25] Although "for the Sikh and Hindus communities there are also State recognised bodies that administer the affairs of these communities" (Jamal 2016, p. 330).

[26] See the UN Declaration on the Rights of Persons Belonging to National or Ethnic, Religious and Linguistic Minorities, 1992. However this Declaration, after affirming in Art. 1 that States have the obligation to protect the existence and identity of minorities, in the following provisions falls back on the traditional notion that only individuals can be right-holders.

[27] The examination of the case-law both of the UN Human Rights Committee and of the European Court of Human Rights confirms that "when religious minorities face discrimination and persecution as a group […] their case is addressed under the "freedom of religion or belief" umbrella in international human rights and not under minority rights" (Ghanea 2008, p. 309).

2. *Personal laws*. A different example of these community-oriented strategies is provided by the systems of personal law that are in force in South Africa, Malaysia and Israel (on systems of personal law see Aoun 2009). They are different from the minority rights systems because they are not restricted to minorities but apply to different groups, be they the majority or the minority(ies) of the population. In other words, it is not a matter of protecting minorities, it is a matter of conceiving society as a group of communities, each of them governed by their own rules. This is clearly expressed by Art. 15(3)(a) of the South African Constitution which states that previous constitutional norms do not "prevent legislation recognizing [...] systems of personal or family law under any tradition, or adhered to by persons professing a particular religion".

   Israel, Malaysia and South Africa reflect well the variety of personal law systems. They may be limited to personal status and family law matters (as in Israel, where a significant process of limitation of the scope of personal law is in progress: see Maoz 2016, p. 217) or extended to some parts of criminal law (as in Malaysia as far as Muslims are concerned: see Adil and Ahmad 2016, p. 269); they may regard religious as well as ethnic communities; they may leave the citizens the possibility to choose between different systems (like in South Africa: see Coertzen 2016, p. 352[28]) or compel them to stick to the one established by their religion[29]; they may be supported by a system of religious adjudication (like in Israel but not in South Africa) which may be exclusive or concurrent[30] with other systems and so on. However, systems of personal law share at least one common feature: the legal status of citizens is not the same but is more or less largely defined by their religious (or ethnic) affiliation. This is true, not only in those areas of personal life and social relations that, in a Western and indirectly Christian perspective, would be considered "religious", but also in areas that (in the same perspective) would be regarded as "secular" and as such subjected to State law and to the principles of equal treatment and non-discrimination.

   Like the minority rights system, the personal law system also presents some problematic features, particularly when the membership of the individual in the group is not based on a personal choice but on involuntary ascription due to birth (for a list of these problematic features see Woodman 2008, p. 36). However, even when the right to leave the group is granted, personal law systems do not

---

[28] For a description of the system of personal law concerning marriage and family in South Africa see van der Vyer (2012, pp. 200–218).

[29] The Malay legal system includes both options: while Muslim citizens cannot conclude a valid civil marriage, as they do not have the option to choose secular laws when the matter falls within the jurisdiction of the *shari'a* courts (see Adil and Ahmad 2016, p. 269), non-Muslim citizens can perform a religious or a civil marriage. On this point see also Thio (2008, p. 79).

[30] In Israel "all religious courts have exclusive jurisdiction in matters of marriage and divorce of members of their respective communities" while "in other matters of personal status some courts enjoy exclusive jurisdiction while others exercise concurrent jurisdiction with the Civil Courts" (Maoz 2016, p. 212). In Malaysia *Shari'a* courts enjoy exclusive jurisdiction (see Art. 121 of the Federal Constitution of Malaysia 2016).

fully conform with the philosophical and legal principles underlying the declarations and conventions on human rights (and the constitutions of many States), based on a concept at the same time universalistic and individualistic of human rights. This concept goes back to the time of the Enlightenment and has been admirably summarized by the French politician Clermont de Tonnerre in 1789 with the sentence "we must refuse everything to the Jews as a nation and accord everything to Jews as individuals". Though formulated more than two centuries ago with reference to a specific religious group, this statement maintains its significance in today's debate and still serves as a reference point for those who believe that "l'émancipation se fait par l'accès à la citoyenneté et donc à des droits universels et abstraits et non pas par la reconnaissance de droits collectives spécifiques" (Woehrling 2007, pp. 134–35, with reference to the French strategy of minority integration).

This notion of citizenship supports the conviction that protection of freedom of religion and belief is better granted through universal rather than particular norms and therefore is unfriendly to the recognition of collective and particular rights connected to group membership.

Individually Oriented Strategies

The legal systems of other countries are more individually oriented, in the sense that center-stage is given to the individual whose rights to religious freedom and equal treatment are granted by the State. This does not mean that collective rights are unknown in these legal systems. However, they do not have a pivotal position, so that religious membership has a limited impact on the definition of the legal status of citizens.

In this book chapters concerning the countries that are part of this group, the statement "there is no system of personal laws based on religious affiliation" is recurrent (see Augsberg-Korioth 2016, p. 180, b; van Bijsterveld 2016, p. 281; Martínez-Torrón 2016, p. 360; Fathally 2016, p. 319; Christians and Overbeeke 2016, p. 103; Holm-García Oliva 2016, p. 381; Schanda 2016, n. 2.2; Adragão and Leão 2016, pp. 298–300; Reis 2016, p. 126; Kiviorg 2016, p. 163). This statement is basically correct but it does not mean that a citizen's religious affiliation is completely irrelevant in the definition of his/her rights and obligations. For example, as noted in the chapter devoted to Portugal, State "law gives relevance to personal religious affiliation of citizens, allowing some degree of "choice of law" concerning marriage" (Adragão and Leão, pp. 298–300): this means that citizens professing some religions can perform religious marriages that are recognized by the State, while members of other religions are bound to celebrate a civil marriage, a religious marriage being impossible or devoid of civil effects. The same system, with some variants, is in force in Italy (see Ventura 2013, pp. 157 and 211–12), Spain (see Martínez-Torrón 2016, n. 1.3) and other countries. In Italy only students professing the Catholic religion have the right to receive the teaching of their religion in public schools: students professing other religions do not enjoy this right but have the mere possibility to receive classes of their religion if a number of conditions are met (see Ventura 2013, pp. 198–208). In the United Kingdom only a member of the Church of England can become the head of the State (see Hill 2007, pp. 12–13). Therefore the declaration that no personal law system is in force in these countries must be understood in the sense that there is no substantial and coherent set of rules encompassing a whole area of legal relations (family, inheritance, etc.) that applies to citizens according to their religious affiliation.

A similar remark can be made with reference to systems of religious adjudication.[31] Also in this case it is frequently noted that the State legal system "does not allot formal jurisdiction to religious courts" (Wieshaider 2016, p. 86; see also Adragão and Leão 2016, pp. 305–06; Schanda 2016, p. 202; Christians and Overbeeke 2016, p. 107; Reis 2016, p. 129; Martínez-Torrón 2016, p. 362; Augsberg-Korioth 2016, p. 182; Kiviorg 2016, p. 163; Holm-Garcia Oliva 2016, p. 385) and also in this case such statement has to be qualified. In Austria, for example, the nomination and dismissal of the professors of the Roman Catholic Theological Faculties (which are part of State Universities) is decided by the competent Catholic bishop and "the professors have legal remedies only within Canon law" (Wieshaider 2016, p. 87). In a number of countries the Roman Catholic court decisions on the nullity of marriage have civil effects in the State legal system, without "any kind of judicial review on the part of State courts" (as in Colombia: Prieto 2016, p. 141) or provided they are confirmed by the competent State courts (as in Italy, Spain, and Portugal). In England and Wales the Church of England courts, which adjudicate upon issues falling within the scope of the Church jurisdiction, "are at the same time State courts" (Holm-García Oliva 2016, p. 385). In the Greek peninsula of Mount Athos "minor offences of common penal law and police violations" are judged by ecclesiastical bodies (Papadopoulou 2014). More generally, the courts of many States are inclined to affirm the exclusive competence of religious courts in matters concerning the relations between the members of a religious community, such as the excommunication of one of them or the dismissal of a minister by the competent religious authority.[32] As in the case of personal laws, the absence of a system of religious adjudication has to be understood in the sense that there are no religious courts with a general competence in a specific legal field, not in the sense that there are no cases in which decisions of religious courts have effects in the State legal system.

However, it is not only a matter concerning the scope of recognition granted by State law to religious provisions and jurisdiction. There is a deeper difference that is highlighted by the distinction between State (or weak) legal pluralism and legal pluralism "conceived as the coexistence of two or more autonomous or semi-autonomous legal orders in the same time–space context" (Twining 2010, pp. 488–89; see also Turner 2016, p. 62). In contrast to the States that follow a

[31] For an overview of the legal systems of the European Union countries see European Consortium for Church and State Research (2014).

[32] The borders of this jurisdiction are sometimes uncertain and disputed. See Adragão and Leão (2016, pp. 305–06).

community-oriented trend, States that implement individual-oriented strategies fall more in the first group than in the second: they try to accommodate some specific religious rules within the State legal system, but are far from recognizing an autonomous or semi-autonomous religious legal order (except perhaps when the internal autonomy of religious organizations is at stake).[33] As noted by Alessandra Facchi in relation to Europe, "apart from cases of long-established communities, in contemporary multiethnic European societies we seldom find ourselves dealing with legal systems, "social bodies" or "semi-autonomous social fields" – namely, groups able to create or apply their own independent legal systems. We are more likely to find individuals who follow rules deriving from different legal systems [...] norms that are neither systems nor institutions" (Facchi 2007).

A second difference between the community- and individual-oriented legal systems is shown by the default role played by State law. As a rule, the States following the latter trend have put in place a default mechanism that is available to citizens of whatever (or no) religious faith: in all these States, for example, it is possible to celebrate a civil marriage that is indistinctly accessible to all citizens, including those who have the option (but, according to the law of the State, not the obligation) to perform a valid religious marriage in compliance with their religious affiliation. This is not the case for a number of States (Israel, for example) included in the first group.

At the end of these remarks, a question is still unanswered. How do the countries of this second group deal with the demand for legal pluralism deriving from the increasing religious diversity of their populations? They do not make use of minority rights, personal laws or religious adjudication. What legal tools are implemented in their place?

To answer this question, we need to identify the main reason behind the rejection of these models of regulation of relationship between State and religions. They are not unknown in the history of these countries: actually, most of them have had a long past of personal statutes, religious courts and special laws for religious minorities. But they were progressively abandoned in connection with the strengthening of the conviction that freedom of religion can be better granted through equal treatment of citizens than through the legal recognition of religiously-based diversity. The most powerful instrument to achieve this goal – that is, to ensure freedom through equality – has been the secularization of the legal system that, expelling from it the rules that are based on and reflect the tenets of one or more religions, can ensure that all citizens are subjected to the same legal provisions.[34] The secularization of the legal system was directed against both confessional States and religiously-based personal laws: both were considered to endanger and limit religious freedom through the pressure put on individuals by the State or the religious communities. In this perspective, a secular legal system did not only grant the equal treatment of citizens: putting an end to the privileges and differentiations that are inevitably con-

[33] See infra, at the end of this section. For a discussion of autonomous and semi-autonomous orders in relation to religious issues see Sandberg (2015, pp. 10–11).

[34] For some consideration on this process of legal secularization see Ferrari 2014, pp. 25–40.

nected to the existence of confessional States and personal laws, it gave citizens the power to make their religious choices in absolute freedom, knowing that their religious decisions had no impact on the enjoyment of their civil and political rights.[35]

At this point it is helpful to consider that the chapters collected in this book show that this individual-oriented strategy is prevalent in the Western countries, that is in the countries where the influence of Christianity has been stronger. Their more or less implicit Christian background was instrumental in developing the idea that it is possible to distinguish two dimensions of human life, presided by two different authorities: one temporal, secular, profane and the other spiritual, religious, sacred.[36] The matters pertaining to the first area are placed under the control of the State, which applies secular rules based on the equality of citizens[37]; the affairs concerning the second are left to the religious authorities' guidance, which enjoy (within limits) the freedom to deviate from non-discrimination and equal treatment rules in their own domain. From this perspective, religious rules maintain their significance in the religious sphere but have only a residual relevance in the secular sphere. And, as the practical distinction between the two spheres took shape at a time when nation States wanted to affirm their undisputed sovereignty over their subjects, most of the subject matters that were at the border of the two spheres – *res mixtae* in the language of Canon law: family law, marriage, education, welfare, and so on – were attracted into the sphere of competence and regulation of the State (see on this process Modéer 2012, pp. 30–31).

This chain of events explains why, in the countries included in this group, State recognition of religious rules is much less widespread. The State legal system does not give them the power to regulate entire areas of human affairs (as it happens in the countries belonging to the first group) but deals with them on an *ad hoc* basis, through instruments that give effect in the State legal system only to those religious rules that are required to avoid tensions and govern conflicts.[38] In most cases this happens by employing legal techniques that are not specific to State-religions relations but are of general use. State recognition of the private autonomy of citizens and legal entities is a good example: in Austria "partners in commerce may validly

---

[35]This point is nicely made by Sophie van Bijsterveld (2016, p. 282), who underlines the connections between secularization, equal treatment, and freedom of religion: "The Dutch legal system excludes a system of legal pluralism based on religion. That would be contrary to the constitutional norm of equal treatment regardless of religion or belief. Secular law is the law applicable to all; this law guarantees freedom of religion. Being subject to religious law always includes an element of choice".

[36]Adragão and Leão (2016, p. 295) underline that "the constitutional and democratic State of western matrix [...] considers State and religion as "differentiated sphere", autonomous and separated" (n. 3). The impact of this distinction on the building of the modern public sphere as a secular entity is underlined by Asad (2003).

[37]In the past, when confessional States were widespread in Europe, States were largely in control of these temporal matters but had the obligation to manage them through provisions that respected the principles of the State religion. In this sense such provisions could not be regarded as secular rules, at least according to the meaning this expression has in contemporary language.

[38]This is particularly evident in countries with a common law tradition: see Sandberg (2011, pp. 183–84).

agree on closing their shops on certain religious holidays, which are not generally recognized by the State" (Wieshaider 2016, p. 84) and in England and Wales a religious school can establish a preferential channel for the admission of students who are members of the religion professed by that school (see Holm-García Oliva, p. 383). International private law is another (see van Bijsterveld (2016, p. 285); Wieshaider (2016, p. 83); Christians and Overbeeke (2016, p. 103); Adragão and Leão 2016, pp. 302–03): within the limits of public order, a State can give effect to religious rules that are valid in the legal system of another State. Exemptions from the laws of general application is another widely applied legal technique. Many States have enacted laws that exempt students from attending schools on certain days (see Wieshaider, p. 84), citizens from serving in the military, and medical doctors from performing abortions. In all these cases the religious convictions of an individual are considered to be a legitimate reason for claiming an exemption from complying with a law that should otherwise be respected.[39] Close to the case of exemptions from laws of general application is the case of conscientious objection[40]: in those States that recognize a right to conscientious objection, like Colombia (Prieto 2016, pp. 148–49), most claims are based on religious convictions.

In other cases States have created legal tools that are specific to State-religion relations. One of the most frequently used is the conclusion of concordats and agreements between States and religious communities, like those in force in Portugal, Spain, Italy, Germany, the Czech Republic, Austria, Brazil, Colombia and other countries. They usually contain the specific regulation of certain issues – the teaching of religion at school, financing of religious communities, State recognition of religious marriages and so on – in which religious norms are given direct or indirect application in the State legal system. Another frequently employed instrument is the enactment of laws on freedom of religion or religious associations. They may have different content and, unlike concordats and agreements, are of general application and deal with problems that concern citizens of different faiths. However, frequently they also include provisions that answer the needs of the faithful of a specific religion.

Similar remarks can be made when we move from the area of legislation to that of adjudication. While rejecting religious adjudication, some States accept religious arbitration in the framework of their conflict resolution system: in this case a religious body can act "as an arbitration body in relation to matters that are arbitrable" according to the law of the State such as, in England and Wales, wills (Holm-García Oliva 2016, p. 386).[41]

[39] See, among others, Martinez-Torrón (2016, pp. 368–69), van Bijsterveld (2016, pp. 285–86), Adragão and Leão (2016, pp. 304–05). Sometimes these exemptions are very specific, like the English law allowing Sikh construction workers to wear a turban rather than a hard-hat (see Holm-García Oliva 2016, p. 384).

[40] For a discussion of conscientious objection (and its difference from exemption from legal obligations of general applicability) see Martínez-Torrón (2015).

[41] For a detailed examination of the Arbitration Act 1996 and of the limits it places on the adjudication power of religious courts, see Sandberg (2011, pp. 184–88). More generally on Muslim arbitration bodies in Britain see Bowen (2013, pp. 129–45). See also Wieshaider (2016, pp. 86–88).

Religious rules have a stronger position in the State legal system when the internal autonomy and self-administration of religious organizations are at stake. Most States of this group recognize "in general, the right of a religious organization to apply its own rules to the legal relations that take place within the religious organization itself or within institutions that are owned or managed by the religious organization" (Adragão and Leão 2016, pp. 301–02; see also Prieto 2016, p. 138) and, as already mentioned, most State courts recognize the jurisdiction of religious courts in this field (see European Consortium for Church and State Research 2014), sometimes with some limitations (see Papadopoulou 2014, for Greece; Friedner 2014, for Sweden). Here States are ready to accept important deviations from the rules that discipline the internal organization of non-religious associations and corporations, softening – or even giving up – the enforcement of the principle of non discrimination (see Adragão and Leão 2016, pp. 301–02). As a consequence religious organizations can apply rules – for example, excluding women from leadership positions – that could not be applied in other organizations and associations. In many countries this deference to religious rules extends to religiously-inspired institutions like schools and hospitals. Their activity is regulated by State law through particular provisions that reflect their religious orientation and, once more, allow them to apply rules – for example dismissing employees for reasons connected to their private life – that would be unacceptable in the corresponding secular institutions (see Prieto 2016, pp. 146–47). These exceptions are defended as a consequence of the principle of separation and the ensuing State incompetence to regulate the internal organization of religious communities and institutions, considered to be strictly connected to their spiritual mission. Interestingly, the terms 'separation' and 'incompetence' are conspicuously absent in the chapters of this book concerning Israel, Malaysia, Singapore, and South Africa. It is further proof of the cultural roots of legal categories and, in this case, of the weight of the Christian cultural background in the legal systems of Western States.

In conclusion, it would be wrong to affirm that the States pertaining to this second group do not know rules that refer to personal laws and religious adjudication. But it is correct to state that these rules do not have the breadth and the strength that personal laws and religious adjudication have in the countries of the first group. These laws and systems of adjudication are – if not exceptional – at least unusual legal instruments in a context that is dominated by the principle of equal treatment of citizens and of the irrelevance of religious affiliation in the definition of civil and political rights.

For a general overview of the law in force in the European Union countries, see European Consortium for Church and State Research (2014).

Conclusions

In this introductory chapter the dichotomy between individual and community rights on the one hand and equality and liberty on the other has been employed to read and systematize the data concerning the tensions between State law and religious rules, that are provided by the contributions collected in this book. The analysis shows that in some countries the guiding principle that determines the room given to religious rules in the State legal system is the protection of individual rights and equality of citizens, while in others, more emphasis is placed on the respect of community rights and freedoms. The latter group is likely to provide religiously-inspired systems of personal laws and adjudication, that are instead considered with some suspicion in the countries included in the first group, fearful that the equal treatment and individual rights of citizens are jeopardized by the recognition of group rights. This distinction between two groups of countries is largely a distinction between two ideal-types because, as already highlighted, in the legal system of each country these two orientations –individualistic and egalitarian on the one hand, communitarian and libertarian on the other- coexist and combine in different ways. However, drawing on the chapters devoted to national legal systems, it is often possible to identify a prevailing orientation in each country and observe that there is a deepening and widening rift dividing legal systems that privilege individual rights and equal treatment of citizens on the one hand and legal systems that stress community rights and freedoms on the other. This rift is rooted in competing conceptions of religion and religious freedom that are emerging with increasing clarity due to the process of globalization. In other words, the rift has been there for a long time but never before people who have been raised within these two different cultural universes have been so strictly intertwined in the same living space. This intermingling is one of the explanations behind the tensions created by religious diversity in many countries and particularly in the Western ones.

What to do, then? What conclusions can be drawn after reading all the chapters of this book? What suggestions does it offer in regards to managing these tensions? The reader would be disappointed if he/she looks for an answer to the following question: what is the State legal system that grants citizens the best chance to live their lives according to their religious (or non-religious) convictions? There is no answer because the question is wrong. It assumes that legal systems can be compared by abstracting them from their social, cultural, historical, and political background. For this reason the correct question is: what can be done by each legal system to give citizens the opportunity to live according to their religious (or non-religious) convictions without endangering social cohesion and fostering (auto) segregation?

Countries that follow community-oriented strategies are frequently accused of encouraging exclusion and segregation through the perpetuation of separate legal orders and systems of adjudication, endangering the respect of equal treatment of citizens and tolerating more or less serious violations of non-discrimination rules within religious communities (see Zapfl-Helbling 2009, pp. 293–302; Fretwell

Wilson 2012, pp. 253–83). In particular, it has been argued that a modern State cannot "provide its citizens, residents and others subject to its power with a *just* and *stable* legal order by referring them to norms associated with their several religions and enforced by state courts" (Hofri-Winogradow 2010, p. 102). On the other hand, these strategies have historically proved to be helpful in protecting religious minorities and safeguarding collective religious freedom (see Aoun 2009, pp. 11–22).[42] However, they have at least one weak point, their compulsory enforcement: in many cases, through social pressures or legal restrictions, no room is left to individual choice. Granting effective opting-out rights from the religious group, putting in place mechanisms that offer a secular alternative to religiously-inspired legal practices,[43] and encouraging reforms that reduce the level of disparity that affects negatively the weakest group members (see Moller Okin 2008, pp. 587–97) are the first steps to bring under control the components of segregation and discrimination that can easily vitiate these community-oriented strategies. If these conditions are met, systems of minority rights protection or personal laws can be an effective way to satisfy the demand for a thicker and more pervasive notion of religious liberty, not limited to the protection of the freedom to choose and practice a religion but extended to the right to follow one's religious convictions in all areas of individual and collective life (within the limits, of course, set by the respect of public order and the rights of others).

Individual-oriented strategies have also been the subject of a number of criticisms, particularly in the last decades. Basically, they have been accused of adopting, at least implicitly, a conception of religion that is too narrow and considers it only a private affair and a matter of conscience, neglecting its communitarian and public dimension.[44] According to these critics, such an approach has led to the marginalization of religion in the public sphere, namely, the space where decisions of common interest are debated and taken.

These accusations are only partially true, as they do not apply equally to all the countries where equal treatment and individual rights are the main legal principles that inspire the relations between State law and religious rules. In the United States, for example, the vigorous implementation of the separation between Church and State did not prevent the flourishing of religion in civil society. Also, the legal systems of many European countries are far from considering religion only as a private affair, and denying religious organizations a visible presence in the public space. As such, a country-by-country analysis would be helpful to draw attention to the variety of approaches and also to show that the real issue in these countries is not so

---

[42] This same author thinks that personal law systems can still fulfil a positive role if some conditions are met: "Le pluralisme des statuts personnels, du moment où il ne met pas en danger l'état politique et tout ce qui intéresse l'ordre public en général, pourrait représenter, de ce point de vue, une garantie de paix sociale dans une société pluriculturelle et/ou pluriconfessionnelle" (*ibid.*, p. 22).

[43] Adragão and Leão (2016, p. 299), refer to the "default system" constituted in Portugal by legal provisions "available for citizens who do not want to be subjected to religious norms".

[44] For a description of the process of interiorization and privatization of religion see Danchin 2011, p. 663 ff.

much the marginalization of religion in the public sphere as the selective process that characterizes its admission to this sphere (see Ramsted 2016, pp. 54–56). Mainstream religions can access it much more easily than new, small, non-traditional religions (see Ferrari 2003, pp. 232–37). While this difference is frequently due to historical facts that cannot be ignored, it contradicts the neutrality of the public and particularly the institutional sphere and the equal treatment that its secular character is supposed to grant. A careful revision of some unjustified privileges that traditional religions enjoy in their relationship with the State[45] is the first step to give credibility to strategies that focus on individual rights and non-discrimination.

One final question still requires to be answered. What contribution is offered by the analysis of this small tessera –the interplay between State law and religious rules- to the whole mosaic? Is legal pluralism the best strategy to give citizens the opportunity to live according to their convictions without endangering social cohesion and fostering segregation? At first glance one could think that the more religious rules that are recognized and implemented in a State legal system, the more citizens have the possibility to run their lives according to the rules of their choice. The chapters of this book seem to disprove this too simplistic conclusion. Sometimes legal pluralism has encouraged religious conservatism (see Hussain 2015, pp. 151–160), in other cases the legal application of the principle of religious pluralism turned out to strengthen dominant cultural and religious identities (see Gozdecka 2015, pp. 179–195). It is therefore wise to accept Michele Graziadei's remark that "legal pluralism as a theory, or as a set of theories, does not necessarily address how diversity can be turned into a resource for individuals and for society as a whole, rather than becoming a cause of fragmentation and anomie" (Graziadei 2016, p. 38) or a ground for the oppression of the weakest components of society. At the same time the contributions in this book seem to suggest that there is a difference between a legal pluralism of choice and a legal pluralism of constraint (see Sandberg 2014, pp. 268–69). In both cases tensions and conflicts are to be expected in the long process of accommodating religious diversity in the State legal systems, but only the first has a good chance to help build an inclusive and, at the same time, even-handed society.

References

Adil, Mohamed Azam Mohamed and Nisar Mohammad Ahmad. 2016. The status and implementation of Islamic law in Malaysia. In Religious rules, state law, and normative pluralism – A comparative overview, ed. Rossella Bottoni, Rinaldo Cristofori, and Silvio Ferrari. Cham: Springer.

Adragão, Paulo and Anabela Leão. 2016. Portugal: Religious rules and state law. In Religious rules, state law, and normative pluralism – A comparative overview, ed. Rossella Bottoni, Rinaldo Cristofori, and Silvio Ferrari. Cham: Springer.

[45] The remark that State cooperation with religions is selective and privileges some of them over the others is recurring in the chapters of this book devoted to national countries: see for example Wieshaider (2016, p. 89).

Akgönül, Samim. 2009. Le statut personnel des musulmans de Grèce. Vestiges ottomans et réalités contemporaines. In *Les statuts personnels en droit comparé. Evolutions récentes et implications pratiques*, ed. Marc Aoun. Leuven: Peeters.

Aoun, Marc (ed.). 2009. *Les statuts personnels en droit comparé. Evolutions récentes et implications pratiques*. Leuven: Peeters.

Asad, Talal. 1993. *Genealogies of religion*. Baltimore: The John Hopkins University Press.

Asad, Talal. 2003. *Formations of the secular: Christianity, Islam, Modernity*. Stanford: Stanford University Press.

Augsberg, Ino and Korioth, Stefan. 2016. The interplay between state law and religious law in Germany. In Religious rules, state law, and normative pluralism – A comparative overview, ed. Rossella Bottoni, Rinaldo Cristofori, and Silvio Ferrari. Cham: Springer.

Azria, Régine, and Hervieu-Léger, Danièle (eds.). 2010. *Dictionnaire des faits religieux*. Paris: PUF.

Bastian, Jean-Pierre, and Messner, Francis (eds.). 2007. *Minorités religieuses dans l'espace européen. Approches sociologiques et juridiques*. Paris: PUF.

Bijsterveld, Sophie. 2016. Religious rules and the law of the Dutch state. In Religious rules, state law, and normative pluralism – A comparative overview, ed. Rossella Bottoni, Rinaldo Cristofori, and Silvio Ferrari. Cham: Springer.

Bowen, John R. 2013. Sanctity and Shariah: Two Islamic modes of resolving disputes in today's England. In *Religion in disputes: Pervasiveness of religious normativity in disputing processes*, ed. Franz von Benda-Beckmann, Keebet von Benda-Beckmann, Martin Ramstedt, and Bertram Turner. New York: Palgrave Macmillan.

Bradley, Gerard V. (ed.). 2012. *Challenges to religious liberty in the twenty-first century*. Cambridge: Cambridge University Press.

Bradney, Anthony. 2010. Some skeptical thoughts about the academic analysis of law and religion in the United Kingdom. In *Law and religion: New horizons*, ed. Norman Doe and Russell Sandberg. Leuven: Peeters.

Brooks, Thom. 2008. *The global justice reader*. Oxford: Blackwell.

Casanova, José. 2012. Globalization and the free exercise of religion worldwide. In *Challenges to religious liberty in the twenty-first century*, ed. Gerard V. Bradley. Cambridge: Cambridge University Press.

Cavanaugh, William T. 2009. *The myth of religious violence. Secular ideology and the roots of modern conflict*. Oxford: Oxford University Press.

Chew Li Hua, Nurjaanah. 2016. Legal pluralism and conflicts in Malaysia: The challenge of embracing diversity. In *Religious rules, state law, and normative pluralism – A comparative overview*, ed. Rossella Bottoni, Rinaldo Cristofori, and Silvio Ferrari. Cham: Springer.

Christians, Louis-Léon, and Overbeeke, Adriaan. 2016. Religious rules and principles in Belgian Law. In *Religious rules, state law, and normative pluralism – A comparative overview*, ed. Rossella Bottoni, Rinaldo Cristofori, and Silvio Ferrari. Cham: Springer.

Coertzen, Pieter. 2016. Religion and the constitutional experience of South Africa. In Religious rules, state law, and normative pluralism – A comparative overview, ed. Rossella Bottoni, Rinaldo Cristofori, and Silvio Ferrari. Cham: Springer.

Coriden, J.A. 1991. *An introduction to Canon law*. New York: Paulist Press.

Danchin, Peter. 2011. Islam and the Secular Nomos of the European Court of Human Rights. *Michigan Journal of International Law* 42: 663–747.

De Tonnerre, Clermont. 1789. *Speech on religious minorities and questionable professions*. Available at https://chnm.gmu.edu/revolution/d/284/.

Doe, Norman, and Sandberg, Russell (eds.). 2010. *Law and religion: New horizons*. Leuven: Peeters.

European Consortium for Church-State Research. 1994. *The legal status of religious minorities in the countries of the European Union*. Thessaloniki/Milano: Sakkoulas-Giuffrè.

European Consortium for Church and State Research. 2014. *Religious jurisdictions and pluralisation of legal adjudication. The emergence of religious parallel jurisdictions in Europe* (forthcoming).

Facchi, Alessandra. 2007. Customary and religious law: Current perspectives in legal pluralism. *Jura Gentium*. Available at http://www.juragentium.org/topics/rights/en/facchi.htm.

Fathally, Jabeur. 2016. L'application Des Règles Religieuses Dans Le Système Juridique Du Québec. In Religious rules, state law, and normative pluralism – A comparative overview, ed. Rossella Bottoni, Rinaldo Cristofori, and Silvio Ferrari. Cham: Springer.

Ferrari, Silvio. 2002. *Lo spirito dei diritti religiosi. Ebraismo, cristianesimo e islam a confronto*. Bologna: il Mulino.

Ferrari, Silvio. 2003. The legal dimension. In *Muslims in the enlarged Europe. Religion and society*, ed. Brigitte Maréchal, Stefano Allievi, Felice Dassetto, and Jørgen Nielsen, 437–478. Leiden/Boston: Brill.

Ferrari, Silvio. 2006. Nationalism, patriotism and religious belief in Europe. *University of Detroit Mercy Law Review* 83: 625–639.

Ferrari, Silvio. 2013. Constitution et religion. In *Traité international de droit constitutionnel. Suprématie de la Constitution*, ed. Troper Michel and Chagnollaud v. Dominique III, 437–478. Paris: Dalloz.

Ferrari, Silvio. 2014. The Christian roots of the secular state. In *Mapping the legal boundaries of belonging. Religion and multiculturalism from Israel to Canada*, ed. René Provost. Oxford: Oxford University Press.

Ferrari, Silvio (ed.). 2015. *Handbook of law and religion*. London: Routledge.

Ferrari, Silvio and Pastorelli, Sabrina (eds.). 2012. *Religion in public spaces. A European perspective*. Farnham: Ashgate.

Fretwell Wilson, Robin. 2012. The Perils of privatized marriages. *Marriage and divorce*, ed. Nichols A. Joel.

Friedner, Lars. 2014. Religious parallel jurisdiction – Sweden. In *Religious jurisdictions*. Granada: European Consortium for Church and State Research.

Ghanea, Nazila. 2008. Religious or minority? Examining the realisation of international standards in relation to religious minorities in the Middle East. *Religion, State & Society* 36(3): 303–325.

Ghanea, Nazila. 2012. Are religious minorities really minorities? *Oxford Journal of Law and Religion* 1: 57–79.

Graziadei, Michele. 2016. State norms, religious norms, and claims of plural normativity under democratic constitutions. In Religious rules, state law, and normative pluralism – A comparative overview, ed. Rossella Bottoni, Rinaldo Cristofori, and Silvio Ferrari. Cham: Springer.

Gozdecka, Dorota A. 2015. Religious pluralism as a legal principle. In *Religion and legal pluralism*, ed. Russell Sandberg. Cambridge: Cambridge University Press.

Hill, Mark. 2007. *Ecclesiastical law*. Oxford: Oxford University Press.

Holm, Søren and García Oliva Javier. 2016. Religion and law in twenty-first century England: Tradition and diversity. In Religious rules, state law, and normative pluralism – A comparative overview, ed. Rossella Bottoni, Rinaldo Cristofori, and Silvio Ferrari. Cham: Springer.

Hofri-Winogradow, Adam S. 2010. A plurality of discontent: Legal pluralism, religious adjudication and the State. *Journal of Law and Religion* XXVI: 57–89.

Hussain, Amina. 2015. Legal pluralism, religious conservatism. In *Religion and legal pluralism*, ed. Russell Sandberg. Cambridge: Cambridge University Press.

Jamal, Arif A. 2016. Managing religion through "religious harmony": The case of Singapore. In Religious rules, state law, and normative pluralism – A comparative overview, ed. Rossella Bottoni, Rinaldo Cristofori, and Silvio Ferrari. Cham: Springer.

Kiviorg, Merilin. 2016. Accomodation of religious rules in Estonian law and practice. In Religious rules, state law, and normative pluralism – A comparative overview, ed. Rossella Bottoni, Rinaldo Cristofori, and Silvio Ferrari. Cham: Springer.

Laurence, Jonathan. 2012. *The emancipation of Europe's Muslims: The State's role in minority integration*. Princeton: Princeton University Press.

Maoz, Asher. 2016. The application of religious law in a multi-religion nation state: The Israeli model. In Religious rules, state law, and normative pluralism – A comparative overview, ed. Rossella Bottoni, Rinaldo Cristofori, and Silvio Ferrari. Cham: Springer.

Maréchal, Brigitte, Allievi, Stefano, Dassetto, Felice, Nielsen Jørgen (eds.). 2003. *Muslims in the enlarged Europe. Religion and society*. Leiden/Boston: Brill.
Martinez Torron, Javier. 2015. Conscientious objections. Protecting freedom of conscience beyond prejudice. *Routledge Handbook of Law and Religion*, ed. Ferrari Silvio. New York: Routledge.
Martínez-Torrón, Javier. 2016. Striking the balance between religious rules and state law: Spain. In Religious rules, state law, and normative pluralism – A comparative overview, ed. Rossella Bottoni, Rinaldo Cristofori, and Silvio Ferrari. Cham: Springer.
Mazzola, Roberto. 2016. Modifications et Contradictions de la Réalité Socioreligieuse en Italie. Profiles Juridiques et Sociales. In Religious rules, state law, and normative pluralism – A comparative overview, ed. Rossella Bottoni, Rinaldo Cristofori, and Silvio Ferrari. Cham: Springer.
Mehdi, Rubya, Petersen, Hanne, Sand, Reenberg, Gordon, Erik, Woodman Gordon R., (eds.). 2008. *Law and religion in multicultural societies*. Copenhagen: Diøf.
Modéer, Kjell Å. 2012. Public and private, a moving border: A legal-historical perspective. In *Religion in public spaces*, ed. Silvio Ferrari and Sabrina Pastorelli. Farnham: Ashgate.
Moller Okin, Susan. 2008. Is multiculturalism bad for women? In *The global justice reader*, ed. Thom Brooks. Oxford: Blackwell.
Nichols, Joel A. (ed.). 2012. *Marriage and divorce in a multicultural context. Multi-tiered marriage and the boundaries of civil law and religion*. Cambridge: Cambridge University Press.
Papadopoulou, Lina. 2014. Religious jurisdictions and the pluralisation of legal adjudication: The emergence of parallel religious jurisdictions in Greece. In *Religious Jurisdictions*. Vienna: European Consortium for Church and State Research.
Pereira, Jane Reis Gonçalves. 2016. The relationship between religion and state in Brazilian law. In Religious rules, state law, and normative pluralism – A comparative overview, ed. Rossella Bottoni, Rinaldo Cristofori, and Silvio Ferrari. Cham: Springer.
Possamai, Adam, Richardson, James T., Turner Bryan S., (eds.). 2015. *The sociology of Shari'a: Case studies from around the World*. Heidelberg: Springer.
Prieto, Vicente. 2016. The Colombian legal system: Applicable religious rules. In Religious rules, state law, and normative pluralism – A comparative overview, ed. Rossella Bottoni, Rinaldo Cristofori, and Silvio Ferrari. Cham: Springer.
Provost, René (ed.). 2014. *Mapping the legal boundaries of belonging. Religion and multiculturalism from Israel to Canada*. Oxford: Oxford University Press.
Ramstedt, Martin. 2016. Anthropological perspectives on the normative and institutional recognition of religion by the law of the state. In Religious rules, state law, and normative pluralism – A comparative overview, ed. Rossella Bottoni, Rinaldo Cristofori, and Silvio Ferrari. Cham: Springer.
Rivoal, Isabelle. 2010. Minorité religieuse. In *Dictionnaire des faits religieux*, ed. Régine Azria and Danièle Hervieu-Léger. Paris: PUF.
Rohe, Mathias. 2015. *Islamic law in past and present*. Leiden: Brill.
Sandberg, Russell. 2011. *Law and religion*. Cambridge: Cambridge University Press.
Sandberg, Russell (ed.). 2015. *Religion and legal pluralism*. Cambridge: Cambridge University Press.
Sandberg, Russell. 2016. Conclusion: In pursuit of pluralism. In Religious rules, state law, and normative pluralism – A comparative overview, ed. Rossella Bottoni, Rinaldo Cristofori, and Silvio Ferrari. Cham: Springer.
Shachar, Ayelet. 2015. Law, religion and gender. In *Handbook of law and religion*, ed. Silvio Ferrari. London: Routledge.
Schanda, Balázs. 2016. Borders of religious autonomy in Hungary. In Religious rules, state law, and normative pluralism – A comparative overview, ed. Rossella Bottoni, Rinaldo Cristofori, and Silvio Ferrari. Cham: Springer.
Thio, Li-Ann. 2008. Religion in the public sphere of Singapore: Wall of division or public square? In *Religious diversity and civil society. A comparative analysis*, ed. Bryan S. Turner. Oxford: The Bardwell Press.
Thio, Li-Ann. 2012. Relational constitutionalism and the management of religious disputes: The Singapore «Secularism with a Soul» model. *Oxford Journal of Law and Religion* 1(2): 446–469.

Troper, Michel, and Dominique Chagnollaud. 2013. *Traité international de droit constitutionnel. Suprématie de la Constitution, v. III*. Paris: Dalloz.

Turner, Bryan S. 2008. *Religious diversity and civil society. A comparative analysis*. Oxford: The Bardwell Press.

Turner, Bryan S. 2016. Legal pluralism: Freedom of religion, exemptions and the equality of citizens. In Religious rules, state law, and normative pluralism – A comparative overview, ed. Rossella Bottoni, Rinaldo Cristofori, and Silvio Ferrari. Cham: Springer.

Turner, Bryan S., and Adam Possamai. 2015. Introduction. Legal pluralism and Shari'a. In *The sociology of Shari'a: Case studies from around the World*, ed. Adam Possamai, James T. Richardson, and Bryan S. Turner. Heidelberg: Springer.

Twining, William. 2000. *Globalisation and legal theory*. London: Butterworths.

Twining, William. 2010. Normative and legal pluralism: A global perspective. *Duke Journal of Comparative and International Law* 20: 473–518.

van der Vyer, Johan D. 2012. Multi-tiered marriage in South Africa. In *Marriage and divorce in a multicultural context. Multi-tiered marriage and the boundaries of civil law and religion*, ed. Joel A. Nichols. Cambridge: Cambridge University Press.

Ventura, Marco. 2013. *Religion and law in Italy*. Alphen aan den Rijn: Wolters Kluwer.

Ventura, Marco. 2015. Human rights in religions. In *Handbook of law and religion*, ed. Silvio Ferrari. London: Routledge.

von Benda-Beckmann, Franz, von Benda-Beckmann, Keebet, Ramsted Martin, and Turner Bertram (eds.). 2013. *Religion in disputes: Pervasivity of religious normativity in disputing processes*. New York: Palgrave and Macmillan.

Wieshaider, Wolfgang. 2016. Religious rules under Austrian state law. In Religious rules, state law, and normative pluralism – A comparative overview, ed. Rossella Bottoni, Rinaldo Cristofori, and Silvio Ferrari. Cham: Springer.

Weber, Max. 1978. *Economy and society: an outline of interpretive sociology*, vol. 2. Berkeley/Los Angeles: University of California Press.

Williams, Rowan. 2008. Civil and religious law in England: A religious perspective. *Ecclesiastical Law Journal* 10: 262–282.

Woehrling, Jean-Marie. 2007. Les minorités religieuses en droit français. In *Minorités religieuses dans l'espace européen. Approches sociologiques et juridiques*, ed. Jean-Pierre Bastian and Francis Messner. Paris: PUF.

Woodman, Gordon W. 2008. The possibilities of co-existence of religious laws with other laws. In *Law and religion in multicultural societies*, ed. Rubya Mehdi, Hanne Petersen, Sand Reenberg, et al. Copenhagen: Diøf.

Zapfl-Helbling, Rosmarie. 2009. La problématique du relativisme culturel ou religieux, en matière de droit fondamentaux dans les Etats membres du Conseil de l'Europe. In *Les statuts personnels en droit comparé. Evolutions récentes et implications pratiques*, ed. Marc Aoun. Leuven: Peeters.

Part I
Religion and Legal Pluralism. Theoretical Perspectives

Chapter 2
State Norms, Religious Norms, and Claims of Plural Normativity under Democratic Constitutions

Michele Graziadei

Abstract Contemporary democracies are open to cultural and religious diversity, but encounter problems when prevailing values and norms are questioned in the name of religious or cultural beliefs and practices. In many Western liberal democracies, legal pluralism is high on the agenda of law and religion scholars because State centred legality fails to do justice to the complexity of social and normative interactions. Legal pluralism provides the intellectual tools for understanding how cultural and religious identities and norms are shaped in different sectors of society. Nonetheless, legal pluralism provides no direct and clear answer to the question of how social order and equality can be upheld under democratic constitutions. Pluralism alone does not guarantee that coexistence among people who live their lives in different groups can be sustained by prosocial attitudes, rather than undermined by conflict. Social psychology, cultural anthropology, and political science investigate how those attitudes can be nurtured. This chapter argues that to understand and manage the tensions generated by the intersection of state norms and religious norms, the law should also make use of the insights provided by these disciplines on human behaviour in society.

1. - In contemporary liberal democracies, the relations between State law and religions, both as belief systems and as sets of norms and institutions governing the lives of followers, are characterised by certain tensions that are increasingly visible and that demand fresh approaches to new issues (Foblets et al. 2014; Ferrari 2015). These tensions revolve around the constitutional principle of equality and involve an emerging body of antidiscrimination law applicable to a wide range of conducts and institutional practices. The recognition of full personal autonomy underpinning life in modern liberal democracies may collide with religious norms concerning issues such as abortion, end-of life decisions, marriage and the termination thereof, etc.... Modern liberal democracies do not have a stake in the religious beliefs of their

M. Graziadei (✉)
Università degli Studi di Torino, Turin, Italy
e-mail: michele.graziadei@unito.it

R. Bottoni et al. (eds.), *Religious Rules, State Law, and Normative Pluralism - A Comparative Overview*, Ius Comparatum – Global Studies in Comparative Law 18, DOI 10.1007/978-3-319-28335-7_2

citizens and residents, or have moderate claims about them, recognising in principle the value of pluralism in society, despite laws often bearing the traces of a different past. All modern liberal democracies protect religious freedom, which in the contemporary epoch includes freedom from religion. Freedom of religion is indeed an essential part of the constellation of freedoms that modern democracies generally intend to guarantee and uphold. That said, this concept is not always understood in the same way or recognised to the same extent everywhere (Durham et al. 2013).

The essays collected in this volume provide abundant food for thought on these matters by describing and comparing the normative settings governing the relationships between State norms and religious norms. The purpose of this chapter is to explore some of the questions that are left unanswered or are only marginally covered by other contributions in this volume. Among them, the principal one is whether and how the bond of citizenship can be reconciled with the bonds deriving from adherence to a religion, and in particular whether religion is to be considered different from other cultural phenomena in this respect. This is, in a certain sense, a problem that has always existed, since the constitution of the modern States. The advent of democracy, with its promise of the provision of equal legal protection for all, independent of personal and religious beliefs and more broadly culturally determined value orientations, has added an entirely new dimension to this issue, as is demonstrated by a wealth of recent research (see, e.g., Shah et al. 2014; Ferrari and Pastorelli 2013; Alidadi et al. 2012).

2. - To put these issues in perspective, it is necessary to return to the inception of the modern States, and to the reshaping of the relations between political authorities, law, and religions that lies at the origins of modern religious freedom. The making of modern States in the sixteenth century took place amidst bloody wars, vicious fights and controversies that tore the Christian world apart. Here I will concentrate on the French situation, taking as a reference point the ideas of a pre-liberal, non-democratic thinker, Jean Bodin (1530–1596), whose great political and philosophical work on sovereignty – *Les Six livres de la République* – published in 1576, marked a turn in the philosophical and political views of the epoch.

Bodin's world was populated by people who did not understand why civic and religious obligations should be treated as pertaining to different life ambits. This world was marked by intense conflicts that involved religious dimensions, culminating in the massacre of St. Bartholomew's Day (1572), when mass killings of French Calvinists (Hugonots) instigated by the Catholic King of France took place. In those hard times, how to contain violence that resulted or was associated with the plurality of polarized religious beliefs was a question of capital importance. Bodin considered peace as a precondition for the prosperity of a nation, and ultimately preferred peace to religious uniformity across the kingdom. Peace was difficult to achieve as "the people everywhere are most jealous of their religion" and "cannot endure any rites and ceremonies differing from the religions by themselves generally received" (Bodin 1962: III, 7; 381). Many of his contemporaries considered civil wars necessary if the alternative was sharing the country with heretics. Confronted with the deep sectarian divisions of his time, Bodin prudently distanced himself from the opinion that religious uniformity formed the foundation of civil coexistence, and suggested that the King should not try to use force against religious minorities, whenever those minorities were established and rooted on the territory. He also did not accept the *cuius regio, eius religio* principle for France, which was favoured by sectors of the nobility and would have torn the country apart. He rejected the segmentation of France into semiautonomous units, each with its own religion. Civic life in polities traversed by divisions such as those experimented by sixteenth century France required a new solution: each person should have the possibility to practice his or her religion in private. Hence, Kings and rulers should abandon attempts to use violence to impose the true religion, to save souls, or to punish heretics, but rather consider the example of the Romans, who insisted on the public worship of the Roman gods "...yet for all that did they easily suffer every man privately within the city to use his own manner and fashion, and his religion" (Bodin 1962, IV, 7, 538).

The opinions expressed in *Les Six livres de la République* raised the opposition of the *dévots* who condemned Bodin's work as a mischievous defence of religious pluralism. To reject their arguments, Bodin accepted that religion remains a source of legitimacy for temporal powers. Having conceded this, he also maintained that even a false religion can help preserve peace in a kingdom. According to Bodin, repression is not an effective strategy in such matters, as it is self-defeating. Violence will generate further violence: "minds resolved, the more they are crossed, the stiffer they are" (Bodin 1962, III, 7, 382). This line of argument is linked to a wider theme, namely the possibility of strengthening the authority of the State by limiting its jurisdiction, and establishing constraints on its actions. This theme reflects a religious motive, mirroring as it does in the political sense the possibility - accepted by theologians - that God may decide to set limits on his infinite powers in this regard (Holmes 1995). One of the implications of this rational was that Christian kings must keep their promises to the infidels as well, an assumption that was crucial in the formation of modern liberal democracies, as well as for laying down the foundations of an international mercantile society in the medieval and modern period. This stance on the relations between political authority and religions was accompanied by a theory of legislation that was associated with positivism. Bodin held that *voluntas, not veritas, facit legem.* This doctrine worked in a society divided into factions, where endless disputes and fights concerned precisely what "reason" or "religion" required. However, Bodin was careful not to overplay what legislation based solely on sovereignty can achieve, by noting that habits and customs fixed boundaries on sovereign commands and sovereign authority (Holmes 1995).

At its inception, this inchoate form of religious freedom was justified by an eclectic set of considerations concerning religious behaviour. Bodin held that conscience, by natural necessity, cannot be constrained; he maintained that persecution begets hypocrisy, and that tributes coming from pure hearts please God, no matter the religious beliefs implicated in the offering. Ultimately, however, all these considerations are inscribed in the theoretical framework of political philosophy, according to which rational thinking and political prudence is the key to stable political authority.

3. - Legal positivism is thus established as a first response to the problem of how to impose authority in a divided society, and yet realism concludes that civil laws can govern society only insofar as coercion is not used every time they must be applied. This point is not as banal as it appears at first sight. Although religions often provide support to ruling powers, religious beliefs may also hinder the smooth application of civil laws and thus undermine governments.

Legislators and the machinery of the law may fail to persuade on many grounds, but opposition to political power and to the law based on religious grounds is notoriously difficult to overcome or to override, for a variety of reasons, including the possibility that many religions have to call upon beliefs relating to an after world, or to a supernatural world, to take position on every aspect of social life. This move tends to undermine the core tenet of political realism as a method of achieving stable government, namely the possibility to calculate the consequences of individual actions by relying on assumptions that prioritise worldly considerations in the weighing of the pros and cons of each possible choice, or course of action..[1] Major theorists of modern sovereignty, such as Thomas Hobbes, were acutely aware of this aspect of religious dissent and of the dangers associated with it for the political order and the authority of the State. But to be true to Hobbes, his arguments did not apply to religious dissent only. Hobbes pointed to other factors - secular factors - as the source of trouble for the stability of governments, such as the rhetoric based on the readings of classics prevailing in his time at the Universities.[2] Hobbes' work thus stands out in this respect as a manifesto against motivational reductionism, which would instead pick the instinct of self-preservation of a person's life as the granitic foundation of political power (Lloyd 1992; Holmes 1995). According to Hobbes, the basic decisions that reasonable individuals should be able to make regarding the choice between, subjection to sovereign powers or incurring the consequences of disobedience, including death, does not necessarily lead to choosing the first over the second. Surprisingly, contrary to the instinct of self preservation, one may choose death over the violation of religious precepts or the betrayal of a certain ideology, simply because personal choices are shaped by opinions and beliefs, and the prospect of death may in some cases be more attractive than life without dignity or damnation, especially if death promises salvation. Ultimately, as Hobbes makes clear, even political power is dependent on opinion, because the powers of the mighty have no foundations except in the beliefs and the opinion of the people (Hobbes 1990, 16). Therefore, even when not backed by the sword, as Hobbes duly noted, "words" and "breath" have an enormous political impact

[1]This is possibly why Max Weber advanced the distinction between value rationality and instrumental rationality, the former being much more mysterious than the latter. Whether that distinction is defensible in terms of coherence is altogether a different matter, of course (on that distinction, in a critical vein, see: Oakes 2003). In any case, the work of Habermas on the relationship between religious beliefs and civic participation in political debates clearly draws upon it (Habermas 2008). Once more, one can ask whether his work resists criticism.

[2]Although it may be anachronistic to represent Hobbes' position in this way, he was anticipating the argument made in full by Cavanaugh, according to whom the distinction between religious and secular violence is problematic to say the least (Cavanaugh 2009).

(Hobbes 1986, II, Ch. 18, 231). The lesson is that force alone fails to persuade. Political realism suggests that legal positivism is an empty box if public opinion is dominated by passions that may completely destroy respect for the common good and authority, be they religious or secular.

4. - The arguments discussed above concerning the troubles that legal positivism has when confronted with rules of conduct grounded on religious beliefs raise a few uncomfortable questions. I will try to sum them up as follows. Are these rules in any sense different from other normative or cultural manifestations entering the public sphere and governing social interactions? Does the public regulation of conduct conforming to religious beliefs pose any special challenge when compared with the public regulation of other conducts that confront State authority?

Such questions cannot be answered completely here, because just as not all religions are the same, not all States are same, as is made abundantly clear by the contributions collected in this book and other studies (Foblets et al. 2010). Some religions regulate the beliefs and conduct that believers must adhere to with greater severity. On the other hand, contemporary States have been formed under different historical conditions and thus the governments of these States must take into account disparate dynamics and forces in deciding what policies to implement. Even Europe's liberal democracies do not all share the same stance towards conduct that is inspired by religious precepts in the public sphere. Hence, different historical and institutional paths of State formation result in different constitutional settings and governmental policies concerning religious matters. Furthermore, history shows that both civic and religious obligations may change over time, even within a single State, with respect to the same religion. To generalise about the relations between State norms and religious norms is impossible without considering the temporal dimensions of comparisons and how these concepts are construed across time and in different places (in a critical vein: Cavanaugh 2009).

Nonetheless, the fundamental questions posed above remains interesting, despite the variety of models reflecting the relations between State norms and religious norms. To answer them requires understanding religions and how they work in society. Quite apart from what religions hold, sociologists, anthropologists, philosophers, economists and natural scientists, have often highlighted the many positive effects that religious beliefs and rituals bring to believers and more generally, to society. These positive effects include, among other things, improved social cohesion, increased sense of control over one's life, and so on. On the other hand, religions have often been examined in a critical vein, as a pernicious form of superstition, or false consciousness.

I need not to review this evidence, but rather to consider the wider picture concerning the working of religions in society. This includes religious strife with strong destabilising effects on society. This possibility is disturbing because compromise over religious matters - as mentioned above - is often difficult to reach, and religious disputes are thus often left without resolve even in the long run. But why should religions in particular be a source of concern in this respect?

As it often happens, discussing the question from a broader perspective, such as that offered by scholarship relating to conflict studies, will better illuminate this point.

Research in this area points to two key factors that work as powerful leverage for conflicts; scarcity and unequal distribution of resources. Scarcity of resources, or the fear thereof, triggers rivalries and conflicts. Whenever a community or a population, hears that "there is not enough left to satisfy everybody" the possibility of conflict rises. Spreading this message in the canonical form – "the more there is of mine, the less there is of yours"[3] – makes conflict both very likely and very harsh. On the other hand, although resources may abound, such as during periods of rapid economic growth, an unequal or unjust distribution of the surplus can still stir social conflicts, especially if attributed to policies enacted by governments, pressures by mighty social actors and so on, rather than being considered as God given, or the fruit of "chance" or "fate".

Are religions implicated in similar dynamics? Are religions able to produce scarcity (or the impression of scarcity) of some resources, and how they do so? Do they sanction controversial distribution of resources that are not scarce, and if so, how?

To this regard, I am largely unconcerned with the distribution of material resources dispensed through religious institutions, although distribution of material benefits has been a function of some religious institutions. I am focussing instead on religion as a way of gaining access to immaterial resources that are perceived as vital, or at least as very attractive, by a certain community. Whether such resources can make life better in this world by fostering the well-being of believers, or guarantee salvation in the after world, is not really the issue. Rather, it is how religions regulate access to those immaterial resources that can only be gained through adherence to religious beliefs and practices.

To delve further into this point, one has to take a second, less conventional look at what religions do in the socio-cultural sphere. Religions defined as belief systems concerned with transcendent dimensions of life apparently have little to do with distributional problems. Nonetheless, on closer scrutiny, one can argue that religions do regulate access to resources that many people consider essential or precious, as they are considered or perceived as the sources of spiritual or physical well being. An analysis of religions from this standpoint casts light on the nature of the conflicts in which religions or religious affiliations play a role (Avalos 2005, 2012, for a broader coverage of the topic: Jerryson et al. 2012).

Religions offer resources that are often viewed as scarce, and subject to restricted or limited access. Inscripturation, namely the notion that God reveals himself only through a select corpus of texts and to a select group of people, is of course central to this type of discourse. Sacred places or objects that are necessary to believers have this quality as well (think, for example, of descriptions of the sacred land). Scarcity is also the mechanism at the basis of group privileging, a feature of both ethnic and non-ethnic religions. Salvation – be it physical, spiritual, or both – is once more not for all, but for believers only, or for selected believers who share certain qualities. Purity, which is a concept central to many religious discourses, is an instantiation of the same logic, as it sets one condition to be included in a group

---

[3] Also known as the Duchess' law, after the dictum of the Duchess in Lewis Carrol's *Alice's adventures in Wonderland* (1865), ch. IX.

with positive features. One can easily multiply similar examples for a variety of religions.

Some passages in the holy scriptures of religions justify resorting to violence to affirm religious values and norms, but this is not really an essential point in understanding how religions can be instrumental in provoking conflicts and strife. Rather, what should be noted is the tendency to foster a mentality in which religion is considered the (only) way to benefit from resources that are otherwise difficult to obtain, and that are therefore limited. Empirical evidence for this thesis comes from the field of social psychology. Social psychologists have noticed that religions exacerbate in-group bias, namely the tendency to favour members of one's group and to exhibit prejudice towards members of other groups (for a review of the literature, which for the moment does not cover all religions, and the discussion of the state of the art: Galen 2012a, b).

Turning to the second argument mentioned above, namely the adverse social effects deriving from the unequal or unjust distribution of certain resources, the salient point to consider is that the overall growth of available resources for a community does not necessarily result in a more peaceful social coexistence. Analysing the social effects of economic growth in the 1960s, Mancur Olson made an important observation regarding this point (Olson 1963). Economic change fostering growth often brings with it distributional effects that marginalize individuals or social groups, or that reduces their weight and salience in society. Members of the community may perceive new distributive patterns emerging during a phase of growth driven change as unjust, when compared to previously established distributions of wealth. Therefore, economic growth can go hand in hand with social troubles and turmoil because those who suffer the adverse effect of change will resist it. This key observation can also be applied to the religious realm. If society's *mores* change and personal autonomy is expanded, as it happens when previously impermissible conduct becomes legitimate, those who consider legitimacy as a scarce resource may oppose such change, although the range of choices available to individuals and groups expands. Current religious objections to laws on gay marriage reflect this logic. To affirm that these laws uphold marriage as a central institution in society will not appease those who think that legislation introducing gay marriage as a legitimate form of marriage undermines marriage as an institution reserved for heterosexual couples, even though this novel legislation concerns civil marriages only, not religious marriages. It will not appease traditionalists, because they consider the concept of "marriage" as belonging to them, and they do not intend to share it with others.

I have hinted above to the fact that religious beliefs defy empirical validation or falsification through tests applicable to scientific propositions. But the question of why religious struggles are so difficult to control, and why religious confrontations are so enduring and so hard to bring to an end, has perhaps little to do with these aspects of religions as belief systems. Many cultural wars share similar characteristics: they are not easily resolved by rational arguments or by those based on empirical evidence. Oliver Wendell Holmes, a famous US Supreme Court

Justice, once quipped: "you can't argue a man into liking a glass of beer".[4] He was right, many preferences linked to cultural conditioning cannot be changed by resorting to rational arguments, or to empirically grounded observations (and yet they are still part of the normal spectrum of preferences permitted in a community!). Hence, to think over the dilemmas raised by State regulation of religious phenomena requires knowing more about other types of conflicts and confrontations as well; to highlight what can be learnt about these conflicts when they are approached in a broader, cultural perspective. To do so, let us turn to one of the central norms of the constitutions of liberal democracies – namely the principle of equality. One of the biggest challenges faced by legal theorists is the interpretation of this principle and its reconciliation with the increasing diversity of viewpoints related to values and cultural practices that are emerging in contemporary democracies. My point is that equality as a key constitutional principle can only be preserved through the development of new awareness of what cultural differences and conflicts involve for the making or unmaking of social order. Social psychologists and political scientists, among other social scientists, have explored these dimensions of social life in depth. Their finding may help to harness and subdue tendencies that would instead work to escalate cultural conflicts - including religious conflicts - out of control.

5. - The universal recognition of the principle of equality by liberal democracies stands in opposition to ancient regimes that were rooted in the division of societies into estates. Such divisions were sanctioned by social custom and inscribed into law. To overcome them, a State centred notion of legality was designed and joined with the foundation of democratic governments under modern constitutions.[5] In Europe, a uniform national concept of citizenship was the ultimate outcome of this revolutionary project in all States. However, this notion is not universal (see, e.g. Segzin 2013; Parolin 2009, 2014).

This new political bond was forged to overcome the peculiar and different legal conditions of subjects and communities that existed in the territory. Corresponding civil institutions were created *ex novo* to expand the powers of the States to ambits of social life that were previously regulated by religious institutions, such as civil marriage, state schools, public hospitals, cemeteries and so on.

The idea of equality underpinning this new civic status was intended to be inclusive, and the State thus became the key reference point for the life of the entire national community. This process involved the construction of an abstract, egalitarian notion of subjectivity, one that freed people from the bonds held in place by previously existing customary regimes, as well from religiously imposed status. As

[4] Full citation: "Deep-seated preferences can not be argued about - you can not argue a man into liking a glass of beer - and therefore, when differences are sufficiently far reaching, we try to kill the other man rather than let him have his way. But that is perfectly consistent with admitting that, so far as appears, his grounds are just as good as ours." (Holmes 1918).

[5] As far as Europe is concerned, a new concept of citizenship is emerging at the European level, the implications of which are still to be fully worked out.

it often happens with major change, this too turned out to be a mixed blessing (Macdonald 2005).[6]

Detaching law from everyday life to justify the equal treatment of subjects whose life trajectories would otherwise be governed by the accidents of birth or belonging, also meant separating people from their traditional sites and modes of symbolic interaction. As a consequence, this new form of legality - sanctioned by the State - was rather distant from the life experience of communities and individuals. State centred legality denied that the overlapping communities, in which people live their lives as children, parents, spouses, neighbours, workers, etc., are sites rich with normativity, in which personal identities are discovered, negotiated, ordered and reordered. This can only be perceived by individuals as paradoxical given the centrality of the experience gained in those communities for the realisation of personal autonomy (Macdonald 2005). Religious fundamentalism can be understood as an extreme reaction to this state of affairs, purporting, as it does, to impose an idealised model of society that should be governed as if civic bonds did not exist. It is not by chance that some scholars argue that fundamentalism originates in urban, rather than in rural ambiences, because it explodes as a consequence of contact with modernity (Ozzano 2014).

Much time has gone by since the realisation of the constitutional project that led modern democracies to adopt and extol that notion of civil subjectivity. The assimilationist model that backed up the original idea of a national citizenship has softened over the past few decades. It has been rendered more inclusive by mellowing the reference to dominant social values that it implicitly endorsed - a case in point is the evolution of blasphemy laws in modern democracies - and by opening it up to diversity. Recognition granted to minority groups and subordinated identities now takes a variety of forms, from the purely symbolic - such as an apology for past crimes or wrongs, gay pride parades, etc. etc.- to more inclusive policies formulated in terms of reasonable accommodation for practices required by religious beliefs (Bribosia et al. 2013; Alidadi et al. 2012). But the State centred model of legality that is connected to the rise of the nation state has hardly been challenged as far as its core mechanism is concerned. State centred legality still tends to deny the overlapping communities in which people live their lives and in which personal identities take shape, the nature of competing normative communities. For the State those social sites cannot generate competing legal regimes, therefore the order which provides structure to these social spheres is represented by the State in terms of "brute" or "mute" facts (Macdonald 2005). The State may establish coordination mechanisms with those alternative sources of normativity, but this is not to be taken for granted, and for good reason. The strategy of fostering a notion of citizenship based on a very selective approach to the construction of citizens' national identities was considered to be the most inclusive strategy that public institutions could follow at the time. Reluctance to change this model is not too surprising, and should not be

[6] In the history of political thought, Tocqueville's analysis of democracy points to the same conclusion highlighted above: Jaume (2014).

confounded with recent moves such as the enactment of anti-sharia laws, which are the expression of an entirely different political inspiration.

In our epoch this classic model is challenged by the open recognition that a monist notion of legality is not really all we have, even in countries that have traditionally adhered to it.

The dynamics of the law both within State borders and beyond them at the international level, highlight the unmaking of the strong notion of sovereignty, cast light on a renewed interest in legal pluralism at all levels of analysis (see the contribution of Turner 2016, Chap. 4 in this volume; on pluralism on a global scale: Berman 2012; Michaels 2009). In this context, State courts may silently acknowledge the need to coordinate their jurisdiction with that of alternative adjudicatory bodies: if justice is best served by a collaborative approach, implicit recognition of the existence of alternative fora may be the rule of the game. On the other hand, the decline of sovereignty, and the rise of legal pluralism as a form of legality in highly complex democratic societies and at the international level, has not ended the debate over what legal pluralism brings in modern contemporary democracies.

The essays in this collection cast light on this changing landscape, as far as religious norms are concerned, and I do not need to say more on the point. I would rather insist on a point that is all too often neglected in these debates, namely that State legality itself, although often presented as monolithic, is actually rather porous and malleable, being the result of a complex set of social forces, checks and balances, discretions, habits, and values often pointing in different directions. Every lawyer will quickly admit this when considering the wavering of legislatures over controversial and divisive issues, the manifestation of bureaucratic discretions, or judicial dissent linked to different judicial ideologies in difficult and not so difficult cases. State law is in itself a mishmash of very different things.[7]

Captured through the lenses of legal pluralism, State law is not stable, it is constantly made and unmade, it is not self-contained and it is subject to centre-periphery tensions. What is true in Texas may not be true in Massachusetts, and what holds in Jerusalem may be rejected in Tel Aviv. The credibility of State law owes much to the fact that of all the organisations on a certain territory, the State is usually - but not always - the actor with the most resources at its disposal. Nonetheless, when called to operate in conflict-ridden contexts, State officials know that State law, from which their authority stems, has no monopoly of normativity. Rather, as it has been aptly said, it is "...nothing more, and nothing less, than a hypothesis about social life." (Macdonald 2005; Nichols 2015).

6. - Once these points are clarified, the question of how equality should be reconciled with the plurality of identities and competing normativities that exist in society beyond the realm of State law remains open. Legal pluralism as a theory, or as a set of theories, does not necessarily address how diversity can be turned into a resource for individuals and for society as a whole, rather than becoming a cause of fragmentation and anomie. That said it would be an exaggeration to claim that this

[7]The point is well put by Ramsted's contribution Chap. 3 in this volume: "Western law does not constitute universal law, *not even in Western societies*." (emphasis added).

is unchartered territory. By now we know that the State's pretence to rank personal identities, to model them, and to decide in favour of one identity over another, is nothing but a bet on the lasting validity of dominant values and social orientations. In the worst-case scenario, it is a recipe for tragedy, which will materialise when dominant values and social orientations are imposed on people thorough violence. We also know that no catalogue of rights can hope to capture the constant evolution and destruction of identity claims through which agency is asserted in society. A table of values and prescriptions set in stone will not stop change, evolution, and differentiation in society. Personal autonomy and free consent as the rules of the game may be resisted in the name of a secular ideology, or religious beliefs, and they do not necessarily favour social cohesion.

How to address the riddles that are posed by the paradoxical juxtaposition of equality and diversity?

One possibility is to reconsider the role of the State by highlighting that the equality discourse was initiated to cater for increased diversity and inclusion, rather than to enforce exclusion and uniformity. By embracing that principle, the State abandoned policies leading to religious persecutions, forced deportation, oppression of minorities and so on. Equality therefore does not need to be the enemy of diversity. Equality was once the surrogate catchword for more diversity and less exclusion, and to an extent it still is (see Foblets et al. 2014). If new identities introduce more diversity in the public space, this dynamic should not automatically be labelled as an attempt to undermine equality, or the possibility of civic coexistence. Social life becomes troublesome only when one social group is perceived by the others as an obstacle to achieving their own goals. In that case, each group will dislike the other, devalue them and reject the idea of collaborating with them, assuming to have nothing in common with them (Kessler and Mummendey 2008).

Under a naive form of social theory, one would think that individual attitudes determine social interactions among groups. Social psychology shows instead that attitudes towards "the others" are determined by the conditions of group interdependence and interaction, which may be negative or positive (Sherif 1966). Even groups that initially share homogeneous features may end up displaying prejudice and hostility as they interact in a competitive setting (for a review of the literature: Hewstone et al. 2008: 293 ff.). Perhaps, the most startling discovery made by social psychologists was that classifying individuals into arbitrary distinct social categories was sufficient enough to produce in-group–out-group discrimination and bias although they did not share a history of competition or conflict between them (Tajfel et al. 1971; see also Rabbie and Horwitz 1969). Changing the conditions of interdependence and turning negative interdependence into positive interdependency is a way of unlocking prosocial, collaborative behaviour if all groups in society are accorded equal status and are not set in competition one against the others (Allport 1954; Pettigrew and Tropp 2006). One way of establishing positive interdependency is by creating superordinate goals that may unite groups that have otherwise an incentive to compete one against the other (Deschamps and Brown 1983).

One can hope to forge new loyalties to overcome the tendency of social groups to discriminate out-groups also by exploring the notion that social life today takes place in a variety of arenas, facilitating contacts and intersections of various groups that shape the self and self perception in different ways, which would make the most of their positive distinctiveness and mutual superiority across various dimensions (Hewston and Brown 1986; Brown and Hewstone 2005). Another finding by social psychologists illuminates the dynamics of group conflict, namely so-called discontinuity effect. In the presence of a conflict over scarce resources, the competitiveness displayed when individuals interact with other individuals is less intense than the competiveness displayed among groups. This is because the willingness to collaborate at the individual level may be overshadowed by the competitive orientation of a group driven by factors that psychologist are still exploring (Wildschut and Insko 2007).

On the other hand, the dynamics of identity building across social boundaries make it clear that cultural variation happens along a continuous rather than discontinuous line, and that the ecology of the ambience in which an individual or a group operates shapes it, as anthropology and political science show (Barth 1998; Ozzano 2009). Evidence from the legal field, relating in particular to patterns of litigation over wealth distribution upon the dissolution of marriage confirms this observation (Fournier 2010).

Research in the field of social psychology and anthropology thus introduces new ways to understand the dynamics of social conflicts. The theories developed in those fields speak more generally about the limits of the law in addressing problems concerning the coexistence of religious and State norms.

One last reflection concerns the role of political parties and/or movements claiming a religious identity in the making of laws. The literature on law and religion seldom covers this aspect, but political scientists pay attention to it (Ozzano and Cavatorta 2014). The main question is whether the inclusion of radical religious parties in political games contributes to moderation of their discourses and their initiatives, or not. The arguments favouring inclusion of these parties in the representative system, so that they may shift towards moderate positions that are compatible with democratic regimes, rely on a number of factors. The extremist party that participates in the political game is bound to accept political diversity in the first place, and to dilute its ideology to attract outside voters. If a radical party is power-driven, it is also likely to rely on alliances with parties that do not share its extremism whenever absolute majority is not in sight. Lastly, while extremist parties may develop ideas from ideological social movements obsessed with doctrinal purity, the step from niche to mass party usually brings about emancipation from them. The empirical testing of this hypothesis returns a mixed picture, however. Although there are examples confirming the hypothesis, research shows that inclusion of radical political parties in parliamentary regimes does not always result in a stable moderate approach (Jaffrelot 2014), while their exclusion from the political game can sometimes produce moderation (Cavatorta and Merone 2014).

Conclusions

Contemporary democracies are open to cultural diversity, but have problems when prevailing values and norms are questioned in the name of religious or cultural beliefs and practices. In many Western liberal democracies, legal pluralism is high on the agenda of law and religion scholars because State centred legality fails to do justice to the complexity of social interactions. Legal pluralism provides the intellectual tools to understand how cultural identities, including religious identities, are shaped in different sites in society.

Nonetheless, legal pluralism provides no direct and clear answer to the question of how social order respecting equality can be upheld under democratic constitutions. Pluralism as such does not guarantee that coexistence among people who form different groups shall be sustained by prosocial attitudes, rather than undermined by conflict. Social psychology, cultural anthropology and political science investigate how those attitudes can be fostered.

This chapter argues that to understand and govern the tensions generated by the intersection of state norms and religious norms, the law should benefit from the insights about human behaviour in society that these disciplines provide as well.

References

Alidadi, Katayoun, Marie-Claire Foblets, and Vrielink Jogchum (eds.). 2012. *A test of faith? Religious diversity and accommodation in the European workplace*. Farnham: Ashgate.

Allport, Gordon W. 1954. *The nature of prejudice*. Cambridge, MA: Addison-Wesley Pub. Co.

Avalos, Hector. 2005. *Fighting words: The origins of religious violence*. Amherst: Prometheus Books.

Avalos, Hector. 2012. Religion and scarcity: A new theory for the role of religion in violence. In *The Oxford handbook of religion and violence*, ed. Michael Jerryson, Mark Juergensmeyer, and Margo Kitts, 554–570. Oxford: Oxford University Press.

Barth, Fredrik. 1998. Introduction. In *Ethnic groups and boundaries: The social organization of culture difference*, ed. Fredrik Barth. Long Grove: Waveland Press.

Berman, Paul Schiff. 2012. *Global legal pluralism*. Cambridge: Cambridge University Press.

Bodin, Jean. 1962. *The six bookes of a commonweal*, ed. K. D. McRae. Cambridge: Harvard University Press.

Brown, Rupert, and Miles Hewstone. 2005. An integrative theory of intergroup contact. In *Advances in experimental social psychology*, vol. 37, ed. Mark P. Zanna, 255–343. San Diego: Academic.

Bribosia, Emmanuelle, Isabelle Rorive, and Lisa Waddington. 2013. *Reasonable accommodation beyond disability in Europe?* Brussels: European Union.

Cavatorta, Francesco, and Fabio Merone. 2014. Moderation through exclusion? The journey of the Tunisian *Ennahda* from fundamentalist to conservative party. In *Religiously oriented parties and democratization*, ed. Francesco Cavatorta and Luca Ozzano, 857–875. Abingdon: Routledge.

Cavanaugh, William T. 2009. *The myth of religious violence: Secular ideology and the roots of modern conflict*. Oxford: Oxford University Press.

Deschamps, Jean-Claude, and Rupert Brown. 1983. Superordinate goals and intergroup conflict. *British Journal of Social Psychology* 22: 189–195. doi:10.1111/j.2044-8309.1983.tb00583.x.

Durham Jr., W. Cole, Silvio Ferrari, Cristina Cianitto, and Thayer Donlu (eds.). 2013. *Law, religion, constitution: Freedom of religion, equal treatment, and the law*. Farnham: Ashgate.

Ferrari, Silvio (ed.). 2015. *Routledge handbook of law and religion*. London: Routledge.

Ferrari, Alessandro, and Sabrina Pastorelli (eds.). 2013. *The Burqua affair across Europe: Between public and private space*. Farnham: Ashgate.

Foblets, Marie-Claire, Michele Graziadei, and Jacques Vanderlinden (eds.). 2010. *Convictions philosophiques et religieuses et droits positifs. Textes présentés au Colloque international de Moncton (24–27 août 2008)*. Bruxelles: Bruylant.

Foblets, Marie-Claire, Katayoun Alidadi, Jørgen S. Nielsen, and Zeynep Yanasmayan (eds.). 2014. *Belief, law and politics: What future for a secular Europe?* Farnham: Ashgate.

Fournier, Pascale. 2010. *Muslim marriage in Western Courts: Lost in transplantation*. Farnham: Ashgate.

Galen, Luke W. 2012a. The complex and elusive nature of religious prosociality: Reply to Myers and Saroglou. *Psychological Bulletin* 138: 918–23. doi:10.1037/a0029278.

Galen, Luke W. 2012b. Does religious belief promote prosociality? A critical examination. *Psychological Bulletin* 138: 876–906. doi:10.1037/a0028251.

Habermas, Jürgen. 2008. Religion in the public sphere: Cognitive presuppositions for the public use of reason by religious and secular citizens. In *Between naturalism and religion: Political essays*, ed. Jürgen Habermas, 114–148. Cambridge: Polity Press.

Hewston, Michael, and Rupert Brown. 1986. Contact is not enough: An intergroup perspective on the "contact hypothesis.". In *Contact and conflict in intergroup encounters*, ed. Michael Hewstone and Rupert Brown, 1–44. Oxford: Blackwell.

Hewstone, Miles, et al. 2008. *Introduction to social psychology: A European perspective*. Oxford: Blackwell Publishing Ltd.

Hobbes, Thomas. 1986. *Leviathan*. Harmondsworth: Penguin.

Hobbes, Thomas. 1990. *Behemoth or the long Parliament*. Chicago: The University of Chicago Press.

Holmes, Oliver Wendell. 1918. Natural law. *Harvard Law Review* 32: 40.

Holmes, Stephen. 1995. *Passions and constraints: On the theory of liberal democracy*. Chicago/London: The University of Chicago Press.

Jaffrelot, Christophe. 2014. Refining the moderation thesis. Two religious parties and Indian democracy: The Jana Sangh and the BJP between Hindutva radicalism and coalition politics. In *Religiously oriented parties and democratization*, ed. Francesco Cavatorta and Luca Ozzano, 876–894. Abingdon: Routledge.

Jaume, Lucien. 2014. *Tocqueville: The aristocratic sources of liberty*. Princeton: Princeton University Press.

Jerryson, Michael, Mark Juergensmeyer, and Margo Kitts (eds.). 2012. *The Oxford handbook of religion and violence*. Oxford: Oxford University Press.

Kessler, Thomas, and Amélie Mummendey. 2008. Prejudice and intergroup relations. In *Introduction to social psychology: A European perspective*, ed. Hewstone Miles, Stroebe Wolfgang, and Jonas Klaus. Oxford: Blackwell Publishing Ltd.

Lloyd, S.A. 1992. *Ideals as interests in Hobbes's Leviathan: The power of mind over matter*. Cambridge: Cambridge University Press.

Macdonald, Roderick A. 2005. Legal republicanism and legal pluralism. In *Human diversity and the law*, ed. Mauro Bussani and Michele Graziadei, 43–70. Brussels: Bruylant.

Michaels, Ralf. 2009. Global legal pluralism. *Annual Review of Law & Social Science* 5: 243–262.

Nichols, Joel A. 2015. Religion, family law, and competing norms. In *Negotiating state and non-state law: The challenge of global and local legal pluralism*, ed. Michael A. Helfand, 197–214. Cambridge: Cambridge University Press.

Oakes, Guy. 2003. Max Weber on value rationality and value spheres: Critical remarks. *Journal of Classical Sociology* 3: 28–45.

Olson, Mancur. 1963. Rapid growth as a destabilizing force. *Journal of Economic History* 23: 529–552.

Ozzano, Luca. 2009. A political science perspective on religious fundamentalism. *Totalitarian Movements and Political Religions* 10: 339–359. doi:10.1080/14690760903454341.

Ozzano, Luca. 2014. The paradox of the female participation in fundamentalist movements. *Partecipazione e conflitto* 7: 14–34. doi:10.1285/i20356609v7i1p14.

Ozzano, Luca, and Francesco Cavatorta. 2014. Introduction: Religiously oriented parties and democratization. In *Religiously oriented parties and democratization*, ed. Cavatorta Francesco and Ozzano Luca, 799–806. Abingdon Oxon: Routledge.

Parolin, Gianluca. 2009. *Citizenship in the Arab World: Kin, religion and nation-state*. Amsterdam: Amsterdam University Press.

Parolin, Gianluca. 2014. Equality before the law (in Classical Islamic Law). In *The Ashgate research companion to Islamic law*, ed. Peri Bearman And Rudolph Peters, 123–36. Farnham: Ashgate.

Pettigrew, Thomas F., and Linda R. Tropp. 2006. A meta-analytic test of intergroup contact theory. *Journal of Personality and Social Psychology* 90: 751–783.

Rabbie, Jacob M., and Murray Horwitz. 1969. Arousal of ingroup-outgroup bias by a chance win or loss. *Journal of Personality and Social Psychology* 13: 269–277.

Segzin, Yüksel. 2013. *Human rights under state-enforced religious family laws in Israel, Egypt and India*. Cambridge: Cambridge University Press.

Shah, Prakash, Marie-Claire Foblets, and Rohe Mathias (eds.). 2014. *Family, religion and law: Cultural encounters in Europe*. Farnham: Ashgate.

Sherif, Muzafer. 1966. *In common predicament: Social psychology of intergroup conflict and cooperation*. Boston: Houghton Mifflin.

Tajfel, Henri, M.G. Billig, R.P. Bundy, and Claude Flament. 1971. Social categorization and intergroup behaviour. *European Journal of Social Psychology* 1: 149–77.

Wildschut, Tim, and Chester A. Insko. 2007. Explanations of interindividual-intergroup discontinuity: A review of the evidence. *European Review of Social Psychology* 18: 175–211.

Chapter 3
Anthropological Perspectives on the Normative and Institutional Recognition of Religion by the Law of the State

Martin Ramstedt

Abstract The negative effects of economic globalisation and the emergence of a host of post-Cold War political crises, accompanied by a drastic increase of global migration, have in many parts of the world, including the US, Canada, and Europe, spurred social movements lobbying for some or greater normative and institutional recognition of religion by the law of the state. Arguing that the resultant new religion-based legal pluralism must be theorised in the light of the increasing colonisation of the life-world by law (Habermas), I then discuss the different positions scholars have taken in the trans-disciplinary debate on "legal pluralism" since the late 1950s. In the course of this chapter, I seek to make three additional points: (1) once religious norms are accommodated in state law, they usually undergo a significant degree of transformation; (2) the term "law" should be reserved for state law only, not to obfuscate the hegemonic claim of the state and of the international community of nation states in the competition between different normativities; and (3) the common blackboxing of the category of "religion" by law-makers and scholars of "legal pluralism" alike has abetted the obscuration of the unequal treatment of religious communities in many countries.

Introduction

The increasing normative and institutional recognition (Woodman 2012: 137) of "religion" and other non-state forms of normative ordering in the law of many states today has yielded what the American legal anthropologist Sally E. Merry, in her seminal article, "Legal Pluralism", called the "new legal pluralism" paradigm (Merry 1988). She contrasted the latter with the classical legal pluralism research carried out in colonial and postcolonial societies.

M. Ramstedt (✉)
Max Planck Institute for Social Anthropology, Halle, Germany
e-mail: ramstedt108@gmail.com

R. Bottoni et al. (eds.), *Religious Rules, State Law, and Normative Pluralism - A Comparative Overview*, Ius Comparatum – Global Studies in Comparative Law 18, DOI 10.1007/978-3-319-28335-7_3

A poignant example for classical legal pluralism is the Ottoman *millet*-system,[1] a flexible governance framework designed to accommodate the heterogeneity of the multi-religious population of the Ottoman Empire, stretching over Europe, Africa, and Asia (Yetisgin 2007: 138–139). *Millet*-status was granted to three major non-Muslim religious groups (the Greek Orthodox, the Jewish, and the Gregorian Armenian), who were placed under the direct authority of the heads of their respective religious communities. The validity of their respective laws remained circumscribed, though, by both Islamic and customary law. In cases of inter-legal conflicts, it was Islamic law that took precedence (Yetisgin 2007: 141–143, 146–149). The *millet*-system remained in place until the Ottoman Empire's protracted demise in the wake of the "Young Turk Revolution", the Balkan Wars, World War I and the emergence of the Turkish national movement (see e.g. Kinross 1999: 27–159, 524–527). It has continued in a modified form, however, in present-day Israel, where fourteen religious communities are granted exclusive jurisdiction over matters of marriage and divorce as well as concurrent jurisdiction with Israel's civil courts over matters of maintenance and inheritance (Sezgin 2010: 631–633, 636, 654).

"New legal pluralism", so Merry, directs its attention to "noncolonized societies, particularly to the advanced industrial countries of Europe and the United States" (Merry 1988: 872), where legal pluralism has sprung from global migration. New legal pluralism research would no longer center upon intersections between indigenous and European law, like the older paradigm had. Instead, it would conceptualize "a more complex and interactive relationship between official and unofficial forms of ordering" (Merry 1988: 873). In advanced industrial societies, non-state forms of normative ordering would be more difficult to see precisely because of their interconnectedness with the law of the state (Merry 1988: 880; see also Griffiths 1985: 17–18). The task would hence be to describe "the way state law penetrates and restructures other normative orders through symbols and through direct coercion and, at the same time, the way nonstate normative orders resist and circumvent penetration or even capture and use symbolic capital of state law" (Merry 1988: 881).

The new legal pluralism research of the past thirty years has very much followed this line of inquiry. Firmly grounded in ethnographic fieldwork and closely interacting with other academic sub-disciplines, above all the sociology of law, legal geography, critical legal studies, and increasingly also religious studies, anthropological new legal pluralism research has been carried out in Western as well as modern Asian and African countries. For, recent global migration waves and other influences have affected all contemporary societies. The resultant insights challenge us to inquire more deeply into the stark data of the national reports in this volume. I will commence my own account with the proposition that the new global legal pluralism is an effect of increasing juridification. Here, attention will be drawn to the fact that juridification is not only driven by state agents. Various social movements

[1] "*Millet*" means "nation". However, in the Ottoman Empire, "*millet*" did not refer to an ethnically defined nation. In contrast to the Muslim subjects of the Ottoman sultan, who constituted the "*umma*", "*millet*" exclusively referred to specific non-Muslim communities.

have likewise stimulated the expansion of state law to other semi-autonomous social fields, such as the family, business, or, for that matter, religion (Bourdieu 1971; Bourdieu 1987; Moore 1972). As a result, the semi-autonomous social fields have become more juridified, while state law itself has "internally pluralized" (Fitzpatrick 1984).

Conversely, many disputes today are managed through transposition into non-legal social fields. The American anthropologist Thomas Csordas, for instance, related the therapeutic resolution of a dispute between a member of the Native American Church (NAC) and her non-Native American co-workers in the setting of a NAC healing ritual, in which the entheogen peyote was being used in a sacramental fashion (Csordas 2013: 19–23; see also Cookson 2001: 34). And Csordas colleague Ziad Munson showed how the pro-life movement in the United States has consciously engaged the therapeutic field, thereby supplementing their successful instigation of a host of new anti-abortion legislation with non-legal strategies. Activists have established some 2900 crisis pregnant centers (CPCs) throughout the country, in which they have been educating and persuading a raft of pregnant women to prevent abortion (Munson 2013: 37–39). In that fashion the pro-life movement has been able to draw in a large part of its recruits from people outside established constituencies (Munson 2008: 5–6).

These cases highlight the frequent entanglement of a plurality of normative systems, which are sometimes so enmeshed with each other that it is difficult, and indeed meaningless, to differentiate them out in analysis (Benda-Beckmann et al. 2013: ix–x). This is why the projection of narrow categories, such as "law", "religion" or, for that matter, "culture", onto entangled normativities often leads to arbitrary results, which frequently support politics rather than science. The problem is, where to draw the boundaries between the different normativities, so as to distinguish between legal, religious and cultural ones? After having delved more deeply into how new legal pluralism is an effect of juridification, I will pursue this issue in more detail, by discussing relevant anthropological positions that have been proposed since the late 1950s until today. Subsequently, I will zoom in on two major issues usually discussed in connection with new legal pluralism: the unequal treatment of religions and access to justice and its effects in states with plural legal orders. I will conclude this essay, by supporting Paul Schiff Berman's argument that in order to understand the different constellations of legal pluralism today, we need to extend our range of inquiry far beyond black letter law.

In his introduction to this volume, Silvio Ferrari posed the salient question, "What can be done by each legal system to give citizens the opportunity to live according to their religious convictions without endangering social cohesion and fostering auto-segregation?" Let me take this question as point of departure for my discussion of anthropology's take on new legal pluralism in societies of both the Global North and the Global South. Silvio's question first of all attests to a positive view of law as a tool of social engineering, and to a confidence in the power of state law to grant or prevent its citizens to live according to their religious convictions. This positive view of, and confidence in, law has continuously driven juridification efforts by states and international corporations that have occurred in tandem with globalization. The German legal sociologist Gunther Teubner, however, reminded us that, whereas some legal scholars have indeed seen juridification as the hallmark of constitutional democracy and the triumph of the rule of law over despotism, others have criticized juridification for its destruction of self-reproducing life-worlds, and hence for the very thing it has been designed against, social disintegration (Teubner 1987: 24–25, 33–35). He also pointed to a myriad of unintended dysfunctional problems resulting from juridification (Teubner 1987: 19–22). One of these unintended problems has arguably been the worldwide acceleration of legal pluralism (Teubner 1987: 6–7). In other words, the pervasiveness of legal pluralism, including religion-based legal pluralism, in our world today might be seen as an effect of accelerated juridification, which, if we want to follow the anthropologists John L. Comaroff and Jean Comaroff, must again be attributed to the hegemony of neoliberalism and its "hyper-extended, often counter-intuitive deployment of legalities in the social, geographical, political, moral and material reconstruction of our world" (Comaroff and Comaroff 2009: 31–32).

Social Movements as Agents of Juridification

The Comaroffs, in their work, have paid particular attention to the continuous use, by states, of "penal powers, administrative procedures, states of emergency, mandates and warrants to discipline [their] subjects by means of violence", or, in their parlance, "lawfare" (Comaroff and Comaroff 2009: 36–37). However, states have not been the only agents of juridification. The various social movements that have emerged in the modern nation states both of the Global North and the Global South throughout the twentieth century until the present day—the civil rights movement, women's lib, labor movements, the gay movement, environmentalism, animal rights activism, the indigenous peoples movement, Occupy, and, not to forget, religionist ones, like the Khomeini Revolution, the Christian Right, the Saffron Revolution, etc., claiming new rights, responding to threats or violence, seeking political emancipation and gains, promoting or opposing lifestyle choices, and so forth (Goodwin and Jasper 2009: pos. 542–552)—have equally stimulated what could be described as a bottom-up transposition of political struggle to the legal domain, which Teubner called the instrumentalization of law for political ends (Teubner 1987: 7–10).

German anthropologist Julia Eckert, for example, observed that, in India, the use of law has increasingly supplemented or even replaced other strategies of counter-politics (Eckert 2006: 45–49, 53–54, 56). She particularly referred to the use of legal terms in protests against corrupt civil servants and other authorities in India. Here, law would serve as "the weapon of the weak". Eckert furthermore argued that the increasing mobilization of law from below has resulted in the fact that "Today, all non-state [i.e., Hindu, Muslim, caste, customary; M.R.] forums of adjudication apply an amalgamated type of law that is strongly shaped by situational interpretations of state law" (Eckert 2006: 48). It would thus be justified, she said, to speak of a homogenization of the legal sphere(s) in India, at least at the normative level, if not at the level of procedure (Eckert 2006: 71), even though the already extant pluralism of judicial authority has been simultaneously enhanced by NGOs, local strongmen, and so forth (Eckert 2006: 47–49). A similar trend can be observed in Indonesia, where widespread social protest against a corrupt civil service prompted the issuance of a number of anti-corruption laws between 1999 and 2009 (Bunjamin et al. 2012). Moreover, the pervasive and longstanding distrust of the corrupt judicial system has continuously led segments of present-day Indonesian society to call for the normative and institutional recognition of Islam, and, for that matter, customary law, even though complaints about graft at Indonesia's Islamic courts have become louder (Ramstedt 2012: 1–7).

While many social movements strive for the recognition of certain norms and institutions within state law, some critics do fear the corruption of their norms, practices and institutions through juridification. Anthropological research has indeed shown "that in the use of law, law transforms those who use it, their understanding of the world, of their conflicts and their normative orientations" (Eckert et al. 2012: 1). This point has long been central to the Sudanese jurist Abdullahi A. An-Na'im's argument in favor of secularism. In his book, *Islam and the Secular State*, he reasoned that, precisely because the juridification of Shari'a norms makes them obligatory, the free choice of Muslims to comply, which is foundational for the religiosity of Islam, would be taken away. When the Shari'a derives its legitimacy from the state and its coercive power, and not any longer from revelation, religion would turn into a political tool of the state, thus losing its sanctity together with its potential for promoting ethical values through personal pious intention (An-Na'im 2008: 1–7, 232, 250, 268, 282).

Similarly, when customary law principles are accommodated in state law, they usually undergo a significant degree of transformation. A case in point is the integration of the concept of "*sumak kawsay*" (Kichwa for "good living") in the Preamble of Ecuador's Constitution from 2008, brought about by sustained intervention of the Confederation of the Indigenous Nations of Ecuador (*Confederación de Nacionalidades Indígenas del Ecuador*, *CONAIE*): "We are determined to create a new form of civic living together in diversity and harmony with nature, in order to attain a good living, the *sumak kawsay*".[2] While the Preamble lacks an elaborate definition of what "good living" entails, there are several articles throughout the Constitution that refer back to *sumak kawsay*. They interpret the concept as protection of the ecosystems of the world, particularly of the provinces of the Amazonas; as integrated, organized, sustainable and dynamic development of the economic, political, socio-cultural and environmental systems; and as the promotion of scientific and technological knowledge alongside that of the forefathers.[3] Only one article

[2] Decidimos construir una nueva forma de convivencia ciudana, en diversidad y armonía con la naturaleza, para alcanzar el buen vivir, el sumak kawsay"(my translation), http://www.cicad.oas.org/fortalecimiento_institucional/legislations/PDF/EC/constitucion.pdf; accessed May 2015.

[3] See http://www.cicad.oas.org/fortalecimiento_institucional/legislations/PDF/EC/constitucion.pdfon.pdf; accessed May 2015.

gives us some inkling that *sumak kawsay* is rooted in an indigenous cosmology and its associated spirituality, stipulating that "Nature or Pachamama, where life is reproduced and realized, has the right to full respect for its existence and maintenance and the regeneration of its natural cycles, structure, function and evolutionary processes" (Radcliffe 2012: 244; see also Cortez and Wagner 2010: 167–168). In the legal discourse of Ecuador, *sumak kawsay* has thus been largely reduced to environmentalist concerns, thus losing not only its link with the respective indigenous cosmologies it has sprung from, but also its rootedness in indigenous institutions and hence its authority as customary law, applicable to perpetrations of men. In order to recognize *sumak kawsay* as the "law" of its indigenous peoples, the government of Ecuador would have to devolve judicial authority to indigenous institutions and to recognize their practices as "due process". Instead, the juridification of *sumak kawsay* transformed it into a token of political reform.

In order to counteract such reductive legal accommodation of indigenous normative systems, the Australian Aborigine lawyer and activist Christine F. Black offered her book, *The Land is the Source of the Law: A Dialogic Encounter with Indigenous Jurisprudence*, from 2011 "as an alternative legal reading for Indigenous peoples to explore and consider their own culture's legal theory" (Black 2011: 12). Indigenous jurisprudence and law comes in a somewhat different guise than modern state law here. Instead of a constitution, you have a cosmology, instead of laws, you have "law stories", instead of a court, you have a camp, and instead of judges, you have "senior law men and women" (Black 2011: 11–19, et passim).

What Is "Legal Pluralism"?

In 1998, i.e., in the midst of the heated trans-disciplinary debate on the validity of the anthropological concept of "legal pluralism", the American anthropologist Mark R. Goodale resuscitated the pertinent work on "legal levels" by Leopold J. Pospisil, a Czech jurist-cum-anthropologist and legal pluralism scholar working in the United States. In the mid-1950s, Pospisil had departed to Dutch New Guinea in order to carry out his PhD research on the law and economy of the Kapauku Papuans (Goodale 1998: 123–125). In the monograph resultant from this research, which was published in 1958, as well as in later publications, he inter alia proposed the existence of a multiplicity of legal levels, that is to say, the existence of discrete legal systems corresponding to the different subgroups, that is, autonomous and semi-autonomous groups, within a given society (Pospisil 1967: 8). He further argued that, because each member of a given society usually belongs to more subgroups than just one, he or she would be subject to multiple and sometimes contradictory legalities (Pospisil 1958: 273–278, 289; Pospisil 1967: 2–3, 7–9, 14–15, 24–25; see also Goodale 1998: 126–128).

Pospisil received the most valid criticism from Sally Falk Moore, the Grande Dame of legal anthropology who inter alia served as American staff attorney at the International Military Tribunal at Nuremberg. Moore's strongest reservation towards Pospisil's theory of legal layers pertained to Pospisil's assumption of "a rigid pyramidal structure, in which each legal level is nested within ever larger units, with each unit maintaining separate rule-making processes and outputs" (Goodale 1998: 130–131; see also Moore 1978: 24). In her seminal article, "Law and Social Change: the Semi-Autonomous Social Field as Appropriate Subject of Study", she proposed instead "that an inspection of semi-autonomous social fields strongly suggests that the various processes that make internally generated rules effective are often also the immediate forces that dictate the mode of compliance or noncompliance to state-made legal rules" (Moore 1972: 721). In other words, the different normativities generated in the various social fields—religion, business, law, education, and others—impact on and interact with each other, to the extent that they may impede, block out, neutralize, or reinforce each other. This is precisely why social fields in contemporary societies can usually at best be called "semi-autonomous", as both complete autonomy and complete dominion are rare. Moreover, some rules are generated within the different social fields, others through and in the interplay between the different normativities. This kind of dynamic normative pluralism seems to drive, if we understand Moore correctly, social change as well as social differentiation (Moore 1972: 728–729, 742–745; see also Ramstedt 2015: 48).

Taking these dynamics into account, American Professor of Legal Sociology at the University of Groningen, the Netherlands, John Griffiths, in his programmatic article, "What is Legal Pluralism?", from 1986, in turn departed from the notion that all modes of self-regulation within a semi-autonomous field can be more or less called "law" (Griffiths 1986: 38–39). Consequently, he defined "legal pluralism" as the co-presence of more than one "legal order" in one and the same social field (GriffithS 1986: 1). We have to note here that it was Griffiths' subsumption of all normative orders under the category of "the legal" that the American jurist and law and society scholar Brian Z. Tamanaha would, to my mind rightly, target in his detailed criticism of the legal pluralist paradigm seven years later. Griffiths, for his part, further introduced a conceptual distinction still current today, namely the distinction between "strong legal pluralism" on the one hand, and "weak legal pluralism" on the other. He spoke of "strong legal pluralism" in case where state law co-exists with non-state law. The term "weak pluralism" in turn applied in cases where legal pluralism is seen only as a characteristic of the state legal system (Griffiths 1986: 7–8). Two years later, Merry would reformulate Griffiths' terms as "classical" and "new legal pluralism".

In his seminal article, "Law: A Map of Misreading. Toward a Postmodern Conception of Law", published in 1987, the Portuguese legal sociologist Boaventura De Sousa Santos conceptualized the co-existing and interpenetrating plural normativities of contemporary societies as maps with different scales that all represent "reality" in different ways, that is, according to the unique vantage point inherent in each of the scales. These vantage points can be understood as metaphors for the different political interests, frames, and internal arrangements that are contingent on certain power relations (Sousa Santos 1987: 282–289, 291–292). The related metaphors of maps and scales furthermore imply "multiple networks of legal orders forcing us to constant transitions and trespassings" (Sousa Santos 1987: 298), rather than plural legal layers neatly nested into the overall jurisdiction of the state. De Sousa Santos called the intersection of these different legal orders "interlegality", which he defined as "the phenomenological counterpart of legal pluralism" (Sousa Santos 1987: 298).

Directly building on De Sousa Santos' plea for the importance of scales with respect to legal orders, Canadian law and society scholar Mariana Valverde argued against the widespread blackboxing of the scalar differences between jurisdictions. She, moreover, turned against an exclusively territorial understanding of jurisdiction, by alerting us to the fact that different temporalities might also be at play in different jurisdictions (Valverde 2008: 3, 5–7, 12; Valverde 2009: 139–142, 144, 151–155).

De Sousa Santos influential article appeared at a time, when the anthropological concept of "legal pluralism" was on the rise within the broader field of socio-legal studies. A few years later, though, a fierce debate broke out among law and society scholars over the validity of the concept. In 1993, Brian Z. Tamanaha published his provocative article, "The Folly of the 'Social Scientific' Concept of Legal Pluralism", in which he criticized this "precociously successful doctrine" (Tamanaha 1993: 192), as already mentioned above, for its subsumption of all kinds of non-legal normativities, ranging from "pockets within state legal systems", such as indigenous norms and institutions, to "the rule-making and enforcing power of social institutions like corporations or universities" under the category of "the legal" (Tamanaha 1993: 193). Tamanaha insisted that the term "law" would thereby lose its distinctive meaning. He furthermore argued that, despite their rejection of an understanding of law as state law, legal pluralists would nevertheless apply state law as the overriding model for the other normativities, which would ironically emphasize rather than deconstruct the Western statist bias inherent in the conventional concept of "law" (Tamanaha 1993: 193–194, 205–206). He finally posed the salient question, still informing anthropological new legal pluralism research today: "how are concrete patterns of social ordering (…) related to the institutional identification and enforcement of norms (…)?" (Tamanaha 1993: 206).

Within the anthropology of law, Tamanaha's position on or, rather, against legal pluralism was vehemently supported by Simon Roberts, British legal anthropologist and specialist of African law, in his article, "Against Legal Pluralism: Some Reflections on the Contemporary Enlargement of the Legal Domain", from 1998 (Roberts 1998). It was the German legal anthropologist Franz von Benda-Beckmann who rose to the defense of the legal pluralism paradigm in 2002. Together with his wife, Dutch legal anthropologist Keebet von Benda-Beckmann, he had just taken the position of Head of the Project Group "Legal Pluralism" at the Max Planck Institute of Social Anthropology in Halle/S., Germany, after having had a career in the Netherlands for almost twenty years. Von Benda-Beckmann can duly be called a scholar of classical legal pluralism, as his research primarily focused on customary law within the interplay between colonial and national state law, Islamic law and customary law in West-Sumatra, Indonesia (see e.g. Benda-Beckmann and Benda-Beckmann 2009, 2012). The increasing normative and institutional recognition of Islam also in West Sumatra over the past decades was of lesser concern to him. In his article, "Who's Afraid of Legal Pluralism?", von Benda-Beckmann departed from the understanding that legal pluralism is a sensitizing concept, "drawing attention to the frequent existence of parallel or duplicatory legal regulations within one political organization" (Benda-Beckmann 2002: 37). He argued for the deployment of "law" in a sociological sense, that is, as the deployment of a kind of Weberian ideal type, with which one would be able to discover "similarity and difference in cross-societal and diachronic comparison" (Benda-Beckmann 2002: 40, 42–45). Moreover, one would have to further inquire as to what extent legal concepts and norms in certain settings have been institutionalized, become mandatory and differentiated from everyday knowledge (Benda-Beckmann 2002: 49–50).

In principle agreeing with von Benda-Beckmann's emphasis of the importance and classificatory demands of comparison, I would nevertheless like to draw attention to Tamanaha's as yet unaddressed contention that state law "is best seen not as a mechanism for maintaining societal normative order, but as an instrument of power in society, available primarily for the elites" (Tamanaha 1993: 211). Even if we take into account the fact that diverse social movements have quite often vied successfully for legislative power in order to push through their various socio-political and socio-cultural agendas, the main thrust of Tamanaha's argument remains unrefuted, due to the fact that it has been highly educated lawyers, hence elites, who have used law against the state in most contemporary social movements.

I therefore plea that the term of "law" exclusively refers to "state law", not in order to fall back on a conservative scholarly position but to emphasize the hegemonic claim of the state and of the international community of nation states in the competition between different normativities. Non-state law in the form of non-juridified customary law and religious law I propose to call "normativities", without denouncing extant claims to legal validity among them. Like many supporters of an inclusive notion of "law", for the most part associated with the Commission of Legal Pluralism, to which among others Griffiths and von Benda-Beckmann belonged, I transpose Max Weber's definition of "law" to a definition of "normative orders". Accordingly, I define "normative orders" as orders guaranteed by the reasonable expectation, informed by experience and observation, on the part of the members of the respective normative communities that these orders will be enforced or infringements avenged by teams of experts responsible with upholding the stability of the respective norms as well as the stability of the social orders rooted in them. Normative orders are furthermore always linked to a shared imagination of how things ought to be, of an ideal state that is in accordance with the particular rationality of the respective normative order.

I furthermore propose a diversified conceptualization of "legal pluralism", taking into account the respective contributions to the "legal pluralism" debate by John Griffiths, Sally E. Merry, Gordon Woodman and Brian Tamanaha. First of all, I argue for the substitution of Griffiths' term of "strong legal pluralism" and Merry's corresponding concept of "classical legal pluralism" with "normative pluralism". I reserve the term "legal pluralism" for two cases only: (a) intra-legal pluralism characterizing the co-existence of different sources of law within a national state law (called "weak legal pluralism" by Griffiths, "new legal pluralism" by Merry, and "state law pluralism" by Woodman); and (b) inter-legal pluralism referring to the co-existence of different interpretations of international legal norms held by different nation states, which are informed by different legal cultures.

More recently, David Delaney, an American protagonist of the interdisciplinary "legal geography" paradigm, came up with theoretical ideas that have resonated with the respective arguments by Pospisil, Moore, and De Souse Santos, even though references to these authors are completely absent in Delaney's work. He inter alia proposed the concept of the "nomosphere" as referring to the spatialization of various normativities that would differ in terms of the content of their norms, their organization, and their scale (Delaney 2004: 851, 855, 858–859; Delaney 2010: 4–5, 8, 15, 24–27). These different normativities would not necessarily be identical with "the legal". Normativities, such as etiquette, custom and ethics, religious rules, familial rules, rules of professional associations, and the like, would rather fall under the category of "the nomic", even though they would be very similar to "law" in that nomic infringements, too, yield social sanctions (Delaney 2010: 27–30). Environments would hence be replete with different nomic traces (Delaney 2010: 71–74), which would frequently conflict and thereby cause nomospheric disturbances (Delaney 2010: 42, 50–58).

Taxonomy and the Unequal Treatment of Religions

Let me now briefly turn to another taxonomic muddle, the common blackboxing of the category of "religion" among scholars of legal pluralism, which has abetted the obscuration of the unequal treatment of those religions not recognized as such in certain societies. A prominent example is the Scientology Church. Whereas in the US Scientology enjoys the status of a tax-exempt religious community, in Germany it is usually regarded as a dangerous "cult", that is, as something almost antithetical to religion, and has since many years been under the surveillance of the Domestic Intelligence Service. Similarly, the Indonesian state has officially recognized six religions (Islam, Protestantism, Catholicism, Hinduism, Buddhism, Confucianism) as "religion proper", while having regarded the country's host of ethnic religions as backward "tradition" or "culture". Since Indonesian citizenship, and hence enjoyment of Indonesian citizen rights, has until today been predicated upon individual affiliation with one of the recognized religious communities, the religious freedom of adherents of ethnic religions has been seriously thwarted (see e.g. Ramstedt 2012: 4, 13–16).

Also elsewhere have indigenous religions experienced blatant discrimination, because mainstream society has failed to regard them as "real religion". A case in point is the continuous infringement of the religious freedom of Native Americans, granted to them by the American Indian Religious Freedom Act of 1978. The Act, which was signed into law by President Jimmy Carter, accords Native Americans, Native Alaskans, and Native Hawaiians "the right to believe, to express, and to practice their native traditional religions" ("Announcements" 1979: 1). Suffice it to mention here that American authorities have nevertheless continued to harass members of the Native American Church for using peyote in their ceremonies (Cookson 2001: 118 et passim), frequently also rejecting claims to access of sacred sites, or keeping the sanctity of sacred sites, and so forth. Strangely enough, the unequal treatment of indigenous religions has remained absent in most works on religion-based legal pluralism in contemporary societies.

It needs to be stressed here that the afore-mentioned problem of taxonomy with regard to the legal recognition of certain religions differs from other hurdles to state recognition. In Germany, for example, in order for non-established religious communities, e.g. Buddhism, to be able to acquire equal rights with the established religions (Roman Catholicism, Lutheranism, and Judaism), the law requires them to prove that their membership is large and in terms of age diversified enough to likely be continuous into the future, and that their tenets of faith and practices are not in opposition to German law. With regard to Buddhism, for example, this necessitates an unusual degree of cooperation between and coordination of the leadership of the different ethnically largely segregated Buddhist schools in Germany, which in their countries of origin have remained rather autonomous until today.

Access to Justice and Its Effects in States with Plural Legal Orders

Finally, I would like to briefly discuss the frequently overlooked issue of access to justice in countries, where the law of the state is characterized by a high degree of normative and institutional recognition of religion, leaving for a moment aside the problem of unequal treatment. With respect to the issue of access to justice, we first have to distinguish between, on the one hand, states, in which citizens have the option to choose between secular and religious institutions to resolve one and the same dispute, and, on the other hand, states, in which citizens are required to file certain cases only with religious courts. As regards the latter, it is important to note that Islamic courts having absolute jurisdiction over marriage, divorce, and inheritance matters need not be a survival of colonialism in a certain country. In Indonesia, for instance, it is only since 2006 that a new law on religious justice obliges Muslim litigants to bring disputes of matters under Islamic jurisdiction solely to Islamic courts. The same law moreover for the first time also grants Islamic courts jurisdictions over disputes involving Islamic economic transactions and Islamic banking (Ramstedt 2012: 20–21). It is quite obvious that this law boosts the fragmentation of Indonesian society along religious lines. This development, it cannot be stressed enough, is spurred to a large extent by recent global developments impacting on a formerly exceedingly religiously tolerant society, rather than being an effect of longstanding structures with roots in the colonial past.

In continental Europe, the angst-ridden notion of parallel societies is in no small measure informed by Dutch experiences. During the period of the pillarization of the Netherlands from the end-nineteenth Century until the mid-1960s, Dutch society was segregated into three large and seemingly irreconcilable ideological pillars (Protestants, Roman Catholics, secular Social-democrats). This period was characterized by the rule of a cartel of elites, cooperating across pillars, and a severe disenfranchisement of the majority of the population (Lijphart 1990: 11). Such a political arrangement is of course completely out of sync with the political worldview of present-day Europe. Some forty years after the beginning of the depillarization of the Dutch, the murder of the Dutch journalist and Islam critic, Theo van Gogh, in 2004, elevated the concept of "parallel society", originally coined by the German Pedagogue Wilhelm Heitmeyer in 1996, to a major xenophobic frame of reference not only in German mainstream discourse (Halm and Sauer 2006: 18). Dutch public policy has for some years now tackled the specter of parallel societies, by systematically weakening the internal social cohesion of groups in favor of nurturing loose relations between individuals of various backgrounds. It has done so by prioritizing the development of heterogeneous neighborhoods (Duivendak 1998).

In Israel, a country marked by a heavily segregated population, disputants are since 2001 allowed to "forum shop" in matters of marriage and divorce, that is, to choose the jurisdiction deemed most favorable to one's claims (Benda-Beckmann 1981: 117 et passim; Shahar 2013: 147 et passim), not least in order to make communal boundaries more porous. Women wishing to obtain an executable maintenance order have thus now the option to file a claim in two very different courts: a) a civil family court with a strong Israeli and civil ethos rigorously promoting gender-equality, and b) Shari'a courts marked by an obvious Palestinian and patriarchal flavor (Shahar 2013: 149). Israeli legal anthropologist Ido Shahar showed that Muslim women sometimes opt for civil courts and sometimes for the Shari'a courts, cogently arguing that we need to know more about the entire background of litigants to understand their disparate choices (Shahar 2013: 159–161).

Conclusion

Recent legal developments in countries of both the Global North and the Global South in my view suggest that the distinction between classical and new legal pluralism has for the most part become obsolete. The intricacies of the Israeli and Indonesian case rather call for a comparative project of contemporary global legal pluralism. I therefore fully endorse American jurist Paul Schiff Berman's engagement of a number of disciplines, including anthropology, sociology, and cultural studies, in the development of a jurisprudence beyond borders that is capable of making sense of the global pluralism of today (Berman 2012: 20). If we want to take serious his reiteration of the point, already made by Merry, Tamanaha, and others, to inquire more deeply into "which social norms are recognized as authoritative sources of obligation and by whom" (Berman 2012: 56), we will have to pay close attention to the existence and interplay of multiple written and unwritten normativities in a certain social field, their scalar range, their spatialization and temporalization, and the worldviews they are embedded in. This in turn will yield a better understanding of what is recognized as "law", and why. Religion-based legal pluralism must then be linked to research on other modes of legal pluralism, for instance economy-based legal pluralism, so as not to fall into the trap of fixed taxonomies preventing us to better understand the deep meaning of normativity.

References

An-Na'im, Abdullahi A. 2008. *Islam and the secular state: Negotiating the future of Shari'a*. Cambridge, MA/London: Harvard University Press.

Benda-Beckmann, Franz. 2002. Who's afraid of legal pluralism? *Journal of Legal Pluralism* 47: 37–82.

Berman, Paul Schiff. 2012. *Global legal pluralism: A jurisprudence of law beyond borders*. New York: Cambridge University Press.

Black, Christine F. 2011. *The land is the source of the law: A dialogic encounter with indigenous jurisprudence*. London/New York: Routledge.

Bourdieu, Pierre. 1971. Genèse et structure du champ religieux. *Revue Française de Sociologie* 12(3): 295–324.

Bourdieu, Pierre. 1987. The force of law: Toward a sociology of the juridical field. *The Hastings Law Journal* 38: 805–853.

Bunjamin, Hiswara, Tandjung and Herbert Smith. 2012. Indonesia. In *Guide to anti-corruption regulation in Asia*, ed. Herbert Smith, 23–27. Hongkong: www.herbertsmith.com.

Comaroff, John L., and Jean Comaroff. 2009. Reflections on the anthropology of law, governance and sovereignty. In *Rules of law and laws of ruling: On the governance of law*, ed. Franz von Benda-Beckmann, Keebet von Benda-Beckmann, and Julia Eckert, 31–59. Farnham/Burlington: Ashgate.

Cookson, Catharine. 2001. *Regulating religion: The courts and the free exercise clause*. Oxford: Oxford University Press.

Cortez, David, and Heike Wagner. 2010. Zur Genealogie des indigenen 'guten Lebens' ('sumak kawsay') in Ecuador. In *Lateinamerikas Demokratien im Umbruch*, ed. Leo Gabriel and Herbert Berger, 167–200. Vienna: Mandelbaum.

Csordas, Thomas J. 2013. Dispelling dispute in Native American Church healing. In *Religion in disputes: Pervasiveness of religious normativity in disputing processes*, ed. Franz von Benda-Beckmann, Keebet von Benda-Beckmann, Martin Ramstedt, and Bertram Turner, 19–35. New York: Palgrave Macmillan.

de Sousa Santos, Boaventura. 1987. Law: A map of misreading – Toward a postmodern conception of law. *Journal of Law and Society* 14: 279–302.

Delaney, David. 2004. Tracing displacements: Or evictions in the *Nomosphere. Environment and Planning D: Society and Space* 22: 847–860.

Delaney, David. 2010. *The spatial, the legal and the pragmatics of world-making: Nomospheric investigations*. Abingdon/New York: Routledge.

Duivendak, Jan W. 1998. Van verzuiling naar vermenging: Wijkopbouw en opbouwwerk in een multiculturele samenleving. http://www.ethiekenmaatschappij.ugent.be/wp-content/uploads/2012/07/EM_13-1998-Duyvendack.pdf. Accessed May 2015.

Eckert, Julia. 2006. From subjects to citizens: Legalism from below and the homogenisation of the legal sphere. *Journal of Legal Pluralism* 53–54: 45–75.

Eckert, Julia, Brian Donahoe, Christian Strümpell, and Zerrin Özlem Biner. 2012. *Law against the state ethnographic forays into law's transformations*. Cambridge: Cambridge University Press.

Fitzpatrick, Peter. 1984. Law and society. *Osgoode Hall Law Journal* 22(1): 115–138.

Goodale, Mark R. 1998. Leopold Pospisil: A critical reappraisal. *Journal of Legal Pluralism* 40: 123–149.

Goodwin, Jeff, and James M. Jasper. 2009. Editors' introduction. In *The social movements reader: Cases and concepts*, ed. Jeff Goodwin and James M. Jasper, 542–686. Malden/Oxford: Wiley Blackwell.

Griffiths, John. 1985. Introduction. In *People's law and state law: The Bellagio papers*, ed. Antony Allot and Gordon R. Woodman, 13–20. Dordrecht: Foris.

Griffiths, John. 1986. What is legal pluralism? *Journal of Legal Pluralism* 24: 1–55.

Halm, Dirk, and Martina Sauer. 2006. Parallelgesellschaft und ethnische Schichtung. *Aus Politik und Zeitgeschichte* 1–2(2006): 18–24.

Kinross, Patrick. 1999. *Atatürk: The rebirth of a nation*. Frome/London: Phoenix.

Lijphart, Arend. 1990. *Verzuiling, pacificatie en kentering in de Nederlandse politiek*. Haarlem: Becht.

Merry, Sally E. 1988. Legal pluralism. *Law and Society Review* 22(5): 869–896.

Moore, Sally Falk. 1972. Law and social change: The semi-autonomous social field as an appropriate subject of study. *Law and Society Review* 7: 719–746.

Moore, Sally Falk. 1978. *Law as process: An anthropological approach*. London: Routledge and Keegan Paul.

Munson, Ziad W. 2008. *The making of pro-Life activists: How social movement mobilization works*. Chicago/London: The University of Chicago Press.

Munson, Ziad W. 2013. Religion, crisis pregnancies, and the battle over abortion: Redefining conflict and consensus in the American pro-life movement. In *Religion in disputes: Pervasiveness of religious normativity in disputing processes*, ed. Franz von Benda-Beckmann, Keebet von Benda-Beckmann, Martin Ramstedt, and Bertram Turner, 37–53. New York: Palgrave Macmillan.

NARF. 1979. Announcements. *Native American Rights Fund* (Winter 1979) 5(1): 1–19.

Pospisil, Leopold J. 1958. *Kapauku Papuans and their law*. New Haven: Yale University (Publications in Anthropology, No. 54).

Pospisil, Leopold J. 1967. Legal levels and multiplicity of legal systems in human societies. *Journal of Conflict Resolution* 11(1): 2–26.

Radcliffe, Sarah A. 2012. Development for a postneoliberal era? Sumak Kawsay, living well and the limits to decolonisation in Ecuador. *Geoforum* 43: 240–249.

Ramstedt, Martin. 2012. *Islamisation by law and the juridification of religion in Anomic Indonesia*. Halle: Max Planck Institute for Social Anthropology Working Papers (Working Paper No. 140).

Ramstedt, Martin. 2015. Anthropological perspectives on law and religion. In *Routledge handbook of law and religion*, ed. Silvio Ferrari, 43–58. London/New York: Routledge.

Roberts, Simon. 1998. Against legal pluralism: Some reflections on the contemporary enlargement of the legal domain. *Journal of Legal Pluralism* 42: 95–106.

Sezgin, Yüksel. 2010. The Israeli millet system: Examining legal pluralism through lenses of nation-building and human rights. *Israel Law Review* 43: 631–654.

Shahar, Ido. 2013. Forum shopping between civil and Shari'a courts: Maintenance suits in contemporary Jerusalem. In *Religion in disputes: Pervasiveness of religious normativity in disputing processes*, ed. Franz von Benda-Beckmann, Keebet von Benda-Beckmann, Martin Ramstedt, and Bertram Turner, 147–164. New York: Palgrave Macmillan.

Tamanaha, Brian Z. 1993. The folly of the 'Social Scientific' concept of legal pluralism. *Journal of Law and Society* 20(2): 192–217.

Teubner, Gunther. 1987. Juridification: Concepts, aspects, limits, solutions. In *Juridification of social spheres: A comparative analysis in the area of labor, corporate, antitrust, and social welfare*, ed. Gunther Teubner, 3–48. Berlin/New York: Walter de Gruyter.

Valverde, Mariana. 2008. Analyzing the governance of security: Jurisdiction and scale. *Behemoth. A Journal on Civilisation* 1: 3–15.

Valverde, Mariana. 2009. Jurisdiction and scale: Legal 'Technicalities' as resources for theory. *Social & Legal Studies* 18: 139–157.

von Benda-Beckmann, Keebet. 1981. Forum shopping and shopping forums: Dispute processing in a Minangkabau village in West-Sumatra. *Journal of Legal Pluralism* 19: 117–159.

von Benda-Beckmann, Franz, and Keebet von Benda-Beckmann. 2009. Beyond the law-religion divide: Law and religion in West Sumatra. In *Permutations of order: Religion and law as contested sovereignties*, ed. Thomas G. Kirsch and Bertram Turner, 227–246. Farnham and Burlington: Ashgate.

von Benda-Beckmann, Franz, and Keebet von Benda-Beckmann. 2012. Identity in dispute: Law, religion, and identity in Minangkabau. *Asian Ethnicity* 13(4): 341–358. Special Issue: *Law and religio-ethnic identity in post-new order Indonesia*, ed. Martin Ramstedt and Fadjar Thufail, London/New York: Routledge.

von Benda-Beckmann, Franz, Keebet von Benda-Beckmann, Martin Ramstedt, and Bertram Turner. 2013. Introduction: On the pervasiveness of religious normativity in disputing processes. In *Religion in disputes: Pervasiveness of religious normativity in disputing processes*, ed. Franz von Benda-Beckmann, Keebet von Benda-Beckmann, Martin Ramstedt, and Bertram Turner, vii–xx. New York: Palgrave Macmillan.

Woodman, Gordon R. 2012. The development 'Problem' of legal pluralism: An analysis and steps toward solutions. In *Legal pluralism and development: Scholars and practitioners in dialogue*, ed. Brian Z. Tamanaha, Caroline Sage, and Michael Woolcock, 129–144. Cambridge: Cambridge University Press.

Yetisgin, M. 2007. The Ottoman way of governing multi-ethnic and multi-religious communities. *Ankara Üniversitesi Osmanli Tarihi Arastirma ve Uygulama Merkezi Dergisi* 21: 135–168.

Chapter 4
Legal Pluralism: Freedom of Religion, Exemptions and the Equality of Citizens

Bryan S. Turner

Abstract One simple definition of legal pluralism is that it concerns the development of different legal traditions or legal sources within a single sovereign jurisdiction. It is often seen therefore to be a challenge to legal centralism or the thesis that the sovereign state has a monopoly over law making to the exclusion of all other sources. It is helpful to make a distinction between 'weak legal pluralism' and 'strong legal pluralism'. The former refers to a situation where there may be various institutions at the central level of government or jurisdictions covering different regions or communities, which nevertheless remain under the hierarchical oversight and control by a state or empire. The latter refers to legal orders that govern over peoples but are not part of a single, hierarchical and integrated system. In short the weak-strong notion describes the degree of delegated legal authority to social groups, communities and institutions. The underlying question behind both forms is the issue of state sovereignty. Critics of legal pluralism regard the development as a threat to the sovereignty of the state and the coherence of a society. By contrast, it is possible to see legal pluralism as the natural companion of political liberalism allowing peoples and their institutions some protection from centralized authoritarian rule and in that regard legal pluralism is sometimes associated with the right of resistance against tyrannical powers. One historical issue in the debate about legal pluralism is its presence in empires such as the Ottoman Empire and attempts to control or eliminate legal pluralism during the rise of the nation state.

Introduction

One simple definition of legal pluralism is that it concerns the development of different legal traditions or legal sources within a single sovereign jurisdiction (Griffith 1986; Tamanaha 2008; Turner and Arslan 2011). It is often seen therefore to be a challenge to legal centralism or the thesis that the sovereign state has a monopoly

B.S. Turner (✉)
The Graduate Center CUNY and ACU (Melbourne),
University of Western Sydney, Sydney, Australia
e-mail: BTurner@gc.cuny.edu

R. Bottoni et al. (eds.), *Religious Rules, State Law, and Normative Pluralism - A Comparative Overview*, Ius Comparatum – Global Studies in Comparative Law 18, DOI 10.1007/978-3-319-28335-7_4

over law making to the exclusion of all other sources. It is helpful to make a distinction between 'weak legal pluralism' and 'strong legal pluralism'. The former refers to a situation where there may be various institutions at the central level of government or jurisdictions covering different regions or communities, which nevertheless remain under the hierarchical oversight and control by a state or empire. The latter refers to legal orders that govern over peoples but are not part of a single, hierarchical and integrated system. In short the weak-strong notion describes the degree of delegated legal authority to social groups, communities and institutions (Ross and Stern 2013). The underlying question behind both forms is the issue of state sovereignty. Critics of legal pluralism regard the development as a threat to the sovereignty of the state and the coherence of a society (Cohen 2012). By contrast, it is possible to see legal pluralism as the natural companion of political liberalism allowing peoples and their institutions some protection from centralized authoritarian rule and in that regard legal pluralism is sometimes associated with the right of resistance against tyrannical powers (Franklin 1969). One historical issue in the debate about legal pluralism is its presence in empires such as the Ottoman Empire and attempts to control or eliminate legal pluralism during the rise of the nation state (Barkey 2008).

In concrete terms, legal pluralism can take the form of recognizing the right of aboriginal peoples to their own customary or tribal norms and procedures within their own tribal land. The issue of aboriginal rights has arisen primarily in so-called 'white settler societies' in Latin America, North America and Australia. Therefore a more pertinent example would be that member countries of the European Union are subject to European laws that may clash with the laws that emerge from national legislatures or parliaments. More broadly human rights legislation may have to be accommodated within a national legal framework. Another example would concern the impact of international regulations (such as the laws of the sea) that are binding on the community of nations. These laws relate to so-called 'community necessity' where it is in the interests of separate nations to accept mutually binding legal norms to regulate behavior. As we will see in this chapter, in recent years the debate about legal pluralism has centred almost exclusively on the accommodation of religious norms or laws within a secular constitution. This accommodation has been particularly problematic in the treatment of the *Shari'a* within western secular law (Possamai et al. 2015). Thus legal pluralism raises important and often troublesome issues concerning state sovereignty, the treatment of citizens as equal subjects under the law, the question of exemptions for religious groups, and the impact of secularization on the status of previously established churches.

Therefore in contemporary legal discussion regarding 'legal pluralism', the debate has largely focused on how the state might accommodate religious differences in secular and democratic societies. In particular with the growth of Muslim minorities in the West, this debate has in practice principally concerned the needs of such communities in a secular environment where state and church are legally separate. These issues have been especially complex in those societies where the Roman Catholic Church has been historically dominant and has enjoyed a privileged relationship to the state. Paradoxically as societies have become more secular, questions about religion have become more pressing and urgent, and the modern state is drawn into some oversight of religious issues, despite the fact that the state is in legal terms not competent to make judgements about religious matters (Turner 2007a). The debates over same sex marriage and the de-criminalization of homosexually are good examples. Thus the need to analyze and understand legal pluralism has emerged from the fact that, while societies are in many respects more secular, there is growing religious and cultural pluralism as a consequence of global labour migration and the displacement of populations thereby creating religious minorities in the West. In addition there are new religious forces at work in civil society such as the rapid growth of evangelical movements that are broadly known as 'Pentecostal'.

Legal pluralism can be said to be a juridical response to growing social diversity. Legal pluralism attempts to accommodate this diversity by recognizing the competing needs of different communities and often this accommodation takes the form of recognizing exemptions in which the special needs of a religious group (such as the need to wear special garments) are accepted as exemptions from the requirements of the majority of the population. One issue or paradox is therefore that exemptions to cater for special needs often conflict with or erode the notion of equality and equal treatment of citizens by the same rules and laws. We need to consider therefore how legal pluralism sits with the notion of egalitarian secular citizenship as a status enjoyed by all citizens equally.

Contemporary commentary on legal pluralism often assumes that it emerged with post-colonialism that recognized aboriginal customary law and with globalization that has made all modern societies pluralistic and diverse (de Sousa Santos and Rodriguez-Garavito 2005; Twining 2000). This interpretation however lacks historical depth. It is clear that legal pluralism was widespread in early modern societies and that the political writings of Thomas Hobbes, Grotius and others sought to contain legal pluralism in the development of early states out of empires. Thus legal pluralism was well known in the Ottoman Empire. What is true of globalization is that under its impact states become more porous and thus more exposed to the need for some degree of legal pluralism if minorities are to be incorporated without tension and conflict. One persistent issue in modern studies of legal pluralism is that, wherever there is an overt commitment to freedom of religion, there will be pressure to offer legal exemptions to minorities to permit them to practice their religion without too much interference from the state.

Historical Development: State Centralism Versus Legal Pluralism

Legal pluralism is often held to be a challenge to 'legal centralism,' namely, a legal doctrine claiming that the state has a monopoly over law making in its sovereign space. This theory is associated with theory of the state and law as developed by Max Weber and Hans Kelsen. Weber (1978: 657–8) in volume two of *Economy and*

Society argued that modernized law had become disentangled from morals and could no longer retain emotive and subjective notions such as 'justice'. Modern law was rational in the sense that 'legal science' aimed to create a logically coherent and general system of legal propositions resulting in a gapless system of legal norms. His realism promoted him to see what he called the 'social law' as the consequence of social and political conflicts between interest groups. He claimed there was no place for natural law in the modern world and his idea of law as command with the backing of the state via a system of courts and professional lawyers illustrates his understanding of the law as a secular instrument of state power. His idea of the decline of natural law was thus an inevitable conclusion of his broader understanding of the rationalization of the law involving its systematization, its separation from morality and religion, the development of a professional body of university-trained lawyers, the elaboration of a scientific jurisprudence as a system of thought and so forth. I have commented elsewhere (Turner 1974) on the fact that Weber regarded both English common law and what he called with reference to Islam 'kadi-justice' as traditional forms of law that had not been systematically rationalized. In short common law and *Shari'a* were characterized by arbitrary decision making on the part of judges who could be readily manipulated by interested parties. In particular he argued that as a result of social change gaps emerged in the *Shari'a* that were closed by the use of ad hoc *fatwa*. In English common law, legal development on the basis of case law could only result in legal inconsistency.

For Weber, legal formalism requires a coercive apparatus, but not an apparatus that primarily requires the use of physical violence. His famous definition of these conditions 'depends on the availability of an organized coercive apparatus for the nonviolent exercise of legal coercion. This apparatus must also possess such power that there is in fact a significant probability that the norm will be respected because of the possibility of recourse to such coercion. Today legal coercion by violence is the monopoly of the state' (Weber 1978 vol. 1: 314). In short, in a modern society with a sovereign state, the law is proclaimed through the courts with the ultimate guarantee of state enforcement. This vision of legal formalism and centralism excluded the possibility of legal pluralism, because the state was sovereign and legal rationalism was not possible on a hybrid system of custom, morality and law.

Kelsen (1967) adopted a similar position with respect for example to international law. In 1934 Kelsen published the first edition of *Pure Theory of Law*, in which he argued that basic norms (*grundnorm*) are binding and enjoy authority, but do not refer to any higher principle or source of authority. Such norms are the ground of all legal institutions. The pure theory sought to provide a framework by which the basic characteristics of any conceivable manifestation of law might be identified. The legal system would be thus constructed as distinct and autonomous from any political or social values. We can summarize his formalism with two propositions: law is its own creation, and rules validate rules. As with Max Weber's notion of legal rationalization, Kelsen was critical of the common law which in his view is too heavily tied to custom and to natural law which is too heavily dependent on morality. He sought to separate law from morality in particular and from social phenomena in general, and identified the law with the state. With this strong notion of central sovereignty, Kelsen rejected pluralism since any contradiction between two legal norms would mean that they could not both be valid. In *Principles of International Law* (Kelsen 1952) these arguments were extended to international relations. Without a legal framework between states, their foreign relations would be simply power politics. Believing that the rise of a global federation of states was an inevitable outcome of the history of international relations, an international judiciary was a fundamental prerequisite of world peace.

Critics of state centralism based on state sovereignty and a legal monopoly often regard it as an ideology rather than a legal doctrine. In the development of the sociology of law, an alternative to legal centralism is associated with the work of the Austrian sociologist Eugene Ehrlich. Born in Czernowitz (in present day Ukraine) the capital of Bukowina on the edge of the decaying Austro-Habsburg Empire in 1862, his work on customary law reflects the marginality of his birthplace in the imperial power structure. While being subject to the centralized system of law, Bukowina had a rich tradition of customary laws. Bukowina was a multicultural society. Ehrlich called it a 'tribal society' in which diverse groups (Germans, Gipsies, Jews, Hungarians, Romanians, Russians, and more) existed side by side under the political and legal umbrella of the imperial state.

Given this imperial context, he was interested in the gap between the actual practice of law and the formal doctrines of law that were developed in the universities and the formal courts. In *Fundamental Principles of the Sociology of Law* (Ehrlich 2001), he developed the notion of 'living law' in contrast to state-centred theories of law. Rejecting Weber's view of law as a deductive system of legal propositions, he examined the customary practices (the living law of the land) operating at the community level. Law is the 'ordering and upholding of every human association' (Ehrlich 2001: 25) rather than an abstract system of legal propositions. Ehrlich's ideas found a ready audience in the United States where American pragmatism offered a fruitful context for his ideas on living law and his approach was eventually supported by figures such as Roscoe Pound at the Harvard Law School developing his own version of 'sociological jurisprudence'. Formalism was also criticised by Judith N. Shklar (1964) for its narrow artificiality and its inability to give a convincing account of morality. She noted the circularity of these basic ideas in which law are rules that can be enforced. Therefore in legal centralism morality refers to those rules that cannot be enforced. As such Ehrlich's ideas prepared the way for theories of legal pluralism (Nelken 1984).

In this framework, legal pluralism can be seen as a controversial sociological issue, because it can only exist in contrast to the notion that the state has a monopoly over the law. In other words, the idea of legal pluralism also functions as a critique of the state-centred or 'official' view of the law. While this sociological interpretation of legal pluralism is important and plausible, there may be other arguments about the importance of a shared citizenship to guarantee equality (especially equality before the law) that must be taken into account. Ehrlich's view of living law made sense in a society of multiple and distinct ethno-cultural communities with their own customs of normative ordering, but, in societies where the majority shares a common culture and a unified citizenship, can legal pluralism find a place? Can legal pluralism add more fuel to the bonfire of civil unrest, especially where a majority fears the impact of a minority, or does legal pluralism offer a liberal solution to significant religious differences?

In modern societies, the revival of Islam and the demand for the *Shari'a* have become the principal testing ground for the operation of legal pluralism. In societies where there is an unstable or unsettled notion of national identity, legal pluralism can play a role in creating disharmony between conflicting groups. Attempts to impose *Shari'a* in such circumstances is a recipe for civil unrest. Sub-Saharan Africa is an extreme illustration. In November 2002, conflicts around the Miss World Competition plunged Nigeria into violent clashes between Christians and Muslims, thereby deepening the controversy surrounding the revival of the strict criminal code of the *Shari'a* in 12 of Nigeria's 36 administrative regions. As a result there were violent protests from Muslims in Abuja, where contestants awaited the opening of the pageant, and eventually Muslims attacked Christians in Kaduna, which is one of Nigeria's most volatile northern cities. The contemporary problem of Christian–Muslim relations is compounded by the fact that Nigeria is made up of 250 separate ethnic groups, with 400 linguistic groups. The struggle over the law is simply a manifestation of a deeper struggle over the unity of the sovereign state. It has also been associated with radical Muslim movements such as Boko Haram which has also moved to establish *Shari'a* as the exclusive jurisdiction over Islamic territory. Critics have also drawn attention to the *Hudud* laws which contain draconian provisions for any transgression of laws relating to alcohol consumption or illegal sexual intercourse (Clarke 2009). Similar problems have emerged in Malaysia where moves to give the *Shari'a* hegemonic status over common law have alienated Chinese and Hindu minorities.

Shari'a and Legal Pluralism in Secular Societies

After 9/11 and the bombings in London and Madrid, many governments and their security agencies came to see the *Shari'a* as a threat to social stability and more broadly the democratic foundations of liberal society. Popular perceptions of the criminal law components in the *Shari'a* concentrated on those measures that appeared to re-enforce gender inequality. In some conservative states in America, Christian evangelicals have responded to what they perceive as the undesirable spread of the *Shari'a* by demanding that Christians should develop a Christian *Shari'a* in order to impose God's law on society. There are now many issues in the public domain that are being contested by evangelicals. One example comes from the Kansas House of Representatives that introduced a bill to permit individuals or businesses to refuse to provide services to same sex couples when their own religious beliefs are compromised. In modern societies, there is an increasing tendency for the state to engage in the management of religion, thereby often compromising the separation of church and state as the foundation of a secular constitution (Barbalet et al. 2011).

Popular anxiety about Islam has frequently developed into widespread Islamophobia which is also prevalent in the USA among right-wing conservative politicians (Turner and Richardson 2012). Thus various Republican states have passed pre-emptive legislation to cut off any further expansion of references to the *Shari'a* in legal judgements for example in domestic disputes. In the United Kingdom protests against the Archbishop of Canterbury's public lecture in 2008 suggesting that the growth of the *Shari'a* was inevitable is further indication of public hostility. These political and legal moves to prevent the spread of *Shari'a* are unnecessarily alarmist, because there is no evidence of pressure from within the Muslim communities for any comprehensive introduction of *Shari'a* or support for its criminal justice norms. Access to the *Shari'a* is mainly confined to domestic issues such as marriage, divorce, adoption and the distribution of property. Through various exceptions Muslims enjoy provision for customary regulations that cover diet and the production of food that is governed by *halal* certificates.

Evidence of the acceptance of Islam in the West presents a complex picture (Bowen 2010; Cesari 2010). However on balance the scholarly evidence suggests that western liberal governments have gone a long way to offer legal accommodation to Muslim minorities through partial recognition of the role of the *Shari'a* in arbitration cases (Joppke and Torpey 2013). There is considerable evidence that judges in western legal systems are beginning to refer to the *Shari'a* on a regular basis in their deliberations regarding domestic issues (Possamai et al. 2014). For example, these cases typically occur when a Muslim couple who became married overseas according to Islamic norms attempt to arrive at a divorce in a secular western society. In these cases, western legal experts have to refer to the *Shari'a* in determining the appropriate legal outcome. As a result the *Shari'a* is being reformed indirectly by the impact of western legal principles and at the same time undergoing internal reform in response to modernization more generally. This reform is especially evident in the case of family law (Layish 2014).

Clearly many devout Muslims want to conduct their lives in terms of the *Shari'a* as a moral rather than legal system. The *Shari'a* is regarded by pious Muslims as necessary for their religious practice and personal integrity and the principle of freedom of religion in liberal societies means that there is legal pressure to respect religious dress codes, food norms, the use of the *Shari'a,* religious education and so forth. The norm of consistent applications of the law requires 'a level playing field'. Thus if pious Jews have an entitlement to access their own legal traditions through Jewish courts, then it is inconsistent to deny Muslims a similar provision.

There is widespread growth and use of Islamic banking where banks will attempt to follow Quranic rules about interest and investment. In other words there is some application of the *Shari'a* to these commercial and economic institutions although the extent of these arrangements and how far they conform to *Shari'a* norms is unclear. While conservative interests, as articulated in the popular press, object to the growth of the *Shari'a* into the juridical domain, there is less anxiety about the presence of Islam in the economy, where there generally is an indifference to religious differences and where market exchanges are the primary concern. The role of the *Shari'a* with regard to banks and banking regulations has received little attention in academic literature.

With globalization and the expansion of Muslim minorities in the West, there is little to prevent the slow introduction of elements of the *Shari'a* into western legal decision-making processes when judges make legal decisions regarding domestic cases. Where democratic governments have a commitment to freedom of religion and equality before the law, it will be difficult to resist pressures from Muslim communities for access to *Shari'a*. However there is in fact little concerted pressure from within Muslim communities for any systematic introduction of the *Shari'a*. While Muslims may occasionally seek advice by legal judgements (*fetwas*), there is little or no evidence of 'creeping *Shari'a*'. There is therefore – despite references to the growth of international law (such as labour law), human rights interventions, commercial law and so forth – little real evidence to support the idea that legal pluralism is a significant threat to the sovereignty of nation states. Legal pluralism may however be simply one aspect of the general fragmentation of civil society into enclaves or parallel communities.

Equality and the Legal Exemption

Recent research reports suggest that legal protection from discrimination, laws relating to hate speech, rule of law, and protection of equality has been significant in shaping the climate of public opinion in Europe. In the United Kingdom, the *Racial and Religious Hatred Act* 2006, the *Equality Act* of 2006 and the *Equality Act* of 2010 have extended the legal protection of individuals. This legislative momentum came originally not from a concern over religious issues but from equality legislation relating to women's rights and racial discrimination. Contemporary interest in religion and belief was basically a byproduct of the general broadening of equality legislation.

However one consistent negative research finding is that respondents do not in fact support equal treatment or a level playing field. Rather a substantial proportion of respondents from religious organizations clearly favour exemptions from equality laws on matters of gender, marriage and civil partnership, sexual orientation and religion or belief itself (Weller et al. 2013: 213). This conclusion rather confirms the view of critics that modern enthusiasm for defending cultural and religious differences undermines equality as a fundamental value of secular citizenship as a common status with shared duties and entitlements. Thus 'The core of this conception of citizenship, already worked out in the eighteenth century, is that there should be only one status of citizen (no estates or castes) so that everybody enjoys the same legal and political rights' (Barry 2001: 7). Typically religious minorities want exemptions from secular notions of equality in order to adhere to traditional or customary religious practices that clearly contradict secular norms. Obvious examples include exemptions from wearing a crash helmet on motorcycles or tax exemption on charitable activities by religious groups.

While these largely domestic improvements in the legislative framework reinforcing the protection of individuals and groups from discrimination are to be welcome, the international environment has unsurprisingly had adverse effects on domestic politics and policies. Public attitudes towards Islam have been shaped by 9/11, the wars in Iraq and Afghanistan, the bombings in London and Madrid, or the Danish cartoon incident, the rise of ISIS, and the global conflict between Sunni and Shia versions of Islam. These international crises have clearly continued to fuel domestic expressions of Islamophobia and fear of the *Shari'a*'.

Many liberals are of course worried that these developments not only undermine the experience of common citizenship but they also challenge some fundamental principles of equality. Brian Barry (2001) concluded that the privileges ascribed to the special interests articulated by religious minorities could not be reconciled with considerations of justice. He was especially critical of the isolation and special benefits enjoyed by sectarian groups. In particular he was critical of the Amish community and their many immunities from state interference. He argued convincingly that any public acceptance of a religious practice of a minority could only be justified if it could be demonstrated that the practice was pivotal to the beliefs of that religious tradition. For Barry many of the exemptions (from taxation, jury service, military service and so forth) won by Amish communities in legal battles are not in fact essential to the practice of their faith. These immunities and privileges are inappropriately packaged in the language of individual religious freedoms. These questions about what constitutes orthodox belief or correct ritual practice will always be controversial. Is the cult of the Virgin Mary in Catholicism an essential or merely a customary aspect of the Catholic tradition? Barry's argument however offers an additional stringent test for religious organizations. Are these exemptions compatible with the criteria that are essential for liberal democracies – transparency, equality, voluntary membership, the rights of dissent and legitimate internal criticism. The state typically supports groups and institutions that are regarded as voluntary and Barry questions whether societies like the Amish are in fact voluntary associations at all, since the option of leaving the community is severely restricted, where those that leave are often subject to considerable psychological pressures. Joining and leaving religious groups – and hence questions about conversion and apostasy – are hugely controversial issues often resulting in violent conflicts between religious groups. Religious groups of all persuasions are genuinely uncomfortable about the whole question of apostates (Cottee 2015). This is yet another area where the secular law may be drawn into religious disputes to protect religious freedoms that allows individuals to freely leave religious groups. Rigid rules about the conditions for voluntary conversion to and exit from social groups contribute inevitably to the construction of exclusive social groups. Recent criticisms of multiculturalism in Europe have expressed fears that multicultural policies have not resulted in integration but in the creation of parallel communities with their own schools, languages and customs. The danger with parallel legislation, even with a range of safeguards, is that it will simply reinforce the fragmentation of modern societies (Turner 2007b).

Conclusion: Legal Pluralism and the Management of Religion

Legal pluralism was characteristic of complex feudal and early modern societies, but in this chapter I have focused on contemporary issues. Much of the literature of the topic was originally concerned with the special status of canon law in the Roman Catholic Church and how ecclesiastical legal norms could be accommodated within societies that were becoming simultaneously more secular and were forced to recognize the needs of evangelical churches that were competing with Catholicism for recognition. This pattern – the social and religious changes impinging on the historical dominance of Catholicism – was the basic issue in Latin America through much of the twentieth century. These developments – secularization, modernization and religious change – required some degree of legal change and pragmatic flexibility to accommodate new demands.

These processes were clearly intensified by globalization that has produced a world-wide problem of minorities with special cultural and religious needs (Teubner 1997). As liberal democracies in the West have had to accommodate communities with special religious needs, legal pluralism offers some solutions to the process of successful integration. In this chapter I have concentrated on Islam and the *Shari'a* as critical issues in legal pluralism. There are of course other demands bringing about legal change – the growth of human rights, the impact of international law, the consequences of laws relating to trade and navigation – and creating legal pluralism as much by accident as by design. Nation states often seek to resist the demands of these external legal pressures on their national legislatures and many liberal societies such as the United States resist the demands of human rights on their laws for example with respect to capital punishment. In 2014 the new government in Australia rejected criticism from human rights groups regarding its treatment of 'boat people' namely the refugees fleeing crises in their home countries.

While there is often resistance to legal pluralism, in examining the West's response to the *Shari'a* I have argued that there is significant accommodation to the religious needs of Muslim communities. In particular there is a growing acceptance of Islamic legal norms in domestic dispute resolution through arbitration provisions, considering adjustment to dietary requirements under *halal* certificates, recognition of educational needs and widespread acceptance of *Shari'a* compliant mortgages and banking. I have concentrated on Islam because despite attempts to quarantine (so to speak) the *Shari'a* is gaining acceptance in Europe and to some extent in the United States in the management of domestic disputes. In this discussion I have only focused on changes to Islamic law that are being brought about by external pressures from western secular law. I have not discussed the internal reform and modernization of the *Shari'a* (An-Na'im 2008).

Legal pluralism would appear to resolve the issue of religious diversity by recognizing the basic principle of freedom of religion in which the state is typically regarded as not competent to make judgements regarding religious matters. Legal pluralism in this respect can be regarded as a modern platform for political liberalism. However as a solution to diversity, it also raises intractable problems. It often operates by recognizing exemptions from general secular principles. For example the slaughter of animals according to *halal* norms conflicts with the general requirements for the humane slaughter of animals and thereby offends animal rights activists. Religious groups often achieve exemptions that are not fundamental to their faith such as the recognition that Amish do not require standard reflectors on their vehicles. Sikh turbans are obviously inconsistent with rules about hard hats for the rest of the population. Thus the spread of exemptions is typically incompatible with fundamental norms about the equality of citizens in a democracy. In all of these cases, we see the law assisting the state to manage the religious lives of citizens in a manner that is generally inconsistent with the separation of church and state. In other ways the law is shaping religious life indirectly by for example recognizing same-sex marriage. In various contests between religion and law – over homosexuality, marriage, abortion and so forth- the law appears to be a force for secularization in rejecting much of the heritage of religion. In other respects legal pluralism contributes to the erosion of established churches by recognizing a 'level playing field' between Protestants, Catholics and new religious movements. Finally while these generalizations hold true across many western societies, it is important to recognize important national differences. While we can say that the United Kingdom and the United States adopt a pragmatic approach to religious diversity in practice (despite official defence of sovereignty), France appears to take a far more active and occasionally aggressive response to religious diversity. France has conducted a 'War on sects' in which it adopts a relatively broad definition of sectarianism to include Scientology (Palmer 2011). The underlying problem is to what extent is legal pluralism compatible with a common citizenship? To the extent that neoliberalism with its emphasis on individualism and markets has already weakened the collective ties of citizenship, then we can expect the extent of legal pluralism to grow.

Despite these difficulties the days of legal centralism appear to be over and the legal world as described by Weber and Kelsen no longer has much purchase on how actual legal systems operate in a global world of interconnectivity. Legal formalism has been somewhat overshadowed by legal realism and by the idea of 'sociological jurisprudence' in the work of Roscoe Pound (1954), despite his conservative inclinations with respect to legal theory, that legislation is a social function and not an abstract construction of formal legal system. The formal separation of morality and law has also been widely challenged. Insofar as the state has become a more porous political institution with globalization, we can expect that the sovereign basis of national legal systems will be exposed to increasing legal diversity from external sources such as the ILO, the International Court of Justice and similar international bodies.

Note Some aspects of the argument in this otherwise original chapter have appeared in Bryan S. Turner (2014) 'Legal pluralism, state sovereignty and citizenship, in Adam Possamai, James T. Richardson and Bryan S. Turner (eds) *Legal Pluralism and Shari'a Law* London: Routledge pp. 7–27.

References

An-Na'im, Abdullahi Ahmed. 2008. *Islam and the secular state. Negotiating the future of Shari'a*. Cambridge: Harvard University Press.

Barbalet, Jack, Adam Possamai, and Bryan S. Turner (eds.). 2011. *Religion and the state. A comparative sociology*. London: Anthem Press.

Barkey, Karen. 2008. *Empire of difference. The Ottomans in contemporary perspective*. Cambridge: Cambridge University Press.

Barry, Brian. 2001. *Culture and equality. An egalitarian critique of multiculturalism*. Cambridge, MA: Harvard University Press.

Bowen, John R. 2010. *Can Islam be French? Pluralism and pragmatism in a secularist state*. Princeton/Oxford: Princeton University Press.

Cesari, Jocelyne (ed.). 2010. *Muslims in the west after 9/11*. London: Routledge.

Clarke, K.M. 2009. *Fictions of justice: The international criminal court and the challenge of legal pluralism in Sub-Saharan Africa*. Cambridge: Cambridge University Press.

Cohen, Jean L. 2012. *Globalization and sovereignty. Rethinking legality, legitimacy and constitutionalism*. Cambridge: Cambridge University Press.

Cottee, Simon. 2015. *The apostates. When Muslims leave Islam*. London: Hurst & Company.

de Sousa Santos, B., and C.A. Rodriguez-Garavito (eds.). 2005. *Law and globalization from below: Towards a cosmopolitan legality*. Cambridge: Cambridge University Press.

Ehrlich, E. 2001 [1936]. *Fundamental principles of the sociology of law*. New Brunswick: Transaction.

Franklin, Julian H. (ed.). 1969. *Constitutionalism and resistance in the sixteenth century*. New York: Pegasus.

Griffith, John. 1986. What is legal pluralism? *Journal of Legal Pluralism* 24: 1–55.

Joppke, Christian, and John Torpey. 2013. *The legal integration of Islam: A transatlantic comparison*. Boston: Harvard University Press.

Kelsen, Hans. 1952. *Principles of international law*. New York: The Lawbook Exchange.

Kelsen, Hans. 1967. *Pure theory of law*. Clark: The Lawbook Exchange.

Layish, Aharon. 2014. Islamic law in the modern world. *Islamic Law and Society* 21: 276–307.

Nelken, D. 1984. Law in action or living law? Back to the beginning in sociology of law. *Legal Studies* 4: 157–174.

Palmer, Susan J. 2011. *The new heretics of France. Minority religions, la Republique, and the Government-sponsored "War on Sects"*. Oxford: Oxford University Press.

Possamai, Adam, James T. Richardson, and Bryan S. Turner (eds.). 2014. *Legal pluralism and Sharia law*. London: Routledge.

Possamai, Adam, James T. Richardson, and Bryan S. Turner (eds.). 2015. *The sociology of the Shari'a: Case studies from around the World*. New York: Springer.

Pound, Roscoe. 1954. *A introduction to the philosophy of law*. New Haven/London: Yale University Press.

Ross, Richard J., and Philip J. Stern. 2013. Reconstructing early modern notions of legal pluralism. In *Legal pluralism and empires 1500–1850*, ed. Lauren Benton and Richard J. Ross, 109–141. New York/London: New York University Press.

Shklar, Judith N. 1964. *Legalism. Law, morals and political trials*. Cambridge, MA: Harvard University Press.

Tamanaha, B.Z. 2008. Understanding legal pluralism: Past to present, local to global. *Sydney Law Review* 30: 375–411.

Teubner, Gunther (ed.). 1997. *Global law without a state*. Aldershot: Dartmouth.

Turner, Bryan S. 1974. *Weber and Islam. A critical study*. London: Routledge.

Turner, Bryan S. 2007a. Managing religions: State responses to religious diversity. *Contemporary Islam* 1(2): 123–137.

Turner, Bryan S. 2007b. The enclave society: Towards a sociology of immobility. *European Journal of Social Theory* 10(2): 287–303.

Turner, Bryan S., and Berna Arslan. 2011. Shari'a and legal pluralism in the West. *The European Journal of Social Theory* 14(2): 139–159.

Turner, Bryan S., and James T. Richardson. 2012. Islam and the problems of liberal democracy. In *Applying Shari'a in the west*, ed. Maurits S. Berger, 47–64. Leiden: Leiden University Press.

Twining, William. 2000. *Globalisation & legal theory*. London: Butterworth.

Weber, Max. 1978. *Economy and society*, 2 vols. Berkeley: University of California Press.

Weller, Paul, Kingsley Purdam, Nazila Ghanea, and Sariya Cheruvallil-Contractor. 2013. *Religion or belief, discrimination and equality: Britain in global context*. London/New York: Bloomsbury.

Part II
Religion and Legal Pluralism. National Perspectives

Chapter 5
Religious Rules Under Austrian State Law

Wolfgang Wieshaider

Abstract Austria is a secular State, which accommodates religious needs both of individuals and institutions. Religious rules are applied within the constitutionally guaranteed autonomy of religious communities. Civilly, they produce legal effects on the basis of reference by State law, including private international law. The same applies to religious adjudication. Beyond explicit reference religious communities may create arbitration tribunals according to the Code of Civil Procedure; as in private international law, the application of religious rules is limited by the public policy clause.

Abbreviations

AAS	*Acta Apostolicæ Sedis*
ABGB	*Allgemeines bürgerliches Gesetzbuch* [Civil Code]
Art.	Article
bbl.	*baurechtliche Blätter* (journal)
BGBl.	*Bundesgesetzblatt* [Federal Law Gazette]
BlgNR	*Beilagen zu den Stenografischen Protokollen des Nationalrates* [Supplements to the Stenographic Protocols of the National Council]
BMUKK	*Bundesministerium für Unterricht Kunst und Kultur* [Federal Ministry of Education, Art and Culture]
can.	*canon*
CIC	*Codex iuris canonici*
DRdA	*Das Recht der Arbeit* (journal)
ed.	editor; edition
EC	European Community
ECHR	European Convention on Human Rights
ECJ	European Court of Justice
ECR	European Court Reports
EU	European Union

W. Wieshaider (✉)
University of Vienna, Vienna, Austria
e-mail: wolfgang.wieshaider@univie.ac.at

R. Bottoni et al. (eds.), *Religious Rules, State Law, and Normative Pluralism - A Comparative Overview*, Ius Comparatum – Global Studies in Comparative Law 18, DOI 10.1007/978-3-319-28335-7_5

Eur. Ct. HR	European Court of Human Rights
GlBG	*Gleichbehandlungsgesetz* [Equal Treatment Act]
GP	*Gesetzgebungsperiode* [legislative period]
IPRG	*Bundesgesetz über das internationale Privatrecht* [Private International Law Act]
JGS	*Justizgesetzsammlung* [Justice Act Collections]
LGBl.	*Landesgesetzblatt* [Provincial Law Gazette]
leg. cit.	*legis citatæ*
LVwG Wien	*Landesverwaltungsgericht Wien* [Vienna Administrative Court]
NÖ	*Niederösterreichisch* [Lower Austrian]
öarr.	*österreichisches Archiv für recht & religion* (journal)
OGH	*Oberster Gerichtshof* [Supreme Court]
Oö.	*Oberösterreichisch* [Upper Austrian]
RGBl.	*Reichsgesetzblatt* [Imperial Law Gazette]
SchiedsVZ	*Zeitschrift für Schiedsverfahren* – German Arbitration Journal
StGBl.	*Staatsgesetzblatt* [State Law Gazette]
UG	*Universitätsgesetz* [University Act]
VfSlg.	*Sammlung der Erkenntnisse und wichtigsten Beschlüsse des Verfassungsgerichtshofes neue Folge* [Collection of the Judgements and most important Decisions of the Constitutional Court, New Series]
ZPO	*Zivilprozessordnung* [Code of Civil Procedure]

Introduction

Notes on the Demography

The Federal Statistical Office conducts a census every ten years. Since 2011, and according to the Act on Counting Registers,[1] this census has been compiled from registers of births, marriages and deaths, which do not contain data on religious affiliation. Hence, the latter has not been registered since the 2001 census.[2] According to section 1(3) *leg. cit.*, any minister concerned can request a non-personal survey on religious affiliation, if this seems necessary from a federal perspective. To date, this has never been done. Reliable data for all registered, recognised or otherwise existing religious communities is not available. Rough statistics, mainly based on internal ecclesiastical registers or scientific research, show a general population of 8.5 million inhabitants, of which less than two thirds are Catholics, 6 % are Muslims,[3] 4 % are Protestants, and 4 % are Orthodox Christians and others.

[1] *Registerzählungsgesetz*, BGBl. I 2006/33, as amended.

[2] Potz 2005: 391.

[3] Marik-Lebeck 2010: 5–9.

Historical and Political Processes

In order to better understand the legal development of the country, it is important to refer to its prevailing Catholic tradition on one side, and to the evolution of fundamental constitutional guarantees from the second half of the nineteenth century to date on the other side. Religious bodies are registered or recognised on three levels,[4] namely

- as associations of private law, conveying a general status as bodies corporate,
- as confessional communities, so called by law and conveying a basic status of a religious community, and
- as legally recognised religious societies, so called by law and conveying an enhanced status of public law.

The Catholic Church is considered to be historically recognised in Austria and has the last-mentioned status of public law. Despite the guarantees of equality and the smooth integration of the European Convention into Austrian constitutional law,[5] the Catholic Church generally holds a stronger position than all other legally recognised religious societies.[6] This is not just owed to the fact that a little less than two thirds of the population are affiliated, but to the Church's legal personality in public international law. The Concordat of 1933[7] and its—later amended—supplements to the 1960s on property[8] and schooling[9] provide for a robust legal anchor to accommodate some needs of the Catholic Church. The procedure of adapting the annuities of post World War II restitution may illustrate this. The increased rate is negotiated with the Catholic Church and laid down for all other concerned and entitled religious societies accordingly.[10]

Provisions of general interest do not only serve Catholic purposes. Through the principle of equality, other legally recognised religious societies may have such provisions analogously applied in their favour. This principle is explicitly laid down in section 1(2)III of the Protestant Church Act.[11] At present, public law status is granted to the Catholic Church, the Protestant Church (Lutheran and Reformed), the Orthodox Church (Greek, Serbian, Romanian, Russian, Bulgarian), the Armenian Apostolic Church, the Syrian Orthodox Church, the Coptic Orthodox Church, the Old Catholic Church, the Methodist Church, the Church of Jesus Christ of the Latter Day Saints, the New Apostolic Church, the Israelite Religious Society, the Islamic Faith Community, the Buddhist Religious Society, the Religious Society of Jehovah's Witnesses, the Alevi Faith Community and the Free Churches.

[4] Kalb et al. 2003: 93–135.

[5] BGBl. 1964/59.

[6] For comparisons with the Protestant Church cf. Gampl 1971: 283; Kalb et al. 2003: 546.

[7] BGBl. 1934 II/2.

[8] BGBl. 1960/195.

[9] BGBl. 1962/273.

[10] Cf. e.g. 159 BlgNR 24. GP.

[11] *Bundesgesetz über äußere Rechtsverhältnisse der Evangelischen Kirche,* BGBl. 1961/182 as amended; see Kalb et al. 2003: 549–550.

The Relationship Between State and Religion

The Republic of Austria is a religiously neutral State. Art. 15 of the State's Basic Act on the General Rights of the Citizens[12] stipulates a legal equality for and amongst all religious societies recognised by law.[13] Recognition implies certain elements of co-operation between the State and the recognised religious societies, especially in matters of religious education, theological faculties and institutional chaplaincies in prisons or the like, in order to accommodate religion and religious needs within the framework of public education and institutions of restricted personal freedom of movement.[14]

The Features of the National Legal System

The autonomy of the religious communities—in whatever legal form they are constituted—is constitutionally guaranteed through Art. 15 of the State's Basic Act on the General Rights of the Citizens, and Art. 9 read in conjunction with Art. 11 of the ECHR. State legislation refers to religion in the aforementioned co-operational matters or wherever the relevant constitutional warranties are implemented.

Religious Rules

Religious rules shall be understood as any rules whose normative quality is anchored within a religious system and not set forth by State legislation. In such instances, it does not matter whether these religious rules are attributed to divine origin or made by religious authorities.

It has been argued that certain social practices have been changing from religious to merely traditional or cultural, as in the case of crosses on the walls of kindergartens and schools, which various provisions require to be displayed—as long as the majority of the pupils are Christian. In no. 2(b) of the Final Protocol to the Agreement on Education, it is stipulated that the Republic of Austria will not change this situation without prior mutual agreement. The general application of these rules is defended with cultural and educational references, in the absence of a violation of negative religious freedom.[15] The Constitutional Court held in 2011 that such a law is constitutional.[16]

---

[12] *Staatsgrundgesetz über die allgemeinen Rechte der Staatsbürger*, RGBl. 1867/142 as amended.

[13] Gampl 1971: 160–163.

[14] Kalb et al. 2003: 65–70.

[15] Potz and Schinkele 2010: 406–412.

[16] VfSlg. 19 349.

Legislation

Mentioning of Religious Law, Invoking the Divine in State Law

The Austrian Constitution[17] was designed by Hans Kelsen in the spirit of legal positivism.[18] It simply begins with Art. 1, declaring Austria a democratic republic whose law emanates from the people. No preceding preamble provides room to invoke religion or the Divine.

Contrary to that, only the Tyrolean Constitution[19] commences with a preamble reminding that being faithful to God and to historical heritage is part of the spiritual, political and social foundations of the Tyrol. Art. 1(1) of the Constitution of Vorarlberg[20] states the significance of the legally recognised Churches and religious societies for the protection and consolidation of the religious and moral foundations of human life. In addition to that, Art. 7(5) *leg. cit.* recognises the significance of Sunday and of public holidays as days of rest. The latter is also laid down by Art. 7b of the Carinthian Constitution,[21] adding an explicit respect for the traditions associated with these days. Since the vast majority of public holidays are of Catholic origin, stipulated in the Concordat, such references can be considered religiously relevant. These references are considered compatible with the federal constitution.[22] Art 4/2 of the Lower Austrian Constitution,[23] Art. 15(3) of the Upper Austrian Constitution[24] and Art. 9 of the Constitution of the Land of Salzburg[25] only refer to Sundays as days of rest in this respect.

Amongst the sources of State law, religious laws are not directly mentioned (see below, section "Religious rules").

Personal Status of People

Until 1938, religious societies recognised by the State used to register births, deaths and marriages. Religious marriages had civil effects.

Nowadays, the respective religious societies are still the competent authorities to retain the old registers.[26] The personal status of people is, however, exclusively governed by State law. Neither current religious registers nor religious marriages have any civil effect. Religiously married people are considered unmarried unless they get married before State authorities.

---

[17] *Bundes-Verfassungsgesetz,* BGBl. 1930/1 as amended.

[18] Walter et al. 2007: 28 f.

[19] *Tiroler Landesordnung 1989,* LGBl. 1988/61 as amended.

[20] *Verfassungsgesetz über die Verfassung des Landes Vorarlberg,* LGBl. 1999/9 as amended.

[21] *Kärntner Landesverfassung,* LGBl. 1996/85.

[22] Pernthaler 2000, 181–184.

[23] *NÖ Landesverfassung 1979,* LGBl. 0001–0 as amended.

[24] *Oö. Landes-Verfassungsgesetz,* LGBl. 1991/122 as amended.

[25] *Landes-Verfassungsgesetz 1999,* LGBl. 25 as amended.

[26] Kalb et al. 2003: 165.

Religious Rules

By and large, State law does not apply rules anchored in a specific religion to all citizens, regardless of their personal religious affiliation. An exception to this rule is the majority of public holidays, which are set forth by section 1(1) of the Public Holidays Act[27] and section 7(2) of the Closing Days Act.[28] All but two originate in Art. IX of the Concordat, and apply to everybody, regardless of religious affiliation. In procedural law, dates cannot expire on weekends and public holidays, and on Good Friday as well, despite its restricted quality as a public holiday (see below section "Religiously motivated exemptions from general laws").

In addition to this, a number of provincial acts concerning cinemas and other public events require a particular respect for Good Friday and Christmas Eve, and on these days public events are prohibited from taking place. This is the case in Vorarlberg,[29] Vienna[30] and the Tyrol[31] with regard to Good Friday exclusively. The same goes for Burgenland,[32] Lower Austria[33] and Salzburg[34] provided that the event intended to take place on Good Friday or Christmas Eve is considered offensive to the population's religious feelings.

There are two acts which do not stipulate further conditions and prohibit any public event on a number of special days: section 8(3) of the Carinthian Public Events Act[35] includes Good Friday, Christmas Eve and Easter Saturday until 2 p.m.; section 16 of the Burgenland Cinema Act[36] includes Good Friday, Easter Saturday and Christmas Eve as well as all Sundays and public holidays until 10 a.m. In addition, from Palm Sunday through to Maundy Thursday and on 1 and 2 November, only films with "serious" content are allowed.

Section 10(2) of the Israelite Religious Society Act[37] refers to the Jewish calendar calculation, which differs from the generally used Gregorian, in order to calculate Sabbaths and Jewish holidays. In contrast to the above-mentioned regulations, they enjoy general protection, but are not deemed to be particular public holidays or the like. In an analogous way, sections 13(1, 2) and 20(1, 2) of the Islam Act of 2015[38] cover Muslim and Alevi holidays.

---

[27] *Feiertagsruhegesetz 1957,* BGBl. 153.

[28] *Arbeitsruhegesetz,* BGBl. 1983/144 as amended.

[29] Section 9(1) of the act LGBl. 2002/56 as amended.

[30] Section 17(2) of the act LGBl. 1955/18 as amended and section 26(5) of the act LGBl. 1971/12 as amended.

[31] Section 20(1) of the act LGBl. 2003/86 as amended.

[32] Section 16(1) of the act LGBl. 1994/2 as amended.

[33] Section 2(1) of the act LGBl. 7070–0 as amended.

[34] Section 22(1) of the act LGBl. 1997/100 as amended.

[35] *Kärntner Veranstaltungsgesetz 2010,* LGBl. 2011/27 as amended.

[36] *Burgenländisches Lichtspielgesetz 1960,* LGBl. 1962/1 as amended.

[37] *Gesetz betreffend die Regelung der äußeren Rechtsverhältnisse der israelitischen Religionsgesellschaft,* RGBl. 1890/57 as amended.

[38] *Islamgesetz* 2015, BGBl. I 39.

Another topic is raised by section 5(4) of the Cultural Heritage Protection Act,[39] which refers to ecclesiastical liturgical provisions. Where they motivate or require an alteration of protected heritage, in order to render liturgy more dignified, the competent public authority is obligated to sustain the motion.[40]

Religious Rules Within Religious Organisations

Religious freedom includes the autonomy of religious organisations to apply their own rules within their own organisations. Specific dietary or holiday regulations may serve as examples hereto. Apart from inherent limits, and pursuant to Art. 63(2) of the State Treaty of St. Germain-en-Laye,[41] in junction with Art. 53 of the ECHR, religious freedom can only be restricted, in order to protect public order or good morals.[42]

Ways of Application of Religious Rules in the State Legal System

State Law is generally produced by the federal and provincial Parliaments, whereas customary law is recognised only as an exception. In various cases, State law contains references to religious rules, such as in the above-mentioned case of religious holidays.

Religious rules can apply where international private law provides a reference to the law of States, the law of which itself is based on or consists of religious rules. Pursuant to section 9(1) of the Private International Law Act,[43] the law governing a person's status is defined by this person's nationality, which applies to affairs of family law (sections 16 ff. *leg. cit.*) and to the law of inheritance (sections 28 ff. *leg. cit.*).[44] The application is limited by the public policy clause, set forth by section 6 *leg. cit.* and Art. 12 of Council Regulation (EU) No. 1259/2010, implementing enhanced cooperation in the area of the law applicable to divorce and legal separation.[45] The public policy clause has, however, to be employed with caution.[46] In this respect, two questions have occupied the courts and authorities: polygamy and *talāq*. Whereas *talāq*—or any other unilateral declaration of divorce—clearly conflicts with Austrian public policy,[47] it is held that polygamy does so only in the case

[39] *Denkmalschutzgesetz,* BGBl. 1923/533 as amended.

[40] Wieshaider 2014: 923–924.

[41] StGBl. 1920/303.

[42] Berka 2013: marg. no. 1434 ff.

[43] *Bundesgesetz über das internationale Privatrecht,* BGBl. 1978/304 as amended.

[44] Posch 2010: 66.

[45] OJ L 2010/343: 10–16.

[46] Verschraegen 2004: § 6 IPRG, marg. no. 1.

[47] Posch 2010: 80–83.

of a close connection to the Austrian legal order, which has not been further specified yet.[48] Maintenance obligations can be granted on the basis of polygamy.[49]

Austrian public law does not provide a legal basis for general treaties between the State and religious communities concerning their external status. Only concordats between the Republic and the Holy See are unambiguously anchored in public international law. Yet very recently, this clear-cut framework has been called into question, particularly so by three treaties of the Protestant Church: a general agreement with the Federal Ministry of Justice on the pastoral care of prisoners, an agreement with the Ministry of the Interior on the pastoral care of the police and an agreement with the University of Vienna on the co-operation within the Faculty of Protestant Theology. Although the university is a public law entity different from the State, many of its decisions are still vested with public authority.[50]

Private contracts can be stipulated within the limits of section 879 of the Civil Code,[51] according to which a contract contravening a legal prohibition or good morals is null and void. Fundamental rights serve as guidelines to grasp the content of the provision.[52] There are only a few cases concerning religious issues. In this regard, it has been stated that contracts requiring a change or adoption of a certain religion are void. Here, religious freedom would be violated. Yet on another level, religion can be matter of a contract. The Supreme Court held that partners in commerce may validly agree on closing their shop on certain religious holidays, which are not generally recognised by the State.[53]

Religiously Motivated Exemptions from General Laws

Religiously motivated exemptions can be found in a few distinct cases. As stated above (section "Religious rules"), all but two public holidays originate from the Concordat. In addition to these, members of the Lutheran Church, the Reformed Church, the Old Catholic Church and the Methodist Church are accorded Good Friday as a supplementary public holiday with all legal consequences and benefits pursuant to section 7(3) of the Closing Days Act.[54]

For pupils, section 13 of the Schooldays Act[55] lays down a wider set of exemptions. First, Lutheran and Reformed pupils are exempt from school attendance on Reformation Day. Good Friday is not an issue here, because it falls within the Easter holidays. Second, pupils who are members of the Israelite Religious Society are exempt from attending school on the two first and the two last days of Passover, on

---

[48] Posch 2010: 83–87.

[49] Verschraegen 2004: § 6 IPRG, marg. no. 3.

[50] Kneucker 2011: 293–294.

[51] *Allgemeines bürgerliches Gesetzbuch,* JGS 1811/946 as amended.

[52] Krejci 2000: § 879 ABGB, marg. no. 69.

[53] OGH 24 November 1926, Ob I 801/26; Krejci 2000: § 879 ABGB, marg. no. 81a.

[54] Wieshaider 2008: 108, 112–113.

[55] *Schulzeitgesetz 1985,* BGBl. 77 as amended.

the two days of the Feast of Weeks, on the two days of New Year, on the Day of Atonement and on the two first and the two last days of the Feast of Booths. In addition to this, pupils who belong to a faith, according to which attending school or certain activities are not allowed on Saturdays, are to be exempted from attendance by the director of the school prior to a parents request. This provision currently applies to Jews and Seventh Day-Adventists and differs from the holiday-exemption by its general reference to the characteristics of a faith and not to an affiliation to a recognised religious body. The exempted pupils have to catch up on all missed lessons on their own.[56] For pupils affiliated to other religions, however, the situation is less evident. The minister for education only recommends giving Christian Orthodox,[57] Muslim,[58] Alevi[59] and Shia Muslim[60] pupils time off. All pertaining decrees are based on section 9(6) of the Compulsory School Attendance Act[61] and on section 45(4) of the School Teaching Act.[62]

Interestingly, these documents are not constructed exactly on the same principles. While most of them grant holiday exemptions to the members of the corresponding religious societies and confessional communities, with regard to Islam and Christian Orthodoxy, the guidelines refer to the adherents of the respective religions. Membership is, however, rather group oriented, whereas adherence is closer to the individual approach. Here, the latter seems more adequate in terms of both religious freedom and non-discrimination.

Cemeteries are municipal or run by a legally recognised religious society. According to Art. 12 of the Interdenominational Relations Act,[63] a religious society cannot refuse a non-affiliated person burial in its cemetery, in a family tomb, or if a cemetery of the deceased person's religion is not available in the vicinity. Section 19(2) of the Israelite Religious Society Act exempts Jewish cemeteries from these obligations, taking into account not only the different burial rites and prescriptions but also the consequences of the Holocaust with a whole number of Jewish cemeteries left throughout the country, detached from Jewish communities. For Muslim and Alevi cemeteries sections 15(2) und 22(2) of the Islam Act of 2015 stipulate similar exemptions.

Another issue relates to the slaughter of animals for human consumption. Section 32(5) of the Animal Protection Act[64] aims at accommodating the requirements of

---

[56] Wieshaider 2008: 108.

[57] The most recent decree, BMUKK-21.001/0005-III/3/2013, concerns Christmas, Good Friday, Easter Monday and Whit Monday and their patron saints' festivals according to the Julian calendar and covers three years.

[58] The most recent decree, BMUKK-21.001/0001-III/3/2012, concerns the Sugar Feast and the Feast of the Sacrifice and covers four years.

[59] The most recent decree, BMBF-21.001/0006-III/3/2014, concerns the Fast of *Hızır,* New Year, the Feast of the Sacrifice and *Ashure* Day and covers five years.

[60] The most recent decree, BMUKK-21.001/0002-III/3/2013, concerns the Sugar Feast, the Feast of the Sacrifice, on *Eid al-Ghadeer* and *Ashure* Day and covers five years.

[61] *Schulpflichtgesetz 1985,* BGBl. 76 as amended.

[62] *Schulunterrichtsgesetz,* BGBl. 1986/472.

[63] *Gesetz, wodurch die interconfessionellen Verhältnisse der Staatsbürger in den darin angegebenen Beziehungen geregelt werden,* RGBl. 1868/49 as amended.

[64] *Tierschutzgesetz,* BGBl. I 2004/118 as amended.

legally recognised religious societies,[65] consistently with Art. 4(4) and Art. 26(2)c of Council Regulation (EC) No. 1099/2009 on the Protection of Animals at the Time of Killing.[66]

Accommodation of Religious Needs

Freedom of religion is not binding on anybody but the State, as is the case with any other fundamental right unless explicitly stated otherwise. The courts have, however, expanded their understanding from merely negative to positive aspects, implying that the State is obligated to positively provide for a space to exercise a fundamental right. The Eur. Ct. HR[67] has extensively developed its case law along this line, especially in labour law.[68] This case law has to be heeded by employers. Explicit regulations can, however, only be found in the Equal Treatment Act.[69]

Section 17(1) and section 18(1) *leg. cit.* prohibit any discrimination on the grounds of religion or weltanschauung as to access to employment and promotion, to self-employment or to occupation, to vocational guidance and training, to employment and working conditions (including dismissals and pay), to the membership of an organisation of workers or employers, and to involvement therein. Cases deal with religious garments, religious holidays, the accommodation of prayer times, or food choices in the workplaces.[70] Based on the case of Vivien Prais vs. Council of the EC,[71] there is a common doctrinal agreement that employers are obligated to undertake all appropriate measures to accommodate the religious needs of employees and to prevent conflicts. The employees are bound to facilitate this task by cooperating. The interests of both sides have to be weighed up against each other.[72]

Adjudication

In general, the State does not allot formal jurisdiction to religious courts; the respective legal orders are separate. This holds true for family law as well.

---

[65] Wieshaider 2005: 242–262.

[66] OJ L 2009/303: 1–30.

[67] 15 January 2013; 48420/10, 36516/10, 51671/10, 59842/10; Eweida and others vs. the United Kingdom.

[68] Schinkele 2012: 167–173.

[69] *Gleichbehandlungsgesetz,* BGBl. I 2004/66 as amended.

[70] Windisch-Graetz 2005: § 17 GlBG, marg. no. 26–34.

[71] ECJ 27 October 1976, 130/75, ECR 1976, 1589.

[72] Windisch-Graetz 2005: § 17 GlBG, marg. no. 34.

An exception to this rule is section 38(1) of the University Act,[73] which is based on Art. V para. 3 and 4 of Concordat. Pursuant to the latter stipulations both the nomination of a professor at a Catholic theological faculty and his dismissal depend on the authorised Catholic bishop's consent.[74] The professors have legal remedies only within Canon law.[75] In this respect the ecclesiastical jurisdiction is prescribed and exclusive, and considered already enshrined in the constitutional guarantee of the Church's autonomy by some authors[76]; others however argue a stronger position of the freedom of science and research against which freedom of religion has to be balanced in the individual cases.[77]

Compared to the recognition of such wide powers to the Catholic Church, section 38(2) *leg. cit.* and section 15(4) of Protestant Church Act (above, section "Historical and political processes") just grant the Protestant Church the right to be heard in an analogous situation.[78]

The above (section "Religious rules") mentioned heritage provisions referring to liturgical provisions are interpreted by the ecclesiastical authorities. Here however, their influence is not as strong as in the case of university law, because they just set the framework for a consultative procedure where a compromise is being sought.[79]

Within their constitutionally guaranteed religious autonomy, religious communities may establish conciliation or arbitration boards, resolving internal conflicts, deciding on membership questions and the like. These boards may even be prescribed by an act governing the external relations of a religious society, e.g. sections 3 and 5 of Israelite Religious Society Act (above, section "Religious rules"). When hearing these questions, the arbitration boards act according to their own systems without recognition by the State and its authorities. The State courts are not competent to decide, as long as there are no civil obligations involved, as, for instance, due membership fees.

In other issues, dispute resolution can be handed to arbitration tribunals pursuant to sections 577 ff. of the Code of Civil Procedure.[80] Their decisions are final; they have the same effects as binding and conclusive State court rulings, as section 607 *leg. cit.* stipulates. In exchange, the State provides a basic set of procedural guarantees and two public policy clauses as thresholds beyond which a State court can quash a decision of an arbitration tribunal seated in Austria according to section 611 *leg. cit.*[81] According to section 603 *leg. cit.* the parties can agree on the set of legal provisions to be applied. Underlying them is a broad concept, to facilitate an

---

[73] *Universitätsgesetz 2002*, BGBl. I 120.

[74] Can. 810 CIC 1983; Art. 25–30 Sapientia Christiana, AAS 71 (1979) 469 ff.

[75] Muzak 2010: § 38 UG, no. III.3.

[76] Potz and Schinkele 2002: 418–419.

[77] Hammer 2014: 129–132.

[78] Muzak 2010: § 38 UG, no. III.3.

[79] Wieshaider 2014: 923–934.

[80] *Zivilprozessordnung*, RGBl. 1895/113 as amended.

[81] Hausmaninger 2007: § 607 ZPO, marg. no. 19 and § 611 ZPO, marg. no. 12–20.

agreement on provisions of various origins.[82] In addition, the parties can stipulate that the arbitration tribunal will decide ex aequo et bono—with due regard to the rule of equality and to the public policy clause.[83] Within this framework religious law can serve as the legal basis for arbitral awards.[84]

Social Implementation of Religious Rules (Without Any Official Recognition)

There is no evidence to suggest that a significant number of citizens apply religious rules prescribing acts and behaviour which are in conflict with State law.

A very specific issue is, however, connected to opening shops on Sundays and public holidays. Having closed their shops out of respect for their own religious holidays, members of religious minorities tend to reopen on Sundays or public holidays in order to compensate, even if they risk fines.[85] Public authorities have not yet issued pertinent permissions, which would, however, be allowed by section 5 of the Opening Hours Act.[86]

Religious behaviour other than the mainstream one, however, has been arousing opposition or even hostility in part of the population.[87] This holds true for garments connoting minority religious conviction, especially for Muslim headscarfs[88] or the construction of mosques.[89]

The Supreme Court, no less, once considered prayers during breaks in labour to violate the religious freedom of other, un-concerned workers.[90] This opinion was criticised in literature.[91] The religious method of the slaughter of animals for human consumption has been contested, although it is unmistakably protected by religious freedom[92] and enshrined by the Animal Protection Act (above, section "Religiously motivated exemptions from general laws").[93] The same goes for religious circumcision, which is legal in Austria,[94] yet at times viewed with hostility by many people in no way directly affected.

---

[82] Hausmaninger 2007: § 603 ZPO, marg. no. 13.

[83] Hausmaninger 2007: § 603 ZPO, marg. no. 21.

[84] Adolphsen and Schmalenberg 2007.

[85] LVwG Wien 20 March 2014, VGW-021/019/20066/2014.

[86] *Öffnungszeitengesetz 2003,* BGBl. I 48 as amended.

[87] Zulehner 2014: 949–952.

[88] Pesendorfer 2009: 113–147.

[89] Wieshaider 2007; Pesendorfer 2009: 51–92; Fürlinger 2013.

[90] OGH 27 March 1996, 9 Ob A 18/96.

[91] Mosler 1997; Windisch-Graetz 2005: § 17 GlBG, marg. no. 34.

[92] VfSlg. 15 394.

[93] Wieshaider 2005: 228–239.

[94] Pabel 2013: 469–487.

As mentioned above (3), religious adjudication bodies need to comply with basic rules, in order to produce results recognised by State law. But even beyond that, citizens are free to address religious institutions to resolve their conflicts—still within the limits of public policy.

Conclusion

By and large, the system seems to be satisfactory from a constitutional point of view, i.e. with reference to the respect of human rights and particularly of religious liberty, and to non-discrimination. Nonetheless, it must be admitted that a lack of understanding—which is not always of social nature, but also of statutory quality—rather encourages forms of segregation, because a general disrespect of religious needs forces members of minority communities to live their lives—working activities included—within their own communities, in order to achieve appropriate accommodation. Although various State institutions try to promote an even-handed and fair attitude towards different religions, it cannot be said that all possible means are used to avoid preferential treatment of the religious majority and non-religious individuals over members of most religious minorities. Bestowing legal personality upon religious communities is only the first step towards their inclusion (and particularly minority religious communities) in the social fabric. A solution to create true social cohesion could be the thorough the implementation of religious liberty and non-discrimination in all fields of statutory and regulatory law as well as on all levels of enforcement. Strategies ought to be chosen diligently and in accordance with the various issues, so that attention is paid to ensuring a balanced position of both individuals and groups (above, section "Religiously motivated exemptions from general laws").

References

Adolphsen, Jens, and Franziska Schmalenberg. 2007. Islamisches Recht als materielles Recht in der Schiedsgerichtsbarkeit? *SchiedsVZ* 5: 57–64.

Berka, Walter. 2013. *Verfassungsrecht*, 5th ed. Wien: Verlag Österreich.

Fürlinger, Ernst. 2013. *Moscheebaukonflikte in Österreich, Nationale Politik des religiösen Raums im globalen Zeitalter*. Göttingen: Vandenhoeck & Ruprecht.

Gampl, Inge. 1971. *Österreichisches Staatskirchenrecht*. Wien/New York: Springer.

Hammer, Stefan. 2014. Zur konfessionellen Bindung der Theologie aus Sicht der Wissenschaftsfreiheit. In *Recht – Religion – Kultur, Festschrift für Richard Potz zum 70. Geburtstag*, ed. Brigitte Schinkele, René Kuppe, Stefan Schima, Eva M. Synek, Jürgen Wallner, and Wolfgang Wieshaider, 117–132. Wien: WUV Facultas.

Hausmaninger, Christian. 2007. In *Kommentar zu den Zivilprozessgesetzen IV/2, Schiedsverfahrensrecht §§ 577–618 ZPO*, 2nd ed., ed. Hans W. Fasching and Andreas Konecny. Wien: Manz.

Kalb, Herbert, Richard Potz, and Brigitte Schinkele. 2003. *Religionsrecht*. Wien: Facultas.

Kneucker, Raoul. 2011. Verträge mit Kirchenleitungen, James Alfred Loader zum 65. Geburtstag, Fachtagung: 150 Jahre Protestantenpatent – 50 Jahre Protestantengesetz. *öarr.* 58: 293–327.

Krejci, Heinz. 2000. In *Kommentar zum Allgemeinen bürgerlichen Gesetzbuch*, vol. I, 3rd ed., ed. Peter Rummel. Wien: Manz.

Marik-Lebeck, Stephan. 2010. Die muslimische Bevölkerung Österreichs: Bestand und Veränderung 2001–2009. In *Islam in Österreich*, ed. Alexander Janda and Mathias Vogl, 5–9. Wien: Österreichischer Integrationsfonds.

Muzak, Gerhard. 2010. In *Kommentar zum Universitätsgesetz*, 2nd ed., ed. Heinz Mayer. Wien: Manz.

Pabel, Katharina. 2013. Die religiöse Beschneidung von Jungen im Lichte der Grundrechte in Österreich. In *Neuere Entwicklungen im Religionsrecht europäischer Staaten*, Kanonistische Studien und Texte 61, ed. Wilhelm Rees, María Roca, and Balázs Schanda, 467–487. Berlin: Humblot.

Pernthaler, Peter. 2000. Gott in der Verfassung. *öarr.* 47: 177–201.

Pesendorfer, Paul Simon. 2009. *Staatliche Akzeptanz von religiösen Riten und Symbolen*. Wien: Verlag Österreich.

Posch, Willibald. 2010. Spannungsfelder zwischen Scharia und österreichischem Zivilrecht. *öarr.* 57: 66–89.

Potz, Richard. 2005. State and Church in Austria. In *State and Church in the European Union*, 2nd ed., ed. Gerhard Robbers, 391–418. Baden-Baden: Nomos.

Potz, Richard, and Brigitte Schinkele. 2002. Im Spannungsfeld von kirchlichem Selbstbestimmungsrecht und Universitätsautonomie: Das konkordatäre Zustimmungsrecht des Bischofs. *öarr.* 49: 401–448.

Potz, Richard, and Brigitte Schinkele. 2010. Gutachten zu den religionsrechtlichen Aspekten des Niederösterreichischen Kindergartengesetzes. *öarr.* 57: 395–412.

Rudolf Mosler 1997. Gloss of OGH 27 March 1996, 9 Ob A 18/96. DRdA no. 6.

Schinkele, Brigitte. 2012. Kirchliches Arbeitsrecht in der aktuellen Rechtsprechung des Europäischen Gerichtshofs für Menschenrechte. *öarr.* 59: 155–173.

Verschraegen, Bea. 2004. In *Kommentar zum Allgemeinen bürgerlichen Gesetzbuch*, vol. II, 3rd ed., ed. Peter Rummel. Wien: Manz.

Walter, Robert, Heinz Mayer, and Gabriele Kucsko-Stadelmayer. 2007. *Grundriss des österreichischen Bundesverfassungsrechts*, 10th ed. Wien: Manz.

Wieshaider, Wolfgang. 2005. Iterum: Schächten, Rund ums neue österreichische Tierschutzgesetz. *öarr.* 52: 227–262.

Wieshaider, Wolfgang. 2007. Das harmonische Minarett, Zur Vereinbarkeit von Minaretten mit dem Orts-Straßen- und Landschaftsbild. *bbl.* 10: 209–213.

Wieshaider, Wolfgang. 2008. Religious Holidays in State Law and Directive No. 2000/78/EC. In *State-Church relations in Europe. Contemporary issues and trends at the beginning of the 21st century*, ed. Lucia Grešková, 106–116. Bratislava: Institute for State-Church Relations.

Wieshaider, Wolfgang. 2014. Die Weitergabe von Kultusbauten vor dem Hintergrund des Denkmalschutzrechtes. In *Recht – Religion – Kultur, Festschrift für Richard Potz zum 70. Geburtstag*, ed. Brigitte Schinkele, René Kuppe, Stefan Schima, Eva M. Synek, Jürgen Wallner, and Wolfgang Wieshaider, 923–934. Wien: WUV Facultas.

Windisch-Graetz, Michaela. 2005. In *Kommentar zum Gleichbehandlungsgesetz*, ed. Robert Rebhahn. Wien/New York: Springer.

Zulehner, Paul M. 2014. Kulturchristen, Kommt der "clash of religions"? In *Recht – Religion – Kultur, Festschrift für Richard Potz zum 70. Geburtstag*, ed. Brigitte Schinkele, René Kuppe, Stefan Schima, Eva M. Synek, Jürgen Wallner, and Wolfgang Wieshaider, 935–954. Wien: WUV Facultas.

Chapter 6
Religious Rules and Principles in Belgian Law

Louis-Léon Christians and Adriaan Overbeeke

Abstract Whilst Belgian society is highly secularised, Belgian courts very often use the concept of "religious rules", but its precise content remains undefined. Sometimes the concept of "religious rules" is very narrowly understood as an institutional and formal rule enacted by a religious authority. Sometimes the concept is largely open to include any individual feeling of religious duty. Sometimes the concept is only open to registered religions, sometimes it includes any kind of religious or philosophical groups. This report chooses a generous understanding of the concept, while focusing it on traditional religions.

Introduction

Historical and Political Processes

Since the foundation of an independent Belgian State the position of religion was firmly safeguarded by the 1831 Constitution. The regulations for the relationship between church and state bear the imprint of the Dutch period, preceding Belgian independence in 1830. Belgium did not only establish a regime of exceptional freedom (also on the level of the religious communities) but at the same time upheld a system of financial state support for different religions present in the country (Van Haegendoren and Alen 1992; Shelley 1990).

In the second half of the nineteenth century, Liberals and Roman Catholics, when they were in power, each took political measures that lead to and constantly fuelled a quasi-permanent struggle on issues related to church and state relationship. Liberal school policies were one of the best stimuli for the development of parallel school systems, ultimately leading to a strong Roman Catholic pillar in all possible life domains. The Christian democratic party slowly lost its position as an

L.-L. Christians (✉)
Université Catholique de Louvain, Louvain-la-Neuve, Belgium
e-mail: louis-leon.christians@uclouvain.be

A. Overbeeke
Free University of Amsterdam, Amsterdam, The Netherlands
e-mail: a.j.overbeeke@rechten.vu.nl

R. Bottoni et al. (eds.), *Religious Rules, State Law, and Normative Pluralism - A Comparative Overview*, Ius Comparatum – Global Studies in Comparative Law 18, DOI 10.1007/978-3-319-28335-7_6

inescapable partner in coalitions governments.[1] This made the party powerless in its parliamentary opposition against changing legislation in some highly sensitive issues (abortion, euthanasia).

The integration in broader international institutions did affect the national legal framework that determines different aspects of state-religion relations. The changing position of religious organizations[2] is a topic of discussion, in politics and society, but also in doctrine. At the same time, religious claims of individual believers, especially when their religion is considered as foreign, are on the discussion table. The debate on religious signs is increasingly an issue for the courts. This issue is fuelling a debate on the meaning of the neutrality of the state, neutrality of state institutions in general and state schools in particular.[3]

Features of the National Legal System: Separation and *Cooperation*

The State-religion relationship is – also in a reaction towards the earlier regimes – freedom oriented (Torfs 2005, 2013; Velaers and Foblets 2010; Overbeeke 2011a). The freedom is a state-*supported* freedom while the state budget yearly provides for the payment of the salaries of religious leaders.

The neutrality of the state is not written down in the Constitution itself. The Council of State considers the principle to be linked to the non-discrimination principle.[4] So in principle all religions (traditional religions but also new religious movements) are equal for the law and equally protected. The neutrality *principle* is not discussed anymore, but *the meaning* of neutrality in different domains of state activities is heavily debated.

Where the state operates as a facilitator for religious groups, the Belgian regime is (and has to be in the light of the neutrality principle) open to newcomers, as was proven with the inclusion of the humanist movement in an equal position compared to the traditional 'recognized religions'.

[1] The last Catholic *one party government* dates back from 1950–1954.

[2] They still have a proportionally strong position in some segments of the labour market: approximately two thirds of Belgian education facilities in primary and secondary education are faith based and belong with some exceptions (there are only a small number of Protestant, Jewish and Muslim schools) to the Roman Catholic faith.

[3] In two cases the Council of State has to verify whether a Flemish State School authorities' policy (banning religious dress even for religion teachers is in line with its policy to remain neutral) is acceptable in the light of both the Constitution and of Belgium's international law obligations. Claims based also on art. 9 ECHR: see Council of State nr. 226.345, 5 February 2014; nr. 226.346, 5 February 2014.

[4] Council of State (as advisor in the legislative process) in: Advice 44.521/AG, 20 May 2008, *Parl. Doc*. Senate 2007–2008, nr. 4-351/2, p. 8. (authors' translation).

Since the turn of the century the support regime is permanently under study[5] and critique (Franken and Loobuyck 2013).

Meaning of the Expression "Religious Rules"

Belgian courts very often use the concept of "religious rules", but its precise content remains undefined. Sometimes the concept of "religious rules" is very narrowly understood as an institutional and formal rule enacted by a religious authority. Sometimes the concept is largely open to include any individual feeling of religious duty. This report also chooses a generous understanding of the concept, while focusing it on traditional religions. Along this large continuum, three main issues may be addressed. First, Belgian courts do not seem to clearly distinguish 'culture' and 'religion' nor make a coherent distinction between cultural customs and religious traditions. Islam is one of the main fields that allows such an observation. For example, in addressing the wearing of a veil by pupils, some courts have tried to find some arguments referring to the national origin or the cultural background of the girl's family history. Conversely, it is also possible to observe a strategy of balancing between a *cultural* understanding for previous dominant religious customs (e.g. Sunday rest) and an accentuation on *religious* aspects to describe minority practices. This variation pushes the judge to deem neutral the former but not the latter (Christians 1995). On the other hand, "religious rules" are sometimes (and even wrongly) referred to as norms coming only from recognized religions. The judiciary seems to be reluctant to take into account religious "rules" affirmed by non-recognized churches or traditions. Further, a "deference principle" is classically adopted by Belgian courts in order not to attempt any interpretation of a general religious rule, but to only defer to a religious authority that has previously interpreted the controversial rule. Nevertheless, this "deference principle", which mainly applies within the system of 'recognised' religions, is sometimes extended to other fields of Belgian law which would have required a more individual and subjective approach, i.e. not to submit an individual religious freedom complaint to a collective or institutional church authority's formal appraisal.

[5] Reports, made on government demand: Delruelle and Torfs (2005), Mortier and Rigaux (2006), and Magits et al. (2010).

Legislation

Religion Mentioned in the Legal Texts (Constitution Preambles, Basic Laws, Other Legal Texts) Defining the Principles and Values Inspiring the State Legal System (Van Haegendoren and Alen 1992; Christians 2009; Overbeeke 2007, 2011a; Rigaux and Christians 2011)

The Belgian Constitution does mention "religion" in two different chapters. The chapter on *fundamental rights* contains four relevant sections, guaranteeing full religious freedom on both the individual and the collective level (the level of religious communities): an article guaranteeing freedom of religion (art. 19), an article guaranteeing the negative aspect of this freedom (art. 20) and a section on religious autonomy (art. 21). Religion is also mentioned in art. 24 §1 Constitution (on educational freedom, a sensitive freedom that historically was guaranteed for the Roman Catholic religion in the first place (De Rynck 2005), even if "religious" schools are not specifically mentioned) and education rights. Important in this respect are paragraphs (added in 1988) on the religious rights of parents, including a right to be offered denominational religious education. In 2014 the Council of State asked the Constitutional Court to enlighten the Council on the issue of obligatory religious education in public authorities' schools,[6] a school subject heavily debated (Loobuyck and Franken 2011; Torfs 2011).

Financial state support, already visible in the educational field, is also present in the constitutional chapter on *the State's finances*. Article 181 §1 guarantees state wages and pensions for religious leaders, while 181 §2, introduced in 1993, opens the possibility to finance non-religious beliefs as well. This arrangement created a *constitutional* basis for a further expansion of the already state supported humanist institutions.

Religious Laws/Principles Mentioned in Connection with Specific Parts of the State Legal System

Belgian State legislation does not mention *religious laws* as *legal sources*. Religious 'principles' or religious 'practices' are however present or wilfully taken into account in legislation. In many cases the reasons for this are linked to the intention of the legislator to take religious rights of the citizens seriously. In some cases religion is however considered to be a potential societal threat; so there legislation is meant to be a protection against religious manifestation. Both sides of the coin are prominent in criminal law. In almost all the domains discussed below the law does not differentiate between the religions involved. In this respect (state supported) 'recognized' and 'non-recognized' religions are treated on equal foot.

[6] See: Council of State, nr. 226.627 6 March 2014.

Family Law (See Christians 2010)

The legislation on adoption explicitly includes religion and belief (the religious background of the child) into the elements to be taken into consideration when deciding on an adoption, in order to respect the best interest of the child and its fundamental rights.[7]

The Civil Code contains the exceptional possibility that, if both parents do not agree on a child's *religious upbringing* after separation, a judge has the authority to make one parent responsible for major religious choices (for the child).[8]

Belgian Private International Law (PIL) allows religious personal status created abroad through a local State recognition to have some indirect effects in Belgium through the mechanism of a simplified public order control. Through this mechanism, widows validly married abroad in a polygamous marriage get an equal and proportional share in survival pension rights (Alofs and Cuypers 2009; Francq and Mary 2013). No express mention of a religious rule is provided: this is a common PIL mechanism at least implicitly accommodating religious norms.[9] In 2014 this mechanism was applied in the case of 190 survivor's pensions.[10]

The Constitution contains in its art. 21 a paragraph on the position of religious marriages: "A civil wedding should always precede the blessing of the marriage (…)". Here we find a 'negative' reference to a religious principle (and for the Roman Catholic church a canonical law), religious marriage. This requirement was included in art. 267 Penal Code as an offence for the religious minister. Courts often hesitate between civil and religious interpretation of the concept of "benediction" : are the religious manifestations under scrutiny religious marriage, or only a betrothal for instance?[11]

Criminal Law (See Brems 2013)

The 1867 Penal code protects a series of religious manifestations, penalizing the disturbance of religious ceremonies,[12] insulting sacred objects used in religious ceremonies,[13] or insulting or attacking religious ministers acting in those ceremonies[14] (Clesse and De Pooter 2012a). No formal reference to a religious rule is made

[7] Art. 362.3, 3° Law 24 April 2003 on adoption, *State Gazette* 16 May 2003.

[8] Art. 374 §1 Civil Code.

[9] Constitutional Court, nr. 96/2009, 4 June 2009.

[10] *Parl. Questions* House of Representatives 2013–2014, Bulletin 150, 3 March 2014, p. 239 (Question nr. 130 Bracke). This is a consequence of the Belgian-Moroccan Convention on social security, Rabat, 28 June 1968, *State Gazette* 1970, p. 8113.

[11] For an example see Mons Court of appeals, 16 June 2009, *Revue générale de droit civil.*, 2011, 361.

[12] Art. 143 Penal Code.

[13] Art. 144 Penal Code.

[14] Art. 145 Penal Code; Art. 146 Penal Code.

in the Penal Code. Nevertheless, the public prosecutor's office seems to act here on the basis of notice by religious authorities even where a non-recognized denomination is concerned.[15]

Article 458 Penal code protects the privacy of the individual believer by including religious ministers in the category of persons penalized for breach of professional secret. Only in exceptional cases the law obliges them to disclose these secrets (see also 458bis Penal Code). The case law progressively broadened the scope of the offence in order to protect every religious confidence, without reference to any specific religious norm.

The Penal Code protects against pressure of a religious nature as well against pressure on a person who wants to manifest his religion or belief.[16] So both aspects of religious freedom (positive and negative freedom) are guaranteed.[17]

For a number of offences criminal law considers it to be an *aggravating circumstance*, provoking higher sentences, if the motive for which the criminal acts are committed are *hate, contempt or hostility* toward a person for, amongst other grounds, this person's *religion or philosophical worldview* (Brems 2013).[18]

Since 2001 an offence of *female genital mutilation*, understood as an intervention with a cultural and religious background, is introduced in art. 409 Penal Code (Wattier 2010).[19]

The Penal Code stipulates[20] that religious ministers, when exercising their function in public, are prohibited to "directly" attack the government, an act of parliament, a royal decree or any other public authorities' act. This ban on political speech for one specific category of the population – a *limitation of 'religious speech'* – is considered to be incompatible with fundamental rights obligations (Brems 2013; Clesse and De Pooter 2012b).

Penal law gives the *people's jury* judging power in serious criminal cases. Exempted from the obligation (or even excluded, the law is introducing an incompatibility) to participate in a jury are the "ministers of a recognized religion and

[15] Some difficulties may arise from the lack of consensus between diverse religious authorities of a single denomination (for example, it seemed difficult to prosecute a photographic exhibition of a naked Virgin Mary organized in a church, morally condemned by the Holy See Nuncio but authorized by the rector of the church where the exhibition is organized. *La Libre Belgique*, 16 February 2006, www.blaspheme.be, bulletin de la label, n°38. See also: ECtHR, 7 July 2009 (Skiba v Pologne), n°10659/03.

[16] Art. 142 Penal Code.

[17] Negative religious freedom is already protected in the 20 Constitution.

[18] Articles 372-377*bis*, 393-405*bis* and 405*quater*, 422*bis*, *ter* & *quater*, 434-437 j° 438*bis*, 442*bis* & *ter*, 443-452 j° 453*bis*, 510-514*bis*, 521-525*bis*, 528-532*bis*, 534*bis*, *ter* j° *quater* Penal Code.

[19] Art. 29 Law 28 November 2000 on the criminal protection of minors, *State Gazette* 17 March 2001. See: *Parl. Doc* House of Representatives, 1998–1999, 1907/1; *Parl. Doc.* Senate 1999-2000, nr. 2-280/5, pp. 103 et seq. Report D. Dubourg & F. Richard (2011), *Etude de prevalence des femmes excises et des filles à risqué d'excision en Belgique*, Brussels : Federal Government, 49 p. This offence does not include male circumcisions, as explicitly stated by the Parliament Drafting Committee.

[20] Art. 268 Penal Code.

persons providing moral assistance according to a non-denominational philosophical concept".[21] This functional exemption did apply to "religious ministers" in general, but was limited since 2009 to persons involved in recognized religions or humanist counsellors since.

Federal discrimination law protects persons or groups against incitement to discrimination, hatred or violence on the basis a number of non-acceptable, problematic criteria. One of the forbidden discrimination grounds is 'religion and non-religious world views'.[22]

Since 2012 a new offence has been introduced in criminal law, intended to penalize abuses by sectarian organizations (Hanoulle and Marlier 2014; Kuty 2012).[23] To that end a new chapter on "Abuse of a person's vulnerability" has been added to the Penal Code,[24] introducing article 442quater, stipulating in §1: "Will be sentenced to a jail term going from one month to two years and a fine (…), anyone who, knowing the situation of physical or psychological weakness of a person altering seriously her capacity of discernment, has fraudulently abused of this situation so as to get that person to do an act or refrain from doing an act, this act or omission being highly detrimental to her physical or mental integrity or to her patrimony".[25] In October 2013 the Constitutional Court upheld the legislation.[26]

Civil Procedure Law

The legislation on the *seizure* of goods of persons in debt contains a list of basic goods that are exempt from seizure. This list includes the "objects in use for religious manifestation".[27]

[21] Art. 224, 12° Code judiciaire. See: L.-L. Christians, "Nouvelle cour d'assises, jury et cultes". http://belgianlawreligion.unblog.fr/2010/01/30/nouveaux-jurys-dassises-et-cultes/

[22] Law 10 May 2007 combating certain types of discrimination, *State Gazette* 30 May 2007; art. 444 Penal Code.

[23] The intention was to criminalise "acts of mental destabilisation", committed by *sects. Parl. Doc.* House of Representatives, Session 2010, nr. 80/1.

[24] See Art. 35 and 36 Law 26 November 2011, *State Gazette* 23 January 2012.

[25] Some new aggravating circumstances are defined, two of which are important for the present report : (a) "the fact that the act or abstention mentioned in § 1 is the result of a *physical or psychological destabilization by exercising serious or repeated pressures or specific acts aimed to impair the individual ability of discernment*"; (b) "abuse referred to in § 1 constitutes an act of participation in the *principal or secondary activity of an association*", a circumstance that can require a specific analysis by the courts of the association's statutes. If "religious norms" are included in these statutes, they also could be put under judicial scrutiny.

[26] Constitutional Court nr. 146/13, 7 November 2013.

[27] Art. 1408 §1, 4° Code of Procedure.

Penitentiary Law

Penitentiary law includes *guarantees for religious freedom* for detainees in penal institutions, including food regulations (Overbeeke 2005).[28] The rising number of Muslim detainees necessitated a change in food policies (halal food on some occasions offered to all prisoners) and the introduction of state financed Muslim counsellors.[29]

Electoral Legislation

The Belgian electoral system is based on a right to vote that is based on a civic duty. The obligation for the voter to present himself on election day is sanctioned by penal law. The different electoral Codes contain an important exception for those voters not able to show up at the ballot bureau for religious reasons. This is one of the rare Belgian rules explicitly requiring a religious decision from religious authorities.[30]

Medical Law, Medical Profession

In medical law, more precisely with regard to the medical professions, the introduction of new legislation on ethical questions that potentially come in conflict with certain personal religious viewpoints, created room for conscientious objection, but this without an explicit reference to religion. This is the case for the legislation on *abortion* (1990)[31] and on *euthanasia* (2002).[32] Where medical professionals are confronted with religious objections of patients (or their relatives), there is an obligation to respect these objections. This is visible in legislation regarding *autopsy.*[33]

In order to get a recognition as a general practitioner[34] or other specific medical functions the professional skills include the *knowledge of the impact of religious*

---

[28] Law 12 January 2005 on penitentiary institutions and the rights of detainees, *State Gazette* 1 February 2005.

[29] Royal Decree 25 October 2005, *State Gazette* 10 November 2005.

[30] "Has the right to mandate another voter to vote in his name: (…) 5° the voter who, for religious reasons, is unable to present himself at the ballot bureau. This inability has to be proven in a written document, *issued by religious authorities*" Art. 147bis §1, (federal) Electoral Code. See also: Art. 212bis, §1, 5°, Flemish Act on local authorities; Art. 205bis, §1, 5° Flemish Act on Provinces; Art. L4132-1 § 1, 5° Code for local democracy and decentralisation (Wallonia).

[31] Art. 350, lid 2, 6° Penal Code.

[32] Art. 14 Euthanasia Act 28 May 2002, *State Gazette* 22 June 2002.

[33] Art. 6 Royal Decree 20 August 1996 holding the recognition criteria for local neonatal care functions, *State Gazette* 1 October 1996. Idem: art. 5§2,6° Royal Decree 20 Augustus 1996 holding the recognition criteria for regional perinatal care, *State Gazette* 1 October 1996.

[34] Ministerial Decree 1 March 2010 holding the criteria for the recognition of general practitioners, *State Gazette* 4 March 2010.

beliefs for their patients.[35] *Male circumcision* (see Meyer 2013) is part of the 'nomenclature' of medical interventions but not labelled as being religious in nature.[36]

Disposal of the Dead

Burial legislation leaves some room to accommodate religious principles (Dehert 2006)[37] but *not* the Jewish religious norm concerning eternal rest (Evers 1998),[38] what explains the existence of cemeteries of Antwerp Jewish communities on foreign soil, namely in the Netherlands. Since 2004, new regional legislations progressively have allowed burials with linen cloth (shroud) instead of a coffin. The debates show the explicit ambition of parliament to accommodate Islamic burial requirements. The legal texts however do not explicitly mention Islam, nor limit the use of the shroud to a religious use.[39] Legislation has the municipal cemetery as the general rule, but still leaves some room for burials in special religious cemeteries.[40]

Animal Welfare Legislation

Animal welfare legislation gives religions, in fact Jewish and Muslim minorities, the opportunity to follow religious prescriptions for slaughter (Velaers and Foblets 2012; Saers and Foblets 2012).[41] A religious certification by a recognized religious authority is required. On a parliamentary level, proposals were tabled to ban slaughtering without stunning. The Council of State advised to leave room for exceptions in order to respect religious freedom principles.[42]

---

[35] Ministerial Decree 28 January 2009 holding the criteria for recognition of nurses as nurses specialised in oncology, *State Gazette* 18 February 2009.

[36] Royal Decree 29 September 2002 implementing article 138 of the Hospital Act 1987, *State Gazette* 29 October 2002.

[37] See federal legislation: Law 20 July 1971 on the cemeteries and the disposal of the dead, *State Gazette* 3 August 1971. Flemish Region: Parl. Decr. 16 January 2004 on the cemeteries and the disposal of the dead, *State Gazette* 10 February 2004.

[38] For the Flemish Region: Art. 7§1 Parl. Decr. 16 January 2004.

[39] Art. 11 Parliamentary Decree Flemish Parliament 16 January 2004. Recently: Art. 2 Ordonnantie Brussels Parliament 26 July 2013, changing the 20 July 1971 law in order to allow a burial in other coverings than the coffin, *State Gazette* 3 September 2013.

[40] See for instance: Art. 21§1 Parl. Decree German Community 14 February 2011 on the cemeteries and the disposal of the dead, *State Gazette* 28 March 2011.

[41] Art. 16§1 Law 14 August 1986 on the protection and wellbeing of animals, *State Gazette* 3 December 1986; Royal Decree 11 February 1988 on ritual slaughtering, *State Gazette* 10 March 1998.

[42] Council of State, advice nr 40.350/AV, *Parl. Doc.* Senate 2005–2006, nr. 3-808/6. A recent proposal to ban religious slaughtering: House of Representatives 2010–2011, nr. 581/001.

Legislation on Public Servants

Religious belonging or identity may not be a reason not to appoint someone as a public servant (art. 10-11 Constitution). This does not answer questions concerning religious rights on the job, for instance *the right to wear religious apparel*. Here a conflict of interests is possible, and thus a balancing of interests, the appearance of government neutrality on the one side and freedom of religion on the other. Belgian legislation does not contain a general prohibitions to ban religious signs or dress by civil servants (Mathieu et al. 2013). In March 2014 an attempt to vote such a prohibition in the Walloon Parliament failed.

For some specific occasions the right on a day off is well established in general labour law. This legislation is accommodating only a specific segment of the religious market, namely Roman Catholicism and Humanism.[43] These accommodations are not built by a *general* reference to religious rules or humanist traditions, but through an exhaustive list of day-off causes specifically recognized by the law.

Legislation on the police force stipulates that objections against certain tasks "for philosophical or *religious reasons*" are a motive for an immediate dismissal.[44]

Education Law

Education law is a legal battlefield when it comes to the accommodation of the wish to accomplish religious rules in the school environment. The focus in Belgian education law is on *visible religious signs*. Public school teachers in Flanders are submitted to a general prohibition of wearing religious signs (Mathieu et al. 2010; Overbeeke et al. 2009). Within the French speaking Community, each school is free to adopt a prohibitive measure (for teachers and even pupils). In the Flemish education system the ban on religious signs for teachers – even religion teachers – and pupils in Flemish government schools provoked many court cases, one of which is still waiting for final adjudication on the level of the Council of State, who has to decide on the constitutionality of a ban for Muslim religion teachers to wear the headscarf on the school premises.[45]

Education law provides for denominational *religious education* in all government schools, including a course on humanist non-confessional ethics. In the educational system an *exemption system* exists, in order to respect the religious choices of the parents not belonging to the recognized religions.

---

[43] See Art. 376, 10°-12° Civil Servants Code Wallonia 18 December 2003, *State Gazette* 31 December 2003.

[44] The objection has to be made in writing. See: Art. 81 Law 26 April 2002 holding the basic rules applicable on the police force, *State Gazette* 30 April 2002.

[45] See Council of State, nrs. 226.345 and 226.346, 5 February 20014.

In order to accommodate the different recognized religious groups, the law allows pupils from non-Catholic traditions to take *holidays* on special religious feasts (enumerated in the legislation).[46]

Media Law

Public media are an important instrument for the State to protect, advance or even guarantee religious pluralism. The three (Flemish, French and German speaking) broadcasting regimes offer airtime to recognized religious groups on public channels. Guaranteeing access to radio and television channels does not, however, necessarily go hand in hand with full State funding. As things stand, national legislation provides for extremely poor airtime and limited budgets.[47] The law protects this category by banning commercial advertising during religious broadcasting programmes.[48]

Privacy Law

Religious privacy has, due to historical reasons a strong position in Belgian law. Since 1856 the censuses had to leave aside questions on religion, due to a formal decision of the legislator, as a too sensitive issue. It is no surprise in the Belgian context to see religious data labelled as *sensitive data* in the Privacy Data Act of 1992.[49] With an exception for religious organizations (who are in need of person-related information for religious purposes)[50] all activities that include checking for or collecting data on personal religious (or belief) convictions is in general

---

[46] Jewish holidays: (French Community) Government Decree 1 August 2000, *State Gazette* 28 October 2000. (Flemish Community) Ministerial 'Circulaire' BaO/2002/11.

[47] For Flemish Community public television: maximum 50 h television per year for all religious and non-religious groups (Flemish Community). Roman Catholic Sunday mass broadcasting is, however, kept outside this maximum.

[48] See for instance: Art. 34§5 Law 30 March 1995 on the cable distribution of broadcasting programs and television broadcasting activities in the bilingual region Brussels-Capital, *State Gazette* 22 February 1996; Art. 5§6 Parliamentary Decree Flemish Parliament 12 June 1991 regulating advertisement and sponsoring on radio and television, *State Gazette* 14 August 1991.

[49] *Sensitive data* relate to race, political opinions, religious or philosophical beliefs, trade-union membership, health, sex life, prosecutions or criminal or administrative convictions See Art. 6§1 Privacy Law 8 December 1992, *State Gazette* 18 March 1993.

[50] Art. 6§2 Privacy Law 8 December 1992, *State Gazette* 18 March 1993: "The prohibition to process the data referred to in § 1 does not apply in the following cases: (…) d) the processing is carried out in the course of its legitimate activities by a foundation, association or any other non-profit organization with a (…) philosophical, *religious*, (…) aim and on condition that the processing relates solely to the members of the organization or to persons who have regular contact with it in connection with its purposes and that the data is not disclosed to a third party without the data subjects' consent;". Law 11 December 1998 on the implementation of EU-Directive 95/46 of the European Parliament and of the Council of 24 October 1995 on the protection of individuals with

anathema. This is reflected by the legislation on the duties of the *national statistics institute* INS-NIS,[51] on the profession of *private detectives*[52] and of *private security agencies*.[53] Protection of religious data is also taken into account in legislation on the deployment of *surveillance cameras*.[54] The Privacy Data Act itself also contains a number of limitations on privacy, in order to attain specific (legitimate) aims.[55] Religious radicalisation (probably even leading to terrorism or assistance to terrorism) is a more recent topic, leading to a closer surveillance of some religious activities[56] of harmful sects.[57]

Labour Law (Alidadi 2012; Christians 2011; Cuypers et al. 1993)

The Labour Act 1905 implicitly includes a Christian day of rest in labour law by having the *Sunday as the regular day of rest* for employees. The introduction of this legislation gave rise to debates on the question if this legislation did not force employers/employees to conform to a specific religious belief. In 1992 the Constitutional Court concluded that the legislator in 1905: "took into account the religious and family traditions and also the importance of cultural and sport activities. The legislator could arguably suppose that employees had chosen for the Sunday, if they had the freedom to choose themselves."[58] The religious aspect of the Sunday as a day devoted to religious activities has been pushed into the background. Nevertheless, the choice for the traditional Christian day of rest is of course facilitating Christian churches.

As for civil servants, general labour law includes a *right on a day off* for some specific religious occasions, a regime that is limited to a specific segment of the

---

regard to the processing of personal data and on the free movement of such data, *State Gazette* 3 February 1999.

[51] Art. 24*quinquies* Law 4 July 1962 on public statistics, *State Gazette* 20 July 1962.

[52] Art. 7 Law 19 July 1991 regulating the profession of private detective, *State Gazette* 2 October 1991.

[53] Art. 11§1 (b) Law 10 April 1990 regulating private and special security services, *State Gazette* 29 May 1990.

[54] Art. 10 Law 21 March 2007 regulating the deployment and use of surveillance cameras, *State Gazette* 31 May 2007.

[55] See Art. 6 §2 Privacy Law 8 December 1992, *State Gazette* 18 March 1993.

[56] Federal Ministry of the Interior, Ministerial 'Circulaire' GPI 78 31 January 2014 on data processing in the context of police action combatting terrorism and violent radicalization, *State Gazette* 17 February 2014.

[57] Art. 7-8 Law 30 November 1998 regulating the information and security service, *State Gazette* 18 December 1998. Art. art. 8 e) of the law says that a harmful sectarian organization («organisation sectaire nuisible») is « each group with a philosophical or religious aim, or pretending to be one, that in its organization or practices undertakes illegal and harmful activities, causes damage to individuals or at the society, or violates human dignity».

[58] Constitutional Court, 12 November 1992, nr. 70/92, B.2.5, *State Gazette*, 19 December 1992.

'recognized' religious market.[59] The discriminatory character of this regulation was put on the agenda in the Senate in 2007.[60]

Religious groups often are in need for religious leaders coming from abroad. This is problematic for those religions who have to engage people who live outside the European Union. Belgian legislation facilitates religious groups in this respect, by *exempting* this category from having the obligation to apply for a *work permit*. Until 1999 this special regime was available for all religions, since then the legislation limited the scope to recognized religions only,[61] creating problems for non-recognized religions employing people from other continents.[62]

Personal Law Based on Religious Affiliation

The Belgian legal system does not include any religious personal status for Belgian nationals. Nevertheless, Belgian PIL allows application of a foreign "religious" personal status if the applicable foreign law provides this for their own citizens (Christians 2010). Nevertheless, some exceptional cases may be found where Belgian court take into account the *virtual possibility* for religious rules to be applied to Belgian citizens, with potential civil recognition in Belgium. One famous example is about the effect in Belgium of an ecclesiastical sentence of matrimonial nullity hold in Italy between to Belgian citizens, previously married in Italy through a religious concordatarian marriage. The Court of Appeal of Brussels[63] hold that any abusive financial pressure organized by the husband against his wife in order to influence her participation to the canon law nullity procedure, would be deemed illegal as a tort against the *civil* status of Belgian citizens (see Rigaux 1976 for a general analysis on indirect influence of the Italian concordat for Belgian citizens).

---

[59] See for example: Art. II Royal Decree 28 August 1963, *State Gazette* 11 September 1963.

[60] Proposal for a resolution *Parl. Doc.* Senate 2007–2008, nr 2018/1 (proposal to extend the system for a day off in order to end discriminatory treatment between the recognized religions).

[61] Art. 2, 6° Royal Decree 9 June 1999 implementing the 1999 Foreign workers law, *State Gazette* 29 June 1999.

[62] See the critical remarks (concerning the Mormon church) in the US State Departments *International Religious Freedom Report 2002* on Belgium: http://www.state.gov/j/drl/rls/irf/2002/13924.htm

[63] Court of Appeal Brussels, 11 May 1994, *Revue générale de droit civil*. 1996, p. 120, comment V. Marquette; *Rev. trim. dr. fam.*, 1996, p. 25, comment. J-L. Van Boxstael.

State Law with a Religious Origin, Applicable to All Citizens

The legislation on the weekly day of rest or on public holidays are examples of State law including rules that have a clearly identifiable religious origin/background, applicable to all citizens, regardless their religion. The general application of these rules is defended with reference to *tradition*, not on religious grounds. In some circumstances, in order to accommodate the practice of religious festivities for minority religions, specific exemptions are present: this is the case, for instance, for ritual slaughtering on Sundays for Jewish and Islamic holidays or festivities.[64]

Also traditional heterosexual marriage has been discussed in public debates as being a civil norm with a strong religious background, but the legislator did not argue along this line. Same-sex marriages have been introduced in legislation as a part of equal treatment policies (banning discrimination on the basis of sexual orientation).

The Right of a Religious Organization to Apply Its Own Rules in the Internal Sphere

Organisations owned or managed by religious groups in many cases are responsible for functions in society that relate strongly with the religious ethos of these institutions (schools, hospitals). In order to guarantee the religious identity, these 'faith based organisations' do have an interest to apply specific, religiously inspired rules in the internal sphere, not in the least with regard to personnel policies (hiring and firing). The Anti-discrimination Law (2007) provides faith-based organizations, in order to enable them to maintain their religious ethos, with a specific status allowing for a difference in treatment based on religious principles.[65] They have the right, in this context, to expect from employees, an attitude of "good faith and loyalty to the ethos" of the employer. The boundaries of this right are not clear cut, but in balancing the right of the employers against employees' rights by the judiciary, the privacy rights of employees are gaining weight.[66]

Religious communities did receive a strong position in art. 21 Constitution, guaranteeing the institutional freedom, especially with regard to the selection of religious leaders.

---

[64] Art. 1 Royal Decree 13 July 1988 allowing ritual slaughtering on the regular day of rest, *State Gazette* 17 November 1988.

[65] (on a federal level:) Art. 13 Law 10 May 2007 to combat certain forms of discrimination, *State Gazette* 30 May 2007.

[66] Privacy rights of employees, e.g. matrimonial religious status and rules, even within Catholic schools or hospitals, have been enforced by the Belgian Supreme Court of Cassation since 1976. Any immediate firing based on religious matrimonial status is deemed invalid (Demeester 1976).

Applicability of Religious Rules in the State Legal System

Religious rules are neither applicable nor enforceable as such in the State legal system and will not be uphold as such by Belgian courts. Legislation that 'translates' rules with a religious origin into general rules is not per se intended to import any religious connotation. The legislation on the day of rest provides us with a good example of a norm that is considered to be '*cultural*' in nature and not the acceptance of a specific (Christian) religious normative system.[67] Even through PIL foreign religious norms would be qualified as foreign *state* norms.[68]

Special treaties with the Holy See (mainly the 1801 French Concordat) were already revoked by the National Congress in 1831, as incompatible with the new constitutional order. Prenuptial agreements (based on religious norms) are not legally enforceable in Belgian legal systems. In 1982, the Court of cassation hold that a purely religious Jewish divorce, even agreed by both spouses, does not allow nor excuse adultery relations subsequently initiated by the husband, since their civil marriage was still in force.[69] At the best, religious agreements are considered as a factual matter, and might be taken into account among other contextual characteristics of the case, at least if the law admits such a subjective approach.

While private autonomy is not applicable to personal status, some contractual references to religious rules would be held as valid in some other areas, such as association status or some for profit businesses (Christians 2010).

One has however to make a distinction between the applicability of religious rules in general and the fact that civil courts take into account *decisions* taken by *religious authorities* (e.g. dismissal of ministers, chaplains, religious teachers, in public institutions). The public regime of recognized religions makes this unavoidable. In other (private law) matters, courts are more reluctant to take into account religious decisions. A definite conclusion is not easy to draw since Belgian case law remains unclear and heterogeneous.

Religiously Motivated Exemptions from Laws of General Application

Section "Religious laws/principles" shows the existence of religiously motivated exemptions in different fields of legislation: *education law* (exemption form religious courses), *animal welfare legislation* (exemption in order to accommodate Islamic and Jewish slaughter methods), *electoral law* (voting obligations on religious holidays). In *medical law* a general conscientious objection clause is present

---

[67] Constitutional Court decisions: nr. 70/92, 12 November 1992; nr. 45/93, 10 June 1993; nr. 19/94, 3 March 1994.

[68] See for *talaq*: Barbe (2003).

[69] Cass., 15 June 1982, *Pasicrisie* 1982, I, p. 1186.

in the legislation on abortion (Christians and Minette 2010) and euthanasia, leaving room for *religiously motivated objections* in the first place (Montero 2012); a rather obvious exemption for religious organisation in *privacy law* concerns the registration of religious personal data. These requirements for recognising conscientious objections have been relaxed. Conditions have been alleviated in a *subjective* way : individual intent should be progressively considered as sufficient—provided that some neutral conditions are met – (communication of refusal, respect of deadlines, alternative obligations, ...). More specifically, no evidence is needed of religious obligations, rules or motivations, subject only to few exceptions.

In exceptional cases legislation is putting a religious category under special obligations, thus creating a difference in treatment. This is the case notably for religious leaders coming from abroad (non EU nationals). Flemish integration policy legislation[70] introduced an special obligation for religious leaders to enter *citizenship courses* on the grounds that religious leaders are key-figures in the lives of the members of the religious communities formed by their fellow-nationals and thus crucial in the integration success of the religious group as such (De Pooter 2005). This exception to the 'ministerial exception' is connected (in fact, but not formally) with the policies regarding the Muslim minority in Belgium.

Reasonable Accommodation (Alidadi 2013; Bribosia et al. 2010; Christians 2006a)

Belgian State law does not contain a *general obligation* requiring people in positions of authority (for example, employers) to accommodate religious needs of the individual who is in a subordinate position (for example, employees), neither in private law nor in public law.

In labour law however already since a law of 10 March 1900 (and now: the 1978 Law on labour contracts[71]) the employer has to offer his employee the *time* necessary to fulfil his religious obligations outside the firm building (Cuypers et al. 1993). It is also worth noting a systemic interaction between labour law and unemployment law (Alidadi 2013; Trine 1982). Whilst the former does not provide any general obligation of accommodation, such an accommodation seems to be provided in an earlier stage for the unemployed. Since the 1960s, Belgian unemployment regulations allowed the refusal of job offers for religious reasons. If an unreasonable refusal was not accepted, the unemployed could consequently be deprived of unemployment benefits. Religious objections received by the Court include for example a job in a pork butchery offered to a Muslim, a job of religion teacher to an atheist, a job including work on Friday and Saturday offered to an Adventist etc. Not all

[70] Now: Decr. Fl. Parl. 7 June 2013 on Flemish policies regarding integration and citizenship education, *State Gazette* 26 July 2013.

[71] Art. 20, 5° Law on Labour Contracts: "The employer has to: 5° allow the employee the time needed to fulfill his religious duties".

religious objections were admitted. For example, a Muslim woman refusing contacts with male employees in the workplace has been deprived of unemployment benefits (Ringelheim 2012). The judicial interpretation of the reasonability of the objection is largely open as a matter of fact, context and proportionality, but the general principle explained above remains: whilst some religious rules and prohibitions have been accepted as factual arguments by the courts, no objective religious rule has to be explicitly evidenced as a formal condition.

In private law, it is worth to note that the Civil Code (art. 1135) classically obliges contractors to a "bona fide" implementation of their contractual duties. Case law and literature are divided on whether any more precise obligations facing *religious* rules might be *required.*[72]

A strange example of reverse-accommodation may be observed where the Belgian Constitutional Court, in its 2012 Burqa case, pointed out that the Muslim female plaintiffs would perhaps have been able to find some religious self-exception to the wearing of the burqa (Brems and Ouald-Chaib 2013).[73] The plaintiffs lost the case in part because they failed to prove the lack of such an exception in their own religious traditions.

Adjudication

Religious Adjudication

The Belgian legal system does not allot formal jurisdiction to religious courts existing alongside State courts and does not recognize dispute resolution systems that act according to religious laws. At the same time there is no formal or penal prohibition of such courts.

No "individual option" to refer a dispute to religious courts has ever been *explicitly* allowed or even discussed before civil courts. In non PIL matters, for example in some dismissal cases concerning religious ministers, Belgian civil local courts seemed to take into account the existence of some internal religious review system in order to address the respect of due process requirements : if the plaintiffs did not appeal within their own religious system, this intentional abstention is understood as waiving every due process rights, even from a civil point of view. Anyway, the Belgian Supreme Court of cassation refused to upheld such a specific solution.

[72] Labour Court Brussels, 15 January 2008, *Journal des tribunaux du travail* 2008, p. 140 (a bookshop branding charter defining the core "openness" of the bookshop may be interpreted as implicitly prohibiting employees to wear the Islamic veil, but the reverse hypothesis is still controversial in the literature – i.e. the possible legal recognition of a branding charter imposing the wearing of some religious dress in a general bookshop).

[73] Constitutional Court, 6 December 2012, *Journal des tribunaux* 2013, p. 234, comment L.-L. Christians, S. Minette & S. Wattier.

The Court of cassation has until now[74] confirmed an absolute hands-off principle when rules drawn by religious authorities (canon law for instance) play a role in a case brought before the courts : civil courts are prohibited to interpret religious rules—even on due process issues—when facing an internal religious issue, such as the dismissal of a minister of religion. This position, strongly influenced by the organisational freedom guaranteed in art. 21 Constitution, has been under doctrinal critique since the end of the twentieth century (Vuye 2009).

In PIL matters, the exclusive jurisdiction of Belgian courts on the Belgian territory is classically confirmed and excludes any civil recognition of any Belgian religious authority whatsoever.

Criteria for Religious Adjudication Set by State Law

Religious court decisions are not bound to respect fundamental rules/principles adopted by the State legal system. Within the public law regime of recognized religions, it is unclear whether even general protection of privacy rights would be ensured by the Council of State as a test of validity or legal relevance.[75]

In private matters, such as labour law[76] or tort law,[77] privacy rights are progressively enforced even against a religious decision, at least as a cause for compensation.

State courts still don't have any competence to *review* religious court decisions nor to impose a specific interpretation of a church's decision. This is still clearly affirmed within the public law regime of recognized religions.

Religious Courts/Institutions: Interpreting Laws of the State/ Assessing Their Conformity to Religious Rules?

Religious courts/institutions do not benefit of any opposable authority to interpret the laws of the State and to assess their conformity with religious rules. In religious matters and especially within the public law regime of recognized religions, State courts have no competence to review church decisions. Outside these specific fields, other kind of compromises may arise between denominations and States. In 2010, during the sexual abuse crisis (within the Roman catholic church), the Prosecutor

---

[74] Cass. 20 October 1994, *J.L.M.B.*, 1995, p. 503, comment L-L Christians; *Revue critique de jurisprudence belge* 1996, pp. 124–129, comment F. Rigaux; Cass., 3 June 1999, *Chroniques de droit public* 2000, p. 110, comment K. Martens.

[75] Council of State, 20 December 1985, nr. 25.995, *Rechtskundig weekblad* 1986–1987, p. 246, comment W. Lambrechts.

[76] Cass. 12 January 1977, *Pasicrisie* 1977, I, p. 520.

[77] Liège Court of Appeals 12 June 2007, *Journal des tribunaux* 2007, p. 780, comment M.-F. Rigaux.

Office, supported by Parliament, decided that religious authorities cannot oppose their own understanding of the civil statute of limitations applicable on public penal sexual offences, and by consequence, religious authorities should have to inform the Prosecutor Office of any indications of a possible offence, even dating back far into the past.[78]

Social Implementation of Religious Rules

Citizens Following Religious Rules Conflicting with State Law

Belgium is a secularized country where religion, with the exception of Islam, seems to have become irrelevant in societal debate. The most prominent debate is on the visibility of Islam, focusing on the wearing of the veil by Muslim women (and schoolgirls), a manifestation of belief that seems to be widespread now in the Muslim communities. This creates not only tensions but also many court cases (as new state law bans visible religious signs), until now without a clear legal outcome.

The right to wear religious symbols in public spaces and in public building as schools and government offices, in particular when civil servants are in contact with the public, remains heavily debated (Mathieu et al. 2013).

A famous example is the controversy regarding the law banning face coverings (and thus: the burqa). The law was reviewed and confirmed by the Constitutional Court in 2012.[79] The Court based its decision on arguments of public safety and on a (controversial) link between the visibility of the face and human dignity (Vrielink et al. 2013).

Following Religious Rules that, Although not Forbidden by State Laws, Cause Problems or Hostility

Religious behaviour in the public sphere is encountering growing societal hostility, especially where this behaviour has its source in Islamic traditions (Foblets and Overbeeke 2004). In Belgium like in other European countries, one of the explanations being given consists of a misunderstanding of these dress codes, assigning to them a moral extremist aim. Along this line, the religious normativity attributed to these dress codes seems a more social-friendly explanation than any controversy on cultural habits and facts.

[78] Montero (2013).

[79] Constitutional Court nr. 145/2012, 6 December 2012, *State Gazette* 25 January 2013.

Services Provided by Religious Adjudication Bodies That are Devoid of any State Recognition and Civil Effects or Even Forbidden by State Law

Roman Catholic ecclesiastical courts continue to deliver judgments regarding the validity of religious marriage, but their decisions do not get civil recognition. Sociological research/surveys are suggesting the existence of similar phenomena in Muslim or Jewish communities (Foblets et al. 2009). Religious adjudication bodies seem able to pacify and regulate an important part of family litigation. These evolutions remain more or less unknown by mainstream media. Belgium is therefore not facing hostility against "sharia court" or "sharia rules" like in the US or the UK (Christians 2012; Foblets 2012).

Conclusion

Respect for Human Rights, Particularly of Religious Liberty, Equality, and Non-discrimination?

The neutrality affirmed by the Belgian legal system was historically built on a pillarized pluralism, including the Roman Catholic, socialist and liberal traditions and their institutions on a more or less equal basis. Secularization and an increasing uncertainty about the position of Islam (even a fear for "islamisation") have progressively destabilized these traditional pluralist policies.

In particular, through a kind of methodological turn, Islam seems to become more and more a standard test for questions regarding the legal or judicial acceptance of any kind of religious rules, irrespective the religions concerned: these rules, perhaps traditionally taken into account in the past, will be admitted in the future only if this would be also tolerated for similar Islamic rules (Christians 2006b).

This "Islamic test" explains why even the application of *prima facie* neutral rules seems unable to fill the vacuum left by the process of depillarization of the Belgian system. Some politicians hesitate to extend to Islam the benefits previously opened to Christian rules and traditions. They prefer to abolish these laws, rather than to apply them to the Muslim minority. This could perhaps indicate the existence of implicit discriminatory tensions (Saroglou et al. 2009).

Government action, legislation included, in different domains (dress codes in schools, choice and qualities of ministers of religions, structuring of the religious communities, the conditions for 'integration' of religious communities in society) could easily be interpreted as forms of security-oriented 'Islam-policies', touching first and foremost this specific religion.

In general however the system in force is respecting in a large measure the rights and freedoms guaranteed in national constitutional law and with the international human rights obligations.

There are also some remarks to be made in the light of *equality and non-discrimination*, when it comes to smaller religious communities, not belonging to the special category of "recognized" religions or non-religious life stance movements. There are three categories to be distinguished

(a) There are, in the first place, legislations that create a different treatment between religions on the basis of their "recognition" status, but *not on purpose*. (see: labour law: legislation on religious holidays)
(b) Then there is the possibility that legislation, initially treating all religions on an equal foot, was changed later, disfavouring non recognized religions (see: labour migration law: 1999 legislation on work permits for non-EU ministers of religion).
(c) And finally: legislation intentionally benefits the recognized religions only. In some cases there is no justification for the unequal treatment (Penitentiary law: 2005 legislation on chaplaincies).

The division of religions in the '*recognized*' and '*non-recognized*' categories was judged, in a recent academic advisory report, to be too dualistic. The introduction of a new category of '*registered*' was proposed, in order to close the gap between the existing categories (Magits et al. 2010; Overbeeke 2011b).

Fostering Inclusion or Causing Segregation?

Does the Belgian legal system foster inclusion of different religious communities (and particularly minority religious communities) in the social fabric or is it causing forms of segregation and communitarian isolation? The system has *both* characteristics. The support system for religions has proven to be open to newcomers and was even applied to nontheistic belief systems (inclusion of Humanism). This aspect of the system is considered to be a quality. Improving the position of the Islamic religion – its formal recognition in 1974, on an equal foot with Christian and Jewish denominations – was considered to be one of the cornerstones of the integration of the second largest religious group in Belgian society. Formal recognition opened the door in education law to denominational religious education. One could argue that the existing system (giving birth to the pillarization earlier on) also contains elements that could encourage forms of communitarian segregation. State funded freedom of education opened the door to parallel school systems for minorities. In fact, only the small Jewish community was able to build a complete school system of its own.

Even-Handed Attitudes or Preferentialism?

Does the law promote an even-handed and fair attitude of State institutions towards different religions or does it strengthen forms of preferential treatment of religious over non-religious individuals or of the members of a particular religious community over the members of other religious communities?

The Constitution guarantees religious freedom, and does not permit discrimination on the basis of religion or belief (nonreligious belief included). State law has to respect the constitutional principles under the control of the Constitutional Court. A preferential treatment of the members of specific religious groups is, in this context impossible. There is only one major exception: *state supported religious spiritual care* is only guaranteed for adherents of recognized religions. Individual members of non-recognized religions who are staying in penitentiary institutions are disfavoured, because they remain in a second class position when it comes to spiritual care. A similar situation was (till 2015) existing in the French and Germans speaking communities, where *religious education courses* of recognised religions were part of the school program, without the possibility of exemption.

References

Alidadi, K. 2012. Muslim women made redundant: Unintended signals in Belgian and Dutch case law on religious dress in private sector employment and unemployment. In *Test of faith? Religious diversity and accommodation in the European workplace*, ed. K. Alidadi, M-Cl Foblets, and J. Vrielink. Aldershot: Ashgate.

Alidadi, K. 2013. Redelijke aanpassingen voor religieuze praktijken op de belgische werkvloer : van "goodwill" naar afdwingbaar recht?. In M.-Cl. Foblets and J.-Ph. Schreiber (eds), *The round tables on interculturalism*, 301–341. Bruxelles: Larcier.

Alofs, E., and D. Cuypers. 2009. De doorwerking van polygamie in de Belgische rechtsorde, in het bijzonder in de Belgische sociale zekerheid: een status quaestionis na de arresten van het Grondwettelijk Hof van 4 mei 2005 en 4 juni 2009. *Revue de droit social*.

Barbe, C. 2003. Un nouvel arrêt de la Cour de cassation dans le domaine de la reconnaissance des répudiations. Note sous Cass. 29 avril 2002. *Revue Divorce*, nr. 7.

Brems, E. 2013. Religion in Belgian criminal law. In *Religion and criminal law – Religion et Droit Pénal*, ed. N. Doe and M. Kotiranta, 21–26. Leuven: Peeters.

Brems, E., and S. Ouald-Chaib. 2013. The Belgian Burqa-Ban, Legal aspects of local and general prohibitions on covering and concealing one's face in Belgium. In *The Burqa affair across Europe: Between public and private*, ed. A. Ferrari and S. Pastorelli. Franham: Ashgate.

Bribosia, E., J. Ringelheim, and I. Rorive. 2010. L'aménagement raisonnable pour motif religieux: un concept issu d'Amérique du Nord en voie d'intégration en Belgique et en Europe? In *Actualités du droit de la lutte contre la discrimination*, ed. C. Bayart, S. Sottiaux, and S. Van Drooghenbroeck. Brussels: La Charte.

Christians, L.-L. 1995. Le juge entre le théologique et le politique : les paradoxes normatifs du concept de trouble. *Journal des tribunaux*, 720–727.

Christians, L.-L. 2006a. Le principe de non discrimination religieuse en droit belge et comparé : entre obligations du législateur et obligations des contractants. In *Le principe de non discrimination en droit des obligations*, ed. Patrick Wéry and Sophie Stijns. Brussels: Kluwer.

Christians, L.-L. 2006b. Droit et islam en Europe: quelles globalisations? *Recherches sociologiques* 37: 2.

Christians, L.-L. 2009. Les tensions du régime des cultes dans la Constitution belge : l'actualité des débats du Congrès national de 1830. In *Le droit ecclésiastique en Europe et à ses marges (XVIII-XXe siècles)*, ed. B. Basdevant and F. Jankowiak. Leuven: Peeters.

Christians, L.-L. 2010. Les prescriptions convictionnelles en droit belge (1830–2008). In *Convictions philosophiques et religieuses et droits positifs*, ed. J. Vanderlinden and M-Cl Foblets. Brussels: Bruylant.

Christians, L.-L. 2011. Diversité au travail. Entre cultures et consciences, entre identité et éthique. Enjeux juridiques des recompositions postmodernes du religieuxé. In *Le droit et la diversité culturelle*, ed. J. Ringelheim. Brussels: Bruylant.

Christians, L.-L. 2012. Les références belges à l'ordre public comme standard de régulation et révélateur de conflits de valeurs dans le statut des personnes musulmanes en dehors du droit international privé: l'exemple belge. In *Ordre public et droit musulman de la famille. En Europe et en Afrique du Nord*, ed. N. Bernard-Maugiron and B. Dupret. Brussels: Bruylant.

Christians, L.-L., and S. Minette. 2010. Avortement et objection de conscience en Belgique. Aborto y objeción de conciencia en Bélgica. Abortion and conscientious objection in Belgium. *Revista General De Derecho Canonico Y Eclesiastico Del Estado.*

Clesse, Ch-E, and P. De Pooter. 2012a. Les délits relatifs au libre exercice des cultes. In *Les infractions – Volume 5: Les infractions contre l'ordre public*, ed. H.-D. Bosly and C. De Valkeneer. Brussels: Larcier.

Clesse, Ch-E, and P. De Pooter. 2012b. Des délits commis par les ministres du culte dans l' exercice de leur ministère. In *Les infractions – Volume 5: Les infractions contre l'ordre public*, ed. H.-D. Bosly and C. De Valkeneer. Brussels: Larcier.

Cuypers, D., M. Kempen, and C. Meeusen. 1993. Culturele minderheden in het sociaal recht. In *Recht en verdraagzaamheid in de multiculturele samenleving*, ed. J. Velaers. Antwerpen: Maklu.

De Pooter, P. 2005. Inburgeringsbeleid van bedienaren van erediensten: een "verlicht" idee of een gallicaanse oprisping?. *Nieuw juridisch weekblad*, 690–695.

De Rynck, S. 2005. Regional autonomy and education policy in Belgium. *Regional and Federal Studies* 15(4): 485–500.

Dehert, P. 2006. Sterven als vorm van integratie. Een republikeinse halt tegen actief pluralistische begrafeniswetten. In *Recht en minderheden. De ene diversiteit is de andere niet*, ed. R. Stockx, 107–134. Brugge: Die Keure.

Delruelle, E., and R. Torfs. 2005. *Commissie voor Interculturele Dialoog. Eindverslag en getuigenissen*. Brussels: CGKR.

Demeester, H. 1976. La morale catholique devant les juridictions du travail en Belgique. *Mélanges Mgr Wagnon, Etudes d'histoire et de droit*, Fac. Int. Dr. can., UCL.

Evers, R. 1998. Moge uw ziel gebundeld worden. Joodse voorschriften bij overlijden en begraven. Kampen: Kok, 254 p.

Foblets, M-Cl. 2012. Les juges belges et l'application de la loi étrangère en droit de la famille. In *Ordre public et droit musulman en Méditerranée*, ed. N. Bernard-Maugiron and B. Dupret. Brussels: Bruylant/Larcier.

Foblets, M-Cl, and A. Overbeeke. 2004. Islam in Belgium: The search for a legal status of a new religious minority. In *Islam and the European Union*, ed. R. Potz and W. Wieshaider. Leuven: Peeters.

Foblets, M-Cl, M. Deklerck, S. Desmet, E. Kusters, and J. Vrielink. 2009. Limits of human rights protection: Drawing upon the findings of (four) legal anthropological field studies. In *Facing the limits of the law*, ed. E. Clae, W. Devroe, and B. Keirsbilck. New York: Springer.

Francq, S., and J. Mary. 2013. Les effets sociaux du mariage polygamique : pour une appréciation en context. *Revue trimestrielle de droit de la famille*, nr. 4.

Franken, L., and P. Loobuyck. 2013. Is active state support for religions and worldviews compatible with the liberal idea of State neutrality? A critical analysis of the Belgian case. *Journal of Church & State* 55: 3.

Hanoulle, K., and G. Marlier. 2014. Une législation forte pour des personnes faibles? *Journal des Tribunaux*, 161–169.

Kuty, F. 2012/11. L'abus de la situation de faiblesse d'autrui (article 442quater du Code pénal). *Rev. dr. pén.* 972–1006.

Loobuyck, P., and L. Franken. 2011. Religious education in Belgium: Historical overview and current debates. In *Religious education in a plural, secularised society a paradigm shift*, ed. L. Franken and P. Loobuyck. Münster: Waxmann Verlag.

Magits, M., L.-L. Christians, C. Sägesser, and L. De Fleurquin. 2010. La réforme de la legislation sur les cultes et les organisations philosophiques non confessionnelles. Brussels, 177 p.

Mathieu, C., S. Gutwirth, and P. De Hert. 2010. Liberté religieuse : vers un devoir de neutralité de l'Etat dans l'enseignement public ? (à propos de l'affaire Lautsi). *Journal de droit européen*, 133–139.

Mathieu, C., S. Gutwirth, and P. De Hert. 2013. Le port de signes convictionnels par les agents publics. In *The round tables on interculturalism*, ed. M-Cl Foblets and J-Ph Schreiber. Brussels: Larcier.

Meyer, D. 2013. Expliquer la circoncision. *J.L.M.B.*, 144–146.

Montero, E. 2012. La loi contre la conscience: réflexions autour de l'objection de conscience. In *[Droit et religion] Jérusalem, Athènes, Rome. Liber amicorum Xavier Dijon*, ed. J. Fierens. Brussels: Bruylant.

Montero, E. 2013. Le Centre d'arbitrage en matière d'abus sexuels: une solution inespérée pour les victimes de faits prescrits. *Journal Recht, religie, Samenleving*, nr. 1.

Mortier, F., and M.-F. Rigaux. 2006. *De federale financiering van de bedienaren der erediensten en de afgevaardigden van de Centrale Vrijzinnige Raad*. Brussels: Verslag van de Commissie van Wijzen.

Overbeeke, A. 2005. God achter de tralies: vrijheid van godsdienst en levensovertuiging in detentiesituaties. In *Vrijheden en vrijheidsbeneming: mensenrechten van gedetineerden*, ed. E. Brems, S. Sottiaux, and P. vanden Heede. Antwerp: Intersentia.

Overbeeke, A. 2007. Levensovertuiging en onderwijs in de Belgische Grondwet. In *De Grondwet in groothoekperspectief. Liber amicorum discipulorumque Karel Rimanque*, ed. B. Peeters and J. Velaers. Antwerp: Intersentia.

Overbeeke, A. 2011a. Kerk en Staat in België: scheidingsregime én state support. In *Overheid, recht en religie*, eds. A.B. Terlouw & J.L.W. Broeksteeg. Deventer: Kluwer.

Overbeeke, A. 2011b. Minderheden, minder recht? De rechtspositie van minderheden in het door de Werkgroep-Magits ontworpen stelsel. *Recht, Religie en Samenleving*, nr. 1.

Overbeeke, A.J., Foblęts, M.-C.L. & Brems, E. (2009). *Culturele diversiteit in het onderwijs. Een werkboek*. Leuven: Acco. (110 p.).

Rigaux, F. 1976. L'article 34 du Concordat du Latran et le droit international. *Mélanges Mgr H. Wagnon, Etudes d'histoire et de droit*, Louvain-la-Neuve : Fac. Int. Dr. can., UCL.

Rigaux, M.-F., and L.-L. Christians. 2011. La liberté de culte. In *Les droits constitutionnels de la Belgique*, 2, ed. M. Verdussen et al. Bruylant: Ashgate.

Ringelheim, J. 2012. Religion, diversity and the workplace. What role for the law? In *Test of faith? Religious diversity and accommodation in the European workplace*, ed. K. Alidadi et al. Aldershot: Ashgate.

Saers, J., and M. Foblets. 2012. Godsdienstvrijheid en het onbedwelmd slachten van dieren. In *Een leven van inzet: liber amicorum Michel Magits*. Mechelen: Wolters Kluwer.

Saroglou, V., B. Lamkaddem, M. Van Pachterbeke, and C. Buxant. 2009. Host society's dislike of the Islamic veil: The role of subtle prejudice, values, and religion. *International Journal of Intercultural Relations* 33(5): 419–428.

Shelley, T.J. 1990. Mutual Independence: Church and State in Belgium: 1825–1846. *Journal of Church and State* 32(1): 49–63.

Torfs, R. 2005. The permissible scope of legal limitations on the freedom of religion or belief in Belgium. *Emory International Law Review* 19: 637–683.

Torfs, R. 2011. Religious instruction in public education in Belgium. In *Religion in public education, Proceedings of the 22nd annual conference of the European Consortium for Church and State Research*, ed. G. Robbers, 63–71. Trier, 11–14 November 2010.

Torfs, R. 2013. New aspects in the relationship between state and religious communities in Belgium. In *Neuere Entwicklungen im Religionsrecht europäischer Staaten. Kanonistische Studien und Texte*, ed. W. Rees, M. Roca, and B. Schanda. Berlin: Duncker & Humblot.

Trine, A. 1982. Liberté de conscience et réglementation de chômage. *Revue de droit social*, 325–345.

Van Haegendoren, G., and A. Alen. 1992. The constitutional relationship between church and state. In *Treatise on Belgian constitutional law*, ed. A. Alen. Deventer: Kluwer Law International.

Velaers, J., and M-Cl Foblets. 2010. Le fait religieux dans ses rapports avec l'Etat en droit belge. In *Religion and the secular state: National reports*, ed. J. Martinez-Torron. Provo: ICLR.

Velaers, J. and M.-Cl. Foblets. 2012. Godsdienstvrijheid en het onbedwelmd slachten van dieren. In Een leven van inzet: liber amicorum Michel Magits, 375–402. Mechelen: Wolters Kluwer.

Vrielink, J., Brems, E., and Ouald-Chaib, S. 2013. The Belgian Burqa-Ban, legal aspects of local and general prohibitions on covering and concealing one's face in Belgium. In The Burqa affair across Europe: Between public and private, ed. A. Ferrari & S. Pastorelli, 143–170. Farnham: Ashgate.

Vuye, H. 2009. Scheiding Kerk en Staat in een multi-levensbeschouwelijke maatschappij. Historische en prospectieve studie van artikel 21 van de grondwet. *Chroniques de droit public*.

Wattier, I. 2010. Les mutilations des organes génitaux féminins. In *Les infractions contre les personnes-Les infractions*, vol. 2, ed. Marie-Aude Beernaert et al. Brussels: Larcier.

Chapter 7
The Relationship Between Religion and State in Brazilian Law

Jane Reis Gonçalves Pereira

Abstract This paper offers an overview of the current relation between State and religion in Brazil. It focuses on the descriptive examination of the legal context compared to the practices of public institutions regarding to secularism, pluralism and religious freedom in Brazil.

Introduction

Statistical Portrayal of Religion in Brazil

Brazil is still the largest Roman Catholic nation in the world, but its religious profile has been undergoing major changes (IBGE 2012).

The 2010 census showed the gradual decline in the ratio of Roman Catholics, while the number of Protestants (both traditional and Pentecostal) has been steadily growing. Between 1960 and 2010, the number of people who have declared themselves Roman Catholics has fallen from 93.1 to 64.6 %. In the same period, the percentage of self-declared Protestants has grown from 4 to 22.2 %.

This statistical change comes from the expansion of the so-called Pentecostalism, which represents an emerging societal and political force.

Recent data indicates the continuing dominance of the Roman Catholic Church and the prevalence of Christianity. But the same data indicates the gradual growth of religious diversity in the country as well. This diversity is found mostly inside Christianity itself, because Protestantism is pulverized amongst traditional denominations (4 %) and a great number of Pentecostal churches (18.1 %). Outside Christianity, both Spiritism (2 %) and those who claim to have no religion (8 %) have gained ground.

Amongst minority religions, African-Brazilian religions (Umbanda and Candomblé) amass 0.3 % of the population. In spite of their small statistical representation, religions of African origin are quite significant in the Brazilian

J.R.G. Pereira (✉)
Universidade do Estado do Rio de Janeiro, Rio de Janeiro, Brazil
e-mail: janergp@gmail.com

R. Bottoni et al. (eds.), *Religious Rules, State Law, and Normative Pluralism - A Comparative Overview*, Ius Comparatum – Global Studies in Comparative Law 18, DOI 10.1007/978-3-319-28335-7_7

religious and cultural scenario. For one thing, by way of syncretism, they have influenced the liturgies and practices of other religions. Secondly, they have been stigmatized and been the object of much intolerance, a fact that has had important implications in the public realm and has stimulated demands for secularism[1] and religious liberty (Giumbelli 2008).

Brazilian syncretism started with the Christianization of African slaves, in which several elements from their own traditions were incorporated into the dominant Christian matrix, fashioning a highly complex scenario of interaction between different liturgies, symbols and beliefs.

Historical Background

Under the Brazilian Imperial Constitution, the relationship between state and religion was confessional and based on the union of Church and State. In 1824, after forcibly dissolving the Constitutional Assembly of 1823, Dom Pedro I proclaimed the first Brazilian Constitution. The constitutional text imposed by him confirmed the establishment of the Roman Catholic Church (Art. 5), claimed that the monarch should be crowned 'by the grace of God' and should swear to maintain the state's religion (Art. 103), assigned political rights to Roman Catholics only (Art. 95) and enshrined the system called *padroado*, according to which priests were to be nominated and paid for by the state, having a status akin to that of civil servants (Art. 102, II). It also determined that Papal bulls and other rulings and decrees of the Holy See should be subject to approval by the monarch, to be valid in Brazil (Art. 102, XIV). Religious freedom was provided for, but in a very limited way: the text assured the right to free worship in the privacy of one's home, without the use of temples and with no implied disrespect for the established religion or public morality (Art. 179, V).

The Proclamation of the Republic, in 1891, inaugurated the separation between Church and State, a model that was followed by all subsequent constitutions. The Constitution of 1891 – strongly influenced by the US Constitution – established a presidential federal republic overcoming the traditional parliamentary monarchy

[1] There is no language uniformity in the international debate over the relations between State and religion. In English speaking countries is usual the use of the words secularism and secularity to express the separation of government and society from religious institutions and dogmas, or, more broadly speaking, the progressive loss of social influence by religions (HUACO 2008, 46). The terms laicism and laicity are more commonly used in Europe, Africa and Latin America to define the institutional and legal dimension of the secularization phenomena. In Latin American scholarship, the expression laicism (*laicismo*), is used to refer to a militant kind of *laicitè*: hostile or indifference towards religion in the public sphere. Laicity, on the other hand, expresses state institutional neutrality towards complex and heterogeneous social structures, open to the growing demands related to religious liberty and pluralism (HUACO 2008, 47). In this report, I will use the expression secularism to refer to the regulative ideal of state neutrality, institutional separation, secular justification of law and prohibition of state confessionalism. The expression laicism is used only in reference to the constitutional text of the first Republican Constitution (1891), to stress its singularity.

and the unitary state. Furthermore, it determined a secular framework for the relationship between the state and the church, which can be noticed, amongst other constitutional provisions, by: the ban on the establishment of, financing of, and interference with worship on the part of the state (Art. 11); the protection of religious freedom for all individuals and confessions (Art. 72, §3); the official recognition of civil marriage only (Art. 74, §4); the secularization of cemeteries (Art. 72, §5); the secularization of all public education (Art. 72, §6); and the requirement that no religious belief can be claimed as an excuse for the non-performance of a legal obligation binding upon all (Art. 72, §§28–29).

Nevertheless, in real life, the degree of separation between state and religion advocated by those provisions was not as great as expected; it did not fit in with the majoritarian societal understanding of how the secular and the religious spheres should interact (Giumbelli 2003; Leite 2011). Actually, the model of strict separation posited by the 1891 Constitution was strongly resisted by the Roman Catholic Church and a large part of Brazilian society (Giumbelli 2008). As time passed, the ongoing interpretation of the constitutional provisions, along with social practice and the enactment of statutory laws, gradually mitigated the laicism of the 1891 Constitution, paving the way for the model of the Constitution of 1934, which brought state and religion together once again and defined the outline of the 'moderate secularism' that has influenced subsequent Brazilian constitutions.

The current Brazilian model of secularism stems from the framework of the 1934 Charter, which combined the principles of secularism and religious freedom with the recognition of the religious realm within the public sphere and the state. The constitutional text banned discrimination on the basis of religious belief (Art. 113), disallowed the divesting of political rights by reason of political or religious convictions (Art. 113, §4), declared the inviolability of conscience and creed and guaranteed freedom of worship subject to the respect for public order (Art. 113, §5). But it enjoined the loss of political rights on those who, by reason of religious, philosophical or political belief, should refuse to abide by legal obligations binding upon all (Art. 111, b). That Charter enshrined important aspects of religious recognition in the public sphere, replacing the strict laicism of 1891 Constitution by a framework of moderate secularism. It provided for the right to religious assistance in government institutions (Art. 113, §6), the freedom of worship in public cemeteries and the right to burial at private cemeteries (Art. 113, §7), the possibility of state recognition of religious marriages (Art. 146) and religious education in public schools (Art. 153).

The guidelines of this flexible or 'soft' secular model were confirmed by subsequent constitutions. The Constitution of 1946 introduced full tax exemption for temples of any religion (Art. 31) and the possibility of conscientious objectors rendering alternative services (Art. 141, §8). The 1988 Charter, now in force, has followed the same general pattern.

Many controversies about the boundaries between state and religion in Brazil arise precisely because of the tension between the principle and those constitutional provisions that incorporate religion into the State. That is the case regarding disputes related to religious education and the constitutionality of the 2008 Agreement between Brazil and the Holy See.

Politically speaking, questions about religious freedom and secularism in Brazil follow three general lines of conflict: (i) the challenges to secularism predicated on the historical prevalence of the Roman Catholic Church and its traditional influence on the public sphere and the State; (ii) the growing demand for the recognition and influence of Neo-Pentecostalism in the public sphere and the state; (iii) the threats to secularism and to religious minorities that result from the strong predominance of Christianity.

A Note on Terminology and Concepts

In the present report, the phrase 'religious rules' refers to commands and injunctions posed by religion as understood according to a predominantly functional point of view, i.e., as including all demands posited by conscious manifestations of belief that may or may not have to do with traditional religions (such as Roman Catholicism, Protestantism and Judaism), but that play, in the lives of people, a role analogous to that played by traditional religious commandments. Although I am aware that such a conception may turn out to be hyper-inclusive and give rise to interpretive difficulties, I am also convinced that, as a working concept, it is the most suited one to the dynamic character of religious phenomena. Besides, an inclusive concept of religion is most adequate to the requirement of neutrality on the part of law and the state in an increasingly plural and diversified social scenario.[2] The concept of religious rules assumed here is based on a quantitative and gradational view that takes indicative hints from elements traditionally connected to the study of religion (such as the antiquity of the belief, the degree of institutionalization, the number of adherents, ethical and moral requirements, the existence of a form of priesthood, the presence or absence of ritual, ceremony and dogma and so on), but it is not exclusively limited to them. What we are looking for, then, is an understanding of religious rules that, whilst clearly detaching itself from its originally Christian matrix, does not include manifestations that fail to conform unequivocally to the idea of religious phenomena.

Political, Normative and Doctrinal Context

General Aspects

The relationship between religion and the state in Brazil is deeply marked by the ancient prevalence of the Roman Catholic Church and by the growing social and political influence of Pentecostal churches. Roman Catholicism is the dominant

---

[2]As Machado (1996) points out, the concept of religion must be reasonably open and dense, so it can answer the demands for state neutrality in a pluralist and democratic society.

religion, and its historical dominance has had structural implications that disclose themselves in major controversies, such as those involving religious education, the presence of crucifixes in courtrooms and the signing of the agreement with the Holy See in 2008. Pentecostalism, for its part, has seen its own political influence grow steeply in recent decades. Such a growth is no mere result of the quantitative increase in the number of Protestants in Brazil. Pentecostal groups have been organizing themselves with the specific aim of entering the political arena; churches support candidates drawn from their numbers, and parliamentary groups have been formed on the basis of 'religious identity as an electoral attribute' (Giumbelli 2008; Oro 2003). Political action by Pentecostals is intense and combative. In an attempt to influence public debate, they sometimes join forces with the Roman Catholic Church – in matters over which there is no disagreement, such as sexual and reproductive rights – but in other issues they distance themselves from it and demand from the government a treatment analogous to that given to Roman Catholics, as in the case of the failed General Religious Bill, which tried to extend to all confessions the terms of the agreement between the Brazilian government and the Holy See, officially internalized by the country in 2010.

The emphatic presence of religious discourse in politics is part of a complex legal-normative scenario. The Brazilian constitution enshrines the principle of secularism and enjoins the separation between religion and the state, but at the same time recognizes religious freedom in its multiple dimensions and contemplates the incorporation of religious manifestations into the public and government realms, providing for the possibility of cooperation between the government and religious groups in matters of public interest (Art. 19, I) and in such instances as religious education in public schools (Art. 221) and the civil ratification of religious marriages (Art. 226, §2).

We can say that the Brazilian constitution enshrines a model of inclusive secularism, because the institutional separation between religion and the state and the requirement of neutrality are linked with normative mechanisms that recognize and assimilate religious phenomena. Our main challenge is to prevent these channels of inclusion from becoming means by which 'comprehensive doctrines' (Rawls 1993) should be enforced, especially in view of the growing influence of the majoritarian religious confessions in the political sphere.

The Constitutional Framework of Secularism and Religious Liberty in Brazil

Although the 1988 Constitution does not explicitly refer to secularism, the ensemble of norms that discipline the relations between the state and religion allows us to identify it as the guiding principle of Brazilian law in this domain. As such, the state cannot 'establish or finance churches or religious sects, interfere in their functioning, or maintain relations of dependence or alliance, with the sole exception of cooperation in matters of public interest on the terms of the law' (Art. 19, I). This provision for cooperation on the basis of a concept as fluid as that of 'public interest' may conflict with the principle of separation, raising some controversy in the legal doctrine (see Silva 2013; Huaco 2008; Zylbersztajn 2012).

Secularism is recognized by the Brazilian Supreme Court as 'an essential postulate of the institutional organization of the Brazilian state' (STF ADI 3510/DF, 558), operating in two dimensions: it prevents the state from 'interfering in religious matters, both as a referee and as a censor,' and keeps 'religious dogmas from determining the content of government acts' (STF ADPF 54/DF, 44).

For present purposes, I take the conceptual core of the secular principle to include the commands of formal separation, institutional independence and state neutrality towards religious confessions. On the basis of this ideal concept, we can say that the secular principle has been in conflict with the dynamics of Brazilian politics ever since the birth of the Republic (Giumbelli 2008; Leite 2011). The propensity to soften the concept of secularism in order to make it more 'religion-friendly' is driven forward by the traditional political weight of the Roman Catholic Church and by the emerging power of Protestantism. The degree to which religion influences the State has led some commentators to say that Brazil is 'secular, but not that much'.[3]

In that sense, the idea of secularism in the Brazilian context has two aspects that should be highlighted. On the one hand, it has always functioned more as a regulatory ideal – a legal principle that may be applied with differing levels of strictness – than as a strict, binary rule. On the other hand, the constitutional text itself stipulates mechanisms of recognition and cooperation between the state and religion, opening the doors for connections that potentially threaten state neutrality and equality amongst religions.

The Preamble to the 1988 Constitution invokes the protection of God, bespeaking the influence of religiously-minded representatives during the workings of the constitutional assembly (Leite 2008). The Brazilian Supreme Court has already ruled that the Preamble has no normative value and is not binding on statutory Lawmakers (STF ADI 2.649/DF; STF ADI 2.076/AC).

In political and academic debate, it is said that the Brazilian state 'is secular but not atheist,' in a bid to show that the position of neutrality and equidistance which must be maintained by public authorities should not automatically entail the rejection of religiosity. The 1988 Constitution enshrines freedom of conscience, freedom of belief, freedom of worship and the protection, in compliance with the law, of the places wherein worship is performed and of its liturgies, as fundamental rights (Art. 5, VI). It also states that no one shall be deprived of any rights by reason of religious belief or philosophical or political conviction, unless he invokes it to exempt himself from a legal obligation required of all and refuses to perform an alternative obligation established by law (Art. 5, VIII).

The order in which fundamental rights are stated in the Constitution suggests that religious freedom is an implication or a specification of freedom of conscience, which may be understood as an original right, i.e., a right from which other rights

[3]As coined by Walter Ceneviva, see Martel 2007; also, Leite 2008, for whom Brazil is more of an agnostic country.

naturally spring (Leite 2008, 284; Neto 2006, 93). Thus, freedom of religion involves both the right to profess a given religion and the right not to guide oneself by any religious beliefs whatsoever. It is generally agreed that the Constitution protects atheism, agnosticism and strictly philosophical convictions (Silva 2013; Leite 2008).

Religious freedom is protected both in its individual and in its institutional dimensions, covering three related kinds of freedom: freedom of belief, freedom of worship and freedom of religious association or organization (Silva 2013).

An aspect of the institutional dimension of religious freedom is exemption from taxation, which applies to temples of all religions. This provision is interpreted in a broad sense by the Brazilian Supreme Court, as applying not only to the buildings wherein religious rites are performed, but also to all properties, income and services related to the essential activities of religious institutions, such as rented buildings and cemeteries (STF RE 578.562/BA).

Constitutional Clauses That Bring the State Closer to Religion

The Brazilian Constitution textually contemplates three hypotheses of assimilation of religion into the government sphere: (i) the provision for religious assistance in the army, prisons and hospitals; (ii) the provision for religious education as an optional discipline in public schools; and (iii) the civil recognition of religious marriage.

(a) *Religious assistance* in the army, prisons and hospitals

The constitutional provision for religious assistance in the army, prisons and hospitals is connected to the constitutional status of freedom of religion, which should be respected, even in a context of seclusion from social spaces.

The Federal Law 9.982/2000 provides for religious assistance in public and private hospitals and civil and military prisons. Such assistance is also assured in confinement facilities for juvenile offenders (Federal Law 8.024/1990). Legal experts have not devoted much attention to the question of religious assistance at such places. Anthropological studies, however, indicate a clear institutional bias in favor of Christianity in those environments (Simões 2010).

There is also another kind of institutionalized religious assistance: that given to the military. It is contemplated in the Federal Law 6923/1981, which institutes military chaplains 'selected amongst priests, pastors or religious ministers belonging to any religion which does not violate discipline, morals, and the law.' This law predates the 1988 Constitution, which only provides for religious assistance in prisons. The wording of the law is biased towards majoritarian religions, so that in recent years the armed forces have hired only Catholic priests and Protestant ministers. With some reason, commentators have suggested that this law offends the present Constitution and, as such, should not go on being applied (Zylbersztajn 2012, 170; Leite 2008).

(b) *Religious education*

The question of the structure and scope of religious education in public schools is one of the most controversial issues in the interaction between religion and the public sphere in Brazilian law. The complexity of this topic arises from the conflict between the general framework of the secular principle and the constitutional rule that establishes religious education as an optional discipline in public schools. Furthermore, Brazil is a federal state and both states and the federal government have regulatory power over education, which adds intricacy to the problem. According to the 1988 Constitution, religious education should be provided as a discipline amongst others during regular school hours in elementary public schools, although student attendance is optional (Art. 210, §1). The very open-endedness and indetermination of this provision gives rise to a string of questions which have not as yet been answered by the Brazilian legal system (Leite 2008, 312): (i) Can religious education be confessional, or should it be non-confessional? (ii) Are statutory law-makers free to determine the content of religious education? (iii) If religious education is to be confessional, who exactly should hire and pay the teachers?

In an effort to achieve simplicity, two answers are suggested to determine which limitations the secular principle imposes upon the state in this matter. Some scholars understand that the only form of religious education that is consistent with the model of separation between religion and state is the non-confessional form, and that teachers should be tested, selected and hired by the government. According to this view, to offer confessional pedagogical content, even if attendance is not compulsory to students, is to violate the principles of equality and freedom of belief (Zylbersztajn 2012). Another view is that statutory law-makers can authorize confessional religious education, but should also provide some guiding principles to assure the neutrality of the state, such as letting students choose which confession they wish to be taught about. The school should also offer alternative activities for non-religious students in the same timeframe. If the confessional model should be adopted, teachers should not be hired nor paid by the state. As a variable, the state should do no more than to provide rooms for the classes to be taught in (Leite 2008, 331; Ferraz 1997).

The National Educational Bases and Guidelines Law, in force since 1996, provided in its first draft for the possibility of confessional religious education with no use of public money. Debates about a possible violation of the secular principle by that clause motivated the revision of that law in 1997. In its new version, the law banned all proselytism and suppressed the provision for confessional religious education, but transferred to the federated states the power of determining and disciplining the structure of religious education (Art. 33).

The states have adopted widely different systems (Zyllbertsztajn 2012). Five of them have embraced the confessional model, with different mechanisms for the payment of teachers. Seven favor the interconfessional (ecumenical) model, and nine have adopted the supraconfessional model (which approximates to the history and anthropology of religion). The question became more complex when the agreement between Brazil and the Holy See was incorporated into the Brazilian legal system with statutory status. Article 11 of the agreement provides for 'religious education, both Catholic and of other religious confessions,' stipulating therefore a confessional system. In that normative context, the Prosecutor General's Office filed an unconstitutionality suit at the Supreme Federal Court, asking the court to issue an interpretation according to the Constitution of the Federal Act for Guidelines and Fundamentals in Education, therefore making it clear that religious education cannot be confessional.

(c) *Attribution of Civil Effects to Religious Marriages*

The Federal Constitution stipulates that religious marriage shall have civil effects in compliance with the law (Art. 226, §2). According to the Civil Code, any religious marriage that meets the requirements of civil marriage may be registered as such, and produces civil effects from the date of its celebration (Arts. 1513 and 1516). Besides compliance with civil requirements, the Public Registrars Act (Federal Law 6.015/1973) also demands that 'the document of religious marriage, signed by the celebrating authority or minister, the bride and groom and two witnesses,' be presented at a Public Registrar's Office.

The possibility of civil recognition of marriages performed in the context of Spiritism and African-Brazilian religions has been a topic of controversy.[4] Hesitation stems from the fact that those religions do not possess the kind of hierarchical structure and institutionalized religious leadership that characterize Roman Catholicism, Protestantism and Judaism. The use of the concept of religious authority in the wording of Federal Law 6.015/1973 has been invoked as a reason to reject the possibility of civil recognition of unions performed in the context of Spiritism – a faith where there are no formal priests. Such interpretation, nevertheless, is not consistent with the principle of secularism, which should assure that all religious confessions be treated equally and in a non-discriminative way (TJRJ/0023741-26.2007.8.19.0000).

Recently, both legal scholars and the courts have tended to recognize the possibility of validating marriages celebrated by any religion whatsoever. Some authors, though, argue for the non-recognition of religious marriages that differ too much from the model of civil marriage, such as in the hypothetical case of multiple marriage bonds based on religions that admit polygamy (Berenice 2007, 143).

[4] The struggle for legal recognition of Afro-Brazilian religious groups has a long story of persecutions and discrimination. These groups face innumerous difficulties to be qualified as religions. For example, most of the Umbanda and Candomblé temples (called *terreiros*) do not obtain tax exemptions due to the difficulty of proving their religious status by their ministers. Recently, a federal judge delivered a very criticized decision in which it was argued that "Afro-Brazilian cults do not constitute religions". A few days later, under strong public disapproval and great media attention, the judge modified the content of the decision (Ação Civil Pública 2014.51.01.004747-2 – JFRJ). Spiritism, differently, faced less hostility in the public sphere. Scholars pointed out that this group has been less vulnerable to state repression in the past. Moreover, they were entitled to benefits legally conceded to ordinary religious associations (Giumbelli 2008). Nevertheless, some spiritist centers prefer not to register themselves as religious associations.

Courts have understood that exclusively, religious marriages of any faith – such as the Jewish faith and religions of African origin – can be alleged as evidence of a kind of civil union called *união estável*. In Brazil, the 1988 Constitution treats *união estável* as a familial entity (Art. 226, §3).

The Relationship Between Religious Affiliation and the Applicable Legal Regime

The adoption of secularism and the formal separation between state and religion in Brazil excludes, as a general rule, the existence of particular legal regimes related to religious affiliations. Generally, a system of laws referring to natural persons, on the basis of their religious affiliation, does not exist in Brazil.

Nevertheless, complex questions have arisen after the incorporation into the Brazilian legal system, in 2010, of the 'Agreement between the Federative Republic of Brazil and the Holy See Regarding the Legal Status of the Catholic Church in Brazil' (Legislative Decree 698/2009; Presidential Decree 7.107/2010). This agreement, which governs several topics of law, was incorporated into the domestic legal system with statutory status. The document regulates the legal personality of ecclesiastical institutions, the protection of the church's historical, artistic and cultural heritage, the guardianship over places of worship, religious assistance in prisons and religious education, amongst other subjects.

Some of these subjects have been, or will be, examined in other parts of this report. Right now, only a brief overview of the legal incorporation of the agreement will be given, together with the legal implications of the provisions governing the recognition of religious rules.

The agreement with the Holy See was signed in 2008 by representatives of both sovereign states and moved swiftly through legal channels. Discussions relating to the legal appropriateness and viability of its approval followed two opposite views: one side argued for its rejection on the basis of its posing a threat to secularism and to equality of treatment for all religious confessions; the other, favorable to its approval, argued that it did no more than 'consolidate in one legal instrument all provisions already in force dealing with the institutional life of the Catholic Church in the country.' As Giumbelli reports, the agreement, although swiftly approved, was met with multiple negative reactions.

In at least three areas, the agreement establishes a clear connection between religious affiliation and the legal regime that is applicable: (i) in its provisions regarding the Military Ordinariate; (ii) in recognizing the autonomy of the church to establish its own internal organization; and (iii) in providing for a differentiated voluntary work regime for church clerics.

First of all, the agreement mentions the Military Ordinariate, which is not regulated by its provisions, but had been the object of another agreement not duly incorporated into Brazilian law, signed in 1989 (Zylbersztajn 2012). The 1989 agreement establishes the rank of military ordinary for clerics with the dignity of Archbishop, nominated by the Holy See and approved by the Brazilian government; their activity is subject to Canon Law and paid for by the Brazilian Armed Forces. As Joana Zilbersztajn remarks, "there is a clear intermingling of religious and state organization" which violates the constitutional clause of secularism.

Another factor that favors the infiltration of religious rules into the legal system is the recognition of the power of the Roman Catholic Church to 'freely create, modify or extinguish all ecclesiastical institutions' mentioned in Art. 1 of the Agreement. It establishes an asymmetric regime in which Catholic entities are immune to the state's regulatory activity, automatically validating church decisions and giving them a privileged treatment in comparison to that applied to other faiths.

The agreement also recognizes the non-existence of an employment relationship between the Catholic Church and its ordained ministers and consecrated laypeople (Art. 16, I), creating a special regime in this domain. Its aim is to except those relationships from the legal framework that governs work relations in general in Brazil.

Rules with a Clearly Identifiable Religious Background but Applicable to all Citizens

In Brazil, the legal rules that have a traditional Christian background but are applicable to all citizens concern religious holidays. There are many national and local holidays of Catholic origin. As Martel (2007) points out, until very recently 'the existence of religious holidays in a secular republic didn't give rise to major controversies'. Nevertheless, the rise and growth of political prominence of Evangelicalism has changed this scenario. For example, a Federal District law that instituted the Day of Evangelicals has had its constitutionality called into question. Courts have deemed it valid and characterized that holiday as a regular exercise of the right to religious freedom.

Religious Rules and the Autonomy of Religious Entities

There is no specific legislative provision regarding the enforcement, by religious organizations such as schools and hospitals, of their own rules inside their premises. All exceptions or accommodations will be based on the general system that governs relations between religion and the state, and not on a legal regime specifically relevant to those organizations. The most remarkable exception to this general rule is the recent agreement between Brazil and the Holy See, analyzed above. For example, 'religious ministers and consecrated laypeople' are not to be considered bound by employment relationships with 'Dioceses and Religious Institutes,' so that the rules of employment law do not apply to them; and the legal personality of ecclesiastical institutions should be established by Canon Law, so long as it does not go against Brazilian laws (Art. 3, §1°).

Channels for the Enforcement of Religious Rules in Brazilian Law

Considering that Brazil follows a lay model of separation between state and religion, all religious rules should be applied indirectly. In other words, they can be applied: (i) through the homologation of judicial rulings from countries where religion is established; (ii) by means of agreements with religious entities, as in the agreement with the Holy See, that stipulated a legal regime for the Catholic Church in Brazil (as analyzed above); and (iii) as an element of private autonomy, since religious organizations are legally described as legal entities under private law, and as such, according to the Civil Code (Art. 44), can be freely created, structured and operated. In this case, it is worth mentioning that churches publish statutes which define their internal organization and state the kind of conduct they can demand from their members.

General Rules and Reasonable Accommodation for Religious Minorities

The Brazilian constitutional system recognizes the possibility of accommodating exceptions to general rules in view of particular norms issued by religious groups. Admission exams for public appointments and public schools that take place on Saturdays are a good example. Some religions impose upon their faithful to keep Saturdays as a holiday, which means that, to be present at the exam, the candidate would have to disobey that religious rule. In Brazil, state courts have recognized the need for accommodation in such cases and, taking into account freedom of religion, have decided to keep the candidate in isolation during the regular hours of the exam and to allow him or her to take the test after sunset (Leite 2011; Martel 2007). Another relevant example involves Jehovah's Witnesses and blood transfusions against their will. In such cases, most countries recognize that, if the believer rejects the transfusion with full autonomy (being an adult with plain mental capacity), the state has no reason to impose it. This is the dominant understanding amongst Brazilian scholars, but courts are still making the transfusion imperative in most cases, disregarding the autonomy of the individual and freedom of religion (Leite 2011; Barroso 2010).

Adjudication: Connections Between Religious Adjudication and State Jurisdiction

A Single-Jurisdiction System

The constitutional text establishes that 'the law shall not exclude from the consideration of the judiciary power any injury or threat to any right.' (Art.5, XXXV) Brazil adopts a single-jurisdiction system: only the Judiciary has the power to state the law in a binding and non-revocable form and the jurisdiction of courts cannot be set aside in any case under the law.

This means that adjudication by religious courts is always challengeable in the country's judiciary courts. Courts can consider, in the light of the country's legal system, the validity of the solutions adopted by religious authorities. Nevertheless, courts can defer in a greater or lesser degree to demands related to the rulings of religious authorities.

Some deference from courts to decisions taken by religious organizations, applying their own particular rules, can be noticed. There are precedents according to which no moral damages are due for the decision, made by a religious institution, to divest a minister from his administrative and pastoral roles, on the grounds that no acts practiced on the basis of the church's internal statutes can be declared illicit (TJRS/70044235885). Similarly, a state court has ruled that the annulment of a religious marriage, decided in accordance with the rules of the religious confession to which both parties are affiliated, cannot result in moral damages (TJSC/2007.064090-8). According to another ruling, a sentence pronounced by a religious congregation, banning certain individuals from their religious services, is not a cause for legal action to seek damages (TJPR 490713–7).

There are instances in which state courts do take into consideration the acts of religious courts, on the grounds that Brazilian procedural rules admit all legally and morally legitimate means of proof (TJSP/0007514-34.2002.8.19.0000). For the same reason, ecclesiastical certificates (along with testimonial evidence) are acceptable as evidence in suits that seek to correct the date of birth included in the birth certificate.

State Homologation of the Rulings of Religious Courts

Traditionally, and based on the normative context described above, the Brazilian legal system did not contemplate the validation of the rulings of religious courts. The only exception to this rule was the homologation of sentences pronounced by religious courts in countries that recognize this kind of jurisdiction (STF SE 5.529/Syria; STJ SE 3.917/Lebanon).

The Brazilian Supreme Court did not admit the homologation of religious court rulings pronounced in Brazil, even when those rulings were confirmed by foreign authorities. This rule was adopted, for instance, in cases involving divorce, in which it was understood that 'no divorce granted by a religious authority to any spouse living in Brazil, or to any Brazilian national living abroad, will be homologated by the Supreme Court. Regarding foreign nationals living outside our territory, an exception applies to the nationals of those countries whose law extends to clerical authorities the granting of divorces' (STF, SE 2.838 AgR/Lebanon).

According to this reasoning, only the acts of foreign state courts could be homologated in Brazil. The Brazilian Supreme Court understood that there could be no homologation of a decision of the 'Sacra Romana Rota' which dispensed parties from a marriage *rato et non consummato* (legally performed but not consummated); but it did accept the ruling of the Civil Court of Genoa which recognized the same decision as having civil effects (STF, SE 2.004/Vatican).

The Brazilian Supreme Court has homologated dissolutions of marriages ruled on by ecclesiastical courts, when they were previously homologated by civil courts of countries which have signed a concordat with the Vatican. That is the case of SE 2501 (Portugal), SE 2613 (Spain) and SE 2041 (Italy). On the other hand, in SE 2852 (Spain), the Supreme Federal Court refused to homologate a ruling by an ecclesiastical court located in Brazil on the grounds that 'family relationships are subject to the jurisdiction of civil courts'. According to section 15 of the Introductory Act to the Civil Code, a foreign ruling is only to be carried out in Brazil in the case of having been pronounced by a competent judge, having the status of *res judicata* and complying with all requirements laid out in sections 216 and 217 of the Brazilian Supreme Court's Rules of Court.

The legal framework on this topic was altered by the incorporation into Brazilian law of the controversial 2008 Agreement between the Holy See and Brazil, which lays down that 'the homologation of ecclesiastical rulings relating to marriage, when confirmed by the higher control organ of the Holy See, will be effected according to the terms of Brazilian law governing the homologation of foreign legal rulings in general' (Art. 12, §1).

Based on the Agreement, the Brazilian Supreme Court has now homologated a judgment pronounced by the ecclesiastical court of the city of Vitória and confirmed by the competent organ of the Holy See in the Vatican. It was stated that, according to the Agreement, 'ecclesiastical rulings confirmed by the higher control organ of the Holy See are equivalent to foreign legal rulings in matters pertaining to homologation' (STF SE 6.516/Vatican).

The main question arising from judicial homologation of the Holy See rulings is the injury to the principle of secularism that stems from the violation of equal treatment to all religious confessions. The Roman Catholic Church is privileged, since there are no equivalent provisions relating to other faiths (Giumbelli 2011).

Social Implementation of Religious Rules (with no Official Recognition)

Faith Healing and Animal Sacrifice

The conflict between religious commands and abstract state norms is a problem that mostly concerns minority religions, and affects, in its most intense form, the religions of African origin.

There are two practices in African-Brazilian religions that bring up legal questions. These are the conflict between abstract legal commands and the exercise of freedom of religion: (i) the practice of healing rituals; and (ii) animal sacrifice.

The Brazilian Criminal Code, drafted in 1940, stipulates that it is a crime to 'practice faith healing' (*curandeirismo*) and describes such a practice as one involving the prescription of substances, the use of words and gestures, and the making of a diagnoses. This crime is defined in the chapter that deals with crimes against public health.

The criminalization of such acts stemmed originally from a context of discrimination against Spiritism and persecution of African-Brazilian religions. Prior legislation (of 1890) criminalized both 'Spiritism' and 'magic and its spells' (Giumbelli 2008, 84). Nevertheless, recent theoretical approaches and legal rulings emphasize that, given the constitutional protection to freedom of belief and freedom of worship, it is not possible to criminalize religious practices as instances of 'faith healing'. Thus, in a ruling over whether the faith healing that took place during a Spiritist séance could be criminalized as *curandeirismo*, the court made it plain that criminal law 'cannot be used as a sieve to interfere in people's religious choice. In other words, it is not up to the Judiciary to stipulate which religions are false, because that would imply disrespect towards those who believe or have believed in them' (STJ HC 97.236/PB).

Another important issue is animal sacrifices in religious rituals, a practice that is intrinsic to religions of African origin. In Article 225, §1°, VII, the Federal Constitution bans all practices that involve cruelty against animals. Also, Article 32 of federal law 9605/1998 criminalizes the abuse and mistreat of animals.

The Supreme Federal Court will face this issue in the judgment of RE 494.601/RS, which is aiming for the reversal of a ruling that affirmed the constitutionality of the provision that exempts the sacrifice of animals in the liturgies of African religions from the State Code for Animal Protection.

Proselytism and Religious Use of Public Spaces

The widespread use of religious symbols in public facilities has also been a controversial topic. In hospitals, schools, police stations and even in the Brazilian Supreme Court (STF) main courtroom, one can come upon a crucifix hanging on the wall. In

2007, complaints were filed with the National Justice Council (CNJ) against the use of crucifixes in Brazilian courtrooms. Facing contradictory opinions about the topic, the CNJ decided that the existence of crucifixes in courtrooms does not violate secularism. Nonetheless, Rio de Janeiro's State Court decided, in 2009, to administratively remove all crucifixes from its courtrooms, being followed by Rio Grande do Sul's State Court in 2012. In the Executive Branch, President Dilma Rousseff removed both the Bible and the crucifix that adorned the Presidential Office.

Finally, the practice of proselytism, so common in Pentecostalism, arouses debates around the use of public and social spaces. There are abundant examples of public nuisance suits involving religious services of different faiths based on noise pollution. To solve this problem, the courts usually have invoked the right to a balanced environment, which is granted in the Federal Constitution (Art. 225).

Conclusion

The treatment of religious matters by the Brazilian State can be assessed as not neutral from a descriptive point of view, but as striving to reach normative neutrality. Christianity has a strong historical influence in Brazilian society, which inclines the state to give it preferential treatment.

Some issues are still looked upon as neutral, but in reality they bespeak the accordance of preferential treatment to one religion over others, such as crucifixes in classrooms and public spaces and religious education in public schools, just to mention two of them. Debate and criticism regarding ingrained assumptions that unwittingly end up privileging Christians in some matters have been steadily increasing.

In conclusion, Brazil still has a long way to go, but it seems to be gradually giving concrete form to the principles of pluralism, democracy, freedom of religion and neutrality – principles that are prescribed in the Constitution and that should regulate the relationship between the secular state and religious groups.

References

Barroso, Luis Roberto. 2010. Legitimidade da Recusa de Transfusão de Sangue por Testemunhas de Jeová: dignidade humana, liberdade religiosa e escolhas existenciais. Instituto Ideas.

Berenice, Maria. 2007. *Manual de Direito das Famílias*, 4th ed. São Paulo: Revista dos Tribunais.

Ferraz, Anna Candida da Cunha. 1997. O Ensino Religioso nas escolas públicas: exegese do §1° do art. 210 da CF de 05.10.1988. *Revista dos Tribunais – Cadernos de Direito Constitucional e Ciência Política* (July/Sept): 20 (5): 19–47.

Giumbelli, Emerson. 2003. O 'baixo espiritismo' e a história dos cultos mediúnicos. *Horizontes Antropológicos* 19(9): 247–281.

Giumbelli, Emerson. 2008. A presença do religioso no espaço público: modalidades no Brasil. *Religião & Sociedade* 28(2): 80–101.

Giumbelli, Emerson. 2011. O Acordo Brasil-Santa Sé e as relações entre Estado, sociedade e religião. *Ciencias Sociales y Religión* 13(14): 119–143.

Huaco Palomino, Marco Antonio. 2008. A laicidade como princípio constitucional do Estado de Direito. In *Em defesa das liberdades laicas*, ed. Roberto Arruda Lorea, 33–80. Porto Alegre: Livraria do Advogado.

IBGE. 2012. Características gerais da população, religião e pessoas com deficiência. In *Censo Demográfico 2010*, ed. Roberto Arruda Lorea. Rio de Janeiro: IBGE.

Leite, Fábio Carvalho. 2008. *Estado e Religião no Brasil: a liberdade religiosa na constituição de 1988*. Doctorate's thesis, Universidade do Estado do Rio de Janeiro (UERJ).

Leite, Fábio Carvalho. 2011. O Laicismo e outros exageros sobre a Primeira República no Brasil. *Religião & Sociedade* 31(1): 32–60. http://dx.doi.org/10.1590/S0100-85872011000100003.

Machado, Jónatas Eduardo Mendes. 1996. *Liberdade religiosa numa comunidade constitucional inclusiva – Dos direitos da verdade aos direitos dos cidadãos*. Coimbra: Coimbra Editora Limitada.

Martel, Letícia de Campos Velho. 2007. Laico, mas nem tanto: cinco tópicos sobre liberdade religiosa e laicidade estatal na jurisdição constitucional brasileira. *Revista Jurídica Brasileira* (Aug/Sept): 9(86): 11–57.

Neto, Jayme Weingartner. 2006. *A Edificação Constitucional do Direito Fundamental à Liberdade Religiosa: um feixe jurídico entre a fundamentalidade e o fundamentalismo*. Doctorate's thesis, Pontifícia Universidade Católica do Rio Grande do Sul (PUC-RS).

Oro, Ari Pedro. 2003. Igreja Universal: um poder politico? In *Igreja Universal do Reino de Deus – os novos conquistadores da fé*, ed. Ari Pedro Oro, André Corten, and Jean Pierre Dozon. São Paulo: Paulinas.

Rawls, John. 1993. *Political liberalism*. New York: Columbia University Press.

Silva, José Afonso da. 2013. *Curso de Direito Constitucional Positivo*, 37th ed. São Paulo: Malheiros.

Simões, Pedro org. 2010. *Filhos de Deus: assistência religiosa no sistema socioeducativo*. Rio de Janeiro: ISER.

Zylbersztajn, Joana. 2012. *O Princípio da Laicidade na Constituição Federal de 1988*. Doctorate's thesis, Universidade de São Paulo (USP).

Chapter 8
The Colombian Legal System: Applicable Religious Rules

Vicente Prieto

Abstract For centuries, the relationship with the Catholic Church has been in Colombia the only model. Thus, it is understandable that despite the new sociological situation of religious plurality (particularly with Christian non-Catholic denominations), the only-known system inspired the model of relations between the State and non-Catholic Churches. Actually, the development of the legal autonomy of religious entities has had as its main point of reference the situation of the Catholic Church and particularly the relationship between Canon law and the State legal system. Concordats, for example, reflect the existence and recognition from the State of an autonomous legal system (Canon law), with important consequences in civil life, such as recognition of a specific legal marriage system and legal personality for Canon Law entities.

The full extension to other denominations of a relationship like the one established with the Catholic Church has not been easy in some aspects. Marriage and civil recognition of legal personality requires the existence of a consistent law system in which the relevant matters have adequate legal regulation. It is not the case at least for the non-Catholic entities that signed in 1997 an Agreement with the Colombian State. These examples show that the simple approach of "giving the same" treatment, to the Catholic Church as well as to minority religions, besides being unrealistic, raises serious concerns from the standpoint of equality, understood not in terms of identity, but as proportion. Actually, the real equality cannot forget the different structure and organization of religious denominations. In some areas the extension of norms previously recognized only to the Catholic Church has been easier. This is the case of the rules related to religious ministers, holidays or conscientious objection.

V. Prieto (✉)
Universidad de La Sabana, Bogotá, Colombia
e-mail: vicente.prieto@unisabana.edu.co

R. Bottoni et al. (eds.), *Religious Rules, State Law, and Normative Pluralism - A Comparative Overview*, Ius Comparatum – Global Studies in Comparative Law 18, DOI 10.1007/978-3-319-28335-7_8

Introduction

The Colombian territory covers 1,140,000 km^2 of land. The Colombian population has approximately 46 million inhabitants (75 % urban, 25 % in rural areas) and falls into two major religious groups: the faithful of the Catholic Church (80–90 %) and non-Catholic Christians of various denominations. This second group is not homogeneous, but includes diverse religious communities (differing in number of members, doctrine, structure, etc.). A small minority of Jews and Muslims also reside in Colombia. Finally, the presence of indigenous tribes who retain their original religious beliefs should be remembered.

Colombia is a secular State. At the origin of the system, adopted by the 1991 Constitution, is great sensitivity towards the different manifestations and consequences of the fundamental right to freedom of religion. This sensitivity is linked to the remarkable increase in recent decades of different Christian denominations other than the majority religion, Catholicism. Colombia is no longer homogeneously Catholic, as was the case until the second half of the twentieth century. Religious plurality demanded new approaches and resulted in the 1991 Constitution and subsequent legislation and jurisprudence.

In Colombia, however, religious plurality is held within the framework of western cultural roots, common to Catholic and non-Catholic Christians. As a result, categories commonly accepted (religious freedom, secular state, equality, etc.) have been specifically applied to all in legislation and case law within the same legal system. Minorities with different roots, such as Jews or Muslims, have had no problem in integrating in this common law, with no need of a particular legal status. A different situation appears in relation to indigenous communities that retain their original religious beliefs. The Constitution (articles 7, 8, 10, 68, 72) assures their culture a special protection that implies serious exceptions to the common regime of religious freedom (see n. 3).

Until 1991, respect for individual and collective religious freedom was guaranteed. However, the State offered special status to the Catholic Church. Catholicism was the majority religion, and was therefore regarded as "the Nation's religion" and as a fundamental element of social order. In this scheme, the government limited the recognition of minority faiths to the regime of private law associations, very different from the status accorded to the Catholic Church.

The system established by the 1991 Constitution is remarkably different. As said before, it welcomes the prospect of the "secular State", in which the State does not adopt or protect any religion, even if it is the religion of the majority. The State also declared itself incompetent in religious matters. Furthermore, all religious denominations are equal before public authorities, and the State facilitates and promotes public cooperation with all religions.

Secularity and Legal Autonomy of Religious Entities

The current regime derives mainly from the Constitution of 1991, from the *Ley Estatutaria de Libertad Religiosa* (Law 133, 1994, *Religious Freedom Act*, RFA), from the Agreements signed with the Catholic Church (Concordat of 1973) and with some non-Catholic Christian entities (Internal Public Law Agreement n. 1, 1997, see Decree 354 of 1998). In brief, the Colombian system, within a framework of full religious freedom, welcomes the principles of equality, secularity and cooperation with churches and religious denominations (Prieto 2008, 120–136).

Colombia's adoption of the 1991 model left behind two other alternatives that were common in countries with a Catholic tradition, and also in Colombian history. One alternative was some form of confessional state. The latter was the secularism that seeks to relegate religion to the strictly private sphere, often with hostile demonstrations towards the institutional and public presence of churches in social life.

Article 19 of the Constitution states: "Freedom of worship is guaranteed. Everyone has the right to freely profess his religion and to disseminate it individually and collectively. All faiths and churches are equally free before the Law". RFA repeats the same principles and, in Article 2, it is stated that "No church or religious denomination is or will be official or established. However, the State is not atheist, agnostic or indifferent to the religious sentiments of Colombians. The government will protect individuals, as well as churches and religious groups, in their beliefs, and will facilitate their participation in achieving the common good. Similarly, the government will maintain harmonious relations and common understanding with the churches and religious entities existing in Colombian society".

Freedom of religion means that the State should recognize and guarantee full immunity of coaction (from the State itself, or from any other individual or social organization) in religious matters for individuals and entities. As a result, freedom of religion implies the recognition of an autonomous framework, in which the State is simply incompetent (Viladrich and Ferrer Ortiz 2004, 96–97; Minnerath 2004).

Secularity is the logical consequence. Individuals and religious entities are subjects of religious freedom, but the State cannot be subject of the act of religious faith. For this reason, the State cannot assume any faith or religious beliefs or undertake actions related to these. The State power is limited to those norms that are necessary to guarantee that individuals and entities could exercise the right to religious freedom without coaction, and obviously within due limits (Martín de Agar 1995, 200).

According to RFA, Article 4, those limits are the following: "The exercise of rights deriving from freedom of religion and worship is limited only by the protection of the rights of others to exercise their public liberties and fundamental rights, as well as the safeguarding of security, health, and public morality, which are constituent elements of public order protected by law in a democratic society".

Actually, secularity does not mean only the autonomy from religion in State activities. It also means autonomy of religious entities in its own. In brief, secularity is the result of double incompetence: the State is incompetent in religious matters, and religious entities are incompetent in secular ones. The emphasis on this second aspect has perhaps deflected the attention from the first.

In Colombia, the right of religious entities to have their own norms and rules (legal autonomy) is recognized by RFA, article 13: "Churches and religious denominations have, in their religious affairs, full autonomy and freedom. They can establish their own rules of organization, internal rules, and dispositions for members. In these rules, as well as in those governing the institutions created by churches and religious denominations for their own ends, could be included provisions for the safeguard of their religious identity and their own nature, as well as due respect for their beliefs, without prejudice of the rights and duties recognized by the Constitution (especially those of freedom, equality, and non-discrimination). The State recognizes the exclusive jurisdiction of the ecclesiastical courts to decide the validity of acts or religious ceremonies that affect or may affect the civil status of persons".

To this general norm it should be added the specific legislation provided by Agreements between the State and religious denominations. In the first place the Concordat with the Catholic Church. It was signed in 1973 and approved by Law 20, 1974. In Articles I–III the autonomy of the Catholic Church is recognized. Article I states: "The State, in deference to the traditional Catholic beliefs of the Colombian Nation, considers the Catholic, Apostolic and Roman Religion as a fundamental element of common good and of integral development of the national community. The State guarantees to the Catholic Church and to Catholic faithfuls full exercise of religious rights. Religious freedom of other religious denominations and its members, as well as freedom of religion of any citizen, is guaranteed". Article II: "The Catholic Church will enjoy full freedom and independence from civil powers. Therefore, the Catholic Church will exercise freely all its spiritual authority and ecclesiastical jurisdiction, according to its own rules in government and administration". Finally, Article III states: "Canon law is independent from State law, and it is not a part of it. However, it will be respected by the authorities of the Republic".

Decision C 027, 1993 (Constitutional Court, CC), declared the non-conformity of some articles of the Concordat with the 1991 Constitution. It was not the case of Articles I-III, that were declared in full conformity with the Constitution. Consequently there is no doubt about their legal force (Prieto 2010a, 1–50).

Article 15, RFA, extended the possibility of signing Agreements with the State to other religious denominations, that enjoy personality and offer a warranty of stability (see also Decree 782, 1995, Article 14). According to these norms, in 1997 a Public Law Agreement was signed with some non-Catholic Christian entities (approved by Decree 354, 1998). The Agreement includes norms about marriage (Articles I-VI), religious teaching in schools (Articles VII-XIII), religious assistance to members of the security forces and in prisons and hospitals (Articles XIV-XVIII), places of worship (Articles XIX-XX) and social assistance programs (Article XXI).

Article XXIII refers only to the Seventh Day Adventist Church. It states that, by agreement between the parties (employee and employer), Saturday can be established as the weekly day of rest. In addition, students are exempt from submitting exams and attending classes on Saturday.

In some CC decisions the incompetence of the State and the legal autonomy of religious communities has been stressed, particularly in relation to the autonomy of the Catholic Church in the administration of sacraments (Baptism, Eucharist, Marriage), that had been denied by church authorities according to internal norms. The affected persons claimed for the application of human rights and requested that civil courts ordered such religious acts. See CC decisions T 200, 1995; C 609, 1996; T 946, 1999; T 998, 2002; T 1083, 2002. All decisions confirmed the autonomy of the Catholic Church in the application of its own rules. However, in a recent decision (T 658, 2013) the State intervened in the internal organization of a Catholic monastery.

Civil Relevance of Religious Rules

For historical and sociological reasons, the civil relevance of religious rules has been developed in Colombia in relation to canon law. This framework is similar to other countries in which three elements can be recalled: a predominantly Catholic population, concordats with the Catholic Church and a civil law system (Ibán 2013, 262–263). It is the case of Italy, Spain, and many Latin American countries (Navarro Floria and Milani 2010).

The Colombian model recognizes the independence of canon law (see Concordat, Article III). Therefore, the relationship with State law is understood as a relationship between autonomous legal systems. The model assumes the connection techniques used by private international law (Lombardía and Fornés 1994, 371–375; Monroy Cabra 1995, 204–216; Rodríguez García 1999, 1010–1011). Amongst these techniques, the different ways of referencing canon law rules by State laws has a special importance.

In jurisprudence we may recall two benchmarks: a decision of the Supreme Court (May 15, 1954) and a recent decision of the Constitutional Court (SU 540, 2007). The first explicitly underlines that canon law is a legal system independent from the State. However, canon law can generate some effects within the scope of civil law when the latter refers specifically to the law of the Church in certain subjects.

The decision explains that there are two ways of referencing canon law rules. First of all, the *material reference*, in which canon law rules are incorporated into State law. They are no longer "external" rules to which some effect is recognized, but civil norms with all the consequences. In the *formal reference*, canon law rules remain external to civil law. Their nature and interpretation belong to canon law. In Colombia, according to this decision, the references to canon law are always *formal*. This is the case in Articles II, III and IV of the Concordat of 1887 (the Concordat in force on the date of the decision, 1954). In cases of formal reference to canon law, the State assumes the canonical regulation in matters like marriage, legal personality, etc. The same criteria can be applied to the Concordat of 1973 (Articles I-III are very similar to the norms contained in the Concordat of 1887).

More recently, decision SU 540, 2007 (see also *Auto* 143, 2007) confirmed the principles of formal reference to canon law. The decision has a special importance in relation to the application of an ordinary labor regime in the case of religious ministers (see 6, c).

In relation to the Catholic Church, the Concordat is the first source that allows the identification of the canonical rules recognized by the State. In addition to the Concordat, some of the ordinary laws include various forms of reference to rules of the Catholic Church. Occasionally, the interpretation of these rules by the Constitutional Court has meant the extension of its content to all religious denominations.

In the case of non-Catholic denominations, it may be said, first, that religious pluralism in recent decades has been developed in Colombia following the growth of Evangelical confessions, heirs of the Protestant Reformation. They are relatively numerous, heterogeneous communities of diverse nature and structure, born frequently around the figure of a preacher or pastor. Their regulatory system is often basic and it is not easy to distinguish between real legal rules and other sort of norms (doctrinal principles, worship, etc.) (Prieto 2011, 254–259). The law of the State takes the place, in many respects, of a real legal system created by a religious community (Stamm 2012; Roca 2012, 807–809).

At the same time, since 1991, the minority confessions have searched a legal status similar to the Catholic Church. This claim is obviously the consequence of the new system, in which all confessions are equal before the law. However, the differences in nature, structure and legal system to the Catholic Church do not always allow the simple extension of the legislation that, until now, has been applied to the Catholic Church. This does not prevent that, in principle, the technique of formal reference could be applied to minority faiths. Actually, as we will see later, this is the case of some rules contained in the 1997 Agreement with non-Catholic entities.

In relation to other faiths (Judaism and Islam), their presence in Colombia is minimal and to date they have not expressed any intention to hold Agreements with the State that recognize their own religious rules with civil effects. Furthermore, their relationship to the civil powers is conceived in very different terms from those that characterize confessions with Christian roots (Ferrari 2004, 274–294; Ciáurriz 2013). The recognition of civil relevance to religious rules with social impact (marriage, inheritance, holidays, etc.) has been granted through the application of State laws, when necessary and possible. In any case, to date, these confessions have operated within the wide margins of the RFA and the courts have not had to rule on particular conflicts.

As stated before, a particular situation arises in relation to the indigenous population. According to the last official census (2005) this population is estimated at 1.4 million. Their culture enjoys special legal protection. As a result, the Constitutional

Court has limited some relevant manifestations of religious freedom that could endanger the indigenous culture. Particularly, in the case of people converted to Christianity, the Court has limited their right to spread their religion in their indigenous community, and their right to have public worship places (see decisions T 257, 1993: T 342, 1994; SU 510, 1998; T 1022, 2001; T 009, 2007; T 349, 2008; Prieto 2010b). As a consequence, the special legal status recognized to indigenous communities (self-government, criminal law, etc.; see Constitution, Articles 246 and 330) has been extended to religious matters. However, the relevance of these norms is limited, mainly because the number of indigenous communities that retain their ancestral beliefs is quite limited (actually, most of the indigenous population professes some form of Christianity, Roman Catholicism or Evangelicalism).

Marriage

Law 57, 1887, can be taken as an initial reference point. The Law recognized civil effects to Catholic marriages. The following year, the Concordat of 1888 established that it was a condition for civil recognition that Catholic marriages were celebrated according to the norms of the Council of Trent (Article 17). It was understood that Catholic marriage was compulsory for those who professed the Catholic religion. As a result, it was forbidden for Catholics to celebrate civil marriage, unless they had formally abandoned the Catholic Church (Law 54, 1924).

This situation lasted until the Concordat of 1973, currently in force, which explicitly abolished Law 54, 1924. Thereafter there were two forms of marriage supported by Colombian law, both indissoluble (up to Law 1, 1976, which allowed divorce only for civil marriage), and with full freedom to celebrate any of them: civil marriage and catholic marriage. There were recognised civil effects given to the latter: according to the Concordat of 1973, Article VII: "The State recognizes full civil effects to marriage concluded in accordance with the norms of canon law. For the effectiveness of this recognition the competent ecclesiastical authority shall transmit a certified copy of the record to the appropriate State official, who shall register it in civil record".

Additionally, according to Article VIII, cases concerning "the nullity or the dissolution of the canonical marriages (…) belong to the exclusive competence of the Ecclesiastical Courts and Holy See Congregations. Decisions and Judgments of these, when they are firm and executive according to canon law, shall be forwarded to the Judicial District Court having territorial jurisdiction, which shall decree civil execution and will order its civil registration". Therefore, there is no need of any kind for judicial review on the part of State courts.

In 1991, the Constitution (Article 42) extended this regulation to all religious marriages: "religious marriages will have civil effects in the terms established by law". Additionally, civil effects recognise "decisions of annulment of religious marriages issued by the authorities of the respective faiths, in the terms established by law". Divorce is admitted for all marriages, including Catholic ones.

Similar norms appear in Article 6, (d) RFA. The starting point is the right "to contract and celebrate marriage and to establish a family according to religious beliefs and according to the rules of the church or religious denomination". It is stressed, according to the Constitution, that "religious marriages and nullity decisions issued by religious authorities will have civil effects, without prejudice of the State's power to regulate them".

The specific regulation has been issued through Law 25, 1992, Articles 1–4. Particularly (cf. Article 1), the recognition of civil effects is limited to religious entities that have "special" legal personality recognized by the Ministry of Internal Affairs (see RFA, Article 9), have signed Agreements with the State, have demonstrated that their matrimonial law provisions are not contrary to the Constitution, and have ensured the reliability and continuity of their religious organization (see also Decree 782, 1995, Articles 13–14). Articles 2–4 establish procedural rules to implement the recognition of civil effects to religious marriages and decisions of annulment.

As noted above, in Colombia there are two Agreements with religious entities: the Concordat with the Catholic Church (1973) and the Internal Public Law Agreement n. 1 of 1997, between the Colombian Government and some non-Catholic religious entities (Decree 354, 1998). In the first (cf. Article VII), the recognition of civil effects of marriage is established in short terms, with a large referral to canon law.

The latter is instead quite wide (Articles I-VI). Civil effects are given to marriages celebrated by the respective ministers (Article I); Article II establishes the conditions to be met to be recognized as a minister; the marriage should be celebrated in the religious district in which the bride has her residence (Article III); content of the marriage record is defined in Article IV. Article V deals with registration of the marriage, and Article VI includes a general final clause: "Everything related to the cessation of civil effects, separation and property, annulment and dissolution of non-Catholic Christian marriages covered by this Agreement, is the exclusive competence of the ordinary courts and therefore will be under civil law established for this purpose". The Agreement makes no reference to civil recognition of decisions of annulment issued by the respective religious authorities.

Actually, the Agreement does not refer to the legal system of the religious entities, as it does with the Catholic Church in the Concordat. Instead, rules are agreed to replace the lack of internal rules (a definition of marriage very similar to the Civil Code, formal requirements for the celebration, and the conditions to be met by ministers). This is probably due to the desire to establish default rules that could guarantee the minimum conditions of civil validity for marriages when these matters are not sufficiently regulated by the internal rules of the religious denomination. In fact, the study of the rules of each entity leads to the conclusion that they can hardly be classified as an autonomous legal system. Except moral or worship norms, they refer directly to civil law. Sometimes there are rules about some prohibitions, like celebrating marriage with persons belonging to other faiths, or limitation of divorce grounds. In all cases, the legal regulation of the substantive aspects of the marriage is absent: capacity, impediments, defects and vices of consent, etc. (Prieto 2011, 254–259).

In conclusion, it seems that we cannot properly speak of recognition of civil effects. Rather than religious marriages recognized by civil law, they are civil marriages held in religious form, and therefore regulated in substance by the rules of the State. Actually, substantial regulation of consent, and much of the formal requirements, is offered by civil law (Prieto 2011, 251–266).

Instead, in Catholic marriages the recognition of civil effects is not limited to the form of celebration. Civil law assumes and recognizes the substance of the marriage relationship, as understood and regulated by canon law (Otaduy 2012, 547). This is a consequence of the nature of canon law, for which marriage is a sacrament, as the law of the Church is competent to regulate the substance and form of marriage.

Recognition of Religious Entities

The starting point is Article 9, RFA: the Ministry of Internal Affairs recognizes legal personality to churches and religious denominations, federations, and confederations of ministers, who have requested it. The Ministry will hold the Public Record of religious entities. The request shall be accompanied by reliable documents in which it shall be indicated the foundation or establishment of the entity in Colombia, as well as its name and other identifying information; its statutes, that shall include the religious purposes, functioning system, organization scheme and representative bodies including powers and conditions for valid designation. Churches, and religious denominations, as well as their federations and confederations, may retain or acquire legal private personality according to general provisions contained in civil law.

It is added in Article 10 that the Ministry of Internal Affairs will automatically perform registration in the Public Record of Religious Entities when the grant of legal personality for churches or religious denominations or their federations or confederations is done. Legal personality will be recognized when the requirements are duly fulfilled, and its recognition does not violate any of the provisions of RFA.

According to the Concordat, Article IV, "The State recognizes true and proper legal status to the Catholic Church. Similarly to the Dioceses, religious communities, and other Church entities to which canon law grants legal status, represented by their legitimate authority. Equal recognition will be granted to the ecclesiastical entities who have received legal status by an act of the legitimate authority, in accordance with canon law. For civil recognition of the latter to be effective, it is enough to prove existence by canonical certification".

RFA, Article 11, recognizes the same principle: "The State continues to recognize public ecclesiastical legal personality to the Catholic Church and the institutions erected or to be erected in accordance with what is established in paragraph 1 of Article IV of the Concordat, approved by Law 20, 1974. For the registration of these in the Public Record of Religious Entities, the decree of canonical erection or approval will be notified to the Ministry of Internal Affairs".

Through recognition of canonical legal persons, the State recognizes civil effects to the canonical act of constitution. This act follows entirely the rules of canon law. The recognition from the State simply assumes the legal persons "as they are" in canon law (constitution, legal qualification, organizational characteristics) (Otaduy 2012, 547). As a consequence, the State does not *give* legal personality to canonical entities, but recognizes their existence and their capacity to act in the civil sphere (see Decree 1396, 1997, Article 2).

With non-Catholic entities the legal regime is different. The recognition from the State has constitutive character and RFA establishes the conditions to obtain legal personality (see also Decree 782, 1995, Articles 1–6, and Decree 1319, 1998, Articles 1–8). Therefore, personality is *given* by the State, and it is not possible to speak of civil recognition of a religious entity and its legal personality as it is disciplined in a religious legal system regulated by religious norms.

Ministers and Religious Personnel

As a result of the exercise of religious freedom, there are religious services guaranteed by the State. These services are provided by persons and designed by religious authorities. Thereby, the State recognizes the particular relationship existing between the religious entity and the appointee. At the same time there are aspects of the religious service in which there is an obvious connection with labor law, administrative law or civil law (Otaduy 2006, 453–454).

RFA, Article 16, states that "The status of minister of cult will be certified by a document issued by the competent authority of the church or religious denomination with legal personality to which the minister belongs. The exercise of ministerial religious functions will be guaranteed by the State". The civil relevance of a religious ministers' appointment has three main grounds of application: (a) Spiritual assistance in military facilities, hospitals and prisons; (b) Nomination of religion teachers in public schools; (c) Labor regime applicable when performing predominantly religious missions. Additionally (d), there are norms regulating the activity of ministers in situations in which freedom of testation could be compromised. Briefly each of these aspects will be explained.

Spiritual Assistance

According to RFA, Article 6, (f), "Freedom of religion and worship guaranteed by the Constitution covers, with the consequent legal autonomy and immunity from coercion, among others, the rights of any person (…): (f) to receive religious assistance from their own church in any place, mainly in health care, public facilities, and in military and penitentiary facilities". In Article 8 it is added that "For the real and effective application of these rights, the authorities will take the necessary measures to ensure the religious assistance offered by churches and religious denominations to their members, when they are in public schools, military facilities, hospitals, and penitentiary facilities. This care may be offered by chaplaincies or by similar institutions, organized with full autonomy by the respective church or religious denomination".

In relation to the Catholic Church, the Concordat of 1973 in Article XVII establishes that: "The spiritual and pastoral assistance for the members of Armed Forces will be provided through the Military Ordinariate, following norms and regulations issued by the Holy See in agreement with the Government".

In the case of entities that subscribed to the Public Law Agreement of 1997, religious ministers are defined as "individuals who are engaged in a stable way in the functions of worship or religious assistance and demonstrate this condition through certification issued by the religious entity according to its statutes and regulations" (Article II). According to Article XIV, the religious entities that subscribed to the Agreement have the right "to provide under request spiritual and pastoral assistance to members of Armed Forces and to persons in schools, hospitals and penitentiary facilities. The spiritual assistance will be provided by ministers appointed by the religious entities. Ministers will receive collaboration from authorities so they can perform their duties under the same conditions as ministers of other religious entities officially recognized by the Colombian State. The way to provide religious assistance will be coordinated with the respective authorities".

Article XV refers in a more concrete way to spiritual assistance in Armed Forces; Article XVI deals with assistance in penitentiary facilities and Article XVIII regulates assistance in hospitals and social centers.

Decree 1519, 1998, established specific rules relating to religious freedom in penitentiary facilities. According to Article 1, the religious assistance will be provided by ministers of the religious entity to which each person belongs. The exercise of the right to religious freedom includes the right to worship and to receive religious assistance, the communication with ministers and representatives of the religious entity, and the existence of suitable places for the exercise of the right to freedom of religion (Article 2). See also Law 65, 1993 (Penitentiary Code), Article 152.

Teachers of Religion in Public Schools

The RFA recognizes the right of parents (or children themselves, if they have reached the age of majority) to choose the religious and moral education for their children according to their own convictions (Article 6, (h) RFA). Schools shall provide religious education of the religion to which the student belongs, and the student has the right not to be obliged to accept such religious education.

Religion teachers are required to possess a certificate of suitability from the respective church or denomination: "In the case of admission, promotion, or permanence in chaplaincies or as religion teachers, certification of suitability issued by the church or religious denomination to which the teachings belong should be required" (Article 6, (i) RFA).

Similar rules are contained in Article XII of the Concordat with the Holy See. It reaffirms the right of Catholic families to have their children religiously educated according to their faith. The Catholic religion is to be taught in public schools (not compulsory for Catholic children whose legal representatives have requested waivers for the Catholic religion classes, or for over eighteen years old Catholic students that submit a request to the same effect). Belonging to the ecclesiastical authority means the responsibility to develop programs, approve textbooks, and monitor the way religious education is taught. Teachers must have a suitability certificate issued by the ecclesiastical authority.

The Internal Public Law Agreement n. 1, 1997 (Decree 354, 1998), Chapter II deals with "teaching and non-Catholic Christian education and information". Article VII ("The freedom to choose non-Catholic Christian religious education") warrants to the faithful of the confession's party to the Agreement the right to choose the kind of education they want for their minor children and the freedom not to be compelled to receive religious education different from their own convictions. Religious entities must provide their plans for education and institutional projects to the competent authorities. The responsibility to monitor the quality of non-Catholic Christian religious education belongs to the religious authorities of the various denominations. The last article of Chapter II contains the requirements to become religion teacher.

In public schools religion teachers receive their salary from the State because they are public employees.

Labor Regime Applicable when Developing Predominantly Religious Missions

According to the CC decision T 495, 1993, in order to determine the status of employees in faith based institutions, it is necessary to apply the following general criteria: (1) In profit activities, the contract of employment is governed by the general rules of labor law; (2) In nonprofit work, rules of nonprofit entities are applied; (3) If the person's situation is a direct result of the exercise of a spiritual or pastoral function, internal rules of each church are applied.

Recently, decision SU 540, 2007 decided the case of a former Catholic priest who had held various important positions in a Catholic University. After his retirement, the plaintiff asked for full application of ordinary labor rules. For the

University, the appointments had been the direct result of him being a priest and a member of the Dominican Order. His relationship with the University was not the consequence of a normal employment contract but the result of a religious commitment, ruled by the norms of the religious community.

The decision recalls Articles II, III and IV of the 1973 Concordat with the Holy See. The autonomy of religious entities is stressed and full respect of religious commitments and rules is guaranteed. In the case the elements of an ordinary labor relationship were not present. Therefore, the applicable rules were those of Canon law (formal reference). In brief, the decision recognizes that predominantly religious employees may be ruled by a special regime. The State should respect the particular norms of religious entities and ensure the religious commitments that arise between them and their members.

Other Norms Involving Religious Ministers

Article 1022 of the Civil Code states that the Catholic priest that has been the confessor of someone during two years prior to his death, or in his last condition, cannot receive any inheritance or legacy. Neither can the Order, Convent nor brotherhood to which the priest belongs, or his close relatives. However, this prohibition does not include the parish of the testator. Article 1060, 16, of the Civil Code establishes that in the solemn will the confessor cannot act as a witness.

In both norms, the Code assumes and incorporates into the civil legislation the canonical concepts of confessor, Order, parish, etc., with the meaning they have in canon law. Moreover, the Code assumes what confession means for Catholics, particularly in situations such as those described.

The cited norms were analyzed by decision C 266, 1994. The point made was that only Catholic priests were included, and therefore there could be a case of discrimination compared with ministers of other religious entities. The decision justifies the norms as a way of protecting freedom in the act of will. Therefore, they are fully compatible with the Constitution. To prevent any possible discrimination, the decision extended the norm to other ministers. Actually, the trust included in the relationship between religious minister and faithful (excluding obviously what is specific for Catholics in the Sacrament of confession) could be present in other religious groups, other than the Catholic Church. It is the case of the diverse forms of spiritual direction, to which the norms of the Civil Code should be applied.

Something similar took place with the concept of "parish". Decision C 094, 2007, applied a similar idea to worship places or communities belonging to religious entities different from the Catholic Church, in accordance with their own structure and organization. Actually, the exception included in Article 1022 is applied to all religious entities in the domicile of the testator.

Religious Holidays

As a result of the Catholic tradition of the country, a number of religious holidays are recognized by the State as non-working days, with the appropriate employment consequences (non-labor days, increased wages in the event of unavoidable work on those days, etc.).

In Article 177 of the Labor Code (modified by Articles 1 and 2 of Law 51, 1983) the following Catholic holidays are listed: January 6, March 19, June 29, August 15, December 8 and December 25, Thursday and Good Friday, Ascension, Corpus Christi and Sacred Heart of Jesus.

Law 51, 1983, was challenged as unconstitutional, invoking the principles of equality and State secularity. In decision C 568, 1993, the Constitutional Court declared the Law's full conformity with the Constitution. Catholic holidays are not against freedom of religion, because no one is bound to worship according to the Catholic faith on those days. Furthermore, the goal of the Law is exclusively to encourage the needed rest for workers, and does not seek to promote or protect a particular religious denomination. In the same sense, see decisions C 107, 1994, and C 1261, 2000.

The civil recognition of religious holidays has been extended to other faiths. It is the case of the Seventh Day Adventist Church. The Public Law Agreement n. 1 of 1997, Article XXIII, recognizes that Saturday is the weekly day of rest for the faithful of this Church. In addition to the appropriate consequences in employment contracts, students in public or private schools are not required to attend classes and take exams on Saturday.

Decision T 448, 2007 extended the same right to all denominations recognized by the State, with or without Agreement: "Especially in public educational institutions but also in private ones [authorities] are bound to seek an agreement with the students who, because of their religious beliefs, cannot meet regular academic calendar or other obligations (...)". The request of the student shall be presented in due time, demonstrating he is "an active member of a church or religious denomination previously recognized by the Colombian State". There are similar dispositions in decision T 044, 2008.

Conscientious Objection

According to Article 18 of the Colombian Constitution, "nobody can be forced to act against his conscience". Although conscientious objection does not appear in an explicit way in the text, the Constitutional Court has issued numerous decisions that recognize it. Most of them deal with religious rules and motivations that are accepted by the State with relevant effects in the civil sphere.

It is the case, for example, of Jehovah Witnesses and their refusal to blood transfusions; some evangelical denominations that refuse to honor the flag or other patriotic symbols; opposition to swear by God by some Christian groups; rejection of abortion or military service for religious or ethical reasons. See decisions T 411, 1994; T 075, 1995; T 474, 1996; C 616 de 1997; T 588 de 1998; T 877, 1999; T 659, 2002; T 823, 2002; T 447, 2004; T 471, 2005; C 355, 2006; C 728, 2009; T 018, 2012.

Concluding Remarks

The influence of Catholicism in Colombian life has been evident for historical and sociological reasons. This can be seen in areas as diverse as cultural heritage, holidays, symbols that preside private and public activities, and ceremonies (civil and military) in which society is in any way represented. It is impossible that this reality, which in its various aspects has been the "mirror" of a predominantly Catholic country, is not reflected in the legal system.

For centuries, the relationship with the Catholic Church has been the only model. Thus, it is understandable that despite the new sociological situation of religious plurality (particularly with Christian non-Catholic denominations), the only-known system has inspired in Colombia the model of relations between the State and non-Catholic Churches.

For these reasons, the development of the legal autonomy of religious entities has had, as its main point of reference, the situation of the Catholic Church and particularly the relationship between Canon law and the State legal system. Concordats, for example, reflect the existence and recognition from the State of an autonomous legal system (Canon law), with important consequences in civil life, such as recognition of a specific legal marriage system and legal personality for Canonical entities.

In Colombia, the full extension to other denominations of a relationship like the one established with the Catholic Church has not been easy in some aspects. Marriage and civil recognition of legal personality requires the existence of a consistent law system in which the relevant matters have adequate legal regulation. It is not the case at least for the entities that signed the 1997 Agreement. These examples show that the simple approach of "giving the same" treatment, to the Catholic Church as well as to minority religions, besides being unrealistic, raises serious concerns from the standpoint of equality, understood not in terms of identity, but as proportion. Actually, in the search for real equality one cannot forget the different structure and organization of religious denominations.

In some areas the extension of norms previously recognized only in the reference to the Catholic Church has been easier. This is the case of the rules relating to religious ministers, holidays or conscientious objection.

The Colombian system allows a realistic approach to different situations through the path of the Public Law Agreements (see RFA, Article 15). There is no need to look for egalitarianisms with the Catholic Church, because the figure of the

Agreement allows a special treatment for each entity, and the identification of the internal religious rules that can be recognized in the civil sphere.

However, the possibility of concluding Agreements depends on the number of members and the tradition and history of a religious group (Article 15, Decree 782 of 1995). In practice, this possibility is reduced to the most representative churches and denominations. Actually, the religious entities that have signed some kind of Agreement are relatively few (the Concordat with the Catholic Church, and the 1997 Internal Public Law Agreement with 13 non-Catholic Christian entities).

If the agreements are understood (among other possible goals) as the means to adapt the general rules to specific situations, it is clear that this possibility cannot be denied to minority institutions. The experience of Spain can be useful, given its similarity to the Colombian system. In recent years the trend is to interpret more benignly the meaning of the expression "deeply-rooted", with the result of providing a number of religious institutions the possibility of signing cooperation agreements with the State. It has been taken into account not only the numerical factor, but above all the stability and permanence of the entity and its ability to take over rights and obligations (Fernández-Coronado 2009, 694–696).

The same experience could be applied in Colombia, allowing a wider and more effective development of religious freedom (Prieto 2012, 307–308). After all, the challenge is to reach a successful relationship between religious legal systems and State law as a consequence of the effective implementation of human rights. In the development of religious freedom it has to be considered not only the individual dimension, but the characteristics and legal structure that each religious entity has as a consequence of its autonomy (Lombardía 1982, 17–18).

References

Ciáurriz, María José. 2013. «Islam y Derecho musulmán». En *Religión, matrimonio y derecho ante el siglo XXI*. Estudios en homenaje al Profesor Rafael Navarro-Valls, coord. J. Martínez-Torrón-S. Meseguer Velasco-R. Palomino Lozano, I, 129–152. Madrid: Iustel.

Fernández-Coronado, Ana. 2009. «Sentido de la cooperación del Estado laico en una sociedad multirreligiosa». En *La libertad religiosa y su regulación legal. La Ley Orgánica de Libertad Religiosa*, editado por Rafael Navarro-Valls, Joaquín Mantecón Sancho, y Javier Martínez-Torrón, 679–698. Madrid: Iustel.

Ferrari, Silvio. 2004. *El espíritu de los derechos religiosos. Judaísmo, cristianismo e islam*. Barcelona: Herder.

Ibán, Iván. 2013. «Relevancia en los ordenamientos civiles de la función judicial canónica». En *Religión, matrimonio y derecho ante el siglo XXI*. Estudios en homenaje al Profesor Rafael Navarro-Valls, coord. J. Martínez-Torrón-S. Meseguer Velasco-R. Palomino Lozano, I, 259–273. Madrid: Iustel.

Lombardía, Pedro. 1982. «La relación entre derecho canónico y derecho eclesiástico». *Ius Canonicum*, n.º 43: 11–30.

Lombardía, Pedro, y Juan Fornés. 1994. «Las fuentes del Derecho Eclesiástico Español». En *Tratado de Derecho Eclesiástico*, 321–376. Pamplona: Eunsa.

Martín de Agar, José Tomás. 1995. «Libertà religiosa, uguaglianza e laicità». *Ius Ecclesiae*, 199–215.

Minnerath, Roland. 2004. The right to autonomy in religious affairs. In *Facilitating freedom of religion or belief: A deskbook*, T. Lindholm, C. Durham, B.G. Tahzib-Lie, Editors. E. A. Sewell and L. Larsen, Associate Editors), 291–319. Leiden: Martinus Nijhoff Publishers.

Monroy Cabra, Marco Gerardo. 1995. *Tratado de Derecho Internacional Privado*. 4.ª ed. Bogotá: Temis.

Navarro Floria, Juan Gregorio, y Daniela Milani. 2010. *Diritto e religione in America Latina*. Bologna: Il Mulino.

Otaduy, Jorge. 2006. «Relación jurídica de los profesores de religión en España. La dimensión canónica». *Ius Canonicum*, n.º 92: 445–489.

Otaduy, Jorge. 2012. «Efectos civiles de los actos canónicos». En *Diccionario General de Derecho Canónico*, III: 545–548. Cizur Menor (Navarra): Universidad de Navarra-Aranzadi.

Prieto, Vicente. 2008. Libertad religiosa y confesiones. Derecho Eclesiástico del Estado Colombiano. Bogotá: Ed. Temis-U. de La Sabana.

Prieto, Vicente. 2010a. «El Concordato de 1973 y la evolución del Derecho Eclesiástico colombiano». *Revista General de Derecho Canónico y Derecho Eclesiástico del Estado*, n.º 22: 1–50.

Prieto, Vicente. 2010b. «Libertad religiosa y culturas indígenas». *Anuario de Derecho Eclesiástico del Estado* 26: 121–151.

Prieto, Vicente. 2011. *Estado laico y libertad religiosa. Antecedentes y desarrollos de la Constitución colombiana de 1991*. Bogotá: Universidad de La Sabana-Diké.

Prieto, Vicente. 2012. «Reconocimiento jurídico de las entidades religiosas en el derecho colombiano: análisis crítico de la Ley Estatutaria de Libertad Religiosa». *Díkaion* 21(1): 285–314.

Roca, María José. 2012. «Reforma protestante». En *Diccionario General de Derecho Canónico*, VI, 804–813. Cizur Menor (Navarra): Universidad de Navarra-Aranzadi.

Rodríguez García, José Antonio. 1999. «El Derecho Canónico como Derecho estatutario en el ordenamiento jurídico español». En *Escritos en honor de Javier Hervada*, 1009–1020. Pamplona: Instituto Martín de Azpilcueta-Facultad de Derecho Canónico, Universidad de Navarra.

Stamm, Heinz-Meinolf. 2012. «Derecho de las confesiones evangélicas». En *Diccionario General de Derecho Canónico*, III, 786–791. Cizur Menor (Navarra): Universidad de Navarra-Aranzadi.

Viladrich, Pedro Juan, y Javier Ferrer Ortiz. 2004. «Los principios informadores del Derecho Eclesiástico Español». En *Derecho Eclesiástico del Estado español*, 5.ª ed., 87–113. Pamplona: Eunsa.

Chapter 9
Accommodation of Religious Rules in Estonian Law and Practice

Merilin Kiviorg

Abstract The article explores the extent of application of religious rules according to the law in Estonia. It is argued that religious rules are applied both de jure and de facto in Estonia, for example, within contractual freedom between parties, in the framework of exemptions from generally applicable laws and autonomy of religious communities. There is a certain amount of individual and collective freedom to choose to live life according to one's conscience and religious rules.

Introduction

While legal pluralism and possible recognition and application of religious rules has been debated in many parts of Europe and elsewhere, it has not so far emerged as a major public concern or legal issue in Estonia. No case has yet reached a civil court. Additionally, there has been very little qualitative or empirical research done in this area. There is very little (and no official) data available as to the use of religious rules in the daily lives of believers and about possible (*de facto*) parallel application of civil and religious rules.

Only in a couple of instances, described in this contribution, has the issue even emerged as a matter of public interest. For example, there has been some debate over exemptions and autonomy given to religious organizations and over potential problems related to the possible growth in immigration and any resultant increases in religious diversity. It is probably not an exaggeration to say that there is a phobia in Estonia regarding pressure from Europe to accept more refugees and immigrants. In this context "alien" customs and traditions have been discussed which may affect traditional state-religions relationships and peaceful co-existence of diverse communities in Estonia. As to religious autonomy, in theory, the resolution of purely religious disputes in Estonia is solved via the traditions of the affected religious associations. As will be discussed below, since the Estonian Constitution

M. Kiviorg (✉)
School of Law, University of Tartu, Tartu, Estonia
e-mail: merilinkiviorg@hotmail.com

R. Bottoni et al. (eds.), *Religious Rules, State Law, and Normative Pluralism - A Comparative Overview*, Ius Comparatum – Global Studies in Comparative Law 18, DOI 10.1007/978-3-319-28335-7_9

(*Põhiseadus*)[1] ensures the right of religious associations to conduct their affairs in accordance with their particular religious traditions, collective religious autonomy is respected.[2] However, the extent of this autonomy is debated. Most recently it was debated in the context of the Co-habitation Law (*Kooseluseadus*), which applies also to homosexual couples,[3] and in the context of draft amendments to the definition of hate speech in the Penal Code (*Karistusseadustik*).[4]

Religious rules are broadly understood in this contribution as rules stemming from religious authority. Examples include Christian canon law, Islamic law (sharia), Hindu law, and Jewish halakha. More broadly it includes acts adopted by religious bodies (for example acts adopted by the Estonian Evangelical Lutheran Church or other churches); norms and beliefs determining religiously motivated behaviour by groups or individuals (such as conscientious objection to military service, insurance, blood transfusion, etc.) or practice of religious beliefs and traditions (such as Sunday observance, observance of certain holidays, dietary restrictions and wearing of specific religious garb or item, such as a cross or kirpan).

Some indication is also needed as to what is meant by legal pluralism and/or application of religious rules by State law. It is quite likely that the first reaction of any lawyer in Estonia would be that state law does not allow any application of religious rules meaning there is no legal pluralism, Estonian law applies. A closer look, however, reveals that religious rules are applied *de facto*, for example, within contractual freedom between parties, in the framework of exemptions from generally applicable laws and autonomy of religious communities. There is a certain amount of individual and collective freedom to choose to live life according to one's religious conscience and rules. The following will try to give some more details about this matter in Estonia. However, firstly a brief account of relevant social and historical facts and state-religions relationships is needed.

---

[1] RT 1992, 26, 349. "Riigi Teataja" (RT) stands for State Gazette. Most Estonian laws are also available in English at the official site of the Riigi Teataja, accessed June 3, 2015, https://www.riigiteataja.ee

[2] Estonian Constitution does not *expressis verbis* mention autonomy or self-determination of religious communities akin to German Basic Law. However, the general right to self-determination of persons (both individuals and groups) stems from Article 19 of the Estonian Constitution. The right to religious autonomy is also considered to be an essential part of collective freedom of religion enshrined in Article 40 of the Constitution. RTL 2001, 82, 1120.

[3] RT I, 16.10.2014, 1. The law will enter into force on 1 January 2016.

[4] Estonian Penal Code has been going through a major review. There was a proposal to extend the scope of the hate crime provision. In response, religious organisations expressed their concerns about the future of religious speech especially regarding possible restrictions on voicing what doctrine says about same sex unions. The proposal was disregarded in the amendment process. Currently, incitement to hatred, violence or discrimination on account of race, religion, nationality or sexual orientation, political ideas or economical or social status is forbidden by §151 of the Penal Code only if the incitement has caused risk to person's life, health or property. RT I 2001, 61, 364.

Social Composition and Religious Demography

With respect to the prevalent religious traditions in Estonia, according to the last population census 54 % of the adult population (those aged 15 and above, or 1,094,564 from a total population of 1,294,455) declared that they do not adhere to any particular creed.[5] Only 29 % considered themselves to adhere to any creed. Of this figure, about 10 % (13.6 % in 2000) declared themselves to be Lutheran. The largest religious tradition in Estonia currently is the Orthodox Church, with 16 % of the population considering themselves as Orthodox (12.8 % in 2000). Since the census in 2000 the Orthodox community has grown in numbers and has become bigger than the historically dominant Lutheran Church.

There is a small and slowly growing Muslim community. Muslims have lived on the Estonian territory since approximately the eighteenth century. The majority of Estonian Muslims are still ethnic Tatars. Although migration is on a steady increase, there have only been a limited number of new arrivals so far. These arrivals are from different regions globally, and do not form any significant ethnic religious communities. There is also an interesting recent trend among ethnic Estonians and Russians to convert to Islam. For a long time after the collapse of the Soviet Union the Muslim community was mainly engaged with preservation of their ethnic rather than religious identities (as e.g. Tatars, Uzbeks etc.). This dynamic has been changing.

There is a small but active Jewish community in Estonia with a synagogue and one secondary school (gymnasium) with an Orthodox Jewish ethos. Although official statistics do not give a full picture, according to the last population census from 2011 only 355 declared that they adhere to Judaism.[6]

All other Christian and non-Christian religious communities have adherents of approximately 3 % of the adult population.[7] The largest religious communities among those are Roman Catholics, Old Believers, the Baptists, Pentecostals and Jehovah's Witnesses.

Since 2000 there has been growth in the number and diversity of registered religious organisations, but not in the overall religious affiliation of the population. One of the major surveys conducted in 2014 indicates that there is a high degree of individualisation of religion. More than half of the people questioned said they have their individual beliefs, which are not dependant on a specific religion or church (58 %), and little less than a half (48 %) said that although they do not consider themselves believers they have great interest in religions and spiritual practices (New Age).[8]

---

[5] *Population and Housing Census 2011 – 'Usk'*, accessed July 1, 2014, http://pub.stat.ee/px-web.2001/Database/Rahvaloendus/REL2011/07Rahvastiku_demograafilised_ja_etno_kultuurilised_naitajad/09Usk/09Usk.asp.

[6] Ibid.

[7] Ibid.

[8] "Uuring: eestlased usuvad vaimsesse enesearengusse ja maavälisesse ellu", accessed January 29, 2014, http://www.ut.ee/et/uudised/uuring-eestlased-usuvad-vaimsesse-enesearengusse-maavalisesse-ellu.

Historical and Political Processes

The independent Republic of Estonia was born in the aftermath of World War I (1914–1918), when it broke away from the Russian empire.[9] The Proclamation of Independence was followed by the War of Independence in 1918–1920. The date of Estonian independence is 24 February 1918. The first Estonian Constitution (ratified in June 1920) was influenced by the liberal thinking prevalent in Europe after the First World War.[10] The 1920 Constitution emphasized the principle of a state based on the rule of law. One of its essential components was the acknowledgement of the fundamental rights of the person. As a result, it was one of the most democratic constitutions in Europe at that time. The 1920 Constitution set forth the principle of a strict separation of State and Church. It stated that 'there is no State religion'. The Constitution was followed by the 1925 Religious Societies and their Associations Act, which reaffirmed the principle of equal treatment of all religious organizations, and the separation of state and religion.[11] The 1930s saw significant political changes in Estonia, characterized by the centralization of the state administration, the concentration of power, a decline of democracy and the expansion of state control. This period is commonly called 'the era of silence' which lasted from 1934 to 1939. In 1934 the Churches and Religious Societies Act was enacted, not by Parliament but by decree of the State Elder (President). This Act established different legal treatment for churches and for other religious societies, and it set out special provisions for churches. Churches were given additional rights, but also restrictions; the government of all churches was subjected to control by the state. The second Estonian constitution (1938) introduced a number of amendments on fundamental rights. It laid down a new philosophy, according to which the legal rights and duties of an individual emanated from his or her status as a member of a commonwealth. This reflected the more collectivist (communitarian) orientation of the era. According to section 84(1)(b) of the 1938 Constitution, the leaders of the two largest churches (the EELC and the EAOC) gained ex officio membership in the *Riiginõukogu* (Upper House of Parliament).[3]

The outbreak of World War II disturbed the peaceful development of the country, which was subsequently occupied by the Soviet Union (1940–1941, 1944–1991) and Nazi Germany (1941–1944). A resurgence of Estonian national identity began in the late 1980s, preceding the break up of the Soviet Union and Estonian independence in 1991. When the Estonian Constitutional Assembly held heated discussions over each provision and meaning of the draft Constitution of the Republic of Estonia at the beginning of 1990, there was no real discussion about the

---

[9]Estonia became part of Russian Empire in 1710/1721 as a result the Great Northern War defeating Swedish rule on Estonian territory. A more detailed overview of Estonian law and religion in Estonia is presented in Merilin Kiviorg, *Law and Religion in Estonia* (The Netherlands: Kluwer Law International BV, 2011).

[10]RT 1920, 113/114, 243.

[11]RT 1925, 183/184, 96.

provisions relating to freedom of religion or belief and State and Church relationships. In the process of re-building the Estonian Republic immediately after the collapse of the Soviet Union, there were more urgent issues to be dealt with. Although many aspects of the relationship between State and religious communities are still under discussion, the relationship between religious communities and the State is generally amicable and cooperative.

The Constitution of Estonia that came into force in 1992 is, in a number of ways, a compilation of aspects of Estonia's previous constitutions. It has continued the democratic spirit of the 1920 Constitution, with some added mechanisms to maintain the balance of power of the state. In drafting the document, great attention was paid to fundamental rights. International treaties, the European Convention on Human Rights (ECHR) and constitutions of other democratic states were taken as models. Estonia joined the European Union on 1 May 2004.[2] Estonia is also a member of many international organizations, including the United Nations, Council of Europe, Organization for Security and Cooperation in Europe (OSCE), North Atlantic Treaty Organization (NATO) and Organisation for Economic Co-operation and Development (OECD), and has ratified key conventions protecting freedom of religion or belief. The religious freedom clauses in the 1992 Constitution were followed by the 1993 Churches and Congregations Act (*Kirikute ja koguduste seadus*, hereinafter CCA).[12] On 1 July 2002, the 1993 law was entirely replaced by the new Churches and Congregations Act (CCA).[13]

State – Religions Relationship

The Estonian constitution expressly protects freedom of religion for individuals and religious communities. The Estonian Constitution encompasses several important principles determining freedom of religion and the relationship between State and religious communities. These principles are neutrality, equality and self-determination/autonomy. There is no State Church, but cooperation between state and religious communities has been accepted within the limits of law.

The fact that the Estonian Constitution provides that there is no State Church, and the 2002 Churches and Congregations Act addresses all religious communities equally, has not been seen by the State as providing grounds for a rigorous policy of non-identification with religion. As to identifying where Estonia stands in terms of the classification of the Church and State relationship, it probably fits most comfortably into the category of cooperation systems. In cooperation systems the law separates but allows collaboration between state and religion. In Estonia this cooperation tends to be more visible regarding Christian churches. In this regard the reality of Church and State relationships in Estonia may not be so different from the most common European model guaranteeing religious freedom as such at one level, but

[12] RT I 1993, 30, 510.

[13] RT I 2002, 24, 135.

granting certain (additional) advantages and privileges to a limited number of religious groups.

Legislation

The current legal and political framework of religion in Estonia was designed by the Constitution adopted by the referendum of 28 June 1992. This Constitution meets entirely the standards of freedom characteristic of Western democracies, European and international law and was a clear indication of how Estonia wanted to identify itself after years of Soviet occupation. Various national, international and supranational sources of law determine the normative framework for religious freedom. From international/regional human rights instruments the European Convention on Human Rights is the most influential along with the Charter of Fundamental Rights of the European Union. Both instruments are legally binding in Estonia. Individual and collective religious freedom are also protected by Article 40 of the Estonian Constitution and Part II of the 2002 Churches and Congregations Act sets further guarantees for this freedom. Like the international instruments, the Constitution and the CCA protect both the right to have/choose and the right to manifest one's religion or belief both alone and in a community with others, in public or in private, unless this is detrimental to public order, health or morals.[14] The Constitution also provides for conscientious objection. Article 124 (2) of the Constitution stipulates that those who refuse service in the defence forces for religious or ethical reasons are obliged to participate in alternative service. Article 41(2) of the Estonian Constitution specifically stipulates that 'beliefs shall not constitute an excuse for a legal offence'. However, no person can be held legally liable just because of his or her beliefs.

There is no reference to religion in the constitution or laws regarding the principles and values that should inspire the State legal system. The preamble of the Constitution states that the idea behind strengthening and developing the state is to guarantee the preservation of the Estonian nation, language and culture through the ages. The latter is a reflection of the classical German constitutional model, which presupposes the prior existence of a people, united by culture, language and ethnicity (Ringelheim 2008). However, in (legal) scholarly interpretation of the constitution the emphasis is on individual rights (Eesti Vabariigi Põhiseadus: Kommenteeritud väljaanne, from now on EVPKV 2012). The Estonian Constitution is perceived to be a liberal constitution based on natural and inalienable individual rights (Nartis 2009). Moreover, the Estonian Constitution recognizes collective religious freedom (e.g., Articles 40, 9, 19 and 48) and provides protection for cultural/ religious minorities and for their autonomy (Article 50). However, some policy papers adopted by the Government (not law) have made a link between preservation

[14] For a comprehensive overview of law and religion in Estonia see Merilin Kiviorg, *Law and Religion in Estonia*.

of culture in the preamble of the Constitution and preservation of Christian Churches.[15]

Religious laws *per se* are not mentioned among the sources of the State law. Religious laws and principles are not mentioned in connection with specific parts of the State legal system (for example criminal law, family law, etc.). There is no system of personal laws based on religious affiliation. In Estonia State laws do not *expressis verbis* include religious rules applicable to all citizens (of course, this does not exclude the possibility of historic influence of religious traditions on some parts of legislation).

As a rule, religious acts as such do not have a civil legal effect. Furthermore, it is not possible for secular institutions to enforce religious rules. Historically, the possibility of enforcing decisions of religious bodies by secular institutions (Ministry of Internal Affairs and the Court) existed under Articles 24 and 25 of the 1934 Act on Churches and Religious Societies.[16] Today this kind of option is not provided by law.

Despite the previous, there are some areas where religious communities are exempt from generally applicable laws and very limited areas where the State may recognize religious laws (e.g. in the case of application of private international law/conflicts of laws). There is also freedom of contract that parties can use to determine some of their civil relationships. Furthermore, religious communities themselves and their affiliated organisations (such as schools) have autonomy to regulate their own affairs and their membership.

Exemptions from Generally Applicable Laws

Currently, most exemptions from generally applicable laws concern anti-discrimination legislation in employment situations. There is also some room for accepting religious laws where a legal relationship falls under private international law. Religious organisations are allowed certain exemptions from the Equal Treatment Act (*Võrdse kohtlemise seadus*).[17] In the case of occupational activities within religious associations and other public or private organizations, the ethos of which is based on religion or belief, a difference in treatment based on a person's religion or belief shall not constitute discrimination where, by reason of the nature of these activities or of the context in which they are carried out, a person's religion

[15] On 11 March 2003 the Estonian government approved a programme/policy paper "*Pühakodade säilitamine ja areng*" (Preservation and Development of Sacred Buildings). Although not a law, the paper provides a basis for several legislative and financial actions to support development of churches over the period from 2004 to 2013 (the programme has been renewed and revised for 2013–2018). "Programm 'Pühakodade säilitamine ja areng' 2013–2018", kinnitatud kultuuriministri käskirjaga nr. 371, 28.11.2013 (Tallinn: Kultuuriministeerium, 2013).

[16] RT 1934, 107, 840.

[17] RT I 2008, 56, 315.

or belief constitutes a genuine, legitimate and justified occupational requirement because it is directly related to the organization's ethos (Equal Treatment Act, §10(2)). The law also does not prejudice the right of these organizations to require individuals working for them to act in good faith and with loyalty to the organization's ethos (§10(3)).[18] These exceptions are based on the EU anti-discrimination directives.[19] The explanatory note to the Equal Treatment Act also refers to Declaration No. 11 on the status of churches and non-confessional organisations, which was added to the Amsterdam Treaty. It needs to be noted that international and transnational developments in anti-discrimination law have become increasingly challenging for religious communities. However, the effects of the interplay between anti-discrimination legislation and collective freedom of religion or belief in Estonia remain to be seen. Currently there is no case law in relation to this matter. Although there have been no court cases yet in relation to employment disputes there was an incident involving application of the Equal Treatment Act within religious communities. In 2010 the Estonian Evangelical Lutheran Church decided to exclude from the ranks of its priesthood a minister who had openly expressed his views in support of gays and had become a board member of the Association for Gay Christians.[20] The incident fuelled some internal discussions in the church, but also attracted public attention. The minister turned to the Gender Equality and Equal Treatment Commissioner to investigate the matter. The post of Gender Equality and Equal Treatment Commissioner had been established to monitor compliance with the requirements of the Gender Equality Act and the Equal Treatment Act. Some church members were furious about the enquiries and demanded the resignation of the Commissioner for violating church autonomy. In its official response the consistory of the EELC explained that the minister's sexual orientation as such was not the ground for the dismissal but the fact that he broke his oath by not following and obeying internal regulations of the church (including its 2009 declaration on homosexuality).[21] No further legal action was taken by the church or the Commissioner. As to further exemptions, the Gender Equality Act (*Soolise võrdõiguslikkuse seadus*) does not apply to the professing and practising of faith or working as a minister of a religion in a registered religious association (§2(2)).[22] However, commentaries to the Gender Equality Act (commissioned by the Ministry of Social Affairs) state that it would be reasonable, in the future, to extend the application of the law to religious organisations (Albi et al. 2010). The future development of this controversial idea still needs to be seen.

As to family law, there are currently no exemptions that explicitly recognize religious family law in Estonia. Changes in family status (such as marriage, divorce,

[18] Ibid.

[19] Council Directive (EC) 2000/78 on Employment Equality [2000] OJ L 195/16; Council Directive (EC) 2000/43/on Racial Equality [2000] OJ L 180/22.

[20] "EELK praost nõuab võrdõiguslikkuse voliniku ametist lahkumist", *Delfi*, 07 November 2011.

[21] "EELK selgitas soovolinikule, miks tagandati üks vaimulik ametist", *Meie Kirik*, 11 October 2011.

[22] RT I 2004, 27, 181.

heritage, subsistence, etc.) need to be conducted according to the civil law to be legally recognized. In accordance with the law a clergyman who has received authorization from the Minister of Regional Affairs is entitled to perform civil marriages. Thus, the state has not recognized the concept of religious marriage *per se* but, rather, has established the possibility of delegating the obligations of the register office to a clergyman of a church, congregation, or association of congregations.[23] It needs to be mentioned that if held separately, the religious marriage as such can be conducted before the civil registration. But only civil registration has a legal effect.

However, application of religious family law as such is not prohibited either. It seems that, in principle, application of some religious family law is possible if it is not against law and does not exceed limits of freedom of contract. There is no official information available as to what extent parties *de facto* resort to religious family law. There have also been no known cases of conflict of interests/rights in applying religious family law. It can be pointed out that the Estonian version of a Muslim journal Iqra has made readers aware of the opportunities to solve family issues without interference of the state authorities. Further details will be provided below when discussing social implementation of religious rules. Estonian law also allows some exceptions in a specific case where a legal relationship falls under private international law. The Private International Law Act (*Rahvusvahelise eraõiguse seadus*)[24] regulates legal relationships which are connected with the law of more than one state. For example, a marriage contracted in a foreign state is deemed to be valid in Estonia if it is contracted pursuant to the procedure for contraction of marriage provided by the law of the state where the marriage is contracted, and the material prerequisites (such as age, consent, etc.) of the marriage are in compliance with the laws of the states of residence of both spouses (§55 of the Private International Law Act). A previous marriage of a spouse does not hinder the contraction of a new marriage in Estonia if the previous marriage has been terminated on the basis of a decision made or recognized in Estonia, even if such a decision is not in accordance with the law of the state of residence of the prospective spouse (§56(3) of the Private International Law Act). Although religious family law may be recognized in Estonia (in cases where religious family law is recognized by the relevant State), there is one general restriction. The Private International Law Act sets forth that a foreign law should not be applied if the result of such application would be in obvious conflict with the essential principles of Estonian law (public order). In such cases Estonian law applies (§7). For example, this would most certainly be true in cases involving child or forced marriage or polygamy. Where gender equality is at issue, it is possible that courts may consider Estonian law to take precedence, for example when ruling on subsistence, custody or inheritance. However, at the moment this is only speculative as there is no case law to rely on.

---

[23] On 7 November 2013 there were 135 persons with the right to conduct religious marriages with civil validity. The information is obtained from the Ministry of Internal Affairs, accessed March 31, 2015, http://www.siseministeerium.ee.

[24] RT I 2002, 35, 217.

Accommodation of Religious Needs

The State law does require some accommodation of religious needs of the individual. One can argue that this requirement comes from the constitutional principle of equality and non-discrimination. The principle of equality is explicitly set forth in the first sentence of the first paragraph of Article 12 of the Constitution, which states that all persons shall be equal before the law. The second paragraph of Article 12 of the Constitution sets forth the principle of non-discrimination, prohibiting discrimination *inter alia* on the basis of religion or belief. Application of these principles is not difference blind. The concept of substantive equality has been endorsed by the Estonian Supreme Court (EVPKV 2012). Additionally, the understanding of direct and indirect discrimination in Estonia has been influenced by and has evolved alongside its development in European Union law and in the case law of the ECHR.[25] The exact application of the equality principle in relation to religion has not been tested in Estonian court.

Further requirements are set forth in the already mentioned Equal Treatment Act. The Act, for example, prohibits discrimination against persons on the grounds of religion or other beliefs, age, disability or sexual orientation in relation to conditions for access to employment, to self-employment or to occupation, including selection criteria and recruitment conditions, whatever the branch of activity and at all levels of the professional hierarchy, including promotion. The Act also applies to membership of, and involvement in, an organization of employees or employers, or any organization whose members exercise a particular profession, including the benefits provided for by such organizations, social protection, including social security and healthcare, and social advantages (§1). In addition to above, Article 3 of the Employment Contract Act (*Töölepingu seadus*) requires an employer to ensure the protection of employees against discrimination, follow the principle of equal treatment and promote equality in accordance with the Equal Treatment Act and Gender Equality Act.[26] Thus there are positive obligations to provide equality. Estonia has not confronted any similar cases to those seen in the European Court of Human Rights, for example *Eweida and others versus United Kingdom.*[27] There has been some public debate over wearing religious symbols, especially over the meaning and impact of different attires worn by Muslim women in many parts of the world. Currently, the wearing of religious symbols is not prohibited in Estonia. Religious symbols, like crosses or headscarves, have been worn by public figures or even civil servants, for example at talk shows in television. As previously discussed, Estonia is not a country of extensive immigration, thus the symbols (if warn at all) tend to belong to those of a predominantly Christian background. Some pagan symbols, Jewish yarmulkes and Muslim headscarves occasionally figure in public space as

[25] *Thlimmenos v. Greece* (App no 34369/97) (2001) 31 EHRR 411; DH and Others v the Czech Republic (App no 57325/00) (2008) 47 EHRR 16.

[26] RT I 2009, 5, 35.

[27] *Ewaida and others v. UK* (App. no. 48420/10; 59842/10; 51671/10; 36516/10).

well. Cultural diversities regarding religious symbols have not produced any major conflicts yet. However, there was a non-publicised incident at one of the schools in Tallinn involving a girl who was dismissed from her class by her teacher because she was wearing a hijab. Some statistics paint a rather worrying picture of Estonia not being a very tolerant country in regards to minorities. For example, the 2011 OECD survey indicated that Estonia is one of the least tolerant regarding minorities (OECD 2011). Hopefully, it is not indicative of how the society, legislature and courts will react to possible future conflicts of interests/rights. As to further accommodation of religious needs, according to the Identity Documents Act (*Isikut tõendavate dokumentide seadus*)[28] a person has the right, on religious grounds, to submit a photo with a head covering for identification documents. This specific provision was added to the law in 2009.[29] However, the face from mandible to upper forehead should be uncovered. This applies both to Muslim women and Christian nuns, as well as to the followers of other traditions for whom the head covering is mandatory.

The Churches and Congregations Act specifies the rights of an individual in medical institutions, educational institutions, social welfare institutions, custodial institutions and military units. Persons staying in named institutions have the right to perform religious rites according to their faith unless this violates public order, health, morals, the rules established in these institutions or the rights of others staying or serving in these institutions. The Churches and Congregations Act also sets forth that every person has the right to be buried according to his or her confession (§8(6)). In the absence of relatives, guardians or curators, and if it is known that a deceased person was a member of a congregation, the congregation of the deceased person is required to take care of the confessional funeral service (§8(7)).

Adjudication

The State itself does not provide any formal religious adjudication and does not give religious courts/institutions the power to interpret the laws of the State or to assess their conformity to religious rules. However, the State has recognized religious adjudication within the autonomy of religious organizations. For example, the state has recognized the existence and activities of the ecclesiastical court of the Estonian Evangelical Lutheran Church. The church's state registered by-laws include provisions relating to the institution of the Church Court (*kirikukohus*, Ecclesiastical Court). According to the by-laws the Church Court is entitled to review internal decisions of the church including, for example, disciplinary matters. The court consists of three members. At least one has to have a higher theological and another a higher juridical education. The members of the court are elected for 4 years. Article 9 of the by-laws of the Estonian Apostolic Orthodox Church sets forth a detailed

[28] RT I 1999, 25, 365.

[29] RT I 2009, 27, 166.

description of the institution of their Church Court. According to the statutes it has jurisdiction over internal disputes that fall under church law. There are lower courts (*alam-kirikukohtud*) and a higher (appeal) court (*ülem-kirikukohus*). The court may invite experts with juridical qualifications to consult the court. The *alam-kirikukohus* consists of three members (bishop and two *ad hoc* members appointed by the bishop, one of which has to be a priest). The Bishops Council (*piiskoppide kogu*) carries out the tasks of the *ülem-kirikukohus*. The state registered statutes of the Jewish Congregations do not include any provisions on adjudication or dispute settlement. There are provisions on review of complaints about the activities of the board of the congregation. The by-laws of the Muslim Congregation, on the other hand, set forth that disputes between members are solved in the court of honour (*aukohus*). The board of the congregation nominates two representatives for each party and a mediator (*vahemees*). Disputes must be resolved within 30 days. The decision is reviewed and approved by the board of the congregation. The statutes specify that the decision is final and must be executed. Interestingly it emphasises that the congregation solves disputes. This means that disputes are deemed to be solely an internal matter and should not be publicised. The statutes specifically point out that unnecessary disclosure of the disputes may result in temporary or permanent exclusion from the membership of the congregation. As there have been no cases in Estonian civil courts regarding the scope of autonomy of religious communities it is hard to predict what would be the scope of religious autonomy in specific cases when an individual, for example, disputes the decision made by the religious organisation or Church Court in a civil court. The individual would not be barred from taking his or her case to a civil court if the case has significance in terms of the State law. Everyone whose rights and freedoms have been violated has the constitutional right of recourse to the courts.[30] However, the civil court will not enter into a purely religious dispute. In that regard some matters may be unjudiciable. The European Convention on Human Rights became legally binding for Estonia on 16 April 1996. The ECHR is part of the Estonian legal system and is directly applicable.[31] Although the jurisprudence of the European Court of Human Rights (hereinafter ECtHR) regarding conflicts between individual rights and collective autonomy has not been consistent itself, it is likely to be used if cases come before Estonian courts. There is an increasing amount of case law in the ECtHR, which essentially concerns conflicts between individual rights and autonomy of religious communities especially in employment matters. How this type of case law evolves and interacts with Estonian domestic solutions is a matter for future study and analysis.

[30] Article 15 of the Estonian Constitution.

[31] Estonia became a member of the Council of Europe on 14 May 1993. The same day Estonia signed the European Convention for Fundamental Rights and Freedoms (ECHR). The Estonian Parliament ratified the ECHR on 13 March 1996.[2] The letters of ratification were deposited on 16 April 1996. The Convention became legally binding for Estonia from that date.

Social Implementation of Religious Rules (Without any Official Recognition)

There is no information available as to what extent parties *de facto* resort to religious law and adjudication. According to the Department of Religious Affairs of the Ministry of Interior there is no data collected or available in this regard. Only on a very few occasions have cases brought before, for example, church courts or institutions captured media or public attention. One of these cases concerned an accusation of infidelity of a minister of an Evangelical Lutheran Church. There was only one incident that brought out tensions between civil and religious jurisdictions in employment matters. The incident concerned dismissal of a minister due to his sexual orientation. This incident was discussed earlier in this contribution.

There is no exact data available as to what extent parties use freedom of contract to solve their issues according to religious law, for example, in family matters. As mentioned earlier, the Estonian version of Iqra, a Muslim journal, made readers aware of the opportunities to solve family issues without the interference of state authorities. Additionally, in 2012 twelve marriage contracts (*nikah*) were signed under the supervision of an imam. Inheritance can be apportioned according to Islamic regulations provided it is accepted by all parties involved (Ringvee 2013). In the case of legal disputes, civil law applies in Estonia. In addition, laws applicable to all may set certain limits to use of religious law, for example, if they contradict some fundamental constitutional principles or go against public order, health or morals.

Conclusion

Both individual and collective religious freedom is protected in Estonia. The relationships between religious communities and the communities and the State have not produced significant conflicts. As noted above, alternative religious adjudication or issues related to the emergence of parallel jurisdictions has not really been discussed in Estonia. Occasionally media reflects on examples in other countries without any analytical connection to the Estonian situation. Furthermore, religious communities themselves have not voiced any specific problems (apart from one exception that was mentioned above). There is no case law in civil courts to provide material for criticism or praise of the State's approach. The above seems to be an indication that the law generally respects the autonomy of religious communities to decide over internal matters (e.g. employment or appointment in accordance with the religious ethos of the community). There also seems to be room for accommodating alternative dispute settlements when all parties agree and there is some room for contractual freedom. On the other hand, the public silence on this matter may also be a reflection of the religious composition of the State, low institutional membership of religious organisations and a high level of individualisation of beliefs.

At the outset Estonian laws are flexible enough to take into account religious needs, both individual and collective. However, there have been no court cases to bring out challenges, for example, regarding the interpretation of anti-discrimination principles and possible need for accommodation of religious differences. The future of state and religious communities' relationship continues to evolve. Changes in the societal attitudes, law and policy regarding religion may occur if Estonia faced changes in the religious composition of the population, for example, due to migration. Currently there exists the need to conceptualise and learn from other countries' experiences to prevent and tackle potential future problems.

References

Albi, K., et al. 2010. *Soolise võrdõiguslikkuse seadus, Kommenteeritud väljaanne*. Tallinn: Juura.

Eesti Vabariigi Põhiseadus. 2012. *Kommenteeritud väljaanne*. Tallinn: Juura.

Kiviorg, M. 2011. *Law and religion in Estonia*. Netherlands: Kluwer Law International.

Narits, Raul. 2009. About the principles of the constitution of the Republic of Estonia from the perspective of independent statehood in Estonia. *Juridica International* XVI: 56–64.

OECD. 2011. Tolerance. In *Society at a glance 2011: OECD social indicators*, OECD Publishing. http://dx.doi.org/10.1787/soc_glance-2011-30-en. Accessed 1 June 2015.

Reingelheim, J. 2008. Minority protection and constitutional recognition of difference. In *The framework convention for the protection of national minorities: A useful Pan-European instrument*, ed. Annalies Verstichel Bruno De Witte, Paul Lemmens, and André Alen, 33–49. Antwerp: Intersentia.

Ringvee, R. 2013. Estonia. In *Yearbook of Muslims in Europe*, vol. 5, ed. J.S. Nielsen et al., 229–236. Leiden: Brill.

Chapter 10
La France Face à Ses Religions

Jacques Robert

Abstract The author focuses on France's legal framework and ecclesiastical policy towards the religions existing and operating in the national territory. The constitutional principle of secularism (laïcité) and the separation between State and religious denominations, which characterize the French legal system, are examined in a two-fold perspective: firstly, which past issues have helped to settle and how; secondly, the way they are currently contributing and may contribute in the future to manage the country's religious diversity.

Après s'être – au long d'une existence heurtée, tragique et glorieuse – efforcée de pratiquer toutes les formes possibles de relations entre les Églises et l'État, la France envisagea (en désespoir de cause ?) de s'arrêter au début du XXe siècle à une combinaison toute simple : *la séparation* entre le pouvoir politique et l'institution ecclésiale. Chacun, de son côté, emplirait un espace distinct. L'État serait seul souverain en son domaine : le public. La religion, de son côté, se contenterait du gouvernement des âmes (la conscience individuelle et la vie privée).

Il fallut cependant attendre le début du XXème siècle pour qu'une telle idée s'imposât. Non sans mal. On pensait alors – avec raison – qu'en supprimant (en théorie !) toute occasion obligée de contact entre l'Église et l'État, on conjurerait la survenance de conflits qui avaient dans le passé fait tant de mal à la France.

Mais deux problèmes se poseraient dès l'origine de cette novation fondamentale : la liquidation du passé; la construction de l'avenir.

Liquider le passé, c'était modifier la nature des Églises. Elles cessaient d'être des services publics, et même d'assurer la moindre mission de service public. Elles ne pouvaient plus qu'être considérées comme des groupements privés. Précisément avait été votée quelques années à peine auparavant une grande loi républicaine sur les associations. Allait-on les intégrer dans ces dernières ? Mais une association « cultuelle » (à créer de toutes pièces) pouvait-elle se mouler dans le cadre général de toutes les associations, quels qu'en soient la forme, l'objet, la destination ?

J. Robert (✉)
Panthéon Assas University, Paris, France
e-mail: voinnesson@legiscompare.com

R. Bottoni et al. (eds.), *Religious Rules, State Law, and Normative Pluralism - A Comparative Overview*, Ius Comparatum – Global Studies in Comparative Law 18, DOI 10.1007/978-3-319-28335-7_10

Signalons ici, seulement, que l'on se décida à mettre sur pied une telle association « cultuelle » dont la structure allait être très voisine de la structure des autres, simplement adaptée au monde religieux dont il était difficile, dès cette époque, de prétendre qu'il n'était pas différent de l'« autre ».

Mais le régime des biens allait susciter de tout autres problèmes. À qui appartiendraient les Églises une fois supprimés les services publics qui leur servaient de supports juridiques ? On décida que les cathédrales seraient propriété de l'État, les autres églises étant attribuées aux collectivités locales.

Que serait alors la nouvelle configuration géo-politico-religieuse de la France ?

Pour exprimer et définir le nouvel agencement des relations juridiques des Églises et de l'État, on découvrit le mot *laïcité*. On pensait qu'il résoudrait le problème en séparant les deux mondes, en supprimant tout lien institutionnel entre eux, en les laissant se gérer l'un l'autre en toute autonomie.

La loi en France ne pouvait être que française, applicable à tous ceux résidant sur notre territoire. De la même manière qu'elle ne s'appliquait qu'à l'intérieur de son pays, la loi étrangère de son côté ne pouvait – sauf accord international ne s'appliquer que sur le sien.

Dans un pays comme la France où vit une écrasante majorité de catholiques romains et où l'Islam se trouve, aujourd'hui, être la seconde religion du pays, il est bien évident qu'affirmer juridiquement et solennellement la séparation des cultes et de l'État par une loi française ne suffit point à bannir toutes les occasions de frictions nées d'une cohabitation qui n'est point toujours douce….

La situation peut s'avérer d'autant délicate que le Vatican représente à la fois une Église et un État et que des relations diplomatiques existent, depuis des lustres, entre la Papauté et l'État français.

La France fille ainée de l'Église ? Comment imaginer un système de relations inexistantes juridiquement entre la mère et la fille alors qu'elles résident l'une et l'autre dans des pays voisins et que l'esprit de l'une inspire l'esprit de l'autre ?

Les dramatiques vicissitudes qu'ont traversées dans l'Histoire les relations entre la France et la Papauté démontrent à l'envi qu'une concurrence a toujours existé entre le pouvoir spirituel et le pouvoir temporel et qu'il n'est sans doute pas facile de mettre sur pied une formule harmonieuse de coexistence quotidienne.

La notion de laïcité a-t-elle utilement servi à l'éclaircissement d'un tel paysage où se sont pendant des siècles toisées l'autorité pontificale et la prétention impériale ?

Elle a fait tout de même admettre par les deux parties en cause un certain nombre de principes qui n'allaient pas de soi et posé les conditions d'une séparation qui aurait pu être vécue comme un schisme contre-nature.

La loi de séparation de 1905 a explicité, le mieux qu'elle a pu, les grandes lignes de cet équilibre entre les deux protagonistes que ne facilitait point le double visage du Vatican, à la fois autorité religieuse universelle et État temporel souverain.

Comme tout État souverain, le Vatican entretenait des relations diplomatiques avec les Nations qu'il souhaitait proches de lui, comme le faisait n'importe quel État dans le monde.

N'en demeurait pas moins que les dignitaires de l'Église catholique universelle qui occupaient en France des postes non négligeables étaient désignés par Rome même si – dans la réalité – leur nomination se faisait en étroit accord entre Rome et Paris. Mais le Nonce, qui était en France le représentant du Vatican (possédant en général la position enviée de Doyen du Corps diplomatique) traitait à la fois des problèmes politiques généraux d'État à État et des questions « religieuses » entre la Curie romaine et les dignitaires ecclésiastiques en poste en France.

Sur le plan institutionnel on coupait donc toute relation entre l'Église de Rome et la France mais, au point de vue historique, on ne pouvait occulter des siècles d'alliance fidèle du Trône et de l'Autel.

Séparation complète et définitive ? Allons donc ! On se quittait officiellement pour l'avenir en vivant désormais chacun sa propre vie; mais on se gardait bien d'oublier des siècles de cohabitation douce, voire affectueuse.

En plus, les questions d'intérêt matériel imposaient des réponses nécessaires acceptées par les deux parties.

*

Le statut des hommes de Dieu devait être en premier révisé pour l'avenir.

Jusqu'à la séparation, l'Église était un service public et donc les ministres du culte étaient des agents de l'État, rétribués par lui. C'était pour les Églises un considérable privilège. Du jour au lendemain, les voilà tenus de subvenir aux besoins de leurs prêtres (sauf en Alsace-Lorraine).

Il en allait de même pour les édifices du culte. Là, on opéra un délicat partage. On distingua, on l'a noté plus haut, les cathédrales des autres églises. Les premières restaient propriété de l'État. Les autres tombaient dans le patrimoine des collectivités locales.

Le budget de l'État ne pouvait évidemment plus contenir la moindre disposition concernant une aide quelconque aux Églises. Mais en France, le ministre de l'Intérieur restait encore celui des cultes… À quel titre et pourquoi faire ?

Les textes étaient clairs et durs. La pratique – elle – s'adaptait à des évènements changeants mais tous étaient conscients du fait qu'il fallait que, même séparés, les anciens « époux » acceptâssent de se voir encore, de se parler, de se comprendre, voire même – et pourquoi pas ? – de s'aimeraprès s'être aidés?....

Mais en cas de litige ?

Disons d'abord qu'en France l'idée que la justice est rendue au nom du peuple français implique qu'elle le soit sur la base des lois qui sont votées par lui. Pourrait-on donc, sans soulever une légitime polémique, admettre qu'en France, un citoyen pût être jugé sur la base d'un texte étranger qui s'appliquerait d'office à lui ?

On peut, certes, toujours passer contrat avec un État étranger; et le Vatican en est un. Mais il ne s'agit point d'une loi étrangère s'appliquant directement sur le territoire d'un État étranger.

En France, les prêtres catholiques sont en général, des citoyens français et, à ce titre, ils relèvent de la loi française. Ils ne sauraient relever d'un autre droit commun qui s'appliquerait spécifiquement à eux et uniquement à eux : au pénal comme au civil.

Le ministre du culte catholique qui, en France, commet un délit ou un crime relève des juridictions pénales françaises. Sur le plan disciplinaire, il relève en revanche de l'institution ecclésiale. Et là réside la subtilité du système. Souvent la « suspension » par l'Église du prêtre indigne règle définitivement le problème. Le prêtre coupable frappé disciplinairement par l'Église et suspendu par elle, disparait. Le plus souvent, la justice de l'État de résidence n'intervient pas. Car elle est rarement saisie par l'institution ecclésiale et répugne à se saisir elle-même.

À la Libération de la France, l'épuration ne s'appliqua guère au personnel ecclésiastique. Le gouvernement français fit simplement savoir qu'il estimait que tel dignitaire haut placé n'avait point eu, pendant l'occupation, l'attitude qui convenait et que son remplacement ne susciterait aucune protestation officielle française. La diplomatie régla directement les cas litigieux.

En fait une double sanction s'appliqua. L'une, la première dans le temps, « disciplinaire » ou mieux « administrative » quoiqu'aussi politique, prise par l'institution ecclésiale. La seconde – implicite – corollaire de la première – par le pays de résidence qui ne s'opposa pas au rappel du prélat concerné.

Dans la réalité, dès l'instant qu'il n'existe pas de juridictions ecclésiales en France et que les tribunaux français ont toujours eu quelque réticence à s'immiscer dans un domaine qui n'était point le leur, les affaires « religieuses » susceptibles d'être traitées par les juges du territoire concerné étaient peu fréquentes… ou secondaires !

Il est bien évident cependant que quand deux paroisses se disputaient la jouissance du même lieu de culte et que cette opposition – souvent brutale – qui se manifestait chaque dimanche sur le parvis du lieu convoité risquait de susciter de graves troubles à l'ordre public, l'autorité publique de l'État concerné ne pouvait point ne pas intervenir. Mais la justice elle n'était point saisie. Si elle l'était d'aventure, et qu'une question de droit canonique se posât à elle, les juges, par le biais de la procédure de la question préjudicielle, demandaient son avis au Vatican.

Alors seulement, il y a tout lieu de penser que la juridiction française saisie au départ se rangerait à l'avis du Vatican et statuerait conformément à ses vues officiellement exprimées. Mais s'agirait-t-il de l'application *ipso facto* en France d'une loi vaticane ? En aucune façon. L'avis demandé n'était que consultatif. Mais le juge français, en possession d'un avis officiel, serait couvert par cet avis et donc ravi de l'avoir reçu et d'en suivre la solution proposée.

Pourrait-on aujourd'hui écrire comme le fit un éminent juriste français une longue et passionnante étude sur « *Le Conseil d'État et la vie paroissiale* » ? On peut en douter. En tous cas, elle n'a jamais été actualisée.

Reste que ce n'est point toujours par l'application immédiate et automatique d'une loi étrangère sur un territoire donné que la puissance d'un législateur peut s'imposer à un autre.

S'agissant d'un État qui est aussi le siège d'une puissance religieuse universelle, les textes religieux qui émanent du Souverain Pontife (qui ne sont pas seulement des « lois nationales » mais des « encycliques universelles ») n'ont-ils pas – sinon une force juridique dans le monde – du moins un impact moral international ? Dans une nation majoritairement catholique, comme la France, peut-on admettre que les normes posées par le Pape n'aient qu'une valeur morale, affective ? Le législateur français peut-il ne tenir aucun compte de ces règles quand un Pape – comme Jean-Paul II – peut se permettre d'écrire que le chrétien ne devrait point obéir à une règle contraire à la morale chrétienne ? Ainsi cette morale ne s'appliquerait-elle pas *ipso facto* dans tous les grands pays catholiques ?

N'a-t-on pas vu en France, ces dernières années, des projets de loi retirés de l'ordre du jour des Assemblées sous la pression de manifestants intégristes qui s'opposaient, par des cortèges impressionnants, au vote de textes qui n'avaient pas l'aval des autorités religieuses ?

Alors la « loi » vaticane en opposition avec la législation française ?

On ne saurait répondre sans nuances à une telle interrogation.

Dans une atmosphère où se côtoient journellement les hommes de Dieu et les gouvernants mais où la République s'affirme laïque et se veut séparée de l'Église, chacun se doit d'agir avec prudence, tact et intelligence.

Certes, aucun mouvement religieux – quel qu'il soit – ne saurait être au-dessus des lois et la France laïque s'estime parfaitement compétente pour légiférer, comme elle le désire, sur des questions religieuses qui ont un retentissement sur sa vie sociale et son opinion publique. Aussi légiférera-t-elle par exemple sur le voile islamique ou la burka mais elle le fera en toute liberté sans se croire tenue par aucune norme ecclésiale. Qu'elle tienne compte des opinions de ses citoyens catholiques qui s'efforcent d'obéir aux incitations du Vatican, quoi de plus naturel ! Mais aucune norme vaticane ne vient entraver la totale liberté du gouvernement. Ce dernier peut toujours s'en inspirer mais à aucun égard il en est tenu.

Quand de difficiles questions internes se posent à l'Église catholique dans un pays donné, la France notamment, celui-ci – surtout quand il est juridiquement séparé de l'Église – se garde bien d'entrer dans la querelle.

L'État français n'avait pas à entrer dans la délicate question du schisme créé par la rébellion de Monseigneur Lefebvre et des évêques institués par lui. Il ne le fit d'ailleurs pas. Ce fut au Vatican de négocier – lui et lui seul – avec les schismatiques. L'État français fut, certes, attentif à la question mais ne s'estima pas compétent pour la trancher.

De la même façon, quand le Vatican crut devoir prendre ses distances avec Monseigneur Gaillot dont les initiatives et les prises de position ne lui semblaient guère acceptables, le gouvernement français ne fit aucune opposition à sa désignation dans un diocèse inconnu ou fictif qui ne le regardait point.

Ce n'est point d'aujourd'hui – on l'a vu plus haut – que date seulement cette éventuelle « concurrence » entre l'ordre spirituel et la vie séculière.

Mais les conflits ouverts et féroces de naguère n'ont plus, à notre époque, droit de cité.

Le pape n'est-il pas – de nos jours – un pêcheur d'hommes, plus qu'un homme d'État? Et les dirigeants des grands États du monde ont d'autres problèmes à résoudre que ceux d'un combat avec l'ange !...

Alors halte au feu !

*

Il semble malheureusement que cet appel à la paix n'ait point aujourd'hui reçu le moindre début d'exécution si l'on en juge par les drames qui, depuis quelques semaines, ensanglantent de nombreux pays. Mais il ne s'agit plus aujourd'hui seulement d'un conflit entre les Églises et l'État mais d'une lutte, souvent barbare, entre les religions elles-mêmes ou du moins entre les extrémistes de certaines d'entre elles.

On semble, en effet, ne s'être sortis des querelles d'école que pour se lancer dans une lutte ouverte et sans nuances entre les tenants des principaux courants de pensée qui traversent le monde. *Guerres saintes ?* Certains iront jusqu'à utiliser ces termes. Pas tous, bien heureusement. Mais il suffit qu'une des parties en conflit n'hésite point à s'en servir pour que le combat devienne féroce et pousse à d'injustes et néfastes amalgames.

Les religions se dressent les unes contre les autres, se lançant de dangereux anathèmes alors que, fondamentalement, elles se proposent toutes officiellement de rapprocher les hommes et de les faire s'aimer.

Chacune va jusqu'à reprocher à l'autre l'ambiguïté de ses discours, l'hypocrisie de sa terminologie, les sous-entendus terrifiants de ses déclarations. On juge chaque communauté à l'aune de ses proclamations les plus fanatiques, voulant oublier que, de chaque côté, les majorités ne partagent point toujours les outrances de leurs dirigeants. Les discours s'aigrissent; les vieilles rancœurs réapparaissent. Au profit de qui ? Sûrement pas des masses qui subissent les dommages de ces affrontements fratricides alors qu'elles sont avides de toutes les nourritures du monde (terrestres et spirituelles).

Chacun se sent mal dans son être... et sur le territoire du pays dans lequel il vit.

Les juifs se sentent mal à l'aise en France et songent de plus en plus à retourner dans cet Israël qui les fascine mais où ils seront sans doute moins heureux et tranquilles – quoiqu'ils disent ! – que dans cette France qui ne les comprend point comme ils le souhaiteraient... D'ailleurs, comment, objectivement, les Juifs souffriraient-ils d'une discrimination quand leurs représentants les plus doués peuplent les coulisses du pouvoir ou les salles de réunion des grandes entreprises ou les plateaux les plus connus de la télévision ? Sans doute, leur sentiment profond n'est-il point celui d'être discriminés, mais d'être l'objet d'un désamour implicite qui les ronge parce qu'il les humilie et les déçoit. Ce peuple « fier de lui et dominateur » comme le disait de Gaulle, se considèrerait-il aujourd'hui comme la vraie victime du destin après avoir eu l'honneur – pendant des siècles – d'être l'élu de Dieu ?

Et pourtant combien de bons esprits juifs parfaitement ancrés dans notre culture et notre civilisation sans pour autant renier les leurs, m'ont-ils confié qu'ils ressentaient encore chez nous ce sentiment de réserve à leur égard de leurs compatriotes français ? Hostilité ? Non pas. Mais une certaine réticence. Comme celle que l'on éprouve à l'égard de ceux qui ne sont pas « du même monde », qui viennent d'autres horizons, qui adorent sans doute le même Dieu mais au travers de rites dissemblables !

Si les juifs de France en sont là, comment les Arabes, de leur côté, ne seraient-ils pas touchés par cette même désaffection cruelle à leur égard ?

Ne soyons pas pour autant angéliques. Nous ne parviendrons jamais à effacer les différences doctrinales ou organisationnelles entre les confessions mais l'objectif n'est-il pas seulement de les faire vivre en paix et d'œuvrer pour qu'elles cohabitent sans heurts ?

On ajoutera que l'interprétation des textes sacrés permet toutes les audaces. On trouvera dans les évangiles et les bibles diverses le « pour et le « contre », le bien et le mal, la tolérance et le pardon comme la guerre sainte et la « loi du talion ». L'amour des autres mais la haine de l'infidèle, l'hospitalité généralisée et l'aumône institutionnelle comme le rejet du mécréant ou simplement – on l'a vu récemment – le dessinateur irrespectueux ou le caricaturiste provocateur.

La liberté nécessaire est difficile à faire vivre. Mais elle en vaut la peine. Comme la solidarité, n'est-elle pas prêchée par la quasi-totalité des religions ? Si cet indispensable combat pour elle est prescrit par les croyants, quelle que soit leur croyance, pourquoi ne s'uniraient-ils pas pour la sauver des périls, puis la faire triompher ?

Parler d'un « apartheid » en France est non seulement absurde mais injuste. Ceux qui en parlent sans doute imprudemment n'ont jamais vécu dans un pays qui le pratiquait. Et ils ne savent pas ce que c'est !

Chapter 11
The Interplay Between State Law and Religious Law in Germany

Ino Augsberg and Stefan Korioth

Abstract Traditionally, German debates on "law and religion" deal with the topic in two ways. On the one side, it is considered a fundamental rights issue. "Law and religion", in this perspective, is all about freedom of religion, and this freedom is conceived of primarily as an individual right. On the other side, the topic is viewed on an institutional level. Thus, it is basically about the church-state-relationship (or, to be more precise and less traditionally but more generally speaking: about the relationship between the state and religious communities). However, a closer look at the constitutional arrangements shows that the provisions of the German *Grundgesetz* need not be limited to this classical twofold perspective. By contrast, it might be worthwhile to analyse the constitutional mechanisms, in particular the fundamental rights, in a different, functionalist perspective, describing them as a tool that enables legal pluralism. This is what we intend to do.

Introduction

Traditionally, German debates on "law and religion" deal with the topic in two ways: On the one side, it is considered a fundamental rights issue. "Law and religion", in this perspective, is all about freedom of religion, and this freedom is conceived of primarily as an individual right. On the other side, the topic is viewed on an institutional level. Thus, it is basically about the church-state-relationship (or, to be more precise and less traditionally but more generally speaking: about the relationship between the state and religious communities).[1] However, a closer look at

[1] On this account, the German debate incorporates both the individual and the community oriented approach that Silvio Ferrari (2015) has identified as a distinctive feature in the national reports on "Applicable Religious Rules according to the Law of the State".

I. Augsberg (✉)
University of Kiel, Kiel, Germany
e-mail: augsberg@law.uni-kiel.de

S. Korioth
University of Munich, Munich, Germany
e-mail: korioth@jura.uni-muenchen.de

R. Bottoni et al. (eds.), *Religious Rules, State Law, and Normative Pluralism - A Comparative Overview*, Ius Comparatum – Global Studies in Comparative Law 18, DOI 10.1007/978-3-319-28335-7_11

the constitutional arrangements shows that the provisions of the German *Grundgesetz* need not be limited to this classical twofold perspective. By contrast, it might be worthwhile to analyse the constitutional mechanisms in a different, functionalist perspective, describing them as a tool that enables legal pluralism. In the following, this is what we intend to do.

Our argument consists of six steps. First, we explain briefly the historical development and sociological background of the current situation in Germany (section "Historical background and religious demography"). Second, we present a short summary of the above-mentioned traditional perspective on freedom of religion and the relationship between the state and religious communities (section "Basic features of freedom of religion and the state-religion relationship according to the Grundgesetz"). The third step scrutinises the question whether state legislation is influenced by religious conceptions or even religious rules (section "The relevance of religion and religious law within state legislation"). Against the background of these analyses, the next step presents the decisive aspect with regard to the leading question of how state law and religious law interact within the German legal order. We analyse the possibilities as well as the limits for a non-state system of mediation and arbitration, that is to say, for a system of religious adjudication that is not only recognised by state authorities but indeed may rely on these authorities in order to enforce its decisions (section "Adjudication according to religious rules"). In addition to this analysis of officially recognised forms of religious adjudication, the last step asks whether there are other, more informal ways of deciding issues on a religious law basis (section "Social implementation of religious rules without official recognition"). A short conclusion will summarise once again the general idea that it is worthwhile to conceive of the relationship between the state and religious groups as a phenomenon of legal pluralism (section "Conclusion").

Historical Background and Religious Demography

In the more than 65 years since the foundation of the Federal Republic of Germany (FRG) with its *Grundgesetz* (Basic Law of 1949) Germany's religious demography has changed dramatically (Waldhoff 2010, 13 et sqq.; Korioth 2009). In 1950, more than 96 % of the population in the FRG belonged to one of the major Christian churches. About 50 % were Protestants, about 46 % belonged to the Roman-Catholic Church. Beginning in the 1960s the Christian confessions witnessed a continuous decline. The number of persons leaving the churches increased. This process of an increasing secularisation and moving away from the churches can be regarded as a fairly typical phenomenon of almost the entire Western world.[2] Yet within the specific German context another crucial aspect has to be taken into account: the existence of a second, politically completely distinct state from 1949 to 1990. While the West German *Grundgesetz* established a legal framework that firmly supported and gave broad freedom to religion and religious confessions the socialist regime in the East German Democratic Republic (GDR) practiced a policy that was deliberately

[2] See Taylor 2007. The US mark perhaps the one important exception, see e.g. Pally 2007.

anti-religious. This campaigning for atheism was remarkably successful. When the GDR collapsed in 1990 and the two German states were re-unified, barely 30 % of the population in the GDR still belonged to one of the great Christian confessions (Pollack 2003, 77). Currently about 60 % of the German population belong to the Catholic or the Protestant church. There is a further decline of about 1 % per year.

Thus the first remarkable tendency regarding religion in Germany is an ongoing process of moving away from the churches. It is accompanied by a second tendency, religious pluralisation. The importance of Islam in particular is increasing. Though there is hardly any reliable data, it is estimated that approximately 5 % of people currently living in Germany are Muslims, most of them being immigrants or descendants of immigrants. Due to specific demographic effects – the average birth rate among Muslim immigrants and their descendants is significantly higher than the one among the "autochtonous" Christian (or: former Christian) German population – and to an ongoing process of immigration not only, but also from countries with a predominantly Muslim population, this number will increase in the years to come.

This appearance of non-Christian religious groups causes specific problems for the legal system, which was framed when these new religious phenomena were by and large irrelevant. Against the background of a changed social context the question arises as to whether the old constitutional background is still adequate to meet the current challenges (Heinig 2008; Walter 2008). This becomes even more questionable when the historical background of the existing constitutional framework is taken into account. The present relationship between religion, church and state has to be seen as the product of century-long conflicts between the different confessions existing side by side (Korioth 2007). The Peace of Augsburg (1555) was the first major step to provide a legal basis for a peaceful co-existence of Catholicism and Lutheranian Protestants. By establishing the principle *cuius regio, eius religio* it guaranteed the aristocratic leaders of the separate states within the old *Reich* a *ius reformandi* (that is, a right to freely choose their own confession and thereby also to determine the confession of their citizens). Its aim was to prevent religious war by preserving a uniform religious belief within a given territory; at the same time a *ius emigrandi* was granted to those citizens with a different belief. We can consider this *ius emigrandi* as a first step towards individual religious freedom; but it took until the end of the eighteenth century before full individual religious freedom was finally achieved. Through the following centuries one can detect a certain tendency: The general idea is to establish peace by banning religion from the field of politics, in a first step by means of state sovereignty, and then in a second step which sees the state withdrawing from the religious field. At the same time religion was to move away from politics (Ladeur and Augsberg 2007; Roellecke 2004). This process of differentiation between politics and religion had important modifying effects on the general idea of religion. Religion became an increasingly private affair and much less of a public affair. But, and this is also a feature of the specific German way, religion was not completely banned from the public area. Churches – and later on other religious communities as well – remained part of the public order. They were and indeed still are seen as social forces in society.

Basic Features of Freedom of Religion and the State-Religion Relationship According to the *Grundgesetz*

Despite the federal organisation of Germany the present relationship between state and religion is fundamentally constituted by provisions of the *Grundgesetz*. The relevant norms have a double function. Firstly, there is the fundamental individual right of religious freedom (a), strengthened by rights of equal treatment forbidding any discrimination with regard to religion (b). Secondly, constitutional rules determine the relationship between the state and the various religious communities (c). This context can define the meaning of "religious rules" (d).

(a) The right of individual religious freedom is laid down in article 4 paragraph 1 and 2 GG. It obliges the state to respect the religious activities of its citizens and to secure their free exercise. Freedom of religion in this sense includes freedom of confession and worshipping. Furthermore, it guarantees the right to lead a life according to the rules of one's personal religious belief (BVerfGE 32, 98, 106). With regard to the question of how to define religion in the legal sense and to the problem of which kind of behavior deserves to be called religiously motivated, the fundamental aspect that state authorities must take into account is the self-understanding of the respective group.[3] Religious freedom also comprises a negative dimension, the freedom not to have any religion. As a human right freedom of religion is not limited to German citizens, but pertains to all persons within the German state. Not only individuals, but also religious communities as such are subjects of religious freedom.

The importance of this basic right is underlined by the specific character of the legal provision concerning the possibility to interfere in and thus to restrict the freedom of religion. Whereas most other basic rights explicitly concede that they may be restricted by or pursuant to a law, the text of article 4 GG contains no such possibility. However, that does not mean that religious activities are beyond any state control and restriction. Yet the state may only restrict religious freedom in the pursuit of specific purposes. These purposes must be the protection of other constitutional rights of equal importance, e. g. basic rights of the citizens.

(b) This freedom to have or not to have a certain religious creed is strengthened by the basic right of equality before the law. According to article 3 paragraph 3 GG no person shall be favored or disfavored because of his or her personal religious opinions. Article 33 paragraph 3 GG specifies this general rule by stating that neither the enjoyment of civil and political rights, nor rights acquired in the public service, nor eligibility for public offices shall be dependent upon religious affiliations.

[3] See for a closer account of this specific technique as developed by the German Constitutional Court Augsberg 2012; for its relevance with respect to the question of religious adjudication *infra*, at 5 b dd.

(c) Secondly, with respect to the relationship between the state and religious communities the *Grundgesetz* uses a special technique. Article 140 GG refers and thereby incorporates the relevant norms from the constitution of the former Weimar Republic (*Weimarer Reichsverfassung, WRV*). According to the *Bundesverfassungsgericht* (Federal Constitutional Court), this technique does not imply an inferior status of the incorporated norms. Rather, they are a fully effective, integral part of the constitution (BVerfGE 19, 206, 219). In contrast to the individual approach of article 4, these incorporated rules constitute the institutional aspect of the German law concerning religion and religious communities. They establish an intricate balance between a separation as well as a cooperation of the state and religious communities. The fundamental rule states that there shall be no state church (article 140 GG and article 137 paragraph 1 WRV). It determines a basic separation of religion and state. Confirming their autonomy, article 137 paragraph 3 WRV declares that all religious societies shall regulate and administer their affairs independently within the limits of the law that applies to all. The fundamental separation of church and state thus established is not to be seen as a conception of *laicité* in the strict French sense. The so called "friendly" separation does not exclude fields of cooperation between the state and religious groups – as long as the state does not interfere or determine what "religion" means (concept of state neutrality) (BVerfGE 12, 1, 4; 19, 206, 216; 104, 337, 353; Huster 2002).

(d) The fundamental right of religious freedom (article 4 GG) and autonomy of religious societies concerning their own affairs (article 137 WRV) includes the self-determination of religious groups by means of religious rules. These are rules which derive from religious authorities and form a set of rules strictly separated from the law of the state. They mostly concern religious items (rules of belief and behaviors, membership in a religious community or church, regulations of worship et al.) Yet they do not necessarily have a direct religious content. They may support religious activities by regulating the organisation or finance of the religious group. The constitution guarantees and protects this self-determination within the limits of the law valid for all.

The Relevance of Religion and Religious Law Within State Legislation

(a) Religion is not mentioned in the legal texts which define the principles and values that should inspire the state legal system (especially in the *Grundgesetz*). There are two exceptions: The preamble of the *Grundgesetz* mentions the "responsibility before God", in which the German people gave this constitution. But this has no legal meaning and binding force; Germany is neither a Christian state nor a state founded on religious roots, but a secular state. The second exception can be found in the constitutions of some *Länder* (states). The

Grundgesetz places the responsibility for education with the state governments; some state constitutions incorporate either specifically Christian or simply general religious references regarding the aims of education in state-run schools. But viewed in the light of state neutrality this does not allow the presentation of Christian or religious values as binding for all. As the Constitutional Court put it in 1975: "The elimination of all ideological and religious references would not neutralize the existing ideological tensions and conflicts, but would disadvantage parents who desire a Christian education for their children and would result in compelling them so send their children to a lay school [...]. As a result, the state legislature is not absolutely prohibited from incorporating Christian references when it establishes a state elementary school, even though a minority of parents has no choice but to send their children" (BVerfGE 41, 29). However, the Court also stressed that this kind of school may not proselytize, that no one may be forced to attend religious classes, and that Christianity in secular disciplines should be limited to references to it as a formative cultural force in occidental, Western society.

(b) In Germany, there is no system of personal laws based on religious affiliation. The state legal system is wholly secular. Religious activities are protected, but there is no part of the law which adopts religious rules as a source of law. In family law, for example, citizens cannot choose between a civil or a religious marriage. Family law is part of the civil law; if a couple wants to have a religious ceremony of marriage, it may opt for it after the civil marriage. Yet from a legal point of view, it is only the civil ceremony that matters.

(c) In general, state laws do not include religious rules applicable to all citizens. This kind of application is excluded by the principle of state neutrality, rooted in article 4 paragraph 1 and 2 GG and article 137 paragraph 1 WRV, which states: "There shall be no state church". There are only few examples of norms with a clearly identifiable religious, i.e. Christian background. Article 139 WRV protects Sunday, the day of religious services and prayer in the Christian tradition as a day of spiritual improvement and rest from work. But in present times the guarantee is understood not only in terms of respect for the Christian tradition, but also as part of the principle of the social state (article 20 paragraph 1 GG). The double function was stressed by the constitutional court in 2009, when it restricted state legislation in Berlin, aimed at allowing trading hours of shops on a certain number of Sundays a year (BVerfGE 125, 39). The problem continues, however, with regard to the laws regulating official holidays, since these holidays have an either secular or, as in most cases, decidedly Christian background. There is an ongoing debate whether this situation corresponds both to the legal requirements of the neutrality principle and to the political idea of sending a signal to the Muslim communities that, as a former President of Germany expressed, Islam indeed has become an integral part of the German society.

(d) Article 137 paragraph 3 WRV respects the right of religious organisations to establish and apply their own rules for their internal affairs. The rules for the content of religious confession, organisation, membership, finances, education of priests and preachers lie within the autonomy of churches and other religious organisations. This autonomy also allows the foundation and running of schools, hospitals, kindergartens, old people's homes and homes for disabled citizens. But all of these activities must take place within the limits of the laws applying to all. In cases of conflict – e. g. when a religious organisation requires the conformity of religious confession of their employees – article 137 paragraph 3 WRV enables a solution by means of proportionality between the (legally protected) position of the individual and the religious aims of the organisation.[4]

(e) Religious rules are applicable in the state legal system only through a reference made to them by state laws – in general by article 137 paragraph 3 WRV, in some cases through the channel of international private law – a case relevant in particular when legal norms of a religious community have been incorporated into the legal order of a foreign state – and on the basis of treaties between the state and religious communities. In Germany, there is a long tradition of treaties between the state and the Catholic church, represented by the Holy See, and the Protestant churches. They mainly repeat constitutional clauses protecting the liberties of churches, but furthermore guarantee e.g. general state protection and financial donations to the churches. Once again, this kind of cooperation of state and churches is not regarded as an infringement of the neutrality principle, since it applies just as well to other religious denominations. In recent years, similar treaties have been made with the Jewish communities and, for instance in Hamburg in 2012, with Islamic groups.

(f) There are some religiously motivated exemptions from laws of general application. A very prominent and general exception is stated in section 9 of the *general act of equal treatment* (2006), which reads: "(1) [...] a difference of treatment on the grounds of religion or belief of employees of a religious community, facilities affiliated to it [...] or organisations which have undertaken conjointly to practice a religion or belief, shall not constitute discrimination where such grounds constitute a justified occupational requirement for a particular religion or belief, having regard to the ethos of the religious community or organisation in question and by reason of their right to self-determination or by the nature of the particular activity. (2) [...]." Labor law is the main field for exemptions from the laws valid for all. Other exemptions concern tax laws. All exemptions have in common that they concern all religious communities equally, irrespective of the content of their faith or belief. This stresses the overall friendly openness of German law to religious activities.

[4] BVerfGE 70, 185 – A Catholic hospital had dismissed a doctor because he had publicly stated that he opposed the church's doctrine on abortion. The constitutional court decided that the hospital was an "affair" of the church (article 137 paragraph 3 WRV) and thus under church regulation, including its special rules concerning labor contracts. "By laying down such duties of loyalty in a contract of employment, the ecclesiastical employer not only relies on the general freedom of contract, but he simultaneously makes use of his constitutional right to self-determination, permitting churches to shape their social activity, even when regulated by contracts of employment according to a particular vision of Christian community service shared by their members."

Adjudication According to Religious Rules

The German legal system does not provide for religious adjudication in an explicit, deliberate manner. Yet it recognises and accepts such dispute resolution systems, both in the form of mere mediation between the parties and in the form of an arbitration by an appointed court-like institution, as long as the solutions and also the proceedings leading to these solutions do not interfere with certain indispensable requirements established by state law. What is more, this acceptance includes the possibility to rely on state authority in order to enforce settlements agreed upon or decisions made within these private dispute resolutions systems.[5]

The obvious problem arising from this position is the question in which cases we may speak of an interference between religious rules and state law which is so severe that it will prevent the free exercise of religious adjudication. In answering this question, we can differentiate between two forms of this general recognition: one being indifferent towards the religious background (a) and one being explicitly based on the religious aspects (b).

(a) In the first, for our general topic less interesting sense religious adjudication is accepted neither because of nor in spite of its religious character but with simply no attention being paid towards the religious aspects of the case in question. Its recognition is merely a part of the general acceptance of private resolution systems. In this respect, religious arbitration panels are accepted to the extent to which they fit into the general framework of private law based on the general concept of private autonomy. If both parties agree to have a dispute settled by a private arbitrator, this settlement is generally permitted (Funke 2011, 47 et sq.). In order to fulfil the parties' will to a maximum extent, the legal regime under which the arbitration process is supposed to work does not need to belong to any (foreign) state law. Rather, the rules applied to a given case can be part of non-state law, be it in the form of a private agreement or of a religious system of belief (for an overview on this – disputed – topic Hötte 2013, at 206 et sqq.).

The precondition for this allowance is, however, that both the proceedings and the solution found at the end of the proceedings pay tribute to the general norms and values of state law, namely the fundamental rights of the citizens (Hötte 2013, 209 et sqq.). Thus e.g. an adjudication system neglecting the equality of men and women – for instance by weighting the testimony of men and women unequally – cannot be accepted.

The same holds true if religious law is incorporated into the German legal order as a part of International Private Law (IPL). In this context, it may be necessary to apply religious rules, for instance the sharia, if the legal order of a foreign state already has integrated these religious rules into its own legal system. Yet from the point of view of IPL this religious origin has no decisive influence on the general practice. The limits of this form of incorporation are set by the general ordre-public-principle (Unberath 2009). With regard to the practical

[5] See generally, with a comparative view on the situation in the United States, in the UK and in Canada, Hötte 2013; with a focus on the German situation Wittreck 2014.

relevance of this IPL solution, one should mention that its logic is one of nation states and their citizens. Hence it cannot be applied if the person that refers to this kind of foreign state law is not a foreigner, but a German citizen. In consequence, inasmuch as the integration of previous "foreigners" into the German society succeeds, IPL tools lose their relevance (on general terms: Ferrari 2015).

Moreover, some of the classical legal topics covered by state law are generally excluded from private dispute settlement solutions. This primary exemption from the rule applies of course to criminal law which cannot be substituted by any private agreement or adjudication by a private arbitrator or an arbitration panel. In addition to that, another important exemption applies to most questions of family law, especially to those questions that deal with the legal status connected with family law arrangements, for instance marriage and divorce – indeed the German Federal Court of Justice speaks with regard to divorce of an "absolute state monopoly" (Bundesgerichtshof 2008) –, and even more specifically with the status of children. The Federal Court has explicitly stated that the German legal order does not recognise an autonomous regulation of family law, law of persons and law of inheritance by religious communities. Emphasising this position, the Court goes on to explain that in this respect the only possible way for German courts to decide upon a case on the basis of religious rules is according to the rules of International Private Law. On this account, what is needed is the law of a foreign state which has incorporated certain religious rules, thus transforming them from merely religious norms to (foreign) state law, and that as such state law has been declared applicable by German courts according to German conflict of rules legislation (Bundesgerichtshof 1980). Apart from this International Private Law scenario, within the context of family law the only legal issues suitable for private arbitration or mediation are questions concerning proprietary aspects of divorce etc. (Hötte 2013, 196 et sqq.).

(b) In the more interesting second sense the idea of recognising religious adjudication is based on the concept of religious freedom. On this account, it is not only the general possibility of relying on religious rules that is strengthened by this fundamental right. Rather, the possible interference of state courts in religious adjudication itself also has to be interpreted and applied against the background of the legal provisions protecting religious freedom.

(aa) The main legal norms establishing religious freedom in the German *Grundgesetz* have already been mentioned above. Apart from the general principle that religious freedom may not be violated, as stipulated in Article 4 GG, we also find a more specific constitutional provision dealing with the subject of religious adjudication in Article 140 GG which refers back to Article 137 paragraph 3 WRV. This norm guarantees all religious societies the freedom to regulate and administer their affairs independently within the limits of the law that applies to all. It is commonly understood that part and parcel of this freedom is not only the right to internal law-making procedures but also the right to have religious courts applying these laws (e.g. von Campenhausen and Unruh 2010, no. 113). In this sense, the constitutional provision establishes a legal pluralism that allows for both state law and religious law.

This interpretation is confirmed by a certain reading of the freedom of religion according to the German *Grundgesetz*. Given its broad interpretation as developed by the Federal Constitutional Court, that is to say, given that religious freedom is said to guarantee the right to lead a life according to the rules of one's personal religious belief (see *supra*, at 3a), religious freedom also covers the idea of leading a life according to religious rules (e.g. Hötte 2013, 229; Wittreck 2003, 519). On this account, the task of religious freedom is to solve the dilemma of individuals who find themselves caught up between a rock and a hard stone, that is to say, between the social (or, from the point of view of the respective community: indeed legal) rules established by their religious group (and hence the social pressure imposed on them to conduct their life accordingly) and state law provisions that are opposed to these rules. In this perspective, freedom of religion constitutes, as Robert Cover has put it, "a refuge not only *from* persecution, but *for* associational self-realisation in nomian terms" (Cover 1993, 128). Accordingly, the fundamental rights perspective also stresses the point that religious freedom not only allows for but indeed calls for legal pluralism.

A historical perspective on Article 137 paragraph 3 WRV supports this understanding. Yet it also points to possible difficulties for its interpretation in today's society. The focus of this norm, introduced in 1919, was obviously the law of both the Catholic and the Protestant Churches which included an internal system of adjudication. One may ask whether the legal solutions found with respect to this specifically Christian situation are equally applicable to other religious denominations.

From the constitutional point of view, however, there is in principle no reason why the general conception of Article 137 paragraph 3 WRV should not be extended to other religious denominations, too. In fact, the state's obligation to the neutrality principle requires such an extension. Neutrality in this sense means that the state must not offer special privileged treatment to certain religious groups exclusively. On the contrary, it has to treat all of them equally. Thus what applies to the Catholic and the Protestant Churches must in principle also be valid for e.g. Jewish or Muslim communities. Indeed, for these religious communities the said constitutional conception seems even more relevant, since both the Jewish and the Islamic system of belief include a complex set of ethical as well as legal rules that affect not only the spiritual field but intend to cover all areas of life within the religious community.

(bb) Hence this norm, Article 137 paragraph 3 WRV, allows for an internal system of religious adjudication for all religious denominations. Yet it applies only to the internal affairs of religious communities. With regard to their external status, and that is to say, as far as their relationship with the rest of society is concerned, the relevant legal regime is that of the state alone. The problem, then, is how to decide the question of which issues remain inside the religious community and which, by contrast, turn to the outside, and even more importantly, who has the last say in this matter – religious or state courts?[6]

[6] See on the intricate movement of in and out from a more theoretical point of view Van Praagh 2014.

Looking at the two extreme positions, the answer to this question seems fairly clear-cut. First, obviously purely doctrinal questions within a particular religious belief are not for the state to decide, even though they might take a legal form. State courts must not decide upon questions concerning how and what one has to believe in order to be a faithful member of a specific religious group.

Second, to take the other extreme, external effects of religious rules are undeniable if and when they touch upon the rights of non-members of the respective religious community; and of course the same holds true if such internal rules and their application by religious courts affect other religious communities or the secular society as a whole in a negative way. Religious freedom does not allow for the violation of other persons' rights.

(cc) Yet what happens if a conflict arises between members of a specific group? Is it necessary that state courts take into account the specific cultural or religious background of the respective group – a background which may also include a specific legal understanding? Does the legal pluralism as enabled by the constitutional provisions of the *Grundgesetz* oblige state courts to interpret the state law in light of possibly conflicting religious rules dealing with the same matter at hand?

This topic has been discussed mainly with regard to criminal law, although it is obviously not limited to this area. As far as criminal law is concerned, the question can be put in this way: Supposing that a certain cultural or religious background may lead to a different understanding of a criminal offence, do we have to recognise this background by way of commuting the sentence? German state courts have denied this possibility. In particular the so called "honour-killings" are not to be explained and partly legitimised against the background of a particular understanding of family and honour. On the contrary, they are to be considered offences committed on the ground of base motives (a constituent fact of murder according to the German penal code). The courts have held that religious reasons are no excuse for committing a crime (Bundesgerichtshof 2002). What apparently follows from this is that state courts not only need not but in fact may not engage with any other than the state law provisions.

In principle, the same also holds true with respect to other areas of state law, e.g. family law. The exception proving this rule was a decision by a state court which stirred the general public as well as the legal system. In a divorce proceeding, the deciding judge sitting singly held that a woman who had married a Muslim husband had implicitly agreed to the cultural and religious standards of Islam which, as the judge asserted, included the right to use corporal punishment. According to the judge's argument, the woman could therefore not complain about having fallen victim to domestic violence practiced by her husband.[7] The decision was not only widely criticised by jurists and feminists

[7] See specifically on this case but also more generally on the practice of German courts in applying Islamic law Unberath 2009.

as well as by Islamic organisations but was also immediately overruled within the state court system.

(dd) Both examples point to a legal position supporting general standards of legal decision-making instead of promoting a special treatment for religious minorities. Yet as much as this is a correct description of the current legal situation in Germany, it is not the last word the German legal system has to say on this matter.

In order to understand the final solution to the problem, it is worthwhile to explain the difficulties connected with the legal provisions described so far in more detail. To restrict the internal affairs of religious communities to doctrinal aspects and the internal organisation of the community, but to deny them any right to have a say in respect to matters with any influence on their social surrounding, would reduce religious adjudication to an extremely limited area of activity. The same holds true if in answering the question what is "inside" and what is "outside" the religious community one simply pointed to the "limits of the law that applies to all" explicitly mentioned in Article 137 paragraph 3 WRV. Taken literally, this would mean that in any conflict-of-laws-scenario state law would automatically supersede the opposing religious rules. Once again, this would leave hardly any relevant leeway for religious adjudication.

Therefore, given the general description of the German *Grundgesetz* in terms of a "religion-friendly" conception as developed by the Constitutional Court, it will come as no surprise that the Court practices a different, less restrictive reading of Article 137 paragraph 3 WRV. In order to enable a wider range of religious adjudication it applies a technique which is very characteristic for the entire German concept of religious freedom (in more detail Augsberg 2012). Because of this technique, the most important aspect of religious adjudication can be found, somewhat paradoxically, in the state court's adjudication. On the one hand, in cases of conflict between state law and religious law the state courts have the last say. The German State does not give religious courts or institutions direct power to interpret the laws of the state and to assess their conformity to religious rules. Insofar, religious provisions conflicting with state law will be overruled.

Yet on the other hand, in finding their judgements the state courts must take into account what is referred to as the "religious self-concept" of the respective religious community.[8] The questions of what a religion is and what a religiously motivated behaviour is have to be explained against the background of this self-concept (Morlok 1993, 78 et sqq.; Isak 1994). In elaborating on this self-understanding, religious rules and their interpretation are a decisive tool for state courts. Accordingly, state courts in finding their judgements have to pay attention to religious adjudication. Since they may not interpret religious rules

[8]The strategy was introduced into the legal discourse by BVerfGE 24, 236 (247 et sq.) and has been one of the most decisive aspects for the realisation of religious freedom ever since; see e.g. BVerfGE 33, 23; 53, 366 (401); 66, 1 (22); 70, 138 (167); 72, 278 (289).

independently without endangering the principle of state neutrality, state courts have to rely on religious jurisdiction as a source of knowledge and understanding. Hence, insofar as the state courts have to pay attention to religious views in applying state law concerning religious issues, the religious courts and institutions have an indirect impact on state court decision-making. Using sociological terminology this technique may be called a strategy of "second order observation" (Luhmann 2002, 155): state courts observe religious courts observing (i.e. in this case: reading and interpreting) their religious rules.

A practical example demonstrating this kind of interplay between state courts and religious rules and adjudication bodies is labour law. Although it is ultimately for the state courts to decide whether e.g. a dismissal of an employee by the Catholic or Protestant church as his or her employer is valid or whether the employees have a right to organise and effect an official strike, the state courts in deciding the case have to pay tribute not only to the text of the state law, but thereby also to the self-understanding of the church which may include a different understanding of the general relationship between employer and employees (Richardi 2009; Thüsing 2006).

(ee) Yet this restricted access to religious rules and their interpretation does not exclude all forms of state control. State courts have to control whether or not a religious doctrine is violating the law of the state (BVerfGE 83, 34). In this context, the constitutional guarantee of religious freedom does not merely constitute the legal foundation for independent religious adjudication, it also sets limits to religious rules and religious courts applying them. The difference can be explained with regard to the question of membership in a religious community. First and foremost, since this is a core element in the process of the self-constitution of a religious community, the definition of membership has to be protected by religious freedom. Thus it is not for the state and its courts to decide whether religious membership necessarily includes an act of will or, by contrast, can be based on genealogical aspects deprived of any individual will – as for instance in the general principle of matrilinearity as practiced in Judaism. Yet it would infringe upon the negative aspect of religious freedom if a community prevented its members from giving up their religious belief and forced them to stay in the community.[9]

Social Implementation of Religious Rules Without Official Recognition

While the mechanisms organising the interplay between state law and religious law were developed with regard mainly to the Christian churches, the current debate on this interplay is focused on Islam and the possible integration of Islamic law into the

[9] See on the general problem of membership in religious communities and state law Augsberg 2013.

secular legal order (Funke 2011). Since in Germany Islam is a religion practiced mostly by immigrants – especially, but not only from Turkey –, the question is whether such forms of adjudication endanger or support the process of integrating the immigrants into the German society. Some claim, for instance, that Muslim "justices of peace" – religious courts of arbitration which mediate and eventually decide cases of contestation between members of a specific religious community – jeopardise the normative idea of both the rule of law and of the "unity of the legal order", as these "justices of peace" establish a jurisdiction beyond statutory as well as constitutional norms of the state, thereby creating a "parallel world", segregated from the rest of society.[10] The opposing opinion claims that prohibiting religious adjudication will only lead to the problematic phenomenon of "'back-alley' forms of dispute settlement", while the state recognition of religious adjudication could "enhance personal autonomy" of the believers (Ahmed and Luk 2012, with regard to the Anglo-American context).

The problem is, however, discussed on a rather abstract level, as there is hardly any reliable data telling us how many Muslims in Germany indeed rely on religious arbitration panels. Given the multifold and highly complex structure of Islam and due to the fact that the immigrants living in Germany differ from those living in other countries, for instance in the UK, with regard to their predominant country of origin and thus typically also with regard to their specific predominant version of Islamic faith, it is also hardly possible to rely on experiences made in other countries. What is more, the discussion leads away from the genuinely legal aspects of the problem.[11] Of course there may be extreme cases of proceedings effected by such "justices of peace" which infringe upon norms of state law, in particular criminal law, e.g. by urging members of the respective community to suppress their testimonies towards state officials, thereby obstructing criminal trials. Yet beyond these extreme forms the debate focuses on two different but likewise rather extra-legal aspects: First, on the general preconditions for integration, and second, on the question whether Islam and the Muslim communities will be able to adapt themselves to a decidedly secular society which allows for religious activities, but only in limited fields with the main focus on the private life of its citizens, not as a common ground for all social activities.

Conclusion

Our analyses have shown that the German legal system, with its general "friendliness" and openness towards religion as established by the constitutional provisions, is well-suited to recognise religious rules and their application by adjudication bodies. Looking at the current situation, one should mention that at least up till now this

[10] See with regard to the German situation in a polemical account Wagner 2012. For a critique of this kind of argument: Wittreck 2014. For a differentiated scepticism An-Na'im 2010, 27.

[11] See for a legal debate on the question of integration and religious freedom Augsberg 2015.

question is of a rather academic nature, since in Germany we find hardly any relevant religious arbitration panels with a significant number of cases (Hötte 2013, 193 et sq., with a comparison to the situation in the US). However, taking into account the growing Muslim population, this situation might change in the years to come. Against this background the question if religious legislation and arbitration bodies basing their decision-making on religious rules should play a greater role in contemporary society can be reformulated in the general form of "what can be done by each legal system to give citizens the opportunity to live according to their religious convictions without endangering social cohesion and fostering (auto)segregation?" (Ferrari 2015). Put in this way, the question is one that lawyers alone will hardly be able to answer. It points to a not predominantly constitutional but rather to a sociological, if not even political issue.

However, the relevance of the subject can also be emphasised from a rather theoretical point of view. From this perspective, the role of religious rules and rule applying bodies stresses an understanding of religious freedom which takes the constitutional guarantee not only as an individual fundamental right.[12] Rather, the focus on religious rules as opposed to state law reveals the entire subject as a conflicts-of-law-scenario (Janssen 2001; Schuppert 2012, 112 et sqq.). In this context, the discussion reveals that religious freedom can and indeed should be re-constructed as an exercise of legal pluralism.

References

Ahmed, Farrah, and Senwung Luk. 2012. How religious arbitration could enhance personal autonomy. *Oxford Journal of Law and Religion* 1: 424.

An Na'im, Abdullahi Ahmed. 2010. The compatibility dialectic: Mediating the legitimate coexistence of Islamic law and state law. *The Modern Law Review* 72: 1.

Augsberg, Ino. 2012. Taking religion seriously. On the legal relevance of religious self-concepts. *Journal of Law, Religion and State* 1: 291.

Augsberg, Ino. 2013. Wer glauben will, muss zahlen? Erwerb und Aufgabe der Kirchenmitgliedschaft im Spannungsfeld von Kirchenrecht und Religionsverfassungsrecht. *Archiv des öffentlichen Rechts* 138: 493.

Augsberg, Ino. 2015. Soziale Integration durch Religionsfreiheit? Zur Neubestimmung des Religionsverfassungsrechts im Horizont eines reflexiven Rechtspluralismus. In *Religionsverfassungsrechtliche Spannungsfelder. Interdisziplinäre Perspektiven*, eds. Hans Michael Heinig and Christian Walter. Tübingen: Mohr Siebeck, forthcoming.

Bundesgerichtshof. 1980. *Neue Juristische Wochenschrift*, 1221.

Bundesgerichtshof. 2002. February 20 2002, – 5 StR 538/01 –, Available at http://juris.bundesgerichtshof.de/cgi-bin/rechtsprechung/document.py?Gericht=bgh&Art=en&nr=19128&pos=0&anz=1.

Bundesgerichtshof. 2008. Neue Juristische Wochenschrift – Rechtsprechungs-Report, 1169.

Campenhausen, Axel von., and Peter Unruh. 2010. Art 137 WRV. In *Grundgesetz*, vol. III, 6th ed, ed. Hermann von Mangoldt, Klein Friedrich, and Starck Christian. Munich: Vahlen.

[12] See for a respective critique of the FCC's judicature Ladeur 2009.

Cover, Robert. 1993. Nomos and narrative. In *Narrative, violence, and the law. The essays of Robert Cover*, ed. Martha Minor, Michael Ryan, and Austin Sarat, 95. Ann Arbor: University of Michigan Press.

Ferrari, Silvio. 2015. Applicable religious rules according to the law of the state, in this volume.

Funke, Andreas. 2011. Parallelwelten des Rechts? Die Anerkennung des Rechts und der Gerichtsbarkeit von Religionsgemeinschaften durch den Staat. In *Herausforderung Islam*, ed. Anja Bettenworth et al., 42 Paderborn: Schoenigh.

Heinig, Hans Michael. 2008. Ordnung der Freiheit – das Staatskirchenrecht vor neuen Herausforderungen. *Zeitschrift für evangelisches Kirchenrecht* 54: 235.

Hötte, Franziska. 2013. *Religiöse Schiedsgerichtsbarkeit. Angloamerikanische Rechtspraxis, Perspektive für Deutschland*. Tübingen: Mohr Siebeck.

Huster, Stefan. 2002. *Die ethische Neutralität des Staates. Eine liberale Interpretation der Verfassung*. Tübingen: Mohr Siebeck.

Isak, Axel. 1994. *Das Selbstverständnis der Kirchen und Religionsgemeinschaften und seine Bedeutung für die Auslegung des staatlichen Rechts*. Berlin: Duncker & Humblot.

Janssen, Albert. 2001. Staatskirchenrecht als Kollisionsrecht. In *Verfassung – Philosophie – Kirche. Festschrift für Alexander Hollerbach zum 70. Geburtstag*, ed. Joachim Bohnert et al., 707. Berlin: Duncker & Humblot.

Korioth, Stefan. 2007. Die Entwicklung des Staatskirchenrechts in Deutschland seit der Reformation. In *Staatskirchenrecht oder Religionsverfassungsrecht?*, ed. Hans Michael Heinig and Christian Walter, 39. Tübingen: Mohr Siebeck.

Korioth, Stefan. 2009. Jeder nach seiner Facon: Grundgesetz für die multireligiöse Gesellschaft. *Kritische Justiz, Beiheft* 1, 175.

Ladeur, Karl-Heinz. 2009. The myth of the neutral state and the individualization of religion: The relationship of state and religion in the face of fundamentalism. *Cardozo Law Review* 30: 2445.

Ladeur, Karl-Heinz, and Ino Augsberg. 2007. The myth of the neutral state. The relationship between state and religion in the face of new challenges. *German Law Journal* 8: 143.

Luhmann, Niklas. 2002. *Einführung in die Systemtheorie*. Heidelberg: Carl-Auer-Verlag.

Morlok, Martin. 1993. *Selbstverständnis als Rechtskriterium*. Tübingen: Mohr Siebeck.

Pally, Marcia. 2007. *Die hintergründige Religion. Der Einfluss des Evangelikalismus auf Gewissensfreiheit, Pluralismus und die US-amerikanische Politik*. Berlin: Berlin University Press.

Pollack, Detlef. 2003. *Säkularisierung – ein moderner Mythos?* Tübingen: Mohr Siebeck.

Richardi, Reinhard. 2009. *Arbeitsrecht in der Kirche. Staatliches Arbeitsrecht und kirchliches Dienstrecht*, 5th ed, Munich: Beck.

Roellecke, Gerd. 2004. Die Entkoppelung von Recht und Religion. *Juristenzeitung*, 105.

Schuppert, Gunnar Folke. 2012. *When Governance meets Religion. Governancestrukturen und Governanceakteure im Bereich des Religiösen*. Baden-Baden: Nomos.

Taylor, Charles. 2007. *A secular age*. Cambridge, MA: Harvard University Press.

Thüsing, Gregor. 2006. *Kirchliches Arbeitsrecht. Rechtsprechung und Diskussionsstand im Schnittpunkt von staatlichem Arbeitsrecht und kirchlichem Dienstrecht*. Tübingen: Mohr Siebeck.

Unberath, Hannes. 2009. Die Anwendung islamischen Rechts durch deutsche Gerichte. Bemerkungen zum Verhältnis von kultureller Identität und Grundgesetz. In *Muslime im säkularen Staat. Untersuchungen anhand von Deutschland und Österreich*, ed. Martina Haedrich, 83. Stuttgart: Boorberg.

Van Praagh, Shauna. 2014. Inside out/Outside in: Coexistence and cross-pollination of religion and state. In *Mapping the legal boundaries of belonging. Religion and multiculturalism from Israel to Canada*, ed. René Provost. Oxford: Oxford University Press.

Wagner, Joachim. 2012. *Richter ohne Gesetz. Islamische Paralleljustiz gefährdet unseren Rechtsstaat. Wie Imame in Deutschland die Scharia anwenden*. Berlin: Ullstein.

Waldhoff, Christian. 2010. *Neue Religionskonflikte und staatliche Neutralität – Erfordern weltanschauliche und religiöse Entwicklungen Antworten des Staates?* Gutachten für den 68. Deutschen Juristentag. Munich: C. H. Beck.

Walter, Christian. 2008. Religiöse Freiheit als Gefahr? Eine Gegenrede. *Deutsches Verwaltungsblatt*, 1073.

Wittreck, Fabian. 2003. Religionsfreiheit als Rationalisierungsverbot. Anmerkungen aus Anlaß der Schächtentscheidung des Bundesverfassungsgerichts. *Der Staat* 42, 519.

Wittreck, Fabian. 2014. Paralleljustiz in ethnischen Minderheiten? – Die bundesdeutsche Perspektive. In *Zak Spezial – Migration, Familie und Vermögen: Vom Europäischen Erbrecht bis zu binationalen Ehen* , ed. Astrid Deixler-Hüber and Martin Schauer. Lexisnexis.

Chapter 12
Borders of Religious Autonomy in Hungary

Balázs Schanda

Abstract Hungary has no system of personal laws. Marriage became secular with the civil marriage law of 1895. State laws do not include religious rules in the strict sense. The autonomy of religious communities is respected by the state. This autonomy includes the respect of the identity of institutions run by religious communities. Internal rules of religious communities would qualify as "religious rules". Religious rules are generally not applicable in the state legal system but in certain cases the state law does refer to the internal rules of religious communities. The internal jurisdiction (like on the issues of marriage in the case of the Catholic Church or other internal decisions) have no significance of any kind for the state. Traditional religious minorities are well integrated into society and the challenge of integrating large numbers of migrants with a diverse religious background has not gained much relevance yet. There are no indications in Hungary that a significant number of citizens apply religious rules in conflict with state laws.

Introduction

Since the Reformation, Hungarians have been divided between Catholicism and Protestantism (mainly Calvinism). There is no exact data on religious affiliation. Whereas the census in 2001 showed that only 11 % refused to answer the question on religious affiliation, ten years later, 27 % did not provide an answer. The percentage of those declaring not to have a religious affiliation has risen from 14.5 to 18 %; and amongst the younger generations, 20 % do not belong to any denomination. Data is difficult to compare, as in 2001 "religion" was the question, whilst ten years later the question was the religious community to which one "felt a sense of belonging". Consequently the number of those who declared to belong to a religious community has dropped vis-à-vis with those who – ten years earlier – declared to have a religion. Denominational proportions, however, did not change significantly. Ten years ago, within a population of around 10 million people, 5.55 million declared to

B. Schanda (✉)
Pázmány Péter Catholic University, Budapest, Hungary
e-mail: schanda@jak.ppke.hu

R. Bottoni et al. (eds.), *Religious Rules, State Law, and Normative Pluralism - A Comparative Overview*, Ius Comparatum – Global Studies in Comparative Law 18, DOI 10.1007/978-3-319-28335-7_12

be Catholic, while more recently only 3.87 million declared to belong to the Catholic Church. The number of Calvinists has dropped from 1.62 million to 1.15 million. Ten years ago, 304,000 people declared to be Lutherans, now only 214,000 declared to be a member of the Lutheran Church. Other traditional communities, like the Jews and the Orthodox, have also lost (declared) adherents. Today 167,000 people belong to other religious communities. The figure was at 96,000 ten years ago, but the change is also due to the fact that some minor communities have changed their policy with regard to the census. Whereas ten years ago they recommended that their adherents should not answer the question on religion, now they urged them to declare their belonging. The estimated number of Jews, however, could be ten times higher than the number of those declaring their belonging (10,000). Within younger generations, the percentage of those unaffiliated has risen but that of declared atheists has not. Elder generations (those over 60) show a higher affiliation to religion (the figure of those who declared themselves to belong to a religious community was almost ten times more than those declaring to belong to none). Under the age of 40, the number of those who declared a belonging was only twice as many as those with no affiliation; data, however, does not show secularization on the rise. That means that the generations born in the 1960s and those born in the 1980s have a similar level of religiosity. Amongst other religious communities, the most significant are the Jehovah's Witnesses with 31,000 declared adherents (the elderly and less educated are overrepresented); 18,000 declared to belong to the Faith Church (an Evangelical congregation with a relatively young membership), over 9000 are Buddhists (dominantly urban adherents with higher education), 18,000 Baptists, 6000 Adventists, 9000 Pentecostals, 2400 Methodists, 6800 Unitarians; traditional small Christian communities are ageing. The number of Muslims has risen from 2907 in 2001 to 5579. 2300 Muslims declared to be Arab, 2200 stated other ethnicities. As a multiple ethnic affiliation is possible, 4000 Muslims also claimed to be ethnic Hungarians. Hungary is probably the last country in Europe where Jews outnumber Muslims.[1]

Religiosity is not especially high in Hungary, but no other social entity has a vital and complex role in society comparable to the one of religious communities. Approximately half of the population has an active adherence to a traditional church (by assigning a percentage of one's income tax to a church or opting for religious education at public schools). The three major Christian denominations (Catholics, Calvinists and Lutherans) and the Jewish Communities receive special attention as mainstream religious communities. This attention can be seen both in governmental relations and in public speech. For example the leaders of these communities are regularly invited to public celebrations, like the opening session of the parliament and also the public media provides for a regular coverage of their activities.

The percentage of resident aliens is under 2 % of the total population, with over 80 % coming from other European countries. Many of them are ethnic Hungarians from neighboring countries. The Chinese community is the largest minority with a

[1] Census data available at: http://www.ksh.hu/nepszamlalas/vallas_sb

non-European background (the estimated number is between 10,000 and 15,000).[2] As the immigration of non-Europeans has been rather limited in the country, non-integrated religious communities do not seem to have much social relevance. The social attitude towards immigrants is rather one of mistrust, rather than welcoming.

Legislation

Constitution

The Basic Law (the new constitution), in force since 1 January 2012, portrays a conservative view of society, underlining the value of family, nationhood and responsibility. At first glance, the text is also characterized by a religious rhetoric as it begins and ends with the mentioning of God, but this is done in a particular way. The very first words of the preamble are a quote, without quotation marks, of the national anthem ("God bless the Hungarians"), a poem from 1823 that was the anthem even during the communist period. The anthem is sometimes sung at the end of church services, and in this context it has a religious content. At soccer games or other public events, however, it is likely that many Hungarians sing it (or listen to it) without any religious feelings. In this case the national anthem is the manifestation of patriotism, with a text that is deeply rooted in the national culture. At the very end of the Basic Law there is a solemn declaration which recalls the wording of the preamble of the Basic Law of Germany, where the members of Parliament passing the Basic Law declare to be aware of their responsibility before God and man. It can be noted that the everyday Hungarian language has preserved a religious vocabulary (literary "happy birthday" translates as "God shall make you live"; "Welcome" is "God has brought you"; in most cases these expressions do not imply any religious sentiments).

The preamble of the Basic Law ("national avowal") contains an acknowledgement of the role of Christianity:

> We recognize the role of Christianity in preserving nationhood. We value the various religious traditions of our country.

This is on the one hand the acknowledgement of an historical fact, on the other hand it is not the religious content of Christianity that is endorsed, but its role in forming the nation. The preamble also shows respect to the various religious traditions of the country through a general reference that does not call any of them by their name. A reference to non-religious, secular or agnostic heritage is missing; the omission makes the text less inclusive than, for example, the preamble of the Polish Constitution of 1997 (Jakab 2011). The mention of Christianity in the preamble

[2] Data available at: http://www.bmbah.hu/index.php?option=com_k2&view=item&layout=item&id=492&Itemid=1259&lang=en#

exclusively refers to the historical role of religion, and not to its present role in society (Horkay Hörcher 2012). In this way, the historical acknowledgement is not a prescriptive provision but a descriptive statement, which does not compromise the neutrality of the state with regard to religion (Csink and Fröhlich 2012).

Doctrine on Religion and State

The doctrine on neutrality, elaborated by the Constitutional Court on the basis of the previous constitution (1949, revised in 1989), may be seen as providing the most important principle governing the State in its relationship with religions and other ideologies. The State should remain neutral in matters concerning ideology; there should be no official ideology, be it religious or secular. Neutrality means that the State should not identify itself with any ideology (or religion); consequently it must not be institutionally connected to any churches or to one of them, nor to any organization based on an ideology. This shows that the underlying doctrine behind the principle of separation (as explicitly stated in the Basic Law) is the neutrality of the State. It is to be noted that neutrality has to be distinguished from indifference, which is not what the new Basic Law implies. Neutrality is neither secularism nor something like the French doctrine on 'laïcité'; the State may have an active role in providing an institutional legal framework as well as providing funding for the churches to ensure the free exercise of religion effectively. There are positive and negative sides to freedom of religion; freedom to religion and freedom from religion are equally protected. All public institutions, including schools, universities, hospitals, etc., are bound by the principle of neutrality.[3] There are no religious symbols at public institutions.

Church autonomy can be seen as the most important difference between entities registered as religious communities and other registered legal entities[4] such as associations, political parties, or trade unions. Autonomy in the stricter legal sense means that the internal acts of organizations registered as 'churches' are not subject to any kind of state interference. This means that whereas an internal decision of an association can be brought before court (and courts have the power to strike down internal decisions that are unlawful or violate the charter of the association), an internal decision of a church entity, like a bishop or a synod, cannot be challenged before state courts. Churches are also not bound by the principle of democratic internal structure, while associations have to be democratic. Churches determine their structure independently from the State; neither consent nor notification is required, for example, in the case of creating new dioceses.

---

[3] Decision 4/1993. (II. 12.) AB. In English: L. Sólyom & G. Brunner (eds.): Constitutional Judiciary in a New Democracy: the Hungarian Constitutional Court. Michigan, 2000.

[4] Decision 8/1993. (II. 27.) AB.

A General Legal System

Hungary has no system of personal laws. Marriage became secular with the civil marriage law of 1895. There have been severe discriminations against Jews from 1938 to 1945 – and from 1941 to 1945 a ban on marriages between Christians and Jews (latter defined on racial criteria) was also enforced.

State laws do not include religious rules in the strict sense. "Thou shall not kill" could have been regarded as a religious norm but has become a generally accepted legal prescription. The right to life as a human right can also be seen as a fundamental value affirmed by all religions and all religious legal systems – from a certain perspective even Constitutions, human rights documents, and criminal codes could be seen as reproducing religious norms. Some elements of state law may have religious origins – or may be rooted in natural law. For example the fact that marriage is only possible between one man and one woman – as it is also stated by the Basic Law – could be seen as a "reproduction" of a religious norm whereas others would regard it as an evident element of natural law. The legislator, however, does not refer to religious norms.

In a very broad sense, the public recognition of holidays or the protection of Sunday as a day of rest could be seen as provisions having a clearly identifiable religious background, motivated now by secular purposes and a general social acceptance. Therefore, a number of public holidays do not qualify as special religious festivities (i.e. Easter Monday or Pentecost Monday), whereas a number of religious festivities are not recognized as days of rest (i.e. Assumption or Epiphany). Since 2015 the protection of Sundays as general days of rest has been strengthened as most shops have to close on Sundays. In the debate on the changes in the legislation, religious arguments were hardly articulated. In the forefront of the discussion the employees' rights were emphasized. Concerning Sunday laws, a case was brought before the Constitutional Court in the early 1990s by a group of observing Jews in Hungary who challenged the provisions of the Labour Code,[5] arguing that the free exercise of their religion was not assured by legislation to an equal extent as that of the Christian religion, as the Labour Code establishes only Christian holidays as days of rest (the 25 and the 26 of December, Easter Monday, and Pentecost Monday). Furthermore, Saturdays could be designated as days of work by the Minister of Labour in order to provide 'long weekends'. For example, if a public holiday fell on Thursday or Tuesday, the day between the holiday and the weekend was made a day of rest, whereas the Saturday of the previous or the following week became a working day. Instead, Sundays were not to become working days. The Constitutional Court stated that the constitutional obligations of the state prohibit the privileged treatment of one religion (i.e. by declaring all of its holidays as days of rest). However, the state must ensure the free exercise of all religions. Historically, religious motives did determine the state decision in picking the holidays; however,

[5] At the time of the case: Act XXII/1992 §125. The new labor code contains similar regulations: Act I/2012 § 102 (1), (5).

the present holidays are the ones the vast majority of society (not only practicing Christians) celebrate. Christmas and Easter, for example, are closely connected to family and folk traditions. No Jewish holiday gained such popular acceptance. The protection of Sunday used to have a religious background; however, nowadays it has lost that background. Sunday as a general day of rest is almost universal. The uniformity of this day of rest has a secular purpose.[6] This means that it is not a majority claim that is accommodated.[7] As employees have the right to decide on one-fourth of their paid leave without the consent of the employer,[8] this ensures that religious minorities are able to observe their holy days (these, however, are not extra days of rest). Certainly, the calendar itself is determined by religious rules. For example. almost all countries in Europe follow the Gregorian calendar, but some countries in Eastern Europe continue to follow the Orthodox calendar determining Easter day and other holy days. Originally the calendar had an evidently religious significance, but nowadays it is endorsed by the state without deeper theoretical considerations.

Conscientious objection is generally regarded as an individual right. A person seeking a religiously motivated exemption has to refer to his individual conscience rather than to his membership in a religious community. Exemptions based on conscience motives could apply to military service (at peacetime they are no longer relevant as national service has been abolished), to the carrying out of abortions by medical staff or to other delicate matters where the convictions of the individual are of paramount importance. Whether convictions are based on a religious faith or on other grounds is irrelevant. Religious slaughter can be carried out when it is religiously motivated: the exemption is not granted to religious communities but depends on the religious nature of the claim. In this way the law does not mention any religious community.[9]

Church Run Institutions

The autonomy of religious communities is respected by the state. This autonomy includes the respect of the identity of institutions run by religious communities. The special loyalty required from employees may also be determined by the respect of religious laws stipulated by internal regulations of religious communities.

---

[6] Decision 10/1993 (II. 27) AB.

[7] The solution the Constitutional Court has reached in this case is similar to the one the Supreme Court of the United States of America reached in the *McGowan v. Maryland* : 'There is no dispute that the original laws which dealt with Sunday labor were motivated by religious forces. [However], the present purpose and effect ... is to provide a uniform day of rest for all citizens; the fact that this day is Sunday, a day of particular significance for dominant Christian sects, does not bar the State from achieving its secular goals.' [366 U.S. 420 (1961)].

[8] Act XXII/1992. (Labour Code) §134(3). According to the current legislation seven days per year can be decided by the employee unilaterally: Act I/2012. § 122 (2).

[9] Act XXVIII/1998 §19 (d).

Church Autonomy – "Internal Law" of Religious Communities

The meaning of separation may be defined, on the one hand, as the respect of the autonomy (or self-determination) of the churches ('the State must not interfere with the internal organisation of any church'),[10] and, on the other hand, as the principle stated in the law on religious freedom that no State pressure may be applied to enforce the internal laws and rules of a church.[11] Religious communities are not allowed to make use of State power. In the relationship between the individual and his or her church, governed by church internal rules, the State plays no role. The State has no competence concerning the nomination of religious authorities or ministers.

Internal rules of religious communities would qualify as "religious rules". Cultural traditions and other customs may have religious origins as well (e.g. Sunday as a day of rest) but would not be regarded as religious rules.

The state law does not refer to religious laws or principles. Religious rules are generally not applicable in the state legal system but in certain cases the state law does refer to the internal rules of religious communities. In this way, the internal statutes of religious communities may have relevance. The 'internal law' of the churches is regarded to be law by the state, though lacking the enforcement of state authorities. State law makes a number of references to the internal laws of the churches, even through the 'reception' of them. That is, the legal character of the 'internal law' (like Canon law) is acknowledged by the State in certain cases. The most important case of the application of the internal church law by state authorities is the acknowledgment of legal entities by the state. According to the law, if the 'charter' of the church provides so, the organizational units of the church with an independent organ of representation (dioceses, parishes and institutions like a church run university, hospital or else) are legal entities in the State legal system.[12] This means that the internal law of the religious communities determines whether legal entities acknowledged by the state come into existence or not – no further state registration of these entities is required (in the case of the Catholic Church, the Code of Canon Law and the Code of Canons of the Eastern Churches determine which church entities have legal personality in the Hungarian legal system). If there is any doubt, the representatives of a Church can refer to their charter, and judges may need to study Church law to find out about the status of Church entities in state law.

For example, the entities of religious communities that enjoy legal personality according to the internal rules of a religious community (like parishes according to the Code of Canon Law in the case of the Catholic Church) are recognized by the state as legal entities.

[10] Decision 4/1993. (II. 12.) AB.

[11] Act CCVI/2011. §8 (2).

[12] Act CCVI/2011. §12(1).

According to a leading case decided by the Supreme Court, separation of church and state does not mean that religious ministers are not liable for infringing personal rights in the course of religious activities. In the given case the plaintiff argues that a statement in a judgment issued by a church court has infringed his good reputation. Lower courts declared to have no jurisdiction in the case, invoking Article 15, section (2) Act IV/1990, on the Freedom of Conscience and Religion, and the Churches stating that 'No state pressure may be applied in the interest of enforcing the internal laws and regulations of a church.' The Supreme Court, however, held that in the given case there were no internal laws at stake, but personal rights that can be invoked without regard to the fact that the alleged infringement (a church trial) has happened in the framework of a church.[13] Certainly, the church trial itself could not be appealed with a state court. The same would apply to sermons delivered at churches. Church premises do not constitute a lawless territory.

The 'vocational secret' embraces the seal of confession, but goes beyond it in a religion-neutral way. Vocational secrets cannot be made public.[14] In civil[15] and administrative[16] procedures, clergy may make use of a provision that allows for a refusal to testify in the case of 'professional' secrets. In this way, the confessional secret is protected as a professional secret, equal to the protection that medical doctors or lawyers enjoy concerning those secrets with which they are entrusted in the practice of their profession. This means that clergy may refuse to answer questions that fall under professional secrecy. According to the criminal procedure code, clergy enjoy a qualified protection, as they may not be questioned about issues on which they invoke the seal of confession.[17] This means that it is not for the clergy to refuse to testify, but the court and the public prosecutor must not interrogate them. No state authority has the right to challenge the scope of professional secrecy.

A few more examples where state law refers to the internal law of churches can be found in tax law and the law on social security. In these two fields the term 'ecclesiastical person', referring to persons subject to some special regulations, is employed (Szuromi and Ferenczy 2009). This definition is determined by the internal law of churches, that is, the internal law of the churches determines which people fall under this definition provided by the secular state law. The same applies in the case of the law on national defence that grants privileges to clergymen acting in their religious capacity[18] (they are not drafted for example). It lies within Church competence to determine whom they regard as clergy. As mentioned above, procedural laws accept the protection of vocational secrets. Church regulations decide what kind of secrets need special protection.

The law dealing with compensation for people unjustly deprived of their life and liberty for political reasons under the regimes between 1939 and 1989 uses the term

[13] BH 2004.180.

[14] Act CCVI/2011. §13(3).

[15] Act III/1952. §170(1)c).

[16] Act CLX/2004. §53(3)b).

[17] Act XIX/1988. §81(1)a).

[18] Act CXIII/2011. §12(2)f).

'ecclesiastical person under the ban of marriage'.[19] Besides Catholic clergy, the members of religious orders would qualify under this category – the law does not call the Catholic Church by its name but in fact the provision only applies to Catholic victims. Whilst with other victims, compensation was provided to family members, in the case of 'ecclesiastical persons' their diocese was entitled to receive the compensation as in their case there was no descendant. The constitutionality of this provision was challenged under the separation clause of the Constitution. The Constitutional Court refused the petition in its 'seventh compensation decision'. As the Court stated:

> in the case of ecclesiastical persons under the ban of marriage, the persons usually referred to in the cases of those who died having a wife and children are missing. The legislator made the diocese – applying a legal fiction – a quasi relative. This is the reason of the compensation and not that the legislator wanted to grant compensation to the church legal entity. The basis of equal treatment in this case is that the law entitles an entity to be compensated also for the death of ecclesiastical persons killed unjustly, who did not have a wife and descendants due to their ecclesiastical wow. The law does not violate the constitutional declaration of the separation of church and state 'as the state takes into account the independence of churches while taking their specialties into consideration where necessary and guarantees their freedom.[20]

The compensation of far-right and Communist crime is almost history now, but taking the 'ban of marriage' as an exclusively internal rule into consideration in state legislation is still relevant.

In a similar way, the canonical provisions on the ban of marriage are taken into consideration in the criminal procedure. When 'ecclesiastical persons' become victims of crimes, the rights recognized to the relatives of victims can be exercised by their superiors.[21] This way the law pays attention to a special personal circumstance.

The examples above show that, under certain circumstances, state law makes references to the internal law (such as Canon law) of the churches. In some cases, this is due to practical considerations, as for the legislator it is easier to refer to internal rules instead of setting up a general framework, e.g. to require all communities to have a similar internal structure. In other cases, the principle of separation (the respect of church autonomy) sets a limit on how far the state law can go. Consequently, the acknowledgment of the right of the churches to make internal laws is an important sign of the acknowledgment of their autonomy. These internal laws can have relevance under state law and can be applied by state organs in actual procedures.

[19] Act XXXII/1992. §2(4).

[20] Decision 1/1995. (II. 8.) AB.

[21] Act XIX/1998. § 51.§(3).

Social Accommodation?

There are no special prescriptions calling for the accommodation of religious needs in private legal relations (including labor relations). A positive attitude towards religious needs could be derived from general principles of tolerance, the cooperation principle in private law. The workplace, the school and all other kinds of public spaces are supposed to be characterized by tolerance. Individuals and communities would be expected to welcome or tolerate religious expressions and practice. Eventually however, as a consequence of the communist regime, religion has been privatized to a high extent. Citizens, under most circumstances, tend to by shy about their religion, as they do not stand up for their beliefs.

Adjudication

Under the principle of separation (Basic Law Art. VII (2)), churches administer the issues they regard to be within their competence independently. As a consequence of the same principle, the internal jurisdiction (like on the issues of marriage in the case of the Catholic Church or other internal decisions) have no significance of any kind for the state.

Doctrine on Internal Disputes

The relation between internal and external jurisdictions was demonstrated in a remarkable case. A professor – a pastor of the Reformed Church – was sent into retirement by the Faculty of Theology of Debrecen in 1995, following a request of a group of students. He first accepted the decision but later challenged it and started an internal church procedure. First he turned to the Synod Court of the Reformed Church and appealed against his rejection to the presidency of the synod. After having lost his case within the Church, he sued the Church as well as the University at the local State court for damages caused by retirement (in Hungary pension is usually significantly less than the salaries earned before). The local court of Debrecen rejected his petition, affirming that the separation of church and state ruled out the possibility that breaking internal church rules could constitute the payment of financial damages according to state law.[22] The court of appeal quashed the decision and transferred the case to the Synod Court as the court of appeal came to the conclusion that the Synod Court was competent according to internal church regulations.[23] The Supreme Court withdrew the transfer of the case to the church court as such transfers

[22] 7.P.21.766/1997/5.

[23] 4.Pf.22.069/1997/4.

are only possible between state organs for competence reasons and a state court had no competence to interpret church regulations.[24] By then the Synod Court had already addressed the case again and decided to transfer it to the local Labor Court.[25] This court decided it had no competence as the internal church service of a pastor was not based on a labor contract. The court of appeal upheld this decision[26] and so did the Supreme Court.[27]

After three decisions of church organs and six decisions delivered by state courts the retired professor filed a constitutional complaint. Different courts took different positions about their jurisdiction over a dispute between a church and its pastor, as section 15 (2) of the Act IV/1990 on Freedom of Conscience and Religion and the Churches states that, as a consequence of the constitutional separation between church and state, "No state pressure may be applied to enforce the internal laws and regulations of a church." The Constitutional Court – while dismissing the application – stated that the separation of church and state cannot be interpreted in a way that leaves without remedy those getting into a legal relationship with a church. The remedies, however, can only apply to those aspects regulated by state law. Aspects regulated by internal church law (Canon law or the statutes of a religious community) cannot be the subject of disputes in State courts. The Constitutional Court expressly referred to the possibility of private individuals to waive their right to seek legal remedy in some legal relations.[28] Generally, private law allows contractual provisions which exclude litigation while in labor relations, however access to courts cannot be restricted by contracts.

The new law on religious freedom (Act CCVI/2011) reflects the results of the dispute about the autonomy of religious communities, more precisely the autonomy concerning internal church disputes. Church and State are supposed to operate separately under the Basic Law.[29] As the law states:

> No state power may be used to enforce decisions made on the basis of the principles of faith, the internal laws, the statutes or the rules of organization and operation of a religious community, or other rules equivalent to them (hereinafter jointly referred to as Internal Rules); public authorities may not examine such decisions. Public bodies may not modify or override decisions made by a religious community based on Internal Rules, and they shall have no competence to adjudicate legal disputes arising from internal legal relationships not regulated by the laws.[30]

Consequently, in the relationship between a religious community and its members, legal instruments of public power may not play a role. For example, the system that is in place in Germany applies to the collection of the church taxes of major religious communities by the state taxation authority and this could not be

[24] Pfv.VI.21.240/1998/2.

[25] 3.M.554/1998/9.

[26] 2.Mf.21.703/1999/3.

[27] Mfv.I.10.168/2000.

[28] Decision 32/2003. (VI.4.) AB.

[29] Basic Law Art. VII.(3).

[30] Act CCVI/2011. §8(2).

introduced in Hungary (Marré 1995). Internal canonical obligations with regard to the financial support of the church, the religious upbringing of children or the attendance of religious services cannot be enforced with the help of state organs. Certainly if these parties enter into a contractual relationship under state law, this relationship is subjected to state remedies.

The new Church Law also mirrors a dispute over the jurisdictional autonomy of churches. Béla Szathmáry, professor of church law at the Reformed Theological College of Sárospatak repeatedly argued in favour of "apellatio ab abusu", the possibility to appeal to state courts against decisions taken in internal church disputes (Szathmáry 2010 and Schanda 2011). The main concern surrounding the argument was the lack of an effective remedy for religious ministers. According to his suggestion not only church decisions contrary to state law, but also church decisions violating internal church regulations should be subjected to scrutiny by state courts. The new law clearly rejects the possibility of the internal regulations becoming the subject of litigation before State courts due to the principle of separation.

The state ignores internal disputes within religious communities; in other words it respects the jurisdictional autonomy of religious communities. Neither marriage cases of Catholic courts nor disciplinary cases from Protestant churches have any relevance for state courts. As church jurisdiction is regarded as an internal issue without legal relevance, due process/fair trial principles are not relevant in the internal procedures of religious organizations. Certainly, church courts are also bound by the generally applicable laws: a judge of a church court can be found guilty of defamation if his statements qualify as such. Respecting freedom of religion and self-determination of religious communities means that the State does not interfere with internal alternative jurisdictions of religious communities.

Religious communities generally appreciate the separation model that emerged in Hungary and churches are keen on their autonomy. When center-to-right wing governments suggested the acknowledgement of church marriages (or weddings) within state law, churches were not particularly happy, pointing to eventual dangers arising from a divergent understanding of marriage and to legal conflicts (Ferenczy and Szuromi 2002). Autonomy seems to be higher on the Church agenda than entanglement.

The Praxis of Religious Communities with Regard to Internal Disputes

No religious community has an internal jurisdiction system comparable to the Catholic Church. Almost all cases discussed at Catholic Church courts are related to marriage issues. As the Primate of Hungary has a court of third instance, practically all annulation cases are concluded in Hungary and do not arrive to the Rota Romana (in this way saving heavy translation expenses). As the annulations of canonical marriages have no civil effects, in most cases the process is started after a civil divorce, often when parties have entered into a new relationship and try to settle their status in the Church. The number of annulments per year could be between 100 and 200 in the whole country, but there is no public data on annulment procedures. Decisions on annulations have no relevance in state law.

Other denominations have no similarly developed internal adjudication. The judicial concept of the Reformed (Calvinist) Church is based on the notion of universal priesthood of all faithful. Theoretically all members of the congregation share the judicial power. The Church has an established internal judicial structure dealing with various disciplinary cases and internal disputes, and handle recourses against administrative and synod decisions. Judges at the parish level can be members of the congregation who could warn another member of the congregation. This warning would already be considered as a kind of judicial act as in its theological understanding it would be regarded as passing a judicial decision. Separate church courts are organized at the level of dioceses, church provinces and at the level of the national synod. Courts always consist of panels where the number of ordained pastors and lay members (non-clerics) has to be equal. Lay members of church courts have to be trained lawyers who are otherwise active in any field of legal practice, including legal scholars (Szathmáry 2004b). Diocesan courts operate as courts of first instance in administrative cases concerning parishes and disciplinary cases against pastors (the lawyer of the diocese acts as prosecutor in such cases). Provincial courts examine the appeals against judgments of diocesan courts as well as the cases of the institutions maintained by the church province. The Synod Court handles disciplinary cases of bishops, professors of theology, national institutions and appeals against administrative decisions of the church pension fund. The Synod Court can also issue decisions to ensure the coherence of court practice when different courts pass diverging decisions. The church courts should focus on educating the faithful. The theoretically well-structured court system covers, in practice, just a handful of disciplinary cases or cases related to the service and retirement of pastors. A widely reported case was a procedure against a far-rightwing pastor of central Budapest who displayed a statute of Admiral Horthy, governor of Hungary from 1920 to 1944 at the entrance of his church. The case finished with a written reprimand. More common disciplinary cases are about financial misconducts of pastors – cases that would be handled in the Catholic Church through an administrative procedure. Doctrinal cases are rare, whereas cases regulated by state law cannot be brought to a church court.

Also, the Lutheran Church has a similar court system composed of diocesan and provincial courts as well as a national court. Cases relate to disciplinary issues and administrative recourses against decisions of various church bodies (Szathmáry 2004a).

Smaller religious communities did not establish an internal judicial system, although some may have disciplinary procedures to handle disputes.

Internal disputes of religious communities only receive media coverage when the case has political relevance like the one of the above-mentioned Calvinist pastor. As the scope of religious adjudication is generally narrow, public attention is not significant either.

Traditional religious minorities are well integrated into society and the challenge of integrating large numbers of migrants with a diverse religious background has not gained much relevance yet. There are no indications in Hungary that a significant number of citizens apply religious rules in conflict with state laws. It is a heritage of the socialist regime that religion has become highly privatized and most citizens rather avoid conflicts than stand for their beliefs. There are no significant signs of religious conflicts or hostilities raised by religious practices. A few cases were occasionally reported when parents mistreated their children and explained their behavior with religious motivations.

Conclusion

In Hungary religious communities and the state carry out their functions entirely separated. Internal (religious) norms have no relevance for the state, whereas the autonomy of religious communities is respected. The consequent legal separation of religious communities and state law does not mean that cooperation between church and state is not important in many fields of social life. Religion may also play an important role in fostering social cohesion. Religious practice for adherents of mainstream religious communities may be easier than for members of minority communities. This, however, has practical explanations and is not the result of a state discriminatory regulation but of a social reality. In general, the practice of any religion (traditional or non-traditional) may be more burdensome than practicing no religion. Religious communities are 'left alone' in handling their internal disputes but their internal law, its interpretation and practice may have relevance concerning State legal procedures and remedies.

References

Csink, Lóránt, and Fröhlich, Johanna. 2012. Egy alkotmány margójára. Alkotmányelméleti és értelmezési kérdések az Alaptörvényről, 117. Budapest: Gondolat Kiadó.

Ferenczy, Rita, and Szuromi, Szabolcs. 2002. Az egyházi házasság mint államilag elismert házassági kötelék (Kritikai megjegyzések jogtörténeti, civiljogi és kánonjogi szempontból). *Jogtudományi Közlöny 57*: 184–189.

Horkay Hörcher, Ferenc. 2012. The National Avowal. In *The Basic Law of Hungary. A first commentary*, ed. Lóránt Csink, Balázs Schanda, and András Zs. Varga, 25–45. Dublin: Clarus Press.

Jakab, András. 2011. Az új Alaptörvény keletkezése és gyakorlati következményei, 181. Budapest: HVG-ORAC.

Marré, Heiner. 1995. Das kirchliche Besteuerungsrecht. In *Handbuch des Staatskirchenrechts der Bundesrepublik Deutschlands*, vol. 1, ed. Joseph Listl and Dietrich Pirson, 1001–1147. Berlin: Dunker & Humblot.

Schanda, Balázs. 2011. Egyházi önállóság és vallásszabadság. Válasz Szathmáry Béla: Az appellatio ab abusu a magyar jogrendszerben c. cikkére. *Magyar jog* 58: 148–151.

Szathmáry, Béla. 2004a. Református Egyházjog. In *Felekezeti egyházjog*, ed. Lajos Rácz, 373–422. Budapest: Atlantisz.

Szathmáry, Béla. 2004b. *Magyar egyházjog*, 367–378. Budapest: Századvég.

Szathmáry, Béla. 2010. Az apellatio ab abusu a magyar jogrendszerben. *Magyar jog* 57: 416–422.

Szuromi, Szabolcs Anzelm, and Ferenczy, Rita. 2009. A katolikus egyházi személyek foglalkoztatásának sajátos helyzete a mai magyar jogban. *Jogtudományi Közlöny* 64: 379–381.

Chapter 13
The Application of Religious Law in a Multi-Religion Nation State: The Israeli Model

Asher Maoz

Abstract The Israeli legal system may serve as a laboratory for the application of religious law in a multi-religious state. While defined as a Jewish State so many religions are represented here, some embracing large communities others having a little numbers of followers in some cases no more than a handful. It would be wrong however to view the Israeli system as a classic model. The approach to religion in the State of Israel is inherently eclectic. It combines traditional and new theories, communal and individual rights, freedom from religion and religious coercion, freedom of religion from state intervention, equality among religions and differential treatment of them. These eclectic principles are rooted in historical, theological, political and national grounds. Perhaps the most significant factor contributing to the complexity of relations between religion and state in Israel is that this part of the world – the Holy Land – is the birthplace of monotheism. It occupies a central place in the theology of many religions, including the three main monotheistic religions, each religion having its own view of the relationship between state and religion, which sometimes come into conflict. Moreover, the principles and practices of previous regimes that governed the Holy Land still have their influence, even though today Israel is predominantly Jewish in culture and religion. This essay aims to give a comprehensive yet concise overview of the status of the application of religious law in the State of Israel against this complex background.

Introduction

The approach to religion in the State of Israel is inherently eclectic. It combines traditional and new theories, communal and individual rights, freedom from religion and religious coercion, freedom of religion from state intervention, equality among

A. Maoz (✉)
Peres Academic Center, Rehovot, Israel
e-mail: maoza@post.tau.ac.il

R. Bottoni et al. (eds.), *Religious Rules, State Law, and Normative Pluralism - A Comparative Overview*, Ius Comparatum – Global Studies in Comparative Law 18, DOI 10.1007/978-3-319-28335-7_13

religions and differential treatment of them. These eclectic principles are rooted in historical, theological, political and national grounds. Perhaps the most significant factor contributing to the complexity of relations between religion and state in Israel is that this part of the world – the Holy Land – is the birthplace of monotheism. It occupies a central place in the theology of many religions, including the three main monotheistic religions, each religion having its own view of the relationship of state and religion, which sometimes come into conflict. Moreover, the principles and practices of previous regimes that governed the Holy Land still have their influence, even though today Israel is predominantly Jewish in culture and religion.

Religious Demography and Structure

On the eve of its 67th anniversary (April 2015), the State of Israel had a population of 8,345,000 people, including the Golan Heights and territories annexed to Jerusalem after the 1967 war. By religious affiliation, 74.9 % (6,251,000) were Jews (including Israeli settlers in the West Bank, known also as Judea and Samaria) and "others" (non-Arab Christians and those not classified by religion) and 20.7 % (1,730,000) Arabs, including Lebanese who were not classified by religion at the Population Register (1,700 at the end of 2014).

At the end of 2014, the population de jure – *i.e.* the legally resident population including residents temporarily absent and excluding temporary residents – of the State of Israel totaled 8,296,900 people: 74.96 % (6,219,200) were Jews, 17.52 % (1453800) Muslims, 1.97 % (163,500) Christian and 1.63 % (135,400) Druze. Additionally, there were 74,567 legal foreign workers; 15,315 illegal foreign workers and 90,000 tourists without a valid visa. There were also 46,437 illegal immigrants from Africa, mainly from North-Sudan and Eritrea.

Alongside the Jewish population, there are two small communities: the Karaites, a movement that abide by the Written Torah and rejects the Oral, or Rabbinic, Law (about 31,200 members) and the Samaritans, an ethno religious group that asserts their religion to be the authentic religion of the ancient Israelites (some 760).

The Muslim population in Israel is diverse: most of the Muslims adhere to the Sunnite rite. Out of the four schools of faith within Sunnite Islam, the Shafi'i mazhab is most common among rural Muslims while the Hanafi mazhab is prominent in urban areas. The latter is also followed in the State recognized *sharia* religious courts.

Most Muslims are Arabs. There exists, however, the Circassian community (4000) and the Ahmadis (1500). Two communities which stem from Islam and are no longer considered Muslim are the Druze community (135,400), and the Bahai faith, which includes approximately 650 members, most of them foreign citizens who serve in the community's institutions.

Many Muslims live in villages. There are also towns with a large Muslim population. There are a few mixed Jewish – Arabic townships. The Muslims live mainly within a traditional community and are characterized by strong religious sentiments that might have been strengthened via nationalistic motivation. The fundamentalism which flooded the Muslims, especially in this part of the world, did not skip over Israeli Arabs. A political religious movement, called "The Islamic Movement", was created. It combines religious fundamentalism with nationalistic ideology. The movement gained strength and heads the local councils in some of the largest Arab settlements. Its southern, more moderate, faction is represented by three members in the *Knesset*, the Israeli parliament. In spite of their relatively small number, the Christians are divided into some 35 different churches and denominations. The variety of churches in Israel should not be of a surprise in view of the central role of the Holy Land in Christianity, and of the vast number of holy Christian sites in Israel.

The various churches may be classified into four main groups: the Catholic Churches, with the largest number of adherents; the Orthodox Churches, the most important of which is the Greek Orthodox; the Monophysite, or pre-Chalcedonian Churches, who originated in the fifth century following a theological split regarding Christ's nature; and the Anglican Church, which is new in the Holy Land and dates back to early 19th century.

There are several estimations as to the division of the Christians among the various churches, but no exact figures are available. The largest churches are the Greek Catholic and the Greek Orthodox. According to the Jerusalem Center for Jewish-Christian relations ("JCJCR"), more than 70 % of the Christian population is either Greek Catholic or Greek Orthodox. Another large community is the Latin (Roman Catholic) Church (15 %). Next, though much smaller, is the Maronite Church (8 %). Other Christian denominations have a rather small number of followers, in some cases no more than a few dozen, and in other cases even fewer. Smaller churches include Jehovah's Witnesses, Seventh-Day Adventists, Baptists, Mormons, Quakers and Lutherans. There are also representatives of several overseas churches, which do not enjoy a local following – Assyrians, Coptic Orthodox, Presbyterians. In the past years, dozens of churches opened to serve the foreign workers and illegal immigrants currently in Israel.

Historical Background

A key to understanding the position of the State of Israel towards religion and towards the State and religion relationship is the *status quo*, the preservation of the existing status. The basic structure of State – Church relations is the legal position laid down during the Ottoman era (1517–1917), which preceded the British occupation of Palestine.

During that period Islam was the established religion of the Empire. Islamic religious law, the *sharia*, was applied in the area of personal status, being family law in its broad sense, by Muslim religious courts which enjoyed the status of State courts. As to non Muslims, a distinction was drawn between "the heathens" on one hand and on the other hand religions based on the Sacred Book (the *Kitabaia*), namely Jews ("The people of the book") and the Christians. With respect to the latter the Ottoman Sultan adopted a system of *millet* or "nation". Under this system, organizational autonomy and jurisdiction in matters of personal status were granted to recognized religious communities. The law applicable was the religious law of the concerned community.

The basic structure of law and jurisdiction in the area of personal status – including the wide jurisdiction of the Muslim courts, save for the fact that they stopped functioning as State courts – was preserved by the British and by the State of Israel. There were eleven recognized religious communities: the Islamic, the Jewish and nine Christian Communities the Eastern (Orthodox) Community, the Latin (Catholic) Community, the Gregorian Armenian Community, the Armenian (Catholic) Community, the Syrian (Catholic) Community, the Chaldean (Uniate) Community, the Greek (Catholic) Melkite Community, the Maronite Community and the Syrian Orthodox Community. The State of Israel added to this list the Druze Community as well as the Evangelic Episcopal Church and the Bahai Community.

At present, all religious courts have exclusive jurisdiction in matters of marriage and divorce of members of their respective communities. In other matters of personal status some courts enjoy exclusive jurisdiction while others exercise concurrent jurisdiction with the civil courts. Moreover, the Knesset has removed several matters from the application of personal law and has applied civil law to them.

The judges of both the Rabbinical and Muslim courts, as well as the Druze courts, are appointed by the President of the State upon the recommendation of election committees similar to the committee for the election of civil court judges. The committees consist of members of the relevant religious court, government and Knesset representatives and representatives of the Israeli Bar and are headed by the Minister of Justice. Recently the Knesset passed a law requiring that four of eleven members of the Rabbinical Court Judges Election Committee must be women. There exist no similar provision regarding the Muslim and Druze religious courts. No statutory provisions exist as to the appointment of judges to the Christian religious courts and to their procedure and administration. They remain at the discretion of each community.

The law provides for the structure of the Jewish religious institutions. The legal structure and authority of the Chief Rabbinate is set in the Chief Rabbinate of Israel Law of 1980. Similarly, statutory law provides for the establishment of Jewish religious councils and defines their powers. The form of electing the Chief Rabbis of the State, the Council of the Chief Rabbinate, the Religious Councils and City Rabbis is provided for by statutory law. There is a large proportion of public representation in the electoral assemblies of not necessarily devout people. The Supreme Court ruled that the qualifications for membership in Religious Councils are not based on *halakha* since they cater for the entire Jewish community not merely for religious Jews.[1] It ruled moreover that persons who do not belong to the Orthodox religious streams may not be disqualified from membership in the Religious Councils.[2] In another case the Supreme Court ruled that women may not be disqualified from serving in electoral assembly of rabbis.[3] Following the Supreme

[1] HCJ 153/87 Shakdiel v. Minister of Religious Affairs, IsrSC 42(2) 221 [1988].

[2] HCJ 4733/94 *Naot v. Haifa Municipal Council*, IsrSC 49(5) 111 (1996).

[3] HCJ 953/87 *Poraz v. Mayor of Tel-Aviv – Jaffa*, IsrSC 42(2) 309 [1988] (In Hebrew).

Court decisions the Knesset intervened and ordered that half of the representatives of the government, as well as the Knesset and the Bar in the election committee of religious judges must be women. Likewise half of the representatives of the municipal council and of the Religious Services Minister to the electoral assemblies of municipal rabbis must be women. No similar provisions exist for any other religious communities. On the other hand no rabbi who belongs to non-Orthodox religious streams might be elected for official rabbinical positions as well as sitting on the Rabbinical Courts bench. This is so since their eligibility must be conferred by the Council of the Chief Rabbinat, which is Orthodox by composition.

Religious institutions and services are financed by the State, though the form of support of the different communities differs (Maoz 1996, 366–373). Recently, the Ministry for Religious Affairs agreed to finance non-Orthodox rabbis following petitions to the Supreme Court.

The communal structure of family law in Israel left members of non-recognized religious communities and persons, which adhere to no religion, at a limbo. Not less problematic was the situation of spouses who belonged to different religious communities. Only in 1969 did the Knesset intervene to enable such people to dissolve their marriage, and only in 2010 did the Knesset provide for the registration of civil unions. However, even this narrow venue is open to persons that are not affiliated to recognized religious communities, thus frustrating the possibility of mixed unions.

Israel as a Jewish State

Israel does not lend itself easily to the traditional classification of state and religion relationship. While it was established as a "Jewish State" it would be most accurate to define the State of Israel as a multi-religion state where various religions are recognized, yet none enjoys the status of official state religion.

The Declaration of the Establishment of the State of Israel specifically states that Israel will be "a Jewish state". This is in line with the Balfour Declaration of 1917 and the Resolution of the League of Nations of 1922 calling for the establishment of "a national home for the Jewish people" in Palestine and the U.N. General Assembly Resolution of 1947 about the establishment of independent Arab and Jewish States in Palestine (the "Partition Resolution").

The Declaration had no constitutional status, yet as expressing "the aspirations of the people and their basic credo" it served as an important instrument in interpreting written law and in introducing extra-legal principles. In 1994 the principles of the Declaration were raised to a constitutional level when the Basic Laws dealing with human rights were amended to state that "[h]uman rights in Israel … will be safeguarded in the spirit of the principles contained in the Declaration of Independence". The Jewish nature of the State of Israel has moreover been fortified by the Basic Laws declaring that "the values of the State of Israel as a Jewish and democratic State" are the basis of human rights in Israel.

Basic Law: The Knesset further prevents a list or candidate whose aims or actions negate the existence of Israel as a Jewish and democratic state from participating in the Knesset elections.

The "Jewish and democratic" formula is wide enough to embrace both freedom of religion and freedom from religion. However, *Basic Law: Human Dignity*, which was enacted in 1992, provides that it shall not affect the validity of any law, including religious laws, in force prior to the commencement of the Basic Law. Thus, any law negating the provisions of the Basic Law remains in force though the court will interpret it in accordance with its values.

Furthermore, the 1980 Foundation of Law Act declares "the principles of freedom, equity and peace of Israel's heritage" to serve as a complimentary source of the Israeli legal system.

The meaning of the 'Jewishness of the State' is highly controversial, spanning from strict religious interpretation to a mere demographic one. There is no doubt however that when speaking about a Jewish State, the Knesset did not have in mind a *halakhic* State. After all, the Zionist movement, which led to the establishment of the State, emerged as a reaction to life in the traditional religious communities in the Diaspora. When speaking of Jewish values the Knesset had in mind national as well as universal values of Judaism, yet these cannot be detached from their religious origin. Judaism is a national religion. National and religious components of Judaism are inseparable. It seems therefore impossible for a Jewish State to divorce religion. It is no coincidence that the Zionist Movement chose the traditional prayer shawl as its flag just as it seems only natural that the founders of the State chose the seven branched candelabrum of the Second Temple as the State's emblem. The Jewish character of the State is further emphasized in its national days of rest and festivals and in State education.

In spite of all these, there is nothing in Israeli law to confer upon the Jewish religion the status of State religion. There are also no provisions for the preferable treatment of Jewish religion.

The Jewishness of the State of Israel does not contradict its democratic nature. Alongside it being a Jewish State, Israel was declared a democratic State dedicated to equality and basic freedoms. The synthesis of the national and democratic nature of the State may pose difficulties; yet, as constantly stated by the Supreme Court, these values are not contradictory and every effort must be made to enable their co-existence (Maoz 2011).

Religion and Legislation

The Knesset has a dual function, both as the legislative body of the State and as its constituent assembly.[4] In both of its capacities it endeavors to balance the Jewish identity and the democratic nature of the State. The goal of such legislation is to allow Jewish teachings to have an impact on the Israeli legal system in a manner which characterizes the State, without infringing upon the rights of minorities and the democratic values. Jewish law serves as an important source of legislation and adjudication. There is a special department in the Ministry of Justice that advises the Ministry, as well as the Knesset, on the views of Jewish law on pending legislation. This seems only natural given that Jewish law is the national legal system of the Jewish people and has moreover influenced other legal systems (Maoz 2004).

As a representative of the citizens, the Knesset serves as the source of all authorities including State authority over religious institutes. This occasionally creates a clash, since religious bodies regard their powers as deriving from God Almighty. On the practical level, however, this clash is resolved in favor of State authority. The Supreme Court ruled that no secondary legislature or administrative body may take into account religious considerations if not explicitly authorized to do so by primary legislation. Moreover, since the enactment of the Basic Laws on human rights, the Knesset cannot use its legislative power to enact statutes, which negate the provisions of the Basic Laws.

As we turn to review the religious considerations of the Israeli legislator we should differentiate between two possible types of effects religion may have on legislation. Some laws may be regarded as religiously motivated, while others may take into consideration a reality that stems from religious factors. Yet, even here the situation might be complex. Take for instance the Pig-Raising Prohibition Law, which prohibits raising pigs, save in certain restricted areas. Religion serves as the major engine behind this statute. Yet pork occupies a central role in Jewish culture and most secular Jews abstain from consuming it. The fact that pigs are also regarded as an unclean animal in Islam may ease the implementation of the law.

The Role of the Judiciary

The Israeli Supreme Court serves two functions. It is an appellate court of last resort, and it is also a court of first instance for petitions against the State and its institutions in matters of administrative law. The role of the Supreme Court is of special importance in the absence of a comprehensive constitution, and especially a complete bill of rights. The Israeli Supreme Court has developed civil rights out of thin air. Thus, in spite of the fact that freedom from religion was not declared in

[4]CA 6821/93, 1908/94, 3363/94, *United Mizrahi Bank* v. Migdal Cooperative Village, [1995] IsrSC 49(4) 221.

constitutional documents, the Court declared it through judge-made law. Most of the Court's decisions in this area lack solid constitutional foundation, however today no one would question them. The Supreme Court plays a major role in supervising other courts, including religious courts. Though authorized to supervise merely their formal jurisdiction, the Court enlarged the scope of its intervention, declaring decisions of religious courts made on improper grounds ultra vires. It is impossible to exaggerate the significance of the role the Supreme Court plays in furthering human rights and advancing freedoms, including freedom from religious coercion. At the same time several judges will consult Jewish law when writing their opinions.

Law of Return

Israeli citizenship serves as a vivid illustration of the relations between the Jewish and democratic components of the State of Israel. Whilst as a democratic State Israel guarantees equality to all its citizens, it defines itself as a Jewish State and the homeland for the Jewish people. This dichotomy extends to citizenship and immigration laws. While one path to citizenship open to all is naturalization, Jews may acquire citizenship through the gate of the Law of Return. This statute enables Jews to immigrate to Israel and automatically be granted citizenship. It reflects a conception of Israel as a safe haven for Jews from the persecutions they have suffered throughout history and of restoring Jewish sovereignty in the land where Jewish statehood existed.

Several scholars justify the statute based on the privilege of each country to set its rules regarding immigration, as long as that policy does not discriminate against a particular national group (Lapidoth 1986 121–122; Lerner 1985 92–93). It is also justified by universal principles of justice based on the right of national self-determination. Such nations have a moral *license* to prefer, by means of State mechanisms, the members of their own national group on matters of immigration and citizenship (Gans 1995). Another proposed justification for the right to nationality-based immigration priorities bases itself on the principle of affirmative action (Kasher, 107–112). Yet these theories offer merely a limited scope for nationality-based immigration (Ganz 2008, 111–133). The philosophy behind the statute goes beyond these justifications. As stated by the founder of the State, David Ben-Gurion: "It is not the State that confers upon the Diaspora Jews the right to settle in the State; rather this right is enshrined within him in that he is a Jew." (Maoz 2011, 224)

The Law of Return also demonstrates the interplay between religious and nationalistic components. While the definition of a Jew is semi-*halakhic*, the right is coffered also upon the children and grandchildren of a Jew and upon their spouses. Direct offspring of Israeli citizens are also eligible for citizenship even if they do not reside in Israel. However, the children of these offspring will not be eligible unless they were born in Israel. In such situations applicants usually request citizenship based on the Law of Return or submit a special request to the Israeli Minister of Interior.

The preferential treatment stops, however, at the borders of the State since all citizens and residents are equal before the law. Thus the Supreme Court overruled a plan to establish a Jewish settlement through the Jewish National Fund and ordered that it must accept Arab applicants.[5]

Penal Law

The Protection of Holy Sites Law further safeguards the sites of all religious denominations. The Penal Law grants specific protection to holy sites and declares their desecration a criminal offense. Historic sites, many of them of religious significance, are further protected by the Antiquities Law. The penalty for maliciously damaging religious, historical, or cultural artifacts is significantly heavier than damaging other properties.

Another set of offences relating to religion is hate offences. They are defined as offences committed "out of a racist motive… or out of enmity toward a public because of their religion, religious group, community of origin, sexual inclination or because they are foreign workers". The punishment for offences with such motive is twice that of an ordinary offence. The Penal Law also includes provisions against blasphemy, insult to religion, disturbing worship, unauthorized entry to a place of worship with the intention of hurting a believer's feelings or of reviling his religion and making a publication or voicing in public any word or sound that are liable crudely to offend the religious faith or sentiments of others.

Religious conversion is permitted and given legal effect when moving between recognized religious communities. The religion of a minor may not be changed against the wish of either parent save with the court's approval. Also, while missionary work and proselytizing are permitted, the granting and accepting of material benefits to entice religious conversion constitutes a criminal offence.

Family Law

Family law stands at the crux of State-religion relations in Israel. Much of family law in Israel is regulated by the personal (religious) law of the concerned persons. Nevertheless, over the years civil law has gradually replaced religious law in many areas and excluded them from the jurisdiction of religious courts.

The subjection of secular people to religious law and jurisdiction infringes their freedom from religion. This is true both on the ceremonial level imposing a religious marriage and in substantive matters. Several religions – such as Judaism – regard mixed marriages as void. They moreover impose restrictions on marriages even within members of the community. Thus *halakha* prohibits marriage of an

[5] HCJ 6698/95, *Ka'adan v. Israel Land Administration*. IsrSC 54(1) 258 [2000].

adulterous wife with her adulterer or of a divorcee with a *Cohen*, a person of priesthood origin.

Religious law might also discriminate between sexes. Thus while according to Jewish law both husband and wife might not remarry without the granting of a *get* (bill of divorce), this obstacle is especially severe for the wife. This is so since an offspring of an adulterous relation by a married woman is regarded a *Mamzer*, as is the offspring of incestuous relations. Though popularly translated bastard, a *Mamzer* is a unique *halakhic* term. Under Jewish law a child born out of wedlock is not regarded illegitimate. However the marriage between a *Mamzer* and a "legitimate Jew" is prohibited. This prohibition also applies to the offsprings of the *Mamzer*. Since civil divorce has no *halakhic* validity, this rule applies also where civil divorce has been executed. It is therefore that a married woman who did not obtain her *get* is termed an "anchored woman" (*Aguna*). On the other hand *halakha* favors the mother in granting her guardianship over her minor children. Moreover, a husband must pay maintenance to his wife regardless of their relative wealth. He must also supply the basic needs of his children.

An interesting example of State-religion relations lies in the area of divorce. While divorce matters among Jews are within the exclusive jurisdiction of the Rabbinical Courts, the court is incapable of carrying out the divorce. This is so, since the divorce will take place only upon the granting of the *get* by a willing husband to a willing wife. In order to induce the reluctant spouse to cooperate in the execution of the *get*, the Knesset has empowered the Rabbinical Courts to issue an injunction against him or her preventing them from leaving the country, holding an Israeli passport or a driving license, having a bank account, holding a public position or office, or running a business. The court may also confiscate their pension or annuity as well as their property. In the most severe cases a reluctant spouse, practically the husband, might be imprisoned until he cooperates with the divorce.

The Supreme Court intervenes to mitigate some of the hardships stemming from the application of religious law and jurisdiction. Thus, it has ruled that the validity of personal status – such as marriage and divorce – will be determined in accordance with the prevailing law of the couple at the time of marriage or divorce. This rule is applied even when the spouses later become citizens or permanent residents of the State of Israel. It is, moreover, irrelevant whether the religious law of the spouses, which applies at the time of the court proceedings, recognizes their marriage or divorce. This rule has been extended also to Israeli citizens and residents who got married abroad. At the beginning, the civil courts recognized the overseas marriages merely for their registration in the Population Registry without passing on their validity. This is so since "the registration itself is incapable of creating or changing status".[6] Later, the Court extended the application of the rule to spouses who married abroad by proxy.[7] Finally, it has been applied to same-sex

---

[6] HCJ 143/62, *Funk-Schlesinger v. Minister of Interior*, IsrSC 17, 225 [1963]. (In Hebrew).

[7] CA 778/77, *Farkash v. Farkash*, IsrSC 33(2) 469 [1979]. (In Hebrew).

marriages.[8] A further revolutionary step took place in 2006. While all the above mentioned cases referred merely to the registration of the marriages by the Population Registrar, which "may be correct and it may be incorrect", the Supreme Court recognized the ceremonial validity of marriages celebrated abroad.[9] Finally, the Court, by majority rule, extended its recognition to the substantial validity of such marriages.[10]

The Supreme Court also ruled that marriages performed in Israel should be recognized even if they violate a *halakhic* prohibition, insofar as *halakha* does not regard them as null, such as the marriage of a divorcee and a priest, and the marriage of adulterous spouses. [11]

A constant area of conflict between the Rabbinical Courts and the civil courts relates to rulings, which are ancillary to divorce proceedings such as children's custody. Arguments are frequently made that the religious courts tend to grant custody to the parent that will ensure the religious upbringing regardless of the child's best interest. In such cases the Supreme Court will intervene and set aside the Rabbinical Court's decision.

The religious restrictions imposed on marriages led to the wide recognition of the institute of de facto marriages or reputed spouses. This institute developed as a result of young soldiers who were killed in the 1948 War of Independence leaving behind spouses whom they did not marry yet. The State nevertheless recognized the status of the spouses and granted them financial support. Later the *Knesset* substantially extended its recognition of the status. Thus, Israel has been the first legal system to recognize inheritance rights of reputed spouses. The Supreme Court pushed further the institution of de facto marriages. Ironically, the insistence on religious marriages led to their circumvention.

Obviously, when State law clashes with religious commandments, the former prevails. Thus it has been maintained that the statute banning bigamy interferes with the dictates of Islam while restricting the age of marriage infringes both Jewish and Muslim tradition. However, these prohibitions and restrictions have been upheld by the court.

Labor Law

The connection between labor law and religion takes place on two levels: statutory provisions that derive from Jewish principles; and considerations of religious requirements. The first aspect is exemplified by the entitlement of an employee to severance pay upon dismissal. This right has its roots in the obligation of the master to confer a grant upon his released slave (Elon 1994, 1367–1370).

[8] HCJ 3045/05, Ben- Ari v. Commissioner of the Population Registry, IsrSC 61(3) 537 [2006].

[9] HCJ 2232/03, 2232/03, Anonymous v. District Rabbinical Court in Tel Aviv, IsrSC 61(3) 496.

[10] Fam. App. 9607/03, *Anonymous v. Anonymous*, IsrSC 61(3) 726 [2006]. (In Hebrew).

[11] CA 238/53, *Cohen v. A.G.*, IsrSC 8, 4 [1954].

The other aspect is expressed in the Jewish Sabbath as well as Jewish holidays, which are State official days of rest and are compulsory for Jewish employees. Arguably, this provision might pass the blue pencil rule. The same goes for the provision that non-Jewish employees may choose Sabbath or their religious day of rest. However, the fact that the duration of the rest is dictated by the *halakhic* definition of Sabbath, as well as the fact that the committee authorized to grant a permit to engage employees on Sabbath includes the Minister of Religious Services, exposes the religious motives behind this provision. The same goes for the statute empowering municipal councils to order the closure of shops and businesses on Sabbath and Jewish holidays. At present, cinemas and other entertainment as well as restaurants operate on Sabbath in a great number of municipalities, and in some of them shopping centers operate as well. Yet, most supermarkets and most shops close on Saturday even where permitted to operate in order not to lose their Kashrut certificate. Public transportation does not operate in most of the State.

Kashrut

Halakha prohibits the consumption of forbidden animals and contains special regulations for preparing and consuming kosher food. In a liberal community, religious dietary laws should be a private concern. However, in Israel, State regulation is dominant. Only kosher food is served in public institutions, as well as in the army. State legislation, moreover, prohibits businesses from declaring their food to be kosher unless it has obtained a certificate from the Chief Rabbinate. Occasionally the Rabbinate takes advantage of its monopoly to dictate religious behavior beyond the requirements of kashrut proper, such as requiring that no "immodest performances" will take place where kosher food is being served. The Supreme Court rejected this practise providing that only strict rules pertaining to the food may be enforced.[12]

The issue of kashrut is a good example of the price paid by religious institutions for state entanglement with religious issues and for state-sanctioned monopoly. This is evident in the *Aviv Delicatessen* case.[13] In this case the Chief Rabbinate threatened to withdraw the kashrut certificate from a poultry slaughterhouse should it continue selling chickens that were found to be non-kosher to a Jewish non-kosher meat producer. Though acknowledging that selling non-kosher products to Jews is forbidden by *halakha*, the Supreme Court ruled that this prohibition is not part of the hard-core *halakhic* rules of kashrut and revoked the condition. Following the court's ruling the Chief Rabbinate issued a warning that its omission to withdraw the kashrut certificate is merely because of the court's order yet reaffirmed that by selling non-kosher poultry to Jews the slaughterhouse violates the kashrut rules of

[12] HCJ 465/89 *Raskin v. Jerusalem Religious Council*, IsrSC 44(2) 673 [1990] (In Hebrew).

[13] HCJ 77/02 *Aviv Delicatessen v. The Chief Rabbinate Council*, IsrSC 56(6) 249 [2002], (In Hebrew).

the Chief Rabbinate. In a furious decision the Supreme Court declared that the Chief Rabbinate blatantly and knowingly breached the court's order and infringed the rule of law. The Supreme Court called upon the Attorney General to consider disciplinary measures against the rabbis. The Court made clear that the authority of the Chief Rabbinate in issuing kashrut certificates stems from the civil legislature and not from *Halakha*. The Court called moreover upon the Knesset to consider revoking the Rabbinates authority in view of the fact that the Chief Rabbinate uses its power in order to enforce religious norms. The Court expressed the view that the protection of observant Jews from being misled when purchasing kosher food is fully being taken care of by the Consumer Protection Law provision that a dealer may not mislead a consumer as to any matter material to the transaction.

Education

The Israeli education system is divided into three main categories: State schools; recognized schools and exemption institutions. State schools are divided into regular – or, general – schools and religious schools (Maoz 2006, 683–684). State Education Law declares the objectives of State education as educating the students to respect their heritage, their cultural identity and their language. The law specifically provides that these objectives include "teaching the *Torah* of Israel, the history of the Jewish people, Israel's heritage and Jewish tradition", considering the religious text to constitute a part of Jewish culture and history beyond its religious significance. Religious education is defined as "State education, yet its institutions are religious according to their way of life, their curricula, their teachers and inspectors." It is reserved and destined for those who desire a religiously orientated curriculum.

In 2008 the State Education Law was amended, and a new category of State schools was created – the combining State school. This is a State school which "combines in its curriculum intensified Judaic studies and emphasizes Jewish identity teaching". A school may be declared a combining State school if parents of at least two thirds of the student body have so requested.

Arab, Druze and Circassian schools operate as part of State schools. They are not regarded as religious schools, however the law provides for a curriculum that will fit "their special conditions." In practice, the curriculum is adapted to the religion of the student body, whether Muslim or Christian. The same goes for the Druze and Circassians. The main language of instruction in these schools is Arabic and Arab culture is taught. The use of Arabic represents a characteristic of cultural autonomy, the language being related to cultural, historical, and religious attributes of the Arab minority in Israel.

Alongside the State schools, there are schools that are recognized by the State, yet they are "non-official." This definition includes mainly religious (both Jewish and Christian) schools. The latter include schools that are operated by the Melkite Greek Catholic Church, the Latin Patriarch and the Anglican Church. Muslim and

Druze students also study in these schools and at times they form a substantial proportion of the student body. There is also a Druze network of recognized schools. A third category includes "exempt schools". These are neither State nor recognized schools; however parents of children attending them are exempt from the obligations of the State Education Law. These institutions belong to ultra-Orthodox Judaism and are run in old fashion as prevailed in the Diaspora.

State schools are fully funded by the State and by local authorities. Recognized schools need to comply with some regulations for budget participation; however two of the main streams of the recognized schools are fully financed by the State. "Exempt" schools also get State funding. There is an ongoing heated debate regarding a compulsory core curriculum, including mathematics, sciences and literature for those schools. The Orthodox community fiercely opposes them. Following a Supreme Court decision (*Paritzky* Case), the Minister of Education established a Commission for Examining the System of Budgeting, which recommended a core curriculum that must be taught at all primary educational institutions in order for them to be eligible for State funding: State schools must teach the whole of the curriculum, while recognized schools must teach 75 % of the curriculum and exempt schools only 55 %.

The issue of teaching the core curriculum in Orthodox schools has been examined by the Supreme Court, also in regards to high schools (grades 9–12). In a decision from 2008,[14] the Court stated that the core curriculum creates a balance between the privilege of the parents to educate their children according to their viewpoints and beliefs, and the State's duty to provide basic common educational values to all students, prepare them for life, and enable them to participate in society. Accordingly, the Court was going to order the Ministry of Education to implement without further delay the core curriculum in all recognized non-official high schools and to withhold any financial support from these schools as well as the exempt schools that did not teach the core curriculum. However, on the eve of handing down the decision, the Knesset passed a statute creating "unique cultural education institutions… where… systematic education stemming from the compulsory way of life of the unique cultural group is provided in accordance with its unique characteristic". The Knesset openly stated that the statute has been designed for the ultra-Orthodox high schools enabling them to shape their own curriculum. The constitutionality of the statute has been confirmed by a majority vote by the Supreme Court.[15] While basing their decision on liberal grounds of objecting paternalism, the Court emphasized that the introduction of a curriculum that negates the creed of an ethnic group should take place via social gradual developments rather than by legal means. It was even stated by one of the judges that a court order would be futile in such circumstances.

The autonomy of private schools, especially religious schools, as well as the extent of State supervision, varies. While the Minister of Education may regulate the basic curriculum of recognized schools, as well as their administration and

[14] HCJ 4805/07 The Center for Jewish Pluralism v. Ministry of Education [2008].

[15] HCJ 3752/10 *Rubinstein v. The Knesset* [2014] (In Hebrew).

inspection, the autonomy of exempt institutions is much wider. Christian religious communities' schools operating under the rules of pre-statehood legislation enjoy the widest autonomy; the State refrains from all interference in the conduct and management of those schools, unless absolutely necessary for the maintenance of order and good Government.

In this spirit, the Supreme Court upheld the refusal of a Melkite Greek Catholic school to enroll a female Muslim student who insisted on wearing a hijab and refrained from participating in co-gender physical education activities whilst wearing a gym suit.[16] The Supreme Court indicated that had it been a State school the student would have been entitled to cover her head because "it is right to grant every student the freedom to express in her dress the principles of her religion. Rules regarding the uniformity of dress should not prevail over the student's freedom of religion"; yet in a private school belonging to a religious community, which is by definition entitled to reject students who are not part of the community, the situation is different.

In the same vein, the labor court refused to issue an injunction against a church school, which would have refrained it from preventing a Muslim female teacher from wearing a hijab in school.[17]

In another case, the Supreme Court ruled that the right of each community to educate its children in light of its unique cultural and religious beliefs is recognized by Israeli law alongside the official educational institutions. However, the school may not base its admittance policy on ethnic discrimination.[18]

Religion in the Army

Since their inception the Israeli Defense Forces have not had separate units for religious soldiers. Military service has moreover been considered a melting pot for Israeli society, a cohesive element which should be as inclusive as possible. The need to integrate religious soldiers in general units has required the introduction of conditions that would enable them to preserve their religious commandments. Thus, only kosher food is served and provisions for the observance of Sabbath have been adopted. Yet, army rules go beyond enabling religious soldiers to preserve religious behavior by introducing a "Jewish atmosphere" in the camp, thus interfering with the freedom of non-observant soldiers. In this vein, on Sabbath the canteens are closed and no desecration of Sabbath is permitted save for compelling emergencies.

The army operates a special unit headed by the Chief Chaplain, who holds the rank of brigadier general. He heads the Army Chaplaincy, which is Orthodox in its composition and rulings. The unit does not satisfy itself with providing for needs of

[16] HCJ 4298/93, *Jabareen v. Minister of Education*, IsrSC 48(5) 199 [1994]. (In Hebrew).

[17] LD (Jer.) 9022-06-10, *Nameri v. Scmid Girls School*. (In Hebrew).

[18] HCJ 9106/11, "Noar Cahalakha" v. Ministry of Education, [2013]. (In Hebrew).

religious soldiers and regards itself as catering for all soldiers and for the army in general. One of the recent Chief Chaplains regarded the role of the Army Chaplaincy as "promoting Jewish consciousness among officers and soldiers". As an example, towards the High Holidays, the Army Chaplaincy runs an "observation campaign" for all army units. In the past it was named "spiritual revival project". Following complaints that this project advocated repentance amongst the soldiers, the title has been changed and its content has been described as "a campaign to improve the self". One cannot overlook, however, the fact that this campaign is being led by chaplains and takes place in days of repentance in the Jewish calendar. On the same token, all soldiers who are stationed in an army base during the Festival of Passover must participate in the Seder led by a clergy. Such participation is being justified on both the national nature of the feast and the need for uniformity within the army. Similarly, military funerals for Jewish soldiers are of religious nature, unless the bereaved family expressly objects. Due to all of this, and to the fact that the composition of the army is almost entirely Jewish (with a relatively small number of soldiers from minority groups whose religious needs are also provided for by the Army Chaplaincy), it may be said that Orthodox Judaism is the religion of the Israeli Defense Forces. It is therefore no wonder that the Chief Chaplaincy stated, in past publications, that its goals were enabling soldiers to preserve religious precepts and "to ensure maintenance of religious, spiritual and moral values, based on the Jewish Torah, by all soldiers and units, as this is the basis for a unified Jewish character of the army, and according to it, it would be feasible to maintain a unified forum in which all Jewish soldiers of whatever religious convictions may live together".

Religious Coercion in the Public Sphere

Accommodating a religious way of life with liberal views in the public sphere poses a special challenge. The clash is indeed between two philosophies: from a liberal point of view the public sphere should be neutral, while from a Jewish Orthodox perspective it should reflect a religious atmosphere. It should be stressed that we are not relating to the European dispute as to whether religious people are entitled to behave in public according to the precepts of their religion, such as wearing the burka, or whether places of worship might be built. The French *laïcité* is not an option. Neither is the Swiss ban on the erection of minarets. We are not dealing either with the American issue of displaying religious items in public. In Israel the debate is whether secular people might be prevented from acting freely in public and whether the public sphere might be blended with religion.

A religious way of life might moreover clash with basic human rights. A good example might be the Festival of Matzoth (Prohibition of Leaven) Law. The Law prohibits the public display of leavened products for sale or consumption in Jewish neighborhoods during the Passover festival. At the same time it does not apply in areas where the majority of the population are non-Jewish. However it does apply in Jewish secular neighborhoods. Two main justifications have been raised in favor of the Matzoth Law. One relates to the nationalistic significance of the festival symbolizing the redemption of the Jewish people from slavery. The other is protecting the feelings of religious people. The practical solution has been that the law remains in the books but it is rarely enforced. Moreover, when examining the limits of the statute, a modus vivendi has been offered by the court: the display of leavened product is prohibited in public areas but not within the store or restaurant.[19]

Another good example is the prohibition of opening entertainment venues on the ninth of Av. This prohibition has *halakhic* roots as it is a religious fast commemorating the destruction of the Temple; however, nationalistic justifications have been raised as on this day the Jews lost their sovereignty and were expelled from their homeland.

Yet, the main area of conflict lies in practical enforcement of religious norms in the public sphere, not by virtue of law and even contrary to law. This includes signposts in Orthodox neighborhoods requiring women to respect the Orthodox dress code and dress modestly. One may even find warnings demanding women to walk on a separate sidewalk, to prevent any contact – even eye contact – between men and women, especially near synagogues and yeshivas. This example may raise the issue as to the definition of the public sphere. Is it possible to argue for some special status of neighborhoods with a unique population? Should visitors be obliged to respect the feelings of the local residents even if that means curtailing their freedom?

This exemplifies an important distinction in the matter: while the debate on spaces shared by religious and secular groups requires a mutually accepted solution, should the public sphere in Orthodox neighborhoods, which are nearly homogenous in nature, adhere to the same concerns or is it possible to make concessions for the community's way of life? On the one hand, it is still a public area open to the general public, but, on the other hand, its inhabitants wish to preserve a unique way of life. Take, for instance, the aforementioned segregation of women in the public sphere. This can be seen as an implementation of liberal tolerance towards a minority's culture or as an egregious affront to liberal values. This debate touches upon the core questions of liberal democracy and liberalism as a substantial or as a procedural philosophy. A further argument might be raised that even individuals within the community do not necessarily respect these restrictions voluntarily, but they rather act under social pressure or even social sanctions.

Another instance of the Orthodox exclusion of women from the public sphere takes place in public events. In 2011 the municipality of Jerusalem organized a festival in an ultra-Orthodox neighborhood, with "strict separation of men and women throughout the premises". This occurrence raised a more severe issue as the event was organized by a public body. The municipality justified its action arguing that it was for the "respect of religious sentiments".

The imposed segregation of sexes has expanded to public transportation. A public transportation company has signed an agreement with Orthodox religious leaders to enforce restrictions on people travelling on the buses, which included both

[19] Crim. C (Jerusalem) 4726/07 *State of Israel v. Terminal Twenty One* [2008].

gender segregation and imposed a "modest" dress code for women. Although these lines travel through Orthodox neighborhoods, they also cross non-religious areas. Several women, both secular and religious, have reported facing hostile reactions when they refused to move to the back of the bus as ordered, as well as being picked on for the way they were dressed. While the Supreme Court ruled that such segregation is unlawful,[20] the enforcement of the decision is far from satisfactory.

The battle over the public sphere shared by secular and religious groups is most heated. While ultra-Orthodox Jews tend to live in separated neighborhoods, their high birthrate combined with the housing shortage forces them to move to the outskirts or even to new settlements which are not religious. Moreover, some religious groups take pride in moving into secular neighborhoods in order to create a religious atmosphere. This is being met by secular opposition. Such opposition groups fight for "maintaining a neighborhood's pluralistic character and safeguarding the values of democracy without religious coercion". They have succeeded more than once in preventing the establishment of religious institutions in their vicinity, such as ritual bathhouses (*mikve*) and *yeshivas* or even religious kindergartens aimed at attracting non-religious parents.

A symbolic case of the courts' stance on the seam between religious and secular public areas concerned the Bar-Ilan Street in Jerusalem. This is a main road, which goes through Orthodox neighborhoods; Orthodox elements demanded its closure for traffic during the Sabbath, while the secular population of the city asked to keep it open. The issue was brought before the Supreme Court and resulted in a landmark decision. It ordered a partial closure of the street during prayer times as an appropriate balance between freedom of movement and the ultra-Orthodox local residents' lifestyle.

In his decision, President Barak offered the following formula:

> [C]onsideration of feelings, including religious sensibilities, as proper grounds for infringing on human rights is most problematic from the point of view of a democracy. Democracy finds itself trapped in an internal conflict, which it must naturally address with great care. The Israeli solution is the following: considering feelings as grounds for restricting human rights is only permissible when the following three conditions are met: First, taking feelings into account conforms to the specific objective underlying the legislation. Second, it is permitted to take religious feelings into account only if doing so does not involve any religious coercion. Third, religious feelings may only be considered when the harm to these is so severe that it is said to exceed the proper threshold of tolerance. This threshold shall vary from right to right.[21]

[20] HCJ 746/07, Ragen v. Ministry of Transportation, [2011].

[21] HCJ 5016/96, *Horev v. Minister of Transportation*, IsrSC 51(4)1 [1997].

A Word of Summation

As demonstrated throughout this essay, State-religion relations in Israel are indeed complex. I have tried to explain the complexity along historical, political and sociological grounds. The complexities of these relations derive to a great extent from the nature of the Jewish religion. Judaism does not confine itself within the walls of synagogues and *yeshivas*; rather it plays a significant role in all aspects of human activities. Both Judaism and classical Islam differ from the Christian definition of religion. They are "integrated civilizations" rather than mere religions, embracing all aspects of human life (Schwarzchild, 915). This aspect, coupled with the national nature of Judaism, may largely account for the Israeli stance on State-religion relations.

References

Elon, Menachem. 1994. *Jewish law: History, sources, principles*. Philadelphia: The Jewish Publication Society.

Gans, Chaim. 1995. The law of return and affirmative action. *Iyunei Mishpat* 19: 683–697 (Hebrew).

Gans, Chaim. 2008. *A just Zionism – On the morality of the Jewish State*. New York: Oxford University Press.

Lapidoth, Ruth. 1986. The right of return in international law, with special reference to the Palestinian refugees. *Israel Yearbook on Human Rights* 16: 103–125.

Lerner, Natan. 1985. Inter-group tensions in Israel: Are legal solutions effective? *Israel Yearbook on Human Rights* 15: 88–100.

Maoz, Asher. 1996. Religious human rights in the State of Israel. In *Religious human rights in global perspective – Legal perspectives*, ed. Johan D. van Vyyer and Witte John Jr., 349–390. The Hague: Martinus Nijhoff.

Maoz, Asher. 2004. Can Judaism serve as a source of human rights? *Heidelberg Journal of International Law* 64: 677–722.

Maoz, Asher. 2006. Religious education in Israel. *University of Detroit Mercy Law Review* 83(5): 679–728.

Maoz, Asher. 2011. The values of Israel as a Jewish and democratic state. In *Israel as a Jewish and democratic state: Jewish law association studies XXI*, ed. Asher Maoz, 149–237. Liverpool: Deborah Charles Publications.

Chapter 14
Modifications et Contradictions de la Réalité Socioreligieuse en Italie. Profiles Juridiques et Sociales

Roberto Mazzola

Abstract This chapter intends to describe the controversial principles regarding the relationship between the Italian Republic and religious denominations. In particular, this analysis concerns the effects of the incoherent legal system about religious freedom and its weakness.

Introduction

Profils sociologiques

La société italienne a connu et elle connaît aujourd'hui une profonde transformation de la réalité socioreligieuse. En moins d'une génération, la carte religieuse en Italie a changé: d'un pays à majorité catholique, l'Italie est devenue une société caractérisée par une diversité religieuse très composite et entièrement nouvelle. C'est un phénomène qui s'est développé très rapidement au cours des dernières années, principalement en raison de la migration non-européenne forte et persistante, toutefois ce phénomène n'explique que partiellement les raisons de ce changement. D'autres facteurs, et non des moindres, sont intervenus pour modifier la géographie religieuse italienne: tout d'abord la disparition du modèle géopolitique de Yalta en Europe et, en second lieu, les profondes transformations au sein du catholicisme même en Italie. En effet les flux migratoires provenant de l'Afrique et de l'Asie ont permis non seulement l'enracinement des communautés religieuses en dehors de la tradition chrétienne, mais aussi un changement de la composition interne de la communauté catholique si fort, que l'on peut aujourd'hui, sans aucun doute, traduire au pluriel le mot «catholicisme»: l'on trouve de fait des catholiques africains de langue anglaise, des catholiques africains de langue française, des catholiques albanais,

R. Mazzola (✉)
Università degli Studi del Piemonte Orientale, Vercelli, Italy
e-mail: rmazzola961@gmail.com

R. Bottoni et al. (eds.), *Religious Rules, State Law, and Normative Pluralism - A Comparative Overview*, Ius Comparatum – Global Studies in Comparative Law 18, DOI 10.1007/978-3-319-28335-7_14

chinois, philippins, indiens, catholiques de rite latin de l'Eglise syro-malabare, lituanien, malgache, vietnamien, hongrois. C'est un processus de grande diversification à l'intérieur de la *communion fidelium* qui donne également lieu à des formes d'interaction très fortes entre les personnes de différentes traditions religieuses: des catholiques africains qui, pour des raisons de langue, fréquentent des néo-pentecôtistes et les églises charismatiques, ainsi que des catholique srinkaises qui, au fil du temps, ont développé des relations toujours plus étroites avec les communautés bouddhistes, ou des catholiques roumains qui sont de plus en plus liées à des églises orthodoxes. Ce processus de changement n'a été pas seulement provoqué par les phénomènes migratoires, mais également par la dissolution de la politique cristallisée avec le Pacte de Varsovie de 1955, qui a généré une transformation de la géographie religieuse en Europe occidentale, et tout particulièrement en Italie, en renforçant la présence des églises chrétiennes-orthodoxe.

Mais le phénomène qui se développe n'est pas uniquement d'ordre quantitatif: il concerne aussi des aspects de nature substantielle qui touchent à la phénoménologie même du religieux, comme le démontre le lien plus faible qu'entretiennent les fidèles avec la dimension hiérarchique et institutionnelle des organisations religieuses au profit, au contraire, des mouvements religieux.

Ces données peuvent se traduire en chiffres, et, à cet égard, le Centre d'études et de la recherche IDOS a estimés dans le Rapport publié le 31 Décembre 2011, la présence régulière en Italie de 5.011.000 citoyens étrangers, ainsi partagés en fonction de leurs appartenances religieuses: avant tout les chrétiens dépassent la somme totale (53.9 %).

Cette donnée montre donc bien combien le spectre d'une «invasion» de personnes de religions différentes en Italie est irréel: en effet, les musulmans ne représentent qu'un tiers (32.9 %) de la part totale, tandis que les fidèles des traditions religieuses orientales (les hindous, les bouddhistes et autres) représentent un peu plus d'un vingtième (5.9 %). En Italie, l'on peut donc dénombrer environ deux millions sept cent mille chrétiens, un million six cent mille musulmans, trois cent mille fidèles qui appartiennent aux traditions religieuses orientales, cinquante mille immigrés que l'on peut rattacher aux religions traditionnelles, trois cent mille personnes entre juifs, athées, agnostiques et autres. À cet égard, les pays d'origine les plus représentés dans chacun des groupes religieux sont, parmi les orthodoxes: la Roumanie, l'Ukraine, la Moldavie, la Macédoine et l'Albanie. Pour les catholiques: les Philippines, la Pologne, l'Équateur, le Pérou, l'Albanie, la Roumanie, la Macédoine, le Brésil, la France, la République dominicaine, la Colombie et la Croatie; chez les protestants: la Roumanie, l'Allemagne, le Royaume-Uni, le Ghana, le Nigéria, le Pérou, les Philippines et le Brésil; parmi les musulmans: le Maroc, l'Albanie, la Tunisie, le Sénégal, le Pakistan, le Bangladesh, la Macédoine, l'Algérie, et le Kosovo. A cet égard il faut souligner que, au cours des dernières années, on a assisté à une baisse en termes de pourcentage mais pas de nombre, des musulmans: cinq points de pourcentage de moins respect aux années précédentes et, dans le même temps, une augmentation correspondante des chrétiens orthodoxes à la suite, comme déjà mentionné, des grands flux migratoires de l'Europe de l'Est.

Le cadre décrit oblige donc à interpréter avec un regard nouveau plusieurs normes du système juridique italien, dont avant tout l'art. 9 second alinéa de la l. du

25 mars 1985, n. 121 où sont soulignées l'identité et les racines catholique de la nation et du patrimoine historique italien. Une formule, sans doute crédible il y a trente ans, mais désormais très critiquable face un décor socioreligieux qui a totalement changé et qui est encore en train de subir de profondes modifications structurelles (cf. plus bas).

Profils historiques et réglementaires

Le contexte religieux et social décrit pose plusieurs défis sur les plans politique et institutionnel. L'esprit de l'ensemble des principes juridiques qui réglementent les relations entre l'Etat et les confessions religieuses ne correspond plus aux changements du cadre religieux présent aujourd'hui en Italie. En effet, le système juridique fondé sur le Concordat (art. 7 Const.) et les accords entre l'Etat et les confessions religieuses minoritaires conformément à l'art. 8 troisième alinéa de la Constitution, exprime un horizon religieux homogène caractérisé par une Eglise majoritaire, l'Eglise Catholique, et des cultes minoritaires qui relèvent généralement de la tradition judéo-chrétienne. Malgré la fracture réalisée en 1984 avec le Traité de *Villa Madama* avec l'abandon du modèle de l'Eglise d'Etat dans l'abrogation de l'art. 1 du Traité de Latran par la loi 25 mars 1985, n. 121, et l'ouverture de la saison des accords incluant également les confessions religieuses minoritaires qui ne relèvent pas de tradition judéo-chrétienne (bouddhisme, indouisme), la politique ecclésiastique italienne a été caractérisée par une forte continuité, comme témoigne l'insertion dans le tissu normatif constitutionnel des normes approuvées pendant le précédent régime fasciste: les Accords de Latran de 1929, la loi sur les cultes admis du 1929 (l. 24 Juin 1929, n 1159) et, encore, les normes d'application contenues dans le Décret Royal 28 février 1930. Toutes ces règles régissent encore la position juridique des minorités religieuses sans accord en démontrant la nature obsolète d'une part du système juridique italien. C'est un appareil législatif qui, bien que modifié par les interventions de la Cour Constitutionnelle, manifeste une architecture conçue pour satisfaire avant tout la nécessité du pouvoir politique de garantir l'ordre établi, c'est-à-dire les exigences fondamentales de la société et de l'Etat, et, seulement après vérifié l'absence de périls potentiels pour l'ordre publique, se charge de répondre aux exigences fondamentales des minorités religieuses. Ce cadre normatif est donc généralement soupçonneux devant les minorités religieuses et pourtant fondé sur la reconnaissance d'un grand pouvoir discrétionnaire à l'administration publique et d'un pouvoir politique, comme le démontrent les norme du 1929-1930 qui règlent la reconnaissance de la personnalité juridique des organisme exponentiels des confessions religieuses. Il s'agit d'un système de contrôle progressif où la décision administrative est organisée par le pouvoir politique, et où la volonté du Gouvernement, est, à son tour, assujettie, dans certains cas, à la volonté du Président de la République, lequel, dans le décret pour la reconnaissance de la personnalité juridique des organismes avec but de religion et de culte, peut prévoir d'autre limites aux dépends des organismes religieux. Il s'agit surtout d'un système où la reconnaissance de la personnalité juridique des organismes exponentiels devient une manière de sélectionner, parfois arbitrairement, les confessions religieuses, d'une vraie procédure de crédit des sujets religieux envers l'Etat italien.

A la lumière de ces considérations il faut donc réfléchir sur la compatibilité entre cet appareil normatif et l'esprit qui anime, en général, la culture juridique des droits de l'homme. En d'autres termes, il faut se poser la question de savoir si le résultat global des efforts de négociation sont ou non compatibles avec la philosophie qui anime l'idée des droit de l'homme. L'idée que le système italien ne satisfait pas l'esprit de ces droits est forte. La raison est simple: la norme bilatérale, développée comme elle l'est dans le système juridique italien, subordonnée au pouvoir discrétionnaire de l'administration étatique (cf. plus bas), semblerait ne pas satisfaire un requis essentiel des droits de l'homme, c'est-à-dire, la nature générale et universelle de ces droits. En effet, les droits de l'homme, pour demeurer ce qu'ils sont, doivent être pour tous, et non pas seulement pour quelques-uns. Ceux-ci doivent être requis pour tous. Au contraire, le choix fait par le législateur de subordonner la règlementation du droit de liberté religieuse à l'existence des accords, produit un résultat exactement contraire, parce qu'il engendre d'une part une mentalité égoïste entre les sujets religieux: chacun pense seulement à soi-même, c'est-à-dire recherche exclusivement sa propre liberté religieuse, de l'autre côté, ce choix légitime la possibilité de l'Etat de sélectionner les interlocuteurs religieux selon un logique arbitraire. Le résultat final est donc évidemment contraire à la substance des droits de l'homme. Comme le souligne une partie de la doctrine politique contemporaine, la liberté religieuse revendiquée seulement en vertu de la foi est d'une nature « triviale », car seule la revendication d'une garantie étatique de la liberté religieuse étendue à des fois qui ne s'acceptent pas les unes et les autres correspond au but authentique des droits de l'homme.

Le système juridique qui régule les politiques des rapports entre Etat et églises pour toutes ces raisons est donc présent comme un système complexe et contradictoire fondé sur la concurrence entre sources normatives unilatérales et sources juridiques bilatérales, nationales ou régionales, unies par le but de réglementer la liberté religieuse des individus et des associations. Ce cadre normatif, toujours en présence de la législation de droit commun de 1929, a produit un résultat paradoxal du point de vue constitutionnel : il a en effet permis aux accords bilatéraux entre l'état et les confessions religieuses des minorités de développer une fonction de division, loin de la logique inclusive pensée par la Constitution. Loin d'être un instruments d'égale liberté pour toutes les confessions religieuses, ces accords sont devenus les sceaux de conditions différentes d'une confession à l'autre en fonction de ces accords, c'est-à-dire entre les organisations religieuses qui ont eu la force politique de signer l'accord et celles qui n'en n'ont pas eu la capacité. Cette situation justifie et explique l'image de la pyramide, c'est-à-dire d'un modèle où les organisations sans aucun accord se trouvent désavantagées face aux autres organisations religieuses qui occupent le degré le plus avantageux dans le système parce-que pourvues des accords, et, entre elles, la position d'absolu privilège de l'Eglise catholique.

Les choses n'ont que peu changé après la réforme en 2001 du titre V de la Constitution : l'article 117 Const. a partiellement redéfini la relation entre la législation de l'Etat et celle des Régions en matière de liberté religieuse. Le nouveau système prévoit, en effet, que les régions puissent contribuer, dans les limites et les indications politiques du Gouvernement national et du Parlement qui conservent la compétence exclusive en la matière (ex art. 117 alinéa 2 lett. c), de participer à la définition des politiques entre l'État et les confessions religieuses. Ainsi, parmi les matières de compétence exclusives des Régions, beaucoup d'entre elles présentent des profils intéressants sous le point de vue ecclésiastique: l'éducation, la santé, la nutrition, la valorisation du patrimoine culturel et de l'environnement, et encore, la promotion et l'organisation d'activités culturelles. Á ce propos on peut dire que la réforme du titre V de la Partie II de la Constitution a jeté les bases et créé l'espace nécessaire à la mise en place d'un véritable droit ecclésiastique régional. Ce cadre est confirmé par l'arrêté n. 406 du 2005 de la Cour Constitutionnelle, dans lequel le juge des lois a souligné que le pouvoir législatif est exercé par l'État et les régions dans le respect de la Constitution et des obligations mises en place par l'Union européenne et le droit international. À cet égard, les profils de droit de l'Union européenne et du droit international ont pris, au niveau de la législation nationale, un rôle de plus en plus important et significatif dans la régulation des politiques sur la liberté religieuse, comme en témoignent les deux arrêtés de la Cour de Cassation du 2006, les n. 401 et n. 402, pour lesquels la CEDH a une position hiérarchiquement supérieure à celle des lois ordinaires tout en reconnaissant l'autonomie de chacun des États membres de l'Union européenne de réglementer et de définir les contenus, dans le respect de la Déclaration n.11 annexée au Traité d'Amsterdam des politiques ecclésiastiques. Ces normes, qualifiées de normes interposées ou sub-constitutionelles, bien qu'elles respectent formellement la marge d'appréciation accordée à chaque État membre individuellement, confirment en fait le rôle croissant de l'Union européenne dans le domaine de la liberté religieuse. Comme la Cour constitutionnelle l'a souligné plusieurs fois (arrêtés 349/2007 et 227/2010), il est important de prendre conscience que le pouvoir législatif italien devrait être exercé dans le respect, non seulement celui de la Constitution en tant que source de rang supérieur interne, mais aussi en ce qui concerne les obligations prévues par les normes internationales et communautaires, pourvu qu'elles soient compatibles avec les principes fondamentaux du système constitutionnel italien, et donc dans le respect du principe général de marge d'appréciation qui, par exemple, dans l'arrêté relatif au cas Lautsi c. Italie prononcé par la Grande Chambre de la Cour EDU a été utilisé de nouveau de manière extensive.

Signification de l'expression «normes religieuses» et distinction entre les normes religieuses et les normes culturelles

Du point de vue de l'interprétation des sources juridiques, les normes religieuses sont généralement placées dans la famille des «sources-fait», expression qui inclut à la fois soit les comportements reconnus par la société comme juridiquement contraignants, comme par exemple les coutumes, soit les actes de production normative extérieurs à l'Etat comme, par exemple, les traités internationaux, les règlements de l'UE, et ainsi les normes religieuses.

En ce qui concerne les normes religieuses, la nature confessionnelle de celles–ci dépend en général de l'autorité d'où elles proviennent, c'est-à-dire que le caractère confessionnel de l'autorité législative donne la substance à la règle religieuse, quel que soit le contenu de celui-ci. Cela signifie qu'une simple règle d'organisation totalement dépourvue de profils sacramentels, par le simple fait d'avoir été promulguée par un sujet confessionnel devrait être classée comme «norme religieuse». On obtient une confirmation ultérieure de cette règle si l'on considère le principe de «réserve de statut» prévu par l'art. 8 second alinéa de la Constitution. En vertu de cette norme, l'Etat ne renonce pas seulement à toutes ses ingérences dans la détermination des statuts des confessions religieuses, mais aussi à réguler les rapports entre eux à travers des actes normatifs unilatéraux. Autrement dit, la réserve de statut, et donc la reconnaissance de la nature religieuse d'une règle, exclut toutes les possibilités d'ingérence de l'État dans la question des dispositions statutaires des groupes religieux, de sorte que ces derniers résistent aux règles qui découlent des lois de l'État, ou des lois régionales.

Il va de soi que la règle mise en place par l'autorité religieuse et caractérisée par des contenus explicitement théologiques sera *a fortiori* classée dans la famille des sources de droit religieux.

Cette classification semble simple, mais en réalité, elle est beaucoup plus complexe et contradictoire. Il est vrai que tous les systèmes juridiques européens, compris l'ordre juridique italien, connaissent différemment le principe de séparation entre le pouvoir religieux et le pouvoir temporel. Cela signifie que les juges étatiques, même lorsqu'on leur reconnaît un compétence juridictionnelle dans certains domaines de nature confessionnelles, doivent toujours appliquer le droit de l'Etat, comme l'expliquent très clairement les Sections Unies de la Cour de Cassation italienne dans l'arrêté n. 1824 du 1993. L'on pourrait dont affirmer que le problème d'application du droit religieux par les juges étatiques est un faux problème, puisque celui-ci ne peut l'appliquer, conformément au principe de séparation des pouvoirs, un droit religieux.

Cette interprétation se vérifie probablement dans plusieurs cas, mais ne peut être généralisée, car dans d'autres contextes, particulièrement lorsqu'il s'agit d'appliquer des normes relatives au droit musulman, ce schéma ne fonctionne pas, puisqu'il ne prend pas en considération la distinction entre les droits religieux et étatique, ce dernier étant mis en parallèle avec le droit religieux. Cela signifie donc que l'application de ce droit pose généralement un problème de coordination dans le système normatif étatique, et non pas un problème de droit religieux. Oublier ces aspects veut dire pas connaître l'évolution et la nature de certains droits contemporains en dehors de la civilité juridique européenne, mais surtout, cela signifie ne pas aborder correctement le problème du rapport entre les systèmes juridiques étatiques et les droits religieux. L'on peut donc dire que la complexité du système des sources juridiques, où il y a un lien très étroit entre droit religieux et droit séculier, comme, par exemple, dans les Etats musulmans, rend difficile pour les juges nationaux l'application du droit religieux, et, pourtant, le respect de l'obligation prévue par la Cour de Cassation italienne dans l'arrêt 2791 de 2002 d'interpréter et d'appliquer le droit étranger de la même façon que le juge du pays étranger. Ce principe pose un problème fondamental: comme appliquer cette règle, quand il y a de la part des juges une faible connaissance de droit étranger, spécifiquement dans le cas religieux, et ce bien que la violation ou la fausse application de droit étranger expose celui-ci à une responsabilité actionnable avant la justice, comme il a été prévu en Italie par la Cour de Cassation dans les arrêtés nn .6664/2001 et 2791/2002. Il est vrai que l'art. 14 de la l. 218/1995 prévoit que les juges italiens puissent utiliser leur science ou différents instruments d'évaluation, telles que les attestations consulaires concernant les lois et les coutumes en vigueur dans le pays de résidence du Consul, et autres instruments prévus par les conventions internationales. Il est aussi vrai que le législateur italien a reconnu aux juges le droit de poser des questions relatives au droit étrangères, dans ce cas musulman, par l'intermédiaire du Ministère de la Justice, ou encore de consulter des experts ou des institutions spécialisées, ou, dans le cas où il est impossible de vérifier le contenu de la loi étrangère, d'appliquer une autre loi étrangère indiquée par les facteurs de rattachement qui contiennent une norme semblable.

Ces solutions sont sans doute raisonnables, mais en aucun cas satisfaisantes, parce qu'elles ne prévoient pas une formation générale et constante en droit comparé en rapport avec les pays dont la culture juridique n'est pas occidentale. En dehors de l'initiative isolée de certains tribunaux, notamment ceux qui s'occupent de la justice des mineurs, qui ont organisé il y a quelques années de brèves formations pour les magistrats en droit musulman, l'Ecole Supérieure de la Magistrature, c'est-à-dire la Haute Ecole de formation des juges italiens, ne prévoit rien en matière de droit musulman dans le programme des cours de l'année 2014, et plus généralement, elle ne prévoit aucune formation de droit comparé en dehors de l'espace juridique européen. Le péril pour les juges consiste donc dans une connaissance superficielle et statique du droit religieux, comme le démontrent les distorsions interprétatives de certains arrêtés. Il est vrai que l'on peut pas demander aux juges européens d'être des anthropologues, mais on peut toutefois leur conseiller de s'en remettre pendant les phases d'instruction des procès ou pendant les débats processuels aux spécialistes; en effet, il faut toujours vérifier que les argumentations utilisés pour justifier une action illicite ont ou non des aspects objectifs, ou si au contraire, ces arguments doivent être mis au nombre des comportements individuels et détachés de toute motivation de nature culturelle. Il faut donc vérifier d'un cas à l'autre si les motivations physiologiques sont enracinées dans des valeurs culturelles du groupe d'appartenance, et si les interprétations données sont en cohérence avec les traditions encore en vigueur. En d'autres termes, il est nécessaire de s'assurer qu'il y a ce qu'on appelle «coïncidence de réaction» entre l'inculpé et le groupe et si la ligne de défense fondée sur des arguments culturels est sincère. Les approches de cette nature sont extrêmement rares dans la jurisprudence. Il existe une certaine résistance à l'utilisation d'outils interprétatifs qui sortent du droit positif. Dans ce genre de cas, le risque majeur consiste à produire des arrêtés conditionnés, consolidant le préjudice en sous-estimant la rigoureuse application du concept de culture conditionnant. Des approfondissements sociologiques anthropologiques sont donc toujours plus indispensables, autant pour les juges que pour les avocats, afin de rechercher une solution à ce problème et c'est ce que démontre l'arrêté tout à fait pertinent du tribunal de Reggio Emilia du 21 novembre 2012, dans lequel le juge souligne le fait que les délits culturellement motivés ont besoin de procès interprétatifs capables de prendre en considération - en ce qui concerne la détermination de la culpabilité - des spécificités culturelles relatives aux cas concret. Un effort de compréhension par le juge qui le rende capable de fuir l'évidence qui produit une manière univoque de penser la réalité est nécessaire. Sortir de l'évidence, cela signifie avoir une chance de se détourner du préjugé. Il est vrai que l'on perd en certitude, mais on gagne en capacité d'adaptation dans l'intérêt d'une justice meilleure.

A cet égard, l'autre question posée est celle du problème de la traduction, que les juges européens sont obligés de faire pour appliquer la *lex causæ*. Traduire, cela signifie déplacer certaines différences culturelles d'un espace de dissemblance étrangère presque totale à un espace de plus grande familiarité et de connaissance. C'est une opération qui repose sur un effort de connaissance du contexte social où les différences se sont générées. En d'autres termes, traduire c'est comprendre la vision du monde qui a produit les différences, c'est comprendre l'imaginaire culturel qui constitue le panorama où celles-ci se sont développées, c'est donc un rapprochement cognitif vers les choix des autres et leurs motivations. Pour assurer le bon fonctionnement du système, sont nécessaires une sensibilité, une culture, et un intérêt pour la traduction culturelle.

À travers la traduction on peut en fait réduire progressivement les distances de sorte que les autres sont toujours moins étrangers, et, dans une certaine mesure, nous deviennent plus semblables, alors que nous leur ressemblons plus: c'est-à-dire qu'entre nous et les autres il n'y a plus de différence: on fini par vivre dans un «nous» commun, qui est différent des « nous » de départ.

Le contexte est complexe parce qu'au-delà des aspects anthropologiques, on est également confrontés à des profils juridiques concrets. En effet, il est nécessaire de comprendre qu'en traduisant un terme d'une manière plutôt que d'une autre, on influe de manière pratique sur la décision du juge. Les mots utilisés dans le langage juridique ne sont pas toujours neutres émotionnellement. Le lexique juridique produit souvent des émotions, il fait référence à un monde et à un système de valeurs. Dans la traduction juridique, le choix d'un mot plutôt que d'un autre peut avoir des conséquences concrètes sur la décision du juge. Quelques fois, on trouve sans problème dans les autres langues le correspondant juridique du mots, à tout le moins du point de vue technique: car il peut entrer en dissonance du point de vue émotif surtout si la traduction se fait entre deux univers culturels différents.

Cette difficulté est illustrée par le cas paradigmatique de la décision prononcée en 2011 en Italie par le tribunal d'Aoste à propos de la reconnaissance d'un jugement de divorce pour *šiqāq*, ainsi qu'il est régulé par le code de la famille marocain de 2004. Sans entrer dans les détails techniques, du point de vue juridique, et bien que dans la doctrine marocaine cette réglementation ne soit pas unanimement partagée, on peut toutefois affirmer que la procédure pour *šiqāq*, c'est-à-dire le divorce pour discorde, est le seul moyen de dissolution du mariage parfaitement égalitaire puisque les femmes comme les hommes sont en droit de le demander en condition d'égalité. Cette question est particulièrement importante pour le gouvernement marocain qui a le souci de faciliter la résolution des problèmes de ses ressortissants à l'étranger, les soi-disant Marocains Résidents à l'Etranger (MRE). En effet la procédure de *šiqāq*, met le droit marocain en matière de divorce dans une position de totale compatibilité avec la réglementation européenne en la matière. On peut alors se demander ce qui s'est passé au tribunal d'Aoste, et se demander pourquoi le juge italien a établi que cette forme de divorce était incompatible avec l'ordre public italien. La réponse est simple: l'arrêté reposait sur une faute de traduction de l'arabe au français par le « Code marocain de la famille ». En effet, le traducteur en traduisant le *šiqāq* comme divorce, n'a pas clairement fait la distinction entre *talaq* et *tatliq*, c'est-à-dire entre le divorce qui dépend de la volonté privé de mari, et le divorce judiciaire, en refusant d'utiliser, donc, la catégorie de 'répudiation' pour le premier cas et de 'divorce' dans le second. L'équivoque a conduit, donc, le juge italien à des conclusions inadmissibles pour les juges marocains. Le Tribunal d'Aoste a, en effet, considéré, en se trompant, le *šiqāq* comme une forme de *talaq* et pas de *tatliq*, ou bien, comme un vrai forme de 'répudiation, donc un acte juridique contraire à l'ordre public italien.

Il est évident que cet arrêté se fonde sur une mauvaise connaissance du droit marocain qui produit une mauvaise traduction en français et donc une désorientation des juges italiens. On a donc l'impression que le juge n'a pas donné de poids à ces extravagances, acceptant la nature exotique et pourtant irrationnelle de la loi étrangère. L'irrationalité, on le sait, est pour les juristes un aspect très négatif. En conséquence, le refus de donner une interprétation dans cette direction signifie qu'au fond du raisonnement du juge italien il y a eu un préjugé négatif contre le système normatif marocain, et, indirectement, contre le système normatif musulman en général. Cet exemple représente peut-être le cas où le traducteur devrait toujours faire beaucoup plus attention dans l'efforce de traduction et avoir plus de courage dans l'application du droit étranger. Dans le cas examiné, cet approche aurai permis d'arriver dans le même temps à deux résultats tout à fait désirables: d'une part conserver la distinction entre les deux catégories de dissolution du mariage prévue par le droit musulman et ainsi de garder l'organisation binaire du discours: à l'opposition *talāq / tatlīq* du texte arabe, répondrait la distinction *répudiation / divorce* dans la version française. L'autre résultat auquel on pourrait parvenir avec une traduction plus attentif, c'est celui de réduire l'impact émotif de certaines mots par les juges. Une avancée dans ce sens a été faite avec l'expérience du mot *ghet* puisque les problèmes créés par cette forme de divorce prévu par le droit juif sont traités par les juges avec plus d'équilibre et moins émotivité par rapport aux répudiations islamiques, malgré l'évidente analogie de ces deux règles. Cet exemple démontre donc que traduire est une opération très difficile mais essentielle. Seule la traduction, et pas seulement la traduction juridique, est en mesure de réduire progressivement l'écart entre nous et les autres, afin que les autres soient toujours de moins en moins autres et de plus en plus nous. La question initiale reste donc ouverte : l'image de l'islam renvoyée par les arrêtés des juges européens est-elle ou non une image déformée? Il y a certainement eu et il y a encore un effort important de compréhension du droit musulman par la magistrature des Etats européens; toutefois cet effort est encore trop désorganisé, et l'approche relève encore trop de l'amateurisme. Il faudrait au contraire un changement de direction vers une vision interculturelle du droit. Dans les faits, plus la distance culturelle est grande, plus l'ignorance à combler est grande, sachant que cette distance est à la fois le symptôme et la cause de l'ignorance. Pour traduire correctement, pour donner une image qui ne soit pas fausse de ce qui est différent, il faut en d'autres termes nécessairement traverser le bassin de l'ignorance qui nous sépare les uns des autres, qui sépare les univers culturels, parce-que la traduction, la reconnaissance, une critique juste, le choix des réglementations qu'il faut appliquer, tout cela exige un effort de compréhension et, sans doute, cet effort est-il toujours un acte de justice. Il est donc toujours plus essentiel que les opérateurs du droit dans le système italien s'ouvrent à ce que la doctrine définit comme un «équivalent fonctionnel», c'est-à-dire la capacité de retrouver dans d'autres cultures, principes, valeurs et critères normatifs autant de catégories valides bien qu'elles soient définies par des critères différents des nôtres. Ce cheminement de l'intégration n'est pas facile à réaliser et la bonne volonté se heurte souvent à la défiance. A certains moments elle se heurte même à la prétention d'une supériorité morale qui contraste avec le laxisme de certaines coutumes et la décadence générale de l'Occident.

Législation

Le renvoi explicite à la dimension religieuse dans le système juridique italien

La dimension religieuse dans ses formes individuelles et collectives est présente dans la plupart des sources juridiques italiennes. Avant tout elle est explicitement mentionnée dans la Partie I de la Constitution entre les principes fondamentaux prévus par les articles 7, 8, 19, 20. Si l'art. 19 règle spécifiquement le droit à la liberté religieuse, les articles restants traitent des profils politiques et procéduraux du phénomène religieux, soit en appelant la dimension contractuelle des relations entre l'Etat et les organisations religieuses, soit en formalisant le principe de distinction des ordres (artt. 7 et 8 troisième alinéa Const.) et de réserve statutaire.

Malgré la référence commune au facteur religieux, l'esprit de ces règles n'est pas homogène, parce-que s'y reflètent les différentes positions culturelles et idéologiques qui ont alimenté le débat à l'intérieur de l'Assemblée constituante: si les artt. 7 et 8, second et troisième alinéa rappellent, en effet, la dimension institutionnelle des relations entre religion et politique unilatéraliste au-delà de la logique d'inspiration libérale des politiques ecclésiastiques du XIXe siècle, le premier alinéa de l'art. 8, ainsi que l'art. 20, se réfèrent au principe général de l'égalité entre les citoyens et les institutions, quelle que soit leur forme, et plus particulièrement, à la nécessité de l'État d'assurer l'égalité et la liberté religieuse de toutes les organisations religieuses, et là où l'art. 19, en particulier dans les régions qui rappellent la dimension individuelle du droit à la liberté religieuse, est inspiré par le principe personnaliste contenu dans l'art. 2 de la Constitution voulu par le constituant comme soutien de l'ensemble du cadre constitutionnel, comme un véritable centre de l'organisation sociale et politique. Le droit à la liberté religieuse rappelle une position juridique subjective antérieure à l'État. L'État porterait son attention sur le sujet, non seulement dans son individualité, mais aussi dans son relationnel ou bien dans l'ensemble des situations, des combinaisons de collectif et organisations, comme les groupes religieux, dans lesquels il avait ses intérêts et ses besoins.

Il y a bien sûr d'autres dispositions constitutionnelles qui se réfèrent directement ou indirectement à la dimension religieuse: il suffit de questionner l'art. 18 concernant le droit d'association, l'art. 21 sur la liberté d'expression, l'art. 29 sur la reconnaissance des droits de la famille comme société naturelle fondée sur le mariage.

La législation ordinaire, en plus de la norme constitutionnelle, contient elle aussi des références explicites au phénomène religieux. La loi du 24 juin 1929, n. 1159 contient les dispositions relatives aux cultes admis dans l'Etat et les dispositions relatives au mariage célébré devant les ministres des cultes eux-mêmes mis en œuvre par le Décret Royal du 28 février 1939, n. 289, dont on fait spécifiquement mention dans l'art. 1 pour les cultes non catholiques. Ces derniers sont admis à condition qu'ils ne soient pas contraires à l'ordre public et à la moralité. Dans la législation ordinaire il faut rappeler, encore, la l. 669/1967 relative à l'assurance en faveur des prêtres et des ministres d'autres confessions minoritaires, la l.194/1978 en matière d'avortement, ou la l. 85/2006, qui a introduit les amendements au Code pénal en matière de délits d'opinion.

De même, dans le contexte de la législation bilatérale on ne peut pas oublier la loi exécutive des accords de Villa Madama entre le Saint-Siège et le gouvernement italien (l. 25 mars 1985, n. 121) et les lois du 20 mai 1985, n. 206 et 20 mai 1985, n. 222 à propos des biens ecclésiastiques et du financement du clergé catholique en service dans les diocèses, ainsi que les différentes lois d'approbation des accords entre les confessions religieuses non catholiques et le gouvernement italien (par exemple: loi 449/1984 modifiée par la loi 68/2009; loi 516/1988 modifiée par la loi 637/1996; loi 517/1988; loi 101/1989; loi 116/1995 modifiée par la loi 34/2012; loi 126/2012; loi 127/2012; loi 245/2012; loi 246/2012).

Dans le contexte général des sources il faut aussi rappeler qu'au sein de la compétence concourante et exclusive des régions ex art. 117 Const. il y a des matières qui sont pertinentes d'un point de vue religieux, on peut penser aux secteurs de l'éducation, de la santé, de la nutrition, de la valorisation du patrimoine culturel et de l'environnement, ainsi qu'à ceux de la promotion et de l'organisation d'activités culturelles.

L'exclusion des sources des droits d'origine religieuse dans le système juridique étatique

Le dispositif de séparation adopté par le constituant exclut qu'entre les sources du droit de l'État, il y ait des sources de nature religieuse. En d'autres termes, sur le plan de la légalité formelle, dans le système juridique italien il ne peut pas exister une effectivité directe et immédiate des règles religieuses. Il y a cependant des cas où les normes de l'État se réfèrent, par l'institut du 'renvoi', aux normes religieuses. Il suffit de penser à l'art. 7.5 de l'Accord de *Villa Madama* de 1984, en vertu duquel l'État prévoit que «l'administration des biens appartenant à des entités ecclésiastiques est soumise aux contrôles prévus par le droit canonique», ainsi que l'art. 1085 du code civil dans la régulation de l'exercice de la servitude des eaux, qui établit que la fruition de ce bien les jours festifs correspond aux jours des fêtes religieuses.

Or les normes d'origine religieuse contribuent souvent à la formation des éléments constitutifs des objets des lois étatiques. On peut penser, à cet égard, à l'art. 498 du code pénal qui punit toute personne qui utilise illégalement des vêtements ecclésiastiques en public; on peut encore penser aux nombreuses normes d'État qui font référence aux systèmes juridiques religieux pour certains types de qualifications comme, par exemple, la notion de ministre du culte, des choses sacrées ou destinées à la fonction culturelle. Autrement dit, le législateur d'État, peut introduire, dans la qualification normative, des références «externes» au système juridique étatique, en réalisant ainsi, une intégration «hétéronome» de la norme civile.

La reconnaissance de l'effectivité juridique des sources religieuses se manifeste aussi à propos des contrôles canoniques. La norme concordée reconnaît certainement l'effectivité civile aux contrôles canoniques à propos des actions des organismes ecclésiastiques. Enfin il faut souligner que les normes confessionnelles ne peuvent pas être utilisées pour raison d'État. À cet égard l'arrêté du juge constitutionnel 334/1996 a en effet établi que le renforcement des obligations normatives étatiques par le renvoi aux préceptes religieux est absolument interdit, interdiction qui trouve sa justification dans le principe de séparation entre pouvoir temporel et pouvoir religieux.

Droit d'option entre le système civil et le système confessionnel

Le système des accords, prévu par les normes constitutionnelles italiennes, donne la possibilité de choisir, dans certains secteurs, par exemple le secteur matrimonial, entre une norme d'origine religieuse et une autre d'inspiration étatique. Le système, en effet, reconnait aux sujets de sexes différents le droit de manifester dans la forme prévue par le législateur, leur volonté de perfectionner un mariage civil ou, différemment, de choisir, en cohérence avec leurs propres convictions de foi, un mariage de forme religieuse avec des effets civils. Il ne faut pas oublier, entre autre, les formes de mariage célébré face au ministre du culte d'une organisation confessionnelle qui n'est pas réglementée par un accord avec l'État. Dans ce cas l'art. 83 cc. prévoit que le mariage perfectionné face aux ministres des cultes admis par l'État sera régulé par les normes relatives au mariage civil.

Mais le choix entre normes d'inspirations religieuses et séculaires peut se manifester aussi à travers le schéma de l'opposition, pour des raisons éthico-religieuses, au droit étatique. Dans certains cas sous la forme d'objection de conscience *contra legem*, c'est-à-dire comme véritable manifestation de désobéissance à la loi de l'Etat, à l'avantage de la table des valeurs d'inspiration religieuse choisie par le citoyen-fidèle. Là où cet choix comporte la violation des droits fondamentaux et des principes constitutionnels de base, la jurisprudence a toujours considéré ces comportements comme l'expression de la liberté religieuse, ou plutôt, comme des formes de manifestation publique des convictions propres, que l'on ne peut rattacher à la catégorie des causes de justification prévues par les articles 51-55 c.p. du code pénal italien. C'est-à-dire que la motivation religieuse ne justifie pas, dans ces cas, les comportements contraires à la loi. A cet égard, l'orientation donnée par la Cour de Cassation italienne de 2008 est très claire. Dans l'arrêté n. 44561 le juge de légitimité a en effet souligné que les principes pivots du système juridique italien, dans le cas particulier du droit de la famille, devaient rester intacts, parce-que, souligne la Cour, ils constituent un barrage infranchissable contre l'introduction dans la société civile du point de vue juridique ou factuel d'habitudes contraires au processus de civilisation réalisé pendant des siècles pour l'actuation de droits inviolables de la personne. Cette position claire ne prévoit pas les fluctuations de la jurisprudence comme le démontre le cas de l'application de l'art. 583 bis du code pénal italien, introduit par la loi n. 7 de 2006 en matière de MGF. En effet, si le Tribunal de Vérone en 2010 reconnaît dans l'intervention de la femme nigérienne une hypothèse d'infibulation, la Cour d'Appel de Venise, deux ans après, donnera une autre interprétation des faits renversant le précédant arrêté en absolvant la femme parce-que l'infibulation n'a pas été perfectionnée, en raison du fait que l'incision a été faite par rapport aux intérêts de la communauté. Ce cas démontre que les ouvertures sont plus faciles lorsque la question est plus proche de la sensibilité culturelle des juges, pour cette raison la circoncision masculine est moins problématique que l'infibulation.

Au contraire, l'on rencontre aussi des cas où l'État autorise une dérogation, pour des raisons religieuses, aux lois générales. Cela se vérifie dans tous les cas où le législateur autorise à pratiquer l'objection pour des raisons religieuses (objection *secundun legem*). L'art. 9 de la loi 22 mai 1978, n. 194 prévoit, par exemple, que les médecins et les auxiliaires qui travaillent dans le domaine sanitaire ne sont pas obligés de réaliser les pratiques relatives à l'avortement dans le cas où l'on fait objection de conscience dans les formes prévues par la loi, une objection souvent argumentée par des motivations de nature religieuses. Et encore, pour les citoyens de religion juive en force de l'art. 6 de la loi 8 mars 1989, n. 101, le système juridique italien autorise, en introduisant une exception à la norme générale, à utiliser le chapeau pendant le serment devant le juge.

Dans la seconde hypothèse on peut relier le cas réglementé par l'art. 4 de la loi 121/1985 à propos du droit des ministres de culte catholique qui ont eu l'ordination sacerdotale, d'obtenir, en conséquence de leur requête, une exonération du service militaire, ou l'assignation au service civil substitutif. On peut retrouver le même modèle en matière des festivités religieuses. Ainsi, l'art. 4 de la loi d'approbation des accords entre la République et l'Union des communautés juives reconnaît aux juifs le droit d'observer le repos sabbatique.

Les exemples démontrent que surtout dans le domaine public et dans les rapports de travail subordonnés, l'appartenance à un système de valeurs et de normes religieuses, justifie le non-respect de la loi générale, à condition que les intéressés manifestent de manière claire leur désir d'être soumis à une discipline différente.

La référence générale à la dimension religieuse dans les normes de l'État

Sur ce point il est nécessaire de bien comprendre le problème afin d'éviter des malentendus. A été mis en évidence le fait que l'État ne peut pas utiliser, dans le respect du principe de laïcité et de séparation entre l'État et les organisations religieuses, aucune référence au droit religieux pour réaliser ses propres intérêts. Au contraire le lien avec la norme religieuse n'est pas interdit, si celui-ci ne vise pas à renforcer l'efficacité des normes étatiques. Le deuxième alinéa de l'article 9 de la loi 121/1985, où l'on justifie l'obligation de l'État d'organiser l'enseignement de la religion catholique dans les écoles publiques semble tomber dans cette seconde hypothèse. La République italienne, en effet, reconnaît la valeur de la culture religieuse et en considérant que les principes du catholicisme font partie du patrimoine historique du peuple italien, continuera à assurer, dans le cadre des objectifs de l'école publique de chaque degré, à l'exception du système universitaire, l'enseignement de la religion catholique sans préjudices pour les autres croyants ou non-croyants qui pourront décider de ne pas choisir cet enseignement.

Autonomie normative des organisations religieuses

L'autonomie normative enracinée sur le principe de réserve exclusive de compétence en matière du statut reconnue aux organisations religieuses non catholiques par le second alinéa de l'art. 8 Const., ainsi que la nature du système juridique primaire reconnu à la Eglise catholique, permettent à celles-ci de régler de façon autonome ses propres rapports juridiques. Toutefois, puisque les normes statutaires s'appliquent sur le territoire de l'État italien, il faut que ces normes soient compatibles et non pas en contraste avec le système juridique italien. Dans les faits les lois civiles prévaudront sur les normes religieuses, seulement dans le cas où les droits fondamentaux seront en péril.

Il est attribué aux organisations ecclésiastiques reconnues du point de vue du droit civil le pouvoir de régler de façon autonome leurs rapports à l'intérieur de l'organisation selon leurs propres normes statutaires. La seule limite est constituée par le respect de certaines normes, c'est-à-dire, les dispositions de droit civil prévues pour la reconnaissance de la personnalité juridique selon le droit étatique: appartenance confessionnelle, finalité de religion et de culte, siège administratif en Italie. Faute de reconnaissance, le législateur italien prévoit l'application de la norme relative aux entités de fait, ou bien de la norme prévue pour les personnes morales privées ou encore, celle prévue pour les personnes juridiques privées ou celles statuées par la typologie d'organisation choisie par l'entité afin d'opérer dans notre système. L'art. 7 alinéa 5 de la l. 121/1985 prévoit la forme juridique choisie par le corps moral.

Lutte contre les formes de discrimination pour raisons de nature religieuse

Dans les relations de travail subordonné, il existe depuis longtemps des normes fonctionnelles qui visent à interdire chaque forme de discrimination religieuse et de limitation d'exercice de la liberté de religion et de conscience. À cet égard, les articles 8 et 15 du Statut du travailleur; l'art. 43 du d. Lgs 286 du 1998 et le d. Lgs 216 du 2003 ont introduit plusieurs interdictions aux employeurs dans le but d'assurer la liberté religieuse et de conscience aux travailleurs subordonnés. L'employeur a tout particulièrement le devoir de: (i) ne pas limiter les facultés d'expressions de la liberté religieuse; (ii) ne pas s'informer sur l'appartenance religieuse des travailleurs subordonnés; (iii) ne pas traiter un travailleur de façon différente en raison de son appartenance religieuse; (iv) ne pas licencier pour raisons de nature religieuse; (v) ne pas soumettre à des décisions limitatives de la liberté religieuse le travailleur que se refuse à réaliser des comportements contraires aux prescriptions dictées par sa conscience, ou qui décide de suivre des habitudes et des comportements, dans le domaine privé, qui ne sont pas conformes aux normes et percepts religieux, à moins que ces comportements soient un obstacle pour le déroulement régulier du travail.

Il va de soi qu'une partie de ces obligations ne seront pas appliquées dans le cas où l'employeur puisse être qualifié comme «organisation de tendance», c'est à dire une organisation pour laquelle la production des services ou des biens est liée à la réalisation d'objectifs particuliers de nature idéologique ou religieuse. Il est évident aussi que dans ces situations l'exigence de protéger les droit humains indisponibles des individus prévoit à propos des intérêts des organisations de tendance que les individus ne pourront pas exiger une protection de leurs instances au point de justifier le sacrifice du droit de l'organisation à demander l'accomplissement des devoirs de solidarité librement choisis, mais également que l'Etat doit assurer un protection juridictionnelle à tous ceux qui décident d'abandonner l'organisation et de considérer inacceptables les violations des droit des travailleurs qui déroulent des activités neutres.

Profils jurisprudentiels

Le devoir de choisir entre les juridictions religieuse et étatique se pose à propos de la discipline du mariage où les épouses peuvent décider de travailler à résoudre le mariage, ou bien en choisissant les procédures de séparation ou de divorce régulées par la l. 898/1970, ou, au contraire, en appelant le juge religieux pour obtenir la nullité matrimoniale, et à travers le processus de délibération, obtenir la cessation des effets civils du mariage canonique. En réalité la question est très complexe sous le point de vue juridique, comme en témoignent les différentes solutions proposées par les juges: d'une part la Cour de Cassation à Sections Unies avec l'arrêté 13 février 1993, n. 1824 a affirmé l'existence d'une concurrence entre la juridiction civile et celle ecclésiastique, compensée par le principe de prévention, selon lequel une fois choisie une juridiction entre les deux, l'autre ne peut plus être élue comme juridiction compétente. D'autre part le juge constitutionnel se positionne avec un *obiter dictum* présent dans l'arrêté 421/1993: dans ce cas les juges des lois ont défendu la réserve de juridiction des tribunaux ecclésiastiques soutenant que le mariage, réglementé par le droit canonique, doit être soumis à la juridiction des juges ecclésiastiques.

Il est clair que si l'hypothèse où l'interprétation de la Cour de Cassation est prédominante, le problème du droit à appliquer se pose: le droit civil et les lois relatives au mariage civil, ou les canons prévus par le droit canonique en raison de ce qui est établi par le droit international privé?

La jurisprudence de mérite (Trib. Milan, 17 juin 1996, n. 6101) a confirmé sur ce point que l'application par juges civils du droit canonique serait en opposition avec le principe suprême de séparation entre les deux ordres, prévu par l'art. 7 Const. Cette dernière interprétation a été acceptée par les juges ordinaires qui se sont prononcés pour la nullité du mariage canonique transcrit pour une des causes prévues par le Code Civil en application de l'art. 122 alinéa 2 et 3 c.c.

Efficacité des actes juridictionnels de nature religieuse dans le système juridique de l'État

Il faut encore se pencher sur la question de savoir si l'administration de la justice dans le domaine religieux doit respecter les principes du système juridique de l'État. Ainsi, dans ce cas, l'on ne peut pas déroger au principe qui concerne la séparation entre l'ordre étatique et l'ordre religieux prévu par l'art. 7 Const. En conséquence de ce principe, dans le système juridique italien, la justice confessionnelle sera administrée seulement à travers les normes de droit interne de nature religieuse. Les normes de l'État seront efficaces seulement si elles sont reçues par le système juridique religieux.

C'est un cas différent celui des effets civils des arrêtés déclarés par les juges religieux. Le problème s'est présenté, en particulier, dans les procédures de délibération des arrêtés en matière de nullité matrimoniale réglementées par l'art. 8 aliéna 2 de la l.121/1985 et intégrées par les dispositions de n-4 lett. b du protocole additionnel. En force de cette norme, l'efficacité civile des arrêtés de nullité pourra se manifester seulement si les conditions prévues par la loi sont satisfaites. Ces conditions sont: i) le respect du principe du contradictoire pendant le procès face au juge ecclésiastique ; ii) la non - contrariété au principe de l'ordre publique italien.

Compétence de l'autorité confessionnelle pour évaluer la légitimité des normes de l'État

Il faut enfin se demander si l'État permet à l'autorité religieuse d'interpréter les lois de l'État et d'évaluer leur conformité avec les règles religieuses. En vertu du principe de distinction entre les ordres, l'autorité légale ne peut pas se substituer à la religion, en correspondance de celle religieuse ne peut pas entrer dans les mérites des normes étatiques, au plus elle pourra exprimer des jugements de nature éthique ou morale en suggérant aux fidèles de désobéir, ou d'agir politiquement afin d'obtenir l'abrogation de ces dispositions.

Les processus sociaux

Politiques et pratiques qui ne sont pas conformes à la tradition et leur discipline

Les processus de migration et la croissance du pluralisme religieux ont certainement augmenté les cas des comportements et des pratiques non conformes aux canons culturels et comportementaux de la tradition italienne; toutefois, ces comportements, comme la jurisprudence en témoigne, n'ont jamais pris des formes aussi enracinées et répandues au point que l'on puisse configurer un réel processus de transformation sociale. Dans le contexte italien, ces phénomènes ont généralement pris une dimension épisodique, parfois répétée au fil du temps, mais jamais cela n'a été le signe d'un véritable changement de coutumes.

Les cas de l'infibulation, ainsi que les préoccupations liées à l'utilisation de la *burqa* font montre d'une forme d'instrumentalisation politique, qui n'est tout de même pas l'expression d'une véritable urgence sociale. Le cas de l'art. 6 de la loi 9 janvier 2006, n. 7 qui a introduit l'art 583-bis c.p qui élève au niveau du délit la «clitoridectomie, l'excision, l'infibulation et toutes autres pratiques produisant les mêmes effets» est symptomatique. D'autre part les chiffres judiciaires de la nouvelle infraction sont ridicules, si l'on prend en compte que, jusqu'à ce jour, il y a eu un seul arrêté de condamnation. Tout cela confirme la valeur éminemment symbolique de la loi vouée à qualifier un fait comme «mauvais».

Le même discours peut être fait à propos de la *burqa*. En effet, face aux cas d'utilisation extrêmement limitée d'un tel vêtement, les propositions de lois visent à en interdire l'utilisation, comme dans le projet de loi n. 2422 d'initiative Sbai-Contento du 6 mai 2009 «Modification de l'art. 5 de la loi du 22 mai 1975, n. 152 concernant l'interdiction de porter des vêtements connus comme la *burqa* et le *niqab*»; le projet de loi n. 2769 d'initiative Cota et d'autres du 2 octobre 2009 «Modification de l' art. 5 de la loi du 22 mai 1975, n. 152, relatif à la protection de l'ordre public et au caractère identifiable de la population» ont été construits, encore une fois, en termes de règle-affiche, invoquant des raisons d'ordre public, de sécurité et d'alarme sociale, ce dernier ayant été suscité à dessein par certaines forces politiques.

En un mot, l'on peut dire qu'en Italie il y a effectivement des cas où certains comportements motivés religieusement, ne souffrant pas des limitations de nature réglementaire, soulèvent des problèmes sociaux qui suscitent l'hostilité de certaines parties de la population, mais ils ne constituent pas la possibilité réelle d'urgence sociale.

Services de nature religieuse des confessions sans accord

Les citoyens italiens et aussi les résidents appartenant à une organisation religieuse dépourvue d'un accord bilatéral bénéficient de certains services qui leur sont fournis par ces mêmes organisations religieuses, parfois grâce à des accords conclus avec les autorités régionales ou locales. À ce sujet, on peut rappeler l'exemple du Plan des services, qui fait, conformément à l'art. 9, paragraphe 4 de la l.r. Lombardie 12/2005, «une évaluation en priorité de tous les équipements au service des fonctions établies dans le domaine municipal [...] et, en cas de défaillance ou d'insuffisance de l'équipement, quantifie les coûts de leur adaptation et identifie les moyens d'intervention».

En vertu des articles 71 et 72 de la même l.r. 12/2005, les «installations d'intérêt commun visant à des services religieux» font partie des services que le Plan doit également garantir. Il faut planifier sur la base des demandes formulées par toutes les confessions religieuses qui ont une présence généralisée, sont organisées et stables dans la municipalité, indépendamment de l'existence d'un accord, et dont les statuts expérimentent le caractère religieux de leurs fins institutionnels et dont l'activité principale consiste à fournir des services religieux. Dans d'autres cas c'est la loi même qui permet aux représentants des confessions religieuses classées comme cultes admis, de fournir certains services. Dans ce sens, on peut souligner les dispositions de l'article 6 du Décret Royal n. 230/1929, qui prévoient que «les ministres des cultes admis par l'État peuvent être autorisés à fournir l'assistance religieuse aux détenus en prisons chaque fois que les intéressés en font la requête». De plus, grâce aux dispositions de l'article 100 du décret présidentiel du 10 septembre 1990, n. 85 concernant le plan de réglementation des cimetières qui autorise la création d'espaces spéciaux d'enterrement séparé pour les cadavres de personnes professant une religion non catholique, certaines confessions religieuses sont en mesure de fournir des services funéraires conformément aux exigences fixées par les traditions religieuses et leur communauté.

Conclusions

Le pluralisme religieux en Italie depuis 1947 a été construit sur la base de deux critères distincts mais connexes: celui de la «précédence » et celui de la «conformité». En force du premier principe, aucun accord avec une minorité religieuse n'aurait été possible en l'absence d'un précédent accord convenu avec l'Église catholique. Tout cela est bien connu de la communauté vaudoise - méthodiste, dont les représentants ont dû attendre 1984 pour voir signer, trois jours après la signature du nouveau Concordat avec l'Eglise catholique, l'accord avec l'État, bien que le texte de l'accord fût prêt depuis 1978. Le critère de la «précédence», cependant, ne garantit pas l'accès à l'accord, pour cela il est nécessaire que la minorité religieuse réponde au critère de conformité, c'est-à-dire que la confession religieuse minoritaire doit accepter de réglementer ses rapports avec l'État selon le modèle du concordat. Autrement dit, l'État italien exige que les minorités religieuses s'organisent selon des modèles reconnaissables par l'État et, en particulier, selon le modèle fondé sur la séparation entre le pouvoir séculaire et le pouvoir spirituel propre à la culture chrétienne occidentale qui est habituée à une distinction claire entre les activités religieuses et laïques et que est aussi habituée à penser la religion organisée à travers le model hiérarchique et avec la présence de professionnels du spirituel.

Il est évident qu'une revendication de cette nature crée des problèmes dans un large éventail d'organisations religieuses, loin d'un modèle ecclésiologique de type constantinien, et ces organisations religieuses ont des difficultés à établir, comme certaines confessions l'ont fait ou tentent de le faire, un organe représentatif unitaire. Je pense au processus de fédération complexe et laborieux qui a conduit, entre 2009 et 2011, plusieurs organisations islamiques à converger dans les fédérations régionales et après dans la Confédération islamique italienne (CII) explicitement liée au gouvernement, et à un certain nombre d'institutions religieuses et cultuelles du Maroc sans avoir, ainsi, aucune chance d'obtenir un accord formel avec l'État.

Les accords auraient dû introduire une norme spéciale relative à la liberté religieuse motivée des caractéristiques uniques des différentes organisations religieuses, ces caractéristiques ne pouvaient pas trouver l'hospitalité dans une loi générale sur la liberté religieuse. Si pour les constituants, l'État aurait dû donner plein effet à l'art. 19 de la Constitution au-delà des limites de la loi sur les cultes admis de 1929, thèse confirmée par la Cour constitutionnelle dans l'arrêté n. 59 de 1958, en réalité, ce qui est arrivé a suivi un autre parcours. Les accords ont fini par être chargés d'un rôle qui n'était pas le leur. À travers le pouvoir discrétionnaire de l'exécutif, les accords ont eu la fonction de faire sortir d'une condition normative d'inconstitutionnalité, celle de la l .1159/1929, les minorités religieuses. En ce sens l'institut des «intese» (conventions) a été très séduisant parce qu'il suggérait aux confessions minoritaires le seul moyen de sortir des limites de la loi sur les cultes, et en même temps il a rendu moins intéressant le projet sur le droit de la liberté religieuse.

Autrement dit, la question de la réforme/abrogation de la loi sur les cultes admis était destinée à tomber dans l'indifférence générale des deux forces politiques et dans de nombreux cas, des confessions religieuses mêmes, fortement attirées par la perspective de bilatéralité. L'utilisation parcimonieuse et sélective des «intese» peut également être partagée, mais là où la prudence devient déraisonnable en raison de traitements et de moyens de distribution des privilèges, les «intese» sont transformées en instrument d'injustice à l'encontre des hypothèses du pluralisme et du principe d'égalité si fortement nécessaire au niveau européen, d'un côté par la cour de Strasbourg, et, de l'autre par l'art. 19, paragraphe 1, du traité sur le fonctionnement de l'Union européenne. Cependant, l'odieux problème de la discrétion est également lié à un aspect plus technique: l'absence d'une loi réglementant l'accès aux «intese». Pendant cinq législatures, de 1990 jusqu'au projet de loi n. 3613 de 2010, diverses conceptions et propositions de loi sur la liberté religieuse ont toujours attendu une norme qui vise à réglementer l'accès aux conventions, le fait que ces dernières ne soient jamais transformées en loi a signifié la permanence dans la question d'une grave anomie.

De ce fait, au niveau législatif, on ne dit rien sur les modalités d'activations des négociations, de leur conduite, de l'implication et de la présentation au Parlement du dessein de loi d'approbation. La justice administrative est intervenue pour compenser ces lacunes réglementaires. Le Conseil d'État dans la prononciation n. 6083 du 18 novembre 2011, confirmé par la Cass. Civ dans l'arrêté n. 16305 du 28 Juin 2013, a voulu introduire le principe en force duquel le gouvernement a le devoir d'entamer des négociations pour la conclusion des accords. En réfutant l'argument avancé par le tribunal administratif régional du Latium, dans son arrêté n.12539 de 2008, le Conseil d'État a estimé que l'article 8 troisième alinéa Const. ne légitime pas l'interprétation de la décision du gouvernement d'activer ou non les négociations comme un simple acte politique. Il s'agit là d'un jugement très questionné et qui ne convainc pas encore le gouvernement. Dans le but de surmonter l'inertie du pouvoir exécutif relativement à l'homologation des accords, la Résolution de la Commission parlementaire sur les règlement de la Chambre des Députés du 28 février 2007, en faveur de la recevabilité de l'initiative législative parlementaire pour ce qui concerne le projet de loi pour réglementer les relations entre les confessions religieuses et l'État mérite également qu'on y prête attention. C'est une mesure qui a permis de surmonter, dans la dernière série d'accords, la résistance et les retards du pouvoir exécutif dans la présentation des dessins et des projets de lois ratifiés depuis longtemps, mais pas encore approuvés. Le système juridique italien en ce qui concerne la liberté religieuse a toujours préféré le régime dell'*aut-aut* à celui de *et-et* dans la régulation de la relation entre le droit à la liberté religieuse et le principe d'égalité. Il l'a fait en 1929 avec la loi sur les cultes admis en sacrifiant la liberté en faveur de l'égalité, il réitère cela avec les politiques d'accès discrétionnaires aux accords, en sacrifiant l'égalité au nom d'une liberté plus grande et qualifiée. Tout n'est évidemment pas propice au pluralisme religieux, mais surtout notre système n'apparaît pas comme étant conforme aux standards des normes exigées par l'Union européenne, dans lesquels les quatre valeurs fondamentales sur lesquelles a été structurée la Charte de Nice, échappent à l'esprit libéral qui veut que traditionnellement ces droits soient en concurrence entre eux. L'égalité et la liberté, la dignité et la solidarité constituent maintenant des valeurs indivisibles mises en lien sur le même plan. Cela aura des conséquences importantes en termes de pluralisme religieux, parce qu'on ne pourra plus accepter, dans le futur, une politique sélective à propos de la reconnaissance de la liberté de religion et de conscience comme droit fondamental.

En conclusion, le processus de transformation qui est en train de modifier rapidement et inexorablement le paysage religieux italien, demande, au-delà de la sensibilité culturelle différente, une adaptation rapide des instruments normatifs. Cela signifie que les institutions de la République ont le devoir d'examiner de façon différente un certain nombre des paramètres liés à la redéfinition de la frontière entre ce qui est négociable et ce qui ne l'est pas, parce que contraire aux droits fondamentaux de l'homme; la définition de ce qui peut être compris et ce qui doit être exclu du système de relations sociales; la capacité, enfin, de transformer l'étrangeté en solidarité, par la gestion des relations complexes et difficiles entre les sociétés multi-ethniques et les valeurs fondamentales de la République. C'est seulement à ces conditions les défis du pluralisme religieux pourront être vaincus par les institutions de la République.

Chapter 15
Legal Pluralism and Conflicts in Malaysia: The Challenge of Embracing Diversity

Nurjaanah Chew Li Hua

Abstract The historical background of colonization and the resulting diversity of communities in Malaysia is reflected in the legal framework which comprises of multiple parallel legal systems. Nevertheless, there are conflicts when the issues straddle over to more than one legal system. The conflicts with regards to jurisdiction of the respective courts, the enforcement of religious laws and the individual's fundamental rights which at first blush seem to be highlighting religious tensions within the society are, it is submitted, part and parcel of the developing legal pluralism. The judiciary plays an essential role in resolving legal conflicts which arise from the existing legal pluralism by remaining true to the letter and spirit of the Federal Constitution which guarantees fundamental liberties to the individuals.

Introduction

In the multi-racial, multi-cultural and multi-religious society that forms Malaysia, legal pluralism is not just a theory. It is a reality, one which is very much alive, as evidenced by the numerous conflicts that have been brought before the courts of Malaysia over the past decades. Although such challenges before the courts may be perceived as the tip of the iceberg, highlighting the religious tensions within the society, it is the author's submission that these are part and parcel of the growing process of legal pluralism. One may even consider these as the 'growing pains'. The challenge in resolving such conflicts is in embracing the diversity inherent to the Malaysian context, guided by the wisdom, spirit and principles encapsulated in the Federal Constitution itself, the document which gave birth to the nation state called Malaysia.[1]

In 2010, Malaysia's population of 28.3 million consists of Malays, Chinese, Indians, other ethnic groups as well as numerous groups of indigenous peoples in

[1] This is not to deny the existence of a state or nation prior to the achievement of independence of the country from the British in 1957.

N. Chew Li Hua (✉)
University of Malaya, Kuala Lumpur, Malaysia
e-mail: janetchew@um.edu.my

R. Bottoni et al. (eds.), *Religious Rules, State Law, and Normative Pluralism - A Comparative Overview*, Ius Comparatum – Global Studies in Comparative Law 18, DOI 10.1007/978-3-319-28335-7_15

the Peninsular, Sabah and Sarawak. In Malaysia, 61.3 % of the population practices Islam, 19.8 % Buddhism, 9.2 % Christianity, 6.3 % Hinduism and 1.3 % practice Confucianism, Taoism, and other traditional Chinese philosophies and religions. 2.1 % consists of those with other religions, unknown religions and those with no religion.[2] Thus, the four main religions in Malaysia today are Islam, Buddhism, Christianity and Hinduism.[3]

Malaysia is a federation of 13 states, with 9 states having a Ruler from the respective royal families and 4 states with *Yang di-Pertua Negeri* or Governor.[4] Malaysia is governed by a Parliamentary democracy, with a federal government and respective state governments. The Federal Constitution of Malaysia sets up the whole structure of the nation; the executive, the legislature and the judiciary. It is the supreme law of the land.[5] Malaysia currently maintains a multi-legal system due to historical factors, as formalized in the Federal Constitution.

The Supreme Head of the federation is known as the *Yang di-Pertuan Agong* or the King of Malaysia, a constitutional monarch elected by the Conference of Rulers for a 5 year term.[6] Only the nine traditional State Rulers are eligible to be so elected. The Conference of Rulers consists of all the nine Rulers and the Governors.[7] The King acts on the advice of the Cabinet and may only act in his discretion on limited matters, such as the appointment of the Prime Minister.[8] He is the head of the religion of Islam in the states without the traditional Rulers and in his own home state, whereas the Rulers of the states are the head of the religion of Islam in their respective states.[9]

[2] Malaysia, Department of Statistics Malaysia, *Population Distribution and Basic Demographic Characteristic Report 2010*, last updated: 5 August 2011, accessed on 23 January 2014 http://www.statistics.gov.my/portal/index.php?option=com_content&id=1215. The Population and Housing Census is conducted once in every 10 years. The last Census was conducted in 2010, using face to face interview. Information collected includes the number of persons and households together with a wide range of demographic, social and economic characteristics. https://www.statistics.gov.my/index.php?r=column/cone&menu_id=ZHJlbWFBSTVEcHY1ait6akR3Wmt VUT09

[3] It is to be noted that inter-racial marriages are not uncommon in Malaysia. Legally, the classification of the ethnicity of the children follows that of the father. However, it is a common practice to state the ethnicity as Malay if the religion is Islam even if either spouse or even neither spouse is not a Malay ethnically. This ensures the privileged status of *bumiputera* or 'sons of the soil' in Malaysia. A Malay is defined in Article 160 of the Federal Constitution as a person who professes the religion of Islam, habitually speaks the Malay language and conforms to Malay custom. See Bashiran Begum and Ainul Jaria, "*Who is Malay: Defining 'Malayness'*", *Current Law Journal* 5 (2008), at pp i–lv for a detailed discussion on the definition of Malay.

[4] Article 1, Federal Constitution of Malaysia.

[5] *Ibid.*, Article 4(1).

[6] *Ibid.*, Part 1, Third Schedule.

[7] *Ibid.*, Article 38 and Fifth Schedule.

[8] *Ibid.*, Article 40.

[9] *Ibid.*, Article 3.

Constitutional Construct

The Malaysian legal system is a combination of secular, religious and customary systems. It comprises of the civil courts, Syariah courts and native courts (in the two states of Sabah and Sarawak in East Malaysia). The national legal system is a combination of the federal and states' legal system. Whilst the civil courts come under the purview of the federal legal system, both the Syariah courts and native courts are under the respective state's legal system.[10] The divisions of legislative matters are laid down in the Ninth Schedule of the Federal Constitution.[11] The subject matters enumerated in the Federal List are exclusively under the legislative power of the Federal Parliament whilst those set out in the State List are exclusively within the purview of the State Legislative Assemblies. For subject matters in the Concurrent List, both the federal and state governments are competent to legislate on said matters. In the event of any conflict between federal and state law enacted over a subject stated in the Concurrent List, the federal law would prevail and the state law, to the extent of the inconsistency, would be void.[12]

Civil, criminal law, procedure, and the administration of justice fall under the Federal List, whereas Islamic law and personal and family law of persons professing the religion of Islam fall under the State List.[13] The organization and procedure of the Syariah courts are under the jurisdiction of the respective states. Similarly, for native courts in Sabah and Sarawak, native laws and customs and the determination of matters of native laws or customs, the constitution, organization, and procedure of native courts (including the right of audience in such courts), and the jurisdiction and powers of such courts fall under the jurisdiction of those two states.

It is to be noted that the word 'law' means written law, the common law in so far as it is in operation in the Federation or any part thereof, and any custom or usage having the force of law in the Federation or any part thereof.[14] Although Syariah is not mentioned in the above said definition, Islamic law is implemented *via* the numerous state legislations and rules passed by the State Legislative Assemblies on

---

[10] *Ibid.*, Ninth Schedule.

[11] *Ibid.*, Article 74.

[12] Ibid., Article 75. See the case of *The City Council of George Town & Anor v The Government of The State of Penang & Anor[1967]* 1 MLJ 169.

[13] The State Legislative Assembly of Kelantan passed the Syariah Criminal Code (II) (1993) 2015 Enactment or better known as the *Hudud* Bill on 19 March 2015, an amendment to the Syariah Criminal Code (II) 1993 in its effort to pave the way for the implementation of Islamic criminal law in the state. See http://malaysianlaw.my/general/news/hudud-is-unconstitutional-discriminatory-and-divisive-says-bar-MY11996.html for Malaysian Bar Council's immediate response to the unanimous passing of the state enactment. A few days before the Bill was tabled, the Sultan of Kelantan, the ruler of the state expressed support for the Bill. See http://www.thestar.com.my/News/Nation/2015/03/16/Kelantan-Sultan-Syariah-Criminal-Code/ . Despite its clear unconstitutionality, the total support for the Bill by all members of the State Legislative Assembly, both the ruling state party and the opposition parties raised the question of how transgression by the state into federal matters are to be dealt with.

[14] Federal Constitution, Article 160.

Islamic law, matters as listed in the State List, which include personal and family law.[15] The subsequent discussion on the conflicts of law is confined to the federal law and the applicable Islamic law at state level.[16] It does not include native and customary laws.[17]

Brief Historical Background

Prior to Islam, early societies in Peninsular Malaya were influenced by Hinduism and Buddhism. The conversion of the Malays to Islam, which began in the early 14th century, was accelerated with the rise of the state of Malacca under the rule of a Muslim prince in the 15th century. The Portuguese came seeking the wealth of spices and conquered Malacca in 1511.[18] It was subsequently overrun by the Dutch in 1641. The British later gained a foothold over Malaya when the early Malay rulers sought aid from the East India Company to resolve succession disputes as early as 1771, when the majority of the people were Malay Muslims.[19] The need for cheap labour to exploit the natural resources of the land drove the British to embark upon a policy of actively encouraging alien immigration into Malaya.[20] Starting in the 1820s, Indians from South India were brought in for the large-scale rubber plantation. The British encouraged the migration of the Chinese from China for the purpose of tin-mining in the later part of 19th century. The Chinese and Indians began to settle in Malaya. They built their own communities, including schools and temples in various parts of the country. The Chinese brought with them Chinese philosophies, practices and culture, whilst the Indians were mainly Hindu and Sikh. This resulted in the distribution of religion along racial lines. It is to be noted that there were earlier Chinese and Indian communities who had settled and assimilated within the Malay community centuries earlier, prior to

[15] *Ibid.*, State List, Ninth Schedule. The Federal Constitution, Ninth Schedule is available at http://www.agc.gov.my/images/Personalisation/Buss/pdf/Federal%20Consti%20(BI%20text).pdf, at p193–p202.

[16] Article 75 of the Federal Constitution provides that if any State law is inconsistent with a federal law, the federal law shall prevail and the State law shall, to the extent of the inconsistency, be void.

[17] In no way does this mean that conflicts of law between federal law and native and customary laws are insignificant or unimportant. A proper analysis of the numerous and diverse native and customary laws is beyond the scope of this chapter.

[18] *Malaysia Country Study Guide*, (Washington DC: USA International Business Publications, 2008), at http://books.google.com.my/books?id=vBm2b0BwU9EC&pg=PA21&dq=history+of+malaysia+%2B+the+British+first+came+%2B++malacca+%2B+Malay+Muslims&hl=en&sa=X&ei=AZv1Ur2bHc3jkAXy-YG4Aw&ved=0CD8Q6AEwBA#v=onepage&q=history%20of%20malaysia%20%2B%20the%20British%20first%20came%20%2B%20%20malacca%20%2B%20Malay%20Muslims&f=false

[19] See Andaya & Andaya, A History of Malaysia, 1982, Macmillan at p. 109.

[20] Parmer JN, Colonial Labour Policy and Administration: A History of Labour in the Rubber Plantation Industry in Malaya, 1960, JJ Augustin Inc, p. 16.

the migration in the 19th century, mainly due to early trade relations. These include the Baba and Nyonya community.

One of the prerequisites set by the British for the transfer of power to the Malayans in the negotiation for independence was interethnic co-operation. This was to ensure a smooth political transition, and to counter the threat posed by the Malayan Communist Party, which played a significant role in the fight against the Japanese during the Second World War. One of the striking features of the Reid Commission's Report and the Federal Constitution are the inter-communal compromises which sought to safeguard the rights and interests of all the communities. The White Paper issued by the British Government in June 1957, shortly after the London Conference, Paragraph 57 reads[21]:

There has been included in the Federal Constitution a declaration that Islam is the religion of the Federation. This will in no way affect the present position of the Federation as a secular State, and every person will have the right to profess and practice his own religion and the right to propagate his religion, though this last right is subject to any restrictions imposed by State law relating to the propagation of any religious doctrine or belief among persons professing the Muslim religion.

The root of religious demography in Malaysia, formed during the British colonial era, was thus formalized in the Federal Constitution. In declaring that Islam is the religion of the Federation, the status of Malaysia as a secular State was emphasized.[22] The only caveat imposed on the freedom of religion are the restrictions on propagation of other religions amongst Muslims.[23]

Brief Legal Background

There were three Charters of Justice which governed the colony of the Straits Settlement.[24] Decided cases held that English law was to be the only law in the various settlements, but it was to be applied only in so far as the religions, manners and

[21] Stockwell, A. J., Political testament of the Alliance': Memorandum by Tunku Abdul Rahman for the Reid *Commission*, (London: HMSO, 1995).

[22] In the case of *Che Omar bin Che Soh v Public Prosecutor Wan Jalil bin Wan Abdul Rahman & Anor v Public Prosecutor* [1988] 2 MLJ 55 at pp 56–57, His Lordship Saleh Abas LP traced the constitutional history of Malaya then and put in perspective the proper meaning of 'Islam' referred to in art 3(1). It was concluded that all laws including administration of Islamic laws had to receive validity through a secular fiat. Thus, it can be seen that during the British colonial period, through their system of indirect rule and establishment of secular institutions, Islamic law was rendered isolated in a narrow confinement to the law of marriage, divorce, and inheritance only (see MB Hooker, Islamic Law in South-east Asia, 1984).

[23] Article 11(4), Federal Constitution.

[24] The first was granted to the East India Company in March 1807 and this set up the judicial administration in the Presidency of Penang. The second was granted to the East India Company in November 1826 and extended the jurisdiction of the Court to cover Singapore and Malacca. The third Charter was granted in August 1855.

customs of the inhabitants would permit it.[25] Inadvertently or otherwise, English law has been the law of general application in Malaysia since the earliest periods of colonial occupation. In a limited aspect, it has undergone a process of adaptation and modification which, in significant measure, has been an accommodation to the various personal laws.[26]

Article 3(1) of the Federal Constitution of Malaysia declares that Islam is the religion of the Federation; but other religions may be practiced in peace and harmony in any part of the Federation. Article 4 affirms the Federal Constitution as the supreme law of the land. Part II (Articles 5 to 13) of the Federal Constitution guarantees the fundamental liberties of all Malaysians. Article 11 guarantees freedom of religion by stating that every person has the right to profess and practice his religion and, subject to Clause (4), to propagate it. Clause (4) allows state law and in respect of the Federal Territories of Kuala Lumpur, Labuan and Putrajaya, federal law, to control or restrict the propagation of any religious doctrine or belief among persons professing the religion of Islam. Article 74(2) of the Federal Constitution read with State List, item 1, of the Ninth Schedule empowers State Legislatures to legislate on matters pertaining to the religion of Islam. It is clear that all State legislation, including Islamic laws passed by State Legislatures, must be consistent with Part II of the Federal Constitution.

Scope of Applicable Islamic Law

The scope of the applicable Islamic law in Malaysia does not include commercial law and covers only a limited range of criminal law.[27] Syariah criminal offences include offences by persons professing the religion of Islam against precepts of that religion, and the offence of propagating doctrines and beliefs amongst persons professing the religion of Islam. It is also clearly stated that the Syariah courts shall only have jurisdiction over persons professing the religion of Islam and only on matters enumerated in paragraph 1 of the State List.[28] In the light of the supremacy of the Federal Constitution, the State Legislative Assembly should only pass Syariah laws which are not inconsistent with the Constitution.[29] Any inconsistency with the Constitution results in the state law being void. The Federal Court reiterated this

[25] See *R v Willans*[1858] 3 Ky 16 and *Fatimah v Logan* [1871] 1 Ky 255 and the Civil Law Act 1956, sections 3 and 5.

[26] For an overview of the Malaysian legal system, see Sharifah Suhana Ahmad, *Malaysian Legal System*, 1999, Butterworths Asia and Wan Arfah Hamzah & Ramy Bulan, *An Introduction to the Malaysian Legal System*, 2003, Penerbit Fajar Bakti Sdn Bhd, Shah Alam.

[27] In the context of Syariah or Islamic law proper, which encompasses all aspects of the lives of its believers, it is conceded that the Islamic law applicable in Malaysia is actually limited in its application.

[28] See footnote 16.

[29] Article 4(1), Federal Constitution of Malaysia.

point in *Latifah bte Mat Zin v Rosmawati bte Sharibun & Anor*, when it observed as follows[30]:

> Actually if laws are made by Parliament and the Legislatures of the States in strict compliance with the Federal List and the State List and unless the real issues are misunderstood, there should not be any situation where both courts have jurisdiction over the same matter or issue.

The reality is, of course, messier than anticipated by the framers of the Federal Constitution. There are provisions in numerous state laws which may go beyond the limited scope provided in the State List of the Federal Constitution. The recent passing of the Islamic criminal law in the form of the Syariah Criminal Code (II) (1993) 2015 Enactment by the Kelantan State Legislative Assembly is an example of this transgression by the state into matters in the Federal List.[31] In addition, the enforcement and overzealous implementation of such provisions, which encroach upon the fundamental liberties of individuals, have over the years increasingly been seen as the rise in moral policing.[32]

Of Conversions and Courts' Jurisdiction

It is inevitable that conflicts will arise in a multi-legal system, especially when the neat compartmentalization of race and religion breaks down. This is highlighted in cases of mixed marriages and conversions to Islam. Although these conflicts are personal and emotive at the individual level, in the public sphere, these exercises of individual fundamental liberties can and has been seen as an affront to Islam and the Malays. Such a public stance is fodder for political mileage in the highly racial

[30] [2007] 5 MLJ 101, at pp. 107–108.

[31] See footnote 16.

[32] The raiding of the premises of the Bible Society by the religious authority of Selangor (JAIS) and the confiscation of 351 copies of translated bibles in early January 2014 precipitated the legal challenge on the validity of such action. This is better known as the "Allah" controversy as the apparent basis for the raid and confiscation of the copies of the bibles was the use of the term Allah. See http://www.thestar.com.my/News/Nation/2014/01/02/Jais-raid-Bible-Society/, last accessed on 16 March 2015. This issue has been hotly debated and discussed, to the extent that even the Prime Minister made references to it. See http://www.thestar.com.my/News/Nation/2014/01/07/Najib-Tackle-issues-via-dialogue-and-engagement/. See also http://www.thestar.com.my/News/Nation/2014/01/07/NUCC-Raid-on-Bible-Society-regrettable-Move-a-blatant-disregard-for-10point-solution/, http://www.thestar.com.my/News/Nation/2014/12/08/BSM-disappointed-over-desecration-of-returned-Bibles/ and http://www.thestar.com.my/News/Community/2014/01/04/Selangor-Jais-raid-draws-more-flak-from-state-politicians/. Other issues include the participation of Muslim women in beauty pageants and even the practice of yoga. See http://www.thestar.com.my/story/?file=%2f2008%2f11%2f30%2ffocus%2f2683235&sec=focus whereby *fatwas* were issued. The relentless prosecution by the religious authority of a Muslim woman who is the store manager of the bookstore Borders for the offence of selling a book which was subsequently banned is another case in point. See http://www.freemalaysiatoday.com/category/nation/2015/03/15/jawi-pursues-nik-raina-with-notice-of-appeal/

political system in Malaysia. The major political parties compete to be seen as more Islamic. There is a growing dis-ease on the secularity of the law and the state, resulting in the government of the day insisting on many occasions that Malaysia is an Islamic state, albeit a moderate one.[33]

Nevertheless, the jurisdiction of the Syariah Courts remains limited in two ways; subject-matter and person-matter. This was elaborated upon earlier and is stated in the State List of the Ninth Schedule in the Federal Constitution. The subject matter within the jurisdiction of the Syariah Courts is as enumerated in the said List and legislated upon by the individual states. The said state legislation must be in line with the Federal Constitution itself.[34] Additionally, the person-matter is limited to persons professing the religion of Islam only. This clearly means that the Syariah Courts do not have any jurisdiction over non-Muslims. Yet, cases affecting non-Muslims are increasingly reported.

In the highly publicized case of *Indira Gandhi a/p Mutho v Patmanathan a/l Krishnan (anyone having control over Prasana Diksa)*,[35] the husband, who converted to Islam, took the action of converting his three minor children as well. The conversion of the children was later held to be null and void by the High Court.[36] The wife filed for a divorce at the Civil High Court and was granted custody of the children. Unknown to her, the husband had earlier obtained a custody order from the Syariah Court for the children. The tussle for custody of the children resulted in the husband absconding with the youngest child who was at that time 11 months and was still being breastfed. The plaintiff wife successfully commenced contempt action against the respondent husband only to be faced by the refusal of the Inspector General of Police to enforce the warrant of committal and recovery order.[37]

---

[33] See "Legislating Faith in Malaysia", Nurjaanah Abdullah, Singapore Journal Of Legal Studies [2007] 264–289, at pp. 270–272 for comments on the Malaysian government's claim that Malaysia is an Islamic State. This article looks at the position of apostasy and freedom of religion in Malaysia in the light of the conflict between state legislation which makes apostasy a crime and Article 11 of the Federal Constitution which guarantees freedom of religion.

[34] In *Majlis Agama Islam dan Adat Melayu Perak Darul Ridzuan v Mohamed Suffian bin Ahmad Syazali & Anor* [2014] 3 MLJ 74 the Court of Appeal held that when a question of whether the Syariah Court has jurisdiction over a matter, one must proceed first to consider whether the state has legislative competency before considering whether the courts have jurisdiction. Here, the state has no legislative competency to enact any state laws where the Syariah Courts may adjudicate a dispute involving a non-Muslim. The State List in the Ninth Schedule in Item 1 List II does not allow that to begin with.

[35] [2015] 7 MLJ 153.

[36] *Indira Gandhi a/p Mutho v Pengarah Jabatan Agama Islam Perak & Ors [2013]* 5 MLJ 552.

[37] The IGP declined to take any action to enforce the warrant on the basis that there are two conflicting custody orders, the husband having obtained a custody order from the Syariah Court and the wife having obtained a custody order from the civil High Court. See http://www.thestar.com.my/News/Nation/2014/09/10/Indira-Gandhi-custody-contempt-appeal-by-Mohd-Riduan-dismissed/. Such a refusal is unprecedented and warrants another article to be written. See http://www.thestar.com.my/News/Nation/2014/09/13/Court-orders-IGP-to-arrest-dad-Khalid-must-detain-Muslim-convert-who-abducted-child-from-exwife/

Although a mandamus order was later obtained by the wife against the IGP, the mandamus order was subsequently discharged by the Court of Appeal on the ground of public policy.[38] The dissenting judge was however clear that the IGP had a well-defined duty under the law to execute the warrant of committal, to apprehend the father, and to give effect to the recovery order. The latter was the final remedy available to the mother to recover the child, as there was no other avenue that the mother could resort to.[39] In dismissing the argument that the matter concerns private rights as opposed to public rights, the learned judge held that whilst the case commenced as a private dispute in a civil matter, the police was now thrust into the dispute by the application of the law. The involvement of the police thus relates to the administration of justice as a whole. More importantly, the full bench agreed with the trial judge in respect of the jurisdictional issue of the two courts. It was reiterated that in matters of custody involving a non-Muslim married couple whose marriage was dissolved on grounds of conversion to Islam, the Syariah Court does not have exclusive jurisdiction.

This position had in fact been clarified at an earlier occasion by the Federal Court in *Latifah bte Mat Zin v Rosmawati bte Sharibun & Anor*, when it observed as follows[40]:

> … if in a case in the civil court, an Islamic law issue arises, which is within the jurisdiction of the Syariah Court, the party raising the issue should file a case in the Syariah Court solely for the determination of that issue and the decision of the Syariah Court on that issue should then be applied by the civil court in the determination of the case. But, this is only possible if both parties are Muslims. If one of the parties is not a Muslim such an application to the Syariah court cannot be made. If the non-Muslim party is the would-be plaintiff, he is unable even to commence proceedings in the Syariah court. If the non-Muslim party is the would-be defendant, he would not be able to appear to put up his defence. The problem persists. Similarly, if in a case in the Syariah court, a civil law issue e.g. land law or companies law arises, the party raising the issue should file a case in the civil court for the determination of that issue which decision should be applied by the Syariah court in deciding the case…

This was further confirmed by the Federal Court in *Subashini a/p Rajasingam v Saravanan a/l Thangathoray and other appeals*.[41] It was held that there is no impediment for the converted spouse, i.e. the husband, to appear in the divorce proceedings in the High Court, albeit as a respondent, as the jurisdiction of the High Court extends to him unlike the Syariah High Court which restricts its jurisdiction to persons professing the religion of Islam only. The wife, being a non-Muslim, has no locus in the Syariah Court.[42] It is clearly stated in the State List that Syariah Court's jurisdiction extends only to Muslims.

---

[38] [2014] MLJU 1139, by a majority decision of 2:1.

[39] [2014] MLJU 1140.

[40] [2007] 5 MLJ 101, at pp. 117–118.

[41] [2008] 2 MLJ 147.

[42] Although there are cases which supported the proposition that Syariah Courts have jurisdiction over non-Muslims by implication such as the Court of Appeal case of *Kaliammal a/p Sinnasamy v Majlis Agama Islam Wilayah Persekutuan (JAWI) & Ors* [2012] 3 MLJ 694, *Soon Singh a/l Bikar*

The wider adverse implications of seeking a custody order from the Syariah court, when the other spouse remained a non-Muslim, were observed by the trial judge in *Indira Gandhi's* case:

> Any perceived advantage of wanting one's new personal law to apply to the disadvantage of the unconverted parent is illusory and more importantly, inimical to the fostering of healthy race relations in the social context of a multicultural and multi-religious state where unity in diversity should be our strength and not our shame… The end of all our seeking and searching must be that we should approximate to that which is fair, just and reasonable in the conflicts that would invariably arise even in the closest of human and filial relationships within a family. However one looks at the problem of custody whether with or without the change of one's religion, the common ground must surely always be the welfare of the child.

Unfortunately, the impact of the Court of Appeal's majority decision in *Indira Gandhi's* case is that to date, the child remains with the father despite the affirmation of the decision regarding the lack of exclusive jurisdiction of the Syariah Court. This is a very significant case which condoned the IGP's inaction under the cloak of public policy. Thus, despite having the law on her side, the remedy obtained by the mother was not enforceable. A very unsatisfactory and unacceptable position indeed. That is the current reality in Malaysia.

Of cross-dressing, right to life, equality and freedom of expression

Article 74(2) of the Federal Constitution, read with item 1 of the State List, empowers State Legislatures to legislate on matters pertaining to the religion of Islam. One of the provisions enacted under numerous state legislation is the offence of cross-dressing by Muslim men. This is part of the creation and punishment of offences by persons professing the religion of Islam, against the precepts of Islam. Article 74(3) of the Federal Constitution stipulates that the legislative powers of the States are exercisable subject to any conditions or restrictions imposed with respect to any particular matter by the Federal Constitution. This means that the exercise of State legislative powers is still subject to the fundamental liberties stated in Part II of the Federal Constitution.

Section 66 of the Syariah Criminal Enactment 1992 (Negeri Sembilan) makes it an offence for any male person to wear a woman's attire or to pose as a woman in

---

Singh v Pertubohan Kebajikan Islam Malaysia (PERKIM) Kedah & Anor [1999] 1 MLJ 489 and *Majlis Ugama Islam Pulau Pinang dan Seberang Perai lwn Shaik Zolkaffily bin Shaik Natar dan lain-lain* [2002]4 MLJ 130; [2003] 3 CLJ 289, the subsequent Federal Court's decision of *Latifah Mat Zin* and *Abdul Kahar bin Ahmad v Kerajaan Negeri Selangor (Kerajaan Malaysia, intervener) & Anor* [2008] 3 MLJ 617 have clearly and categorically stated that the jurisdiction of the Syariah Court must be expressly provided for by law enacted by the Legislature. When two decisions of the Federal Court conflict, on a point of law, the later decision prevails over the earlier decision.

any public place. The offence carries a punishment, on conviction, of a fine not exceeding one thousand ringgit or to imprisonment not exceeding six months or to both. In the case of *Muhamad Juzaili Bin Mohd Khamis & Ors v State Government Of Negeri Sembilan & Ors*,[43] an application for judicial review was filed for a declaration that section 66 of the Syariah Criminal Enactment 1992 (Negeri Sembilan) ("section 66") is void by reason of being inconsistent with Articles 5(1), 8(1), 8(2), 9(2) and 10(1)(a) of the Federal Constitution.[44] The High Court dismissed the application by the three Muslim men, resulting in an appeal before the Court of Appeal. The Court of Appeal held section 66 of the said enactment to be invalid on grounds of its unconstitutionality, being in breach of Article 5(1), 8(1), 8(2), 9(2) and 10(1)(a) of the Federal Constitution which embodies the right to life, equality, freedom of movement and freedom of expression respectively.

The applicants have a medical condition called Gender Identity Disorder (GID). As a result of the medical condition, they have since a young age been expressing themselves as women and showing the mannerisms of the feminine gender such as wearing women's clothes and using makeup. They have been repeatedly detained, arrested, and prosecuted by the religious authority of Negeri Sembilan acting pursuant to section 66 for the offence of cross-dressing. The injustice and humiliation that they are subjected to moved them to apply to the Court for the declaration that the said provision is unconstitutional.

The Court of Appeal found merit in the submission that the said provision punishes gender expression of transsexuals, degrades and devalues persons with GID, resulting in a life of continued uncertainty, misery and indignity, directly affecting their right to live with dignity as guaranteed under Article 5(1). It also prohibits the appellants and other sufferers of GID who cross-dress from moving in public places to reach their respective places of work, thus rendering their right to livelihood/work illusory, another facet of the right to life. It also restricts their freedom of movement and freedom of expression. They are constantly at risk of being arrested and punished under section 66 of the Act.

This is a surprisingly bold stance by the judiciary in the light of the continuous pressure and exercise of powers by religious authorities to implement and enforce religious rules that have been passed as state legislation.

[43] [2014] MLJU 1063.

[44] Art. 5(1) of the Federal Constitution guarantees that no person shall be deprived of his life and personal liberty save in accordance with law. The right to life has been held to include the right to live with dignity by the Court of Appeal in *Lembaga Tatatertib Perkhidmatan Awam Hospital Besar Pulau Pinang & Anor v Utra Badi K Perumah* [2000] 3 CLJ 224. Article 8(1) of the Federal Constitution guarantees equality before the law and the equal protection of the law. Article 9(2) of the Federal Constitution guarantees freedom of movement within the Federation. Art. 10(1)(a) of the Federal Constitution guarantees freedom of expression.

Conclusion

Whilst more conflicts are faced due to the existence of legal pluralism in Malaysia, the clear constitutional construction remains the compass resorted to by judges when the matter comes before them. Despite the growing insistence for a wider scope of Islamic law to be applicable in Malaysia by politicians and groups championing the Malay and Islam, the diversity of race and religion embraced and protected by the Federal Constitution is given life by the judiciary rising to the occasion in clearing the confusion and stating the legal position succinctly.

Chapter 16
The Status and Implementation of Islamic Law in Malaysia

Mohamed Azam Mohamed Adil and Nisar Mohammad Ahmad

Abstract In the Federation of Malaysia, Islam is the religion of the Federation but this does not extend to the legal perspective. In other words, Islamic law is not the supreme law of the Federation because the Federal Constitution has clearly stated that the supreme law of the country is the Constitution itself. This article aims to examine the status and implementation of Islamic law in Malaysia. At the onset, the article analyses the historical background of Islam in pre-Malaysia era with particular focus on its Islamic law perspective. The independence of Malaya in 1957 led to the formation of the Federal Constitution which is considered the main source of law in the country. This article assesses a number of provisions in the Constitutions and some related cases that touch on Islamic affairs. Also, the divisions of jurisdictions for both civil laws and Islamic laws is analysed against the backdrops of the Federal Constitution and other relevant legislations. To sum up, it can be said that despite the fact that Islam is given a special position under Article 3(1) of the Federal Constitution, Islamic law is not fully implemented in Malaysia. The jurisdiction awarded by the Ninth Schedule, List II State List is very limited, only confined to Muslim followers and is mostly related to personal laws, including amongst others: marriage; divorce; inheritance and other offences that are against the precepts of the religion of Islam. Civil laws, on the other hand, are subject to federal jurisdiction, which cannot interfere with the State laws such as the Islamic laws which fall under the State jurisdiction.

M.A.M. Adil (✉)
International Institute of Advanced Islamic Studies Malaysia/Universiti Teknologi MARA, Kuala Lumpur, Malaysia
e-mail: mazamadil@hotmail.com

N.M. Ahmad
Universiti Sains Islam Malaysia, Nilai, Malaysia
e-mail: nisar.usim@gmail.com

R. Bottoni et al. (eds.), *Religious Rules, State Law, and Normative Pluralism - A Comparative Overview*, Ius Comparatum – Global Studies in Comparative Law 18, DOI 10.1007/978-3-319-28335-7_16

Introduction

Malaysia is a country with a predominant Muslim population. A demographic overview of the country suggests that, out of its estimated population of 28.9 million,[1] approximately 60.4 % belong to the Islamic faith.[2] In addition, the Federal Constitution of Malaysia (the "Constitution"), under Article 3, designates Islam as the religion of the country while at the same time guaranteeing the principle of freedom of religion to its multi-ethnic communities. Despite Islam being named as the religion of the Federation, Islamic law or *Shari'a Law*, has never been considered by the same Constitution as the law or legal system of the federation. In other words, the status of Islam as the religion of the Federation does not reflect its legal dimension. The Constitution, as mentioned under Article 4, is considered to be the supreme law of the country which shall always prevail over any other laws passed after the Independence Day, whereas Islamic law is only made a subordinate law falling under the States' jurisdiction with a very limited jurisdiction confined to personal matters and offences relating to morality only.[3]

Even though special provision is given to Islam in the Federal Constitution,[4] Islamic law in Malaysia is not practised in such a manner that reflects the traditional principles of Islamic law. Rather, the scope and jurisdiction of Islamic law has been made smaller in Malaysia than what it is supposed to be. This is because the Constitution has specified that Islamic law is confined to certain spheres such as matrimonial matters and minimal criminal jurisdictions empowered by the State authorities.[5]

Historical Background

Islam came to the Peninsula of Malaya by the fourteenth century (al-Attas 1969). It is assumed that Parameswara had converted to Islam because of his marriage to a Pase (*Pasai*) princess (Tan et al. 1996). Parameswara was later known as Sultan Iskandar Shah. Malacca was well known as a trading port between India and China. One of the factors that promoted the rapid growth of Malacca was its acceptance of Islam. Its strategic geographical position and Chinese patronage, which helped in resisting the claims of nearby Siam, were other factors that contributed to its rapid

[1] Economic and Planning Unit (EPU), Prime Minister's Department of Malaysia. Socio-Economic statistic. (2000) Accessed on 20 November, 2013 from: http://www.epu.gov.my/html/themes/epu/images/common/pdf/eco_stat/pdf/1.2.5.pdf

[2] US Department of State. Background Note: Malaysia. (2011) Accessed on 22 November 2013, from: http://www.state.gov/r/pa/ei/bgn/2777.htm

[3] Ninth Schedule, List II, State List, the Federal Constitution.

[4] Article 3(1), the Federal Constitution.

[5] Ninth Schedule, *supra*.

growth.[6] Islam spread rapidly in Malacca and in the entire Peninsula of Malaya, perhaps due to the conversion of Parameswara to Islam.

Since Islam came to the soil of Malacca, it rapidly changed the law. Historians and legal scholars have unanimously agreed that the influence of Islamic law together with Malay customs largely contributed to the application of Islamic law in Malacca. *Hukum Kanun Melaka* or the Malacca law, is one of the best examples that could prove this claim. The significance and contribution of this law, to certain extent, largely shaped the drafts of other Malay laws in other respective States in the Peninsula of Malaya. This can be seen in Johore Law, Pahang Laws, Kedah Laws and the *Undang-undang Sembilan Puluh Sembilan* (Ninety-nine Laws of Perak), where most of the provisions mainly originated from the *Hukum Kanun Melaka* (Ibrahim and Joned 1995).

The collapse of the Malacca Sultanates and the invasion of the Portuguese in 1511 AD marked the end of the rule of the Malacca Kingdom. Malacca was ruled by the Portuguese from 1511 to 1641 until it was surrendered to the Dutch. The Dutch later ruled Malacca from 1641 to 1795. From 1801 to 1824, there was an exchange of control between the Dutch and the British. In 1824, the Dutch officially surrendered Malacca to the British (Ibrahim and Joned 1995; Hassan 1996 and others).

History has witnessed that although both the Portuguese and the Dutch ruled Malacca for quite some time, their influence on the law was hardly apparent. This was due to their non-interference policy with the local customs and practices (Buang), unlike the British who had not only successfully ruled Malaya, but had also introduced their laws in order to maintain power. In fact, the British intervention in Malaya had left behind a great deal of influence in the way laws should be administrated. They had successfully shaped the laws to such a great extent that Malaysia still applies them today (Abdul Majid 1997). Some of the laws that are still applicable are the Penal Code, the Evidence Act, the Contract Act, the Civil Procedure Code, the Criminal Procedure Code and the Land Code (Ibrahim and Joned 1995). It must be noted that except the Land Code, the other laws are similar to the Indian ones.

The Federal Constitution

The formation of a Federal Constitution is based on the local culture, which consists of different ethnic and religious identities. It was a manifestation of tolerance amongst the three major political parties, namely UMNO, MCA and MIC for the sake of stability and a united government (Noor et al. 2006).

The Reid Commission was set up by the British in 1956 to draft a new constitution for an independent Malaya. Hundreds of memorandums were submitted to the Commission. In addition, the Commission had also attended hundreds of meetings

---

[6] Ibid.

with various parties and individuals. In the end, a White Paper (Report) was issued and there was a new Constitution that took effect on 31 August 1957 just after mid-night.

It must be noted that there are four protected matters in the Federal Constitution: the position of Islam as the religion of the Federation; *Bahasa Malaysia* as the national language; the Malay Rulers (Sultans)[7]; and the Malay rights and privileges. These were four compromised matters agreed by the three major parties, also known as the "social contract". The Chinese and Indians gave up their "rights" simply because they were more concerned about getting citizenship by *jus soli*.

Article 3: Islam in the Federal Constitution

When the Reid Commission first revealed the White Paper, there was no provision on Islam as the State religion. It was the idea of Justice Abdul Hamid of Pakistan, a member of the Commission, who made a note of dissent with regard to this matter. It was later accepted by the Alliance party that a provision on Islam as the religion of the Federation should be inserted into the Constitution. In the first place, however, the Malay Rulers rejected such an idea, fearing that they could lose the only power left for them, i.e. matters pertaining to Islam. In the end, after a series of explanations, the Malay Rulers agreed to the idea, after the Alliance had made it clear that this provision would not jeopardize the prerogative and rights of the Rulers (Adil 2014).

The White Paper has indicated that the provision, "Islam is the religion of the Federation; but other religions may be practised in peace and harmony in any part of the Federation" would not prevent the country from being a secular State. This last part of the report has led to a series of debates amongst practitioners and scholars. For some scholars, Malaysia is a secular state, while others suggest that Malaysia is an Islamic state. The endless debate on this matter will not bear any fruitful result (Adil 2007). Except for the Pan-Malaysian Islamic Party (PAS) – the Islamist political party in Malaysia, the majority of Muslims in Malaysia believe that Malaysia is not a secular state (Faruqi 2004).

As already said, Article 3 (1) provides that "Islam is the religion of the Federation; but other religions may be practised in peace and harmony in any part of the Federation". Such provision has been re-emphasised in Article 11 (1). No other religions have been specifically mentioned in the Federal Constitution. As such, despite the fact that the religion of Islam is given a special place in it, the Federal Constitution guarantees that the right to freedom of religion is enjoyed by individuals, Muslims and non-Muslims alike.

[7] The Malay Rulers, also called the Sultans, are the constitutional heads of the nine Malay States in Malaysia.

The interpretation of the position of Islam is very crucial. Islam seems to be placed above other religions in the Federation.[8] Even though some legal commentators agree to the higher position given to Islam, it was decided otherwise in *Che Omar bin Che Soh v Public Prosecutor.*[9] The Supreme Court held that "although there can be no doubt that Islam is not just a mere collection of dogmas and rituals but it is a complete way of life covering all fields of human activities, may they be private or public, legal, political, economic, social, cultural, moral or judicial", Article 3(1) merely provided for a ritualistic and ceremonial role of Islam.[10] Sheridan also seems to agree with the *Che Omar* decision. He posits that Article 3(1) does not mean anything except that it imposes an obligation on the participants in any federal ceremony to regulate any religious parts of the ceremony according to Muslim rites (Sheridan 1961). However, according to Abdul Aziz Bari, this case does not provide a clear picture of the position of Islam as stated in the Reid's Commission Report and the White Paper (Bari 2005; Bari 1999, 2001). Thus, he further argues that the *Che Omar* decision merely ruled that Article 3(1) should not become the basis to challenge the legality of statutes. In other words, it only limits the operation of Islam to what is stated in the provision. It must also be noted that the extent and implementation of Islam in the Constitution should not be assessed or interpreted solely from the context or point of view of Article 3(1). But, it is also contended that the *Che Omar* decision merely differentiated the position of Islamic law as prescribed by Article 3(1) of the Federal Constitution. It is argued that since Islam is the religion of the Federation,[11] and since the Constitution is the supreme law of the Federation,[12] the imposition of the death penalty upon drug traffickers, not being an Islamic law *per se*, i.e., not in accordance with *hudud* or *qisas* laws, is contrary to the Islamic injunction and is therefore unconstitutional (Tan et al. 1996).[13] The Supreme Court (as it then was) rejected this argument, saying that provision in Article 3(1) does not actually mean that Malaysia is an Islamic state, but in reality Islamic law only applies to Muslims merely on matters that related to personal laws. Since the Constitution makes a clear distinction between private law and public law,[14] offences like drug trafficking are under the Federal List which defines the Federal government's jurisdiction, and are therefore constitutional (Harding 2002).

---

[8] See judgement in *Meor Atiqulrahman bin Ishak & Anor. v Fatimah Bte Sihi & Anor*, [2000] 5 MLJ 382; In this case, the learned judge, Dato' Mohd Noor Abdullah interpreted Article 3(1) that states "Islam is the religion of the Federation but other religions may be practised in peace and harmony in any part of the Federation" which means that Islam is the supreme religion and its position is not on par with other religions such as Christianity, Buddhism, Hinduism and others. It is placed beyond other religions in the Federation.

[9] [1988] 2 MLJ 55.

[10] Ibid.

[11] Article 3(1) of the Federal Constitution.

[12] Article 4(1) of the Federal Constitution.

[13] See Che Omar bin Che Soh v Public Prosecutor [1988] 2 MLJ 55.

[14] Ninth Schedule, List 1, Federal List; List 2, State List, and List 3, Concurrent List.

Islamic Law: Its Jurisdictions and Adjudication in Malaysia

As mentioned above, Article 3(1) of the Federal Constitution provides that:

> Islam is the religion of the Federation; but other religions may be practised in peace and harmony in any part of the Federation.[15]

However, Article 4 of the Constitution provides that:

> This Constitution is the supreme law of the Federation and any law passed after Merdeka Day which is inconsistent with this Constitution shall, to the extent of the inconsistency, be void.[16]

Generally speaking, both Articles 3 and 4 of the Federal Constitution connote the key issues that reflect the nature and status of Islam and Islamic law in Malaysia. Despite acknowledging Islam as the religion of the federation, the Constitution however does not mention the superiority of Islamic law in the Malaysian legal system. Rather, Article 4 emphasises that the Constitution itself is the highest and supreme law of the country. As such, the implementation of Islamic law in Malaysia should always be observed in accordance with the provisions of the Constitution.

Despite the limited jurisdiction vested by the Constitution, Islamic law or *Shari'a* law is the only religious-based law which constitutes part of the Malaysian legal system, laid down in the Constitution. The Constitution provided and placed a list of *Shari'a* law jurisdictions and the establishment of the *Shari'a* adjudication system or *Shari'a* courts under List II,[17] which lies under the State government's jurisdiction. The administration of Islamic law is further detailed in the Islamic enactments applied in every state in the Federation of Malaysia.

Nevertheless, despite the recognition of Islamic law as part of the Malaysian legal system, the term 'Islamic law' has never been defined. In the clear wording of the Federal Constitution, the word 'law' in Article 160 does not mention Islamic

---

[15] See *The White Paper*, Article 3 (1), p. 33; See also Article 3(1) of the Federal Constitution.

[16] See Article 4(1) of the Federal Constitution.

[17] It says that 'Except with respect to the Federal Territories of Kuala Lumpur, Labuan and Putrajaya, Islamic law and personal and family law of persons professing the religion of Islam, including the Islamic law relating to succession, testate and intestate, betrothal, marriage, divorce, dower, maintenance, adoption, legitimacy, guardianship, gifts, partitions and non-charitable trust; *Wakafs* and the definition and regulation of charitable and religious trusts, the appointment of trustees and incorporation of persons in respect of Islamic religious and charitable endowments, institutions, trusts, charities and charitable institutions operating wholly within the State; Malay customs; *Zakat*, *Fitra* and *Bait al-Mal* or similar Islamic religious revenue; mosques or any Islamic public places of worship, creation and punishment of offences by persons professing the religion of Islam against precepts of that religion, except in regard to matters included in the Federal List; the constitution, organisation and procedure of *Shari'a* Courts which shall have jurisdiction only over persons professing the religion of Islam and in respect only of any of the matters included in this paragraph, but shall not have jurisdiction in respect of offences except in so far as concerned by federal law, the control of propagating doctrines and beliefs among persons professing the religion of Islam; the determination of matters of Islamic law and doctrine and Malay custom'.

law at all.[18] It is a pity that the word law in this Article only 'includes any written law, the common law in so far as it is in operation in the Federation or any part thereof, and any custom or usage having the force of law in the Federation or any part thereof'. Similarly, no provision is traced in the Federal Constitution providing for the jurisdiction and powers of the *Shari'a* Courts. The only provision where the Federal Constitution does state the word '*Shari'a* Courts' is in Article 121 (1A), where it takes away the jurisdiction of the Civil Courts on matters that are within the jurisdiction of the *Shari'a* Courts (Harding 1996).

In addition, *Shari'a* laws enjoy a very limited jurisdiction under the Federal Constitution. The only jurisdiction of Islamic law is specially provided in the Ninth Schedule, List II – State List, which amongst other things, covers only persons professing the religion of Islam. In other words, Muslims in Malaysia shall have no options but to abide by the Islamic law jurisdiction as prescribed by the Constitution. Matters that are provided under this jurisdiction are strictly confined to personal laws such as marriage, divorce, and all ancillary matters related to them, and succession. With regard to criminal laws, only punishment of offences by persons professing the religion of Islam against precepts of that religion such as offences of eating and drinking in public during the month of *Ramadan*, neglecting from performing Friday prayer, committing *zina* (fornication) and *khalwat* (close proximity) and other matters that are strictly provided in various respective States' Islamic Criminal Laws can be subjected to Islamic law jurisdiction.[19]

In the case of lacuna, English laws apply. In fact, Section 3 (1) and 5 (1) of the Civil Law Act 1956 provides:

> 3. (1) Save so far as other provision has been made or may hereafter be made by any written law in force in Malaysia, the Court shall – (a) in Peninsular Malaysia or any part thereof, apply the common law of England and the rules of equity as administered in England on the 7 April 1956;
>
> 5. (1) In all questions or issues which arise or which have to be decided in the States of Peninsular Malaysia other than Malacca and Penang with respect to the law of partnerships, corporations, banks and banking, principals and agents, carriers by air, land and sea, marine insurance, average, life and fire insurance, and with respect to mercantile law generally, the law to be administered shall be the same as would be administered in England in the like case at the date of the coming into force of this Act, if such question or issue had arisen or had to be decided in England, unless in any case other provision is or shall be made by any written law.
>
> As a result, unless there is a specific written law in Malaysia, the basic law that would be applicable and referred to would be English law, at both the federal and state level (Ibrahim 1997).

[18] Prof. Harding suggests that "there is no provision for the *Shari'a* to be a source, or the basic source, of legislation".

[19] Ninth Schedule, List II – State List.

Divisions of Jurisdictions Between *Shari'a* and Civil Courts

In accordance with the dual judicial system applied in Malaysia i.e. Civil law (under Federal Government jurisdiction) and *Shari'a* law (under the State Government jurisdiction), the powers to make laws related to both systems are accorded to Parliament and State legislative assemblies respectively. In other words, Parliament makes laws for all the matters listed under List I – which include Civil Law, whereas the State legislative assemblies make law for all matters listed under List II – which include *Shari'a* Law. Because the question of Islamic law is confined under the jurisdiction of respective states, except in the Federal Territories of Kuala Lumpur, Labuan and Putrajaya, Parliament cannot make laws with respect to any matters of Islamic law or the custom of the Malays, and no Bill for such a law shall be introduced into either House of Parliament until the Government of any concerned State has been consulted.[20] This includes the purpose of promoting uniformity of the laws of two or more States,[21] or if so requested by the Legislative Assembly of any state.[22] Although the Yang di-Pertuan Agong is the supreme Head in the Federation, there is no paramount head of Islam in the entire Federation. This is because all Malay States have their own head of Islam, namely their respective Sultans. Thus, apart from merely being the Head of Islam in his own state, the Yang di-Pertuan Agong is the Head of religion in the Federal Territories of Kuala Lumpur, Labuan and Putrajaya; and also in the states of Malacca, Penang, Sabah and Sarawak, other than the nine States which have Sultans.[23] Since Islam is the States' matter, there is no head of Islam in the Federation as the respective Sultans are the head of Islam.

It must be also noted that Parliament has no power to legislate on matters that have been awarded to the Ninth Schedule, State List – II. In *Mamat bin Daud & Ors. v Government of Malaysia*,[24] Section 298 of the Penal Code makes it an offense to wound other people's religious feelings with deliberate intent. In this case, although the Supreme Court recognised the competency of Parliament to restrict the right of the practice of a religion on grounds of public order, section 298A of the Penal Code which criminalizes any act that will cause or is likely to cause disharmony in the practice of religion is nevertheless void because such power is specifically confined to the state's jurisdiction and out of the framework of the Federal Constitution.

---

[20] Article 76 (2).

[21] Article 76 (1) (b).

[22] Article 76 (1) (c).

[23] Article 3 (1192) of the Federal Constitution.

[24] [1988] 1 MLJ.

Legal Areas Where Religious Rules Are Prescribed

Non-Criminal Jurisdictions

Most jurisdictions that Islamic law is provided for by the Constitution are related to personal and matrimonial affairs. These jurisdictions are detailed in List II under the Ninth Schedule of the Constitutions.[25]

All in all, it can be said that the implementation of Islamic law is purely under the jurisdiction of State government, and the power to legislate on matters laid down in List II (above) lies with the States legislature i.e. the State legislative assembly (Jusoh 1991).[26] The Islamic law, being positioned under the jurisdiction of State government, is therefore territorial in nature. It only governs Muslims in the respective state borders based on the respective State's Islamic law enactment. Despite the power given to the State legislature to enact law on Islamic matters, it cannot create any law that is contrary to the Federal law. In other words, religious rules and Islamic law are bound to respect the superiority of the Federal Constitution. This is because, where any state law is inconsistent with that of the Federal law, the Federal law shall prevail, and the State law shall, to the extent of the inconsistency, be void.[27]

Criminal Jurisdictions[28]

The scope of *Shari'a* criminal law is stated under the Ninth Schedule of the State List of the Federal Constitution.[29]

The Schedule clearly indicates that the Federal Constitution gives the power to the State legislative body to create laws for persons professing the religion of Islam and punish them for offences that are against the precepts of that religion. However, the power of the state to enforce Islamic criminal law is limited by the words "except in regard to matters included in the Federal list" or "dealt with by federal law" as in the above list. As a result, should there be a redundancy, inconsistency or conflict with the federal law – for example with provisions under the Penal Code which is the prime statute of criminal law– the state law would be *ultra vires*, null and void. This can be seen in the case of capital punishment which is listed under the Federal List of the Federal Constitution. Therefore, only federal law can provide such punishment for serious crimes like homicide. Consequently, offences related to *qisas*

---

[25] *See* note 31.

[26] Article 74 (2).

[27] Article 75 of the Federal Constitution.

[28] The discussion of this subheading is entirely based on Siti Zubaidah Ismail, "Islamic Criminal Law: The Reality of Implementation in Malaysia", in Kamali and Adil (2016).

[29] *See* note 31.

involving the death sentence do not fall within the jurisdiction of the *Shari'a* Court. The Civil High Court has the power to hear homicide cases based on the homicide provision under the Penal Code of Malaysia (Act 574). By the same token, *hudud* crimes like theft (*sariqah*), highway robbery (*hirabah*) and rebellion (*bughah*) should also fall within the civil court's jurisdiction.

However, the provisions for those offences – at present – are not in accordance with *hudud* punishment. This is no surprise due to the fact that the Penal Code of Malaysia was originally transformed from the Indian Penal Code. Since Malaysia embraces a dual legal system comprising of Civil and *Shari'a* Courts, matters of Islamic law fall within the jurisdiction of *Shari'a* Courts exclusively, and consequently the Civil Courts have no jurisdiction over Islamic criminal offences except in offences like *liwat* (sodomy) where both the Civil and *Shari'a* Courts have a parallel jurisdiction over the same act.[30] This is by virtue of Article 121(1A) of the Federal Constitution which explicitly explains that the Civil Courts shall have no jurisdiction in respect of any matter within the jurisdiction of the *Shari'a* courts.[31]

The jurisdiction of *Shari'a* Criminal law is also confined to persons professing the religion of Islam. The *Shari'a* Courts Act 1965 (Criminal Jurisdiction) gives a jurisdiction to the *Shari'a* Courts to punish with up to 6 months imprisonment, or fine up to RM1,000.00, or a combination of both. The *Shari'a* Courts jurisdiction pertaining to criminal matters was amended in 1984 and the *Shari'a* Courts obtained a wider jurisdiction to sentence up to 3 years imprisonment, or fine up to RM5,000.00 or caning up to 6 strokes, or any combination of these punishments.[32] As a result, even though offences like *zina* (illegitimate sex) and *shurb* (drinking) are categorised under *hudud* offences, the punishment for those offences is limited by the 1984 Act. As the limitation of this jurisdiction is awarded to the *Shari'a* Court, it could be said that punishment for drinking (and other Islamic criminal law) in Malaysia is *ta'zir* in nature.[33]

Social Implementation of Religious Rules

It has to be noted that despite the true Islamic law being based on the traditional Islamic teaching and covering the whole aspect of Muslim life, the provisions of Islamic law applicable in Malaysia as prescribed by the Constitution does not reflect

[30] Sukma Darmawan Sasmitaat Madja v Ketua Pengarah Penjara Malaysia & Anor (Sukma) [1999] 2 MLJ 241 (FC); [1999] 1 MLJ 266 (CA); [1998] 4 MLJ 742 (HC).

[31] Article 121 (1A) of the Federal Constitution, as amended in 1988. Ninth Schedule, List II – State List of the Federal Constitution.

Sukma Darmawan Sasmitaat Madja v Ketua Pengarah Penjara Malaysia & Anor (Sukma) [1999] 2 MLJ 241 (FC); [1999] 1 MLJ 266 (CA); [1998] 4 MLJ 742 (HC).

[32] Section 2 of the *Shari'a* Courts Act (Criminal Jurisdiction) of 1965 (Amended in 1984).

[33] Ta'zir are offenses that are given to the judge or authority to make punishments. They are also offenses which are prescribed under hudud but due to lack of evidence, the punishment is subject to the discretion of the judge.

such spirit. Therefore, there are instances where there have been conflicts between the manifestation / observance of Islamic principles and the compliance with the Constitution. In this regard, the Constitution has clearly put some restrictions on the implementation and observances of Islamic laws.

There are at least two articles- Articles 11(5) and 10(2) (a)- that are inherently concerned with these restrictions. Article 11 (5) of the Federal Constitution seems to create a restriction on religious freedom. It states: "this Article does not authorise any act contrary to any general law relating to public order, public health or morality". In other words, this provision clearly signifies that religious freedom in Malaysia is not absolute, but conditional and restricted (Bari 2000 and others). This means that religious activities can be freely carried out but must not go against the general law, public order, public health and morality (Groves 1964).

In sum, there are at least four restrictions on religious freedom under Article 11 (5) of the Federal Constitution:

First, religious freedom is subject to general law. It means that the government is empowered to enact or introduce laws that restrict or control religious activities including profession, practice and propagation. Second, public order is the second restriction. Because of the importance of the state to ensure the maintenance of public order and preservation of order in a society, the government can restrict religious freedom. As such, the government through Article 11 (5) of the Federal Constitution could restrict pursuance of freedom of religion if it perceives a threat to public order (Tan 1997). The third and fourth restrictions concern health and morality. It means that any acts that are claimed to be religious but contradict morality or health could be restricted and may be banned by the government. Thus, if a group of people walk naked in public in the name of a religion, then the government can bar such action on the ground of immorality.

Article 10 (2) (a) states that "Parliament may by law impose on rights conferred by paragraph (a) of Clause (1), such restrictions as it deems necessary or expedient in the interest of the security of the Federation or any part thereof, friendly relations with other countries, public order or morality and restrictions designed to protect the privileges of Parliament or any Legislative Assembly or to provide against contempt of court, defamation, or incitement to any offence". However, restrictions on religious freedom, though introduced in the name of Parliament, cannot be passed, in respect to Articles 149[34] and 150[35] of the Federal Constitutions.

In *Halimatussaadiah v Public Service Commission, Malaysia & Anor* (McGoldrik 2006),[36] the Supreme Court rejected the claim by the appellant that wearing purdah

[34] Article 149 deals with legislation against subversion, action prejudicial to public order, etc. Article 149 deals with legislation against subversion, action prejudicial to public order, etc.

[35] Article 150 is proclamation of emergency which excludes the power of Parliament to enact law pertaining Islam.

[36] [1992] 1 MLJ 513. In another development in Singapore, three pupils were banned from wearing *tudung* (veil) during school hours. The Singapore government had directed that all pupils should conform to school regulations, among others, not allowing Muslim schoolgirls to wear *tudung* in school. The parents have apparently, threatened to take legal action against the school authority as well as the Singapore government, see *Utusan Malaysia*, 4 February 2002, p. 1; In France, a law

(full-face veil) was a religious right in practicing her religion. In this case, the Public Service Commission (JPA) issued a circular prohibiting any attire that covers a female public servant's face whilst on duty. The appellant apparently refused to comply with the circular, arguing that wearing a veil was part of her religious duty. The Supreme Court upheld the decision made by the subordinate courts. Moreover, the Supreme Court accepted the testimony of the then Mufti of Federal Territory that suggested the mode of dress that covered the face of female Muslims was not a mandatory requirement in Islam. It appears that the Supreme Court accepted the circular because it was for the benefit of public order. The dismissal of the appellant from office simply indicates that the right to practise one's religion is subject to the Constitution, and in this case Article 11(5). However, the judgement has been criticised by many experts, including Prof. Aziz Bari and a prominent lawyer, Zainur Zakaria, who questioned how wearing a veil could be held as contravening public order, since she had been putting it on for several years without any incident of such nature. Indeed, the issue of whether wearing a veil was a mandatory requirement in Islam or not was not the subject concerned since Islam did not prohibit anyone from wearing it (Zakira 1993; Bari 2005).

In *Meor Atiqulrahman bin Ishak & Anor. v Fatimah Bte Sihi & Anor,*[37] three pupils were expelled from school after ignoring the order issued by the headteacher (the first defendant). The headteacher had apparently asked the pupils to remove their serban (turbans) and substitute it with a songkok (black hat). The Seremban High Court, however, ruled that the dismissal was void, invalid and ineffective, and the pupils should have been reinstated to the same school. In the judgement, the learned judge ruled that wearing a turban is accepted in Islam though it is not obligatory. It was also in line within the provision of Article 11 (1) that guarantees an individual the right to profess and practice a religion. To prohibit such an act would be regarded as contrary to Articles 3 (1) and 11 (1) of the Federal Constitution. Furthermore, such prohibition has nothing to do with general law that relates to public order, public health and morality. Referring to the case of Halimatussa'adiah, the learned judge also made a distinction between wearing a turban and veil. The learned judge ruled that whilst wearing a veil during work would make it difficult to identify a staff member and may lead to breach of public security, the same could not be said about wearing a turban.[38]

However, the Court of Appeal overruled the High Court judgement merely on the grounds that the head teacher was right to dismiss the pupils from the school

---

was passed in 2004 that prohibits the use of conspicuous religious symbols (including the headscarf) in all public schools, except at universities. This development has prompted Muslims around the world to protest in public, arguing that the right of religious freedom should not be violated, since wearing a veil is part of the religious practice under Islam; see *The Independent*, 18 January, 2004, p. 1; In Turkey, two students were expelled from their university on the ground that they wore a headscarf within the university campus; see European Court of Human Rights Press Release Issued by The Registrar in Chamber Judgements in The Cases of *Leyla Sahin v Turkey* and *ZeynepTekin v Turkey*, *http://press.coe.int/cp/2004/330a(2004).htm*, www.coe.int

[37] [2000] 5 MLJ 375.

[38] *Ibid*, at p. 383.

because they did not conform to the school regulations. The issue of the right to freedom of religion, according to the Court did not arise at all.[39] The judgement has been widely criticised by human rights activists and opposition parties, particularly by PAS. They claimed that such ruling seemed similar to the one in France, where Muslim girls were forbidden to wear the veil in schools.[40]

In the Federal Court, the judges upheld the judgment of the Court of Appeal. Abdul Hamid Mohamad FCJ, who wrote the judgment, pointed out that not all the Prophet's deeds must be complied with by Muslim followers. The turban, according to him, was an Arab tradition which had nothing to do with the teaching of Islam. However, he Abdul Hamid Mohamad FCJ had gone far out of the context of the case by saying that Muslims should not imitate the Prophet's life, and he gave examples such as building a clay house, travelling by camels and so on.[41]

Conclusion

From the above discussion, it could be said that despite the fact that Islam is given a special position under Article 3(1) of the Federal Constitution, Islamic law is not fully implemented in Malaysia. The jurisdiction awarded by the Ninth Schedule, List II State List is very limited, only confined to Muslim followers and is mostly related to personal laws, including amongst others: marriage; divorce; inheritance and other offences that are against the precept of the religion of Islam.

Except in the Federal Territories of Kuala Lumpur, Labuan and Putrajaya, Islamic law in Malaysia is a State law due to the fact that such laws are made in the respective States' legislative assembly. As for the Federal Territories, laws relating to Islam must be passed by the Parliament. As such, Islamic criminal law is not under the jurisdiction of Federal law but it is a competence of the respective states.

As for non-Muslims, they are governed by the Civil laws including matters pertaining to marriage and divorce which are inherited from the British reign. In general, Civil laws are subject to federal jurisdiction, where it cannot interefere with the State laws such as the Islamic laws which fall under the State jurisdiction. However, the Islamic laws only extend to matters pertaining to marriage and divorce, and certain offences punished under the precept of Islam, whereas matters other than these are subject to Civil Laws.

[39] See Fatimah Bte Sihi & Ors v Meor Atiqulrahman Bin Ishak Ors [2005] 2 MLJ 25.

[40] See "Islamists Denounce Malaysian Court's Decision on Muslim Headgear" in www.harakhdaily.net, 23 November 2004.

[41] Civil Application No. 01-3-2005 (N) Federal Court, July 12, 2006.

References

Abdul Majid, Mahmood Zuhdi. 1997. *Pengantar Undang-undang Islam di Malaysia*, 52–53. Kuala Lumpur: Penerbit Universiti Malaya.

Adil, Mohamed Azam Mohamed. 2007. Law of apostasy and freedom of religion in Malaysia. *Asian Journal of Comparative Law* 2: 145–147.

al-Attas, Syed Muhammad Naguib. 1969. *Preliminary statement on a general theory of the Islamization of the Malay-Indonesia Archipelago*, 11. Kuala Lumpur: Dewan Bahasa dan Pustaka.

Bari, Abdul Aziz. 1999. Murtad Dalam Konteks Kebebasan Beragama. *MJLS* 3: 55.

Bari, Abdul Aziz. 2000. Islam in the Federal Constitution: A commentary on The decision of *Meor Atiqulrahman*. 2 *MLJ* at cxxxviii.

Bari, Abdul Aziz. 2001. Negara Islam dan Kerangka Perlembagaan Malaysia. *Dewan Masyarakat, Dewan Bahasa dan Pustaka* 39: 22.

Bari, Abdul Aziz. 2005. *Islam Dalam Perlembagaan Persekutuan*, 21–23, 80–81. Petaling Java: Intel Multimedia and Publication.

Faruqi, Shad Saleem. 2004. Constitutional perspectives on freedom of religion, secularism and theocracy. In *Islam, democracy and good governance – The Malaysian experience essays in Honour of Tun Dr. Mahathir Mohamad*, 88. ed. Ibrahim Abu Ashah. Shah Alam: UPENA, UiTM.

Groves, H.E. 1964. *The Constitution of Malaysia*, 215. Singapore: Malaysian Publications Ltd.

Harding, A. 1996. *Law, government and the Constitution in Malaysia*, 136–137. London: Kluwer Law International.

Harding, A. 2002. The *Keris*, The crescent and the blind goddess: The State, Islam and the Constitution in Malaysia. *Singapore Journal of International and Comparative Law* 154: 166–167.

Hassan, Abdullah Alwi Haji. 1996. *The administration of Islamic law in Kelantan*. Kuala Lumpur: Dewan Bahasa dan Pustaka.

Ibrahim, Ahmad Mohamed. 1997. *Pentadbiran Undang-undang Islam di Malaysia*, 61–74. Kuala Lumpur: Institut Kefahaman Islam Malaysia (IKIM).

Ibrahim, Ahmad, and Joned, Ahilemah. 1995. *The Malaysian legal system*, 2nd ed, 15–16. Kuala Lumpur: Dewan Bahasa dan Pustaka.

Jusoh, Hamid. 1991. *The position of Islamic law in the Malaysian Constitution with special reference to the conversion case in family law*, 35. Kuala Lumpur: Dewan Bahasa dan Pustaka.

Kamali, Mohammad Hashim, and Adil, Mohamed Azam Mohamed. (ed.). 2016. *Islamic law in Malaysia: Major themes and developments* (Forthcoming). Kuala Lumpur: IAIS Malaysia.

McGoldrick, D. 2006. *Human rights and religion: The Islamic headscarf debate in Europe*, 140–172. Oxford: Hart Publishing.

Mohamed Adil, Mohamed Azam, and Nisar Mohammad Ahmad. 2014. Islamic law and human rights in Malaysia. *Islam and Civilisational Renewal*: 43–67. IAIS Malaysia.

Noor, Mansor Mohd, Abdul Rahman Abdul Aziz, and Mohamad Ainuddin Iskandar Lee. 2006. In *Hubungan Etnik di Malaysia*, 124. Petaling Jaya: Prentice Hall Pearson Malaysia Sdn. Bhd.

Sheridan, L.A. 1961. *The Federation of Malaya Constitution – Text, annotations and commentary*, 4. Singapore: University of Malaya Law Review.

Tan, Poh-Ling. (ed.). 1997. Asian legal systems – Law, society and pluralism in East Asia, 267. Sydney: Butterworths.

Tan, K., et al. 1996. Constitutional law in Malaysia and Singapore. *Malayan Law Journal Sdn. Bhd.*

Zakaria, Zainur. 1993. Religious freedom – Right to wear *Purdah* 3 *MLJ* xxv–xxx.

Chapter 17
Religious Rules and the Law of the Dutch State

Sophie Van Bijsterveld

Abstract Against the background of the thought-provoking lecture Rowan Williams, the former Archbishop of Canterbury, delivered in 2008 on the relationship between civil and religious law in England, this contribution explores the relationship between civil and religious law in the Netherlands. It analyses the various legal mechanisms through which this relationship is established in Dutch law, with special attention to the relationship between religious and civil arrangements of conflict resolution and the social acceptance of religious behavior and the acceptance of state law by religious believers. The conclusion is that the mechanisms through which Dutch law accommodates religious rules are satisfactory. With regard to some topics, however, a development can be discerned that religiously informed ethics or social traditions no longer run parallel with the generally applicable norms, but are acknowledged through legislative exemptions or even no longer accommodated by the law. Processes of value change both outside and within religious denominations play a role in these developments.

Introduction

In a thought-provoking lecture delivered in 2008, entitled 'Civil and Religious Law in England: a religious perspective' (Williams 2008), Rowan Williams, then Archbishop of Canterbury, addressed the question of 'what level of public or legal recognition, if any, might be allowed to the legal provisions of a religious group'.[1] Although the presence of Muslims in British society had prompted this question, the Archbishop made it clear that the issue had much wider relevance. '[B]eyond the specific issues that arise in relation to the practicalities of recognition or delegation,'

[1] It is interesting to note that the particular lecture was not included in his book, *Faith in the Public Square* (London [etc.]: Bloomsbury, 2012) a collection of lectures and essays published just before he left office.

S. Van Bijsterveld (✉)
Radboud Universiteit Nijmegen, Nijmegen, The Netherlands
e-mail: s.vanbijsterveld@ftr.ru.nl

R. Bottoni et al. (eds.), *Religious Rules, State Law, and Normative Pluralism - A Comparative Overview*, Ius Comparatum – Global Studies in Comparative Law 18, DOI 10.1007/978-3-319-28335-7_17

the Archbishop stated, 'there are large questions in the background about what we understand by and expect from the law, questions that are more sharply focused than ever in a largely secular social environment.'

The lecture provoked enormous reaction and even led to an official explanation of what the Archbishop had actually said. Part of the consternation can certainly be attributed to the attention that had been devoted to the Islamic faith and the notion of 'Sharia' as religious law. The lecture not only reverberated in the media, but also gave rise to fundamental academic debate (Ahdar 2010).

The Archbishop's lecture showed that fundamental legal issues are at stake in the question of the relation between civil and religious law (even in England, where the law of the Church of England is part of the law of the land). The reaction it provoked make it clear that these are sensitive issues. But what exactly is the relationship between civil and religious law?

This contribution deals with the relationship between civil and religious law in the Netherlands. Against the background of the social, historical, constitutional, and political aspects that have shaped this relationship (2), its various dimensions will be analysed as well as some recent trends and developments. This will be done through assessing the use of mechanisms through which such a relationship may be established (3). Special attention will be paid to the relationship between religious and civil arrangements of conflict resolution (4) and social acceptance of religious behaviour as well as social acceptance of state law by religious believers (5). This is followed by a conclusion (6).

A note on the terminology: for the purposes of this contribution, the term 'religious law' includes statutes[2] of religious bodies (such as churches) in the strict sense, norms and beliefs underlying directly religiously motivated behaviour by groups or individuals (such as conscientious objection to all forms of insurance on religious grounds) or underlying the practice of religious beliefs and traditions in daily life (such as Sunday observance, observance of dietary restrictions). In the absence of a specification in the text, it will be clear from the context in what sense the term 'religious law' is referred to.

Background

In his lecture on the relationship between religious and civil law, the Archbishop of Canterbury suggested ways in which public or legal recognition of religious law could be strengthened and subsequently proposed rebuttals to possible objections against these suggestions. Through his lecture, the Archbishop contributed to a broader public debate on the place of religion in the 'public domain'. Such a debate in being conducted in the Netherlands as well. This debate started at the end of the 1990s and quickly became one of the dominant public themes in the first decade of the new century.

[2] The word 'statutes' is a literal translation from Dutch; this notion refers to the Constitution and bylaws of the organization.

In the Dutch debate, at one end of the spectrum, a certain level of accommodation of religion in the public domain is favoured. Opinions at the other end argue that religion is or should be a merely private matter and, subsequently, see no role for religion in the public domain. Both sides use arguments to support their point of view which are based on the religious make-up of the country, on the constitutional arrangements with regard to religion, and on the developments in these fields over the last decades.

The Netherlands has always been a religiously diverse country, almost proverbially so. Traditionally, religious pluralism has manifested itself predominantly within the Jewish faith and within Christianity, notably within Christian Protestantism. Currently, the religious landscape is much more diverse. A recent statistical survey mentioned figures of 58 % of the population regarding itself as having a religious affiliation, 29 % Catholic; 19 % Protestant Church in the Netherlands (a union, since 2004, of two large reformed churches and the Lutheran Church in the Netherlands); 5 % Islamic; and 6 % affiliated with another religion or belief.[3] Such figures on the religious make-up of the country are quite rough.[4] They must be supplemented with the general 'awareness' of religion, and that is one of a thoroughly secularized country, with a weak public visibility of the larger mainstream Christian denominations, a more outspoken visibility of small orthodox Christian denominations and – a quite recent development – a fairly high level of visibility of Islam. The visibility is a reference to a combination of factors such as active participation in the public debate, being the subject of public debate, or visibility in terms of fostering distinct values (such as concerning male/female relationships or attitudes towards homosexuality) or religious practices (wearing headscarves, maintaining practices such as ritual slaughtering, or observing particular days of rest) which depart from mainstream societal values or practices.

Church and state are separate in the Netherlands. Two other principles that govern the constitutional relationship between church and state are those of state neutrality with regard to religion and belief, and of freedom of religion and belief. The latter principle is explicitly guaranteed in the Dutch Constitution (Article 6)[5];

[3] See Centraal Bureau voor de Statistiek [Statistics Netherlands], *Religie aan het begin van de 21ste eeuw*, Heerlen 2009, pp. 14 and 7.

[4] Reasons for this are that a uniform and well-defined notion of membership of religious denominations or religious organizations does not exist. Each denomination has its own criteria for membership, and these may differ widely from one church to another. These criteria, in turn, may differ from affiliation or non-affiliation as experienced by believers or non-believers. There is no census in the Netherlands either. Depending on the way statistical surveys are set up, these may also differ quite significantly from one to another.

[5] Art. 6 Dutch Constitution: '1. Everyone shall have the right to profess freely his religion or belief, either individually or in community with others, without prejudice to his responsibility under the law. 2. Rules concerning the exercise of this right other than in buildings and enclosed places may be laid down by Act of Parliament for the protection of health, in the interest of traffic and to combat or prevent disorders.' See http://www.rijksoverheid.nl/documenten-en-publicaties/brochures/2008/10/20/the-constitution-of-the-kingdom-of-the-netherlands-2008.html

the principle of neutrality is considered to be embodied in the combination of Article 6 and Article 1 (which guarantees equal treatment and non-discrimination, *inter alia*, on the grounds of religion and belief).[6] Separation of church and state is not explicitly proclaimed in the Constitution or any other legislation, but is commonly accepted as a norm implicit in a number of constitutional provisions and must be interpreted in the light of these provisions. Apart from those already mentioned, Article 23 is relevant in this respect. This Article guarantees freedom of education (private education alongside public education) and states that private elementary education is funded on the same footing as public education.[7] This funding system is extended to all other forms of education as well, including academic education. The Constitution guarantees freedom to establish schools, freedom to administer a school, and freedom of denomination. Private education in this sense is practically always denominational education. In elementary education, denominational schools (publicly funded) make up about two thirds of the entire school system.

The system of education is exemplary of the Dutch way of dealing with organizations based on a religion or belief. A traditional feature of Dutch society is the strong presence of the voluntary sector, which are often organizations based on a religious denomination. In the field of health care, housing, education, and welfare (poor relief), many non-profit or volunteer organizations have traditionally existed on a denominational basis. With the expansion of public activity in these fields – the 1970s were the peak of the social welfare state -, the state took the policy of accommodating these non-profit organizations into the system, often subsidizing or supporting them on the same footing as the public alternatives.

For some denominations, this societal self-organization was also a way to 'emancipate' themselves socio-economically. As mentioned above, this broader societal pattern of organization along denominational lines has become known in the Netherlands as 'pillarization.'[8] It included newspapers, mass media associations, youth clubs, employers' and employees' organizations, and leisure organizations, such as football clubs. After the Second World War, in the run-up to the social welfare state, pillarization diminished; in many existing organizations, the religious identity became less pronounced, with the exception perhaps of those establishments

[6] Art. 1 Dutch Constitution: 'All persons in the Netherlands shall be treated equally in equal circumstances. Discrimination on the grounds of religion, belief, political opinion, race or sex or on any other grounds whatsoever shall not be permitted.'

[7] This Article deals with education; it guarantees freedom of education and establishes the dual system of education with public schools and private (usually denominational) schools, which are funded on an equal footing as public schools.

[8] 'This term is a translation of the Dutch word Verzuiling, first used by the political scientist J.P. Kruyt to describe the peculiar nature of the social structure and political institutions in the Netherlands, although it has since been applied elsewhere (for example with reference to Belgium). For much of the twentieth century, Dutch society was divided by cross-cutting class-based and religious cleavages into four dominant interest groups or blocs – Catholics, Protestants, Socialists, and Liberals – around which formed 'virtually all politically and socially relevant organizations and group affiliations' (Lijphart 1968).

that have a strong educational character and deal with younger children, such as elementary schools (Van Bijsterveld 2010a).

This background leads some to argue in favour of a substantial degree of accommodation of religion by the law. The model of separation of church and state which, in practice and in principle, has always provided scope for such accommodation is pointed at, as is the fact that the system of pillarization has functioned as a method of emancipation and integration and of assuming societal responsibility for the various religious groups in society. Besides, in a liberal democracy which fosters private choice, pluralism, including religious pluralism, should be respected. Developments such as the repositioning of the state at a greater distance vis-à-vis society and societal organizations are consistent with this point of view.

The same background leads others to point at the desirability or even necessity of relegating religion to the private domain. Arguments used in favour of this position include the model of separation of church and state, the development over the last two centuries of disentanglement of religion and law in various domains, the process of secularization, the need to foster integration and social cohesion through common norms of a secular democracy, the desire not to jeopardize modern, 'hard won' liberal values (sometimes at the expense of religion or the churches), and the necessity to avoid the occurrence of so-called 'parallel societies' (Vestdijk-Van der Hoeven 1991 and Labuschagne 1994).

A characteristic of the Dutch legal system is that the Constitution does not permit the courts to examine parliamentary legislation for compatibility with the Constitution. This means that, in matters of constitutionality, the legislator has the final say. As to the composition of parliament since the last few elections, two developments are relevant. The first is a loss of seats by the Christian Democratic Party (CDA) and the second is the rise of the Party for Freedom (PVV), which has a strong anti-Islam profile.

As in society as a whole, values also develop and change within religious groups, apparently more so in mainstream religious denominations than in smaller and more orthodox ones. Examples are perspectives on marriage and divorce, co-habitation, homosexuality, and observance as Sunday as a day of rest. Such changes are also reflected in law. In terms of the relationship between religious law and civil law as discussed in this contribution, this means that certain topics or issues may move from one category to another (such as rules that are respected by law in general – either as rules with a clear religious background or as cultural heritage – to rules that are respected by way of exemption to general rules or to rules that are no longer respected by law).

Legislation

Religion and Law: Foundations

In assessing applicability of religious law in the law of the state, the most abstract yet fundamental level is that of the referral to religion or religious law in legal texts, whether at the symbolic level of preambles, as a source of general law, as a way of determining the applicability of law to individual persons depending on religious affiliation, or as law which is applicable as general law regardless of a person's religious affiliation.

The Dutch Constitution does not contain any reference to the source of power or the foundation of the state or any reference to any other basic principles that guide the state or the Constitution, neither does it explicitly refer to the sources of law. The Dutch Constitution does not have a preamble. In the articles of the Constitution, no explicit references are made to values, a value system, or the principles of democracy and the rule of law. The values of the Constitution (notably those of democracy and the rule of law) are expressed implicitly, that is, through concrete provisions such as those guaranteeing specific fundamental rights and the independence of the judiciary or containing concrete norms that shape the main features of the democratic system. It is generally acknowledged that the sequence of fundamental rights does not express a hierarchy or prioritization of fundamental rights. The rather sober character of the Constitution is usually explained by the fact that the Netherlands has always been a fairly culturally diverse country. Current debates on pluralism, social cohesion, and values make such an adoption, apart from a departure from the tradition, also politically sensitive and pose a risk of polarization.

The Constitution contains various articles that are directly relevant to religion. First and foremost, this is the fundamental right of freedom of religion and belief. Other fundamental rights also explicitly mention religion, such as the right to equal treatment and non-discrimination and the most elaborate article in the Constitution: that on freedom of education. Needless to say other fundamental rights are important as well and may both protect religious liberty (such as freedom of speech or freedom of assembly) and challenge it when invoked by others against a claim of religious liberty.

Just like the internal rules of secular organizations (e.g., a corporation or a football club), rules established by the competent authorities of churches are acknowledged as internally applicable and as such do have legal relevance. The Dutch Civil Code expressly recognizes 'churches, their independent elements and structures in which they are united' as having legal personality and as being 'governed by their own statutes in so far as they do not conflict with the law' (Article 2:2 Dutch Civil Code). These statues are not a source of generally applicable law within the state.

The Dutch legal system excludes a system of legal pluralism based on religion. That would be contrary to the constitutional norm of equal treatment regardless of religion or belief. Secular law is the law applicable to all; this law guarantees freedom of religion. Being subject to religious law always includes an element of choice.

The types of norms with a religious 'connection' closest to general applicability are norms such as those in labour law that include Sunday as the ordinary day of rest. Although these norms do have a religious (Christian) background, they have become part of the culture. It is in this latter capacity that they are being upheld and that they are currently also being modified and challenged.

Religion and Law: Internal Rules of Religious Organizations

Within the Dutch legal system, the various forms of legal entities have the right to determine their own legal order within the limits of the law. The Dutch Civil Code contains a closed typology of legal entities, e.g., foundations and associations, and determines basic rules for each specific entity as well as general rules that are applicable to all types of legal entities. Apart from these constraints, limitations can be found in many other laws, such as labour law or specific law relating to the social sector in which the organization is active (such as hospitals, schools,[9] mass media, etc.) For organizations based on a religion or belief – of which many examples can be found in the social domain – this is no different; the Equal Treatment Act (*Algemene Wet Gelijke Behandeling*) sets out the limitations to these organizations' liberty to maintain their religious identity in hiring and firing policies.

Churches and specific organizations that are closely related to churches enjoy a special regime. The Dutch Civil Code recognizes churches as legal entities *sui generis*. Article 2:2, paragraph 1, Dutch Civil Code, states that churches, their independent units, and structures in which they are united have legal personality. They are governed by their own statutes 'in so far as they do not conflict with the law'. This liberty is not restricted to the 'spiritual domain', but extends to other (substantive) issues as well: the organizational structure as well as internal legal matters (Pel 2013).

Difference of opinion exists as to the precise meaning of the word 'law' in the clause that churches etc. are governed by their own statutes, 'in so far as they do not conflict with the law'. A recent, in-depth study concludes that 'law' in this context means parliamentary legislation, with the exclusion of subordinate legislation. The Dutch Criminal Code certainly qualifies as 'law' in this context (Pel 2013).[10]

The Civil Code contains a set of general rules applicable to the various types of legal entities. Article 2:2, paragraph 2, exempts churches from these provisions. However, it states that analogous application of these provisions is allowed, in so far as this does not conflict with the churches' statutes or with the nature of their internal relations (Article 2:2, paragraph 2, Civil Code). A ruling by the Netherlands Supreme Court (Civil Division) from 1985 held that analogous application should be the starting point for rulings in this field.[11] Thus, decisions of ecclesiastical authorities can be challenged e.g. on the ground that they have not been taken in good faith.

The law does not provide any definition of a 'church'. It is the organization itself that determines its status. In case of a dispute, the courts need to interpret this notion.

---

[9] As a result of the guarantee of freedom of education (Article 23 of the Constitution), education law contains guarantees relating to founding schools, administering schools, and the denomination of schools (see above, Section 2).

[10] P.T. Pel, p. 212, further includes 'fundamental mandatory rules with pretence of priority, fundamental principles of civil law, fundamentals of the legal system such as the principles of good faith, reasonableness, equity, and public morality, and rules of public order'.

[11] HR 15 maart 1985, NJ 1986, 191.

Cases on this issue are rare. In a 1946 ruling, the Netherlands Supreme Court used a phrase that is sometimes regarded as a definition.[12] It mentioned the purposes of the organization in terms of shared worship by its members on the basis of joint religious beliefs; however, it can be contested whether this clause was actually meant as a definition. In a 1986, ruling the Supreme Court was faced with a disputed claim of an organization to be a 'church'. The Court formulated minimal requirements: there must be a 'structured organization' and 'religion must be involved'.[13] In that particular case (Church of Satan), the qualification was withheld. Dutch law contains no system of prior recognition of churches.

Religious organizations can also opt for organization types other than that of a 'church'. In the Islamic domain, foundations are constituted for the management of a mosque and the employment of an imam. Small Christian communities may organize themselves as a formal or informal association.

Methods of Applicability of Religious Rules in the Secular Legal System

In theory, various ways exist through which applicability of religious rules in the secular legal order can be established. Such applicability can be realised through a general reference to such rules by secular law, through secular norms that reproduce the content of religious norms, through the channel of private international law, through treaties or agreements between the state and churches, or as a part of the autonomy that exists under private law. In the Dutch legal system, applicability of religious rules in the secular legal system can be established in a variety of these ways.

Applicability Through a General Reference by Secular Law In the previous Section, it was shown that Article 2:2 Dutch Civil Code plays a crucial role in the acknowledgement of religious rules in the secular legal system. Article 2:2 Civil Code acknowledges the internal rules of churches and related bodies and determines the way they relate to secular law.

Applicability as a Part of the Autonomy Under Secular Law Within the autonomy that private individuals and legal entities enjoy under secular civil law, religious rules may be applied as well. Freedom of marriage enables people to marry within their own religion should their religion prescribe this. Parents can bring up their children in their own religion, which may be a religious rule. These are just two examples of a wide variety of possibilities.

[12] HR 23 juli 1946, NJ 1947, 1.

[13] HR 31 oktober 1986, NJ 1987, 173.

Applicability Through Private International Law Private international law can also be a vehicle for applicability of religious rules in secular law. For the purpose of this contribution, the most relevant issue is that how the national law of Islamic countries applies in the Dutch legal order. The most relevant aspects of private international law in this context concern acknowledgement in the Dutch legal order of legal acts performed in another country and applicability of foreign rules in the Netherlands itself (Oldenhuis et al. 2007).[14] Issues that attract most attention are those in the field of family law: marriage (including polygamy) and divorce, wills, and the way in which apostasy is dealt with in these contexts. A substantive discussion of these themes would be too detailed in the context of this contribution. In general, it can be concluded that the applicability of Islamic law is fairly limited (Oldenhuis et al. 2007).

The 'statute' of a foreign religious organisation (i.e., a church) can have effect in the Dutch legal order. This was explicitly acknowledged at the time of the establishment of the relevant rules in the Dutch Civil Code. The arrangement is not applicable to Dutch churches as Article 2:2 already regulates the applicability of their internal rules in the Dutch legal order (Pel 2013).

Other Methods The Dutch legal system does not contain norms that reproduce the content of religious rules as such. Obviously, the legal system contains many ethical norms that are part of religious law in the broad sense of the word. These secular norms, however, are not applicable by virtue of their religious background. Examples are standards underlying Criminal Code provisions on issues such as theft or murder.

Agreements between state and church are not a common feature of Dutch church and state relationships. Neither are they a vehicle for the applicability of religious rules in the Dutch legal order. Occasionally, agreements are concluded between the State and churches. An example is the agreement reached by various churches and the Dutch government in the run-up to the abolition of historic financial obligations of the state with respect to income, pensions of clergy, and the like. According to the Constitution, however, the final abolition of these historic financial obligations could only be realised by Act of Parliament. The agreement provided a basis for realising this goal in good harmony.

Religiously Motivated Exemptions from Laws of General Application

The legal force of religious rules within a state must be distinguished from legal norms which may be informed by values with deep roots in religion. Societal values evolve over time and lead to changes in secular law. Opinions within religious communities evolve as well. These processes, however, are seldom clear-cut, and

[14] Strictly speaking this does not concern religious rules as such ('sharia'), but foreign national law, which itself may be considered as an embodiment of religious law.

diversity of opinion exists in society between and among adherents of various religions or world views. Debates take place over what norms laws of general application should contain and what the scope and limit of religiously motivated exemptions from those laws should be. In the Netherlands, these developments can be distinguished in the area of Sunday laws and labour laws relating to shop opening on Sunday or employment on Sunday. Another example is the changing attitude towards the acceptance of homosexuality. In this context, the previously widely recognized right of organizations based on a religion to have their own hiring and firing policies in this respect has become problematic. Similarly, the possibility for conscientious objection to conducting same-sex marriages for civil registrars which was agreed upon when same-sex marriages were introduced has been abolished by law.[15] In the field of confessional education, rights connected with the maintenance of the confessional identity are being challenged through legislative plans and proposals that aim at facilitating the change of identity of a school at the wish of parents, at banning the right to conduct an identity-based admission policy with respect to pupils, the introduction of a system of school planning based on numerical criteria only regardless of religion, and a limitation of the scope of hiring and firing policies.[16]

An example of a religiously motivated exception to general standards that is no longer accepted is the case of the Dutch political party SGP. This reformed protestant party did acknowledge the right of women to vote, but not their right to stand for election for the party. This point of view was rooted in their view of male/female role patterns, based on the Bible. In a civil action against the state on behalf of human and women's rights organisations, the Netherlands Supreme Court ruled that the Dutch state violated an Article from the UN Convention on the Elimination of All Forms of Discrimination against Women.[17]

Exemptions of general law motivated by religion do exist. Well-known examples are the exemptions in the field of obligatory insurances, conscientious objection to military service (currently, there is no conscription, however), and in the field of labour law and equal treatment law for clergy. With respect to the latter category, however, parts of social security law and tax law have been declared applicable 'as if' clergy fall in certain relevant categories (Pel 2013). In the absence of a legislative exemption from general law, it is rare for courts to acknowledge an individual claim to exemption on the basis of religion.

The Employer and Accommodation of Religion

The final issue to be discussed in this Section is whether the employer has an obligation to accommodate the religious needs of employees.

[15] See *Kamerstukken* 33 344; the Bill became law on July 4, 2014 (Stb.2014, 260).

[16] See *Kamerstukken* II, 33400-VIII-164 (Brief van de staatssecretaris van onderwijs, cultuur en wetenschap, 12 juli 2014).

[17] HR 9 April 2010, LJN BK4549; see also ECtHR 10 juli 2012, App.nr. 58369/10.

One traditional way for the court to take religion into account is through the interpretation of open norms in civil law. Thus, in a case concerning the immediate dismissal of a Muslim employee who took a day off on a religious holiday after her employer had denied her this day off, the Netherlands Supreme Court took into account an 1984 ruling that in a situation in which the employee applied for this day off, well in advance and providing reasons, in general no 'urgent reason' for such dismissal could be established, unless specific circumstances in the sphere of the conduct of business could justify this.[18]

Another important way in which religion in the workplace is regulated is through the Equal Treatment Act (*Algemene Wet Gelijke Behandeling*). Under this Act of Parliament, direct as well as indirect discrimination, *inter alia* on the grounds of religion, is prohibited; under conditions specified by the Equal Treatment Act, indirect discrimination may be legitimised This Act is applicable in the public as well as in the private sector. Churches and the clergy are exempt from the applicability of the law. In the private sector, specific exceptions are allowed in order to maintain the confessional identity of schools and other organizations. Not only does the Act cover such issues as wearing religious clothes and symbols and hiring and firing, but it is also acknowledged that the employer must assure a working situation free from discrimination or hostility from other employees. The Act has triggered an enormous number of cases which have been dealt with under the Equal Treatment Committee (currently: Netherlands Institute for Human Rights), a quasi-judicial body set up under the Act.

Adjudication

Secular courts have no role in adjudicating conflicts of a theological nature.[19] The adjudication of conflicts with a civil dimension which arise within churches falls within the competence of secular courts. However, churches may have their own internal systems of conflict resolution as well as part of their 'statutes' within the scope of Article 2:2 Civil Code. In situations in which a secular court is competent, the secular court will dismiss a case if obligatory internal ecclesiastical procedure has not been followed first.[20] Afterwards, the secular court can be addressed, which then tests for reasonableness (Pel 2013 and Santing-Wubs 2002, 2014). In conducting such a test, the religious statutes can also be interpreted, of course only in so far as the issue falls within the competence of the court. The interpretation by secular courts of ecclesiastical rules is not open for cassation by the Supreme Court. The Supreme Court regards the application and interpretation of religious law as a matter of 'fact', not of law (Pel 2013).

[18] HR 30 maart 1984, NJ NJ 1985, 350.

[19] HR 15 februari 1957, NJ 1957, 201 (Hasselt).

[20] See, for example, HR 19 December 2003, NJ 2004, 559; and Hof Arnhem 19 januari 2010, LJN BL0003 and BK9957 (Pel, pp. 67–68).

In their own internal procedures, ecclesiastical authorities must respect fundamental principles of a fair trial (Oldenhuis et al. 2007 and Pel 2013).

Ecclesiastical statutes may provide for internal disciplinary procedures. This does not detract from the full applicability of secular criminal law. Church officials can be removed from office under ordinary law as a subsidiary penalty.

Secular civil law may extend to internal religious matters. The content of a prayer, for example, in which a former member was criticized for leaving the church, can constitute a wrongful act vis-à-vis that person.[21] The violation of fundamental procedural rules in ecclesiastical proceedings can be wrongful as well (Van Bijsterveld 2001).[22]

Social Implementation of Religious Rules

Within the limits of the law, religious believers are free to practice their religion and implement religious rules in their daily lives. As the limits of the law are not static and religious beliefs and practices in society diversify and social attitudes towards religious practice change, conflicts and controversies may and, in fact, do arise. Quantitative figures on violations of the law motivated by religious belief are not available, except in very specific areas and even then the figures are usually estimates.

Hostile encounters of religious believers is equally difficult to quantify, although court rulings and annual reports by complaints mechanisms show that such hostile encounters do occur. Within religious communities, conflicts may and do occur in which religious believers may take recourse to religious (ecclesiastical) institutions for adjudication, in so far as they exist. In this Section, the domains are discussed in which such violations and hostile encounters occur and recourse is taken to religious adjudication.

Outright and open violation of state law on a substantive scale motivated by the will to follow religious prescriptions – the first issue mentioned above – does not occur in the Netherlands, nor are there examples of this from the recent past. So far, the law has always tried to accommodate religion and religious practices through granting exceptions to general rules. Cases in point concern, for example, conscientious objection to military service on religious grounds or conscientious objection to insurances. Because of expected conscientious objections, obligatory inoculations have not been introduced.

Although outright and open violations of state law on a substantive scale have never really occurred in the recent history of the Netherlands, a number of issues have surfaced in the political debate that might lead to real conflict between religious law and state law. In 2011, a proposed change to the Animal Welfare Act, initiated in and adopted by the Lower House of the Dutch Parliament – in effect banning ritual

[21] Vzr. Rb. Arnhem, 24 februari 1989, KG 1989, 114.

[22] Hof Den Bosch, 2 December 1998, rolnr. C971117/ro.

slaughtering of animals –, was defeated in the Upper House.[23] The initiator of the Bill announced that another attempt would follow. A ruling of a German Criminal Court triggered debate on the desirability of outlawing religious male circumcision. The issue was not new. However, the debate is still in its early beginning and has not reached a level of political viability. At the same time, it will certainly resurface sooner or later. Another example is the burka. Two distinct bills regarding a ban on wearing a burka are pending in the Lower House: a bill introduced by the (previous) government aimed at regulating wearing facial covering in public places and a parliamentary initiative restricted to banning the burka in public places. Both bills, which have had a very mixed reception, are not being actively pursued at present.[24]

Recently, public concern has manifested itself with regard to so-called 'informal marriages'. An 'informal marriage' is a 'marriage' of which at least one of the parties wrongly assumes that it is a lawful marriage (Van der Leun and Leupen 2009); such a marriage does not have any civil effect. The Dutch Civil Code recognizes only civil marriage as legally valid and, in order to avoid any misunderstanding with regard to the status of 'marriage' ceremonies, Dutch law stipulates that a civil marriage must precede any religious marriage ceremony. A religious leader who performs them is subject to prosecution.

The concern about informal marriages arose especially with regard to assumed practices in immigrant communities, especially in Muslim communities. The background to these concerns were not so much the religious practice as such, but the protection of the socio-economically weaker party, often the woman, also with regard to her legal status. Concern with informal marriages can also be seen in a broader context, namely, that of so-called arranged or forced marriages. It is generally held that these marriages are not so much expressions of religious practice but of cultural practices, which are far removed from the Dutch cultural value that a marriage should be entered into voluntarily and that one's marriage partner is a personal choice. Forcing someone into marriage is a criminal offence and, even though convictions have never taken place (partly because the offence is hard to prove and the willingness to come forward and press charges is practically non-existent), the maximum penalty for this offence has recently been raised.

A related issue of concern – one that did not, however, involve a violation of civil law – was that of the existence of so-called Islamic courts. This issue surfaced following media attention for Islamic courts in Great Britain and Canada. As we have seen in the previous section, the Dutch Civil Code leaves room for ecclesiastical courts to operate within certain margins and, where issues of Civil Law are involved, without blocking access to the regular civil court altogether. Although public concern focused on the existence of these courts as such, the gist was not so much a strictly legal concern, but rather a concern about the knowledge or ignorance of those involved with conflict resolution about the legal status of these courts and a possible lack of social resistance or reality of access for those who live in non-integrated, tightly knit social communities (Van Bijsterveld 2001).

---

[23] See *Kamerstukken* 31 571.

[24] See *Kamerstukken* 31 108; and 33 165.

The second issue mentioned above, hostility in everyday life towards religious believers as a result of following religious rules or of religious practices does occur. Hostile treatment includes smearing the walls of a mosque and hostile reactions to Jews wearing a yarmulke. Although incidents are reported in the media and anti-discrimination NGOs issue annual reports on such forms of discriminatory behaviour, it is difficult to gain an overall impression of its occurrence. In the area of labour law, hiring and firing issues involving religious practices occur from time to time (direct and indirect discrimination); often they are related to wearing religious symbols. The Equal Treatment Commission (currently: Netherlands Institute for Human Rights), a quasi-judicial complaints body, has determined that the responsibility of the employer also entails the care for a 'discrimination-free' environment, that is, the care that employees treat each other with respect. Though hostile encounters do occur, they seems to be incidental rather than structural. At present, in any case, polarization on the issue of religion (and notably Islam) has quieted to a large extent. Legal norms concerning the treatment of religion in the work place have largely been established. And in society, a process of accommodation with respect to religious symbols has taken place.

The third issue mentioned above is the use of services by religious believers provided by religious adjudication bodies. Such adjudication is made use of within the framework sketched in the previous section. Examples especially include marriage annulment procedures before Roman Catholic ecclesiastical courts. These procedures do not have any civil effect.

Conclusion

The system of legal recognition of religious rules (in the strict sense of the word) in the Dutch legal order is satisfactory. Churches have the liberty to be governed by their own statute, whilst fundamental legal norms of the Dutch secular legal order take precedence, in terms of both substance and procedure. The system facilitates churches which are organized hierarchically as well as those which have a more decentralised structure. The institutional autonomy of churches is furthermore recognized through exemptions from generally applicable law for churches and the clergy in specific labour-related legislation. Religious organizations are not obliged to organize themselves as a 'church'. Especially in the Islamic domain, foundations are used for the maintenance of a mosque or the employment of clergy.

Societal organizations, such as schools and welfare or youth organizations, may organize themselves on the basis of a religion. The self-organization of society along religious lines is even characteristic of Dutch society. It is undisputed that the right to such organization also exists for minority religions, such as Islam. The desirability of this right is disputed. Some see it as a method for emancipation and integration into Dutch society. Others see it as an obstacle to integration and an undesirable development at a time when the traditional 'pillarization' in society has diminished. Dutch law has traditionally respected the religious identity of such organizations, also through exemptions from generally applicable law. The tendency is to limit this institutional autonomy especially where hiring and firing policies are concerned.

The Constitution grants everyone the freedom to manifest his religion either alone or in community with others, without prejudice to a person's responsibility before the law. Law may be based on religiously informed ethics or social traditions or create specific exemptions with respect to generally applicable law in order to accommodate religious beliefs and practices. In the course of time, the law may change from the first category to the second or even stop to accommodate religious beliefs and practices. Over the last few decades, a development can be discerned of less tolerance for religious orthodoxy. The process of secularization, changes in societal value patterns (also within religious denominations) and a certain fear for the still 'unknown' Islam seem relevant factors in this regard.

References

Ahdar, Rex, and N. Aroney. 2010. *Shari'a in the West*. Oxford: Oxford University Press.

Labuschagne, B. 1994. *Godsdienstvrijheid en niet-gevestigde religies: een grondrecht-rechtsfilosofische studie naar de betekenis en grenzen van religieuze tolerantie*. Groningen: Wolters-Noordhoff.

Lijphart, A. 1968. *The politics of accommodation*. http://www.encyclopedia.com/doc/1O88-pillarization.html. Last accessed on 6 July 2010.

Oldenhuis, F.T., et al. 2007. *Schurende relaties tussen recht en religie*. Assen: Van Gorcum.

Pel, P.T. 2013. *Geestelijken in het recht. De rechtspositie van geestelijke functionarissen in het licht van het eigen recht van kerken en religieuze gemeenschappen in de Nederlandse rechtsorde*. Den Haag: Bju.

Santing-Wubs, A.h. 2002. *Kerken in geding: de burgerlijke rechter en kerkelijke geschillen*. Den Haag: Bju.

Santing-Wubs, A.h. 2014. Geschilbeslechting binnen geloofsgemeenschappen. In *Geloofsgemeenschappen en recht*, ed. L.C. van Drimmelen, and T.J. van der Ploeg. Den Haag: Bju.

Van Bijsterveld, Sophie. 2001. Church autonomy in the Netherlands. The distinctiveness of the Church – The interplay between legal, popular and ecclesiastical perspectives. Church autonomy as a test case. In *Legal position of churches and church autonomy*, ed. Hildegard Warnink. Leuven: Peeters.

Van Bijsterveld, Sophie. 2010a. Religion and the secular state in the Netherlands. In *Religion and the secular state: Interim national reports*, ed. W. Cole Durham, and J. Martinez-Torrón. Provo: The International Center for Law and Religion Studies, Brigham Young University.

Van Bijsterveld, Sophie. 2010b. Negotiating the unfamiliar: Reflections from the Netherlands on the Archbishop of Canterbury's lecture. In *Shari'a in the West*, ed. Rex Ahdar, and Nicholas Aroney. Oxford: Oxford University Press.

Van der Leun, Joanne, and Leupen, Avalon. 2009. Informele huwelijken in Nederland. Een exploratieve studie. Universiteit Leiden. http://www.wodc.nl/onderzoeksdatabase/het-voorkomen-van-islamitische-huwelijken-zonder-voorafgaand-burgerlijk-huwelijk-in-nederland.aspx. Last accessed February 22, 2014.

Vestdijk-Van der Hoeven, A.C.M. 1991. *Religieus recht en minderheden: een onderzoek naar de rechtspositie van de leden der minderheden in relatie tot het eigen religieuze recht van deze minderheden in Nederland*. Arnhem: Gouda Quint.

Williams, R. 2008. http://rowanwilliams.archbishopofcanterbury.org/articles.php/1135/sharia-law-what-did-the-archbishop-actually-say. Last accessed February 13, 2014.

Chapter 18
Portugal: Religious Rules and State Law

Paulo Pulido Adragão and Anabela Leão

Abstract This article discusses the relationship between religious rules and State law in the Portuguese legal system. Sociological data concerning religious diversity and a brief description of the Portuguese constitutional and legal system of State/Religion relations (which can be labeled as a model of non-identification with cooperation), are provided in the *Introduction*, where the authors also discuss the meaning to be given to "religious rules". In a second moment, different fields of intersection between religious rules or religiously enacted rules and State law, namely in the domain of family law, are identified. A special focus is given to the relevance of Canon law, due to a tradition of cooperation between the Portuguese state and the Catholic Church through Concordats. Finally, adjudication issues, concerning the relation between civil and religious jurisdictions, are discussed. The authors conclude that the Portuguese legal system is religion-friendly and reveals openness to religious pluralism.

Introduction

1. With a resident population of about ten million,[1] Portugal can presently be characterized as a country with cultural and religious diversity, which can be partly attributed to immigration waves (see Vilaça 2006, 2010). According to the results of the 2011 *Census*,[2] the religion with major presence in Portugal is Roman Catholicism (81 %), notwithstanding the presence of other religions, such as Islam and Judaism (whose presence in the country also dates from ancient times) as well as other non-Christian religions. Following a trend reported in other countries, religious indifference also seems to be increasing (Mucznik 2013).

[1] According to data available at the website of the National Institute of Statistics, the Portuguese resident population in 2013 amounted to 10 427 301. http://www.ine.pt/. Accessed 31/03/2015.

[2] Available at http://censos.ine.pt. Accessed 31/03/2015.

P.P. Adragão (✉) • A. Leão
Associate Professor, Law Faculty, University of Porto, Porto, Portugal
e-mail: pauloadragao@gmail.com

R. Bottoni et al. (eds.), *Religious Rules, State Law, and Normative Pluralism - A Comparative Overview*, Ius Comparatum – Global Studies in Comparative Law 18, DOI 10.1007/978-3-319-28335-7_18

The historical and constitutional evolution of religious freedom in Portugal reveals, according to Adragão (2012c, 70 ff), not only a Catholic majority since the country's formation, but also a relatively peaceful co-existence between religious minorities and the Catholic majority (notwithstanding some episodes of intolerance e.g. the persecution of Jews, the establishment of the Inquisition in the fifteenth century). Recent data seems to confirm the peaceful co-existence of both believers and non-believers and of different religious groups in Portugal.[3]

However, it was only after the democratic turn in 1974, and the approval and enforcement of the present Portuguese Constitution[4] in 1976, that a system of full religious freedom, irrespective of religious denominations, was achieved (see Miranda quoted by Adragão 2012d, 44).[5] Presently, the structural principles of the Portuguese model of relation between State and religion can be systematized as follows (Raimundo 2012, 272 ff): *separation and non-confessionality*, *co-operation*, *equality and non-discrimination*, and *tolerance*.

Religious freedom, both in individual and collective dimensions, is extensively enshrined in the Constitution, which frames a non-confessional State and a model of separation or non-identification between State and religious communities and churches (a limit that must be respected by Laws that modify the constitution, see Article 288). According to CPR, freedom of conscience, religion and worship is a fundamental right, enshrined in Article 41. Discrimination on grounds of religion or belief is prohibited by Article 13, which establishes the principle of equality and the prohibition of discrimination on several non-exhaustive grounds, reinforced in respect to workers rights (Article 59) and in various sets of ordinary rules that are to be applied by diverse authorities. Freedom of conscience and religion shall not be affected in the case of a declaration of a state of siege or of emergency (Article 19/6). Other constitutional norms refer to religion, e.g. stipulating that "the State may not plan education and culture in accordance with any philosophical, aesthetic, political, ideological or religious directives" (Article 43/2) and that "public education shall not be linked to a religious belief" (Article 43/3).

Moving to the infra-constitutional level, in the past decade Portuguese law on religion went through a process of deep transformation and consolidation. A pivotal role was played by the adoption in 2001 of the new Law on Religious Freedom, Law 16/2001, July 22nd (hereinafter, LRF) and by the signature of the new Concordat between the Portuguese State and the Holy See in 2004 (hereinafter, Concordat).[6] Both instruments implement co-operation with religious denominations,

[3] See data for 2012 available at the website of Pew Research Center's Forum on Religion and Public Life, placing Portugal amongst the countries with a low level both of social hostility concerning religion and of government religion-based restriction. http://www.pewforum.org/2014/01/14/religious-hostilities-reach-six-year-high/. Accessed 10/02/2014.

[4] The Constitution of the Portuguese Republic (hereinafter CPR) bears the date of its passage by the Constituent Assembly – April 2nd 1976 – and entered into force on April 25th 1976 (Article 296). The English translation available for consultation at the website of the Portuguese parliament [www.parlamento.pt] has been generally followed in this paper.

[5] For an historical perspective about the relations between State and religions, see Adragão 2002.

[6] Replacing the existing Law on Religious Freedom of 1971 and Concordat of 1940.

suggesting the evolution of the model from relative separation between State and religion towards a model of "non-identification with cooperation" (Adragão 2002, 2007 and 2012a, b, c, d, 45) or "cooperative separation" (Gouveia 2012, 293 ff; Raimundo 2012, 267 ff). The principle of cooperation is presently enshrined both in Articles 1 and 4 Concordat and in Article 1 LRF. The dualism between LRF and Concordat appears to be less significant than it may seem at first glance (Miranda and Marques 2010, 918): besides similarities in content, LRF enshrines some general principles applicable to all religions, Catholicism included, complementing constitutional provisions on religious freedom.

Finally, as stated in Article 1 LFR, protection of religious freedom benefits also from the openness to international and European law (Articles 8 and 16 CPR), e.g. European Convention of Human Rights (1950, hereinafter ECHR) and Universal Declaration on Human Rights (1948).

2. It seems difficult to ascribe an unambiguous meaning to the expression "religious rules".[7] For the purposes of this report, "religious rules" are generally assumed to be rules enacted by a religious authority that are relevant to the Portuguese State law.

The constitutional and democratic State of Western matrix, in which the Portuguese State can be included, considers State and religion as "differentiated spheres", autonomous and separate (Raimundo 2012, 227). Despite this, some degree of juridical regulation is needed, not as an obstacle to the above-mentioned separation, but as a consequence of the pluralism of the State and the specific concept of freedom it entails, therefore assuming itself as an instrument of protection of religious freedom (Raimundo 2012, 231 ff). This seems consistent with the doctrine of positive and negative duties of the State arising from fundamental rights (Canotilho and Machado 2013, 287 ff) as well as with the role ascribed to the State as a promoter of pluralism and tolerance among religious groups (inter alia, Raimundo 2012, 235).

From the point of view we endorse - that of the *law of the State* - religious rules assume relevance to the law of the State under some conditions and through different mechanisms of recognition, suggesting the existence of a certain degree of normative pluralism encompassing religious normative orders (in the same sense, Canotilho and Machado 2013, 295 ff). Canon law is usually seen as a primary legal order (inter alia, Gonzalez del Valle 2005, 41 ff; Adragão 2004), but other religious communities can also be considered to have religiously-based normative orders.[8]

Portuguese LRF often refers to "norms of the religion" and specifies that the content of religious freedom encompasses the right to act or not to act in accordance with the norms of one's religion, with respect for human rights and the law (Article 8). It is not the State's right to determine what is a religion or what are "religious norms" (Miranda and Marques 2010, 911; Folque 2012, 242 ff) nor to give

[7] On this, see the contribution of Silvio Ferrari in this book.

[8] Whether or not meeting the characteristics to be considered as "confessional laws", "private orders" or "primary legal orders" (see Gonzalez del Valle 2005, 86–88; Raimundo 2012, 248), a question which falls outside the scope of this report.

"substantive attention" to the internal norms of a religious denomination, even though some scrutiny of the observance of, for example, constitutional standards is required in the course of State recognition of religious entities and/or their activities (Article 39/c) LRF) or of conclusion of agreements with religious denominations (article 47 LFR) (Raimundo 2012, 323; Folque 2012, 252 ff).

Finally, even though we will generally take "religious rules" as rules enacted by a religious authority, rules regulating the social dimension of the religious factor, whether produced unilaterally by the State or bilaterally through agreements between the State and religious denominations, will also be taken in account when appropriate. These criteria allow for the consideration both of religiously based law through private international law and for the direct or indirect recognition, through substantive State law, of religious norms, procedures and acts. It must be noticed, however, that the religious and/or cultural meaning of some symbols, rituals and practices is sometimes disputed (see bellow 5 and inter alia, Raimundo 2012, 276 ff).

Religious Rules and State Law

3. The importance of religion to society justifies the recognition of (a certain degree of) a regulatory role played by the State through law (on this, see Gouveia 2012, 287 ff and Raimundo 2012, 223 ff). At the constitutional level, besides generally providing for the respect of religious freedom as well as for the separation between State and religion (see above 1): in the Constitution there is no mention of a specific religion or divinity, and it's not granted a specific status. The non-denominational character of the State as envisaged by the Constitution does not preclude the possibility of public recognition of the importance granted to religion by believers, or of the dimension of religiosity as a social fact, provided the principle of equality is observed.[9] It is worth mentioning, concerning the present issue, that both the Concordat (Article 1) and the Agreement between Portugal and the Imamat Ismaili (Preamble and Article 2)[10] recognize that the State, and those religious communities, share and promote the values of human dignity and respect for human rights, which are enshrined in the Constitution.

Concerning *sources of law,* the abovementioned pluralist perspective demands accommodations in the classic, State-centered, theory of the sources of law, a debate that goes beyond the scope of this report. In the Portuguese case, the dogmatic

[9] In Case 423/87, the Constitutional Court sustained that all religions should be treated equally according to CPR, equality of treatment allowing for differentiated treatment of religions according their social representativeness but not for discrimination or privilege (on this, Miranda et al. 2007; Brito 1999; Adragão and Gonçalves 2006, 179 ff).

[10] Agreement between the Imamat Ismaili (the institution representing Shia Imami Ismaili Muslims, according to article 2) and Portugal, signed in Lisbon on May 8th 2010 and approved by Resolution of the Assembly of the Republic 109/2010, hereinafter APII.

elaboration on the subject focuses on Articles 1 onwards of the Civil Code[11] (hereinafter CC), which adopts a classical theory on the sources of law (statutory law as an immediate source, custom, jurisprudence and doctrine as mediate sources). Scholars notice the shortcomings of this approach, emphasizing e.g. the need to take into account the constitutional (Articles 112, 8, 227, among others) or even supranational norms on sources, enriching the theory in a multidimensional way (see Amaral 2004, 343 ff).

None of the aforementioned specific provisions on sources of law refers specifically to religious norms or even religious agreements. However, in a disputed interpretation, some authors interpret the mention (Articles 1/1 and 3/2 CC) to "corporative norms" as "immediate source of law" as internal norms of social corporations, among which the internal law of the Catholic Church, an autonomous and specific law system with its own specific sanctions not enforced by State courts or police (Amaral 2004, 527 ff).

Treaties and other international agreements must also be considered amongst sources of law, their regulation flowing essentially from the CPR (e.g. Articles 8 and 133). The Concordat of 2004 is an international treaty, part of Portuguese law under Article 8 CPR, ranking below the Constitution and above ordinary law as a source of law[12]; it regulates several aspects of individual and institutional religious freedom, containing provisions concerning the interaction of the two legal systems, State law and Canon law (see below). Given the supranational character or scope of other religious communities and churches beside the Catholic one, and despite some controversy, most scholars tend to affirm that international agreements can also be signed between those religious entities and the State, provided they enjoy powers to conclude international covenants under international and internal law (Gouveia 2012, 83 ff; Canas 2007, 293 ff) – a solution that fits the demands of the principle of equal treatment between religious denominations. This seems to have been the case of the abovementioned religious agreement signed in 2010 between Portugal and the Imamat Ismaili (Gouveia 2012, 69 ff; Canotilho and Machado 2010).

Continuing to assume "religious" in the sense of "produced by a religious authority", religious agreements of internal law should be mentioned among sources of law. Following the European trend towards cooperation via agreements between the State and religious denominations, and the possible generalization of a "concordat-based formula" (on the issue, Canas 2007), LRF allows agreements on matters of common interest between the State and churches and religious communities enjoying the status of "settled" (under the conditions of Article 37). These agreements have the form of religious agreements of internal law, regulated by Articles 45 onwards LRF.[13]

[11] Decree Law 47344/66, November 25th, with subsequent amendments.

[12] Therefore, susceptible to judicial review of constitutionality by the Constitutional Court under the terms established by Articles 277 ff CPR (on this, Adragão 2007, 184 ff).

[13] The juridical nature of these agreements, as well as several aspects of their legal regime, are debated, see inter alia Canas 2007, 327 ff and Raimundo 2012, 351 ff. Diversity of legal instruments does not seem to amount to discrimination, rather mirroring the diverse legal nature of the

References to religious laws and principles can be found in infra-constitutional law, in connection with specific parts of the State legal system. That is the case of religious norms specifically mentioned by the Concordat or LRF concerning different profiles of self-organization of religious communities, the professional situation of ministers of religion, or the possibility to conclude agreements (as explained below).

Considering the institutional dimensions, the State acknowledges the competence of Canon law to regulate the internal organization of the Catholic Church, recognizing the civil effects of the creation (as well as modification or extinction), by that legal order, of several corporate bodies. The legal status of canonical entities is subject to Canon law and Portuguese law, applied by the respective authorities, and their civil competence is equal to that accorded by Portuguese law to other legal entities of identical nature (Article 11 Concordat). According to the Concordat, the State recognizes the legal status of the Catholic Church (Article 1) and other canonical entities (Articles 8 and 9), in some cases (Article 10) requiring registration (Costa 2006, 313 ff). For other religious denominations, according to LRF (Article 33 onwards) the State recognizes legal personality to religious corporate bodies through registration in a specific register (Raimundo 2012, 314 ff).

Considering criminal law, the Portuguese Penal Code[14] (hereinafter, PC) does not explicitly refer to religious rules or principles, but it does give relevance to the protection of religious feelings and manifestations of religion, e.g. criminalizing offences motivated by religious belief (Article 251 PC) or protecting acts of worship (Article 252 PC). The relevance of religious norms also needs to be mentioned, since the significance of some of the concepts used e.g. "minister of religion", "in the exercise of their duties" or "profanation", needs to be determined in accordance with religiously-based normative systems (Leite 2012). Although non-confessional, the State cannot help recognizing some degree of relevance of concepts held by religious groups, but this reference must be understood in the context of the criminal protection of paramount social values such as personhood or/and public peace (Leite 2012).

As will be considered in detail below, religious rules are also relevant in other domains of law, namely family law (by regulating marriage), labor law, administrative law and education law.

4. Portugal does not have a system of personal laws based on religious affiliation. The law of the State is generally applicable to Portuguese citizens irrespective of their religious affiliation.

Yet, Portuguese law gives relevance to the personal religious affiliation of citizens, allowing some degree of "choice of law" concerning marriage. Article 36 CPR protects the right to celebrate marriage, as well as the institution of marriage and its dissolution, independently from the form of celebration, referring its regulation to law. Even though it doesn't explicitly refer to religious marriages, there is a

religious denominations (Adragão 2007, 184; Medeiros 2012, 645 ff; Miranda and Marques 2010, 918 ff.).

[14] Decree Law 48/95, March 15, with further ammendments.

general agreement that it allows the celebration of religious marriages, provided that equality and separation principles are respected (Coelho and Oliveira 2008, 188 ff; Martins 2010, 241 ff).

In brief, Portuguese civil law (Articles 1587 onwards CC) recognizes two different legal institutions: *civil marriage* and *canonical marriage*. According to Article 13 of the Concordat, the State recognizes the civil effects of marriages celebrated according to Canon law as long as the act of marriage is registered in the appropriate State Register (transcription). As for civil marriage (Article 1615 CC), it can be celebrated, according to the will of the spouses, in accordance with the procedure established in civil law (see Articles 153 onwards of the Code of Civil Register) or, alternatively, according to the rituals of religious communities with the status of "settled" in Portugal ("civil marriages under religious form"), a possibility introduced in 2001 by LRF (Article 19).

The Portuguese marriage system can nowadays be labeled a system of optional civil marriage.[15] This system allows fiancés to choose between a canonical marriage or a civil marriage, whether or not celebrated under a religious form, and offers the advantage of avoiding a double celebration of marriage, recognizing civil effects to marriages celebrated according to religious rituals, even if it means sacrificing the unity of matrimonial law (Martins 2010, 248). There are laws available for citizens who do not want to be subjected to religious norms, enabling the celebration of a strictly civil marriage (this is, indeed, the "default system").

Scholars underline the difference between canonical marriage and civil marriage under religious form, the first being an autonomous modality of marriage, whereas the second is a form of civil marriage (Coelho and Oliveira 2008, 180 ff; Pinheiro 2010, 424 ff; Martins 2010; Vitor 2010). Canonical marriage is governed by several aspects of specific religious rules concerning formalities but also validity, therefore subject to Canon law. Civil marriages under religious form celebrated before the minister of religion of a church or religious community settled in the country have recognized civil effects (Article 19 LRF), but their regime is the one established in the CC for civil marriages, except that which concerns some aspects of form, including procedure (Article 19 and 58 LRF).

Notwithstanding being an autonomous modality, canonical marriages must also respect conditions established in civil law besides respecting Canon law. Civil law rules concerning capacity to celebrate (Article 1596 CC), and some aspects of the form do apply, and the effects, both personal and patrimonial, of these marriages are regulated by civil law (Article 1588 CC). Both laws also govern the dissolution of marriage: State law regulates dissolution by death or divorce,[16] Canon law regulates

[15] More accurately, Coelho and Oliveira (2008, 186 ff) prefer to call it a system of optional civil marriage to Catholics and members of other religious communities settled in the country and a system of compulsory civil marriage to members of churches or religious communities not having the status of settled in the country, for the law gives no relevance to the religious ceremony eventually performed by these latter.

[16] Divorce is not admitted by Canon Law; the application of civil divorce to canonical marriages was introduced in 1975, by the State, through an Additional Agreement that changed the Concordat of 1940.

nullity and marriage ratified but not consummated (Article 16 Concordat). It is generally assumed that the causes of inexistence or ability to be annulled established in Articles 1627 onwards of the CC do not apply to canonical marriages, which, besides nullity, have a specific cause of dissolution (dispensation).

It is also worth mentioning that, concerning the end of life, religious rituals for the dead are optional. Laws that regulate the destination of corpses,[17] namely inhumation in secular public cemeteries and cremation, recognize the possibility of inhumation in specific places according to the deceased's religious convictions or citizenship[18]

5. Portuguese State laws do not include religious rules applicable to all citizens independent from the fact that they profess a religion and also apart from their particular religious affiliation. However, it is possible to identify some civil rules - applicable to all citizens, since the system does not in general distinguish according to religious affiliation – that have an identifiable religious origin or background.

This is often invoked in some domains of family law, where the influence of religious values and prescriptions is well known. That is the case of marriage, whose present civil configuration, even though revealing religious influence and Judaic-Christian roots, resulted from processes of secularization and full recognition of religious freedom, demanding the existence of a civil matrimonial regime (Machado 2010, 11 ff; Coelho and Oliveira 2008, 172 ff). Also the prohibition of polygamy - by civil and criminal law, in the Portuguese case - is usually connected with religion and, specifically, with Christian roots, but this explanation seems to ignore other reasons underlying the prohibition, as well as the fact that some religions do allow polygamy (Pinheiro 2008).

Other rules, outside family law, reveal religious influence or roots.[19] The case of Sunday closing rules, public holidays or labor rules establishing weekly rest periods for workers, is worth specific mention. Under the Concordat, Portugal recognizes Sunday as festive day (Article 3) as well as other religious festivities. Religious festivities recognized by the State are part of the common calendar, being applicable to all citizens irrespective of their religious beliefs, and are associated with specific legal consequences, e.g. counting of legal deadlines, organization of working periods or opening schedules of public offices (underlining this, Vitali and Chizzoniti 2006, 183 ff).

However, even though these public norms are in accordance with the confessional law, originating from a pact between the State and Catholic Church, they are still laws of the State, having legal force due to a secular title and not to a confessional title, as imposed by the separation principle: they do not signify the State's identification of itself with a certain religious denomination but only that it recognizes a "specific sociological reality" (Raimundo 2012, 248–249). Religious holidays show, nevertheless, how Catholic, national and cultural traditions are

[17] Namely, decree Law 411/98, 30th December, with subsequent amendments.

[18] See Article 11/2, Decree Law 411/98.

[19] E.g. labor rules protecting working conditions (Canotilho and Machado 2013, 292 ff; Raimundo 2012, 248).

inter-twined (Canas 2007, 283; Miranda and Marques 2010, 913; Raimundo 2012, 228) and how religion contributes to the design of individual and collective identities (Canotilho and Machado 2013, 295 ff, 303). Additionally, the religious roots of weekly rest days shall not overshadow its deep cultural, social and symbolic meaning, even to those who are not religious (Canotilho and Machado 2013, 295 ff).

6. Portuguese laws recognize, in general, the right of a religious organization to apply its own rules to the relations that take place within the religious organization itself or within institutions that are owned or managed by the religious organization. The abovementioned principle of separation between State and religious communities also safeguards religious communities from improper interference from the State.

Under Article 41/4 CPR "churches and other religious communities are separate from the State and are free to organize themselves and to exercise their functions and form of worship". Institutional features of religious freedom are further developed both in Concordat (Article 20) and LRF (Article 20 onwards), and can also be developed through agreements (see above 3).

Article 22 of LRF provides that churches and other religious communities are free to organize themselves, having the right to autonomously decide the formation, composition, competence and functionality of their organs, the selection, duties and powers of their representatives, ministers, missionaries and religious auxiliaries, the religious rights and duties of the believers, without prejudice to their religious freedom, the adherence or participation in the creation of federations or interdenominational associations. Under the Concordat, the State recognizes that the Catholic Church shall freely organize itself in accordance with the norms of Canon law, the legal status of canonical persons being subject to Canon and Portuguese laws, applied by the respective authorities (Article 11). According to the APII (2010), the State also recognizes that the Ismaili Community may be freely organized in consistence with the rules of the Constitution of the Shia Imami Ismaili Muslims (Article 4), allowing not only for the protection of religious identity (Article 3) but also safeguarding the autonomy of the Community in several aspects concerning self organization and its educational system (Articles 4 ff). Article 22 LRF also contains the clauses safeguarding religious identity and the specific character of the concerned denomination.[20]

The appointment and training of ministers of religion also belongs to the religious denomination's autonomy (Articles 15 and 22 LRF, Article 20 Concordat and Article 4 APII). LRF provides in Article 16 that the exercise of the ministry is considered a professional activity of the minister of religion when it provides him with a means of support, allowing him to benefit from a general social security system under certain conditions. According to Brito (2012, 280) "the autonomy of churches

[20] EU Directive 2000/78/EC on equal treatment in access to employment or occupation and membership of certain organizations allows for the existence of so-called "occupational requirements" in Article 4. The Labor Code (Law 7/2009, 12th February, with subsequent amendments, hereinafter LC) partially incorporates the regulation of this article in article 25/4 (on the issue, see Brito 2012, 279.

and religious communities in matters of internal organization and cult implies that the selection, the rights and the duties of their ministers are not subject to the rules of the contract of employment, including the prohibition of discrimination".

In the specific field of education, CPR guarantees the "freedom to teach any religion within the ambit of the religious belief in question and to use the religion's own media for the pursuit of its activities" (Article 41/5) as well as the right to create private and cooperative schools (Article 43), subject to inspection by the State (Article 75/2). However, this power does not cover strict religious teaching, e.g. training of ministers of religion (Canotilho and Machado 2007, 615, 906). Besides a private system, religious classes provided by religious denominations can take place in public schools (Article 19 Concordat for Catholic education and Article 24 LRF for other religions[21]), under the State's duty of cooperation with parents in the education of children (Article 67 CPR and Article 8 ECHR and Optional Protocol nr.1). Despite some controversy on the issue, this doesn't seem to impair on the constitutional requirement of a non-confessional character of public education (Article 43/1 CPR): the Portuguese constitution *allows* for this cooperation with parents and religious denominations, as long as classes are not compulsory, remain under the responsibility of religious denominations (and not of the State) and no discrimination between religions occurs (see decisions of the Constitutional Court in Cases 423/87 and 174/93). In accordance with the principle of non-identification, both the Concordat (Article 19/3,4) and the LRF (Article 24/4) stipulate that teachers in charge of religious education will be appointed or hired, transferred and excluded from teaching the subject by the State in agreement with the representatives of the churches, communities or representative organizations (on this, Raimundo 2012, 363 ff).

The existence of religious private healthcare institutions are also constitutionally protected, even though the State is obliged to regulate and inspect entrepreneurial and private forms of medicine and articulate them with the National Health Service, in order to ensure adequate standards of efficiency and quality (Article 64/3/d) CPR).

7. The authors are unaware of religious norms applicable in the Portuguese State legal order through State norms that reproduce their content. Despite this, in a broad sense, religious rules can become relevant to State law by reference.

Besides the application of Canon law through the Concordat or specific legal rules (as seen above, in 3 and 4), LRF and other infra constitutional laws do sometimes take into account norms originating from religious denominations as a mere given or presupposition of fact. This can be seen, for example, when the law refers to "ministers of religion", whose determination does not impend on the State (Articles 15 and 22 LRF, Article 20 Concordat, Article 4 APII). Religious norms can also become relevant to State law in connection with administration (e.g. the appointment of teachers of religious classes in public schools, see above 4) or certificatory (e.g. in case of marriage, see above 3) procedures that take place within religious denominations according to its norms. Finally, as already seen, the State

[21] See also Decree-Law 70/2013 and Decree-Law 329/98, November 2nd.

gives religious communities the power to organize themselves, recognizing legal personality to their freely erected institutions (see above 3 and 6). Likewise, it is also possible that religious norms become relevant through the compliance with general clauses or in the effective carrying out of competences and powers recognized by the law to natural persons, e.g. decisions concerning religious education in the context of parental responsibilities[22] (on this, Fialho 2013, 65 ff).

Also, systems of law influenced by religion can become relevant through the channel of international private law. In this regard, it ought to be noticed that the influence of religious law in a foreign State's legal system namely in States of Islamic majority, can operate through diverse models, expressing different intensities of religious influence, more visible in matters concerning family and personal status (as demonstrated, about Islam and Islamic law, by Tahir Mahmood 2012). In this domain, Portuguese choice of law rules give relevance to the law of nationality of the person in matters concerning *personal law*, which encompasses status and capacity, family relations and succession (Articles 25 and 31 CC); on family issues, the law of the common habitual residence of the spouses or the law of the country with which the family life has the closest connection may also be relevant (Articles 49 ff CC) (for a résumé, Teles and Brito 2007, 287 ff). Foreign law may, however, be excluded if it is deemed to violate fundamental principles of public policy (article 22 CC). Constitutional rules and principles, namely those concerning fundamental rights and equality, stand as a limit to the application of competent foreign law and to the recognition of foreign court decisions (Lima Pinheiro 2009, 323, 584 ss and 691 ss). In line with other European countries, monogamy is generally considered as part of the Portuguese public policy,; this does not preclude the recognition of some effects to polygamous marriages regularly celebrated abroad (Pinheiro 2008).

Religious rules can also become applicable through treaties and agreements between the State and religious communities. The Constitution does not impose but also does not prohibit either specific regulation of religious phenomenon or agreements between the State and religious denominations (Miranda and Marques 2010, 890 ff), a model explained above in 3. As already pointed out, the Concordat regulates several aspects of individual and institutional religious freedom, containing provisions concerning the interaction of the two legal systems, State law and Canon law. Namely, the concordat recognises the latter's civil effects on subjects such as the marriage system or self-organization of religious institutions as well as recognizing the jurisdiction of ecclesiastical courts (this will be further developed bellow). Besides the Concordat and the APII (on this issue, see Article 4), religious agreements with other religious denominations, although extensively admitted by law, have not yet been concluded.

8. Portuguese State law does allow religiously motivated exemptions from laws of general application.

[22] Both parents have the right to educate their children in accordance with their own convictions on religious matters, "with respect for the moral and physical integrity of the children and without prejudice to their health", until minors reach the age of 16 (Articles 11 LRF and 1886 CC).

Apart from guaranteeing freedom of conscience and religion, CPR specifically acknowledges a *fundamental right* to conscientious objection (Article 41), also established in Article 12 LRF. In a broad sense, this right protects the refusal to act in accordance with a legal obligation (originating from law or contract), based on grounds of conscience, namely of religious nature (on this, see Adragão and Leão 2012). Despite some controversy among scholars on the issue, this right is established as a general right, directly evocable in several hypothetical domains, even in the absence of specific prescription in infra-constitutional law (Adragão and Leão 2012). The Constitution also guarantees conscientious objection to perform military service (Article 276)[23] and several ordinary laws establish specific conscience objection clauses, namely guaranteeing medical doctors and other health professionals the right to object to acts concerning lawful abortion,[24] medically assisted reproduction[25] or advance directives on health care.[26]

The specific case of churchmen and ministers of religion is also acknowledged both in the Concordat and LRF. They shall not be questioned by authorities about facts or matters of which they have knowledge by reason of their ministry (Article 5 Concordat and Article 16/2 LRF) and have no obligation to assume jury duties, (Article 6 Concordat and 18 LRF) or become members of courts or similar institutions when considered to be incompatible with their ecclesiastical status by Canon law (Article 6 Concordat).

Besides this, accommodation of religious beliefs is also established in LRF in matters of education or work, as will be seen below.

9. The accommodation of religious needs is determined by law in several fields, something that shall be understood in the light of the equality principle and of the general prohibition of discrimination on religious grounds enshrined in the Constitution (Article 13), enforceable both before public authorities and private entities. In the employment field, the Labor Code (Article 23 onwards), prohibits discrimination conducted by employers against workers or applicants for a job based on several grounds, among which religion or convictions (Brito 2012). Similar principles apply to employees in public functions.[27]

LRF explicitly provides for the accommodation of religious beliefs in labor relations and the organization of the working periods. Article 14 of the law provides that employees have the right to demand their absence from work on days of weekly rest or festivals and during hourly periods prescribed by the religion or belief they profess, under some established conditions concerning, e.g., type of working schedule.[28] Given the fact that the weekly rest day is ordinarily (not necessarily) the Sunday (Article 232 LC) and that some of the festive days recognized as usual

[23] Law 174/99, September 21st, abolished compulsory military service in peacetime, thus reducing the practical importance of this form of conscientious objection.

[24] Law 12/2007, 17th April, article 6.

[25] Law 32/2006, 26th July, article 11.

[26] Law 25/2012, 16th July, article 9.

[27] According to Article 14 of the Law 59/2008, September 11th

[28] Discussing the constitutionality of this requirement, Adragão 2002, 522 ff.

non-working days (Articles 234 to 236 LC) are of Catholic origin (as noticed above in 5), religious duties of Catholics are thereby more easily accommodated than those of believers who observe different religious prescriptions on rest or festive days, therefore subject to indirect discrimination (Canotilho and Machado 2013), even though sociologically justified. Exemptions from classes and rescheduling of assessments on religious grounds are also guaranteed, under some conditions, in Article 14 LRF. The application of this article shows, however, some fluctuation.[29]

The law also determines others types of accommodations concerning diets compatible with religious and spiritual beliefs[30] and religious assistance and worship[31] for detainees, patients in hospitals and health institutions of public National Health Service (SNS) and members of the military and security forces, creating conditions for the institution of services of religious and spiritual assistance of the different religious denominations (on this legal regime, Raimundo 2012, 374 ff). Accommodations are also required both by LRF (Article 28) and the Concordat (Article 25) in urban planning, namely demanding the inclusion of spaces for religious ends in planning instruments as well as establishing a right of the religious communities to be heard concerning those spaces (Raimundo 2012, 404 ff).

Adjudication

10. As noticed above, Portuguese law recognizes that some questions concerning religious entities fall outside the scope of the civil jurisdiction, instead belonging to the ecclesiastical jurisdiction. The principle of separation between State and religious denominations is again relevant in determining jurisdictional boundaries between civil and ecclesiastical jurisdictions. The jurisdiction of the Catholic Church through its courts "in the ecclesiastical sphere" is recognized in the Concordat in Article 2/1 and further developed in Article 11, whose sub-section 1 leads to the conclusion that Catholic Church courts apply Canon law to canonical legal persons, while civil Portuguese courts apply Portuguese law (Adragão 2004, 36). The determination of such jurisdictional boundaries has, however, raised some controversy in Portuguese courts.[32]

Being a domain of shared regulation (in terms explained above, in 4) canonical marriage also poses questions of jurisdiction. On the one hand, legal regulation of canonical marriage admits several causes of extinction of the matrimonial link, different in regime and effects, ranging from nullity (Article 1625 CC and Canon 1103 ff, 1671 ff Codex Iuris Canonici) or pontifical dispensation (Canon 1142, 1697–

[29] Inter alia, Decision 545/2014 of the Constitutional Court and Neto 2009.

[30] Article 11 of Decree-Law 252/09 and aAticle 12 of Decree-Law 253/2009.

[31] Article 18 Concordat, Article 13 LRF, Decree-Law 253/2009 and Decree-Law 252/2009.

[32] See Case 268/04 of the Constitutional Court, annotated by Adragão 2004, and, more recently, the judgment of the Court of Appeal of Coimbra on May 7th 2011 critically reviewed by Adragão (2012a).

1706 Codex Iuris Canonici) to death (Article 1688 CC) or divorce (Article 1773 ff CC). Divorce is the exclusive competence of civil courts, and pontifical dispensation is within the exclusive competence of ecclesiastical courts. Unlike the Concordat of 1940 (Article XXV), the Concordat of 2004 does not expressly reserve to the ecclesiastical courts the appreciation of nullity causes of canonical marriages. However, considering the wording of Article 1625 CC (formulated in accordance with the previous Concordat and not revised under the new Concordat) most scholars consider that the rule of the exclusive competence of ecclesiastical courts to declare the nullity of canonical marriages is still in force (Coelho and Oliveira 2008, 329; Pinheiro 2010, 669 ff; 427, Vítor 2010, 165–166; Lopes 2008).

11. According to the Concordat of 1940 (Article XXV), the decisions of ecclesiastical courts were exempted from revision and confirmation by State courts in order to produce civil effects. Nowadays, according to Article 16/1 of the Concordat of 2004, implemented by Decree Law 100/2009, May 11th, which changed the text of Article 1626 CC, the decisions of the competent ecclesiastical authorities regarding the nullity or dispensation of marriages shall have civil effects at the request of either party, after revision and confirmation within the terms of Portuguese law and by the competent court of the State. The competent court shall verify: (a) that the claims are authentic; (b) that they have been examined by the competent tribunal; (c) that the principles of evidence and counter-evidence have been equally respected; (d) that the outcomes do not contradict the principles of the public international order of the Portuguese State (Article 16/2).[33] The system adopted is no longer a system of automatic civil effect, being instead one of conditioned recognition (Silva and Geraldes 2010, 795 ff).

Apart from this case, ecclesiastical courts' decisions are not subjected to judicial review on the part of State courts.

12. Finally, the authors are not aware of any specific provision through which the State gives religious courts/institutions the power to interpret the laws of the State and to assess their conformity to religious rules. However, both the abovementioned principle of separation between State and Church and the right to religious freedom, in its individual and institutional dimensions, can be invoked, also before a court, by religious institutions in order to protect their sphere of self-determination.

13. Social implementation of religious rules without any official recognition seems difficult to assert, since the authors are not aware of specific data on the issue. Practices like female genital cutting (whose cultural and/or religious grounds are, however, disputed) have been reported in Portugal (see II Programa 2011); leading instruments such as the National Plans on Gender Equality, on the Integration of Migrants and on the Combat of Domestic Violence pursue the goal of combating and eradicating that practice in order to protect the integrity of women.

Grave cases of hostility concerning religious dress codes, practices or religious symbols do not seem to exist. No specific laws or case law regulate religious attire, a question that has revealed to be problematic in many European countries.

[33] The English translation used in the text follows the one available at http://www.concordatwatch.eu/showtopic.php?org_id=1361&kb_header_id=4131

Constitutional admissibility of religious symbols in public buildings, e.g. crucifixes in classrooms, is discussed (Adragão 2012b; Raimundo 2012, 278 ff).

Finally, even though religious courts' decisions are not recognized as such by Portuguese law, outside the case of ecclesiastical courts' decisions mentioned above, it should be pointed out that, given the autonomy recognized to religious denominations, citizens are free to use services provided by their religious communities, including mediation services. This does not preclude the access to civil courts.

Conclusion

The authors consider the Portuguese legal system to be globally satisfactory from the point of view of the respect of human rights and particularly religious freedom, equality and non-discrimination. Besides the constitutional protection afforded to religious freedom in its varied dimensions, the Concordat, APII and LRF converge in the guarantee of religious freedom in individual as well as institutional terms. The evolution of the system towards the full recognition of religious freedom and of equality between religious denominations should be highlighted, as well as the recognition of a moderate degree of normative pluralism.[34]

The cooperation model fosters inclusion of different religious communities and shows sensibility to the specificities of different religious groups, allowing for different levels of institutional recognition (the Concordat, APII, articles 33 ff LRF; Folque 2012; Raimundo 2012, 310 ff). However, the consensual pathway should be further explored through agreements between the religious denominations, Catholic included, and the State, since it enables the adoption of solutions better tailored to the specificities of each religious community (Adragão 2012d, 57–58).

Some points could be nonetheless ameliorated. At the normative level, some of the solutions adopted by LRF could be rethought and/or simplified, concerning e.g. the regulation of agreements (Raimundo 2012, 339 ff; Canas 2007, 308 ff) and the requirements for legal recognition of religious entities (Gouveia 2012, 81–82). At the "law in action" level, a greater sensibility of the legal operators to the demands of religious freedom should be achieved and some administrative obstacles removed. Difficulties are still reported in administering religious assistance, obtaining judicial recognition of the right/duty to respect the Sabbath or obtaining permission by public administration to use buildings for religious purposes (Soares Loja quoted by Adragão (2012d, 51)).

All in all, the Portuguese legal system is religion-friendly and reveals openness to religious pluralism.

[34] On this issue, identifying strategies and tools, see Silvio Ferrari's contribution on this book.

References

Adragão, Pulido. 2002. *A liberdade religiosa e o Estado*. Coimbra: Almedina.

Adragão, Pulido. 2004. Ordem jurídica Portuguesa e Ordem Jurídica Canónica – Um tema invulgar na Jurisprudência Constitucional. *Jurisprudência Constitucional* 4: 30–39.

Adragão, Paulo. 2007. Concordata. In *Dicionário Jurídico da Administração Pública*, 168–191. Coimbra: Coimbra Editora.

Adragão, Paulo. 2010. A Lei da liberdade religiosa portuguesa: Um diagnóstico, 8 anos depois. In *Constitución, leyes de libertad religiosa, acuerdos, derecho común*, 29–45. León: Universidad de León.

Adragão, Paulo. 2012a. A quem pertence a jurisdição nas questões relativas à vida interna das misericórdias? In *Anuário Português de Direito Internacional 2011*, 101–105. Lisboa: Instituto Diplomático – Ministério dos Negócios Estrangeiros.

Adragão, Paulo. 2012b. Disciplina jurídica acerca da exposição (presença) de símbolos religiosos nas salas de aula das escolas públicas: breve parecer sobre Portugal. In *Estudos em homenagem ao Prof. Doutor José Joaquim Gomes Canotilho*, vol. 3, 9–14. Coimbra: Coimbra Editora.

Adragão, Paulo. 2012c. *Levar a sério a liberdade religiosa*. Coimbra: Almedina.

Adragão, Paulo. 2012d. A Lei da Liberdade religiosa: novo diagnóstico, onze anos depois. *Forum Canonicum* VII(2): 41–59.

Adragão, Paulo, and Diogo Gonçalves. 2006. Educação religiosa católica nas escolas estatais, em Portugal: o estado da questão em 2006. In *Estudos sobre a Nova Concordata*, 175–191. Lisboa: Universidade Católica Portuguesa.

Adragão, Paulo, and Anabela Leão. 2012. O direito à objecção de consciência por parte do Chefe de Estado, em questão. In *Estudos em Homenagem ao Prof. Doutor Jorge Miranda*, vol. 3, 133–170. Coimbra: Coimbra Editora.

Amaral, Diogo Freitas. 2004. *Manual de Introdução ao Direito*, vol. I. Coimbra: Almedina.

Brito, José de Sousa. 1999. *A Jurisprudência constitucional em matéria de liberdade religiosa em Portugal*. Report presented at XI Conference of Constitutional Courts of Europe, Poland. http://www.tribunalconstitucional.pt. Accessed 15 Feb 2014.

Brito, José de Sousa. 2012. Portugal. In *Religion and discrimination law in the European union*, ed. Mark Hill QC, 271 ss. Trier: European Consortium for State and Church Research. http://ubt.opus.hbz-nrw.de/volltexte/2012/742/. Accessed 15 Feb 2014.

Canas, Vitalino. 2007. Os acordos religiosos ou a generalização da fórmula concordatária. In *Estudos em Memoria ao Conselheiro Luís Nunes de Almeida*, 281–334. Coimbra: Coimbra Editora.

Canotilho, J.J. Gomes, and Jónatas Machado. 2010. Metódica Multinível: Acordos Internacionais do Estado Português com Comunidades Religiosas. *Revista de Legislação e Jurisprudência* 139(3962): 254–269.

Canotilho, J.J. Gomes, and Jónatas Machado. 2013. Igrejas e Sindicatos e o Dia do Senhor. In *Estudos em Homenagem a António Barbosa de Melo*, 285–319. Coimbra: Almedina.

Canotilho, J.J. Gomes, and Vital Moreira. 2007. *Constituição da República Portuguesa Anotada*, vol. I. Coimbra: Coimbra Editora.

Coelho, Francisco Pereira, and Guilherme de Oliveira. 2008. *Curso de Direito da Família*. Coimbra: Coimbra Editora.

Costa, Elsa Maria Santos. 2006. Estatuto e reconhecimento das pessoas jurídicas canónicas. In *Estudos sobre a Nova Concordata*, 311–327. Lisboa: Universidade Católica Portuguesa.

del Valle, Gonzalez, and José Maria. 2005. *Derecho eclesiástico español*. Madrid: Civitas.

Fialho, António José. 2013. *Guia prático do divórcio e das responsabilidades parentais*. Lisboa: Centro de Estudos Judiciários. http://www.cej.gov.pt. Accessed 15 Feb 2014.

Finocchiaro, Francesco. 2007. *Diritto Ecclesiastico*. Bologna: Zanichelli.

Folque, André. 2012. As pessoas colectivas no novo direito eclesiástico. In *Estudos em Homenagem ao Prof. Doutor Jorge Miranda*, vol. 1, 239–259. Coimbra: Coimbra Editora.

Gouveia, Jorge Bacelar. 2012. *Direito, religião e sociedade no Estado Constitucional*. Lisboa: Instituto do Direito de Língua Portuguesa.

II Programa de Acção para a Eliminação da Mutilação Genital Feminina. 2011. http://www.cig.gov.pt/planos-nacionais-areas/mutilacao-genital-feminina/. Accessed 15 Feb 2014.

Leite, André Lamas. 2012. Direito Penal e discriminação religiosa – subsídios para uma visão humanista. *O Direito* 144(4): 865–908.

Lima Pinheiro, Luís. 2009. *Direito Internacional Privado*, vol. I. Coimbra: Almedina.

Lopes, José Joaquim Almeida. 2008. Direito eclesiástico português no século XXI. *Revista da Faculdade de Direito da Universidade do Porto* 5: 143–213.

Machado, Jónatas. 2010. A (in)definição do casamento no Estado Constitucional. Fundamentos meta-constitucionais da deliberação democrática. In *Família, consciência, secularismo e religião*, 9–37. Coimbra: Wolters Kluwer/Coimbra Editora.

Mahmood, Tahir. 2012. *Diritto e religione nell'Islam mediterraneo*, 29–42. Bologna: il Mulino.

Martins, Rosa. 2010. O reconhecimento da sentença de nulidade do casamento católico dos Tribunais Eclesiásticos em Portugal – a possível contradição dos seus efeitos civis com os da sentença de divórcio dos Tribunais do Estado. In *Família, consciência, secularismo e religião*, 241–273. Coimbra: Wolters Kluwer/Coimbra Editora.

Medeiros, Rui. 2012. Uma leitura constitucionalmente comprometida da Concordata. In *Estudos em Homenagem ao Prof. Doutor Jorge Miranda*, vol. 3, 635–663. Coimbra: Coimbra Editora.

Miranda, Jorge, and José de Melo Alexandrino. 2007. As grandes decisões do Tribunal Constitucional Português. http://www.fd.ul.pt/Portals/0/Docs/Institutos/ICJ/LusCommune/jmjma.pdf. Accessed 15 Feb 2014.

Miranda, Jorge, and Pedro Garcia Marques. 2010. Anotação ao artigo 41. In *Anotada, Tomo I, edited by Jorge Miranda and Rui Medeiros*, ed. Constituição Portuguesa, 890–921. Coimbra: Coimbra Editora and Wolters Kluwer Portugal.

Mucznik, Esther. 2013. Os censos, reflexo da liberdade religiosa. *Publico*, January 7. http://www.publico.pt/opiniao/noticia/os-censos-reflexo-da-liberdade-religiosa-1579808. Accessed 3 Mar 2014.

Neto, Luísa. 2009. *De die ad diem*: os dias úteis ou a utilidade dos dias, Comentário ao Acórdão do TCAN (1.ª secção) de 8.2.2007, P.1394/06.OBEPRT. *Cadernos de Justiça Administrativa* 74: 37–54.

Pinheiro, Jorge Duarte. 2008. Poligamia e uniões paralelas. In *Escritos de direito das famílias: uma perspectiva luso-brasileira*, 55–74. Porto Alegre: Magister Editora.

Pinheiro, Jorge Duarte. 2010. *O direito da família contemporâneo: lições*. Lisboa: AAFDL.

Raimundo, Miguel Assis. 2012. Direito Administrativo da Religião. In *Administrativo Especial*, vol. VI, ed. Tratado de Direito, 223–442. Coimbra: Almedina.

Silva, Paula Costa e, and João de Oliveira Geraldes. 2010. A Concordata de 2004 e o novo artigo 1626.° do Código Civil. In *Estudos em Homenagem ao Prof. Doutor Sérvulo Correia*, 795–816. Coimbra: Coimbra Editora

Teles, Eugénia Galvão, and Maria Helena Brito. 2007. Private international law. In *Portuguese law. An overview*, 287–303. Coimbra: Almedina.

Vilaça, Helena. 2006. *Da Torre de Babel às Terras Prometidas – Pluralismo Religioso em Portugal*. Porto: Edições Afrontamento.

Vilaça, Helena. 2010. Para lá da etnicidade: as comunidades religiosas dos imigrantes de leste em Portugal. In *Religião e Movimento. Imigrantes e Diversidade Religiosa em Portugal e Itália*, 73–91. Porto: Estratégias Criativas.

Vitali, Enrico, and Antonio Chizzoniti. 2006. *Manuale Breve: diritto ecclesiastico*. Milano: Giuffrè.

Vítor, Paula. 2010. A evolução legislativa recente do sistema de casamento português. In *Família, consciência, secularismo e religião*, 155–181. Coimbra: Wolters Kluwer/Coimbra Editora.

Chapter 19
L'Application des Règles Religieuses dans le Système Juridique du Québec

Jabeur Fathally

Abstract In this chapter the author defends the idea that religious rule is not among the legal sources of Quebec's legal system even though some legal rules can find their socio-historical justification in religious beliefs. For the author, the application of a rule with a "religious root" depends on its integration – explicitly or implicitly – by the legislator or the judge. The plurality of "religious roots" and the diversity of "socio-cultural grounds" of Quebec laws are not, according to the author, synonymous with automatic application of religious rules in Quebec.

Résumé. Dans cet article l'auteur défend l'idée selon laquelle la règle religieuse ne fait pas partie des sources du droit positif québécois et cela même si certaines règles juridiques peuvent trouver leurs justifications socio-historiques dans des croyances religieuses. Pour l'auteur, l'application d'une règle «à racine religieuse » dépend de son intégration – explicitement ou implicitement – par le législateur ou par le juge dans le système de droit positif étatique. La pluralité des «racines religieuses» et la diversité des «terreaux socioculturels» du droit québécois ne sont pas, selon l'auteur, synonymes de l'existence d'un système de droit religieux applicable au Québec.

Ce texte, qui fait suite à un rapport présenté au XIXe Congrès de l'Académie international de droit comparé tenu à Vienne entre le 20 et 27 juillet 2014, vise à répondre à la question - posée presque quotidiennement dans les médias québécois et canadiens et dans les sphères juridiques et politiques -portant sur l'application des règles religieuses dans le droit québécois. À vrai dire, la question n'est pas nouvelle. Elle s'est posée depuis les années soixante à l'époque de la révolution tranquille québécoise considérée comme une rupture sociale, politique et juridique avec les pratiques de l'église Catholique et un rejet de son influence sur les différents rouages

J. Fathally (✉)
University of Ottawa, Ottawa, Canada
e-mail: jabeur.fathally@uottawa.ca

R. Bottoni et al. (eds.), *Religious Rules, State Law, and Normative Pluralism - A Comparative Overview*, Ius Comparatum – Global Studies in Comparative Law 18, DOI 10.1007/978-3-319-28335-7_19

de la société québécoise. C'est au début du XXIe siècle que la question va être reposée avec acuité à l'époque de «la prétendue « crise » des accommodements raisonnables»[1] et surtout suite au projet de Loi 60 intitulé « Charte affirmant les valeurs de laïcité et de neutralité religieuse de l'État ainsi que d'égalité entre les femmes et les hommes et encadrant les demandes d'accommodement»[2] et proposé par le Ministre québécois responsable des institutions démocratiques et de la participation citoyenne à l'automne 2013. Afin de répondre à la question, titre du présent texte, nous avons jugé utile de synthétiser nos différentes réponses au questionnaire qui nous a été soumis par le rapporteur international le professeur Silvio Ferrari en trois sections inter-liées pour défendre l'idée selon laquelle la règle religieuse n'a plus de présence voire d'application dans le droit québécois contemporain en dépit des particularités sociodémographiques et juridiques québécoises sans que cela soit en contradiction avec la protection accordée par le droit québécois et canadien à la liberté de religion.

Contexte sociodémographique et juridique québécois

Ce contexte se traduit par des différences linguistiques et religieuses et par une histoire et une réalité juridique particulière.

Spécificités sociodémographiques

Faisant partie de la confédération canadienne et s'étendant sur une superficie de 1 667 441 km2, le Québec n'est pas uniquement la plus grande des dix provinces canadiennes mais, elle est également la province qui dispose de sa propre langue et d'un système juridique de droit privé qui lui est spécifique. Sa population estimée à 8 179 000 personnes, au 1er janvier 2015,[3] est majoritairement francophone au point que certains qualifient le Québec comme étant «la seule terre de la langue française dans un océan anglophone» (Venon, 2011). Cette particularité linguistique est favorisée en grande partie par les origines françaises de la population, par la politique gouvernementale de sélection des nouveaux arrivants ainsi que par l'adoption, en 1977, de la Charte de la langue française (loi 101) qui a fait du français la langue

[1]Gouvernement du Québec, *Document de réflexion: La Charte et la prise en compte de la religion dans l'espace public* , Juin 2008, en ligne,: Commission des droits de la personne et des droits de la jeunesse http://www.cdpdj.qc.ca/publications/charte_religion_espace_public.pdf.

[2]Assemblée nationale, Charte affirmant les valeurs de laïcité et de neutralité religieuse de l'État ainsi que d'égalité entre les femmes et les hommes et encadrant les demandes d'accommodement, Projet de loi no 60, 1[ière] session , 40ième législature, en ligne: http://www.assnat.qc.ca/fr/travaux-parlementaires/projets-loi/projet-loi-60-40-1.html.

[3]Institut de la Statistique du Québec, *Le bilan démographique du Québec*, Édition 2014, en ligne: Institut de la statistique http://www.stat.gouv.qc.ca/statistiques/population-demographie/bilan2014.pdf.

officielle du Québec[4] c'est-à-dire la langue de l'administration, du travail, de l'enseignement, des communications, du commerce et des affaires.

Le recensement de 2011[5] montrent que 78 % de la population a le français comme langue maternelle contre 7,6 % ayant l'anglais comme langue maternelle et 12,3 % de langue maternelle autre que l'anglais et le français (allophones et autochtones).[6]

Le particularisme québécois se manifeste également dans le domaine confessionnel, puisque c'est dans cette province canadienne qu'on trouve la plus grande concentration des chrétiens catholiques.[7] Ainsi, selon le rapport de la Commission des droits de la personne du Québec, 83,4% de la population québécoise est de confession catholique repartie sur les différentes congrégations et églises, telles que l'Église catholique romaine, l'Église catholique ukrainienne ou l'Église catholique nationale polonaise, autres catholiques.[8]

Les chrétiens appartenant aux églises protestantes constituent 4,7 % de la totalité de la population alors que ceux appartenant aux églises orthodoxes ne représentent que 1,4%. Les autres minorités religieuses ne représentent que 3,9% de la population dont 1,5% sont de religion musulmane et 1,3 de religion juive.[9]

Histoire et spécificité du système juridique québécois

Le caractère distinct de la nation québécoise, pour reprendre le contenu de la motion votée, le 27 novembre 2006, par la Chambre des communes du Parlement du Canada,[10] se manifeste dans le statut privilégié accordé à la langue française et surtout dans son système juridique largement inspiré du système civiliste français. D'ailleurs, on ne peut comprendre le système juridique du Québec contemporain sans remonter à la période qui précéda la création du Canada en 1867 puisque la réception du «droit français», plus précisément des coutumes françaises, remonte au

---

[4] *Charte de langue française*, 2e sess., 31e leg., Québec, 1977, (adopté par l'Assemblée nationale du Québec le 26 août 1977, L.R.Q Chap. C-11), art 1, en ligne: http://www.axl.cefan.ulaval.ca/amnord/quebecchartetitre1.htm.

[5] Gouvernement du Canada, *Série « Perspective géographique »: Recensement de 2011*, en ligne: Statistique Canada http://www12.statcan.gc.ca/census-recensement/2011/as-sa/fogs-spg/Facts-pr-fra.cfm?Lang=fra&GK=PR&GC=24 [Série]. Voir également Conseil des relations interculturelles, *Laïcité et diversité religieuse: l'approche québécoise* (version abrégée), 2004, en ligne: Immigration Diversité et Inclusion http://www.midi.gouv.qc.ca/publications/fr/cri/diversite/Avis-laicite-diversite-religieuse-resume-francais.pdf [Conseil des relation interculturelles].

[6] Ibid.

[7] Ibid.

[8] Ibid.

[9] Ibid.

[10] Motion sur la nation de Québécoises et de Québécois dans un Canada uni, 1ière sess., 39e leg., 24 novembre 2006, en ligne: Parlement du Canada http://www.parl.gc.ca/HousePublications/Publication.aspx?DocId=2544166&File=0&Language=F&Mode=1&Parl=39&Pub=hansard&Ses=1#Int-1798655.

XVIIe siècle avec les premières expéditions françaises de 1603 et de 1608.[11] Le roi de France autorisait les premiers colonisateurs de la Nouvelle-France «à légiférer sous la forme de «lois, statuts et ordonnances [...] autant qu'il se pourra conformes aux nôtres»». (Belleau, 2012) Les peuples autochtones rencontrés par les Français avaient certes leurs traditions juridiques coutumières et ancestrales mais les mouvements d'assimilation ou ce que la juge en chef de la Cour suprême du Canada a récemment qualifié de «génocide culturelle»[12] ont fini par faire prévaloir le droit des nouveaux arrivants/colons[13] (Belleau, 2012). Après la conquête anglaise de 1760, «les Britanniques ont choisi de gouverner l'ancienne colonie française en changeant le moins possible les arrangements existants»[14] et en reconnaissant certaines spécificités aux sujets français à travers la garantie notamment la liberté de leurs pratiques religieuses catholiques et leur droit d'être gouvernés en matière de propriété et de rapports de droit privé par leurs lois et coutumes «enracinées depuis des siècles dans la célèbre Coutume de Paris telle que modifiée par les grandes Ordonnances royales de Louis XIV et de Louis XV» (Guy, 1993). L'Acte de Québec de 1764, va codifier et confirmer cette réalité marquée par un dualisme religieux et juridique.

Un siècle plus tard, soit en 1866, le Bas Canada, adopte son premier code civil: *Code Civil du Bas-Canada* grandement inspiré du Code civil français de 1804 (Code Napoléon). Ce code sera appliqué jusqu'au 1994, date d'entrée en vigueur du Code civil du Québec.

En 1867, l'Acte de l'Amérique du Nord britannique, promulgué à Londres par le Parlement britannique, va définir les pouvoirs des provinces et ceux du gouvernement fédéral en accordant à ces deux ordres de gouvernement le droit de gouverner et de légiférer dans leurs champs de compétence respectifs.[15] La loi en question va ainsi réaffirmer la compétence exclusive du Québec en matière de «propriété et droits civils» et de «célébration du mariage» mais tout en réservant au fédéral la compétence en matière de « mariage et divorce» limitant ainsi la compétence antérieure du Québec sur ces matières.[16]

---

[11] Jacques Vanderlinden, «La réception des systèmes juridiques européens au Canada», (1996) 84 Tijdschrift voor Rechtsgeschiedenis 359.

[12] Radio-Canada, «Les Autochtones victimes d'un « génocide culturel », dit la juge en chef de la Cour suprême, en ligne: Radio-Canada.ca http://ici.radio-canada.ca/nouvelles/national/2015/05/29/001-genocide-culturel-beverly-mclachlin-autochtones-premieres-nations.shtml. L'auteur du présent texte n'adhère pas à ce concept de «génocide culturel» puisque les éléments de définition du génocide prévus dans *La Convention pour la prévention et la répression du crime de génocide du 9 décembre 1948* et dans l'article 6 du *Statut de la Cour pénale internationale* sont suffisants pour englober les atrocités physiques et culturelles subies par les peuples autochtones au Canada.

[13] Hélène Belleau, Quand l'amour et l'État rendent aveugle : le mythe du mariage automatique, Québec, Presses de l'Université du Québec, 2012 à la p 11.

[14] Brian O'Neal, « La société distincte: origine, interprétations, implications», décembre 1995, en ligne: Parlement du Canada, Division des affaires politiques et sociales http://www.parl.gc.ca/Content/LOP/researchpublications/bp408-f.htm.

[15] *Supra* note 16. Voir également « Acte de l'Amérique du Nord britannique », dans Gérald-A. Beaudoin: La Constitution du Canada, Montréal, Wilson et Lafleur, 1990, aux p 849-902.

[16] *Supra* note 17.

Par conséquent, cette loi constitutionnelle n'a pas mis en cause l'application du code civil du Bas- Canada.[17] C'est dans les années quatre-vingt du XXe siècle et suite à ce que la littérature juridique et politique québécoise qualifie de révolution tranquille que ce code a connu des vagues successives de modifications.

Ce contexte socio-historique québécois a, indubitablement, influencé aussi bien la signification et le sens à donner à la règle religieuse que la présence de celle-ci dans l'ensemble des sources du droit québécois.[18]

Les significations de la règle religieuse et sa présence dans le droit québécois

L'étude de l'histoire juridique québécoise montre que la règle religieuse semble avoir des significations différentes et qu'elle n'a plus de présence dans le droit étatique québécois contemporain.

Les significations de la règle religieuse dans le droit québécois

Au Québec, la règle religieuse semble couvrir deux significations. La première consiste à définir la règle religieuse comme étant une règle émanant de l'Église. Cela veut dire que la «religiosité» de la règle se définit par l'autorité qui l'a édictée et non par son propre contenu. C'est en d'autres termes la signification qu'on donne au droit canonique. La question du caractère religieux ou humain du droit canonique ne sera pas débattu dans le cadre de ce rapport et ce en dépit du fait que la réalité juridique et religieuse du Québec du XIXe siècle, et même avant cela, peut nous ramener à soulever la question sur la nature de ce droit: S'agit-il véritablement d'un droit religieux ou d'un ensemble de coutumes et de traditions - donc d'un droit d'origine humaine – adopté par l'Église, détentrice d'un pouvoir divin sur les âmes, et en leur conférant un caractère religieux?

À cet égard, il est utile de souligner que pour le groupe de recherche sur les systèmes juridiques de la Faculté de droit de l'Université d'Ottawa-JuriGlobe- dont l'auteur du présent chapitre est le cofondateur et chercheur principal, «le droit canonique n'est pas un droit religieux: il s'agit d'un droit qui, bien qu'informé par des dogmes religieux, est d'origine humaine et appartient sans conteste à la famille de droit civil» (Fathally and Mariani, 2009).[19]

[17] Pierre-André Côté, «La survie du droit préconfédéral: le cas des dispositions relatives à l'interprétation et à l'application des lois du Code civil du Bas-Canada» en ligne: Ministère de la Justice http://www.justice.gc.ca/fra/pr-rp/sjc-csj/harmonization/cote_p/survi.html.

[18] Conseil des relations interculturelles *Supra* note 6.

[19] Voir également JuriGlobe- Groupe de recherche sur les systèmes juridiques dans le monde , en ligne: JuriGlobe www.juriglobe.ca. Dans la majorité des textes consultés le droit canonique est défini comme étant «l'ensemble des lois et des règlements adoptés ou acceptés par les autorités

Cependant, pour les fins de ce texte, nous définissons le droit canonique qui a influencé le droit québécois, comme étant l'ensemble des règles de droit émanant de l'Église.

Cette première signification qui associe la règle religieuse au droit canonique corresponde à la réalité sociale et juridique québécoise depuis le XVIIe siècle jusqu'à la période de la révolution tranquille de la deuxième moitié du XXe siècle.

L'autre signification attribuable à la règle religieuse est celle qui met l'accent sur le lien entre la règle juridique et la culture judéo-chrétienne. Il s'agit certes d'un lien ténu, puisque, à vrai dire « un État confessionnel est un État dans lequel une loi religieuse est applicable par les juges et non, comme certains l'ont écrit, un État dont le droit aurait pris historiquement ses sources dans les valeurs d'une religion» (Saris, 2006) mais, ce lien pourrait, à certains égards, donner certaines indications-aux historiens de droit par exemple - sur l'étendue historique des règles juridiques étudiées.

Cette signification, si on peut l'appeler ainsi, est celle qui illustre le rapport entre le droit québécois et la culture judéo-chrétienne depuis la révolution tranquille.

La religion dans le droit québécois jusqu'à la révolution tranquille

Contrairement à l'expérience française, le Québec n'a pas connu une révolution semblable à celle de 1789. Si en France, la révolution a permis la suppression de tous les privilèges, féodaux et ecclésiastiques et qu'elle a, surtout, permis "l'éjection" de l'Église du champ législatif et politique en séparant les pouvoirs de l'Église et de l'État, expressément traduite en 1905 par la Loi de Séparation qui a mis fin « au système des cultes reconnus qui prévalait sous le régime concordataire» (Kousse, 2011), au Québec, l'Église a gardé une forte présence dans le domaine législatif.[20] Un domaine cardinal comme celui du droit de la famille était quasiment sous l'emprise des orientations de l'Église. À titre d'exemples, le Code civil du Bas-Canada consacrait le caractère sacramental du mariage en prévoyant son indissolubilité du vivant des époux,[21] la plupart des empêchements au mariage reprennent ceux édictés par le droit canonique[22] et la célébration du mariage fut, quant à elle,

catholiques pour le gouvernement de l'Église et de ses fidèles», Voir par exemple, Fabien Davier, *Les écrits catholiques de Tertullien: formes et normes*, History, Université de Franche-Comté, 2009 à la p 219.

[20] *Supra* note 13.

[21] Code civil du Bas-Canada, l'acte 29 Vict., chap 41, 1865 art 185.

[22] *Supra* note 13. Voir également Michel Morin, « Le pluralisme religieux et juridique en matière d'état civil et de mariage, 1774-1921 », dans Lorraine Derocher et al, dir, *L'état Canadien et la Diversité Culturelle et Religieuse, 1800-1914*, Québec, Presses de l'Université Du Québec, 2009 aux pp 3 à 20 [Morin] .

Signalons à cet égard que l'article 127 du Code Civil du Bas-Canada allait même jusqu'à sembler incorporer la totalité des empêchements religieux au mariage. Sa rédaction peu claire donna cependant à une longue controverse judicaire et doctrinale qui ne cessera que dans les années de la révolution tranquille soit avec l'arrêt Ouellette c. Gingras, [1972] C.A. 247 dans lequel la Cour

confiée aux ministres du culte[23] au point que certains iront jusqu'à dire que « le Code ne reconnait de mariage que celui qui est célébré religieusement» (Loranger, 1879). Comme l'a bien résumé un auteur «le mariage existait, encore fallait-il qu'il se conformât au message et à l'éthique dont les théologiens, les juristes et les ministres du culte avaient la charge» (Beaux, 2006).

Autre exemple de cette interférence de l'Église dans le domaine législatif est celui des actes de l'état civil qui relevaient, eux aussi, des pouvoirs de l'Église. Ainsi, «l'enregistrement des actes de naissance, de décès, de mariage est demeuré confessionnel et ses actes sont conservés dans les paroisses» (Moore, 2009). Ce pouvoir ecclésiastique va être, toutefois, restreint avec ce que la littérature sociologique québécoise qualifie de révolution tranquille.

La religion dans le droit québécois contemporain (depuis la révolution tranquille)

Cette révolution consiste dans un mouvement social, économique et politique (activisme des mouvements féministes, réorganisation du système éducatif, urbanisation) qui a permis au jeune «État providence québécois »[24] de prendre en charge des prérogatives qui, jusque-là, relevaient des congrégations religieuses mettant ainsi un arrêt à l'immixtion de l'Église dans le champ juridique québécois et annonçant la «sécularisation» [25]du droit québécois.[26]

Les modifications successives apportées au Code civil du Bas-Canada dans le domaine du droit de la famille, surtout celles introduites en 1980 avec la Loi instituant un nouveau Code civil et portant réforme du droit de la famille, confirment cette démarche de «dissociation/sécularisation». Ces modifications ont, entre autres, permis l'abolition de la distinction entre les enfants légitimes et les enfants naturels,[27] la reconnaissance de la filiation adoptive qui accorde à l'adopté les mêmes droits que la filiation par le sang.[28] Ils ont également permis la reconnais-

---

d'appel a jugé que: « L'article 127 C.C. n'a pas pour effet de sanctionner civilement les empêchements religieux ».

[23] Morin *ibid*

[24] Conseil des relations interculturelles, *supra* note 6.

[25] Nous avons préféré parler de sécularisation puisque, comme l'a bien souligné l'auteur David Koussens, l'usage du mot «laïcité» « était quasiment inexistant (au Québec) avant 1990». Voir *supra* note 24.

[26] Dans la même période le Vatican a confirmé dans la constitution pastorale *Gaudim et spes* de 1965 «que sur le terrain qui leur est propre, la communauté politique et l'Église sont indépendantes l'une de l'autre et autonomes ». Voir Concile du Vatican II: Constitution pastorale sur l'Église dans le monde de ce temps Gaudium et Spes, en ligne: Vatican http://www.vatican.va/archive/hist_councils/ii_vatican_council/documents/vat-ii_const_19651207_gaudium-et-spes_fr.html.

[27] Gouvernement du Canada, *Dates importantes de l'histoire du droit civil du Québec*, en ligne: Ministère de la Justice: http://www.justice.gc.ca/fra/apd-abt/gci-icg/hist/index.html. Voir également Conseil des relations interculturelles, *supra* note 6.

[28] Ibid.

sance de la capacité juridique de la femme mariée en introduisant le concept d'autorité maritale,[29] la célébration civile du mariage[30] ainsi que la possibilité de la dissolution du mariage par le divorce.[31]

Plus encore, même «les appellations à connotation religieuse se laïcisent. Ainsi, la Confédération des travailleurs catholiques du Canada (CTCC) devient la Confédération des syndicats nationaux (CSN); la Corporation des instituteurs catholiques se transforme en Centrale des enseignants du Québec (CEQ)»[32]

Sans déclarer explicitement le caractère laïc de la législation québécoise, la Charte des droits et libertés de la personne (Charte québécoise) de 1975 va consacrer des règles qui ne s'inscrivent pas dans l'idéologie de l'Église telle que l'égalité entre les sexes et l'interdiction de toute discrimination basée sur la religion.[33]

En 1982, le Parlement canadien a obtenu de Londres le « rapatriement » de l'Acte de l'Amérique du Nord britannique et a adopté la Charte canadienne des droits et libertés en l'intégrant dans la Constitution canadienne. Cette Charte a renforcé et a amélioré le dispositif de protection des droits et des libertés fondamentaux tels que, l'égalité entre les sexes et la liberté religieuse.

La révision du Code civil du Bas-Canada qui a donné naissance au Code civil du Québec en 1994 va accentuer ce mouvement de «sécularisation». Comme le résume bien la chercheuse Jane Jenson,

> « En moins de 20 ans, la société québécoise est ainsi passée d'un modèle unique de lien matrimonial – l'union indissoluble, sanctionnée par l'Église – à un modèle multiforme englobant le divorce, la séparation, l'union libre et le mariage entre personnes de même sexe. Comme on l'observe souvent en parlant parfois de « désaffection vis-à-vis du mariage en tant qu'institution ». La toute dernière variante de l'union maritale, celle des personnes de même sexe, a été reconnue en tant qu'union civile en 2002 et comme mariage proprement dit en 2004».[34]

Ces changements sociaux, politiques et juridiques ont réduit la religion à sa sphère spirituelle et privée sans lui accorder une quelconque présence ni dans le droit substantiel, ni dans le droit procédural québécois.

---

[29] Ibid.

[30] Ibid.

[31] *Supra* note 17 à la p 466.

[32] Musée virtuel, «Le début d'un temps nouveau: Le recul de la religion catholique», en ligne: musée québécois d'art populaire http://larevolutiontranquille.ca/fr/le-recul-de-la-religion.php. Voir également Conseil des relations interculturelles *supra note 6*

[33] Charte des Droits et Libertés de la Personne, L.R.Q, c. C-12, art 10.

[34] Gouvernement du Québec « Les familles québécoises depuis la Révolution tranquille », en ligne: Famille Québec www.mfa.gouv.qc.ca.

La présence de la religion dans les textes juridiques

Les règles religieuses ne figurent pas ni parmi les sources du droit canadien et québécois (Constitution, Lois et autres textes juridiques devant définir et inspirer le système juridique québécois) , ni dans les règles de procédures régissant les tribunaux et le déroulement des procès.

La religion dans les sources du droit québécois

Le préambule de la Charte canadienne énonce que « le Canada est fondé sur des principes qui reconnaissent la suprématie de Dieu et la primauté de droit».[35] Il s'agit d'une disposition non seulement, «paradoxale» comme l'ont souligné certains juristes (Fournier, 2013), mais elle est également sans effet juridique. Elle ne peut pas servir de fondement d'une règle de droit. Elle ne peut pas non plus servir comme fondement d'interprétation visant à donner un aspect religieux à une règle de droit positif. Le Dieu mentionné est un dieu abstrait qui n'a aucun rôle dans la création des règles de droit (Fathally, 2013). Cette disposition semble s'inscrire dans la laïcité canadienne qui est une laïcité non-militante et non anti-religieuse.[36] Elle n'a qu'une valeur symbolique.[37]

D'ailleurs, la suprématie de Dieu est utilisée pour défendre la liberté religieuse et non pas pour soutenir un quelconque caractère religieux de la législation canadienne. Comme le rappelle la Cour suprême dans l'arrêt R. c. Big M Drug Mart, le but même de la garantie des libertés fondamentales de conscience et de religion est d'empêcher l'État d'imposer aux citoyens une conception religieuse particulière: « Une majorité religieuse, ou l'État à sa demande, ne peut, pour des motifs religieux, imposer sa propre conception de ce qui est bon et vrai aux citoyens qui ne partagent pas le même point de vue. La Charte [canadienne] protège les minorités religieuses contre la menace de "tyrannie de la majorité". »[38]

Dans un *obiter dictum*, le juge Muldoon de la Cour fédérale du Canada, qui pourtant voulant donner une signification à la suprématie de Dieu, a souligné le caractère ouvert de la laïcité canadienne en précisant que,

> « la reconnaissance de la suprématie de Dieu dans le préambule de la Charte empêche le Canada de devenir un État officiellement athée ; elle ne l'empêche pas d'être un État laïc. Un État laïc ne s'occupe pas de religion, à une exception près: il est obligé d'intervenir pour

---

[35] *Charte canadienne des droits et libertés*, partie I de la *Loi constitutionnelle de 1982*, constituant l'annexe B de la *Loi de 1982* sur le Canada (R-U), 1982 c 11, en ligne: Site Web de la législation (Justice) http://laws-lois.justice.gc.ca/fra/const/page-15.html.

[36] Ibid.

[37] Pierre Bosset, «Pratiques et symboles religieux: quelles sont les responsabilités des institutions? » en ligne: Commission des droits de la personne et des droits de la jeunesse http://www.cdpdj.qc.ca/publications/pratiques_symboles.pdf.

[38] R. c. Big M Drug Mart Ltd., [1985] 1 R.C.S. 295.

> empêcher des pratiques fondées sur des croyances religieuses qui font du tort à autrui physiquement ou mentalement, ou portent atteinte aux droits garantis à autrui par la Constitution. L'histoire des brutalités commises au nom de la religion montre que le caractère résolument laïc de l'État est l'assise solide de la sécurité de chacun, y compris de la protection des croyances religieuses. L'État laïc n'est pas tenu de favoriser toutes les expressions de la liberté de conscience ou de religion, ni autorisé à le faire. La liberté de religion qui est garantie par l'alinéa 2a) de la Charte signifie non seulement que l'État ne peut y porter atteinte, mais aussi qu'il doit la protéger.»[39]

À l'exception de sa mention dans le préambule de la Charte canadienne, la suprématie divine n'est citée nulle autre part dans les textes juridiques québécois. Plus encore le droit québécois ne fait aucune référence au droit canonique comme source de droit et le législateur n'a fait aucun renvoi aux tribunaux religieux.[40] L'existence de certaines règles pouvant être comprise comme perpétuant un lien avec les règles du droit canonique, ne confère aucun caractère religieux auxdites règles et cela même si la doctrine s'aventure parfois de fouiner dans le passé judéo-chrétien de certaine règle juridique telle que l'interdiction du travail pendant certains jours sacrés dans la religion chrétienne (le dimanche ou les jours des pâques et de Noël).[41]

Le droit procédural

D'inspiration britannique,[42] l'organisation judiciaire québécoise relève de l'ordre étatique. Le droit québécois ne reconnait pas les tribunaux religieux. Plus encore, il «interdit l'arbitrage en matière familiale et règlemente de façon précise la médiation, en la réservant aux membres de cinq ordres professionnels (avocats, notaires, conseillers d'orientation, psychologues et travailleurs sociaux) accrédités suite à une formation spécialisée».[43]

Cependant, le recours des justiciables à des procédés extra-judiciaires autre que ceux reconnus par la législation québécoise est un fait social qui nécessite des études sociologiques approfondies. Le recours à ces procédés s'observe au sein de certaines communautés telles que la communauté musulmane ou la communauté juive hassidique. Pour certains, ce recours «sur une base privée aux conseils, à la médiation et à l'arbitrage de l'imam, du rabin ou du curé»[44] s'explique par les problèmes

---

[39] *Supra* note 47

[40] Ibid.

[41] Lucia Feretti, « L'État québécois et les organisations religieuses sous la révolution tranquille: continuités et changements», Réseau d'études des dynamiques transnationales et de l'action collective en ligne: Revue possibles http://redtac.org/possibles/2011/09/11/l%E2%80%99etat-quebecois-et-les-organisations-religieuses-sous-la-revolution-tranquille-continuites-et-changements/.

[42] Lac d'Amiante du Québec Ltée c. 2858-0702 Québec Inc., [2001] 2 R.C.S.743

[43] André Poupart, « Bienvenue au Québec: Réflexions sur les Tribunaux Islamiques » (2006) 8:2, Argument: Politique, Société, Histoire en ligne: http://www.revueargument.ca/article/2006-03-01/348-bienvenue-au-quebec-reflexions-sur-les-tribunaux-islamiques.html.

[44] Ibid.

d'ordre identitaire, éducatifs et économiques rencontrées par certaines catégories d'immigrants.[45]

Le caractère «séculier» du droit québécois a été semble-t-il un outil efficace pour protéger les droits et libertés des citoyens parmi lesquels figurent la liberté de choisir et de pratiquer sa religion.

La protection de la liberté de religion

La liberté de religion (ou religieuse) est garantie par le droit québécois et canadien. L'article 2. a) de la Charte canadienne déclare que «Chacun a les libertés fondamentales suivantes: a) liberté de conscience et de religion;..». L'article 3 de la Charte québécoise stipule quant à lui que « toute personne est titulaire des libertés fondamentales telles la liberté de conscience, la liberté de religion, la liberté d'opinion, la liberté d'expression, la liberté de réunion pacifique et la liberté d'association». Les interprétations faites par la Cour suprême aux dispositions de la Charte portant sur la liberté de religion confirment cette protection. Pour cette Cour, cette liberté s'entend du « droit de croire ce que l'on veut en matière religieuse, le droit de professer ouvertement des croyances religieuses sans crainte d'empêchement ou de représailles et le droit de manifester ses croyances religieuses ».[46] Elle inclut la « liberté de se livrer à des pratiques et d'entretenir des croyances ayant un lien avec une religion, pratiques et croyances que l'intéressé exerce ou manifeste sincèrement, selon le cas, dans le but de communiquer avec une entité divine ou dans le cadre de sa foi spirituelle ».[47]

Les tribunaux québécois ainsi que la Cour suprême du Canada ont eu l'occasion de se pencher sur cette question d'ordre socio-juridique suite à des évènements qui ont suscité des controverses aussi bien politiques que juridiques au sein de la société québécoise. Le port du niqab islamique ou l'érection d'une souccahs juive[48] sur les balcons d'un complexe de condominiums à Montréal, figurent parmi les questions soumises devant les juges de la Cour. C'est par des interprétations évolutives de la Charte Canadienne que ces tribunaux, en « créant » notamment la notion d'accommodement raisonnable, ont tenté de trouver un équilibre entre la liberté de religion et le bon fonctionnement des institutions étatiques. Ainsi, pour la Cour suprême le respect des pratiques religieuses des minorités est «une des caractéristiques essentielles d'une démocratie moderne».[49] Selon la même Cour, l'accommodement raisonnable (religieux) peut être considéré comme un droit

[45] Ibid.

[46] *Supra* note 48.

[47] Syndicat Northcrest c. Amselem, [2004] 2 R.C.S. 551.

[48] Marc Rioux, « Enquête sur un échantillon de cas d'accommodement (1998-2007) » (Rapport remis à Gérard Bouchard et Charles Taylor), en ligne: http://www.accommodementsquebec.ca/documentation/rapports/rapport-1-rioux-marc.pdf.

[49] Syndicat Northcrest c. Amselem, [2004] 2 R.C.S. 551, 2004 CSC 47.

inhérent au droit à l'égalité[50] garantie par la Charte canadienne et également par la Charte québécoise. Cette obligation d'accommodement ne doit pas, toutefois, causer une contrainte excessive.[51]

Plus récemment, à l'occasion d'une affaire qui portait sur la récitation d'une prière catholique au début des séances publiques du conseil municipal d'une ville québécoise (la ville de Saguenay),[52] la Cour suprême a rendu une décision unanime, infirmant la décision de la Cour d'appel du Québec et donnant raison aux appelants, le Mouvement laïque québécois (« MLQ ») et le citoyen Alain Simoneau, en jugeant que la prière en question porte atteinte de façon discriminatoire à la liberté de conscience et de religion des citoyens. La Cour a tout d'abord rejeté l'argument culturel sous-tendant cette pratique en se référant à - et en faisant sienne - «un passage du rapport de la Commission de consultation sur les pratiques d'accommodement reliées aux différences culturelles, *Fonder l'avenir: Le temps de la conciliation* (2008)».[53] Dans ce passage nous pouvons lire ce qui suit,

> « Il faut cependant éviter que des pratiques qui constituent dans les faits une forme d'identification de l'État à une religion – la plupart du temps celle de la majorité – soient maintenues sous prétexte qu'elles ne comporteraient plus aujourd'hui qu'une valeur patrimoniale.»[54]

Elle a, ensuite, précisé la signification de la neutralité de l'État en sa relation avec la liberté de religion en adhérant à une définition stricte à ce concept (la neutralité de l'État). Selon la Cour,

> « Si, sous le couvert d'une réalité culturelle, historique ou patrimoniale, l'État adhère à une forme d'expression religieuse, il ne respecte pas son obligation de neutralité. Quand cette expression religieuse crée, en outre, une distinction, exclusion ou préférence qui a pour effet de détruire ou de compromettre le droit à la pleine égalité dans la reconnaissance et l'exercice de la liberté de conscience et de religion, une discrimination existe».[55]

Conclusions

Au terme de cette étude, nous pouvons dire que le législateur québécois a réussi non seulement à mettre fin à la mainmise de l'Église et à son interventionnisme dans le champs législatif mais, et surtout, à de la sécularisation du droit un moyen pour défendre la liberté de religion pour tou(te)s les québécois (es). Le vote/sanction par lequel les québécois (es) ont défait le gouvernement du Parti québécois et son projet de Charte des valeurs, laquelle comportait des atteintes sérieuses au liberté de

---

[50] Pierre Bosset, «Les fondements juridiques et l'évolution de l'obligation d'accommodement raisonnable», en ligne: Commission des droits de la personne et des droits de la jeunesse http://www.cdpdj.qc.ca/publications/accommodements_fondements_juridiques.pdf.

[51] Ibid.

[52] *Mouvement laïque québécois c. Saguenay (Ville). 2015 CSC 16.*

[53] *Mouvement laïque québécois c. Saguenay (Ville). 2015 CSC 16 au para.87.*

[54] *Ibid..*

[55] *Ibid. au para.78.*

religion, montre, si besoin est, que les québécois (es) veulent sauvegarder cet équilibre entre la sécularisation et la liberté de religion.

Aujourd'hui, le système juridique québécois offre une protection constitutionnelle large et efficace aux droits de la personne et assure une protection institutionnelle à la liberté de religion. La législation québécoise -tout comme la législation canadienne- est basée sur la neutralité de l'État et sur la suprématie de la loi tout en favorisant un multiculturalisme intégrationniste (Palard, 2006) qui permet aux différentes communautés de vivre leurs identités culturelles et spirituelles dans le respect des règles fondamentales d'une société libre et démocratique. D'ailleurs, c'est cette approche qui été choisie par l'actuel gouvernement libéral dans son nouveau projet de loi intitulé « Loi favorisant le respect de la neutralité religieuse de l'État et visant notamment à encadrer les demandes d'accommodements religieux dans certains organismes».

References

«Acte de l'Amérique du Nord britannique. 1990. In La Constitution du Canada, ed. Gérald-A. Beaudoin. Montréal: Wilson et Lafleur.

Dominique, Beaux. 2006. *Se marier: Christianisme, Islam, Judaisme*. Bréal: Rosny-sous-bois.

Hélène, Belleau. 2012. *Quand l'amour et l'État rendent aveugle: le mythe du mariage automatique*. Québec: Presses de l'Université du Québec.

Concile du Vatican II: Constitution pastorale sur l'Église dans le monde de ce temps Gaudium et Spes, en ligne: Vatican http://www.vatican.va/archive/hist_councils/ii_vatican_council/documents/vat-ii_const_19651207_gaudium-et-spes_fr.html.

Fabien, Davier. 2009. *Les écrits catholiques de Tertullien: formes et normes*. History: Université de Franche-Comté.

Jabeur, Fathally, and Mariani Nicola. 2009. *Les systèmes juridiques dans le monde*. Montréal: Wilson& Lafleur.

Fathally Jabeur. 30/09/2013. De la charte des valeurs et de la religion civile. *Gazette*, Université d'Ottawa, 30 septembre 2013

Pascale, Fournier. 2013. *Mariages musulmans, tribunaux d'occident: Les transplantations juridiques et le regard du droit*. Paris: Presses de Sciences Po.

Guy, Marcel. 1993. Le Code civil du Québec: un peu d'histoire, beaucoup d'espoir. 23 R.D.U.S, 454.

Koussens, David,. 2011. La religion «saisie» par le droit. Comment l'État laïque définit-il la religion au Québec et en France». 52: 3 *Recherches sociologiques*.

Morin, Michel. 2009. Le pluralisme religieux et juridique en matière d'état civil et de mariage, 1774-1921. In *L'état Canadien et la Diversité Culturelle et Religieuse, 1800-1914*, eds. Lorraine Derocher et al. Québec: Presses de l'Université Du Québec.

Moore, Benoît. 2009. Culture et droit de la famille: de l'institution à l'autonomie individuelle. 54: 2 *R.D McGill*, 257-272.

Palard, Jacques, Alain-G Gagnon et Bernard Gagnon eds. 2006. *Diversité et identités au Québec et dans les régions d'Europe*. Bruxelles et Sainte-Foy: P.I.E Peter Lang, Les Presses de l'Université Laval.

Saris, Anne. 2006. Les tribunaux religieux dans les contextes canadien et québécois. 40 R.J.T 353.

Vanderlinden, Jacques. 1996. La réception des systèmes juridiques européens au Canada. 84 *Tijdschrift voor Rechtsgeschiedenis*.

Venon, Fabien. *Géographie et religion en France et au Québec*. Paris: L'Harmattan.

Chapter 20
Managing Religion Through "Religious Harmony": The Case of Singapore

Arif A. Jamal

Abstract Singapore is a multi-racial, multi-ethnic and multi-religious country in which one does not have to look very hard to find active engagement with religion among many of its residents. There are numerous churches, mosques, temples and the like that operate in the country as well as religiously-linked charitable and other civil society organisations. While the government of Singapore is formally religiously uncommitted, it does not promote atheism and there is no formal separation of state and religion. Indeed, references to the diverse religious commitments of the peoples of Singapore are made in public speeches and debates, including in Parliament, and, for example, by the recognition of public holidays linked to Hindu, Muslim, Buddhist and Christian traditions. The special status of the Malay Muslim community in Singapore is also recognised in the Constitution of Singapore and in legislation that establishes Sharia (local spelling 'Syariah') courts in the country

Singapore is, however, concerned about maintaining 'religious harmony' and there are frequent, and recent, references to the need not to take racial and religious harmony for granted. As such, the state has equipped itself with strong legislative powers to manage religious harmony. While these powers are not actually exercised often, they make it clear that the state can step in to secure religious harmony if it feels it necessary to do so. While this model may raise concerns in the eyes of some, one should consider it in response to local demographic and other conditions and ask if it fits the context. More generally, perhaps a model of robust management of religious harmony might be salutary for other highly plural environments as well. In addition to outlining the scene in Singapore, this chapter also raises these questions.

A.A. Jamal (✉)
Faculty of Law, National University of Singapore, Singapore, Singapore
e-mail: arif.jamal@nus.edu.sg

R. Bottoni et al. (eds.), *Religious Rules, State Law, and Normative Pluralism - A Comparative Overview*, Ius Comparatum – Global Studies in Comparative Law 18, DOI 10.1007/978-3-319-28335-7_20

Introduction

Singapore is a multi-racial, multi-ethnic and multi-religious country. The fifth national census carried out in 2010 listed a population of just below 5.1 million people, consisting of about 3.8 million residents (citizens or non-citizen permanent residents) and approximately 1.3 million non-residents (i.e., non-citizens or non-permanent residents).[1] Within this population, several major religious traditions are represented, the main ones being Christianity, Islam, Buddhism and Taoism, and Hinduism as indicated below (Table 20.1), with Buddhism/Taoism together being the largest, but not majority, tradition.

Being located in Southeast Asia, some authors have asserted that religion has been an important factor in the social and political landscaping of Singapore for centuries, with various waves of traders and travellers having brought with them Buddhist, Confucian, Hindu, Islamic and, more recently, Christian traditions (Tan, 56). To these influences must be added immigration and consequent settlement, especially from China and India. In addition, many of the religious affiliations have remained more or less stable over the past 30 or so years, however, from 1980 to 2000, there was a notable increase in those identifying themselves as Buddhist and Christian, and a significant decrease in those identifying themselves as Taoist (Table 20.2). Additionally, the substantial economic changes in Singapore and increase in wealth since 1980 had an appreciable effect on the percentage of the population saying that they have 'no religion' (13.0 % in 1980–17.0 % in 2010) but this has not altered the fact that the vast majority of Singapore's residents identify with a religious tradition.

The religious identities of Singapore residents are, however, strongly coloured along racial lines. Thus, the majority of the Chinese population in Singapore are mainly Buddhist/Taoist or Christian (whose affiliations constitute a high majority of the population) with very few Muslims. On the other hand, the Malay community is overwhelmingly Muslim, while the Indian population is majorily Hindu with a significant Muslim minority and much smaller numbers of Christians and Buddhists.

In the case of Islam, this also accounts for a near conflagration of Muslim identity with Malay identity in the Singapore context, which in turn may impinge upon the understanding of differences amongst Muslims, especially those that are non-Malay (e.g., 'Indian Muslims'). This is interesting since Singapore's Muslim population, whilst small in absolute terms, is the largest as a percentage of any of the Muslim minorities in Southeast Asia (Funston, 71).

Issues concerning religion are regulated in a variety of ways in Singapore. Both constitutional and statutory laws are invoked and these are moderated by political principles. Of these measures, the political principles are the most fluid and therefore more difficult to pin down, so the remainder of this discussion will restrict itself mainly to the formally articulated legal norms.

[1] http://www.singstat.gov.sg/Publications/publications_and_papers/cop2010/census_2010_advance_census_release/c2010acr.pdf.

Table 20.1 Key indicators of the resident population[a]

	Total		Chinese		Malays		Indians		Others	
	2000	2010	2000	2010	2000	2010	2000	2010	2000	2010
Demographic characteristics										
Singapore residents ('000)	3273.4	3771.7	2513.8	2794.0	455.2	503.9	257.9	348.1	46.4	125.8
Ethnic composition (%)	100.0	100.0	76.8	74.1	13.9	13.4	7.9	9.2	1.4	3.3
Religion										
Religion (%)	100.0	100.0	100.0	100.0	100.0	100.0	100.0	100.0	100.0	100.0
(Aged 15 years & over)										
Christianity	14.6	18.3	16.5	20.1	0.3	0.7	12.1	12.8	53.3	57.6
Buddhism/Taoism	51.0	44.2	64.4	57.4	0.1	0.2	0.7	0.8	13.9	20.8
Buddhism	42.5	33.3	53.6	43.0	0.1	0.2	0.7	0.8	13.7	20.2
Taoism	8.5	10.9	10.8	14.4	–	–	–	–	0.2	0.6
Islam	14.9	14.7	0.3	0.4	99.6	98.7	25.6	21.7	22.3	9.2
Hinduism	4.0	5.1	–	–	–	0.1	55.4	58.9	1.1	0.8
Other religions	0.6	0.7	0.3	0.3	–	0.1	5.6	4.6	1.3	1.1
No religion	14.8	17.0	18.6	21.8	0.1	0.2	0.6	1.1	8.1	10.6

[a]Ibid (NB: excludes non-citizens and non-permanent residents)

Table 20.2 Resident population aged 15 years and over[a]

Distribution by religion

			Percent
	1980	1990	2000
Total	100.0	100.0	100.0
Buddhism	27.0	31.2	42.5
Taoism/Chinese traditional beliefs	30.0	22.4	8.5
Islam	15.7	15.3	14.9
Christianity	10.1	12.7	14.6
Hinduism	3.6	3.7	4.0
Other religions	0.5	0.6	0.6
No religion	13.0	14.1	14.8

www.singstat.gov.sg/statistics/browse_by_theme/.../religion.xls

Legislation

Freedom of religion is guaranteed under the Constitution of Singapore in Article 15, which stipulates in 15(1) that: "Every person has the right to profess and practice his religion and to propagate it" and, in 15(3), that "Every religious group has the right (*a*) to manage its own religious affairs (*b*) to establish and maintain institutions for religious or charitable purposes; and (*c*) to acquire and own property and hold and administer it in accordance with law."[2]

Article 16(2) of the Constitution also gives religious groups the right to establish and maintain institutions which are to provide religious instruction and education for children. In addition, Art 16(1) states that there is to be no discrimination in public education with respect to admission, fees etc., against any citizen on the basis of religion (amongst other grounds).

Singapore thus guarantees freedom of religion in the context of non-establishment of any religious tradition or 'church', such that: "[Singapore's] brand of constitutional secularism is not anti-theistic but framed along agnostic or benevolent lines, where the state does not favour or disfavour religion(s), nor favour irreligion over religion…" (Thio, 870).

Freedom of religion in Singapore, however, would not be likely to cover atheism and give it the same protection as religious conscience. As discussed below, Singapore is concerned with preserving religious harmony and preventing offence to religious sentiments, but it is very doubtful whether this extends to atheistic sentiments so that a religious perspective could offend atheistic conscience.

That said, there are two articles of the constitution that make special reference and arrangements for Muslims. Article 152 does this in the context of the Malay community, which, as has been noted, is overwhelmingly Muslim, stating that:

[2] Constitution of the Republic of Singapore (Original Enactment: S 1/63) available at: http://statutes.agc.gov.sg.

Minorities and special position of Malays

152. (1) It shall be the responsibility of the Government constantly to care for the interests of the racial and religious minorities in Singapore.

(2) The Government shall exercise its functions in such manner as to recognise the special position of the Malays, who are the indigenous people of Singapore, and accordingly it shall be the responsibility of the Government to protect, safeguard, support, foster and promote their political, educational, *religious*, economic, social and cultural interests and the Malay language.

To this Article 153 adds that:

153. The Legislature *shall by law make provision for regulating Muslim religious affairs* and for constituting a Council to advise the President in matters relating to the Muslim religion. [Emphasis added].

It is on this basis that the Islamic Religious Council of Singapore, known locally by its Malay language acronym 'MUIS', has been established by the Government. MUIS oversees religious affairs such as the maintenance of mosques, halal certification and the provision of religious education and guidance to the Malay (and other) Muslim communities.

Furthermore, for the Muslim community of Singapore, there is the *Administration of Muslim Law Act (AMLA)*,[3] which, as its name suggests, provides a structure for the administration of Muslim Law – including the set-up of MUIS. This Act concerns mainly personal law matters such as marriage, divorce and inheritance, though it primarily leaves the *substantive* law to be decided within the context of the Muslim community itself, and mostly addresses administrative procedures. *AMLA* does, however, also stipulate certain behaviours which are criminal for Muslims in Singapore but would not be for non-Muslims.

Muslim law is also established by the operation of special Sharia Courts, a Board of Appeal (to hear appeals from the Sharia Courts) and the capacity of MUIS to issue legal opinions, *fatwa* (pl. *fatawa)*, through its Legal (Fatwa) Committee (Abdul Rahman, 127). It should be noted, however, that these legal opinions are not binding, though they may be persuasive, on the regular courts in Singapore.[4]

No other religious community has a structure for its religious law established by statute in this manner. Previously, certain religious groups were incorporated via Private Acts of Parliament. For example, the Roman Catholic Church in Singapore was incorporated by the *Roman Catholic Archbishop Act*[5] and thereby allowed to hold property and do other things allowed to corporate bodies. This legislative procedure seems anachronistic now, since, as Gary Bell points out (Bell, 65–66), "More recently, the Singapore Government seems to have required new religious groups to

---

[3] Cap. 3, 2009 Rev Ed. Emphasis added.

[4] On this see the Singapore case of *Shafeeg bin Salim Talib* v *Fatimah bteAbud bin Talib* [2010] 2 SLR 1123 (CA).

[5] Cap. 375, 1985 Rev Ed.

incorporate either under the *Companies Act*[6] or the *Societies Act.*[7]" Bell also states that "…the Constitution of Singapore has provided space for the [Roman Catholic] Church to administer itself according to its own rules and the Roman Catholic Archbishop Act has provided for legal personality ('body corporate') without imposing rules for the management of the internal affairs of the Church (Bell, 68)." This broadly typifies the legislative approach taken in Singapore towards all religious groups and is not inconsistent with *AMLA*. That is to say, generally, Singapore allows religious groups to define and deal with their own 'internal affairs'. It is, however, important to note that by virtue of the legislation noted above, Muslims in Singapore cannot opt out of the application of Muslim law in matters such as inheritance. Thus, section 111 of *AMLA* states:

> 111. (1) Notwithstanding anything in the provisions of the English law or in any other written law, no Muslim domiciled in Singapore shall, after 1st July 1968, dispose of his property by will, or by any nomination under section 49M(2) of the Insurance Act (Cap. 142), except in accordance with the provisions of and subject to the restrictions imposed by the school of Muslim law professed by him.

Similarly, marriages in which both parties are Muslim go through a unique process with a special registration. Thus, there is the general Registrar of Marriages and the specific Registrar of *Muslim* Marriages.[8]

For other religious communities, there is more flexibility since their religious law is not applied by statute in the same manner as Muslim law. For instance, a Catholic or a Hindu would not have the laws of their communities applied by the state in the way that aspects of Muslim law are applied via *AMLA* and so could choose which aspects of their tradition's law to apply more freely. That said, for the Sikh and Hindu communities there are also state recognised bodies that administer the affairs of these communities, and the Government of Singapore holds the power to appoint some members to these bodies. As with MUIS, however, the government does not seek to delve into theological matters per se, but is primarily concerned with administration.

The situation of Muslim law with its particular legislative framework is therefore special in Singapore, but there are other general pieces of legislation which impact religion in Singapore generally. These provisions allow the government to manage the corporate organisation of religious communities by registration (and deregistration), and to manage the religious environment of Singapore by controlling speech or acts that might cause offence to or upset religious communities.

Under the *Societies Act*,[9] religious groups can be denied registration or indeed be deregistered if they are deemed to be acting in a way that is "prejudicial to public

[6]Cap. 50, 2006 Rev Ed.

[7]Cap. 311, 1985 Rev Ed.

[8]Under section 3(4) of the *Women's Charter* (Cap 353, 2009 Rev Ed) Muslims in Singapore cannot get married under 'secular law' but must undertake a Muslim marriage.

[9]Cap 311, 2014 Rev Ed.

peace, welfare or good order in Singapore". Punishments can also be meted out for injuring a place of religious worship, disturbing a religious assembly or uttering sounds to deliberately wound religious feelings under Chapter 15 of the *Penal Code.*[10] Furthermore, under s. 3(e) of the *Sedition Act*[11] it is a punishable seditious tendency "to promote feelings of ill-will and hostility between different races or classes of the population of Singapore", and this could be used to regulate actions with respect to religious communities, especially with the strong co-relation noted above of Malay and Muslim.

Even stronger powers are available to the government under the *Internal Security Act*[12] which allows for 'preventive detention' "...for the internal security of Singapore...the prevention of subversion, the suppression of organised violence against persons and property in specified areas of Singapore" (Preamble). These powers, including the use of arrests, have been used to deal with cases where parties were deemed to be fomenting racial or religious discord (Tan, 65).

Mention should also be made of the *Undesirable Publications Act*,[13] which stipulates offences for the making or distribution of objectionable publications and allows for the search and seizure of objectionable publications. According to section 4(b) a publication may be objectionable if it deals with:

> 4(*b*) matters of race or religion in such a manner that the availability of the publication is likely to cause feelings of enmity, hatred, ill-will or hostility between different racial or religious groups.

Notwithstanding the above, an overarching framework for dealing with disturbances to religious harmony in Singapore is found in the *Maintenance of Religious Harmony Act (MRHA).*[14]

Under this Act, Singapore has a Presidential Council for Religious Harmony that advises the President of the Republic on religious affairs and in particular on conduct that can upset religious harmony. The Act also empowers the Minister to act pre-emptively and issue restraining orders to deal with actions that cause enmity, hatred, ill-will or hostility between different religious groups and the Act is especially concerned with the mixing of 'religion' and 'politics' (Thio, 918). However, the broad language of the Act provides an ill-defined boundary between religion and politics and so there is considerable ministerial discretion that may be exercised. That said, it should be noted that no restraining orders have actually been issued under the *MHRA* as yet, though Thio Li-ann notes that there were three instances when the *MHRA* was almost invoked (Thio, 920 fn. 230).

[10] Cap. 224, 2008 Rev Ed.

[11] Cap. 290, 2013 Rev Ed.

[12] Cap. 143, 1985 Rev Ed.

[13] Cap. 338, 1998 Rev Ed.

[14] Cap. 167A, 2001 Rev Ed.

Adjudication

Mention has been made above of the Sharia courts established under *AMLA*, which have jurisdiction primarily for family or personal law matters as defined by *AMLA*. On some matters such as child custody, divorce, maintenance of a wife and child, the Sharia courts have concurrent jurisdiction with the High Court but, more generally, the Sharia courts are inferior courts and are under the supervision of the High Court. It is important to mention as well that the application of Islamic law in the Sharia courts is moderated via the *AMLA*, such that the Sharia courts can only apply Islamic law as bound by the Act and overseen by the civil courts. Thus, one may say that the overall context for Islamic law is for adjudication by state-defined norms: on the one hand this is done by legislation in which the state defines the scope of Islamic law; on the other, this is done by institutional structure where the state subjects the Sharia courts to the jurisdiction of the civil courts.

Aside from the Sharia courts, there are no other state recognised religiously-defined courts in Singapore. Singapore is, however, very open to arbitration and allows for arbitration to incorporate norms coming from religious traditions, though, in general, family law issues are not matters that may be subject to arbitration.

Social Implementation of Religious Rules

Singapore has a religiously active population. The presence of religious worship as well as religion-linked activities and good works done by religious communities is evident and these evidence the social presence of religion in Singapore. Some of these activities, it might be said, reflect a religious sentiment or motivation and express a type of religiously inspired 'civil society' work. Examples of these types of activities are churches (or other religious groups) helping those in need or organising sporting, camping, social service or other such events for co-religionists. For instance, during the month of Ramadan, some Muslim groups will collect food and other provisions to give to the less fortunate, consistent with the ethos of that holy month, and similar types of work are undertaken by other communities.

Religion is also more or less freely discussed in public fora. For example, lectures are held both within faith communities as well as across them through the Inter-Religious Organisation (Singapore) (www.iro.sg) to promote dialogue and understanding of the varied faith traditions in the country.

In addition to the social expression of religious norms in these ways, there is also the personal application, by members of religious communities themselves, of what may more properly be called 'religious rules'. Prominent examples are dietary rules/restrictions such as sticking to a vegetarian diet, only eating halal foods, foregoing meat on Fridays, restricting one's diet during Lent, temporary fasts out of observance of religious festivals or as a form of prayer or atonement. Singapore allows all of these types of expression of religion and the self-application of religious rules are not uncommon in Singapore society. However, in order to keep to consistent school uniforms Malay girls do not wear headscarves (local terminology 'tundung') in Singapore schools. Where there are no uniform policies, however, for instance amongst university students, they may wear the tudung and some do. Also, while in most parts of the general civil service (e.g., amongst nurses, police officers and immigration and checkpoints authority officers) tudungs may not be worn at present, public school teachers or staff working at the public-supported universities may wear the tudung. Furthermore, there is a general allowances for turbans to be worn by Sikh males.

Finally, the communal ethos within Singapore means that informal mediation by community leaders or family elders with their attendant moral suasion is a live practice in Singapore and some of this relies upon the norms coming from religious traditions or at least the authority of religious 'office'. In particular, family matters are sometimes settled by way of mediated arrangements (for instance, some of this is done as part of the 'litigation' process in the Sharia courts), though commercial matters may also, but less frequently, be settled by these negotiated or mediated means. It is important to distinguish this informal mediation by moral suasion from formal arbitration, which, as noted above, is not generally available for family issues.

Considering Singapore in Theoretical Perspective

The question of the appropriate role that religious convictions may have in public life, and within public political debate, is salient almost everywhere and has attracted much academic consideration. There are, of course, different points of view on this important matter.

One line of argument holds that, to put it basically, there are good reasons for excluding arguments coming from religious outlooks when debating matters of general public concern because these arguments are not shared. The most prominent exposition of this argument probably comes from John Rawls' *Political Liberalism* in which he develops the concept of 'public reason'. Rawls asked: "How is it possible that there may exist over time a stable and just society of free and equal citizens profoundly divided by reasonable religious, moral and philosophical doctrines? This is a problem of political justice, not about the highest good?"

To this question, he famously proposed that:

> …we are to appeal only to presently accepted general beliefs and forms of reasoning found in common sense, and the methods and conclusions of science when these are not controversial…*we are not to appeal to comprehensive religious and philosophical doctrines – to what we as individuals see as the whole truth* – or to elaborate economic theories of general equilibrium, say, if these are in dispute (Rawls (1993), 224). [Emphasis added].

In advancing this position, Rawls advocated – putting it simply but also somewhat roughly – that when it came to fundamental matters of what he termed 'constitutional essentials' religion should be more or less kept out of the debate. Instead, we should use 'public reason', which is a type of reasoning that does not depend upon justifications or arguments stemming from comprehensive doctrines of any type, including but not limited to religious convictions, since such commitments are not shared and cannot therefore be endorsed by all citizens generally. To be fair, later on Rawls modified his position somewhat with what is often referred to as his proviso, stating:

> …reasonable comprehensive doctrines, religious or non-religious, may be introduced in public political discussion at any time, provided that in due course proper political reasons – and not reasons given solely by comprehensive doctrines – are presented that are sufficient to support whatever the comprehensive doctrines are said to support (Rawls (1997), 783–784).

While one cannot suggest that Singapore is choosing to follow a Rawlsian framework, it might be fair to say that Singapore does seek to restrict the reliance of reasoning based on religious commitments in matters of public concern, in a manner that shares some of the concerns of such a framework. That is to say, that just as Rawls' framework was concerned with the potentially stability-threatening consequences of allowing religious (or other comprehensive) doctrines to hold sway on issues of general public concern, Singapore may feel the same concern given the highly plural religious make-up of its people. Thus, it may adopt a similar strategy, namely to keep religious sentiments within the realm of private life and away from public policy discussions. One of the differences, however, is that while Rawls limited his restriction to what he termed constitutional essentials, these restrictions may be applied to a wider ambit of issues in the case of Singapore.

Jurgen Habermas also articulates a theoretical framework that posits limitations on the scope of religious reasons in public decision-making. While, in general, Habermas' theory allows a wider scope for religious reasons in general public debate than that of Rawls, Habermas suggests that there should be institutional limits to religious reasons. Thus he says that only secular reasons will count "beyond the institutional threshold that divides the informal public sphere from parliaments, courts, ministries and administrations" (Habermas, 10). From this a 'translation requirement' is developed in which "[t]he truth content of religious contributions can enter into the institutionalised practice of deliberation and decision-making only if the necessary translation already occurs in the pre-parliamentary domain, i.e., in the political public sphere itself."[15] (Habermas, 11–12). Habermas' concern appears to be that in the venues where policy decisions are made, only reasons that are cast in secular language are appropriate because only these reasons are sufficiently accessible to all i.e., to those with and without religious convictions. In this respect, Habermas' theory might support an outlook that draws a line between religious reasoning in general political speech and religious reasoning in institutional politics (or, one might say, religious and political decision-making). As we will see below, it may be possible to see this tendency, albeit in modifed form, in Singapore, particularly with the policy of 'keeping religion and politics separate'. In this policy,

[15] Ibid., pp 11–12.

religious reasoning is allowed to be expressed in the parliamentary domain but it is made clear in this domain that there is restricted policy scope for such reasons to be the basis of decision-making.

Finally, we can consider a third perspective articulated by Nadia Urbinati. Urbinati argues for a contextually-sensitive approach, saying:

> My conclusion can be rendered as follows: In matters that have a direct impact on the individual freedom of religion and social peace such as the presence of religion in the public sphere, political theorists should pay close attention to the ethical and historical context of a given society instead of applying to it practical conclusions that have been derived from an ideal conception of democratic societies as religious-pluralist *de facto* and *de iure*... Religious-pluralism is the essential condition within which we should situate any discourse on the role of religions in the public sphere. (Urbinati, 16–17)

This "pragmatic suggestion of going back and forth from the ideal norm to the context"[16] (Urbinati, 16) appeals to the need to set our frameworks in light of the realities of religious pluralism in the society with which we are concerned. Pragmatic contextual sensitivity is invoked in the religiously plural and geographical small context of Singapore, as we shall see below. Indeed, a recent study notes that Singapore has amongst the highest, if not the highest, level of religious diversity when considered internationally (Pew Research Centre, 4).

With these perspectives in mind we can consider some examples of the public expression of religiously-informed perspectives in Singapore.

There have been matters of public concern in which voices coming from religious traditions have been expressed, including in Singapore's Parliament and by members of the Cabinet. One example came in the discussion on the 'integrated resorts', which include casinos. Dr Yaacob Ibrahim, then Minister-in-charge of Muslim Affairs (and currently Minister for Communications and Information and Minister-in-charge of Muslim Affairs) spoke as a Muslim raising a concern about gambling, though not in the end opposing the integrated resorts.[17] Dr Yaacob said:

> As Muslims, we are against gambling. Many respected members of the community have rightly expressed concerns on a possible casino because Islam prohibits gambling. Others have also pointed to the possible social ills that this proposal could potentially bring about and have, therefore, opposed the proposal. Hence, having raised our concerns, many in our Muslim community will be disappointed with the decision to proceed with the proposal.[18]

Minister Yaacob's reference to his religious background was echoed by other MPs from different religious affiliations. Thus, Mr R Ravindran, MP for Marine Parade, said:

> Sir, I am a Hindu in my religious beliefs. My religious values and teachings advise on the dangers of gambling. In fact, the great Hindu book, Mahabharatha, explains the downfall of the Pandavas due to a game of dice.

---

[16] Ibid., p 16.

[17] See http://www.mti.gov.sg/MTIInsights/Documents/Ministerial%20Statement%20-%20Yaacob%2018apr05.pdf

[18] *Singapore Parliamentary Reports*, (10th Parliament, 2nd Session) Volume 80, Sitting 1 (18 April 2005) (http://sprs.parl.gov.sg/search/report.jsp?currentPubID=00004697-WA)

> Sir, I thought that only amongst the Chinese gambling had a history. Yesterday, I was looking up the great Indian book written by Thiruvalluvar 2000 years ago and I noticed that, 2000 years ago, he had dedicated 10 couplets on the dangers of gambling. It looks like that the problem not only existed amongst the Chinese, but also amongst the Indians. In fact, Sir, there is a very famous Tamil proverb, "*SoothumVaathumVethanaiSeiyum*", which means gambling and quarrelling bring agony to anyone.
>
> I think all these ancient and religious values highlight that gambling is dangerous and that one does it at his own peril.[19]

Indeed, as the Prime Minister, Mr Lee Hsien Loon, himself mentioned in the Parliamentary debate:

> [M]any Singaporeans, though not all, who oppose the IR [integrated resort] do so on religious grounds. The main religious groups have made their views known. The churches, the Buddhist and Hindu groups, as well as the MUIS [The Islamic Religious Council of Singapore] and Muslim groups, have all stated their views. I have also received letters from many Singaporeans, especially Christians, expressing objection on religious grounds.[20]

At the same time, both the PM as well as other members of Parliament made the point that in public discussion, whilst perspectives from religious commitments may be raised, including in Parliamentary debates, such perspectives could only have a limited role in actual decision making. So, Mr Gan Kim Yong (MP for Holland-Bukit Panjang) stated:

> Religious organisations, for example, have argued strongly against the casino. We accept that the Government cannot make its decisions based on religious grounds as it is a secular Government. But it is important that we engage them and take pains to explain our decision. We must also encourage them to turn their conviction into positive and constructive actions. For a start, I would like to suggest that these organisations can initiate a campaign among their constituent members to voluntarily place themselves into the exclusion list, so that they and their families will abstain from the casino.[21]

Minster Yaacob echoed this point of view, albeit as a Muslim, in saying:

> [T]here are many things that exist around us which we do not agree with as Muslims, but accept as part of the wider landscape. Gambling, drinking and other activities that Muslims consider vices are not banned in Singapore. We understand that in our multi-ethnic and multi-religious society, it is not tenable for Government policies to be dictated by the views of one or any groups.[22]

The role of religious voices in public debates was also raised in the discussions on the Human Organ Transplant Act (*HOTA*).[23] Before *HOTA* was passed, when the legislation was still in Bill form, a Select Committee heard from both Catholic and Muslim groups, who, speaking from their traditions, gave their reactions and raised

[19] *Singapore Parliamentary Reports*, (10th Parliament, 2nd Session) Volume 80, Sitting 1 (18 April 2005) (http://sprs.parl.gov.sg/search/report.jsp?currentPubID=00004697-WA)

[20] Ibid.

[21] Ibid.

[22] Ibid.

[23] Cap 131A, 2012 Rev Ed.

questions about provisions of the Bill.[24] Indeed, when *HOTA* was initially passed it did not extend to the Muslim population of Singapore because of concerns that its terms were not compatible with Muslim doctrine. This was eventually changed in 2008, when an amendment to the Act was passed extending it to Muslims. During the Parliamentary debate on the amendment, several members, Muslim and otherwise, spoke from religious perspectives, either in general or more tradition-specific terms. For instance, Madam Halima Yacob, a Muslim (and the present Speaker of Parliament) said:

> There are several *fatwas* from the MUIS Fatwa Committee on the issue of organ donations by Muslims after death. The key point to note is that Muslims are allowed to donate their organs, subject to the approval of the *waris* after a person's death. A key consideration for the *fatwa* committee's decision is that Islam places a high premium on saving lives and gives priority to the needs of the living rather than the dead. Hence, Islam supports transplants to save lives in emergency situations.[25]

Another example of religious arguments being raised comes from the Parliamentary discussion on the 'policy of keeping religion and politics separate'.[26] Whilst the very language of this policy is indicative of the general Singaporean approach, the nature of the discussion that took place is interesting for our purposes.

Speaking in the debate, the Deputy Prime Minister, Mr Teo Chee Hean, stated:

> Every citizen, regardless of his religious beliefs, *has the same rights to express his views on public issues*. In doing so, a citizen who belongs to a particular religion will often be guided by his own religious beliefs and personal conscience. However, like other citizens, *he should always be mindful of the sensitivities of living in a multi-religious society and the bounds of the law.* [Emphasis added].

This statement succinctly captures important elements of the model adopted in Singapore, recognising the claimed right of all citizens not only to hold but also to express their religious beliefs on public issues, but to do so in a manner that is sensitive to the local environment. The last phrase invoking the 'bounds of law' also alludes to the fact that the boundaries of appropriate sensitivity are effectively set and monitored by law in Singapore. This means that it is the judgment of the law that is the ultimate arbiter of what is appropriate sensitivity and the law can intervene as and when, in its view, the boundaries of sensitivity are breached.

---

[24] Singapore. *Report of the Select Committee on the Human Organ Transplant Bill (Bill No 26/86)*. See Paper 5 from The MajlisUgama Islam Singapura (MUIS, or 'The Islamic Religious Council of Singapore') and Paper 7 from The Catholic Medical Guild of Singapore.

[25] *Singapore Parliament Reports (Hansard)* (10th Parliament, 1st Session) Volume 77, Sitting 1 (5 January 2004) (http://sprs.parl.gov.sg/search/topic.jsp?currentTopicID=00000766-WA&currentPubID=00004650-WA&topicKey=00004650-WA.00000766-WA_1%2B%2B).

[26] *Singapore Parliament Reports (Hansard)* (12th Parliament, 1st session) Volume 89, Sitting 8 (15 October 2012) (http://sprs.parl.gov.sg/search/report.jsp?currentPubID=00078007-WA).

The following exchange in Parliament on the same day as the above statement further illustrates the position taken now, cast in light of the relation of 'religion and politics':

> *Mr Laurence Lien [Nominated Member]*: Sir, I would like to make a point of clarification. My views are a bit more nuanced. They are not clear, not so black and white. Of course, in certain instances, religion should not cross the boundaries, but my question is for the Deputy Prime Minister to consider that, in some cases, a separation of religion from politics is not entirely reasonable.
>
> *Mr Teo Chee Hean [Deputy Prime Minister]*: Sir, the position is very clear between that of an individual practising his religion and carrying through the practice of his religion and his beliefs into his own personal decisions. And that is quite different from getting religious groups involved in politics. I think those are two quite different things and that, in fact, as Mr Lien has suggested, is a nuanced position, and not very different from Mr Lien's. I think we need to keep that separation; otherwise once religious organisations get involved in politics, we then run the danger of having a clash.[27] With many religious groups entering into the political arena, or political groups seeking to use religious groups to further their political agenda, we then begin to have a problem.[28]

Again, here, we can see the repeated themes of religious freedom as a matter of individual belief or conscience but a concern that certain forms of public expressions of religion may engender social tension. This conforms to the language of the Constitution of Singapore. Recall that Art 15 of the Constitution deals with freedom of religion, with Art 15(1) stating:

15.—(1) Every person has the right to profess and practise his religion and to propagate it.

But this is limited by Art 15(4), which states:

15.—(4) This Article does not authorise any act contrary to any general law relating to public order, public health or morality.

Thus, following the commentary of Thio Li-ann and using, as she does, the well-known distinction between *forum internum* and *forum externum* one can say that Art 15(4) provides a constitutional limitation on the *forum externum* aspects of religion in Singapore and that this is reinforced, elaborated and extended by various of the above-noted other laws to address situations when it is felt that the political actions of religious groups might have crossed the appropriate political line (Thio, 869).

---

[27] Ibid. One can note that Mr Lien made the point earlier in the debate of stating that he is a Catholic.

[28] Ibid. Italics added for clarity of identification.

Conclusion

One does not have to look too hard to find a religiously active and diverse population in Singapore. For instance, there are many places of worship, there is openly-worn religious dress, religious education is provided by different groups, lectures on different religious traditions are conducted, politicians are happy to participate in events connected to religious festivals or celebrations by different communities and there are national public holidays connected to the numerically larger major faith traditions of Singapore (Christianity, Hinduism, Islam and Buddhism). In addition, public speech willingly and explicitly recognises the country's multi-religious heritage and culture though not infrequently refers to Singapore as a 'secular state'. Singapore also provides constitutional protection for freedom of religion, within limits. If these indicators are a measure of the accommodating nature of Singapore's society to religious ideas, expressions and practices, including measures of freedom of religion and religious expression, then Singapore ranks well.

At the same time, there is great concern about maintaining harmonious relations amongst Singaporeans and therefore concern not to cause religious offence or hurt. The result is that the government of Singapore is armed with an impressive panoply of legislative powers, under several different acts, to defend and secure 'religious harmony'. These legislative provisions would permit the government to take serious action against speech or acts that, in its view, threaten religious harmony in Singapore. Such powers have been used in the past, though fairly sparingly, and they remain a potent deterrent.

Do such provisions make Singapore a worrying case? In many jurisdictions around the world regulating religion is becoming an increasing challenge. One part of this challenge involves the question of what 'accommodations' might reasonably be provided to those holding religious convictions. In addition, there is also the issue of what restrictions might be placed on religious expression especially in public fora, on the one hand, and expressions about religion (whether from those holding religious views or not), on the other. Indeed, significant political thinkers have noted the potentially divisive nature of religious reasons in public political discussions and thus have posited different forms of limitations on these reasons in particular in terms of their impact on public policies.

One cannot say that Singapore follows any of the theoretical perspectives surveyed above and certainly not that it follows any of them explicitly. However, a sense of needing to balance the expression of positions that derive from religious affiliations in the social and political context of a religiously plural society is evident both in the theory and in Singaporean practice. Singapore expresses this concern in its defence of 'religious harmony' and its allied 'policy of keeping religion and politics separate'. In so doing, Singapore allows for rich religious engagement of its population in the *forum internum*. In the *forum externum*, religious voices are expressed even in Parliament and by Cabinet Ministers; however, it is also made clear that, while they may be aired, they will not be dispositive of government policy.

In the broader perspective, one must keep in mind that political negotiation and soft power plays an important role in the Singapore context. This is facilitated by Singapore's compact geography and relatively small population as well as by the significant role of its government vis-à-vis other jurisdictions.

Some commentators have raised concerns about the consequences, some of which may be unintended, of the managed state of religious relations in Singapore. For example, with respect to Islam or the Muslim community in Singapore, Tim Lindsey and Kerstin Steiner say:

> MUIS is involved in a vast array of areas…This deep reach into the life of Muslims has meant that the inward-looking, traditionalist and state-compliant norms discernible in MUIS' *fatawa* (and so many of its other public statements and programmes) have saturated the official religious culture of Singapore's Muslim community and will probably do so for the foreseeable future (Lindsey and Steiner, 134).

When considered in totality, Singapore offers an environment which recognises, protects and allows for religious identity to be expressed and practised fairly openly. The Republic is a theologically uncommitted state but does not promote atheism; rather, it openly and explicitly embraces its multi-religious nature. In this context, the position of the Muslim community and Islamic law is unique since special provision is made for the Malay Muslim community and for Islam within the constitution of Singapore and, more significantly, the *AMLA*, including special Sharia courts. As part of this wider social compact, however, Singapore manages religious harmony through both informal, political means, and through formal, legal provisions by which the state may take strong action to maintain what it holds to be proper religious harmony.

Acknowledgement My thanks to Eugene K.B. Tan for his review of an earlier draft of this chapter and for highlighting points to be corrected and to Tan Zhong Xing for generously helping me to locate relevant information. What weaknesses errors remain are, of course, solely my responsibility

References

Abdul Rahman and Noor Aisha. 2012. Muslim personal law and citizen's rights: The case of Singapore. *Asian Journal of Comparative Law* 7: 127–152.

Bell, Gary F. 2012. Religious legal pluralism revisited –The status of the Roman Catholic Church and her Canon law in Singapore. *Asian Journal of Comparative Law* 7(49): 49–84.

Funston, Jon. 2006. Singapore. In *Voices of Islam in Southeast Asia: A contemporary sourcebook*, ed. Greg Fealty and Virginia Hooker. Singapore: Institute for Southeast Asian Studies.

Habermas, Jurgen. 2006. Religion in the public sphere. *European Journal of Philosophy* 14(1): 1–25.

Lindsey, Tim, and Kerstin Steiner. 2012. *Islam, law and the state in southeast Asia, volume II: Singapore*. London: IB Tauris.

Pew Research Center. 2014, April. *Global religious diversity: Half of the most religiously diverse countries are in Asia Pacific region*. http://www.pewforum.org/files/2014/04/Religious-Diversity-full-report.pdf.

Rawls, John. 1993. *Political Liberalism*. New York: Columbia University Press.

Rawls, John. 1997. The idea of public reason revisited. *The University of Chicago Law Review* 64(3): 765–807.

Tan, Eugene K.B. 2008. Keeping god in place: The management of religion in Singapore. In *Religious diversity in Singapore*, ed. Lai Ah Eng. Singapore: ISEAS/IPS.

Thio, Li-ann. 2012. *A treatise on Singapore constitutional law*. Singapore: Academy Publishing.

Urbinati, Nadia. 2014. The context of secularism: A critical appraisal of the post-secular argument. In *Constitutional secularism in an age of religious revival*, ed. Susana Mancini and Michel Rosenfeld. Oxford: Oxford University Press.

Chapter 21
Religion and the Constitutional Experience of South Africa

Pieter Coertzen

Abstract The article is about religion and its place in the Constitutional provisions of South Africa. It touches on aspects like the social composition and religious demography of South Africa pointing out the big variety of cultural and religious groups in South Africa who all live together under one constitution. Attention is also given to the historical and political development in the country. The notion of religious rules and the way it is formulated in the Constitution are discussed. Tension between religious rules and State laws and what tools are available to lessen these tensions are also discussed. In this regard there is reference to the *South African Charter of Religious Rights and Freedoms* and the positive role it can play with regard to all the religions in South Africa in their relationship with the State.

All of this provides for a system which shows respect for human rights and especially freedom of religion, equality, non-discrimination and freedom of association. It also provides for religions in South Africa to take ownership of freedom of religion and to formulate their religious identity in terms of their given freedom of religion.

Introduction

Social Composition and Religious Demography of South Africa

South Africa is a country of pluralities. The total population of about 50 million is made up of 80 % black people, 9.1 % whites, 8.9 % brown people and 2.5 % Indians. The plurality of cultures within the different social and ethnic groups is reflected in the fact that eleven official languages are spoken which are here below indicated with the percentage of speakers of each of them in comparison with the total population. The languages are Isizulu (23.8 %); IsiXhosa (17.6 %), Afrikaans (13.3 %), Sepedi (9.4 %), SeTswana (8.2 %), English (8.2 %), SeSotho (7.9 %), Xitsonga (4.4 %), SiSwati (2.7 %), Thsivenda (2.3 %), isiNdebele (1.6 %), other (0.5 %).

P. Coertzen (✉)
University of Stellenbosch, Stellenbosch, South Africa
e-mail: pc@sun.ac.za

R. Bottoni et al. (eds.), *Religious Rules, State Law, and Normative Pluralism - A Comparative Overview*, Ius Comparatum – Global Studies in Comparative Law 18, DOI 10.1007/978-3-319-28335-7_21

As far as religion is concerned 79.8 % of the population declare that they are followers of a form of Christianity. Of this 79.8 % of Christians, Reformed churches make up 7.2 %, Anglicans 3.8 %, Methodists 7.4 %, Lutherans 2.5 %, Presbyterians 1.9 %, Congregational churches 1.4 %, Roman Catholics 8.9 %, Pentecostal churches 7.3 %, other churches 12 %. African Independent Churches have a membership of 40.8 % of the total Christian population. Apart from Christian followers in SA there are also 0.2 % followers of the Jewish religion, 1.1 % followers of the Islamic faith, 1.3 % Hindu followers, and 0.1 % Buddhist believers. There is also a large segment of African Traditional Religion in SA. It is estimated that 12 % of the total of African Traditional Religion followers are in SA.[1]

Not only is there a plurality of cultures as is shown by the fact that the country has eleven official languages, there is also a plurality of religions which all claim their legitimate share of the public space.

The Historical and Political Processes

In 1652 a refreshment post was started at the Cape of Good Hope by the Dutch East Indian Company for their ships underway from the Netherlands to the East-Indies and back again. In 1806 the Cape of Good Hope became a British Colony. A significant section of the Dutch (by 1838 they also called themselves Afrikaners), especially from the eastern parts of the Cape Colony started trekking northwards to found their own republics away from British rule. The discovery of diamonds in 1867 and gold in 1886 brought about a large influx of foreigners and at the same time intensified the subjugation of the black inhabitants as a labour force for the mines. The Boers, as the Dutch was also known by then, resisted British encroachment but were finally defeated in the Anglo-Boer War (1899–1902) (Pretorius 2012). In 1910 the Union of South Africa came into existence, a union in which the British and the Afrikaners, as the Boers came to be known, ruled together until 1961 when South Africa became a republic after a whites only referendum. In 1948 the National Party was voted into power and they instituted a policy of Apartheid – the separate development of races in South Africa (Giliomee 2000). After growing resistance from the black population lead by the ANC under the leadership of Nelson Mandela against their exclusion from politics and the vote since 1910, and after 1948 against the policy of Apartheid, as well as a growing awareness amongst whites that Apartheid was not the answer to the problems of South Africa, a negotiated settlement was contemplated and reached in 1994. This brought about a whole new dispensation in South Africa: a Constitutional Democracy with a new legal system and guaranteed human rights.

---

[1](SouthAfrica.info. The Official Gateway http://www.southafrica.info/pls/procs/iac.page?p_tl=2779&p_t27372&p_t3=0&p_t. 13/4/2011; South African Christian Handbook 2007–2008: 69,74.).

The Notion of Religious Rules

Meaning Given to the Expression "Religious Rules" Plus a Short Discussion of the Difference Between Religious, Traditional and Cultural Rules

The concept of "religious rules" can have more than one meaning. It can mean the rules laid down by the state for all religions within the boundaries of the state. For many years, to a less or a larger extent, this was the case in South Africa. From 1652 until 1994 the political authorities – first the Political Council of the Dutch at the Cape (1652–1806), then the English colonial authorities (1806–1910) and after 1910 the political parties in power – determined the legal position of religions in South Africa through certain state laws that religions had to respect. It is not to say that, during the years mentioned, all religions in South Africa could not make internal rules for themselves; they could, but the state always had the final say and there were times in the history of South Africa when religions were severely hampered by the state in their development. There are many examples in the history of religions in South Africa of how the state made use of this power (Coertzen 2008).

The other meaning of religious rules would be the rules that religions develop for their own internal functioning. These internal rules would concern matters like the place and authority of sacred and confessional texts; the place, number, requirements, function and authority of religious assemblies as well as of office bearers of the religion. The internal religious legal system will also contain the rules and requirements regarding how to become a member and an office bearer; how disciplinary matters are handled; what the rules of the specific religion are with regard to matters like worship, sacraments, rituals, marriage, education, the teaching of the youth, women, mission work and evangelization and also how that specific religion sees itself in relation to other religions, the larger society and the state.

In the case of Christian churches these internal rules are often published as Church Orders.[2] Other religions have similar documents while still others, like African Traditional Religions, make use of oral traditions transferred from one generation to the other as a source for their internal order.

The internal rules of a religion can also be defined as the whole of general stipulations and regulations for a church or a religion, approved by a competent body of that religion (Bronkhorst 1959). These rules are of course only applicable within the specific religious community. Through its rules and regulations a religious community usually manifests itself as a legal person within the legal set up of the state. The rules and regulation of a religion, sometimes the mere tradition of a religion, are thereby also seen by the courts of the land as binding.[3] Seen from a legal

[2] See for instance *The Church Order of the Dutch Reformed Church 2011*. With Bylaws, Policy, Functional Decisions and Guidelines as established by the General Synod of 2011.

[3] There are many examples in the jurisprudence of South Africa which proofs exactly this point. One of the latest examples is the case of Kievits Kroon Country Estate (Pty) Ltd v. Mmoledi and others (LAC) (Unreported case no. JA78/10. 24-7-2012) (Tlaetsi JA).

perspective religious rules are the internal laws of association for either a church or a religion (Pienaar 1984). The internal rules of a religion are recognised by the courts of South Africa and it is seen as part of the religious freedom of religions to draw up such rules. Should it happen that a religion does not have internal rules, it will merely be disciplined through the existing laws of the land. In Taylor v Kurstag[4] the Constitutional Court considered it questionable whether the internal rules of a religious group qualified as "law of general application"[5] in order to legitimately limit the rights of a member. In issue here was the decision of the Beth Din (Jewish Ecclesiastical Court) to issue a "cherem" excommunicating one of the members of the religious community. The question was whether such excommunication infringed or limited the member's constitutional rights. Although the court found that the Beth Din, like any other religious tribunal, was subject to common law review jurisdiction of the courts and the decision of the tribunal was invalid in terms of South African law, its validity under Jewish law, which bound the member, was unaffected. Since the court found that there had been no evidence of bias, bad faith or unfairness on the part of the Beth Din and the right to fair administrative action had thus not been infringed, the application to have the decision of the Beth Din declared null and void was dismissed.

Since 1994/1996 the Constitution of South Africa guarantees freedom of religion which *inter alia* means that religions have the freedom to make their own rules which are applicable to them as a religion and which make them independent from the State. The rules limiting the rights of members may not be in contradiction to the Charter of Rights in the Constitution.[6]

The South African Constitution clearly distinguishes between religion, culture and tradition. Article 15 of the Constitution allows for freedom of religion. This implies that all the religions in South Africa are recognised and are granted the freedom to exercise their religion. Article 30 grants everyone the right to use the language and to participate in the cultural life of their choice as long as it is not inconsistent with any provision of the Bill of Rights while article 31(1) states that "Persons belonging to a cultural, religious or linguistic community may not be denied the right, with other members of that community (a) to enjoy their culture, practise their religion and use their language". They may also "form, join and maintain cultural, religious and other organs of civil society" as long as these rights are not exercised in a manner inconsistent with any provision of the Bill of Rights. Article 211 is about traditional leadership and the status of customary law in South Africa. It reads "(1) The institution, status and role of traditional leadership, according to customary law, are recognised, subject to the Constitution. (2) A traditional authority that observes a system of customary law may function subject to any applicable legislation and customs, which includes amendments to, or repeal of, that legislation or those customs. (3) The courts must apply customary law when

[4] Taylor v Kurtstag 2004 4 All SA 317 (w); 2005 1 SA 362 (W); 2005 7 BCLR 705 (W).

[5] The Constitution of the Republic of South Africa, 1996, article 36.

[6] The Constitution of the Republic of South Africa, 1996, Chapter 2 and article 36.

that law is applicable, subject to the Constitution and any legislation that specifically deal with customary law."

Religion and the Constitution of South Africa

The South African Constitution does not contain extensive rules and regulations for religions and freedom of religions but includes very important statements concerning both subjects. This implies that religion plays a very important role in the South African society as well as in its legal manifestations.

In the Preamble to the Constitution statements with important implications for the laws of the land as well as for the religions in the country are made when it is stated that "South Africa belongs to all who live in it, united in our diversity." This means that also the diversity of religions in South Africa can claim a lawful right to existence in the country. A few lines further in the Preamble we read "God protect our people" and this is followed by the last words of the Preamble "God bless South Africa". Although this is a very general reference to "God", the implication is firstly that "God", and indirectly religion, is recognised as very important for the existence, protection and wellbeing of South Africa and its people. Secondly this very general and rather vague reference to God means a legal recognition of the God of all the religions in South Africa, from the Triune God of Christianity to the God of the Jewish religion, as well as the God of the Muslim, Hindu, Buddhist, African Traditional religion(s) and whatever other religion is present in South Africa. The Constitutional recognition of the "God" of all South African religions does not imply that every religious person must consent to a "multiplicity of Gods". It is a constitutional recognition of the fact that there is a plurality of religions in South Africa with which government and citizens have to live, and all of which have an equal, legitimate and free place in South Africa. It means that government and citizens have to deal with this diversity/plurality in an unbiased, equal and fair way, granting each religion its rights. South Africa is not a secular or a religiously neutral state. To the contrary it is a country in which it is officially recognised that religion plays a very important role. Government can also not be neutral to religion but is obliged to respect, protect, promote fulfill religion as a human right.[7]

In article 15(1) of the Constitution we read "Everyone has the right to freedom of conscience, religion, thought, belief and opinion". Art 15(2) states that "Religious observances may be conducted at state or state aided institutions provided (a) that those observances follow rules made by the appropriate public authorities; (b) they are conducted on an equitable basis; and (c) attendance at them is free and voluntary". Article 15(3)(a) provides that articles 15(1) and (2) "does not prevent legislation recognising (i) marriages concluded under any tradition or system of religious, personal or family law, or (ii) systems of personal and family law under any tradition, or adhered to by persons professing a particular religion." Article 15(3)(b)

[7] The Constitution of the Republic of South Africa, 1996, art 7(3).

states that "recognition in terms of paragraph (a) must be consistent with this section and other provisions of the Constitution." We also read about religion in article 9(3) of the Constitution where it is stated that the state may not discriminate directly or indirectly against anyone on, *inter alia,* grounds of religion. In article 31 of the Constitution it is said

"(1) Persons belonging to a cultural, religious or linguistic community may not be denied the right, with other members of that community – (a) to enjoy their culture, practise their religion and use their language; and (b) to form, join and maintain cultural, religious and linguistic associations and other organs of civil; society.
(2) The rights in subsection (1) may not be exercised in a manner inconsistent with any provision of the Bill of Rights."

The fact is that religion plays a very important part in the Constitution and since legislation must be consistent with the Constitution[8] it results in the fact that religion is mentioned in many of the laws of the country.

Tensions Between Religious Rules and State Law

Article 31(1)(a) of the Constitution states that persons belonging to a religious community may not be denied the right, with other members of that community, to practise their religion. Following this there are various laws in South Africa which allow for the accommodation of religious freedom and the religious needs of people.[9]

This does not mean that there are no tensions between religion and other institutions in the SA society. Taking on these challenges is the challenge for the new South African democracy

At the moment some very interesting developments are taking place on the legal scene in South Africa. The newspaper *Die Burger* of 19 October 2012[10] in an article *Voorvadergeeste is 'n geldige rede (Ancestors are a legitimate reason)* wrote about a woman, Johannah Mmoledi, who had been working for the Kievits Kroon Country Estate for the previous 8 years. During her own time she attended a course to qualify as a traditional healer. After this course she asked for a month's leave of absence from work to attend a fulltime course to qualify as a sangoma (a traditional healer). Her employers refused her request. She decided to attend the course anyway. Before her departure she handed her employers a letter from a traditional healer in which the healer declared that he examined her and found her to be plagued by the ancestors. On her return to work there was a disciplinary hearing, she was found guilty of

[8]The Constitution of the Republic of South Africa, 1996, art 2.

[9]Laws like Childrens Act 38 of 2005; Childrens Justice Act 75 of 2008; Electronics Communication Act 36 of 2005;and the South African Schools Act no 84 of 1996 as amended, Chapter 2(7).

[10]Voorvadergeeste is 'n geldige rede sê die hof. Die Burger 19 Oktober 2012, p.6.

unauthorised absence and fired. She appealed to the CCMA (Commission for Conciliation, Mediation and Arbitration) which found that her dismissal was unfair and reappointed her in her post. The employers appealed to the Labour Court where three judges found that the employers showed contempt to her culture and religion when they rejected her letter from the traditional healer, explaining why she had to attend the course. In their judgement the judges found that the argument that Western standards are opposed to African culture is misplaced. "It would be disingenuous of anybody to deny that our society is characterised by a diversity of cultures, traditions and beliefs. This being the case, there will always be instances where these diverse cultural and traditional beliefs and practices create challenges within our society, the workplace being no exception. The Constitution of the country itself recognises these rights and practices. It must be recognised that some of these cultural beliefs and practices are strongly held by those who subscribe [to] them and regard them as part of their lives. A paradigm shift is necessary by the state and also by the courts of the land, one must appreciate the kind of society we live in. Accommodating one another is nothing else but "botho" or "Ubuntu" which is part of our heritage as society".[11]

Strategies and Tools Available to Lessen Tensions

Under the new constitutional dispensation in South Africa the Constitution is the supreme law of the land (Art. 2) and is binding on all judicial organs of the state (Artt. 2 and 7). The Constitutional Court, which is an important part of an independent judiciary, has the power to decide on the constitutionality of any parliamentary or provincial Bill (Art. 167 (4) (b)). Chapter two of the Constitution is a Bill of Rights. The Bill of Rights applies to all laws and binds the legislature, the executive, the judiciary and all organs of state. Provisions in the Bill of Rights bind a natural or a legal person if, and to the extent that they are applicable, taking into account the nature of the right and the nature of the duty imposed by the right. A legal person is entitled to the rights in the Bill of Rights to the extent required by the nature of the rights and the nature of that legal person (Art. 8). The rights in the Bill of Rights include the right to equality before the law and the right to equal protection and benefit of the law (Art. 9 (1)); the right not to be discriminated against (Art. 9 (2)), the right to dignity, freedom and security (Artt. 10, 11 and 12), freedom of expression (Art. 16), assembly, demonstration, petition and association (Artt. 17 and 18); the right to make political choices (Art. 19); the right to citizenship (Art. 20);

[11] *Changing Traditional view's,*in De Rebus, October 2012, pp 53–54 Both the terms "Ubuntu" and "botho" denotes humaness or human kindness and can also be seen as African ethics The case referred to is *Kievits Kroon Country Estate (Pty) Ltd v Mmoledi and others* (LAC) (unreported case no JA78/10, 24-7-2012) (Tlaetsi JA). Other cases in which the same trend can be found are Bhe v Magistrate, Kayelitsha (Commission for Gender Equality as Amicus Curiae); Shibi v Sithole; South African Human Rights Commission v President of the Republic of South Africa 2005 (1) BCLR 1 (KH); Alexkor Ltd v Richersveld Community 2003 (12) BCLR 1301 (KH).

freedom of movement and residence (Art. 21); as well as freedom of trade, occupation and profession (Art. 22); full access to the courts; and fair and lawful administrative justice mechanisms, including rights concerning detention, arrest, and accusation (Artt. 33, 34 and 35). Other provisions provide for specific rights in areas such as economic activity, labour relations (Art. 23), property and housing (Artt. 25 and 26), environment (Art. 24), health care, food, water and social security (Art. 27), children, language and culture, education (Artt. 28, 29, 30 and 31), and conditions under which a state of emergency can be declared (Art. 37).[12] Article 36 of the Constitution contains the conditions under which the rights in the Bill of Rights can be limited. In one way or the other all of the above mentioned rights relate to religions and their rights too and religions should reflect on this.

Freedom of religion is specifically mentioned in article 15 of the Constitution while religion is also mentioned in articles 9(3); 30; 31 and 185. The religious rights as well as all the other above mentioned rights are guaranteed for every individual as well as for all other legal persons (Art. 7). Apart from that which is said about religion in the articles 9(3); 15; 30; 31 and 185 not much is said about what freedom of religion means in South Africa. About the content of freedom of religion Justice Albie Sachs wrote in 1990, 6 years before the final Constitution of South Africa was approved: "Ideally in South Africa, all religious organisations and persons concerned with the study of religion would get together and draft a charter of religious rights and responsibilities …. It would be up to the participants themselves to define what they consider to be their fundamental rights" (Sachs 1990). This makes article 234 of the Constitution very important. Under the heading "Charters of Rights", it reads: "In order to deepen the culture of democracy established by the Constitution, Parliament may adopt Charters of Rights consistent with the provisions of the Constitution." This provision inspired a group of people from different religions, academic fields and walks of life to formulate a South African Charter of Religious Rights and Freedoms.

The *South African Charter of Religious Rights and Freedoms* was drafted over a period of several years by a Continuation Committee of academics, religious leaders, government commissioners and international legal experts in consultation with all the major religions in South Africa, human rights groups and media bodies. The Charter was publically endorsed at a ceremony on 21 October 2010 at the University of Johannesburg in the presence of the Honorable Mr Dikgang Moseneke, Deputy Chief Justice of South Africa. At that occasion 91 leaders representing religious, academic, legal, human rights and media organizations in South Africa as well as international advisors endorsed the Charter. The signatories included the representatives of the Jewish Religion, 24 Christian denominations, the Muslim Judicial Council, The Ismaeli Community, The Jami'atul 'Ulama (The Council of Muslim Theologians), the Hindu Faith (The Arya Samay SA, The Hindu Co-ordinating Council, the Sri Sathya Sai Baba Council, the Tamil Federation), The National

[12] See also South Africa The New Legal System, http://www.photius.com/countries/south_africa/government/south_government_the_new_legal_system.html. 2013/12/07. Sources: The Library of Congress Country Studies; CIA World Fact Book.

Spiritual Council of the Baha'is of South Africa, African Traditional Religion, African Independent Churches, The National Commission for Culture, Language and Religion, Women's organizations, Youth Movements, The Education Desk of the Dutch Reformed Church, The Griqua National Council, The Griqua Independent Church, The Commission for Religious Freedom of the Evangelical Alliance of South Africa, the Evangelical Alliance of Southern Africa, Trans World Radio, Media Production Houses, The Christian Network, the Jesuit Institute, The Elected School of Amadlosi and the Interdenominational Ministries. Since 2010 many more individuals, large bodies in society as well as large religious groups like the Zionist Christian Church and groups from the African Traditional Religions have endorsed the Charter making the Council even more representative of the religions in South Africa.

The total of practicing religious believers represented by the signatories is estimated to be approximately 10.5 million of the total South African population. At the moment (May 2015) it is estimated that the total number of subscribers of the Charter has grown to about 15 million people. This makes the South African Council for Religious Rights and Freedoms which are the custodians of the Charter the most representative body of religions in South Africa

The charter defines the rights and freedoms that each religion can claim while working together with other religions in the public sphere for the common good of the country. The Charter is also a very useful tool for religions to determine their own identity in terms of the rights and freedoms that they can legitimately claim. If religions do not use this tool they risk that their rights and freedoms are determined by the courts of the country. Even if parliament does not enact the Charter, religions can always make it part of their own body of rules and regulations which will have to be taken into account by the courts.

The Charter consists of a preamble of 8 articles which explains why a charter is needed. This is followed by the 12 articles with sub-divisions of the Charter itself in which the religious rights and freedoms of religious people and communities in South Africa are stated. The Charter expresses what freedom of religion means to religious believers and organizations within the South African context, as well as the daily rights, responsibilities and freedoms that are associated with this right. These include: the right to gather to observe religious belief; freedom of expression regarding religion; the right of citizens to make choices according to their convictions; the right to change their faith; the right to be educated in their faith; the right to educate their children in accordance with their philosophical and religious convictions; the right to refuse to perform certain duties or assist in activities that violate their religious belief.

Currently the Charter is available is Afrikaans, English, Zulu, Xhosa, Suthu, Tswana and also in German.

After the public endorsement of the Charter, a *South African Council for the Promotion and Protection of Religious Rights and Freedoms* was established to oversee and promote the process of the Charter being officially taken note of by Parliament as a document coming out of the religious communities of South Africa.

The Council for the Promotion and Protection of Religious Rights and Freedoms is continuously engaging with more and more religious bodies as well as with financial, academic and cultural bodies and with various trade and labor unions for their support in taking the Charter to Parliament. Political parties are also met to inform them about the Charter and the effort to have it enacted by Parliament.

According to art 15(3) (a) (ii) of the Constitution legislation recognising systems of personal and family law under any tradition or religion is possible. All religions in South Africa can therefore develop a system of personal and family law which reflects their teachings. This system of laws will be recognised as long as it is consistent with all the provisions of the Constitution (Art. 15 (b)).

An example of what these provisions allow is the Act regarding the Recognition of Customary Marriages[13] "The Act recognises customary marriages while seeking to ensure the equal status and capacity of the spouses. Polygyny is permitted as long as the husband has a written contract approved by a court which will then regulate the matrimonial property system of his marriages" (Currie, De Waal, and others 2005).

Given the existence of different systems of personal and family laws in South Africa, article 15(3) also confirms the possibility to convert from one system to another. In South Africa there are different possibilities to marry – civil, religious or traditional. Within the civil category there is also the possibility of civil unions. A conversion from a traditional marriage to a civil one has always been possible as long as the legal requirements of civil marriage are respected, which in such a case would mean that the civil law requirement of monogamy must be accepted.[14] Couples married according to customary or religious law before 1996 were considered not to be legally married, their children were considered to be illegitimate and the parties had to rely on traditional or religious authorities and not on the civil courts to enforce the consequences of their marriage. Today citizens of South Africa can decide under which system of law they want to marry as long as the marriage is consistent with art 15 and the other provisions of the Constitution (Currie, De Waal, and others 2005).

According to art 15 (3) of the SA Constitution there are different systems of law available for citizens who do not want to be subject to religious norms. With regard to marriage, citizens can choose to marry according to civil law[15] (which can include a religious component, as the law provides that a minister of a religion is considered to be a civil servant). People can also choose to marry according to the Civil Union Act,[16] or according to the Recognition of Customary Marriages.[17]

Even before 1996 South Africa did not have a state religion established by law,[18] although it can be said that between 1652 and 1994 the state authorities, at a later

[13] Recognition of Customary Marriages Act 120 of 1998.

[14] See *Seedat's Executors v The Master* (Natal) 1917AD 302, 309 (Innes CJ).

[15] Marriage Act 25 of 1961.

[16] Civil Union Act 17 of 2006.

[17] Recognition of Customary Marriages, Act 120 of 1998.

[18] Aronson v Estate Hart 1950 2 All SA 13 (A); 19501 SA 539 (AD) 561; Buren Uitgewers (Edms) Bpk v Raad van Beheer oor Publikasies 1975 1 SA 446 (C); 1975 1 SA 379 (C) 419; De Waal v Van der Horst 1918 TPD 277 281.

stage through the policies of political parties, had a very strong control over religion. After 1996 the Constitution was established as the supreme law of the Republic of South Africa. The Constitution sets as its aims to heal the divisions of the past and to establish a society based on democratic values, social justice and fundamental human rights. It also has the aim to "lay the foundations for democratic and open society in which government is based on the will of the people and every citizen is equally protected by law." (Preamble). Chapter 2 of the Constitution contains a Bill of Rights which is the cornerstone of democracy in South Africa: it "enshrines the rights of all the people in our country and affirms the democratic values of human dignity, equality and freedom." (Art. 7 (1)).

There are many examples that show that the state and the courts of the land respect the internal rules of religious organisations. The courts of the country have a history that they do not want to get involved in doctrinal affairs of religions. The courts also respect the internal rules and regulations of religious bodies regarding matters like the rules for membership, the election and functioning of office bearers, disciplinary rules etc. The courts however do not hesitate to get involved when religious bodies violate the rules of natural justice or their own rules or when in the absence of their own rules they violate the laws of the land. In terms of guaranteed freedom of religion the courts of the land are obliged to take notice of the official documents of religions.

The South African Constitution and the laws of the land do not contain religiously motivated exemptions from laws of general application. Article 36 of the Constitution does allow for the limitation of the rights in the Bill of Rights. The limitation of these rights are however subject to strict conditions. They are:

(1) The rights may be limited only in terms of law of general application to the extent that the limitation is reasonable and justifiable in an open and democratic society based on human dignity, equality and freedom, taking into account all relevant factors, including –

  (a) the nature of the right;
  (b) the importance of the purpose of the limitation;
  (c) the nature and extent of the limitation;
  (d) the relation between limitation and its purpose; and
  (e) less restrictive means to achieve the purpose

Conclusion

The laws with regard to religions in South Africa start with the Preamble of the Constitution which utters the prayers "May God protect our people" and "God bless South Africa" to be followed by article 1(a) "The Republic of South Africa is one sovereign democratic state founded on the following values: (a) Human dignity, the achievement of equality and the advancement of human rights and freedoms." This is followed by the Bill of Rights in the Constitution[19] which includes amongst others, articles on equality, human dignity, life, freedom of religion belief an opinion, freedom of expression; freedom of association, labour relations, education, language and culture, cultural, religious and linguistic communities, just administrative action, access to courts and the limitation of rights. All of this would be an adequate description of the place of religious liberty, equality and non-discrimination in South Africa.

It is however often found that neither the state nor the religions in the country have an adequate understanding of what religious liberty really entails. Article 185 of the Constitution allows for a Commission for the Promotion and Protection of the Rights of Cultural, Religious and Linguistic Communities. The functions of the Commission are (a) to promote respect for the rights of cultural, religious, and linguistic communities; (b) to promote and develop peace, friendship, humanity, tolerance and national unity among cultural, religious and linguistic communities, on the basis of equality, non-discrimination and free association; and (c) to recommend the establishment or recognition, in accordance with national legislation, of a cultural or other council or councils for a community or communities in South Africa (Art. 185 (1) (a), (b) and (c)). The Commission also has the power to achieve its primary goals including the power to monitor, investigate, research, educate, lobby, advise and to report on issues concerning the rights of cultural, religious and linguistic communities (Art. 185 (2)). Furthermore the Commission may report any matter which falls within its powers and functions to the Human Rights Commission for investigation (Art. 185 (3). This Commission can go a far way to educate the people and the religions in South Africa on what freedom of religion exactly means.

Apart from this there is also article 234 of the Constitution which determines that "In order to deepen the culture of democracy established by the Constitution, Parliament may adopt Charters of Rights consistent to the provisions of the Constitution." This is exactly what religions in South Africa did in 2010 when they developed the SA Charter of Religious Rights and Freedoms. Now the SA Council of Religious Rights and Freedoms is working on a strategy on how to get the Charter officially taken note of by Parliament.

All of this provides for a system which shows respect for human rights and especially freedom of religion, equality, non-discrimination and freedom of association. It also provides for religions in South Africa to take responsibility for their freedom of religion and to formulate their religious identity in terms that are coherent to freedom of religion.

References

Bronkhorst, A.J. 1959. Kerkorde. In *Christelijke encyclopedie*. Kampen: JH Kok.
Coertzen, P. 2008. Freedom of religion – Then and now. *Studia Historiae Ecclesiasticae*, 115–139.

[19]The Constitution of the Republic of South Africa, 1996, Chapter 2. See *supra*, pp. 8–9.

Currie, Iain, and Johan de Waal in association with Lawyers for Human Rights and the Law Society of South Africa. 2005. *The bill of rights handbook* fifth edition. Juta: Landsdowne 7779. p 356.

Giliomee, Herman. 2000. *Apartheid 'n ander blik.* In *Geskiedenis van Suid-Afrika. Van Voortye tot Vandag.* Fransjohan Pretorius (Red). In opdrag van die Geskiedeniskommissie van die Suid-Afrikaanse Akademie vir Wetenskap en Kuns. Tafelberg, Kaapstad, 429–441

Pienaar, G. 1984. (2). *Die Regsposisie van Gereformeerde Kerke in Suid-Afrika.* In die Skriflig 18/71.

Pretorius, Fransjohan. 2012. Fransjohan Pretorius, *Almal se oorlog: die Anglo-Boeroorlog (1899–1902).* In Geskiedenis van Suid-Afrika. Van Voortye tot Vandag. Fransjohan Pretorius (Red). In opdrag van die Geskiedeniskommissie van die Suid-Afrikaanse Akademie vir Wetenskap en Kuns. Tafelberg, Kaapstad, p 238.

Sachs, Albie. 1990. *Protecting human rights in a New South Africa. Contemporary South African debates*, 46 and 47. Cape Town: Oxford University Press.

Chapter 22
Striking the Balance Between Religious Rules and State Law: Spain

Javier Martínez-Torrón

Abstract This chapter examines the interaction between religious and state laws in Spain. After describing the basic normative framework, the author analyses the main areas in which such interaction takes place: the civil effects of religious rules on marriage, State laws and institutions in which an identifiable religious origin can be observed, State laws aimed at offering a specific protection of the autonomy of churches and religious groups, the exemptions from generally applicable laws on religious or conscience grounds, and the wearing of personal religious symbols in public areas or institutions. The author notes that a large part of the reception of religious rules by State laws relies on the Concordat with the Catholic Church and similar cooperation agreements with three other religious communities. Among other criticism to Spanish current law and practice, the author points out that, by failing to extend the agreements system to other religious communities in comparable situation, the Spanish State ignores one of the main provisions of the 1980 Organic Law on Religious Freedom, in breach of the constitutional principle of equality.

Introduction

Spain is a country predominantly Catholic, although religious pluralism has developed in the last decades as a consequence, mainly, of two factors: immigration (which has brought a relatively large number of Muslims, Orthodox Christians and Protestants) and the advance of atheism and agnosticism, as well as the expansion of deinstitutionalized personal belief systems (Martínez-Torrón 2014, paras 1–43).

For almost five centuries Spain was a Catholic monarchy, with only ephemeral interruptions in the 19th and 20th centuries. Catholic religion was the official religion of the State, and was especially protected—and controlled—by the secular political power. As a consequence, many provisions of the canon law of the Roman Catholic Church were part of the Spanish law.

J. Martínez-Torrón (✉)
Unversidad Complutense de Madrid, Madrid, Spain
e-mail: jmtorron@der.ucm.es

R. Bottoni et al. (eds.), *Religious Rules, State Law, and Normative Pluralism - A Comparative Overview*, Ius Comparatum – Global Studies in Comparative Law 18, DOI 10.1007/978-3-319-28335-7_22

The 1978 Constitution

The situation changed radically with the Constitution of 1978 (hereinafter CE, *Constitución Española*), which is in force today. Constituted as a full democracy in the shape of a parliamentary monarchy, the State has no longer an official religion and is supposed to keep a neutral stance towards religions and other worldviews. The constitutional provisions on religion were developed by the Organic Law on Religious Freedom of 1980 (hereinafter LOLR, *Ley Orgánica de Libertad Religiosa*), which is the main statute on religion.

Articles 16 and 14 CE design a system of relations between State and religion defined by four main principles: *religious freedom, equality, State neutrality, and State cooperation with religion* (Ferrer Ortiz 1989; Martínez-Torrón 2014, paras. 44–54 and 75–100).

According to the principle of *neutrality*, the State has no official religion and may not make judgments about the value or merits of different religions or beliefs, and in general about strictly religious issues. Constituted as a democratic secular State, the Spanish legal system is based upon values and principles of exclusively secular nature—although many of them, as usually occurs in most countries, have a religious origin. No specific role is or can be assigned to any particular religion, or to religion in general, in shaping the legal and political system. Spain does not have personal laws based on religious affiliation. On the contrary, according to the Constitution (art. 14), the Spanish are equal before the law and shall not be subject to discrimination on the ground of religion (among others). In addition, art. 16 CE provides that 'nobody shall be obliged to declare about his ideology, religion or beliefs'.

However, the principle of *cooperation* distinguishes Spain from separationist systems, and therefore the reciprocal autonomy of State and churches is not understood in terms of strict separation. Public authorities, at any level, are constitutionally bound to take into account the religious choices of citizens. Implicit in this approach is a constitutional consideration of religion as a positive social factor. This, however, does not imply a lesser protection of atheistic or agnostic beliefs, for it is undisputed that the 'freedom of ideology, religion and worship' recognized by art. 16 CE protects all types of beliefs—theistic, atheistic or agnostic; institutional or strictly personal.

Unilateral and Bilateral Legal Sources

After the 1978 Constitution, the sources of the Spanish legal system are of secular nature, and *no religious law—Catholic or other—is per se a legal source for State law*. However, the Spanish legal system admits bilateral *sources of mixed nature*, in which one of the parties is a religious community.

The first and most important of these bilateral sources is the Concordat with the Catholic Church, composed by four thematic agreements signed in 1979 (on juridical affairs, economic affairs, education and cultural affairs, and religious assistance in the Army), plus another agreement signed in 1976 (Díaz Moreno 1979, Fornés 1980). The Concordat is aimed at regulating the legal status of the Catholic Church in Spain and is binding for the Spanish State as well as for the Catholic Church. It is both a canonical and a secular legal source; and, having being signed by the Spanish State and the Holy See, it has a standing similar to international treaties.

There are other agreements between the State and religious communities whose legal status is less clear. After the Concordat was signed, art. 7 LOLR, inspired by the constitutional principle of equality, opened for other churches or religious communities the possibility to sign cooperation agreements with the State—in particular for registered religious communities that have been recognized 'well-known roots' (*notorio arraigo*) in Spain. Such agreements must be approved by a specific parliamentary statute and are negotiated and signed at the national level; consequently, they are not comparable to international treaties. From a *formal* perspective they are statutory laws, but their *substantial* content is necessarily determined by an institutional agreement negotiated between the government and the relevant religious communities (Martínez-Torrón 1994, 95–116). So far, there are only three cooperation agreements, approved by statute the same day, in 1992, with Protestantism, Judaism and Islam, organized in three respective federations.

Religious legal provisions, definitions or principles are often received implicitly in Spanish law mainly in two ways: through the Concordat with the Catholic Church and the cooperation agreements with religious minorities; and through specific provisions of unilateral State legislation. The tendency is to provide a comparable legal reception of religious laws or legal concepts to all religions within the same *level of State cooperation*. In this respect, we can distinguish, *grosso modo*, the following levels of religious denominations from the perspective of State cooperation: (1) religious communities that have reached a cooperation agreement with the State (Catholic Church; Protestant, Jewish and Islamic communities); (2) religious communities that have been recognized well-known roots in Spain by the Ministry of Justice but have not negotiated a cooperation agreement with the State (Mormons, Jehovah's Witnesses, Buddhists, Christian Orthodox); (3) and religious communities that have been registered in the Registry of Religious Entities but have not been recognized well-know roots in Spain.

In this paper I will explain the main areas in which there is a direct or indirect reception of religious rules, adding, when necessary, some comments about the tensions that may emerge.

Partial Reception of Personal Religious Laws Governing Marriage

Although Spain does not have personal laws based on religious affiliation, personal religious laws may have an influence on the personal legal status under civil law, in particular in the area of marriage. There is a long-standing and almost uninterrupted tradition of recognizing full civil effects to one type of religious marriage, namely the marriage according to the rules of Roman Catholic canon law. The 1978 Constitution (art. 32) adapted this tradition to the new constitutional principles and kept an open mind towards the civil recognition of religious marriage, Catholic or else. This constitutional approach to marriage was confirmed by different laws in the ensuing years. Currently, Spain has a plural matrimonial system whose main characteristics can be described as follows (López Alarcón & Navarro-Valls 2010).

Everybody has the right to marry in accordance to the religious ceremony of his choice (article 2 LOLR) and no civil ceremony, before or after the religious rite, is required by law. However, under the LOLR the right to a religious marriage does not include per se the right to the recognition of civil effects of that marriage. As a general rule, a specific form of religious marriage produces *civil effects only when it has been explicitly recognized by the State*, either by an agreement with the relevant religious community or by State unilateral legislation (arts. 59–60 Civil Code).[1]

Until recently, Spanish civil law had recognized civil effects to religious marriages only by agreement; in particular, the 1979 Concordat and the 1992 Agreements recognized civil effects to Catholic, Evangelical, Jewish and Islamic marriages. However, a 2015 reform of the Civil Code and the Civil Registry has extended—by unilateral State laws—to the religious communities with 'well-known roots' the same type of civil recognition of religious marriage currently applicable to the Evangelical, Jewish and Islamic marriages (art. 60 Civil Code, as modified by Law 15/2015).

In order to obtain civil effects, a marriage celebrated in accordance with one of the recognized religious forms must meet two *requirements*: it must comply with the requisites imposed by the Civil Code on personal capacity and consent; and, once celebrated, it must be registered in the Civil Registry. Civil registrars must scrutinize that the parties to a religious marriage comply with the civil law requisites; this is normally done after the celebration in the case of Catholic marriages and before the celebration in the case of other religious marriages (Martínez-Torrón 2014, paras. 549–550 and 557). It must be noted also that the three 1992 Agreements (art. 7) and the new art. 60 Civil Code provide that, to have civil effects, the religious celebration of marriage must include the expression of the parties' consent in the presence of a religious minister of the relevant religious community and at least two other witnesses of full age. This requisite is particularly significant for Islamic marriages, whose religious form does not require the presence of an imam as a condition of validity; which means that, in practice, the State law imposes an additional requisite on the religious form of celebration of Muslim marriages.

The legal position of *Catholic marriage* is superior to the other recognized religious marriages, in accordance with the international obligations assumed by the State in the 1979 Concordat, which are a consequence of the stronger social rooting

[1]There are two exceptions to this rule, in application of provisions of private international law: the Civil Code accepts the civil validity of marriages celebrated abroad by Spanish citizens in a religious form accepted by the law of the land (art. 49); and of marriages celebrated in Spain by two foreign citizens in a religious form recognized by the personal law of any of them (art. 50). Polygamous marriages, however, are not recognized, for monogamy is considered part of the Spanish public order—although such marriages may be granted some 'peripheral' effects, especially with regard to the rights of wives and children (Juárez Pérez 2012).

of the Catholic Church in Spain and of the well-established historical influence of canonical marriage on the legal concept of marriage in Spain (as in all Western cultures). The most significant difference is that Spanish law recognizes civil effects not only to the canonical form of celebration but also to some types of decisions of *ecclesiastical jurisdiction* on the issue of the termination of marriage—while the other religious marriages are recognized civil effects only as a valid form of celebration. It has been argued that, together with the long-standing tradition of civil effects of ecclesiastical jurisdiction in Spain (as in Italy or Portugal), the main reason for this differential treatment is the certainty and 'reliability' of ecclesiastical jurisdiction vis-à-vis the State: Roman canon law offers a unified and hierarchically structured jurisdiction, with an ancient, consistent and well-known body of jurisprudence and case law.

More precisely, two types of ecclesiastical decisions are recognized by civil law: an ecclesiastical court's judgment declaring the *nullity* of a marriage, and the *dissolution* of a valid but unconsummated marriage by a specific act of the Pope. Both the Concordat and the Civil Code provide that these ecclesiastical resolutions shall have civil effects upon request of at least one of the parties and after a competent civil court declares that the ecclesiastical resolution is 'adjusted to State law'.[2] Normally, the civil courts perform merely a formal control of the ecclesiastical decision and not a substantial control of its merits (i.e., they check that the decision is authentic and final, and that none of the parties oppose to its recognition).

The decisions of *religious jurisdictions other than Catholic* on the termination of marriage, or on any other issue relating to their respective religious marriages, are not recognized civil effects. Of course, nothing prevents the parties from submitting to a religious jurisdiction, by mutual consent, the termination of their marriage and other issues linked to it, such as the economic consequences thereof or questions connected with the custody and future care of the children. However, the judgments adopted by religious courts shall not have civil effects either as judicial decisions or as arbitration awards.[3] Nevertheless, the decisions of religious jurisdictions might have some indirect effects through mediation, if incorporated in the divorce agreement that the parties eventually reach and must later submit to the civil judge for approval. And even in that case, the civil judge is not bound by the parties' agreement when he observes that it is 'harmful for the children or seriously prejudicial for one of the spouses' (art. 90 Civil Code).

---

[2] Moreover, in application of art. 63 of the Council Regulation (EC) No. 2201/2003, of 27 November 2003, ecclesiastical decisions on the nullity or dissolution of canonical marriages, once executed by Spanish civil courts, shall be recognized with civil effects in any Member State of the European Union as if they were decisions of nullity or divorce rendered by Spanish civil courts. The same rule applies to Portugal, Italy and Malta, whose concordats also accept the civil effects of ecclesiastical decisions (Rodríguez Chacón 2005).

[3] Under Spanish law, arbitration is possible only with regard to 'conflicts about matters of free disposal in accordance with the law' (see art. 1 of the *Ley* 60/2003, 23 December 2003, *de Arbitraje*), and family law provisions, save for questions relating to the determination of the economic regime of marriage, are not disposable by the parties.

Religious marriage with civil effects is a *choice* offered by Spanish State laws to the members of some religions, but *not a legal obligation* at all. *Civil marriage is available to all citizens irrespective of their religion*, if they meet the relevant civil law requirements. The same rule applies to *the civil jurisdiction*, which is available to all citizens regardless of the form of celebration of their marriage, civil or religious.[4] The recognition of the civil effects of ecclesiastical decisions declaring the nullity or decreeing the dissolution of canonical marriages does not imply any reservation of jurisdiction in favour of ecclesiastical courts. Civil and religious jurisdictions are separated and autonomous, and each of them applies its respective law. There is not, in principle, mutual interference between civil and religious jurisdictions.

For the rest, religious marriage laws on aspects other than the form of celebration may have some civil effects through the *matrimonial agreements* that the contracting parties may voluntary enter into before or after marrying.[5] These agreements must be solemnized by a notary public and abide by the general norms on contract. They often take place before the celebration of marriage and usually refer to the economic regime of marriage, which under the Spanish law can be freely decided by the contracting parties. Matrimonial agreements may also extend to other aspects of the marital union as, for example, the religious upbringing of the offspring. However, if there is a later disagreement on issues related to the children's education or welfare, prior agreements that are the consequence of a religious legal provision may be appealed to the civil jurisdiction. In any event, the civil efficacy of religious family law through matrimonial agreements is restricted by Article 1328 Civil Code, which declares null and void 'any stipulation contrary to the law or accepted principles of morality, or limiting the equal rights of each spouse'.

With respect to *other aspects of family law*, the most significant aspects of parent–child relationships are regulated by Spanish civil law and do not leave room for the application of religious legal provisions, which, being at stake the rights of minors, cannot prevail over civil law provisions aimed at the protection of those rights. Something similar occurs in the area of *inheritance rights*. Religious law provisions can only be effective through their explicit acceptation by the testator, taking into account that Spanish law follows the Roman law pattern and impose strict limitations on the testator's freedom to decide on the future destination of his properties.

State Laws and Institutions with Identifiable Religious Origin

Being a secular State that does not recognize any religious law directly as a source of law, Spain does not have any religious law applicable to all citizens. However, Spanish law includes some rules, institutions and values with a clearly

[4] See arts. 73, 81 & 85 Civil Code.

[5] See arts. 1325–1335 Civil Code.

distinguishable religious origin—normally Catholic—which, having been 'secularized' with the passage of time, are applicable or available to all citizens irrespective of their religious affiliation.

Thus, for example, the institutions of *civil marriage and Civil Registry* in Spain date back only to 1870, when they were created following the patterns of canonical (Catholic) marriage and of Baptism registries existing in Catholic parishes. In the same line, values such as the monogamy of marriage and the equal position of the spouses vis-à-vis the celebration of marriage were taken from Catholic canon law (the legal equality of husband and wife, however, did not extend to other aspects of marriage law and succession law, in which the woman was depending on her husband's will for many aspects concerning the disposition of her property; full legal equality would not be implemented until the late twentieth century).

Other examples of Catholic religious rules adopted by the State are the recognition of some religious *festivities* as national, regional or local festivities (e.g., Christmas, Good Friday, Corpus Christi, etc.); and the establishment of Sunday as the regular day of rest in the labour environment, in school and in public services. Thus, the Statute of Workers (art. 37.1) provides that, Sunday shall be a weekly day of rest for workers as a rule, although labour contracts may stipulate otherwise; in fact, in most regions in Spain shops and business must be closed on Sundays (and, of course, schools and most public offices).

The legal choice of Sunday as the ordinary day of rest for workers has created some problems in practice for members of religions that do not have any moral difficulty to work on Sunday but, instead, have a strict obligation of religious rest or other religious duties in different days of the week. Spanish law, so far, has not been very receptive with respect to this type of problems (Meseguer Velasco 2012). Thus, the 1992 Agreements (art. 12) do not recognize properly any individual right on this aspect of religious observance. They just contains a sort of 'declaration of good intentions' with regard to the *possibility* of fixing the weekly rest of Jewish, Evangelical or Muslim employees in a way compatible with their religious duties. Such possibility is *subject to an agreement between the parties of the labour contract*. Identical treatment is given to the observance of Jewish and Islamic religious festivities. The need of an agreement between employee and employer gives the latter, in practice, unlimited discretion to accept or reject the requests of his employees, for employers have no legal obligation to search for a reasonable accommodation of the employee's religious duties. Moreover, the Agreements do not distinguish between labour relationships with private employers and with public agencies or companies, which means that the position of civil servants is equally vulnerable.

Not surprisingly, article 12 of the 1992 Agreements has been criticized by scholars (Martínez-Torrón 1994, 153–155), which have pointed out that it is not only redundant, but it also contains a restrictive interpretation of the religious freedom protected by the Constitution, the Organic Law on Religious Freedom and the Statute of Workers, whose art. 17.1 specifically forbids indirect discrimination—a notion that should be interpreted in the light of the European Union's Council Directive 2000/78/EC. The origin of this restrictive interpretation of the employee's religious freedom is to be found in a judgment of the Constitutional Court of 1985,[6]

[6] STC 19/1985.

also criticized by scholars (Castro Jover 1990), which rejected the claim of a Seventh-Day Adventist woman dismissed for refusing to work on Saturdays; the Court's reasoning revolved around the secular character of Sundays as a common day of rest in contemporary Spain—as in other countries of Christian tradition—despite its religious origins.

Article 12 of 1992 Agreements, however, recognizes the *students' right* to the observance of sabbatical rest, the attendance to collective prayer and the commemoration of some holy days of their religion. Upon request of their parents or legal guardians, students of public schools and private schools funded by the State have the unconditional right to be excused from attending classes or passing examinations in those days.[7] The same article of the Agreements contains a parallel rule for *applicants to enter the civil service* that have been summoned for examination in one of their holy days, but their right is subject to practical limitations—their examination shall be transferred to an alternative date if they request it, except when there is a 'good cause' to refuse their petition. In practice, this right is not easy to implement, for typically public examinations to enter most branches of civil service are competitive and in writing, and require that all applicants pass an identical examination, in the same date and under the same conditions.

The Guarantee of Internal Religious Autonomy

Art. 2.2 LOLR guarantees to all religious communities some characteristic expressions of autonomy, such as the right to establish places of worship or meeting, to appoint and train their ministers, to propagate their faith, and to freely communicate with their own organizations or with other churches, inside the country as well as abroad.

Art. 6.1 LOLR guarantees a *reinforced* autonomy for religious communities *registered* in the Registry of Religious Entities (Otaduy 1987). They have 'full autonomy' to establish their own organizational rules, internal regime and personnel regime. Their normative autonomy includes the possibility of enacting, for them and for their internal entities, 'clauses aimed at safeguarding their ethos and religious identity, as well as the due respect for their beliefs'. This provision has been in practice of particular significance for private religious schools, whose religious identity has been protected by the Spanish laws on education; and also for the determination of the legal status of teachers of Catholic religion in public schools, whose qualification depends on the judgment of ecclesiastical authorities.

Religious communities are considered a specific type of entities by Spanish law, and the tendency is to exclude from the common rules of labour law the relation-

[7]As far as I know, there is no sociological study on the level of respect for this exemption in Spanish schools in practice, but occasionally some abuses have been reported (by parents complaining that their children's requests for adapting examination dates coincident in Sabbath or in a religious holy day have been ignored).

ships that take place inside a religious community as far as they refer to its spiritual mission and to its religious ministers.

The type of relationship between a *religious minister* and his respective religious community varies depending on each community. In Spanish law it is normally accepted that this relationship is out of the boundaries of State labour law and governed by the internal rules of the relevant religious denomination. Neither ministers are deemed employees nor religious communities are deemed employers. This is the position of the Spanish courts with particular reference to those activities of religious ministers that are part of their religious compromises and mission, such as worship or spiritual assistance.[8] The Constitutional Court has taken a similar stance with regard to the activities performed by members of religious orders in service of their respective communities, confirming the precedent case law of labour courts.[9] The Constitutional Court has excluded from the scope of labour law even the relationship between a member of a Catholic religious order and a school run by her institution, even though that person worked as ordinary teacher and performed educational tasks comparable to those performed by her lay colleagues in the same school. According to the Court, all the activity done by the religious was permeated by and had to be seen in the light of her religious compromise and vows; she was not just doing a job for the school, she was complying with the religious mission assigned by her superiors, and indeed her religious condition was the very reason why she performed those teaching tasks at the school.[10]

Leaving aside religious ministers or members of religious orders, the relationship between churches and their *employees* is subject to the ordinary rules of labour law, including the prohibition of discrimination contained in the Statute of Workers and in the EU Council Directive 2000/78 EC. The same applies to the employees of institutions run or explicitly inspired by religious communities, such as hospitals or schools. It should be taken into account, however, that the labour relationship in these cases is nuanced by the employees' duty of loyalty and respect for the religious rules or ethos of the relevant community or institution, protected by Article 6 LOLR. In the concrete case of private religious schools, funded or not with public money, Spanish laws on education have always recognized their right to have their own ethos, which must be accepted by the teachers and other staff, as well as by the students and the students' parents.[11]

There has not been much litigation regarding relationships between churches and their employees but some significant conflicts have arisen apropos of the situation of *religion teachers in public schools*, and in particular teachers of Catholic religion. The 1979 Concordat[12] provides that Catholic religion must be offered, as an elective

[8] See STS 3946/2001, 14 May 2001, FJ 3.

[9] See STC 63/1994, FJ 4.

[10] See *ibid.*

[11] See, for the law currently in force, art. 115 of the *Ley Orgánica* 2/2006, 3 May 2006, *de Educación*, which remained untouched in the reform operated by Organic Law 8/2013.

[12] In particular, the 1979 Agreement on Education and Cultural Affairs between Spain and the Holy See.

subject, in all public schools and shall be taught by teachers authorized by the competent diocesan bishop. These teachers are hired and paid by the State but selected by the Catholic Church. Diocesan bishops are competent to propose every year the persons appropriate for teaching Catholic religion, and their proposals are binding for State educational authorities. Once granted, the proposal of a person is automatically renewed every year, but the bishop can remove a teacher that he considers no longer adequate for that task. It is important to keep in mind that religion teachers in public schools are supposed to teach religious doctrines on behalf of the Catholic Church, fulfilling an ecclesiastical mission; they provide a confessional religious instruction and do not teach courses based on a neutral or purely academic approach to religion. Occasionally, problems have arisen when some persons have been deprived from their ecclesiastical permission to teach religion not because of lack of pedagogical capabilities but because their behaviour out of school was known to infringe serious moral principles of the Catholic Church or to be against the interests of the Church—for instance, people that lived in cohabitation or were actively involved in protests, strikes and demonstrations against policies on religion teachers.

The relevant bishops, in those cases, considered that such situations necessarily had an impact on the efficacy of religious instruction, in addition to constituting a scandal, and withdrew their *missio canonica* to teach religion in order to protect the credibility of the Church. Some cases of this type have reached the Constitutional Court (Valero Estarellas 2013), which has almost always decided in favour of the Catholic Church's autonomy to determine when a person was or was not appropriate to teach religion on behalf of the Catholic Church in a public school. However, the Court has also held that, existing a labour contract between the religion teacher and a public institution, the ecclesiastical autonomy is not free from control by the State jurisdiction, whose role is to scrutinize if the reasons that justified the bishop's decision are of religious nature or not.[13] One of those cases, relating to a former priest that contracted civil marriage and was publicly involved in a 'movement pro optional celibacy' of Catholic clergy,[14] attracted particular attention and media cov-

[13] See STC 38/2007; STC 80/2007 to 90/2007, all of them of the same date, 19 April 2007. Nevertheless, in a judgment of 2011 (STC 51/2011), the Constitutional Court decided in favour of a woman that had been removed from the list of persons qualified to teach religion because she had contracted civil marriage with a divorced person, also a Catholic. The Court accepted that the bishop has acted on religious grounds, but counterbalanced religious autonomy with the constitutional rights of the dismissed teacher—in particular her right to the 'free development of personality' (art. 10.1 CE), her right to marriage (art. 32 CE), and her right to the 'respect for private and family life' (art. 8 ECHR)—and gave priority to the latter. This judgment has raised some criticism among scholars (Gas Aixendri 2012) because, among other reasons, it emphasizes the significance of the labour situation of the plaintiff and ignores the constitutional basis of the current system of teaching Catholic religion in public schools. From that perspective, it seems contradictory to permit a person to teach a religious doctrine *on behalf of a church* that has explicitly disqualified her from that task.

[14] STC 128/2007.

erage because it reached the European Court of Human Rights (which confirmed the Constitutional Court's judgment).[15]

An interesting specific case of recognition of religious rules and religious autonomy by the civil jurisdiction in Spain relates to the issue of *apostasy*, which was raised, in the mid 2000s, by persons that, having formally abandoned their Catholic faith, asserted their right to oblige ecclesiastical authorities to completely remove or 'cancel' their data from baptism registries, alleging their freedom of religious choice and their right to privacy, as protected by the data protection laws.[16] To some extent, this was an organized initiative, nurtured by some political and ideological movements, in which several hundred people participated. Catholic bishops rejected unanimously all those claims, based on three concurring grounds. First, religious autonomy includes the inviolability of ecclesiastical archives, as specifically recognized by the Concordat.[17] Second, ecclesiastical registries of baptism cannot be considered 'personal data filing systems' either from the perspective of Spanish law[18] or from the perspective of European Union law,[19] for they are not 'structured sets of personal data which are accessible according to specific criteria'. And third, the entries about the baptism of people do not properly constitute personal data but just records of historical facts that, per se, do not convey information on the current belief or religious choices of baptized persons; from the Catholic Church's perspective, baptism is like a new birth to supernatural life and, therefore, a person's request to erase the record of baptism is as groundless as a request to erase his civil record of birth.

In 2008, the Supreme Court decided in favour of the Catholic Church,[20] on the ground that the ecclesiastical registries of baptism could not be considered 'personal data filing systems' under the current legislation.[21] The Court did not consider necessary to analyse the issue from the perspectives of religious autonomy and the inviolability of ecclesiastical archives guaranteed by the Concordat, thus leaving unresolved two very important legal questions in dispute (Otaduy 2008; González Moreno 2009; Pérez-Madrid 2009).

[15] *Fernández Martínez v. Spain*, 15 May 2012 (Chamber) and 12 June 2014 (Grand Chamber).

[16] The basic law on this matter is the *Ley Orgánica* 15/1999, 13 December 1999, *de protección de datos de carácter personal*.

[17] See art. I.6 of the 1979 Agreement on Juridical Affairs between Spain and the Holy See.

[18] See *Ley Orgánica* 15/1999, art. 3.b).

[19] See Directive 95/46/EC of the European Parliament and of the Council of 24 October 1995 on the protection of individuals with regard to the processing of personal data and on the free movement of such data, especially art. 2.c).

[20] See STS 4646/2008, 19 September 2008. Many other similar judgments have followed.

[21] The reason provided by the Supreme court is that baptism registries are a mere 'accumulation of [personal data] that makes difficult their search, access or identification, for they are not organized either alphabetically or by date of birth, but only by date of baptism, so that it is absolutely necessary to know the parish in which the christening was performed; in addition, [baptism data] are not accessible to any other person different from the baptized, and no third party can request a baptism certificate' (*ibid*., FJ 4).

Exemptions from Laws of General Applicability on Religious or Conscience Grounds

State law in Spain is not particularly receptive to the accommodation of religious or non-religious beliefs in cases of conflict between personal moral convictions and obligations derived from neutral laws of general applicability. The position of the Constitutional Court has not been entirely consistent over time and, from an open approach towards conscientious objections in some judgments of 1982 and 1985,[22] seems to have changed towards more restrictive attitudes since 1987 (Navarro-Valls & Martínez-Torrón 2012, 63–68).[23] Ordinary courts—including the Supreme Court—often tend to declare the undisputed supremacy of ordinary legal provisions over the protection of freedom of conscience and, consequently, are reluctant to recognize exemptions from this type of laws unless there is an explicit exemption granted by statutory law (*interpositio legislatoris*).

The result of this judicial policy has often been that citizens have adjusted their religious practices to the legal obligations, instead of the State accommodating the religious or conscience claims of the citizens. This, however, has known some exceptions. The most remarkable one is the adamant resistance of Jehovah's Witnesses to accept blood transfusions for them or for their children (Cebriá 2005, 23 ff.), although, in the case of the latter, they tend to accept passively the State intervention via judicial orders.

In recent times, State legislation has recognized two main types of exemption from general laws on conscience grounds: conscientious objection to *military service*[24] and conscientious objection to *abortion*.[25] In both cases the exemption clauses applied equally to religious and non-religious objections.

In older times (since the 19th century), Spanish procedural laws recognized the *clergy-communicant privilege*, which continues to be in force. Thus, the Code of Criminal Procedure explicitly excuses religious ministers from the obligation to report crimes they have known through confidential communications (art. 263). The same Code exempts from the obligation to testify in criminal trials 'ecclesiastics and ministers of dissident religions, with regard to facts that have been revealed to them in the exercise of functions of their religious ministry' (art. 417.1).[26] With varying terminology, a similar exemption is guaranteed by the Concordat to Catholic

[22] See especially STC 15/1982, FJ 6 (objection to military service), and STC 53/1985, FJ 14 (objection to abortion).

[23] Especially since STC 160/1987 and STC 161/1987 (objection to military service).

[24] The right to conscientious objection to military service was recognized by art. 30.2 CE, and later regulated (in 1984) by two statutes: *Ley* 48/1984 and *Ley Orgánica* 8/1984 (which experienced several reforms in the subsequent years). Since 2001, military service in Spain is suspended sine die.

[25] See art. 19.2 of the *Ley Orgánica* 2/2010, 3 March 2010, *de salud sexual y reproductiva y de la interrupción voluntaria del embarazo*.

[26] The peculiar terminology of this article ('ministers of *dissident* religions') dates back to the nineteenth century.

priests and members of religious orders,[27] and by the 1992 Agreements to Evangelical, Jewish and Islamic religious ministers (art. 3.2). The exemption contained in these agreements has a more general scope and is not circumscribed to the sphere of criminal procedure. The protection of confidentiality extends not only to the sacrament of penance but also to the exercise of religious ministry or assistance in general (Palomino 1999).

Individuals' right to comply with *religious dietary rules* is commonly understood as being protected by freedom of conscience, although the Organic Law on Religious Freedom does not mention it explicitly. To observe those rules, State cooperation is normally needed when people are confined in places, under the responsibility of public authorities, where they do not enjoy free movement for a variety of reasons (such as in the Army, in penitentiaries or in hospitals).

The general regulations of the Army do not contain specific provisions to protect this aspect of freedom of conscience. Instead, the general Regulation of Penitentiaries provides that meals provided to inmates must be adequate to their 'age, health, work, climate, customs and, as far as possible, personal and religious convictions'.[28] A certain trivialization of religious dietary requirements seems to be present in this provision. On the one hand, religious convictions are put on the same level as other 'personal' convictions, for instance vegetarianism or veganism, which are perfectly legitimate options but often not based on beliefs protected by art. 16 CE. On the other hand, the fact that the proviso 'as far as possible' is referred only to personal and religious convictions indicates that they are put on an inferior level in comparison with other individuals' preferences stemming, for instance, from customs or climate.

The 1992 Agreements envisage the State cooperation with individuals' compliance with religious dietary restrictions in the particular case of Muslims. Article 14.4 of the 1992 Agreement with the Islamic Federation specifically provides that 'meals for persons confined in public centres or military establishments, as well as for Muslim students of public schools and publicly funded private schools, when they so request, shall be adapted to Islamic religious rules. The same policy shall be applied to the schedule of meals during the fasting month of Ramadan'. Curiously, no parallel provision exists in the Agreement with the Jewish Federation, despite the fact that it was included—even in more protective terms—in the first proposal for an agreement that Jewish communities presented to the government in 1981. After that, it disappeared from all subsequent drafts (Martínez-Torrón 1994, 158–159). No parallel provision exists either for Catholics to facilitate their mandatory abstinence from meat in some days of the year (such as Ash Wednesday, Good Friday or Lent Fridays); in this case, the likely reason why the Concordat did not foresee the need to include such provision was the fact that those customs were well-known and respected in State facilities at the time.

---

[27] See art. II.3 of the 1976 Agreement on the renouncement to the presentation of bishops and the benefit of clergy between Spain and the Holy See.

[28] Art. 226 of the *Real Decreto* 190/1996, 9 February 1996, *por el que se aprueba el Reglamento Penitenciario*.

Religious Rules Regarding Personal Symbols

In Spain, the issue of *personal religious symbols* that some people wear to comply with a religious rule, and particularly female Islamic garments, has had a limited impact so far.

In the area of *education*, there is no national or regional legislation on the issue of religious clothing in public schools and therefore its regulation is in the hands of the school boards. Normally, the internal rules of schools refer to clothing in general rather than to religious garments in particular, and tend to be applied with flexibility. Until now, conflicts of this type have been significantly less numerous than in other European countries and, by and large, in public schools there is an atmosphere of tolerance for wearing religious symbols of any kind, including Islamic clothing. There have been only two known cases concerning the wearing of hijab by female Muslims students, in 2002 and 2010 respectively.[29] The two cases, with different nuances, were handled through transferring the student to a nearby school that did not object to the wearing of hijabs. However, the student's father in the second case initiated an administrative review procedure and later a judicial procedure against the school sanction. In 2012, a court of first instance rejected his claim[30] justifying the school board's position—with a poor reasoning—by reference to the Strasbourg Court's case law, and indicating that the board was free to interpret the notion of public order as excluding the use of veils.[31]

In the area of *labour relations* there has been very limited litigation in Spain with respect to the accommodation of personal religious garment while at work, which is probably indicative of a high level of tolerance of personal religious symbols at the workplace (Cañamares Arribas 2009a, 185–188).

In the area of *public security*, the use of Muslim female religious clothing has also raised some issues of diverse significance. On the one hand, Spanish regulations on identification documents (passports, ID cards and driving licenses) is sufficiently flexible as to permit providing personal photographs wearing a hijab and most common religious garments, but not a burka or niqab, which cover the entire face of the woman.[32] On the other hand, the use of full veils such as burka or niqab

[29] The first case is reported by Cañamares Arribas 2009b, 7–9. Information about the second case can be obtained in the Internet pages www.webislam.com (accessed 26 February 2016), searching by 'Najwa Malha' (the student's name).

[30] See *Juzgado Contencioso Administrativo* Nr. 32 of Madrid, Judgment Nr. 35/2012, 25 January 2012.

[31] The decisions of the ECtHR cited by the judgment of the Madrid court are *Dogru*, *Kervanci* and *Dahlab*, which are not, in the view of many scholars, particularly good examples of interpretation of Article 9 ECHR (Martínez-Torrón 2012, 49–59).

[32] See art. 4.1.c) of the *Real Decreto* 896/2003, 11 July 2003, *por el que se regula la expedición del pasaporte ordinario y se determinan sus características*; art. 5.1.b) of the *Real Decreto* 1553/2005, 23 December 2005, *por el que se regula la expedición del documento nacional de identidad y sus certificados de firma electrónica*, according to the modifications introduced by the *Real Decreto* 1586/2009, 16 October 2009; *Reglamento General de Conductores, Anexo* III, A.1.b), approved by the *Real Decreto* 818/2009, of 9 May 2009. The Islamic Federation has been active in reminding

in public places became a controversial question in Spain some years ago, although the debate has been less popular, and less heated, than in other European countries (Camarero 2012). At a national level, the Senate approved in June 2010—by a narrow margin—a motion requiring the government to promote legislative and administrative reforms aimed at banning full-face covering clothes in public spaces or events,[33] but the motion was rejected by the Congress a few weeks later. At a local level, in the last years several city councils have enacted municipal ordinances prohibiting the use of full veil in municipal facilities, mostly in Catalonia. The Supreme Court, in a judgment of 2013,[34] declared the ordinance of one of those cities (Lérida) null and void. The Court's decision focused on the lack of competence of city councils to regulate fundamental rights guaranteed by the Constitution, and held that municipal by-laws may impose limitations on religious freedom only on the bases of a prior ad hoc legislation. At the same time, the Court made clear that the legislator was competent to impose limitations on the use of full veil, if it considered it appropriate, and that the current judicial decision could not be interpreted as conditioning the choices available to parliament.[35]

Concluding Remarks

As indicated in this rapport, a substantial part of the civil effects of religious rules refers to marriage law issues and rely on the State cooperation agreements with religious communities. When this type of agreements were introduced in Spanish law, there was a debate about if that was an appropriate solution or if rather the State should have renounced the system of bilateral sources and have adopted instead unilateral legislation, equally applicable to all religions and previously negotiated with the most relevant religious communities operating in Spain (Martínez-Torrón 1994). The passage of time, however, has demonstrated that bilateral sources have been well accepted by most scholars, by legal actors and, most importantly, by religious communities—not only by the signatories of existing agreements but also by the rest of communities, many of which aspire to sign, one day, a cooperation agreement with the Spanish State.

The most important reason for criticism of the current system of bilateral sources is not its existence but its arbitrary and discriminatory practical application. On the one hand, some expressions of State cooperation with religion, which should have been extended to all registered religious communities, have been reserved to those communities that have a formal agreement with the State (Catholics, Protestants,

---

public authorities the existence of current regulations so that they are not neglected or ignored at the local level, but hardly any problems have been reported.

[33] The motion was tabled by the Popular Party, and the Socialist Party opposed to it. See the oral interventions in *Diario de Sesiones del Senado (Pleno), IX Legislatura*, Núm. 85, 23 June 2010.

[34] STS 693/2013, 14 February 2013.

[35] See *ibid.*, FJ 10.

Jews, and Muslims)—for example, tax benefits or, until recently, the civil effects of the religious celebration of marriage. On the other hand, since 1992 no government has had any political will to negotiate other cooperation agreements—according to art. 7 LOLR, the State *may* negotiate and conclude a cooperation agreement with those religious communities that have been recognized 'well-known roots' in Spain but is not legally *obliged* to do so. As a result, the four other religious communities that have been recognized 'well-known roots' after 1992[36]—i.e., communities that meet all legal requirements to conclude a formal agreement with the State—are excluded from almost all State cooperation channels.

Thus, the misapplication of a system of bilateral sources originally designed to achieve a gradual integration of religious minorities and a proportionate State cooperation with religion has produced, in practice, social fragmentation and discrimination, and has created some privileged categories of religious communities segregated from the rest. Certainly, there are no significant differences between religious communities in Spain from the perspective of the protection of collective religious freedom, and it is undeniable that the privileged categories cover a very high percentage of Spanish population adhering to a religion. However, there is no doubt discrimination of most religious minorities from the perspective of State cooperation. These anomalies could be easily remedied if the two main parties in Spain had the political will to confront the situation and take seriously the implementation of the constitutional principle of equality.

Two other features of the Spanish law related to the application of religious rules in the public sphere could and should be improved, in my opinion.

One is the accommodation of conscience claims in cases of conflict between moral duties and legal obligations (conscientious objections). As indicated above, Spanish courts are often reluctant to decide in favour of freedom of conscience in those cases unless they can rely on an explicit and specific statutory provision—and the Spanish legislator has often shown a lack of sensitivity to provide legislative tools for those accommodations. As laws are based on ethical values, which tend to correspond to values accepted by the largest part of society, the consequence is a certain indirect discrimination of religious minorities or individuals dissenting from the ethical values that inspire legislation.

The other aspect that could be improved is the position of the Spanish Constitutional Court with respect to the protection of the autonomy of religious communities. In general, the degree of respect for religious autonomy has been high in Spain, but the reasoning of the Constitutional Court in cases related to teachers of Catholic religion in public schools, and the outcome of some recent decision (2011), suggests that the Court is allowing some room for the State interference with religious autonomy when labour contracts and the right to privacy are involved. It would appear that in some areas the Court is forcing religious communities to abide, in their internal life and organization, by rules and principles parallel to those of State law.

---

[36] Since 2003, Mormons, Jehovah's Witnesses, Buddhists and Christian Orthodox have been recognized 'well-known roots'.

References

Camarero, Victoria. 2012. *El velo integral y su respuesta en democracias europeas*. Valencia: Tirant Lo Blanch.

Cañamares Arribas, Santiago. 2009a. Religious symbols in Spain: A legal perspective. *Ecclesiastical Law Journal* 11: 181–193.

Cañamares Arribas, Santiago. 2009b. Tratamiento de la simbología religiosa en el Derecho español: propuestas ante la reforma de la Ley orgánica de libertad religiosa. *Revista General de Derecho Canónico y Derecho Eclesiástico del Estado* 19: 1–29.

Castro Jover, Adoración. 1990. Libertad religiosa y descanso semanal. *Anuario de Derecho Eclesiástico del Estado* 6: 299–312.

Cebriá García, María. 2005. *Objeciones de conciencia a intervenciones médicas*. Doctrina y jurisprudencia. Pamplona: Thomson-Aranzadi.

Díaz Moreno, José María. 1979. Acuerdos Iglesia-Estado en España: notas marginales. *Estudios Eclesiásticos* 54: 283–334.

Ferrer Ortiz, Javier. 1989. Los principios constitucionales del derecho eclesiástico como sistema. In *Las relaciones entre la Iglesia y el Estado: estudios en memoria del Profesor Pedro Lombardía* (VV.AA. 309–322). Madrid: Edersa.

Fornés, Juan. 1980. *El nuevo sistema concordatario español (Los Acuerdos de 1976 y 1979)*. Pamplona: Eunsa.

Gas Aixendri, Montserrat. 2012. La declaración canónica de idoneidad para la enseñanza de la religión católica y su control jurisdiccional por parte del Estado. *Revista General de Derecho Canónico y Derecho Eclesiástico del Estado* 29: 1–17.

González Moreno, Beatriz. 2009. El derecho fundamental a la protección de datos personales: su contenido y límites respecto al bautismo y la apostasía. *Revista General de Derecho Canónico y Derecho Eclesiástico del Estado* 19: 1–42.

Juárez Pérez, Pilar. 2012. Jurisdicción española y poligamia islámica: ¿un matrimonio forzoso? *Revista Electrónica de Estudios Internacionales* 23: 1–45.

López Alarcón, Mariano, and Rafael Navarro-Valls. 2010. *Curso de derecho matrimonial canónico y concordado*, 7th ed. Madrid: Tecnos.

Martínez-Torrón, Javier. 1994. *Separatismo y cooperación en los acuerdos del Estado con las minorías religiosas*. Granada: Comares.

Martínez-Torrón, Javier. 2012. Islam in Strasbourg: Can politics substitute for law? In *Islam, Europe and emerging legal issues*, ed. W. Cole Durham Jr, David M. Kirkham, Christine Scott, and Rik Torfs, 19–61. Aldershot: Ashgate.

Martínez-Torrón, Javier. 2014. *Religion and law in Spain*. The Netherlands: Kluwer International.

Meseguer Velasco, Silvia. 2012. La integración de la diversidad religiosa en el ámbito de las relaciones laborales: la cuestión de las prácticas religiosas. *Revista General de Derecho Canónico y Derecho Eclesiástico del Estado* 28: 1–28.

Navarro-Valls, Rafael, and Javier Martínez-Torrón. 2012. *Conflictos entre conciencia y ley. Las objeciones de conciencia*, 2dth ed. Madrid: Iustel.

Otaduy, Jorge. 1987. Las cláusulas de salvaguarda de la identidad de las instituciones religiosas. *Ius Canonicum* 27: 673–696.

Otaduy, Jorge. 2008. Iglesia católica y Ley española de protección de datos: falsos conflictos. *Ius Canonicum* 48: 117–140.

Palomino, Rafael. 1999. *Derecho a la intimidad y religión: la protección jurídica del secreto religioso*. Granada: Comares.

Pérez-Madrid, Francisca. 2009. Protección de datos personales y apostasía. *Revista General de Derecho Canónico y Derecho Eclesiástico del Estado* 19: 1–31.

Rodríguez Chacón, Rafael. 2005. Sentencias matrimoniales canónicas y Unión Europea. *Revista General de Derecho Canónico y Derecho Eclesiástico del Estado* 7: 1–33.

Valero Estarellas, María José. 2013. El derecho de los profesores de religión católica al respeto de su vida privada y familiar. *Revista General de Derecho Canónico y Derecho Eclesiástico del Estado* 33: 1–28.

Chapter 23
Religion and Law in Twenty-First Century England: Tradition and Diversity

Søren Holm and Javier García Oliva

Abstract The chapter provides an account of the many levels of relations between religion and law in England. The first section briefly outlines the historical developments leading to the establishment of the Church of England as the legally established church, and explains the current legal position of the Church of England and its relation to the Monarchy and the State. Subsequent sections analyse and discuss (a) the influence of Christianity on the English legal system, (b) the ways in which the English legal system accommodates other religions and religious organisations, (c) how religious beliefs and actions are accommodated in the work place, and (d) the legal and political response to 'religious adjudication' in Shariah councils or similar bodies. The chapter concludes that the English legal approach to the non-established religions can be described as a form of 'benign neglect'. The State does not grant explicit minority group rights to religious groups, but it does not usually interfere in their internal affairs either.

Introduction: Legal Diversity in the United Kingdom, Sociological Aspects, Establishment in England and General Terminological Considerations

Within the field of Law and Religion, it is not possible to provide a single response from the United Kingdom as a whole. An analysis of any aspect within this field will require us to focus on England and Wales,[1] Scotland and Northern Ireland, separately, since they are separate jurisdictions with widely divergent legislation in the area of Law and Religion. This is indeed the correct approach for the study of

[1] Although it can be argued that the traditional unity between England and Wales has been challenged in the course of the last few years, due to the process of devolution of powers in Wales, particularly as of the enactment of the Government of Wales Act 2006. An emerging Welsh jurisdiction is no longer a fantasy.

S. Holm (✉) • J. García Oliva
University of Manchester, Manchester, UK
e-mail: soren.holm@manchester.ac.uk; javier.oliva@manchester.ac.uk

R. Bottoni et al. (eds.), *Religious Rules, State Law, and Normative Pluralism - A Comparative Overview*, Ius Comparatum – Global Studies in Comparative Law 18, DOI 10.1007/978-3-319-28335-7_23

the applicable religious rules according to the Law of the State, which is the scope of the current chapter. In this contribution, therefore, we intend to deal, mainly, if not exclusively, with England and Wales, and where the law in England and Wales differs, primarily with England. However, despite the four jurisdictions in the UK, the final court of appeal, the Supreme Court of the United Kingdom is the same for all four jurisdictions.

The last census, carried out in the UK in 2011, shows the largest religious group in England and Wales to be Christianity. 59 % of the population in these two nations declared themselves to be Christian; whilst the second largest group, representing 25 % of the population was composed of those who declared themselves not to have any religion. Islam was the second largest religious group, at 4.8 % of the population, followed by Hinduism, Sikhism, Judaism and Buddhism (United Kingdom Government Census 2011).

Unsurprisingly, analysing the figures, the London area comes across as the most diverse region, with the highest proportion of people identifying themselves as Muslims, Buddhists, Hindus and Jews. This clearly shows the cosmopolitan nature of the capital of the United Kingdom. The North-east and the North-west of England have the highest proportion of Christians, and Wales has the highest number of individuals reporting no religion.

By comparison with the previous census, held in 2001, in which 71 % of residents in England and Wales regarded themselves as Christians, there has been a significant decrease in the members of this faith. Furthermore, those who declared not to profess any religion were only a 15 % of the population in 2001, as opposed to the current 25 %. Therefore, whilst the substantial shift is undeniable, the truth is that the majority of the population in those two British nations still professes Christianity. Even though Grace Davie's well-known statement "Believing without belonging" (Davie 1994) was made in the 1990s, is still in our view an accurate description of the current British religious make-up and the response of British citizens to religion.

England is an interesting example of a country successfully embracing religious diversity and pluralism, as stated above, whilst retaining a model of establishment, which finds its historical roots in the English Reformation. Wales is a different system altogether, as the Church (of England) in Wales was formally disestablished by the Church in Wales Act 1914, not coming into effect until 1920. Vestiges of the previous model of establishment remain in the current Welsh framework (Watkin 1990, and Doe 2011, 217 on marriage in England and Wales),[2] arguably rendering the Church partially disestablished or quasi-established, but this discussion is certainly beyond the scope of this contribution.

The Reformation in England was the result of King Henry VIII's determination to annul his marriage with Catalina of Aragon, one of the daughters of the Catholic King and Queen of Spain, Fernando and Isabel. Catalina had been previously married to Arthur, the eldest brother of Henry's, but their marriage had not been consummated before Arthur died, and it had been subsequently annulled. Due to the

[2] See N. T. G. Watkin, "Vestiges of Establishment: the Ecclesiastical and Canon Law of the Church in Wales" (1990) Ecc. L.J. 110–115.

lack of a male heir and Catalina having suffered several miscarriages, Henry decided to marry Anne Boleyn. However, this initiative met with the fierce opposition of the Holy Father, a strong ally of Carlos, the Spanish King and Catalina's nephew. As Roman Catholic Canon Law does not recognise divorce, Henry pursued the annulment route on the grounds of Catalina's first marriage's breach of Divine Law. This annulment was not granted by the Pope, on theological grounds, but clearly motivated by political reasons, and this led to the schism with Rome and the foundation of the Church of England.

The Reformation in England and Wales was, therefore, significantly different from the movement in both continental Europe and Scotland, which was primarily driven by theological, rather than personal interests. It would be over-simplistic to suggest that theological elements did not play any part in the English process, but the personal dimension makes it a substantially different phenomenon and explains the theological proximity of Anglicanism to the Church of Rome. Interestingly, Henry VIII had been awarded a few years earlier, in 1521, the title *Fidei Defensor* (Defender of the Faith), by Pope Leo X and he indeed had been a passionate defender of the Roman Catholic doctrine.

The Church of England is established by law,[3] and its legal framework differs from other denominations in England and the rest of the United Kingdom. There is a wide diversity of definitions of establishment (for a more detailed analysis of the model of establishment, see García Oliva 2010), but for the purposes of this contribution, the definition of Lord Rodger in *Aston Cantlow*,[4] when referring to the Church of England as a denomination that has "certain important links" with the State, is most suitable:

Those links, which do not include any funding of the Church by the Government, give the Church a unique position but they do not make it a department of State [...] In so far as the ties are intended to assist the Church, it is to accomplish the Church's own mission, not the aims and objectives of the Government of the United Kingdom.

Following Carr (Carr 1999, 2–10), a distinction between high and low establishment is helpful. High establishment refers to the visible tip of the iceberg, the special bond between public authorities (e.g. the Crown, the Government and Parliament) and the Anglican hierarchy. Low establishment, on the contrary, alludes to the earthed relationship, or in other words, the ways in which the model of establishment has an impact on the daily lives of English citizens.

The position of the Monarch as Defender of the Faith[5] and Supreme Governor of the Church of England,[6] the appointment of the hierarchy of the Church of England

[3] Act of Supremacy 1534 and 1559.

[4] Aston Cantlow and Wilmcote with Billesley Parochial Church Council v Wallbank [2003] UKHL 37; [2004] 1 A.C. 546 at 156, per Lord Rodger of Earlsferry.

[5] This title was confirmed by parliamentary statute in 1544, through the Third Treason Act of 1544 (35 Hen. 8 c. 3) and it has been maintained by subsequent legislation, such as the Royal Titles Act 1953.

[6] See, for instance, the Thirty-Nine Articles of Religion and the revised Canons of the Church of England, Canon A7, Of the Royal Supremacy: "We acknowledge that the Queen's excellent

by the Monarch on the advice of the Prime Minister,[7] the presence of 26 Archbishops and diocesan bishops of the Church of England[8] in the House of Lords and the approval of measures[9] and other legislation of the Church of England,[10] can all be regarded as features of "high" establishment, whilst the duties of Church of England clergy towards all citizens in terms of education,[11] prisons,[12] marriage[13] and burials[14] are signs of the model of "low" establishment.

However, it would be misleading not to stress that nowadays this model of establishment has become predominantly symbolic, and it comes alongside the recognition of a wider and enriching religious plurality, which has been strengthened by recent legislative developments, such as the Human Rights Act 1998. This statute confirms the principle of religious freedom in the UK, whilst making most provisions of the European Convention on Human Rights justiciable in the domestic courts. Furthermore, a second important trend concerning discrimination law has taken place in recent years in the UK, as the legislature has aimed to combat forms of discrimination on religious grounds, whether direct or indirect. This development in the employment field is exemplified by the Equality Act 2010. However debatable the model of establishment may well be, we would concur with Ahdar and Leigh, leading commentators in the field of Law and Religion, who state that "Establishment, at least in a modern mild form exemplified by the United Kingdom, we believe, is consistent with religious freedom" (Ahdar and Leigh 2013, 123).

Following Sandberg (2011, 10–11), in this introductory section some terminological clarifications may be necessary. "Religion Law" is the State legal branch concerned with the recognition and regulation of certain religious relationships, and 'religion' certainly has meanings outside the legal domain. In a slightly simplistic manner, it could be regarded as the equivalent to "Ecclesiastical Law" in continental Europe. "Religious Law", on the contrary, may be defined as the study of the 'internal'

Majesty, according to the laws of the realm, is the highest power under God in this kingdom, and the supreme authority over all persons in all causes, as well ecclesiastical as civil".

[7]Although since 1976, a Crown's Appointment Commission proposed two names to the Prime Minister, limiting the Head of Government's powers substantially. This was renamed in 2003 as the Nominations Commission and since the Green Paper on the Governance of Britain, published on 3rd July 2007, the Prime Minister's plays a far less significant role and the Commission only passes on to him/her one name, which must then transmit be transmitted by the Prime Minister to the Queen.

[8]Bishopric of Manchester Act 1847.

[9]The Church of England Assembly (Powers) Act 1919.

[10]Submission of the Clergy Act 1533.

[11]Education Act 1996.

[12]Prison Act 1952.

[13]Marriage Act 1753.

[14]Case law (e.g. *Maidman v Malpas* 161 E.R. 526; (1794) 1 Hag. Con. 205 KB) has endorsed the right of parishioners to be buried in the parish churchyard regardless of their faith and the same approach has been taken by the canon law of the Church of England. In fact, Canon B 38 para. 2 states: "It shall be duty of every minister to bury, according to the rites of the Church of England, the corpse or ashes of any persons deceased within his cure".

laws or other regulatory instruments created by religious collectives themselves (Sandberg 2011, 12). This would include the internal legal systems of religious bodies such as the Roman Catholic Church, the Islamic community and Judaism. The Church of England is a hybrid body and it is difficult to classify measures (legislation approved by its General Synod, which requires the subsequent endorsement of the UK Parliament and the Royal Assent)[15] and much of the law affecting the Church of England, as being either Religion Law or Religious Law (Sandberg 2011, 13).

Legislation

Sources of Law in the UK and Religion

Unlike all other European countries and most other States in the world, the UK does not have a codified Constitution, and this has an impact on the way religion has been dealt with.

Acts of Parliament are one of the main sources of the UK Constitution, and there are frequent references to religion in statutes, some of which have been regarded as having constitutional significance by the UK judiciary.[16] As indicated above, some constitutional statutes refer to the Church of England, including the position of the Monarch and His/Her relationship with the Church of England,[17] the appointment of bishops of the Church of England[18] and the approval of legislation of this denomination.[19] However, there are also important references to religion and religious groups, generally speaking.[20]

Alongside Acts of Parliament, other sources of UK Constitutional Law deal with the religious element, particularly case law,[21] conventions[22] and secondary legisla-

[15] See below.

[16] See *Thoburn v Sunderland City Council* [2002] EWCH 195 (Admin) [2003] QB 151, [62]

[17] E.g. The Act of Settlement 1700, The Accession Declaration Act 1910 and The Royal Titles Act 1953.

[18] Appointment of Bishops Act 1534 and the Suffragan Bishops Act 1534.

[19] The Church of England Assembly (Powers) Act 1919.

[20] E.g. The Human Rights Act 1998, the Charities Act 1993 and the Equality Act 2010.

[21] Setting aside the position of the Church of England, with regard to other religious bodies, the UK courts have emphasized the significance of the principle of non-interference. As a sign of the respect for the autonomy of religious bodies, UK courts are usually reluctant to get involved in internal disputes within religious bodies. See *Sant Baba Jeet Singh Maharaj v Eastern Media Group Ltd* [2010] EWHC (QB) 1294. However, where there is a financial interest and in relation to the disposal and administration of property, courts may exceptionally intervene to enforce the laws of a religious group. See *Forbes v Eden* (1867) LR 1 Sc & Div 568.

[22] For instance, it could be argued that a convention has been developed, according to which although the UK Parliament could legislate directly on the Church of England, the expectation will be for the Church of England to legislate itself, by means of measures.

tion.[23] As stated above (see footnote 7), UK case law considers that the mission of the Church of England, which is established by law,[24] is to pursue its own mission and not the aims and goals of the Government of the United Kingdom, differentiating this model from other State Churches in continental Europe, particularly the Church of Denmark.

Measures[25] are an important and idiosyncratic legal source in the UK, as they are approved by the three Houses of the Church of England (Bishops, Clergy and Laity), although requiring the subsequent endorsement of both Houses of Parliament and the Royal Assent. They are bound up together with Acts of Parliament and they are included on the statute law database.[26] Canons of the Church of England are approved by the General Synod and unlike Measures, do not require subsequent endorsement by the bicameral Parliament, but do still need the assent of the Monarch, in Her capacity as Supreme Governor of the Church of England. Measures and Canons could, depending on the legal perspective of the beholder, be conceptualised as a form on internal legal plurality within English law.

The importance of the position of the Church of England should not be underestimated and we concur with Rivers' analysis of the English Law of organised religions, when he states that it "[…] is located between establishment and secularism. The established position of the Church of England has acted as a constitutional paradigm securing certain forms of connection (plural establishment) in a context in which separation is assumed, and ensuring the ongoing public significance of religion in a context in which it increasingly appears irrelevant" (Rivers 2010, 344–345).

The Influence of Christianity on the English and Welsh Legal System Nowadays

It can be argued that English Law is deeply rooted in Judeo-Christian values, and particularly, that the Christian ethos has been historically present in the primary legislation. The recent controversy concerning the approval of the Marriage (Same Sex Couples) Act 2013 and the exemptions provided to the Church of England and other religious denominations illustrate this analysis (as argued by García Oliva and Hall 2013). Religious education in State schools must be non-denominational, but perhaps surprisingly, the syllabus "must reflect the fact that the religious traditions of Great Britain are in the main Christian whilst taking into account the teaching and practices of the other principal religions represented in Great Britain".[27]

[23] E.g. The Employment Equality Regulations 2003., prior to the enactment of the Equality Act 2010.

[24] Acts of Supremacy 1534 and 1559.

[25] See The Church of England Assembly (Powers) Act 1919.

[26] The database easily accessible at: http://www.legislation.gov.uk/

[27] Education Act 1996, s 375(3).

Moreover, the law of the State also alludes to the duty on the part of school authorities to provide religious worship, which must be wholly or mainly of a broadly Christian character, not being distinctive of any specific denomination.[28] In Sandberg's view, "[…] a case could be made that the laws on religious education and worship are now the clearest examples of the favouring of Christianity in religion law" (Sandberg 2011, 159) and "[…] the references to Christianity seem outmoded" (Sandberg 2011, 160).

In addition, there has been a proliferation of legislation on religion ("Religion Law"), in other fields such as a criminal law, and the enactment of the Racial and Religious Hatred Act 2006 illustrates this development. Unlike the law on education, all religious bodies are put on an equal footing in the latter statute, this equality of treatment being a common feature of the vast majority of pieces of legislation within this broader "Religion Law".

The Partial Recognition of Religious Law in England and Wales

In England and Wales there is no system of personal laws based on religious affiliation and all citizens, regardless of their faith or lack of it, are subject to the law of the land. However, it is the case that *some* aspects of Religious Law are already recognized. The hysterical response of the media and commentators to the former Archbishop of Canterbury's lecture (Williams 2008, 262) on the accommodation of some aspects of Islamic Law in Britain ignored this reality. Public authorities in the United Kingdom face a choice which is more complex than just deciding whether to accept all aspects of Islamic Law (or any other Religious Law) or none, as it is popularly presented and misinterpreted. In fact, there is a third possibility, the recognition of some aspects of Religious Law, which is the model embraced by English and Welsh Law. Indeed, there are many examples which illustrate this partial recognition of Religious Law, but perhaps the clearest is the Divorce (Religious Marriages) Act 2002, which aimed to sort out the problems arising in situations in which Orthodox Jewish husbands decide not to provide their wives with a bill of divorce known as a 'get' leaving them as *agunah* unable to marry (Sandberg 2011, 183).

Although religious adjudication will be developed further in section 3 of this contribution, it would be advisable to mention at this stage, however briefly, that in compliance with the Arbitration Act 1996, some disputes can be dealt with by religious arbitration bodies and the decisions enforced by secular courts. It should be noted, however, that the main focus of the Arbitration Act is normal, secular commercial arbitration, and section 1 of this statute declares that secular courts will not enforce a decision if the 'public interest' requires them not to. Importantly, decisions of religious arbitrations are enforced by the secular courts, not because they are decisions of religious courts, but because the parties have agreed to be bound by the decisions in question. In fact, anyone can be appointed as an arbitrator.

[28] School Standards and Framework Act 1998 s. 70 and Sch. 20 para. 3(3).

Furthermore, there are two limitations on the use of arbitration (Rivers 2010, 102): (1) The extent of arbitrability, being individual rights of contract and property within the scope of a possible arbitration procedure, whilst criminal law or cases concerning the public interest or personal status are outside their remit; (2) Party consent is required.

In any event, it is important to emphasize that there is no general recognition of the Religious Law of different religious communities, although the law of the Church of England is *sui generis* and it is part of the law of the land. Furthermore, its diocesan Chancellors are bound to have a 7-year qualification under the Courts and Legal Services Act 1990, and the Dean of Arches[29] has to have a 10-year qualification. Furthermore, the Ecclesiastical Committee of Parliament is a statutory committee appointed under the Church of England Assembly (Powers) Act 1919.

Importantly, the presence of an established Church in England does not mean that the faithful of that denomination are bound to embrace its Religious Law, and certainly there is no attempt on the part of either the State or the Church to limit the freedom of Anglicans. Needless to say, the same is applicable to those citizens who profess other faiths or none.

Moreover, areas which have been traditionally linked with religious bodies, such as education and marriage, also offer a secular version nowadays. For example, parents in England and Wales have a wide range of options in terms of schooling and no citizen in England and Wales is bound to send his/her children to schools with a religious ethos, also popularly known as faith schools (see below). As previously indicated, the truth is that even schools with a religious character must provide non-denominational religious education with a special emphasis on Christianity, but significantly, the law recognizes a parental right to opt-out.

In relation to marriage, according to Bradney "notwithstanding the religious antecedents of family law, current legislators and lawyers work in a secular mode" (Bradney 2009, 98). This secular mindset can also be found amongst members of the judiciary:

> Marriage … [is] a civil institution whose duties and obligations are regulated by the secular courts of an increasingly secular society. For, although we live in a multi-cultural society of many faiths, it must not be forgotten that as a secular judge my concern is with marriage as a civil contract, not a religious vow.[30]

Autonomy of Religious Bodies in England and Wales

Religious denominations in England and Wales (except for the Church of England and the Church in Wales, which retains some marks of establishment) are organised on a private basis, and are treated as voluntary associations. Furthermore, the

[29] The presiding judge in the Church of England Court of Appeal.

[30] Mr Justice Munby in *Sheffield City Council v E and S* [2005] 1 FLR 965 at p 1000.

powers of religious organisations are the result of an agreement amongst their members, who are governed by quasi-contract.

However, due to the absence of a codified Constitution for the United Kingdom, in England a constitutional guarantee of religious autonomy does not exist as such. In Edge's view, this has proved detrimental to religious groups, and he states:

> [...] Islamic organisations do not receive the same constitutional privileges as the Church of England. This has not meant, however, that their autonomy has been protected. Instead, the English absence of a constitutional guarantee of religious autonomy may leave open the path to asymmetrical disestablishment, whereby religious organisations lose, or do not gain, power within the state order; while the state retains, or even increases, its power over these organisations (Edge 2013, 187).

Religious bodies are entitled to establish organisations such as schools, and the State is deferential towards the religious ethos of those bodies, with special rules concerning collective worship, religious education, admissions and employment of staff sharing the school's religious ethos (Ahdar and Leigh 2013, 251). Importantly, religion can be regarded as a factor in terms of admissions, but not race. In fact, in *R(E) v Governing Body of JFS* [2009] UKSC 15, the Supreme Court of the United Kingdom declared, by a majority of five to two, that racial discrimination had taken place, when a child was denied a place in an Orthodox Jewish school, because his mother was a convert to Judaism.

Schools with a religious ethos have been strongly supported by the current Coalition Government and by the former Labour Administration, and their autonomy in terms of admissions (Rivers 2010, 254) has proved controversial, particularly as many of these schools are very popular amongst parents, due to their strong academic credentials. Generally speaking, they have been widely criticised for different reasons, such as their possible indoctrination and proselytism, their funding by the State, their suggested social exclusivity and their enforcement of 'monoculturalism' (Petchey 2008, 179–183).

Legislative Recognition of Religious Exceptions

One of the most controversial aspects in the field of Law and Religion in the last few years has been the recognition of religious exceptions to rules of general application in the employment field and in the provision of goods and services. With regard to the former,[31] employers of an "organised" religion can be entitled to discriminate on the grounds of gender, sexual orientation and religion. For this to happen, three important criteria must be met: (1) The employment must be for the purposes of an organised religion; (2) the 'compliance' or 'non-conflict' principles must be engaged. This requires that the discrimination must be necessary to comply with the doctrines of the religion and in order 'to avoid conflicting with the strongly held convictions of a significant number of the religion's followers'; (3) The employer

[31] Equality Act 2010, schedule 9, second paragraph.

can discriminate either where the employee does not meet the requirement imposed or where the employer is not satisfied that the person meets it and it is reasonable for him not to be satisfied that that person meets it (Sandberg 2011, 119–121; Vickers 2008). Furthermore, organisations relating to religion or belief may enjoy an exception of the general prohibition of discrimination on the grounds of sex, sexual orientation and religion. The conflict between religion and sexuality is one of the most difficult areas in the field of Law and Religion at the moment, and as rightly suggested by commentators, Law is only one of the instruments which may be used to solve these conflicts, and without an intelligent use of human-resources policy, Law will not suffice (Malik 2013, 90).

Accommodation of Religious Beliefs in the Workplace

The importance of religious beliefs has been acknowledged by leading commentators in the Employment Law field:

> Religious belief has crucial significance for individual identity, linked as it is with beliefs about man's nature and place in the universe. Given the gravity of the issues involved in the lives of adherents, they should not have to relinquish their practices too lightly. However, important as they are, religious interests are not absolute. It is accepted that in some circumstances burdens may need to be placed on religious practice, and that at times the rights of others will prevail over religious interests (Vickers 2008, 53).

In the United Kingdom, the State provides statutory conscience exemptions for employees on religious grounds.[32] Unquestionably, employment is an area of considerable significance for minorities, including religious minorities (Knights 2007, 127). Amongst those exemptions, the following can be highlighted: some shop workers have safeguards against being coerced into working on Sundays, Sikh construction workers may continue to wear a turban rather than a hard-hat, and when closed shop legislation formerly existed, people with religious objections to joining a trade union could claim exemption (Ahdar and Leigh 2013, 347–348). Nevertheless, it could be argued that the UK authorities have recently become more reluctant to accept this sort of exemptions, as the controversy concerning adoption agencies opposing adoptions by couples of the same sex illustrates.[33] However, the situation in Scotland has been different, and the Scottish Charities Appeal Panel[34] has overturned a decision of the Scottish Charity Regulator and has decided to maintain the charitable status of a Glasgow-based Adoption Agency, run by the Roman Catholic Church, despite its refusal to place children with same-sex couples.

[32] For instance, the Abortion Act 1967, s 4(1) gives a right of conscientious objection to medical and other health care staff who have been asked to take part in abortion.

[33] http://www.independent.co.uk/news/uk/home-news/catholic-adoption-charity-appeal-dismissed-2275012.html

[34] Scottish Charity Appeal Panel App 02/13

Religion and Adjudication in UK Courts

UK courts are secular. As the current President of the Family Court has expressed it in a judgment:

> We sit as secular judges serving a multi-cultural community of many faiths. We are sworn (we quote the judicial oath) to "do right to all manner of people after the laws and usages of this realm, without fear or favour, affection or ill will." But the laws and usages of the realm do not include Christianity, in whatever form. The aphorism that 'Christianity is part of the common law of England' is mere rhetoric; at least since the decision of the House of Lords in Bowman v Secular Society Limited [1917] AC 406 it has been impossible to contend that it is law.[35]

This means that the courts will, in general, not take religious law into account in adjudication, except in the circumstances discussed below.

UK courts are also reluctant to adjudicate on what they regard as pure matters of religious doctrine. But when a matter involves both doctrine and contract, the courts may adjudicate. In a recent judgment concerning disputed rights to manage the affairs of a Sikh temple, the Supreme Court of the United Kingdom, on the one hand affirmed that:

> But disputes about doctrine or liturgy are non-justiciable if they do not as a consequence engage civil rights or interests or reviewable questions of public law.[36]

And, on the other,stated that:

> But where a claimant asks the court to enforce private rights and obligations which depend on religious issues, the judge may have to determine such religious issues as are capable of objective ascertainment. The court addresses questions of religious belief and practice where its jurisdiction is invoked either to enforce the contractual rights of members of a community against other members or its governing body or to ensure that property held on trust is used for the purposes of the trust.[37]

State Provision of Religious Adjudication

As discussed, Measures passed by the General Synod of the Church of England, and approved by the UK Parliament, have the full force of law. The Church has its own system of consistory courts and other courts which adjudicate issues falling within the scope of the Church's jurisdiction. These courts will apply both the statute law in the measures, as well as general principles of English Common and Administrative law. Although these courts are courts of the Church, they are at the same time State courts.

---

[35] Johns & Anor, R (on the application of) v Derby City Council & Anor [2011] EWHC 375 (Admin) at 39.

[36] Shergill & Ors v Khaira & Ors [2014] UKSC 33 at 46.

[37] Shergill & Ors v Khaira & Ors [2014] UKSC 33 at 45.

There can be a complicated interplay between Church law and adjudication and the secular law of the State. This can for instance be seen in the still ongoing dispute about the burial of the remains of King Richard III, found in 2013 during an archaeological excavation in the city of Leicester. The excavation took place under a license issued by the Home Office, which provides the University of Leicester with authority to decide on the disposition of any human remains found during the excavation. The University consequently decided that the remains of Richard III should be buried in Leicester Cathedral. The issuing of this license in currently being unsuccessfully challenged through judicial review in the High Court by the Plantagenet alliance that wants to have Richard buried in York Minster.[38] The burial of Richard in Leicester Cathedral will require the erection of a tomb or the placement of some other kind of marker in the Cathedral, and separate permission from the Cathedrals Fabric Commission for England will be necessary, as it counts as a significant alteration to the fabric of the Cathedral, under the Care of Cathedrals Measure 2011.

In England, the State does not recognize any other religious dispute resolution systems formally and generally, in their specific guise as religious dispute resolution systems.

Decisions made by other religious bodies can, however, be recognized by the State courts in two circumstances:

(a) If the religious body has acted as an arbitration body in relation to matters that are arbitrable under the Arbitration Act 1996, i.e. mainly commercial matters but also issues relating to wills[39]; or
(b) If the Court gives prior permission for the use of a specific religious body for dispute resolution in a specific case.

In the latter instance, the Court has to be convinced that the religious body uses standards of adjudication that are equivalent to the standards of the UK courts, although the substantive law may be different. In a recent case involving the divorce of a Jewish couple, the Family Court, for instance, allowed arbitration at the New York Beth Din and endorsed the arbitration outcome after having been convinced, *inter alia*, that in relation to matters pertaining to the children of the marriage, the Beth Din would apply a standard equivalent to the English legal standard making the child's interest the paramount consideration.[40]

UK courts will not apply the rules of religious legal systems in cases where the legally relevant acts have taken place in the UK, or partly in the UK and partly in a foreign jurisdiction. A religious divorce or a religious marriage will thus, for instance, only be recognized if it was contracted wholly outside the UK and if it was legally valid in the jurisdiction in which it was contracted (see below). Islamic

[38] See Plantagenet Alliance Ltd, R (o a o) v Secretary of State for Justice & Anor [2013] EWHC B13 (Admin) for the decision to grant judicial review and R (Plantagenet Alliance Ltd) v Secretary of State for Justice [2014] EWHC 1662 for the final judgment.

[39] See, for instance Kohn v Wagschal & Ors [2007] EWCA Civ 1022

[40] AI v MT [2013] EWHC 100 (Fam)

finance and banking is the major exception to this rule, in that the UK courts will have to take account of the fundamental principles of Islamic law when judging in cases involving Islamic finance contracts (Aldohni 2011), but a closer analysis of the jurisprudence in this area lies outside the scope of the current paper.

The UK courts will apply the rules of religious legal systems in cases where the legally relevant acts have taken place abroad and under religious law. The approach that is followed by the courts is essentially the same approach that is applied to any case involving foreign law. The court will hear expert evidence concerning the relevant provisions of the foreign law and their legal effects in the instant case, and will then decide the case under English law, but taking account of the legal effects of acts performed abroad.

If, for instance, a marriage under religious law is legally valid in another jurisdiction and the parties to the marriage later immigrate to England, then the marriage will, as a general rule, be legally valid in England, as well under the doctrine of *Lex Loci Celebrationis*. This means, for example, that although polygamous marriages cannot be legally contracted in England (or by anyone who is resident or domiciled in the UK), a polygamous family can immigrate to England and all the marriages be recognized as valid.

The courts may, nevertheless, still decide not to give legal effect in England to acts that are performed elsewhere and are legally valid under religious law in that jurisdiction. This happens if there are public policy reasons not to accept the outcome, or if the outcome is seen as inequitable. Domestic courts have, for instance, refused to grant legal effect to bare Islamic Talaq divorces declared overseas, unless they are accompanied by some form of legal registration,[41] and have also refused to recognize a marriage as legally valid because one of the parties was severely mentally disabled,[42] despite the fact that the marriage was legally valid in Bangladesh, where it had been contracted.

Another class of cases where the UK courts will enforce religiously based agreements is where these agreements can be understood as contracts. The courts will, for instance, enforce dowry agreements as contracts, even if these relate not to a legally valid English marriage, but to an Islamic *Nikah* marriage contracted in the UK, which is otherwise completely devoid of legal validity as a marriage.[43]

Permission or Prescription of Religious Adjudication

There are in English law no direct permissions or prohibitions relating to the use of religious adjudication bodies by individuals, or relating to the functions of such bodies. And it is known that religious adjudication bodies do deal with cases in many different areas of law (Bano 2007). See, for instance, the descriptions of their

[41] H v S [2011] EWHC B23 (Fam)

[42] XCC v AA & Anor (Rev 3) [2012] EWHC 2183 (COP)

[43] Uddin v Choudhury & Ors [2009] EWCA Civ 1205.

activities on the web-sites of the London Beth Din[44] and the Muslim Arbitration Tribunal,[45] as well as the academic analysis of the function of three different religious adjudication bodies in Douglas et al. 2011.

The lack of direct permission in statute entails that a decision by a religious adjudication body would never be automatically enforceable in cases where it is challenged or not adhered to by one of the parties. Legal enforcement, for instance through seizure of assets, would always require a judicial decision from a State court, although this decision can be summary if there is no dispute between the parties as to whether the arbitration followed the arbitration agreement. This will include many cases of purely commercial arbitration by religious adjudication bodies. The UK courts have also been willing to accept, albeit *obiter*, that judges in religious adjudication bodies possess some aspects of qualified legal privilege in relation to their communications.[46]

The members of any adjudication body adjudicating matters that fall under English Criminal Law may, however, potentially commit a range of criminal offences, including the common law offence of Perverting the Course of Justice and the statutory offence of Assisting an Offender. If a religious adjudication body enforced a physical punishment on a person, it would also commit further criminal offences such as Assault or False Imprisonment. In English law the claim in a criminal case is never between the victim and the alleged offender, but always between the Crown (e.g. State) and the alleged offender. There is, therefore, no legal space in which any other adjudication body could operate in the area of Criminal Law.

Conformity of State Law to Religious Rules

There are no religious institutions in the UK that are authorized by the State to assess the conformity of State law to any particular set of religious rules.

It is, however, worth reiterating that the Church of England is automatically represented in the Upper Chamber of Parliament by 26 bishops. These bishops, and other members of the House of Lords, who sit in a personal capacity (e.g. the, now former Chief Rabbi of the UK and the Commonwealth), but also hold religious offices, can comment on bills going through the legislative process, and may of course comment on such bills from the perspective of their particular religion.

---

[44] http://www.theus.org.uk/the_united_synagogue/the_london_beth_din/about_us/

[45] http://www.matribunal.com/

[46] Maccaba v Lichtenstein [2004] EWHC 1577 (QB).

Brief Thoughts on the Situation in Scotland[47]

As far as Scotland is concerned, Alan Rodger clearly thought that the Church of Scotland was now a private institution: see his *obiter* in the Inner House[48] in *Percy v Board of National Mission of the Church* [2001] ScotCS 65:

> [...] the General Assembly enacts laws which have many of the stylistic and other hallmarks of the kind of legislation which is enacted by Parliament. The procedures of the Church courts are replete with terminology which is familiar to practitioners of Scots law. The language does nothing indeed to conceal the hand which those trained in Scots law have had in guiding such proceedings down the centuries. None the less, despite their outward appearance, the laws of the Church operate only within the Church and her courts adjudicate only on matters spiritual. In other words, the formality and indeed solemnity of all these transactions and proceedings does not disclose an intention to create relationships under the civil law; rather, it reflects the serious way in which the Church regulates the matters falling within the spiritual sphere (at 14).

However, this does not mean that the law of the Kirk is definitively *not* part of the law of Scotland,– not least because the actings of the Kirk (but of no other religious organisation, all of which are merely private voluntary organisations), are not reviewable by the Court of Session. In fact, there are numerous judicial *dicta* to that effect, most recently *Logan v Presbytery of Dumbarton* 1995 SLT 1228, in which the Lord Ordinary (Osborne) declined to interfere in what the Church judged to be a disciplinary case under Article IV, concluding that he had no jurisdiction and adopting the view of Lord Justice Clerk Aitchison in *Ballantyne v Presbytery of Wigtown* 1936 SC 625, that the Church of Scotland Act 1921 "is not an Act of Parliament conferring rights upon the Church, but it is a recognition by Parliament of Articles framed by the General Assembly of the Church as its Supreme Court in the exercise of what it claimed to be its own inherent powers".

So, the answer to the question "is the law of the Kirk part of the law of Scotland?" would be, "yes and no". "No", insofar as it does not apply *outside* the Church and her courts, but "Yes", insofar as the Kirk and its courts have a particular status not shared by other institutions. In fact, the Court of Session has no hesitation in reviewing the actings of the courts of other Churches: see most recently *Macdonald, Re Application for Judicial Review* [2010] ScotCS CSOH 55.

Social Implementation of Religious Rules (Without Any Official Recognition)

The religious composition of the UK is extremely diverse, as explained above; and within all of the major religious groups there will be more orthodox, conservative or fundamentalist groups that adhere strictly to what they see as the true teachings of

[47] We are indebted to Frank Cranmer, for his invaluable assistance on this particular section.

[48] The Scottish Court of Appeal.

their religion in relation to both belief and conduct. This will inevitably bring their conduct into conflict with State law, either because they will require specific accommodations to be able to live in accordance with their beliefs, or because they believe that their religion enjoins them to act in ways that in some way contravene State Law.

There has traditionally been a significant willingness to find accommodations, either politically or legally, especially in cases where the impact on non-members of the religion is minimal. A few examples should suffice to show the breadth of accommodations: the Exclusive Brethren can have their children schooled without the use of IT equipment (although they mostly send them to their own schools), Orthodox Jewish communities can establish *Eruvim* partly using municipal lamp poles and other street furniture in the construction of the *Eruv* wall, and Islamic headscarves that do not cover the face can be worn on passport and other official photographs. However, even here there are limits, for instance in relation to Rastafarian use of cannabis.[49]

Having said that, if the religiously motivated action can be construed as harmful to others, including by being discriminatory, there has been less willingness to read a legal accommodation or compromise in recent years: see, for instance, Bull & Anor v Hall & Anor [2013] UKSC 73 and McFarlane v Relate Avon Ltd [2010] EWCA Civ 880, both cases involving a conflict between actions based on Christian beliefs and direct or indirect discrimination of homosexual persons or couples, as well as Eweida and Others v the United Kingdom [2013] ECHR 37.

Problems in Everyday Life

The wearing of religious symbols has given rise to wide litigation in relation to education and employment. Most UK schools have set school uniforms, described in a set of rules that usually extend to cover use of jewelry and allowable hair styles. A number of cases have been litigated where religious pupils have wanted to wear symbols, clothing or have hair styles that were incompatible with the school rule. The courts have been more reluctant to find unlawful discrimination in cases where the only reason for non-conformance with the uniform rules has been purely religious (e.g. Playfoot (a minor), R (on the application of) v Millais School [2007] EWHC 1698 (Admin) and Begum, R (on the application of) v. Denbigh High School [2006] UKHL 15)), but more willing to find unlawful discrimination where the reasons were at the same time religious and based on belonging to a specific ethnic group (e.g. Watkins-Singh, R (on the application of) v Aberdare Girls' High School & Anor [2008] EWHC 1865 (Admin) (García Oliva and Cranmer 2013, 555–582)). It should be stressed that Sikhs and Jews are defined as racial groups in the UK – which Muslims and Christians are not – and therefore, they attract the provisions of race relations legislation. This is an area of potential future contestation since some

[49] R v Taylor [2002] 1 CAR 519.

expressions of the intertwined religious and racial identity seem arguably to be more religious than racial. The wearing of the 5 traditional Sikh symbols is, for instance, only strongly mandated for baptised Sikhs, but never the less protected as an ethnic trait. The Home Office, for instance in 2014, changed its visiting policies in relation to immigration detention centres in order to allow Sikh ministers and legal advisors to wear the *kirpan* (the Sikh ceremonial knife) when visiting detainees.

In relation to employment, a number of cases have involved the wearing of the Christian cross in contravention of the dress code of the employer, and these have been uniformly lost in the UK courts, although the Court of Strasbourg found a breach of Article 9 of the ECHR when it examined one of them (Eweida and Others v the United Kingdom [2013] ECHR 37). In contradistinction, there are a number of laws specifically exempting turban wearing Sikhs from particular provisions that apply to others (e.g. Employment Act 1989, Section 11 & 12), and cases finding that not allowing Sikh men to wear turbans is discriminatory: Mandla (Sewa Singh) v Dowell Lee [1982] UKHL 7 (see also Vickers 2008).

It is worth mentioning that the rejection of various forms of Islamic clothing that has occurred in other European countries has been strongly identified with the extreme political right in the UK public debate, and that this probably precludes it from becoming an issue for legislation.

Use of Religious Adjudication Bodies

As indicated, English law does not automatically recognize any religious adjudication bodies, except the consistory courts and other courts of the Church of England. But it does, on the other hand, not directly prohibit them either (Malik 2012). There are a large number of Islamic Shariah adjudication bodies in existence in the UK, as well as Jewish Beth Din courts. These bodies are reported to be widely used by the relevant communities to resolve issues in Family and Commercial law (Shah-Kazemi 2001). Unfortunately, there are no good research studies of the extent of their use

Conclusion

The interplay between Law and Religion in England and Wales is complex, and is in some way, despite the establishment of the Church of England and the positive views on religion contained in the UK legislation and case law, characterized by a desire not to interfere directly in religious matters.

The Church of England has significant legal powers to legislate its internal affairs and a court system to adjudicate issues that fall within the jurisdiction of the Church. This jurisdiction interacts in varied ways with the State jurisdiction. The Measures of the Church of England are primary sources of law, and have to be approved by the UK Parliament, but Parliament aims to avoid undue interference in the legislative processes of the Church. Key examples of controversy between Church and State in recent years are the introduction of women bishops the Church of England and the recognition of same sex marriage. Theoretically, Parliament could have forced the Church to recognize female bishops, but it did not do so and instead waited for the Church to make the necessary legal changes.

The Church of England also plays a complicated constitutional role, through the links between the Monarch and the Church, and the Church and the Upper House of Parliament. The Church (of England) in Wales was disestablished in 1920 and all other religious denominations in England and Wales are regarded as voluntary associations by the legal framework.

The English legal approach to the religious jurisdiction of the non-established religions can perhaps best be described as a type of "benign neglect". The State does not in general recognize religious adjudication, but it does not directly prohibit it either. The State does not grant explicit minority group rights to religious groups, and it has set itself firmly against the recognition of any type of "personal law" system. So, recognition is on a piece-meal and case by case basis.

Religious adjudication in the area of Criminal Law will expose the adjudication body to a range of significant legal risks, and can never be enforceable, but even this form of adjudication is not directly prohibited in statute or court decisions.

There has, however, been some public and political disquiet in relation to Islamic Shariah courts and a bill (Arbitration and Mediation Services (Equality) Bill [HL] 2012–2013) was unsuccessfully introduced in the House of Lords in 2012 by Baroness Cox to curtail their functions. A specific issue that is seen as problematic is that these bodies are perceived as discriminatory against women. The perceived discrimination is both in relation to alleged evidentiary standards, i.e. that the testimony of women is not given the same weight as the testimony of men, and in relation to the asymmetry of the Shariah jurisprudence on divorce. The bill has been re-introduced in the current Parliament, but is probably unlikely to pass and become law, since that would require the Government to give it time in the parliamentary schedule.

Acknowledgements We would like to thank Frank Cranmer, Research Associate at the Centre for Law and Religion at Cardiff University and Fellow at St Chad's College at Durham, for his invaluable suggestions and comments on a previous version of this contribution.

List of References

Ahdar, R., and I. Leigh. 2013. *Religious freedom in the liberal state*, 2nd ed. Oxford: Oxford University Press.

Aldohni, A.K. 2011. *The legal and regulatory aspects of Islamic banking*. London: Routledge.

Bano, S. 2007. Muslim family justice and human rights: The experience of British Muslim women. *Journal of Comparative Law* 2(2): 38.

Bradney, A. 2009. *Law and faith in a sceptical age*. Abingdon: Routledge Cavendish.

Carr, W. 1999. A developing establishment. *Theology* 102: 2–10.

Davie, G. 1994. *Religion in Britain since 1945*. Oxford: Blackwell Publishing.

Doe, N. 2011. *Law and religion in Europe: A comparative introduction*. New York: Oxford University Press.

Douglas, G, N. Doe, S. Gilliat-Ray, R. Sandberg, A. Khan. 2011. Social cohesion and civil law: marriage, divorce and religious courts – report of a research study funded by the AHRC. http://www.law.cf.ac.uk/clr/Social%20Cohesion%20and%20Civil%20Law%20Full%20Report.pdf

Edge, P. 2013. Autonomy and established churches: Thoughts on English establishment(s) in the twenty-first century. In *Transformations of church and state relations in Great Britain and Germany*, ed. C. Walter and A. Von Ungern-Sternberg. Baden-Baden: Nomos.

García Oliva, J. 2010. Church, state and establishment in the united kingdom in the 21st century: Anachronism or idiosyncrasy? *Public Law* 3: 482–504.

García Oliva, J., and F. Cranmer. 2013. Education and religious symbols in the UK, Italy and Spain: Uniformity or subsidiarity? *European Public Law* 19: 555–582.

García Oliva, J., and H. Hall. 2013. Same sex marriage: An inevitable challenge to religious liberty and establishment? *Oxford Journal of Law and Religion*. doi:10.1093/ojlr/rwt045.

Knights, S. 2007. *Freedom of religion, minorities, and the law*. Oxford: Oxford University Press.

Malik, M. 2012. *Minorities, pluralism and the law*. London: British Academy. Minority Legal Orders in the UK.

Malik, M. 2013. Religion and sexual orientation: Conflict or cohesion? In *Religion in a liberal state*, ed. G. D'Costa, M. Evans, T. Modood, and J. Rivers. Cambridge: Cambridge University Press.

Petchey, P. 2008. Legal issues for faith schools in England and Wales. *Ecclesiastical Law Journal* 10: 174–190.

Rivers, J. 2010. *The law of organized religions: Between establishment and secularism*. Oxford: Oxford University Press.

Sandberg, R. 2011. *Law and religion*. Cambridge: Cambridge University Press.

Shah-Kazemi, S.N. 2001. *Untying the knot: Muslim women, divorce and the shariah*. London: Nuffield Foundation.

Vickers, L. 2008. *Religious freedom, religious discrimination and the workplace*. Oxford: Hart Publishing.

United Kingdom Government Census. 2011. http://www.ons.gov.uk/ons/rel/census/2011-census/detailed-characteristics-for-local-authorities-in-england-and-wales/sty religion.html

Watkin, T.G. 1990. Vestiges of establishment: The ecclesiastical and canon law of the church in Wales. *Ecclesiastical Law Journal* 2: 110–115.

Williams, R. 2008. Civil and religious law in England: A religious perspective. *Ecclesiastical Law Journal* 10: 262–282.

Chapter 24
Conclusion: In Pursuit of Pluralism

Russell Sandberg

Abstract This concluding chapter returns to the questions posed by Silvio Ferrari in his introductory chapter and his distinction between States that employ individual orientated strategies and those who favour community orientated strategies. Revisiting the arguments of Ayelet Shachar, it is argued that both of these strategies are required. Further, it is not a question of whether or not the State intervenes in religious legal systems but when and how they should do so. The chapter draws upon Shachar's concept of 'joint governance' but rejects her much lauded variant of 'transformative accommodation'. Instead, it draws upon three of Shachar's five variants of joint governance to reach sixteen propositions of how States should proceed.

The Age of Anxiety

A spectre haunts every single page in the book you have just read. Its presence can be found in every paragraph, every line. It is found more often than not in the spaces between the words, rather than in the words itself. The phantom is in the subtext. It is a constant companion ever present but seldom acknowledged. There have been times when it has become visible but these sightings have been exceptional. For the most part the reader has glimpsed it through the corner of their eye but they would not hesitate in affirming its importance to the volume as a whole. It is a, if not the, reason for this volume existing and for the wider literature in which this book finds itself. It is why more and more academics scribble, why politicians seek simplistic solutions and why journalists spread panic.

As convenient short-hand for the poltergeist in question, it may be appropriate to talk about a fear of sharia. In our post 9/11 world, concerns about Islam have become commonplace. These apprehensions existed before 2001 and had previously given rise to moral panics across the globe. However, in the twenty-first century these panics have become more frequent with concerns about fundamentalism overflowing

R. Sandberg (✉)
Cardiff Law School, Cardiff University, Cardiff, UK
e-mail: SandbergR@cardiff.ac.uk

R. Bottoni et al. (eds.), *Religious Rules, State Law, and Normative Pluralism - A Comparative Overview*, Ius Comparatum – Global Studies in Comparative Law 18, DOI 10.1007/978-3-319-28335-7_24

into debates about the wearing of religious dress and symbols in the public sphere, the appropriateness of the publication of words and images that satirise religious imagery and the operation of courts and tribunals who apply religious rules. These examples show that talk of a fear of sharia is simply a convenient short-hand. Our anxieties go deeper than that. For most of the globe, the late twentieth century was a period of accelerated social change which led to widespread uncertainty. The thawing of the cold war diluted distinctive political differences and at the same time other certainties began to crumble. Age hold traditions and forms of employment became increasingly archaic. Old consensuses concerning gender roles and sexual orientation became challenged. Geographic barriers began to be removed. The media became all powerful and all embracive as technological advances allowed mass communication, information overload and instant access to people at all social levels. An 'individuating revolution' (Taylor 2002 p.80) took place. Achieved identities became more important than ascribed identities. A 'subjective turn' occurred with people placing an increased emphasis upon construction and re-construction of personal identities as the main source of significance, meaning and authority.[1] While this might appear to be empowering, the result has actually been increased loneliness as the familial and local bonds of old have been replaced with mass uncertainty and people are left to fend for themselves as the agents of socialisation, including the State, do less than they did in their post-World War Two heyday.

These profound changes, which remain ongoing, have had a significant effect upon religion. It is often asserted that we are living in the age of the 'culture wars' where there is conflict concerning people's 'basic commitments and beliefs that provide a source of identity, purpose, and togetherness for the people who live by them' which is characterised by 'polarizing impulses or tendencies' whereby 'differences are often intensified and aggravated in the way they are presented in public' (Hunter 1991 p.41–43). These 'culture wars' involves the various moral panics concerning religion such as those concerning same sex marriage, the wearing of religious dress and symbols and the operation of religious courts. Even if it may be inappropriate to designate such conflicts as a war, it is clear that the consensus that seemed to exist by the mid-twentieth century has been broken down. Religion is no longer seen as a benign dwindling force. Rather, those who profess adherence to a faith are regarded as the Other and their loyalty to a source of authority other than the State is viewed with suspicion. Commentators have struggled to explain this change. Some still refer to the death of God whilst others speak of the demise of the secularisation thesis. Some paradoxically deny that the secularisation thesis was ever correct but then talk of the 'return' of religion. The only matter of clarity is that simplistic kneejerk reactions cannot capture the complexity and contradictions of what has occurred.[2]

---

[1] See further Sandberg 2014 p.161; Sandberg 2015a p.1; Taylor 1991 p.26; Heelas and Woodhead 2005.

[2] For a full discussion of the secularisation thesis see Sandberg 2014 and Bruce 2011. For two seemingly opposite views compare Bruce 2002 and Stark 1999.

The fear of sharia – or to be more precise, the persistent anxiety surrounding the place of religious manifestations in the public sphere in many Western States – explains the increased frequency in which moral panics concerning the regulation of religion have occurred. The moral panics concerning religious courts, religious dress, religious cartoons and so on are not simply the consequence of the breakdown of the consensus. They are not simply the result of religion becoming controversial. They are also means by which societies (or institutions within them) let off steam. By discussing the claims by litigants or public statements by religious officials, we are able to address major concerns in concrete ways. Simplified public debates allow us to address wider issues such as immigration, national identities and changing attitudes towards gender and sexuality. The fears that unite us are dealt with as discrete issues. Various social actors partake in this conversation, playing different roles. The political and media systems play their part as do religious authorities.

Law plays a role in this. Alongside the education system, it is often the means by which perceived problems are solved, especially in relation to what Martin Ramstedt's chapter in this volume described as the 'new global legal pluralism'. In his introduction to this volume Silvio Ferrari identified two ideal types in terms of the strategy taken by States. The first comprised of 'community orientated strategies' which focus on group rights and obligations by protecting minority rights (as in Greece and Singapore) and personal laws (as in Israel, Malaysia and South Africa). The second were referred to as 'individual orientated strategies' which focus on the religious freedom and equal treatment of individuals by the granting of specific rights or exceptions to generally applicable norms (such approaches are prevalent in Western Europe). As Ferrari rightly states, this does not mean that the second group does not recognise collective rights. Indeed, international human rights instruments protecting religious stress that it is both a collective and an individual right.[3] Moreover, as Ferrari makes clear, the difference between the two ideal types is a matter of degree: the two strategies start from different perspectives but both provide some recognition of religious legal systems. As Ferrari correctly points out, the frequent statements in the country reports in this volume that countries who follow the second strategy have 'no system of personal laws based on religious affiliation' and 'do not allow formal jurisdiction to religious courts' are only true as a result of the words 'system' and 'formal jurisdiction'. While it is true that States that follow the second strategy do not have rules concerning personal laws and religious adjudication that have the breadth and the strength commonly found in the countries of the first group, this does not mean that they do not recognise religious

[3] For example, Article 18 of the Universal Declaration on Human Rights 1948 states that 'Everyone has the right to freedom of thought, conscience and religion; this right includes freedom to change his religion or belief, and freedom, *either alone or in community with others* and in public or private, to manifest his religion or belief in teaching, practice, worship and observance' (emphasis added). The European Court of Human Rights has held that religious organisations are entitled to protection under freedom of religion provisions through the protection afforded to its individual members: *X v Denmark* [1976] 5 ECHR 157; *Metropolitan Church of Bessarabia v Moldova* [2002] 35 EHRR 306. See, further, Sandberg 2008a.

legal systems; the difference is simply that the accommodation is usually much more ad hoc and dependent upon legal mechanisms that are not reserved exclusively for religious and cultural groups.[4] Ferrari's two ideal types are perhaps best understood as the two ends of a spectrum upon which all legal systems can be found. While no countries fall on either extreme side of the spectrum in that they do neither emphasize collective rights at the exclusion of individual rights nor individual rights at the exclusion of community rights, countries can be placed at different places on the spectrum based not only on their guiding principle (that is, which of the two ideal type strategies they adopt) but also in terms of the letter and applications of their laws.

Ferrari's recognition of two ideal type strategies is also useful in terms of answering the questions he set at the end of his introduction. Given that legal systems do not exist as abstract entities in a social, cultural, historical and political vacuum, Ferrari is correct to assert that it would be wrong to ask 'what is the State legal system that grants citizens the best chance to live their lives according to their religious (or non-religious) convictions?' The quest is not for a 'one size fits all' solution but rather to identify ways in which legal systems with different emphases and in differing contexts can balance the needs of religious and non-religious individuals, groups, wider communities and the State. As Ferrari puts it, the question is 'what can be done by each legal system to give citizens the opportunity to live according to their religious (or non-religious) convictions without endangering social cohesion and fostering (auto)segregation?' This chapter attempts to answer that question by revisiting the arguments of Ayelet Shachar (2001), elements of which have been influential in the debates concerning religion and legal pluralism given the discussion of Shachar's concept of 'transformative accommodation' in the controversial lecture by the then Archbishop of Canterbury Rowan Williams (2008).

Distinctions in the Sand

Like Ferrari, Shachar identified two ideal types in terms of how States can manage what she referred to as *nomoi* groups, that is, 'minority communities that generate sets of group-sanctioned norms of behavior that differ from those encoded in state law' (2001 p.2). The first, is the 'religious particularist model' where jurisdictional powers are granted to the group and there exists an'expansive structure of accommodation'; the second, is the 'secular absolutist model' where full jurisdictional powers are granted to the state and religious or customary practices are relegated to

[4]A clear example of this is provided in the chapter by Merlin Kiviorg who notes that: 'It is quite likely that the first reaction of any lawyer in Estonia would be that state law does not allow any application of religious rules meaning there is no legal pluralism, Estonian law applies. A closer look, however, reveals that religious rules are applied *de facto*, for example, within contractual freedom between parties, in the framework of exemptions from generally applicable laws and autonomy of religious communities.' Lawyers elsewhere would make similar initial erroneous reactions.

the "private" realm' in that 'a uniform secular state law is imposed upon all citizens in family law matters, regardless of those citizens group affiliation(s)' and there is 'a strict separation of church and state' (2001 p.13, 63, 72–73). These two models can be seen as roughly aligning to Ferrari's two ideal types, albeit across a different axis. Like Ferrari's ideal types, these models are best understood as being the two ends of a spectrum; Shachar suggests that they represent 'a decisive point on the continuum of accommodation' (2001, p.63).

However, Shachar's identification of the second model with a separation of Church and State is unhelpful, however, for two reasons. First, as Ferrari's elucidation of his ideal types show, the distinctions drawn do not correspond with models of Church-State relations. It has conventionally been thought that three models of Church-State relations exist in Western European States: State church systems, separation systems, and cooperationist (hybrid) systems (Robbers 2005: 578–580).[5] It is not the case that countries that fall under particular models of Church-State relations will share similar models of accommodation. As Ferrari's distinction shows, Greece is an example of a State taking a 'community orientated strategy' while England and Wales fall under the 'individual orientated strategy' label. The fact that both are State Church systems is irrelevant. What matters is not the constitutional position of the majority religion but rather the legal regulation (and the approach to legal regulation) of religious minorities. The second reason why the invocation of the models of Church-State relations is unhelpful is connected to this. A body of scholarship has questioned the usefulness of the conventional models suggesting that while the models describe the letter of the constitutional provisions they fail to take into account sub-constitutional laws and the impact of international norms which have led to a greater degree of homogenisation (see, e.g, Ferrari 1997; Sandberg and Doe 2007; Sandberg 2008b; Doe 2011). It has become clear that referring to a country as an example of a State Church system or as a separation system says very little about the regulation of religion in that State. Indeed, it has been suggested that cooperation with religion is actually the dominant characteristic of European religion-State relations (Doe 2011).[6]

[5] State church systems are those countries characterised by the existence of close links between the State and a particular religious community, which may be styled as a 'State,' 'national,' 'established,' or 'folk' church. Examples include England, Denmark, Greece, Finland, Malta, and Bulgaria. By contrast, separation systems include those countries where there is a constitutional barrier forbidding the financial support and establishment of any one religion. Examples of such a separation are France (with the exception of the three eastern *départements*), the Netherlands and Ireland. Hybrid systems, effectively, are those States whose constitutional provisions concerning religion come in between state church systems and separation systems. Also known as cooperationist systems or sometimes concordatarian systems, these States are characterised by a simple separation of state and church coupled with the recognition of a multitude of common tasks which link state and church activity, which are often recognised in the form of agreements, treaties, and Concordats. Examples include Spain, Italy, Germany, Belgium, Austria, Hungary, Portugal, and the Baltic States.

[6] As Wolfgang Wieshaider points out in his chapter in this volume, 'Recognition implies certain elements of co-operation between the State and the recognised religious societies'. Louis-Leon Christians and Adriaan Overbeeke in their chapter talk of the State operating as a 'faciliator' for

However, the ideal types identified by Shachar are helpful. Indeed, the importance of Shachar's account is that she rejects both models. She claims that both approaches fail to protect what she refers to as 'the paradox of multicultural vulnerability' (2001 p.3): the concern that those who are inside *nomoi* groups are denied the rights that they would ordinarily enjoy by virtue of their citizenship of the State. This is often referred to as the 'minorities within minorities' issue. The 'religious particularist model' in increasing the authority of the group and the 'secular absolutist model' in turning a blind eye to groups that already exist both do little to protect minorities within minorities. Shachar (2001 p.28–29) therefore rejects the 'strong' version of multiculturalism in which the identity group 'are to be granted extensive, formal, legal and constitutional standing so that they may govern themselves in accordance with their *nomos*' and calls instead for a 'weak' version of multiculturalism should be adopted which focuses on 'providing multicultural accommodation without abandoning the protection of individual rights'. This insight is important. In rejecting her two models Shachar also (implicitly) rejects Ferrari's ideal types, making it clear that both individual and community orientated strategies are required.

Shachar is scathing of approaches that claim that the States should not intervene in group affairs (2001 p.12, 68–70).[7] In particular, she is critical of the 'right to exit' argument: that the role of the State should be simply to ensure that every individual has the option to leave the group if they so wish. She asserts that 'this right to exist offers no comprehensive approach at all, … imposing the burden of solving conflict upon the individuals—and relieving the state of any responsibility for the situation' (Shachar 2001 p.41). The right to exit 'forces an insider into a cruel choice of penalties: either accept all group practices – including those that violate your fundamental citizenship rights – or (somehow) leave'. This approach is predicated upon a 'binary' notion of identity whereby individuals can either be an adherent of the group or a citizen of the State – they cannot be both. As Shachar puts it, 'once individuals enter (or choose to remain within) minority communities, they are presumed to have relinquished the set of rights and protections granted to them by virtue of their citizenship'. Shachar is equally contemptuous, however, of approaches that take a purely individualised approach whereby States intervene to protect individual rights and have little, if any, regard to the autonomy and rights of the group (2001 p.12, 65).[8] Such an approach, she writes 'fails to recognize that power dynamics at

religious groups, an idea that has been expressed by the European Court of Human Rights, as shown by the Grand Chamber judgment in *Refah Partisi v Turkey* (2003) 37 EHRR 1 at para 91 that: 'The Court has frequently emphasised the State's role as the neutral and impartial organiser of the exercise of various religions, faiths and beliefs, and stated that this role is conducive to public order, religious harmony and tolerance in a democratic society'.

[7] She highlights the 'unavoidable costs' argument by Kukathas (1992) which she summarises as claiming 'that although tensions can arise between the goals of accommodating differences and protecting rights, a genuinely tolerant state will rarely intervene in minority group affairs- even if that minority group systemically violates certain of its members citizenship rights'.

[8] She highlights the 're-universalized citizenship' response by Okin (1997) which, according to Shachar, 'holds that in a conflict between an individual and a minority group, the state should put

play within cultural groups are not static' by assuming the existence of a 'zero-sum game, in which any strengthening of a minority group's rights implies an accompanying weakening of rights for that minority group's female members'. Shachar criticises such approaches as being 'based on sweeping generalizations about the majority of the world's different cultures and religions' and for casting 'women who remain loyal to minority groups' cultures as victims without agency. Importantly, Shachar notes that although the community orientated 'right to exit' and individualised approaches 'appear to be diametrically opposed', they are based on a similar misunderstanding in that 'they effectively function as mirror images of one another since both are underpinned by the same basic logic' (2001 p.7):

> 'these two theoretical responses are based on a common error: an oversimplified "either-or"- type understanding of legal authority which is not tailored to respect individuals' manifold identities' (2001 p.12).

Shachar's significant achievement is to suggest that we should be more ambitious than this. She contends that the choice is not between 'invention' and 'non-intervention' because '*nomoi* groups are always reacting to the effects of state power, even when they claim to be most isolated from them' (2001 p.40). The question is rather about the kind of accommodation that is needed in order to protect both cultural identities and citizenship rights. Shachar calls for 'an alternative way of practicing multiculturalism' which 'seeks to enhance the autonomy of distinct *nomoi* communities, whilst at the same time providing at-risk individuals with viable legal-institutional tools to enhance their leverage within the group', challenging the power relations encoded within their minority groups' traditions' (2001 p.7, 71). To return to Ferrari's ideal types, it could be said that Shachar is effectively calling for a fusion of both community orientated and individual orientated strategies. The question is how this is to be achieved.

Shachar's *Deus ex Machina*

In his infamous and much misunderstood lecture on 'Religious and Civil Law in England: A Religious Perspective' in February 2008 the then Archbishop of Canterbury Dr Rowan Williams (2008) praised Shachar's 'highly original and significant' work and endorsed her call for 'transformative accommodation'. However, Williams did not place 'transformative accommodation' into the context of Shachar's work and did not mention at all her notion of 'joint governance': the idea that people can belong to, show allegiance to and follow norms from more than one source of authority at any given time.[9] In Shachar's schema 'transformative accommodation'

---

its weight behind the individual, even if in doing so, the State helps to alienate the individual from her group'.

[9] As Shachar (2001 p.81) puts it: 'Joint governance promises to foster ongoing interaction between different sources of authority, as a means of improving the situation of traditionally vulnerable

is just one of five variants of 'joint governance'. It is clearly Shachar's preferred variant as shown by the way in which the other four variants are often presented as 'straw' arguments. However, it has been suggested that three of the other four variants are preferable to 'transformative accommodation' if they are fused together and developed in ways that are consistent with Shachar's notion of 'joint governance' (Sandberg et al. 2013). While Williams and subsequent commentators focused upon 'transformative accommodation',[10] this may actually prove to be nothing more than a *deus ex machina*; an overly simplistic implausible solution of convenience.

The concept of 'transformative accommodation' is not clearly defined by Shachar. She writes that the label 'transformative' has been used because this variant 'is designed to encourage group authorities themselves to reduce discriminatory internal restrictions' (2001 p.14). Later on, however, she seems to suggest that under this approach both the group and the State will transform: transformative accommodation will encourage 'each entity to become more responsive to *all* its constituents. Through an arrangement of non-exclusive competition for the loyalties of those citizens who overlap both jurisdictions, transformative accommodation seeks to adapt the power structures of both *nomoi* groups and state in order to accommodate their most vulnerable constituents' (2001 p.117). This appears to be little more than a general description of joint governance, coupled with an emphasis upon competition which has been criticised for taking a 'rational actor view of the world' and being 'written in the language of the marketplace' (Phillips 2007 p.153). The same is true of the 'four key assumptions' of transformative accommodation identified by Shachar (2001 p.118): one, that 'group members living within a larger political community represent the intersection of multiple identity creating affiliations'; two, that 'in many real-life circumstances both the group and the state have normatively and legally justifiable interests in shaping the rules that govern behavior'; three, that 'the group and the state are both viable and mutable social entities which are constantly affecting each other through their ongoing interactions'; and four, that 'it is in the self-professed interest of the group and the state to vie for the support of their constituents'. Although some assumptions are a little suspect,[11] the first three assumptions clearly underpin joint governance in general (and indeed legal pluralism *per se*) rather than being distinctive to transformative accommodation. The fourth assumption suggests that Shachar sees transformative accommodation as a competitive model. Indeed, she observes that, 'each entity must "bid" for these individual's continued adherence to its sphere of authority' (2001 p.117). This

insiders without forcing them to adhere to an either/or choice between their culture and their rights'.

[10] See, e.g., Jackson 2009 and Malik 2012 p.36. Compare the wider treatment by some political scientists such as in Eisenberg and Spinner-Haley 2005.

[11] The third assumption, though underlining how joint governance is premised on the notion that it is possible to determine whether the group is a viable social entity, is problematic in its use of the words 'constantly affecting' which seems to imply a closeness between systems that does not necessarily exist as shown, e.g., in the empirical findings of Douglas et al. (2011).

reference to competition is unnecessary and culturally loaded. It would also seem to breed conflict and stoke existing anxieties.

In addition to resting on 'four key assumptions', Shachar claims that transformative accommodation is characterised by having 'three core principles': the 'sub-matter' allocation of authority, the 'no monopoly' rule, and the establishment of 'clearly delineated choice options' (2001 p.118–119). It is questionable, however, whether these core principles actually advance matters, especially in light of recent empirical work conducted in the United Kingdom (Douglas et al. 2011). The first principle, the 'sub-matter' allocation of authority, 'observes that contested social arenas (such as education, family law, criminal justice, immigration, resource development, and environmental protection) are internally divisible into "sub-matters": multiple, separable, yet complementary legal components' (2001 p.119). Transformative accommodation allocates 'jurisdictional authority upon sub-matter lines' and this division into sub-matters ensures that both the State and the group need to work together to resolve any dispute since each will only have jurisdiction over one sub-matter only. In other words, both the State and the group will lack pieces of the jigsaw and so will need to work together to complete the puzzle. Shachar gives the example of family law matters (2001 p.119–120). She identifies a distinction between the 'demarcating' function, the role of family law in 'defining and regulating a group's membership boundaries', and the 'distributive' function, 'which shapes and allocates rights, duties, and ultimately powers between men and women within the group' (2001 p.50–55). She notes that divorce proceedings generally involve both of these aspects, 'a change in personal status (the demarcating function) and a determination of property relations between the spouses (the distributive function)' (2001 p.51). Shachar suggests that by affording the group one function and the State another then both will be forced into a dialogue to resolve any dispute.

However, empirical work has suggested that while religious tribunals and the State already exercise different functions, there is little contact or dialogue between the State and religious groups. A UK based study of matrimonial jurisdiction of the Catholic National Tribunal for Wales, the London Beth Din and the Shariah Council of the Birmingham Central Mosque (Douglas et al. 2011) found that each tribunal was for the most part exercising a demarcating function. In all three tribunals, the fundamental rationale for the grant of the religious annulment/divorce was to enable the parties to remarry within the faith. The focus was on the marriage itself, not the ancillaries (children, money and property). The tribunals were ultimately concerned with religious status. The State was responsible for distributive functions and in practice the tribunals were aware of this and advised their clientele that they did not deal with such matters. This 'sub-matter' allocation of authority provided an implicit compromise between group and State but did not provide an incentive for dialogue between. The different functions, if anything, served to keep the group and State separated. The religious tribunals were wary of deciding upon matters where the State alone had competence but there was no dialogue between the State and the group as to these limits. They were rather implied and accepted. In short, there was little evidence of any 'transformative' element.

Shachar's second principle, the 'no monopoly' rule, draws from the separation of powers, stating that 'neither the group nor the state can ever acquire exclusive control over a contested social arena that affects individuals both as group members and as citizens' (2001 p.121). Although this seems similar to the first principle, Shachar seems to suggest that this rule would lead to the blurring of jurisdictional boundaries. She observes that this principle 're-defines the relationship between the state and its minority groups by structurally positioning them as complementary power-holders' and that: 'Thanks to this interdependent balance, decision-makers in contested social arenas can benefit from a broader pool of precedent and autonomy'. It seems implausible and undesirable that religious groups and the State would share precedents given the particular nature of religious rules (as explored by Ferrari in his introduction). Such a fusion of approaches would either require the secularisation of religious rules or the sacralisation of State legal systems. Empirical work has also suggested that religious tribunals do not wish to act like the State. The UK based study (Douglas et al. 2011) found that each tribunal were aware they did not exercise a legal monopoly and did not wish to increase their jurisdiction. The limits to their jurisdiction were shaped by their understandings of state law and the overriding impression given was one of deference. The leaders of religious tribunal did not want to hold 'complete power' and they also did not seem to mind whether they had any 'public legal authority' (Douglas et al. 2011).[12] Shachar's rule seems based on a false presumption that religious tribunals wish to monopolise and does not further matters.

Shachar's third principle, 'the establishment of clearly delineated choice options', refers to the need to establish 'clearly delineated choice options through which constituents can express approval or disapproval of state or group decisions' (2001 p.121). The idea that group jurisdiction should be a matter of choice for members is sound. However, oddly Shachar seems to view this choice as being limited to the choice to move from group to State (or vice versa). This sounds similar to the 'right to exit' argument which she was critical of. Although Shachar seeks to distinguish her scheme on the basis that while 'most accommodation models only allow membership to be "entirely in" or "entirely out", the possibility to "opt in" or "opt out" of specific group positions produces a decisive shift in group influence from dominant power-holders to individual members' (2001 p.123), it is difficult to see how the right to 'opt-out' does not suffer from most of the defects of the right to exit. Moreover, Shachar describes this possibility of opting in or out in such a way that it makes it sound that such movement will be exceptional. She writes that 'such participation must proceed on an issue-by-issue basis, once the initial jurisdictional boundaries have been set, thus allowing *nomoi* members to meaningfully choose between jurisdictions' (2001 p.123). The reference to 'initial jurisdictional

[12] The research underscored that the authority which religious tribunal officials enjoy is not purely 'legal'; rather it seemed to derive from a combination of their position in the court, their standing in the community and their own personality. The majority of those interviewed were also religious leaders and their 'legal' functions are just one part of their much larger pastoral role.

boundaries' here seems to be crucial since for Shachar, 'reversal provisions' are not to be taken lightly:

> The purpose is not to fracture group solidarity so that members can opt out at the slightest opportunity. The initial division of authority between group and state must remain meaningful and presumptively binding on its individual.

This would seem to amount to a presumption that people should remain subject to the authority which they originally found themselves in. Moreover, Shachar seems to be saying that these clear reversal points would become fixed. Although she claims that 'the predefinition of reversal points … relieves the vulnerable insider from the need to negotiate individually the transition between group and state norms on a case-by-case basis' (2001, p.125), it is difficult to see how this overcomes the criticisms she has made of the 'right to exit': surely this is an "either-or"- type understanding of legal authority' (cf. 2001, p.12) which will be of little help to the vulnerable minority who is a matter of fact unable to leave. This also raises the question of how an individual could be said to remain in the group even once they have opted out of significant rules and practices. For the coherence of the group to be un-affected the 'reversal provisions' would need to concern fairly minor matters of doctrine and teaching. But that would undermine the entire point of the exercise.

Generally, it seems that 'transformative accommodation' is defective in that lacks any distinctive attribute and the principles identified are deeply problematic. It has further been suggested that there are five main problems with the concept (Sandberg et al. 2013). First, the concept ignores the fact that there will people are often members of more than one group. There are often groups within larger groups and movement between these groups is possible.[13] Second, Shachar's account employs a too legalistic understanding of authority assuming that 'group leaders may want to hold complete power over all group members [but] can be convinced of the practical advantages of compromise when faced with the alternative of receiving no public legal authority at all' (2001 p.126). Third, Shachar's insistence that transformative accommodation would operate without minimal standards being required by the State (2001 p.127) is objectionable. Without explicit 'minimal standards' to guide interactions between the state and the group, implicit ideas about minimal standards will form anyway but would be hidden and opaque. Minimal standards are required: surely a State would and should be obligated to impose its norms where a group's *nomos* required (say) human sacrifice? Fourth, Shachar's scheme is often aimed at achieving integration rather than accommodation.[14]

---

[13] This was shown clearly in the phenomenon of 'forum shopping' observed in the religious tribunals studied by Douglas et al. 2011. The absence of an appeal hierarchy in the Muslim and Jewish communities means that litigants can, to some extent, choose which tribunal they go to according to the way in which (they think) the law will be applied to them and can then make use of a different religious tribunal if they are not satisfied the first time.

[14] Although there is no consensus as to the exact meanings that are to be attributed to these words (see, e.g., Poulter 1999 p.12), it may be suggested that integration implies a intention to achieve over time a degree of assimilation whereby differences are reduced. In contrast, accommodation

Shachar seems to think that if the right conditions were created then the group will reform itself and will accept the prevailing norms of the state.[15] This is naive and condescending. Fifth, transformative accommodation is politically unfeasible. Shachar concedes that 'transformative accommodation is admittedly limited in terms of immediate and practical judicial economy' (2001 p.131) and that it requires considerable generosity on part of the State.[16] Given current anxieties and the short-term mentality of political leaders, this means that transformative accommodation is unlikely to provide a means forward in terms of reform. It is fortunate, therefore, that three of the other four variants of joint governance identified by Shachar provide a more realistic and plausible approach whereby 'joint governance' can be recognised by a fusion of individual and community orientated strategies. The following section will explore how this could be achieved and how this approach would overcome the five problems with 'transformative accommodation'.

Solutions of Straw

For Shachar (2001 p.7), the 'model of joint governance describes a repertoire of accommodation designs which can be combined and applied in creative ways according to different social needs and arenas'. This repertoire is not intended to provide a 'one size fits all' solution. As Shachar notes, no 'mere legal formula, or even the best of institution's designs, can ever single-handedly resolve all the immensely complex philosophical problems and near-inexorable moral and ethical tensions that arise out of encounters between different cultural communities in shared political spaces' (2001 p.7–8). In short, she is not seeking to answer the question which Ferrari said that we should not (namely, 'what is the State legal system that grants citizens the best chance to live their lives according to their religious (or non-religious) convictions?'). Rather, the model of joint governance provides an answer to the question that Ferrari said that we should ask: what can be done by each legal system to give citizens the opportunity to live according to their religious (or non-religious) convictions without endangering social cohesion and fostering (auto)segregation?' This section will seek to answer this question by developing a series of propositions. This will be achieved by exploring and developing three of the four other variants of joint governance identified by Shachar. However, before doing this, a number of propositions may be identified based on the notion of joint

---

assumes no such intention. The end goal of accommodation is simply the making of space for such difference to exist within the majority culture.

[15] 'Transformative accommodation seeks to create institutional conditions where the group recognizes that its own survival depends on revoking certain discriminatory practices in the interests of maintaining autonomy over sub-matters crucial to the group's distinct *nomos*' (2001 p.125).

[16] She reasons that 'since the state is the most powerful entity, the presumption in the negotiations must be in favor of the group'. This means that 'generosity at the negotiation stage is required from the state as the stronger party' (2001 p129, 130).

governance itself. The first proposition is that: each State should recognise that its citizens belong to, show allegiance to and follow norms from more than one source of authority at any given time. From this a second and crucial proposition follows: States should recognise that religious freedom is both an individual and a collective right and consequentially legal mechanisms need to be both individually and community orientated.[17] This does not mean that every legal mechanism needs to have an individual and a community orientation but the legal framework as a whole needs to balance these focuses.

The three variants of 'Joint Governance' that will be adopted are those based on jurisdictional rather than territorial considerations' (Shachar 2001 p.95).[18] The first, 'temporal accommodation', is 'time bound and issue specific': it holds that 'certain life events crucial to the continuation of the group's collective identity (such as the creation of a family or the early education of children) should be governed by group tradition as the sole and definitive source of authority' and that 'outside of these crucial moments, individuals must turn to state law' (Shachar 2001 p.97). For example, it could be said that the early education of children is a matter for the *nomoi* group whilst the later education of children is a matter for the State. Shachar claims that this takes us beyond the "either/or" trap' in that it recognises a division of authority, 'neither the state nor the group has full and exclusive jurisdiction' (2001 p.98) but this is only true when one looks at the full life of the group member. Furthermore, this model depends on 'a precise definition of time- and issue-based jurisdictional boundaries between the state and the group' (2001 p.97), which Shachar concedes would be difficult to achieve (2001 p.102).

That said, this model does provide a number of insights into how joint governance can operate. It stresses that tensions between states and groups 'typically arise around significant life events' (2001, p.99), a conclusion underlined by empirical studies such as Douglas et al. (2011). Further, Shachar (2001, p.98) notes that temporal accommodation schemes 'must also allow individuals sufficient "inside" knowledge of their culture, so that they can … make a meaningful decision to follow a traditional way of life'. This suggests that choice and education is part of the answer to the paradox of multicultural vulnerability. From this model, two further propositions can be deduced. The third proposition is that: States can accept that

[17]The mention of 'religious freedom', of course, raises the vexed question of the definition of religion. Martin Ramstedt's chapter in this volume rightly raised the issue of how to draw the boundaries between different normalities. The terms 'religion', 'law', 'religious law', 'religious rules' are all contested. Elsewhere I have suggested that the systems theory of Niklas Luhmann may be of help here in defining law (see Sandberg 2015b and 2016). For current purposes the conventional international law definition that freedom of thought, conscience and religion extends to the manifestation of religion or belief and the understanding of belief covers worldviews will be implicitly adopted for convenience. This, however, ignores the fact that cultural groups often have their own nomos, on which see Hussain 2015.

[18]The first variant of joint governance identified by Shachar, federal-style accommodation, occurs 'where power is allocated between several sub-units and among different branches and levels of government'. It can only occur where there is 'a territorial division of authority': Shachar 2001 p.92.

groups may have authority over 'agreed matters' that are time bound and issue specific. The fourth is that: this acceptance must be conditional upon the parameters of these 'agreed matters' being clearly communicated to both members and non-members of the group and both the legal system and the group are responsible for ensuring that this is clearly communicated. The means by which this communication occurs need not be litigation, it could be education. However, there needs to be an agreement between the State and groups as to the parameters. This could take the form of a constitutional provision or concordat agreement. Similar provisions are widely used by States. There are, however, some exceptions to this general trend. For instance, in the context of the UK, these parameters are currently defined negatively. Religious tribunals, such as those studied by Douglas et al. (2011), define their authority in terms of areas where the State currently does not claim authority. Although this is in line with the common law tradition,[19] a preferable approach would be to provide a positive definition. This can be developed into a fifth proposition: the 'agreed matters', that is, the authority exercised by or granted to a group, should be defined in positive terms. This would also remove the stereotype of religious tribunals operating unofficially where State law does not tread. There are clearly gap areas where State law does not provide a remedy, and such gaps are likely to increase given the neo-liberal roll back of the State. The task is to identify what these are and where the dividing line is drawn. These areas may be different to those envisaged by Shachar. Rather than being linked to age, they are more likely to be linked to status. It could be stated that groups have authority to determine questions concerning group status. As the work of Douglas et al. (2011) show this is already occurring. The difference would be that the acceptance of temporal accommodation as a model would lead to discussion as to what aspects of marriage and divorce proceedings are matters for the group and which are matters for the State.

The issue of consent is important and that brings us to Shachar's next variant of joint governance, 'consensual accommodation'. This functions 'to permit individuals with multiple affiliations to exercise choice and make their own determinations about which legal authority – the state or the group, for example – will have their jurisdiction over their personal affairs' (Shachar 2001 p.103). This could easily be combined with temporal accommodation: temporal accommodation could dictate when group authority *can* arise; individuals can then *choose* whether or not to invoke it (Sandberg et al. 2013). Oddly, Shachar criticises consensual accommodation on the basis that it requires a 'one-time choice of [which] legal framework will govern the individual's relevant affairs from beginning to the end' (2001 p.103). However, there is no reason why this should be the case. On the contrary, consensual accommodation should only exist when the choice is on-going. This does not, however, make this model synonymous with the' right to exit'. The choice is not

[19] The classic common law approach is that 'everything is permitted except what is expressly forbidden': *Malonev Metropolitan Police Commissioner* [1979] Ch 344. See also: *AG v Guardian Newspapers Ltd (No 2)* [1990] 1 AC 109,178, Donaldson MR: 'the starting point of our domestic law is that every citizen has a right to do what he likes, unless restrained by the common law … or by statute'.

whether to leave but whether to be subject to the rules of the group in that particular context (the context being one that has been agreed under the principles of temporal accommodation outlined above). This is closer to Shachar's notion of opting in and out but there are a number of legal tools which could be employed to ensure that the group member's choice not to follow or accept a certain rule does not become tantamount to leaving the group. The group member could be afforded an exemption from the rule of the group or a right based on conscientious objection. Alternatively, their rejection of the rule could trigger discussion as to whether the rule ought to be modified; this could mean debating the merits of retaining the rule entirely or it could require the consideration of exceptions to the rule or the recasting of the rule. This underscores how religious rules should be treated as the product of the group in question and the result of consensus. 'Consensual accommodation' stresses that groups operate a voluntary jurisdiction. It may be questioned, however, to what extent being of a particular religion is voluntary in than many people are born into a religion and community pressure may be a significant factor in keeping people within groups. This means that issues concerning how that choice is made and what safeguards need to be in place regarding the nature of consent are important.

From this model, a number of propositions can be developed. The sixth proposition is that: in exercising jurisdiction over the 'agreed matters', groups exercise a voluntary jurisdiction. The seventh is: a voluntary jurisdiction is one based on the consent of the members of the group, including the valid consent of group members to which decisions specifically relate. The challenge here is determining whether or not there has been valid consent. As Shachar (2001 p.105) rightly observes, 'consensual accommodation must still provide an institutional setting that can ensure that vulnerable group members will have the resources to choose'. In short, the group member must have the capacity to choose. This not only requires that there is sufficient information and education; it also requires action where the group member is deemed incapable of making that choice because they are too young, are under duress or are suffering from a mental illness. In the context of English law, it has been suggested that guidance may be derived from the nuanced understanding of consent that has already been developed in English criminal law concerning sexual offences.[20] As Williams (1983 p.227) pointed out, under English law sexual activity is generally lawful but there are two different types of sexual offence: criminal offences concerned with sexual taboo where the act itself becomes unlawful (for example, because of the age of one of the parties) and those concerned with sexual aggression where the act is only unlawful where there is coercion by one party or where one party does not consent. The Sexual Offences Act 2003 effectively follows this distinction. Sections 1–4 provide for crimes of sexual aggression such as rape and sexual assault while the child sex offences found in sections 5–15 are crimes of sexual taboo. In relation to child sex offences, the consent of the victim is irrelevant to the defendant's liability. In relation to the general crimes of sexual aggression, the consent of the victim and whether the defendant should have known that they were not consenting is part of the definition of the crime. The

[20] For a draft Bill implementing this, see Sandberg and Cranmer 2015.

Sexual Offences Act 2003 provides a statutory definition of consent: according to section 74: 'A person consents if he agrees by choice, and has the freedom and capacity to make that choice'. This is buttressed by the use of conclusive and rebuttable presumptions, meaning that a person cannot be said to consent if the defendant intentionally deceived them as to the nature or purpose of the sexual act or if the defendant induced the victim to consent by impersonating a person known to the victim.[21]

These provisions can be used to develop the following propositions concerning valid consent. The eighth proposition is that: valid consent means that the person agrees by choice, and has the freedom and capacity to make that choice. The ninth proposition is that: it is unlawful and a criminal offence punished by the State for groups (and group personnel) to exercise or attempt to exercise a judicial or quasi-judicial function in respect of a person without that person's consent. The tenth proposition is that: evidence of intentional deception as to the nature and purpose of the act or any form of impersonation would provide conclusive evidence of a lack of consent. The eleventh proposition is that: evidence of actual or feared violence or any form of duress (including unlawful detention, stupefaction and the victim's physical and mental state) would provide rebuttable evidence of a lack of consent. The twelfth proposition is that: decisions relating to matters that are not 'agreed matters', including all decisions of a criminal nature and relating to disputes about children, are always be unlawful regardless of whether the parties consent and such decisions may be subject to criminal prosecution by the State.

The third jurisdictional model of 'joint governance', 'contingent accommodation', occurs where jurisdictional autonomy is afforded to groups in certain well-defined legal arenas, 'but only so long as their exercise of this autonomy meets certain minimal state-defined standards' (Shachar 2001 p.109). Where these minimal standards are not met, 'the State may intervene in the group's affairs and override its jurisdiction by applying the state's residual powers'. This may be combined with the temporal accommodation model in defining the legal arenas and the consensual accommodation model in stressing consent as one, if not the, most important minimal standard. The importance of contingent accommodation is that it 'may create far reaching review powers for the state' (Shachar 2001 p.110). Shachar sees this as a disadvantage commenting that 'this accommodation system also requires a complex regulatory regime because information must be gathered (presumably by the state authorities)'. She is wrong. There is no reason why the regulatory regime should be complex. The difficult job will be identifying the legal areas in which groups may exercise authority. By contrast, monitoring the use of such authority and checking that groups do not act *ultra vires* will be much simpler. A range of options exist: decisions by the group could be subject to review by the State and such a review could be automatic or could depend on the decision being challenged

[21] These are examples of conclusive presumptions. The rebuttable presumptions pass the burden of proof meaning that it has to be proved that the victim did consent. These include where violence is used or threatened, where the victim is unlawfully detained, asleep, stupefied or otherwise unconscious, or where the victim is unable to communicate their lack of consent due to a disability.

by a party to a dispute; a system based on registration and regular inspections could be developed tying in with the registration rules for religious groups which are commonplace in many States (see Doe 2011 chapter 4); or it could be achieved through greater education of the limits of the authority of groups and providing a sanction (legal or non-legal) for whistle-blowers. A problem with contingent accommodation is that the model focuses on methodology not principle: it is not clear what the guiding principle is (Sandberg et al. 2013). Consensual accommodation could provide an answer here: the guiding principle could be that 'powers will be allocated between the state and the group in a way which maximizes these members' interests (Shachar 2001 p.113). However, since this is an individual orientated strategy it may be prudent to also expressly state that the objective is also the protection of the religious autonomy of groups. Shachar (2001 p.116) is critical of the imposition of minimal standards on the basis that this raises questions of 'who is allowed to define them and how is one supposed to enforce them in a way consistent with the accommodation of deep cultural differences?' These difficulties are overcome, however, by insisting that the standards themselves are developed (and re-developed) through a on-going dialogue between the group members, other representatives of the group and the State, rather than the State simply 'imposing' the standards found in its law.

A number of propositions can therefore be derived from the contingent accommodation model. The thirteenth proposition is that: any decision by the group in relation to an 'agreed matter' must comply with the minimal standards that are to be agreed with the State as part of the dialogue concerning 'agreed matters'. The fourteenth is that: where minimal matters are not met, the State may override the authority of the group and States will develop ways by which the compliance with minimal standards will be monitored. The fifteenth is that: the 'agreed matters' and minimal standards are subject to review by the State and by groups with any modifications of changes being communicated in ways that are consistent with the propositions laid out. The sixteenth and last proposition is that: the guiding principle which will be adopted will be that powers will be allocated between the State and the group in a way which maximizes the interests of members whilst respecting the religious and cultural autonomy of groups, balancing these interests where they compete in way that is proportionate and ensure that the level and type of protection afforded by State law is provided.

These sixteen propositions provide an example of an approach that fuses and develops Shachar's three jurisdictional variants of 'joint' governance to give both group and State a role to negotiate whilst primarily investing power in individuals. Such an approach overcomes the five main problems with the concept of transformative accommodation (Sandberg et al. 2013). First, the propositions accept that people are often members of more than one group and it places the individual at the heart of the analysis. Second, the propositions underline that groups and States more often than not want authority over different matters; it is not a battle for complete power over all aspects of a person's life. Third, minimal standards are central to the propositions developed. Fourth, the propositions seek to achieve a compromise based on accommodation rather than integration; the role of the State is that of regulator ensuring that the group does not act outside its agreed powers rather than attempting to make groups act in the same way as the State. Fifth, and most importantly, the propositions are more politically feasible than transformative accommodation. As the studies in this book have shown, States already have a great deal in common in how they accommodate religious rules. It is true that some States emphasise collective rights while others stress individual rights; it is also true that the constitutional posture of States differ, usually as a result of historical legacies that are no longer sociologically significant.[22] However, no doubt in part due to common standards and obligations found in international laws, all of the States studied all adopt a basic stance which may be described as 'autonomy within limits'. The attitude of the State may differ slightly: the general stance of '"friendly" separation' described by Ino Augsberg and Stefan Korioth in their chapter in this volume may appear different from the stance of 'benign neglect' described by Soren Holm and Javier Garcia Oliva in their chapter. However, the effect is the same. All States facilitate individual and collective religious freedom without protecting it as an absolute right.

All States respect the autonomy of religious groups, some doing so explicitly in constitutional instruments.[23] Indeed, for Doe (2011 p.263), the principle that 'A religious organization is autonomous, and the State cannot intervene in its internal affairs' is a principle of religion law common to the States of Europe.[24] However, in all States, this recognition of autonomy is not a blank cheque: there are always limits, which again can be expressed explicitly or implicitly.[25] The overall approach, therefore, is one of 'autonomy within limits'. This is often reflects in rules and customs whereby States and State actors are reluctant to interfere in the affairs of religious groups but will do so where they need to in order to ensure public order and the enforcement of State-derived legal rights.[26] As Bryan Turner argued in his

[22]The historical background in Brazil provides a clear example of how Church-State postures are shaped by the sociological position of religion, as described in the chapter to this volume by Jane Reis Goncalves Pereira.

[23]Germany and Hungary provide clear examples of this see Article 137 para 3 WRV as discussed in the chapter on Germany by Ino Augsberg and Stefan Korioth and the Law on Religious Freedom (Act CCVI/2011) as discussed by Balázs Schanda's chapter on Hungry.

[24]This stance is not limited to European jurisdictions. See, for instance, the approach of the Colombian legal system where, according to Vincete Preito's chapter in this volume, 'great sensitivity' is afforded towards the manifestations and consequences of freedom of religions with the State now declaring itself incompetent in religious matters.

[25]For an example of an explicit recognition of limits see the discussion of the Societies Act and other legislation in Singapore as described in Arif A Jamal's chapter in this volume.

[26]See, for instance, the Dutch legal system where internal rules of religious organisations are considered to be binding on members in the same way as secular organisations such as football clubs. As Sophie van Bijsterveld states in her chapter in this volume, churches have legal personality and are governed by their own statutes while the secular courts have no role in determining disputes as to a theological nature but church statutes can only operate 'in so far as they do not conflict with the law' and the adjudication of conflicts with a civil dimension fall within the competence of secular courts even if they arise within churches. Lord Hope in the UK Supreme Court helpfully summed up this approach in two principles: first, that 'It has long been understood that it is not the business of the courts to intervene in matters of religion' and second that 'It is just as well under-

chapter in this volume, legal pluralism is an attempt 'to resolve the issue of religious diversity by recognizing the basic principle of freedom of religion in which the state is typically regarded as not competent to make judgements regarding religious issues'. For the most part, therefore, adopting the sixteen propositions should be a question of codifying current practice but the dialogue needed for codification will result in greater understanding and clarity as notions accepted implicitly become questioned.[27] The notion that such discussion would lead to a watertight consensus that would cover all future eventualities would, of course, be a pipedream but it is worth aspiring to, not least because the dialogue began now would be useful in dealing with unforeseen scenarios in the future even by simply setting a precedent in how States, groups and individuals can discuss these issues.

The Spectre of Sharia

The fear of sharia has limited and contaminated the public debate concerning the extent to which religious rules should be accommodated in Western societies. It is possible to point to a number of detrimental effects caused by the prevalent fear, from the demonization of religious minorities and people of faith more generally to the low often crude level of public debate that reproduces stereotypes, which are at best unhelpful. However, the spectre of sharia has had some positive consequences. Fears make us concentrate; they make us reappraise; they make us responsive to change. The anxieties of the age has meant that increased attention has been paid to the ways in which States regulate, permit, tolerate, acquiesce, accommodate, encourage, discourage and forbid the recognition of religious rules.

This has led to a significant literature, of which this book is a part. The studies in this book have shown that the ways in which State legal systems deal with religious rules is historically and geographically contingent and the differences in history, geography, politics, sociology, culture and so on means that it is ill-advised to seek a one-size fits all solution. Rather, as Ferrari argued in the introduction to this volume, the question is 'what can be done by each legal system to give citizens the opportunity to live according to their religious (or non-religious) convictions without endangering social cohesion and fostering (auto)segregation?' Ferrari provided the tools to answer this question in his identification of two ideal types by which States respond: individual and community orientated strategies. As the work of Shachar (2001) shows, such ideal types can be seen as existing on either side of a

stood, however, that the divide is crossed when the parties to the dispute have deliberately left the sphere of matters spiritual over which the religious body has exclusive jurisdiction and engaged in matters that are regulated by the civil courts': *R v Governing Body of JFS* [2009] UKSC 15 paras 157 and 158.

[27] This will include the questioning of what Javier Martinez-Torron described in his chapter to this volume as 'rules, institutions and values with a clearly distinguishable religious origin … which having been "secularized" with the passage of time, are applicable or available to all citizens irrespective of their religious affiliation'.

spectrum and this reveals how polarised responses to the issue are insufficient. It is not a question of providing individual orientated strategies on their own or community orientated strategies on their own; both are required. It is not a question of whether or not the State intervenes but when and how they should do so. Shachar's work shows that 'joint governance' is the answer to the question that Ferrari posed. States that currently prioritise community orientated strategies need to balance this out by individual orientate strategies and vice versa. Sixteen propositions of how this can be achieved were developed by fusing three of Shachar's five variants of joint governance, rejecting federal-style accommodation which is drawn on territorial rather than jurisdictional lines and the much lauded variant of 'transformative accommodation' which was found to be lacking. The sixteen propositions were:

1. Each State should recognise that its citizens belong to, show allegiance to and follow norms from more than one source of authority at any given time.
2. States should recognise that religious freedom is both an individual and a collective right and consequentially legal mechanisms need to be both individually and community orientated.
3. States can accept that groups may have authority over 'agreed matters' that are time bound and issue specific.
4. This acceptance must be conditional upon the parameters of these 'agreed matters' being clearly communicated to both members and non-members of the group and both the legal system and the group are responsible for ensuring that this is clearly communicated.
5. The 'agreed matters', that is, the authority exercised by or granted to a group, should be defined in positive terms.
6. In exercising jurisdiction over the 'agreed matters', groups exercise a voluntary jurisdiction.
7. A voluntary jurisdiction is one based on the consent of the members of the group, including the valid consent of group members to which decisions specifically relate.
8. Valid consent means that the person agrees by choice, and has the freedom and capacity to make that choice.
9. It is unlawful and a criminal offence punished by the State for groups (and group personnel) to exercise or attempt to exercise a judicial or quasi-judicial function in respect of a person without that person's consent.
10. Evidence of intentional deception as to the nature and purpose of the act or any form of impersonation would provide conclusive evidence of a lack of consent.
11. Evidence of actual or feared violence or any form of duress (including unlawful detention, stupefaction and the victim's physical and mental state) would provide rebuttable evidence of a lack of consent.
12. Decisions relating to matters that are not 'agreed matters', including all decisions of a criminal nature and relating to disputes about children, are always be unlawful regardless of whether the parties consent and such decisions may be subject to criminal prosecution by the State.

13. Any decision by the group in relation to an 'agreed matter' must comply with the minimal standards that are to be agreed with the State as part of the dialogue concerning 'agreed matters'.
14. Where minimal matters are not met, the State may override the authority of the group and States will develop ways by which the compliance with minimal standards will be monitored.
15. The 'agreed matters' and minimal standards are subject to review by the State and by groups with any modifications of changes being communicated in ways that are consistent with the propositions laid out.
16. The guiding principle which will be adopted will be that powers will be allocated between the State and the group in a way which maximizes the interests of members whilst respecting the religious and cultural autonomy of groups, balancing these interests where they compete in way that is proportionate and ensure that the level and type of protection afforded by State law is provided.

Given the widespread acceptance of 'autonomy within limits' by all States despite superficial differences in their constitutional posture towards religion and their preference for either individual or community orientated strategies, Western States are all grappling with the question of how religious and other cultural groups can be afforded autonomy without the writing of blank cheques that could lead to suffering of minorities within minorities.[28] These sixteen propositions are intended to provide a helpful starting point.[29] They provide a means by which fears and anxieties can be conquered by setting out a stance of 'autonomy within limits' which should be conducive to dialogue between groups, individuals and the State. However, the most important thing is not the substance of the propositions or even their existence; it is that the dialogue takes place. The fears of the age, that poltergeist haunting every page of this book and others like it, are therefore welcome in that the apparition has shed light upon these matters, albeit light that has been accompanied by much heat. This book is a product of fear but should also contribute to overcoming fear. The ways in which fears are defeated are by recognising them and by discussing them in rational, cold and considered ways. Clearly, the fight-back has already begun.

Acknowledgment I am grateful to Kelly Stant for her research assistance. This chapter draws upon work completed as part of the 'Social Cohesion and Civil Law: Marriage, Divorce and Religious Courts' project at Cardiff University, funded under the AHRC /ESRC Religion and Society scheme. For further details of the project see Douglas et al. (2011) and http://www.law.cf.ac.uk/clr/research/cohesion.html.

[28] As Balázs Schanda's chapter to this volume puts it, 'Church premises do not constitute a lawless territory'.

[29] It should be stressed, however, that legal only solutions will be inadequate as argued convincingly in Michele Graziadei's chapter in this volume. There is a need for interdisciplinary approaches to law and religion, on which see Sandberg (2014).

References

Bruce, Steve. 2002. *God is dead*. Oxford: Blackwell.

Bruce, Steve. 2011. *Secularization: In defence of an unfashionable theory*. Oxford: Oxford University Press.

Doe, Norman. 2011. *Law and religion in Europe*. Oxford: Oxford University Press.

Douglas, Gillian et al. 2011. *Social cohesion and civil law: Marriage, divorce and religious courts*. Cardiff University. http://www.law.cf.ac.uk/clr/research/cohesion.html.

Eisenberg, Avigail, and Jeff Spinner-Halev (eds.). 2005. *Minorities within ninorities: Equality, rights and diversity*. Cambridge: Cambridge University Press.

Ferrari, Silvio. 1997. The new wine and the old cask: Tolerance, religion and the law in contemporary Europe. *Ratio Juris* 10(1): 75.

Heelas, Paul, and Linda Woodhead. 2005. *The spiritual revolution*. Oxford: Blackwell.

Hunter, James D. 1991. *Culture wars*. New York: Basic Books.

Hussain, Amina. 2015. Legal pluralism, religious conservatism. System. In *Religion and legal pluralism*, ed. Russell Sandberg, 151. Farnham: Ashgate.

Jackson, Bernard. 2009. "Transformative accommodation" and religious law. *Ecclesiastical Law Journal* 11: 131.

Kukathas, Chandran. 1992. Are there any cultural rights? *Political Theory* 20(1): 105–139.

Malik, Maleiha. 2012. *Minority legal orders in the UK*. London: The British Academy.

Orkin, Susan M. 1997. Is multiculturalism bad for women?. *Boston Review* 22: 25.

Phillips, Anne. 2007. *Multiculturalism without culture*. Princeton: Princeton University Press.

Poulter, Sebastian. 1999. *Ethnicity, law and human rights*. Oxford: Oxford University Press.

Robbers, Gerhard. 2005. State and Church in the European Union. In *State and Church in the European Union*, 2nd ed, ed. Robbers, Gerhard, 577. Leiden: Nomos.

Sandberg, Russell. 2008a. Religion and the individual: A socio-legal rerspective. In *Religion and the individual*, ed. A. Day, 157. Franham: Ashgate.

Sandberg, Russell. 2008b. Church-state relations in Europe: From legal models to an interdisciplinary approach. *Journal of Religion in Europe* 1(3): 329.

Sandberg, Russell. 2014. *Religion, law and society*. Cambridge: Cambridge University Press.

Sandberg, Russell. 2015a. The impossible compromise. In *Religion and legal pluralism*, ed. Sandberg, Russell, 1. Farnham: Ashgate.

Sandberg, Russell. 2015b. Religious law as a social system. In *Religion and legal pluralism*, ed. Sandberg, Russell, 249. Farnham: Ashgate.

Sandberg, Russell. 2016. A sociological theory of law and religion. In *The confluence of law and religion: Interdisciplinary reflections on the work of Norman Doe*, eds. Cranmer, Frank, Hill, Mark, Kenny, Celia, and Sandberg, Russell. Cambridge: Cambridge University Press.

Sandberg, Russell, and Doe, Norman. 2007. Church-state relations in Europe. *Religion Compass* 1(5): 561.

Sandberg, Russell and Cranmer, Frank. 2015. Appendix: Non-statutory courts and tribunals (Consent to Jurisdiction) Bill. In *Religion and legal pluralism*, ed. Sandberg, Russell, 273. Farnham: Ashgate.

Sandberg, Russell et al. 2013. Britain's religious tribunals: "Joint Governance" in practice. *Oxford Journal of Legal Studies* 33(2): 263.

Shachar, Ayelet. 2001. *Multicultural jurisdictions: Cultural differences and women's rights*. Cambridge: Cambridge University Press.

Stark, Rodney. 1999. Secularisation RIP. *Sociology of Religion* 60(3): 249.

Taylor, Charles. 1991. *The ethics of authenticity*. Cambridge, MA: Harvard University Press.

Taylor, Charles. 2002. *Varieties of religion today*. Cambridge, MA: Harvard University Press.

Williams, Glanville. 1983. *Textbook of criminal law*, 2nd ed. London: Stevens & Sons.

Williams, Rowan. 2008. Civil and religious law in England – A religious perspective. *Ecclesiastical Law Journal* 10: 262.

Appendix

International Academy of Comparative Law (Vienna 20–27 July 2014) Applicable Religious Rules According to the Law of the State Questionnaire

1. Introduction
   Please provide a short introduction where
   1.1 a description of the social composition and religious demography of your country is provided
   1.2 the historical and political processes that can be helpful to understand the topic of the session are described
   1.3 the features of the national legal system that are relevant to the topic are illustrated, with particular reference to the existing systems of State –religions relationship
   1.4 the meaning you give to the expression "religious rules" is defined (religious because of their content or because of the authority from which they derive? etc.), so that the reader can easily understand which religious rules you are taking into account. If you deem it relevant to your exposition, a short discussion of the difference between religious, traditional and cultural rules could find place here.
2. Legislation
   2.1. Is religion mentioned in the legal texts (constitution preambles, basic laws, other legal texts) which define the principles and values that should inspire the State legal system? If so, what is the legal significance of this according to the courts and scholars?

R. Bottoni et al. (eds.), *Religious Rules, State Law, and Normative Pluralism - A Comparative Overview*, Ius Comparatum – Global Studies in Comparative Law 18, DOI 10.1007/978-3-319-28335-7

2.1.1 Are religious laws mentioned among the sources of State law? In which way (primary source, secondary source, etc.)?

2.1.2. Are religious laws/principles mentioned in connection with specific parts of the State legal system (for example criminal law, family law, etc.)?

2.2. Does your country have a system of personal laws based on religious affiliation? If so, which parts of the legal system are affected by these laws? Which are the religious affiliations that are relevant for the application of personal laws?

2.2.1. Is it possible to opt out of this system? How?
2.2.2. Are secular laws available for citizens who do not want to be subjected to religious norms (for example, can they choose between either a civil or a religious marriage)?

2.3. Do State laws include religious rules applicable to all citizens, independent from the fact that they profess a religion and also apart from their particular religious affiliation?

2.3.1. Do State laws include rules that have a clearly identifiable religious origin/background and are they applicable to all citizens, independent from the fact that they profess a religion and also apart from their particular religious affiliation?
Is the general application of these rules defended with reference to the cultural/traditional heritage of the State legal system?

2.4. Do State laws recognize the right of a religious organization to apply its own rules to the legal relations that take place within the religious organization itself or within institutions (school, hospitals, etc.) that are owned or managed by the religious organization?

2.5. Are religious rules applicable in the State legal system

2.5.1. through a reference made to them by State laws
2.5.2. through State norms that reproduce the content of religious norms
2.5.3. through the channel of international private law
2.5.4. through treaties and agreements between the State and religious communities
2.5.5. as part of private autonomy (as in the case of prenuptial agreements reflecting religious law)

2.6. Does State law include religiously motivated exemptions from laws of general application? Which are the conditions to be exempted? In which fields do exemptions apply?

2.7. Does State law require that people in positions of authority (for example, employers) search for an accommodation of the religious needs of the individuals who are in a subordinate position (for example, employees)?

3. Adjudication

 3.1. Does State provides religious adjudication

  3.1.1. allotting formal jurisdiction in certain fields to religious courts existing alongside State courts or, more generally, recognizing dispute resolution systems that act according to religious laws
  3.1.2. leaving citizens the option to refer a dispute to a religious court in the framework of the State-recognized arbitration system
  3.1.3. directing State courts to apply rules drawn by religious legal systems to some cases

 3.2. In the previous cases, which are the legal areas where religious adjudication is prescribed or permitted?

  3.2.1. In the case 3.1.1 is religious court jurisdiction exclusive or concurrent with State courts jurisdiction?
  3.2.2. In cases 3.1.1 and 3.1.2 are religious courts decisions bound to respect some fundamental rules/principles of the State legal systems?
  3.2.3. In cases 3.1.1 and 3.1.2 are religious courts decisions subjected to judicial review on the part of State courts?

 3.3. Does the State gives religious courts/institutions the power to interpret the laws of the State and to assess their conformity to religious rules?

4. Social implementation of religious rules (without any official recognition)

 4.1. Does a significant number of citizens apply religious rules prescribing acts and behaviors which are in conflict with State law?

 4.2. Do citizens follow religious rules prescribing acts and behaviors that, although not forbidden by State laws, raise problems in everyday life or hostility in a part of the population (wearing some religious symbols, for example)

 4.3. Do citizens make use of services provided by religious adjudication bodies that are devoid of any State recognition and civil effects or even forbidden by State law?

5. Conclusion

Please provide a final assessment concerning the system that is in force in your country.

In particular:

(a) is it satisfactory from the point of view of the respect of human rights and particularly of religious liberty, equality, and non-discrimination?
(b) does it foster inclusion of different religious communities (and particularly minority religious communities) in the social fabric or encourage forms of segregation and communitarian isolation?

(c) does it help to build social cohesion or does it promote divisions and paves the way to forms of social fragmentation?
(d) does it promote an evenhanded and fair attitude of State institutions towards different religions or does it strengthen forms of preferential treatment of religious over non-religious individuals or of the members of a particular religious community over the members of other religious communities?

CPSIA information can be obtained
at www.ICGtesting.com
Printed in the USA
LVOW13*1920170317
527618LV00010B/201/P

9 783319 283333